BASIC TEXTS IN INTERNATIONAL RELATIONS

Also by Evan Luard

BRITAIN AND CHINA
NATIONALITY AND WEALTH
CONFLICT AND PEACE IN THE MODERN
   INTERNATIONAL SYSTEM
THE CONTROL OF THE SEABED
INTERNATIONAL AGENCIES: The Emerging Framework of
   Interdependence
SOCIALISM WITHOUT THE STATE
TYPES OF INTERNATIONAL SOCIETY
THE UNITED NATIONS: How it Works and What it Does
THE MANAGEMENT OF THE WORLD ECONOMY
ECONOMIC RELATIONS AMONG STATES
INTERNATIONAL SOCIETY
A HISTORY OF THE UNITED NATIONS
   Volume 1: The Years of Western Domination, 1945–1955
   Volume 2: The Age of Decolonization, 1955–1965
THE GLOBALIZATION OF POLITICS
THE BALANCE OF POWER: The System of International
   Relations, 1648–1815

Basic Texts in International Relations

The Evolution of Ideas about International Society

Selected and introduced by
EVAN LUARD

St. Martin's Press   New York

First published in the United States of America in 1992
Reprinted 1993

Printed in Hong Kong

ISBN 0–312–06506–X (hardcover)
ISBN 0–312–06511–6 (paperback)

Library of Congress Cataloging-in-Publication Data
Basic texts in international relations: the evolution of ideas about
   international society / selected and introduced by Evan Luard.
        p.   cm.
      ISBN 0-312–06506–X (hardcover). — ISBN 0–312–06511–6 (paperback)
      1. International relations—History—Sources.   2. State, The—
History—Sources.   I. Luard, Evan, 1926–1991.
   JX68.B38   1992
   327'.01—dc20   91–10832
                                                                          CIP

Contents

v

PART TWO THE NATURE OF STATES

Preface

Though international relations is increasingly widely studied at universities and colleges in the US and Europe, many of the texts that are widely referred to by teachers, especially the writings of classical authors, are not always readily available to students. The object of this reader is to put together passages from major writers on this topic over the ages, together with a brief commentary, in a form that may be useful to students and to those who teach them.

In making my selection of texts I have had three considerations in mind.

First, I have sought to present writings that are not confined, as are most of the collections produced in recent years, to those appearing, mainly in academic journals, in the last ten or twenty years alone, but to include relevant passages from important writings over the whole period during which the subject of relations among states has been addressed by serious thinkers: that is, two thousand years or more. It is often the texts of the earlier commentators which are most inaccessible to students and which it is therefore most important should be included in a collection of this kind.

Secondly, I have felt that the selection should not be confined to academic writers on the subject. The authors quoted therefore include thinkers of many kinds, philosophers, historians, strategic writers and politicians. Many of these have not regarded themselves as international relations specialists but have none the less had important and influential things to say on the topic. I have been particularly concerned to include the ideas of leading statesmen, who have themselves been involved in the conduct of international relations and whose views on the subject are thus sometimes of special significance.

Finally, I have wished to make the selection fairly broadly based in terms of the writers' countries of origin. Earlier collections have tended to be confined almost entirely to American writers. In my view European observers have often had at least as much that was of interest to say on the subject, and I have therefore sought to maintain a roughly even balance between European and American authors.

The commentary has been kept to a minimum. But it has been thought worthwhile to point to the historical background against which some of the ideas were put forward and to seek to show how each writer, or set of writers, fits into the general evolution of thinking on international relations over the years.

The collection is divided into three main sections, each concerned with different levels of approach – the individual, the state and the society of states: the three main alternative ways of conceiving the subject. Within these broad themes a series of sub-topics have been chosen, on each of which three or four writers have been presented, sometimes putting forward contrasting views. The presentation is thus not strictly chronological; but within each main section there is an attempt to show the way ideas have evolved over time in response to a changing international environment. In this way the whole volume can perhaps give a reasonable idea of the development of thinking on the subject over the centuries.

It is hoped that the collection may be of value to students in providing, as a complement to the detailed study of individual authors which they will also undertake, a more general view of the wide range of the ideas that have been put forward over the years concerning international society and relationships within it; and that for other readers it may provide an overview of the kind of opinions that have been expressed by a wide range of thinkers about the principal factors affecting international relationships and the means of establishing a more peaceful world.

Acknowledgements

The editor and publishers wish to thank the following who have kindly given permission for the use of copyright material:

Mrs Berdine Ardrey, for the extract from her late husband Robert Ardrey's book *The Territorial Imperative* (Collins, 1967).

Augustus M. Kelley Publishers, for the extracts from Joseph A. Schumpeter's *The Sociology of Imperialisms*, in *Imperialism and Social Classes*, trs. Heinz Norden, edited with an introduction by Paul M. Sweeny (New York: Augustus M. Kelley, 1951), © copyright 1951 by Elizabeth Boody Schumpeter.

Basil Blackwell Publishers, for the extracts from St Thomas Aquinas' *De Regimine Principum* and *Summa Theologica*, trs. J. G. Dawson (Oxford: Basil Blackwell, 1978); and for the extracts from Jean Bodin's *Six Books of the Commonwealth* (1576), trs. M. J. Tooley (Oxford: Basil Blackwell, 1955), Books V and VI.

Mr John Burton, for the extracts from his book *World Society* (Cambridge: Cambridge University Press, 1972).

Carnegie Institution of Washington, for the extract from *On the Indians* (1532), by F. de Vitoria, ed. Ernest Nys (Washington, D.C.: Carnegie Institution, 1917).

Columbia University Press, for the extract from Han Fei-tzu, *Eminence in Learning and the Five Vermin*, © 1964 Columbia University Press; extracts from Hsun-Tzu, *Debating Military Matters*, © 1964 Columbia University Press; and extracts from Mo Tzu, *Against Offensive Warfare*, © 1964 Columbia University Press; all these extracts published in *Basic Writings*, trs. Burton Watson (New York: Columbia University Press, 1964).

Columbia University Press, for the extracts from Kenneth N. Waltz, *Man, the State and War* (New York: Columbia University Press, 1956), © 1954 Institute of War and Peace Studies, Columbia University.

Constable Publishers, for the extract from H. J. Mackinder, *Democratic Ideals and Reality* (London: Constable, 1919).

Croom Helm, for the extract from R. Pettman, *State and Class: A Sociology of International Affairs* (London: Croom Helm, 1979).

J. M. Dent, for the extracts from Aristotle, *Politics*, Book VII, trs. William Ellis (London: J. M. Dent, Everyman, 1912); extracts from St Augustine, *The City of God*, trs. J. Healey (London: J. M. Dent, 1945); also extracts from Joseph Mazzini, *The Duties of Man*, trs. Ella Noyes (London: J. M. Dent, 1907).

Harper & Row Publishers, Inc., for the extracts from J. G. Fichte, *Addresses to the German Nation*, trs. R. F. Jones and G. H. Turnbull, copyright © 1968 George A. Kelly; also extracts from *The Necessity for Choice* by Henry S. Kissinger, copyright © 1960, 1961 by Henry S. Kissinger.

Harvard University Press, for the extracts from Thomas C. Schelling, *The Strategy of Conflict*, copyright 1960, 1980 by the President and Fellows of Harvard College, © 1988 by Thomas C. Schelling; the extract from Immanuel Kant, *Thoughts on a Perpetual Peace*, in *Inevitable Peace* by Carl J. Friedrich (Cambridge, Mass.: Harvard University Press, 1948), copyright 1948 by the President and Fellows of Harvard College, © 1976 by Carl J. Friedrich; also the extracts from R. C. Keohane and J. I. Nye, *Transnational Relations and World Politics* (Cambridge, Mass.: Harvard University Press, 1970), copyright © 1970 by the President and Fellows of Harvard College.

Heinemann, for the extract from Norman Angell, *The Great Illusion* (London: Heinemann, 1909).

Professor John H. Herz, for the extracts from his book *International Politics in the Atomic Age* (New York: Columbia University Press, 1959).

David Higham Associates Ltd, for the extracts from Michael Howard, *Studies in War and Peace* (London: Gower Publishing, 1970).

Holt, Rinehart and Winston, for the extract from H. C. Kelman, "Social-Psychological Approaches to the Study of International

Relations", copyright © 1965, in Kelman, *International Behaviour* (New York: Holt, Rinehart and Winston, 1965).

Lawrence & Wishart Ltd, for the extracts from V. I. Lenin, *Imperialism: The Highest Stage of Capitalism*, in *Lenin: Collected Works*, vol. 22 (London: Lawrence & Wishart, 1964).

Leicester University Press, for the extracts from Martin Wight, *Power Politics* (1946).

Professor Charles A. McClelland, for the extract from his *Theory and the International System* (New York: Macmillan, 1966).

McGraw-Hill Publishing Co., for the extract from Harold Lasswell, *World Politics and Personal Insecurity* (New York: McGraw-Hill, 1935); and for the extract from F. L. Schuman, *International Politics* (New York: McGraw-Hill, 1934).

Macmillan, Inc., and Routledge, for the extracts from Talcott Parson, *The Social System*, reprinted by permission of The Free Press, a Division of Macmillan, Inc., copyright © 1950 by The Free Press, renewed 1978 by Talcott Parsons.

Macmillan Publishing Co., for the extracts from *Louis XIV: Memoire for the Instruction of the Dauphin*, trs. P. Sonnino (New York: Free Press, 1970) copyright © 1970 The Free Press; and extracts from *Foreign Policy Decision-Making* by Richard C. Snyder, H. W. Bruck and Burton Sapin, copyright © 1962 by The Free Press; and extracts from Reinhold Neibuhr, *Moral Man and Immoral Society* (Scribner's Sons, 1932, an imprint of Macmillan Publishing Co.), copyright 1932 Charles Scribner's Sons, copyright renewed © 1960 Reinhold Niebuhr.

Oxford University Press, for the extracts from Plato, *The Republic*, trs. F. M. Cornford (1941); the extract from Hegel, *The Philosophy of Right*, trs. T. M. Knox (1942); the extract from Grotius, *The Law of War and Peace*, trs. F. W. Kelsey *et al.* (1925); the extracts from Machiavelli, *The Prince*, trs. Luigi Ricci, revised by E. R. P. Vincent (1935); the extract from Christian Wolff, *The Law of Nations*, trs. T. J. Hemelt (1934); and the extract from Alexis de Tocqueville, *Democracy in America*, trs. Henry Reeve (1946), all published by Oxford University Press.

Penguin Books Ltd, for the extract from *The Peloponnesian War* by Thucydides, trs. Rex Warne (London: Penguin, 1955), translation copyright © Rex Warner, 1954.

Peters, Fraser and Dunlop Ltd, for the extract from Anthony Storr, *Human Aggression* (London: Allen Lane, 1968), © Anthony Storr 1968.

Prentice-Hall Inc., for the extract from Karl W. Deutsch, *The Analysis of International Relations* (Englewood Cliffs, NJ: Prentice-Hall, 1968); also the extract from K. J. Holsti, *International Politics: A Framework for Analysis* (Englewood Cliffs, NJ: Prentice-Hall, 1967).

Princeton University Press, for the extract from Bernard Brodie, *Strategy in the Missile Age*, copyright © 1959 by Rand Corporation; the extract from Carl von Clausewitz, *On War*, copyright © 1976 by Princeton University Press; the extract from Harold and Margaret Sprout, *The Ecological Perspective on Human Affairs*, copyright © 1965 by Princeton University Press; the extract from Klaus Knorr and Sidney Verba, *The International System: Theoretical Essays*, copyright © 1961 Princeton University Press; the extract from K. W. Deutsch, *Political Community and the North Atlantic Area*, copyright © 1957 Princeton University Press.

Random House, Inc., for the extract from Inis Claude, Jr., *Power and International Relations*, copyright © 1962 by Random House, Inc.; and the extract from Hans Morgenthau, *Politics among Nations*, copyright © 1948, 1954 © 1960 by Alfred A. Knopf Inc.

Professor J. N. Rosenau, for the extract from his *The Scientific Study of Foreign Policy* (New York: Free Press, 1971).

Routledge, for the extract from Friedrich Meinecke, *The Idea of 'Raison d'État'* (1924), in *Modern History*, trs. Douglas Scott (London: Routledge, 1957).

Routledge and Harcourt Brace Jovanovich, for the extract from Konrad Lorenz, *On Aggression*, trs. Marjorie Kerr Wilson, copyright © 1963 by G. Borotha, English translation copyright © 1966 by Konrad Lorenz, copyright © 1983 by Deutscher Taschenbuch Verlag.

The Royal Institute of International Affairs, for the extract from David Mitrany, *A Working Peace System* (London, 1949).

Scott, Foresman and Co., for the extract from G. T. Allison, *Essence of Decision: Explaining the Cuban Missile Crisis* (Boston, Mass.: Little, Brown, 1971).

Simon & Schuster, and St Martin's Press, for the extract from C. R. Mitchell, "World Society a Cobweb", which was published in *Conflict in World Society*, ed. M. Banks (1984).

Stanford University Press, for the extract from Ernest B. Haas, *Beyond the Nation-State: Functionalism and International Organization*, © 1964 by the Board of Trustees of the Leland Stanford Junior University.

Sweet & Maxwell, for the extract from Georg Schwarzenberger, *Power Politics: A Study of War Society* (London: Stevens & Sons, 1964).

UNESCO, for the extract from Raymond Aron, "Historical Sociology as an Approach to International Relations", which appeared in *The Nature of Conflict*, © Unesco 1957.

The University of Chicago Press, and Professor David Easton, for the extract from *A Systems Analysis of Political Life*, by D. Easton, copyright 1965 and 1979 by David Easton.

University of Illinois Press, for the extract from *How Nations See Each Other*, by William Buchanan and Hedley Cantril (1953).

Unwin Hyman, for the extract from J. J. Rousseau, *The State of War*, trs. M. Forsyth, in *The Theory of International Relations* (London: George Allen & Unwin, 1970); the extract from E. Glover, *War, Sadism and Pacifism* (London: George Allen & Unwin 1933); the extract from J. A. Hobson, *Imperialism* (London: George Allen & Unwin, 1902); and the extract from Martin Wight, "The Balance of Power", in H. Butterfield and M. Wight (eds), *Diplomatic Investigations* (London: Allen & Unwin, 1966).

Weidenfeld & Nicolson Ltd, for the extract from Raymond Aron, *Peace and War: A Theory of International Relations* (1966).

John Wiley & Sons Inc., for the extract from M. Kaplan, *System and Process in International Politics* (1957).

The executors of the Leonard Woolf estate, for the extract from *International Government* (London: The Hogarth Press, 1916).

Every effort has been made to trace all the copyright holders, but if any have been inadvertently overlooked the publishers will be pleased to make the necessary arrangement at the first opportunity.

Publishers' Note

Evan Luard died on 8 February 1991 before he was able to correct the proofs of this book.

Part One
The Nature of Man

Introduction

Beliefs about the way relations among states are conducted, or should be conducted, depend partly on beliefs about human nature.

Some have seen humans as naturally aggressive and have tended to conclude that this was the cause of warfare among states. Such thinkers have held that the world is naturally one of conflict, in which all are compelled to fight to defend their own interests. Politically, economically, and if need be militarily, individuals struggle against each other to secure supremacy. Even those who are not naturally aggressive have needed to become so in order to defend themselves against those that are. So mutual suspicion and mutual hatred have condemned mankind to an internecine struggle: a struggle which, it is believed, is reflected in the wider conflicts among states.

Other writers have held a different view of human nature. It is not that they have denied the existence of widespread conflict; nor that many individual humans are prone to aggression, or may even enjoy the delights of war. They have adopted, however, a less sceptical approach to the possibility of containing and redirecting these tendencies. Sometimes they believe that humans are naturally good, or naturally peace-loving, and that only their rulers lead them into war. They denounce the futility and destructiveness of conflict, affirming that it is possible for humans to live in peace with one another if only they transform their own attitudes, or if only they create the right institutions. And they believe it is especially important for the rulers themselves, who control the destiny of their peoples and are often responsible for making war, to reform their conduct so as to establish a more harmonious and peaceful world.

As time went on, a middle view between these over-simplified alternatives began to be put forward. It was increasingly recognised that humans are not necessarily inherently wicked or inherently good, "naturally" aggressive or "naturally" peace-loving. Not only is there a wide variation between individuals but each individual is a mixture of different qualities. The same individual might be sometimes aggressive and sometimes pacific, and it was therefore important to know the reasons for these variations in behaviour. Psychological study might therefore have a role to play in the study of international behaviour.

Moreover, the individuals who influenced or determined the actions of states acted in a social context. Whether or not conflict between states occurred, it was increasingly understood, did not necessarily depend on the fundamental characteristics of human beings – human nature – but on the character of the institutions within which they had organised themselves. It was when they became organised into national states that their duty as citizens demanded that they should feel hostility for the citizens of other states; and it was as leaders of such states that statesmen led them into war. It was therefore not the study of individual psychology that was relevant in the analysis of inter-state relations but social psychology which might demonstrate the social factors which drove individuals to behave in ways quite contradictory to their natural desires and attitudes.

This did not eliminate the human factor. However they were organised, citizens remained human beings, with the same fears and desires as other human beings, yet having interests, individual and collective, which often differed from those of other individuals. There were still some who believed there was a natural conflict of interests among peoples and states that condemned them to war, while others believed that there could be a harmony of interests among them, making it possible to establish a condition of perpetual peace. This basic division of views – between "realists" and "Utopians" – has persisted among those who have spoken and written about international relationships until the present day.

1 The Ancient Chinese View

Some of the earliest writings about relations among states date from more than two thousand years ago. Three or four centuries BC there existed, both in China and in Greece, societies of states which shared a similar language and culture, had regular contact with each other and engaged in frequent conflict. In both areas the philosophers of the age debated the type of political system *within* states which would best promote the welfare of their citizens. In doing so they also considered, at least in passing, the kind of relationship which should be established *among* states.

In China this was the time of the "hundred schools of thought". Different philosophers put forward widely conflicting views about the kind of political system which would best promote the interests of the people in each state, and those of the state as a whole. They differed most radically on the fundamental question described above: whether or not mankind was naturally "evil" and prone to conflict, or on the contrary naturally "good" and so capable of enjoying a socially harmonious existence.

One of the best-known schools, that of the Realists, or "Legalists", held that men were naturally bad and, if unrestrained, were likely to seek only their own ends in conflict with each other. They could be made good only by strong laws and an authoritarian organisation of society. The people, in other words, had to be coerced into conformity: the ruler must see to it that they are "not allowed to be bad", as Han Fei-tzu, the leading writer of this school, put it. Members of this group believed above all in efficient government, with offices held by those of the greatest ability rather than by hereditary right. This efficiency was required by each state in part for external reasons: to make it better equipped to prevail against other states. In an age of constant warfare (this was the so-called Warring States period) only strong and well-run states would survive. War could make them stronger and, in the words of Shang Tzu, it was "a misfortune for prosperous states not to be at war". This is the view put forward by the members of this school quoted below, Shang Tzu and Han Fei-tzu. So Shang Tzu extols warfare, which may be able to secure for a state domination over other states; while Han Fei-tzu praises the ruler who is strong enough not to be attacked himself.

Other schools of thought, however, held an opposite view of human nature. Mencius, a follower of Confucius, believed, like his master, that people were naturally "good" and could live in peace together if only they were provided with benevolent government. They had no natural desire for conflict, and war resulted only from the policies of evil rulers. The enlightened ruler would not make war because it condemned his people to misery. For this reason, Mencius declared, Confucius had condemned those who fought wars on behalf of their rulers: far from praising war – like the Realists – he held that "those who are skilled in war should suffer the severest punishment". A similar viewpoint was put forward by Mo Tzu, another philosopher of this age. Though hostile to the Confucianists, he equally condemned warfare as conflicting with the principle of "universal love" which he upheld above all others. He therefore denounced states which "delight in aggressive warfare" and the rulers who take "delight in the injury and extermination of the people of this world".

Other writers expressed a middle view. Hsun-Tzu, for example, was an eclectic who inherited some of his views from Confucius and his followers and some from the Legalists (as well as being influenced by Taoist writings). He believed, like the Legalists, that people were naturally bad and therefore required moral education (for example, study of classical texts and correct ritual). But he shared the view of Mencius that benevolent government was required to bring out the best in humans. Because the benevolent ruler desired the happiness of his people, he would not himself initiate war against his neighbours. But, because he enjoyed the support of his people, when war did take place such a ruler was likely to prevail.

Writers of the hundred schools therefore expressed a variety of views about the nature of mankind and the causes of war. Those who believed that humans were naturally bad (providing the philosophy of the Ch'in rulers who finally united China and the regime they established) were inclined to regard warfare as inevitable and uphold those policies which would promote success in warfare. Those who regarded mankind as naturally good, on the other hand, generally deplored the prevalence of war and urged on rulers policies of peace.

Both schools, in other words, attributed the fact of war to characteristic features of human nature. The latter believed in the possibility of reforming that nature; the former believed that human attributes and human action could be altered only by the sanction of force.

* * *

Shang Tzu – The Necessity of War*

"Former kings were able to make their people tread on naked swords, face showers of arrows and stones. Was it that the people liked doing it? Not at all; but they had learnt that by doing so they escaped from even worse harm. Therefore I would have the people told that if they want gain, it is only by ploughing that they can get it; if they fear harm, it will only be by fighting that they can escape it. Then everyone within the borders of the land would know that he could get no happiness without first applying himself to ploughing and warfare. The country might be small, but the grain produced would be much; the inhabitants might be few, but their military power would be great. A country that devoted itself to these two ends would not have to wait long before it established hegemony or even complete mastery over all other States. . . .

[It is a misfortune for a prosperous country not to be at war; for in peace time it will breed] "the Six Maggots, to wit, Rites and Music, the Songs and the Book, the cultivation of goodness, filial piety and respect for elders, sincerity and truth, purity and integrity, kindness and morality, detraction of warfare and shame at taking part in it. In a country which has these twelve things, the ruler will not promote agriculture and warfare, with the result that he will become impoverished and his territory diminished. . . .

"Concentrate the people upon warfare, and they will be brave; let them care about other things, and they will be cowardly. . . . A people that looks to warfare as a ravening wolf looks at a piece of

---

* Attributed to Wei Yang (c. 390–338 BC). Chief official and adviser to the Duke of Ch'in. Introduced changes in the law and administration of the state to centralise authority and reduce the power of the feudal lords. Probable author of *The Book of the Lord of Shang*, which emphasises the importance of agriculture and war to a state's success. Quoted from *The Book of the Lord of Shang*, trs. Arthur Waley, in *Three Ways of Thought in Ancient China* (London: Allen & Unwin, 1939).

meat is a people that can be used. In general, fighting is a thing that the people detest. A ruler who can make the people delight in war will become king of kings. In a country that is really strong the father will send his son, the elder brother his younger brother, the wife her husband, all saying as they speed him: 'Conquer, or let me never see you again.'

"If the only gate to riches and honour is battle, then when people hear that there is war they will congratulate one another; at home and in the streets, at their eating and at their drinking, all the songs they sing will be of war. . . . .'"

Mencius – The Iniquity of War*

Mencius said, "While he was chief officer to the head of the Chi family, Jan Ch'iu doubled the yield of taxation without being able to improve their virtue. Confucius said, 'Ch'iu is no longer a disciple of mine. You, little ones, may attack him to the beating of drums.' From this it can be seen that Confucius rejected those who enriched rulers not practising benevolent government. How much more would he reject those who go out of their way to wage war for them? In wars to gain land, the dead fill the plains; in wars to gain cities, the dead fill the cities. This is called showing the land the way to devour human flesh. Such men deserve more than punishment by death. Therefore those who are skilled in war should suffer the severest punishments; those who bring about alliances with other feudal lords come next, and then come those who open up wastelands and increase the production of land."

Sung K'eng was on his way to Ch'u. Mencius, meeting him at Shih-ch'iu, asked him, "Where are you going, sir?"

"I have heard that Ch'in and Ch'u are at war, and I am going to see the king of Ch'u and try to persuade him to cease hostilities. If he is not pleased with my advice, I shall go to see the king of Ch'in and try

* From Mencius (*c.* 390–305 BC). Disciple of Confucius and adviser to the rulers of various states. Sought to find a ruler who would practise benevolent government as, he believed, it had been practised in ancient times. Believed in the essential goodness of humans and the need for an enlightened system of government to allow this natural goodness to flourish. Quoted from Mencius, *The Four Books* (350–330 BC, trs. James Legge (Taipei: Council of Chinese Cultural Renaissance, 1875).

to persuade him to the same end. I shall probably have success with one of the two kings."

"I do not wish to ask about the details, but I would like to hear about the general outline of your plan. How are you going to carry out your persuasion?"

"I shall tell them how unprofitable war is."

"Your aim, Master, is lofty indeed, but your slogan is unconvincing. If you put the profit motive before the kings of Ch'in and Ch'u, and they cease the operations of their armies because of this, it would mean that the soldiers in their armies were similarly disposed. If subjects cherished the profit motive in serving their prince, sons did the same in serving their fathers, and likewise younger brothers in serving their elder brothers, then it would mean that, doing away with benevolence and rightness, prince and subject, father and son, elder brother and younger brother, all cherished the profit motive in their mutual relationships. Never has there been a prince ruling over such a state who has not perished. If, on the other hand, you put benevolence and rightness before the kings of Ch'in and Ch'u, and they ceased the operations of their armies because of their delight in benevolence and rightness, then it would mean that the soldiers in their armies were similarly disposed. If subjects cherished benevolence and rightness in serving their prince, sons did the same in serving their fathers, and likewise younger brothers in serving their elder brothers, then it would mean that, doing away with the profit motive, prince and subject, father and son, elder brother and younger brother, all cherished benevolence and rightness in their mutual relationships. Never has there been a prince ruling over such a state who has failed to become a true King. What is the necessity of mentioning the word 'profit'?"

Lu wanted to make Shen Tzu commander of the army. Mencius said, "To send the people to war before training them is to bring calamity upon them. One who brings calamity upon the people would not have been tolerated in the days of Yao and Shun. Even if Ch'i could be defeated and Nanyang annexed after a single engagement, it should still not be permitted."

Shen Tzu, looking displeased, said, "This is something I do not understand."

"I shall tell you plainly. The domain of the Emperor is a thousand *li* square, without which he would not have sufficient to enable him to treat with the feudal lords. The domain of a feudal lord is a hundred *li* square, without which he would not have sufficient to enable him to keep the archives of the ancestral temple. When the Duke of Chou was enfeoffed in Lu, his domain was a hundred *li* square. There was indeed no shortage of land, but his fief was not more than a hundred *li*. When T'ai Kung was enfeoffed in Ch'i, his domain was a hundred *li* square. There was also no shortage of land, but his fief was not more than a hundred *li*. Today Lu is five times a hundred *li* square. If a true King arises, do you think the territory of Lu will be reduced or enlarged by him? A benevolent man would not even take from one man to give to another, let alone seek territory at the expense of human lives. In serving his lord, a gentleman's aim is simply to lead him on to the right path and set his mind on benevolence."

Mencius said, "Those who are in the service of princes today say, 'I can enlarge the territory of my prince, and fill his treasuries for him.' The so-called 'good subject' of today would have been referred to in antiquity as a 'robber of the people'. To enrich a prince who does not turn towards the Way nor set his mind on benevolence is to enrich a Chieh [tyrant].

"They say, 'I can gain allies and make sure victory in war for my prince.' The so-called 'good subject' of today would have been referred to in antiquity as a 'robber of the people'. To try to make a prince strong for war who does not turn towards the Way nor set his mind on benevolence is to aid a Chieh.

"If a prince follows the Way of today and does not change the customs of the people, he would not be able to hold the Empire for a single morning, even if it were given to him."

Han Fei-tzu – Power Abroad Depends on Order at Home*

"A true king is one who is in a position to attack others, and a ruler whose state is secure cannot be attacked. But a powerful ruler can

---

* From Han Fei-tzu (*c.* 280–233 BC). Probably taught by Wei Yang and Hsun-Tzu. Having tried unsuccessfully to influence the ruler of his native state, he became an adviser to the king of Ch'i, one of the most powerful states of the system, and of its chief minister Li Ssu. Later, suspected of treachery in favour of his native state, he was imprisoned and killed. Advocated a strengthening of central government, the creation of a class of trained officials, strict laws and warfare to expand the frontiers of the state. Quoted from *Eminence in Learning and the Five Vermin*, in *Basic Writings*, trs. Burton Watson (New York: Columbia University Press, 1964).

also attack others, and a ruler whose state is well ordered likewise cannot be attacked. Neither power nor order, however, can be sought abroad – they are wholly a matter of internal government. Now if the ruler does not apply the proper laws and procedures within his state, but stakes all on the wisdom of his foreign policy, his state will never become powerful and well ordered. . . .

"[I]t is easy to become skillful when you have ample resources. Hence, it is easy to scheme for a state that is powerful and orderly but difficult to make any plan for one that is weak and chaotic. Those who scheme for the state of Ch'in can make ten changes and still their plans will seldom fail; but those who plan for the state of Yen can scarcely make one change and still hope for success. It is not that those who plan for Ch'in are necessarily wise and those who plan for Yen are stupid – it is simply that the resources they have to work with – order in one case, disorder in the other – are different.

"Chou deserted the side of Ch'in and joined the Vertical Alliance, and within a year it had lost everything.[1] Wey turned its back on Wei to join the Horizontal Alliance, and in half a year it was ruined.[2] Thus Chou was ruined by the Vertical Alliance and Wey was destroyed by the Horizontal Alliance. Instead of being so hasty in their plans to join an alliance, they should have worked to strengthen the order within their domains, to make their laws clear and their rewards and punishments certain, to utilise the full resources of the land in building up stores of provisions, and to train their people to defend the cities to the point of death, thus ensuring that any other ruler would gain little profit by trying to seize their lands, but on the contrary would suffer great injury if he attempted to attack their states. In that case, even the ruler of a state of ten thousand war chariots would have been unwilling to wear out his armies before their strong walls and, in his exhausted condition, invite the attack of powerful enemies. This would have been the way to escape destruction. To abandon a way which assures escape from destruction, and follow instead a path that leads to certain downfall, is the greatest error one can make in governing a state. Once the wisdom of its foreign policy is exhausted and its internal government has fallen into disorder, no state can be saved from ruin."

Notes

1. In 256 BC King Nan of the Chou dynasty joined with the leaders of the Vertical Alliance in an attack on Ch'in which failed miserably. To make amends, he was obliged the same year to turn over all his territory to Ch'in.

2. The event to which Han Fei-tzu is probably referring occurred in 241 BC, though the details are not known. The names of the two states are romanised the same way in modern Chinese, but the translator has spelled the name of the older state "Wey" to distinguish them.

Mo Tzu – Warfare Harms the State which Conducts it as Well as Mankind as a Whole*

"[W]hen the benevolent men of ancient times ruled the world, they strove for amicable relations among the large states, united the world in harmony, brought together all within the four seas, and led the people to serve and honour the Lord on High, the sacred mountains and rivers, and the spirits. Many were the benefits they brought to mankind, and great was their success. Therefore Heaven rewarded them, the spirits enriched them, and men praised them. They were honoured with the rank of Son of Heaven, enriched with the possession of the world, and their names formed a triad with those of Heaven and earth, enduring to this day. Such, then, are the way of the wise man and the means by which the former kings held possession of the world.

"But the rulers and feudal lords of today are not like this. They all set about to examine the relative merits of their soldiers, who are their teeth and claws, arrange their boat and chariot forces, and then, clad in strong armour and bearing sharp weapons, they set off to attack some innocent state. As soon as they enter the borders of the state, they begin cutting down the grain crops, felling trees, razing walls and fortifications, filling up moats and ponds, slaughtering the sacrificial animals, firing the ancestral temples of the state, massacring its subjects, trampling down its aged and weak, and carrying off its vessels and treasures. The soldiers are urged forward into battle by being told, 'To die in the cause of duty is the highest honour, to kill a large number of the enemy is the next highest, and

---

* From Mo Tzu (c. 450–370 BC). Chinese philosopher. Little is known of his early life, but he probably came from Sung or Lu states. Travelled a great deal, spreading the doctrine of "universal love". Sought to persuade the rulers to abandon war and urged the weaker states to improve their defences so as to deter attack and create a more even balance of power. Quoted from *Against Offensive Warfare*, in *Basic Writings*, trs. Burton Watson (New York: Columbia University Press, 1964).

to be wounded is next. But as for breaking ranks and fleeing in defeat – the penalty for that is death without hope of pardon!' So the soldiers are filled with fear.

"Now to seize a state and overthrow its army, massacre its subjects, and undo the labours of the sages – is this intended to benefit Heaven? Yet it is the people of Heaven who are gathered together to attack a city of Heaven.[1] So they are massacring the subjects of Heaven, driving out the spirits of their ancestors, overthrowing their altars of the soil and grain, and slaughtering their sacrificial animals. This brings no benefit to Heaven on high. Is it intended then to benefit the spirits? But to murder men is to wipe out the caretakers of the spirits, to cause the spirits of the former kings to suffer neglect, to oppress the subjects of the state and scatter its people. This brings no benefit to the spirits in the middle realm. Is it intended then to benefit mankind? But murdering men is a paltry way to benefit them indeed, and when we calculate the expenditures for such warfare we find that they have crippled the basis of the nation's livelihood and exhausted the resources of the people to an incalculable degree. This brings no benefit to mankind below.

•   •   •

"When a state which delights in aggressive warfare raises an army, it must have several hundred high officers, several thousand regular officers, and a hundred thousand soldiers, before it can set out. The time required for the expedition will be several years at the longest, several months at the least. During that time the leaders will have no time to attend to affairs of government, the officials no time to manage their departments of state, the farmers no time to sow or reap, the women no time to spin or weave. So in this case too the state will lose its fighting men and the common people will be forced to abandon their occupations. Moreover, there will be the damage and depreciation to the horses and chariots to consider, while if one fifth of the tents and hangings, army supplies and weapons can be salvaged from the campaign, the state will be lucky. In addition, a countless number of men will desert or become lost along the way, or will die and end tumbled in a ditch due to the starvation, cold and sickness caused by the length of the journey or the fact that supplies do not arrive in time.[2]

Such is the injury which warfare inflicts upon men, the harm it brings to the world. And yet the rulers and officials delight in carrying out such expeditions. In effect they are taking delight in the injury and extermination of the people of the world. Are they not perverse?

"At present the states in the world which are fondest of warfare are Ch'i, Chin, Ch'u and Yüeh. If these four states were in a position to order the rest of the world about, they could easily increase their present populations by tenfold and still have land left over to feed even more. This is because they have too few people and an excess of land. And yet now they go to war with each other over land and succeed only in doing further injury to each other's people. This is simply to destroy what one does not have enough of for the sake of what one already has in excess! . . .

"If you were really able to establish a reputation for righteousness in the world and attract the other rulers by your virtue, then it would be no time at all before the whole world had submitted to you, for the world has for a long time been plagued by warfare and is as weary as a little boy who has spent the day playing horse. Now if only there were someone who would conduct his diplomatic affairs in good faith and would think first of all how to benefit the other feudal lords; who, when a large state committed some unrighteous act, would feel concerned along with others; who, when a large state attacked a small one, would go to the rescue of the small state along with others; who, when the walls and fortifications of the smaller state were in poor condition, would see to it that they were repaired; who, when the smaller state's supplies of cloth and grain were exhausted, would supply more; who, when the smaller state's funds were insufficient, would share his own – if one were to conduct his relations with the large states in this manner, then the rulers of the smaller states would be pleased. If others struggle while one is at ease, then one's own military position will become stronger. If one is merciful and generous, substituting affluence for want, then the people will surely be won over. If one substitutes good government in one's own state for offensive warfare, then one will achieve manifold success. If one weighs the expenditures of one's own army and compares them with the ruinous expenditures of the other feudal lords, one will see that one has gained rich benefits. If one conducts one's affairs in accordance with what is correct, acts in the name of righteousness, strives for lenience in ruling one's subjects and good faith in dealing with one's army, and thus sets an example for the armies of the other feudal lords, then one will have no enemy under heaven and will bring incalculable benefit to the world.

"This is what benefits the world, and if the rulers and officials do not know enough to make use of it, then they cannot be said to understand the most important way of benefiting the world.

"If the rulers and officials and gentlemen of the world sincerely desire to promote what is beneficial to the world and to eliminate what is harmful, they should realise that offensive warfare is in fact a great harm to the world. If they wish to practise benevolence and righteousness and become superior men; if they wish to act in accordance with the way of the sage kings and benefit the people of China, they should not fail to examine what I have said in my condemnation of offensive warfare."

Notes
1. That is, all men are the people of Heaven and all cities are its cities.
2. The text of this paragraph and the preceding one is in poor condition and the translation at numerous points is highly tentative.

Hsun-Tzu – Conquest Will Not Win Control of Territory Unless Accompanied by Righteousness*

"There are three methods by which you may annex a neighbouring state and bring its people under your rule: you may win them over by virtue, by force, or by wealth.

"If the people of a neighbouring state respect your reputation, admire your virtuous actions, and desire to become your subjects, they will throw open their gates, clear the roads and welcome you to their cities. If you allow them to follow their old customs and remain in their old homes, the common people will all rest easy and will willingly obey your laws and commands. In this way you will acquire new territory and your power will increase; you will have added to your population and your armies will be stronger than ever. This is what it means to win over a neighbour by virtue.

If the people of a neighbouring state do not respect your reputation

---

* From Hsun-Tzu (c. 312–230 BC). Adviser to the courts of Ch'i and Chu and teacher of Han Fei-tzu. Differed from Confucianists in believing that man is basically evil. Advocated the abolition of hereditary titles and promotion on the basis of merit. Attacked Mo Tzu as a moralising preacher who was out of touch with the harsh reality of the world. Quoted from *Debating Military Matters*, in *Basic Writings*, trs. Burton Watson (New York: Columbia University Press, 1964).

or admire your virtuous actions, but are awed by your authority and intimidated by force, then, although they will feel no loyalty to you in their hearts, they will not dare to resist annexation. In such cases, however, you will have to enlarge your garrisons and increase your military supplies, and your government expenditures will increase likewise. In this way you will acquire new territory but your power will decrease; you will have added to your population but your armies will be weaker than before. This is what it means to win over a neighbour by force.

If the people of a neighbouring state do not respect your reputation or admire your virtuous actions, but are poor and are looking for some way to get rich, are starving and in search of plenty, then they will come to you with empty bellies and gaping mouths, attracted by your food alone. In such a case, you will have to issue supplies of grain from your storehouses in order to feed them, hand out goods and wealth to enrich them, and appoint conscientious officials to look out for them, and only after three years have passed can you put faith in their loyalty. In this way you will acquire new territory but your power will decrease; you will have added to your population but the state will be poorer than before. This is what it means to win over a neighbour by wealth. Therefore I say, he who annexes a state by virtue is a true king; he who annexes it by force will be weakened; and he who annexes it by wealth will be impoverished. From ancient times to the present it has always been the same.

"It is easy enough to annex territory; the difficult thing is to stabilise and maintain control over it. Ch'i was able to annex Sung, but could not hold on to it, and so Wei snatched it away. Yen succeeded in annexing Ch'i, but could not hold on to it, and so T'ien Tan seized control of it. Han's territory of Shang-tang, a region several hundred *li* square, rich and well inhabited, chose to become part of Chao, but Chao could not hold on to it, and hence Ch'in took it away. He who is able to annex territory but not to hold on to it will invariably be stripped of his acquisitions; he who can neither annex territory nor hold on to what he has will surely be destroyed. He who can hold on to territory will invariably be able to acquire more. When one can both acquire and hold on to territory, there is no limit to the amount he can annex. In ancient times T'ang began with the region of Po and King Wu began with Hao, both of them areas of only a hundred *li* square. The reason they were able to unite the world under their rule and win the allegiance of all the other feudal lords was simply this: they knew how to secure their hold upon their territory.

"Secure your hold on the aristocracy by means of ritual; secure your hold on the people through government. With ritual well ordered, the aristocracy will submit to your rule; with the government fairly administered, the people will feel safe. With the aristocracy submissive and the people content, you will attain what is called a situation of great stability. If you remain within your borders, you will be unassailable; if you march to battle, you will be strong. What you command will be done, what you forbid will cease, and the undertakings of a true king will be complete in you."

2 The Ancient Greek View

At about the same period, in another society of states racked by war, philosophers in Greece were discussing similar topics. As in China their main concern was with the internal organisation of states: the system of government that would best promote the welfare of their peoples. This was the theme of the best known works of the period, *The Republic* of Plato and the *Politics* of Aristotle. Both of these touch only in passing on the relationships that should be established with other states. But neither ignores that question altogether.

In *The Republic* Plato takes a view that is closer to that of the Legalists in China than that of Mencius. He too believed that humans were not naturally inclined to live peacefully together. And he therefore demanded a strong, authoritarian state, with a powerful system of education to indoctrinate citizens in the arts of living. A part of this education should be education for war. For though states should act justly towards each other, war was certain to occur; and one reason for establishing justice within the state was that, by reducing domestic conflict, this would help it to prevail in contests with other states. But warfare among the Greek states, with their common culture and common racial origin, amounted to a form of "civil war" and Plato called for a sufficient sense of solidarity among all Greeks to prevent such conflicts.

Aristotle, on the other hand, came closer to the opinion of Mencius and the Confucianists. He does not believe human nature makes conflict inevitable. He strongly criticises the political system established by the Spartans, who were willing to tolerate an authoritarian and oligarchic system only because they saw victory in war as the prime objective of their state. They failed to understand that the only purpose of war was to restore peace, just as the main objective of labour was to attain rest. War should not be seen as an end in itself, in other words, but should be undertaken only for defensive purposes. The best political system was one which created the conditions for the peaceful life which most people in their hearts desired.

There is thus a certain symmetry between the different views put forward in ancient China and ancient Greece on relations among states. In both places those who held a low view of human nature tended to favour an authoritarian system of government; and though they did so primarily because weak and erring humans required

18

strong government at home, it was also because this would enable the state to be stronger in its relations with other states and to make war more effectively against them. Those who had a more favourable opinion of human nature, on the other hand, were against harsh measures of government. They believed that the welfare of the people should be the supreme goal; and this required not only the establishment of a more lenient system of government at home but abstention from war as an act of policy abroad.

*   *   *

Plato – Justice among States*

"Would you agree that a state may be unjust and may try to enslave other states or to hold a number of others in subjection unjustly?"

"Of course it may; above all if it is the best sort of state, which carries injustice to perfection."

"I understand, said I; that was your view. But I am wondering whether a state can do without justice when it is asserting its superior power over another in that way."

"Not if you are right, that justice implies intelligence; but if I am right, injustice will be needed. . . ."

"Please add to your kindness by telling me whether any set of men – a state or an army or a band of robbers or thieves – who were acting together for some unjust purpose would be likely to succeed, if they were always trying to injure one another. Wouldn't they do better, if they did not?"

"Yes, they would."

"Because, of course, such injuries must set them quarrelling and hating each other. Only fair treatment can make men friendly and of one mind."

* From Plato (428–348 BC). Greek philosopher and disciple of Socrates. Author of *The Republic*, a Socratic dialogue setting out views, attributed to Socrates, about the meaning of justice and the type of political organisation which would establish justice within the state. Proposed a totalitarian system, in which music and other arts were abolished, and occupations allocated to different sections of the population according to their abilities. Quoted from *The Republic*, Books I and V, trs. F. M. Cornford (Oxford: Oxford University Press, 1941).

"Be it so, he said; I don't want to differ from you."

"Thank you once more, I replied. But don't you agree that, if injustice has this effect of implanting hatred wherever it exists, it must make any set of people, whether freemen or slaves, split into factions, at feud with one another and incapable of any joint action?"

"Yes."

"And so with any two individuals: injustice will set them at variance and make them enemies to each other as well as to everyone who is just."

"It will."

"And will it not keep its character and have the same effect, if it exists in a single person?"

"Let us suppose so."

"The effect being, apparently, wherever it occurs – in a state or a family or an army or anywhere else – to make united action impossible because of factions and quarrels, and moreover to set whatever it resides in at enmity with itself as well as with any opponent and with all who are just. . . ."

"And is it of no importance that men who are to be warriors should see something of war in childhood? Is that not worth some danger? . . ."

"Granted, then, that the children are to go to war as spectators, all will be well if we can contrive that they shall do so in safety. To begin with, their fathers will not be slow to judge, so far as human foresight can, which expeditions are hazardous and which are safe; and they will be careful not to take the children into danger. Also they will put them in charge of officers qualified by age and experience to lead and take care of them."

"Yes, that would be the proper way."

"All the same, the unexpected often happens; and to guard against such chances we must see that they have, from their earliest years, wings to fly away with if need be."

"What do you mean by wings?"

"Horses, which they must be taught to ride at the earliest possible age; then, when they are taken to see the fighting, their mounts must not be spirited chargers but the swiftest we can find and the easiest to manage. In that way they will get a good view of their future business, and in case of need they will be able to keep up with their older leaders and escape in safety. . . ."

"Now, as to the conduct of war and your soldiers' relations to one another and to the enemy: am I right in thinking that anyone guilty of an act of cowardice, such as deserting his post or throwing away his arms, should be reduced to the artisan or farmer class; while if any fall alive into the enemy's hands, we shall make them a present of him, and they may do what they like with their prey? . . ."

"We have already said that the brave man is to be selected for marriage more frequently than the rest, so that as many children as possible may have such a man for their father. But besides that, these valiant youths may well be rewarded in the Homeric manner. . . ."

"At sacrificial feasts and all such occasions, we shall reward the brave, in proportion to their merit, not only with songs and those privileges we mentioned but 'with seats of honour, meat, and cups brimful'; and so at once pay tribute to the bravery of these men and women and improve their physique. . . ."

"And next, how will our soldiers deal with enemies?"

"In what respect?"

"First take slavery. Is it right that Greek states should sell Greeks into slavery? Ought they not rather to do all they can to stop this practice and substitute the custom of sparing their own race, for fear of falling into bondage to foreign nations? . . ."

"They must not, then, hold any Greek in slavery themselves, and they should advise the rest of Greece not to do so."

"Certainly. Then they would be more likely to keep their hands off one another and turn their energies against foreigners."

"Next, is it well to strip the dead, after a victory, of anything but their arms? It only gives cowards an excuse for not facing the living enemy, as if they were usefully employed in poking about over a dead body. Many an army has been lost through this pillaging. There is something mean and greedy in plundering a corpse; and a sort of womanish pettiness in treating the body as an enemy, when the spirit, the real enemy, has flown, leaving behind only the instrument with which he fought. It is to behave no better than a dog who growls at the stone that has hit him and leaves alone the man who threw it."

"True."

"So we will have no stripping of the slain and we shall not prevent their comrades from burying them. Nor shall we dedicate in the temples trophies of their weapons, least of all those of Greeks, if we are concerned to show loyalty towards the rest of Hellas. We shall rather be afraid of desecrating a sanctuary by bringing to it such spoils of our own people, unless indeed the Oracle should pronounce otherwise."

"That is very right."

"And what of ravaging Greek lands and burning houses? How will your soldiers deal with their enemies in this matter?"

"I should like to hear your own opinion."

"I think they should do neither, but only carry off the year's harvest. Shall I tell you why?"

"Please do."

"It seems to me that war and civil strife differ in nature as they do in name, according to the two spheres in which disputes may arise: at home or abroad, among men of the same race or with foreigners. War means fighting with a foreign enemy; when the enemy is of the same kindred, we call it civil strife."

"That is a reasonable distinction."

"Is it not also reasonable to assert that Greeks are a single people, all of the same kindred and alien to the outer world of foreigners?"

"Yes."

"Then we shall speak of war when Greeks fight with foreigners, whom we may call their natural enemies. But Greeks are by nature friends of Greeks, and when they fight, it means that Hellas is afflicted by dissension which ought to be called civil strife."

"I agree with that view."

"Observe, then, that in what is commonly known as civil strife, that is to say, when one of our Greek states is divided against itself, it is thought an abominable outrage for either party to ravage the lands or burn the houses of the other. No lover of his country would dare to mangle the land which gave him birth and nursed him. It is thought fair that the victors should carry off the others' crops, but do no more. They should remember that the war will not last for ever; some day they must make friends again."

"That is a much more civilised state of mind."

"Well then, is not this commonwealth you are founding a Greek state, and its citizens good and civilised people?"

"Very much so."

"And lovers of Greece, who will think of all Hellas as their home, where they share in one common religion with the rest?"

"Most certainly."

"Accordingly, the Greeks being their own people, a quarrel with them will not be called a war. It will only be civil strife, which they will carry on as men who will some day be reconciled. So they will not behave like a foreign enemy seeking to enslave or destroy, but will try to bring their adversaries to reason by well-meant correction. As Greeks they will not devastate the soil of Greece or burn the homesteads; nor will they allow that all the inhabitants of any state, men, women and children, are their enemies, but only the few who are responsible for the quarrel. The greater number are friends, whose land and houses, on all these accounts, they will not consent to lay waste and destroy. They will pursue the quarrel only until the guilty are compelled by the innocent sufferers to give satisfaction."

"For my part, I agree that our citizens should treat their adversaries in that way, and deal with foreigners as Greeks now deal with one another."

"We will make this a law, then, for our Guardians: they are not to ravage lands or burn houses."

Aristotle – Peace as the End of War*

"Now life is divided into labour and rest, war and peace. Of what we do the objects are partly necessary and useful, partly noble: and we should give the same preference to these that we do to the different parts of the soul and its actions, as war to procure peace; labour, rest; and the useful, the noble. The politician who composes a body of laws ought to extend his views to everything; the different parts of the soul and their actions; more particularly to those things which are of a superior nature and ends; and, in the same manner, to the lives of men and their different actions. They ought to be fitted for labour and war, but even more for rest and peace; to do what is necessary and useful, but even more what is fair and noble. It is to those objects that the education of the children and of all the youths who want instruction ought to tend. All the Grecian states which now seem best governed, and the legislators who founded those states, appear not to have framed their polity with a view to the best end, or to every virtue, in their laws and education; but eagerly to have attended to what is useful and productive of gain: and nearly of the same opinion

* From Aristotle (384–322 BC). Athenian philosopher, logician and scientist. In his youth a disciple of Plato and author of Platonic dialogues. Author of a wide range of works, covering ethics, politics, biology, psychology and other matters. Best known perhaps today for his *Politics* in which he sought to categorise states according to their constitutions and political structure. While he held that humans had a natural disposition to associate within political communities, he recognised that these might themselves (as in his own day) come into frequent conflict with each other. Quoted from *Politics*, Book VII, trs. William Ellis (London: Dent, 1912).

with these are some persons who have written lately, who, by praising the Lacedæmonian state, show they approve of the intention of the legislator in making war and victory the end of his government. But how contrary to reason this is . . . for it is evident, since the Lacedæmonians have now no hope that the supreme power will be in their own hand, that neither are they happy nor was their legislator wise. This also is ridiculous, that while they preserved an obedience to their laws, and no one opposed their being governed by them, they lost the means of being honourable. These people understand not rightly what sort of government it is which ought to reflect honour on the legislator; for a government of freemen is nobler than despotic power, and more consonant to virtue.

"Neither should a city be thought happy, nor should a legislator be commended, because he has so trained the people as to conquer their neighbours. In this there is a great inconvenience: since it is evident that upon this principle every citizen who can will endeavour to procure the supreme power in his own city (which crime the Lacedæmonians accuse Pausanias of, though he enjoyed such great honours). Such reasoning and such laws are neither political, useful, nor true: but a legislator ought to instil those laws on the minds of men which are most useful for them, both in their public and private capacities.

"The rendering a people fit for war, that they may enslave their inferiors, ought not to be the care of the legislator; but that they may not themselves be reduced to slavery by others. In the next place, he should take care that the object of his government is the safety of those who are under it, and not a despotism over all: in the third place, that those only are slaves who are fit to be only so. Reason indeed concurs with experience in showing that all the attention which the legislator pays to the business of war, and all other rules which he lays down, should have for their object rest and peace. Most of those states (which we usually see) are preserved by war; but, after they have acquired a supreme power over those around them, are ruined. For during peace, like a sword, they lose their brightness. The fault of this lies in the legislator, who never taught them how to be at rest.

"As there is one end common to a man both as an individual and a citizen, it is evident that a good man and a good citizen must have the same object in view; it is evident that all the virtues which lead to rest are necessary; for, as we have often said, the end of war is peace, of labour, rest. But those virtues whose object is rest, and those also whose object is labour, are necessary for a liberal life and rest. For we want a supply of many necessary things that we may be at rest.

"A city therefore ought to be temperate, brave, and patient. According to the proverb, 'Rest is not for slaves'; but those who cannot bravely face danger are the slaves of those who attack them. Bravery, therefore, and patience are necessary for labour, philosophy for rest, and temperance and justice in both; but these chiefly in time of peace and rest. For war obliges men to be just and temperate; but the enjoyment of pleasure, with the rest of peace, is more apt to produce insolence. Those who are easy in their circumstances, and enjoy everything that can make them happy, have great occasion for the virtues of temperance and justice. Thus if there are, as the poets tell us, any inhabitants in the happy isles, to these a higher degree of philosophy, temperance and justice will be necessary, as they live at their ease in the full plenty of every sensual pleasure. It is evident, therefore, that these virtues are necessary in every state that would be happy or worthy; for he who is worthless can never enjoy real good, much less is he qualified to be at rest; but can appear good only by labour and being at war but in peace and at rest the meanest of creatures.

"For this reason virtue should not be cultivated as the Lacedæmonians did. They did not differ from others in their opinion concerning the supreme good, but in imagining this good was to be procured by particular virtues. But since there are greater goods than those of war, it is evident that the enjoyment of those which are valuable in themselves should be desired, rather than those virtues which are useful in war. . . ."

3 The Christian View

Christian thinkers throughout the ages discussed similar themes. Among them too there have been differences of opinion about the nature of mankind and how far this made warfare among states an inevitable feature of human existence.

St Augustine, in his vast work *The City of God*, expressed the belief that men have a natural love of peace. He repeats the view of Aristotle that even when people fight each other their aim is to win peace. But they want peace on their own terms: "to have it as they like". Even conquerors wish ultimately for peace, since they desire to make those they conquer "their own" and to "give them such laws as they like". Wars are made therefore not out of any love of fighting but from the urge to dominate. The implication of such views is that wars are often made not from evil motives, but because one party believes it knows best what is good for the other. Under this view the root cause of war is often reforming zeal.

Thomas Aquinas, writing eight centuries later, was concerned to clarify how far wars could be justified on the basis of motives of that kind. Precisely because all those who made war declared their cause a righteous one, he sought to distinguish more clearly between those wars which had a "just" cause and those which did not. In the first of the two passages reproduced here he describes the responsibility of rulers for establishing conditions that would make possible a good life within their states: for example to promote the welfare of the community and to ensure that it was continually extended. In the second he defines the "just war". Such a war must have been declared by the ruler himself, who alone has the competence to make war; it must be for a just cause (to avenge a wrong, to punish a state for having failed to make amends for a wrong done, or to restore what has been taken unjustly); and it must be undertaken with a right intention. This final condition makes clear that it was not enough for a ruler to *declare* that a war was being undertaken for a just cause (as most rulers habitually did): its true and underlying purpose must be just.

Erasmus, two or three centuries later, also held that human nature did not make war inevitable. By nature humans had a "mild and gentle disposition" and their inclination was to seek peace. But sometimes the human heart was filled with "an insatiable rage for war", to which even ordinary people were driven sometimes by "passion or mistaken interest". As a result, even those who thought themselves most Christian converted "the gentle acts of the gospels to the trumpet of Mars". They would thus willingly make war in the name of religion against other Christians, holding their own conflict always to be a "just" war. Man's true nature, under this view, is to love peace. But that nature is corrupted by passion; and the fact that a people might claim that their cause was just did not necessarily make it so.

William Penn, an early Quaker, reflected the concern of that sect with the prevalence of war. He deplored the fact that the nature of men was often to secure their ends by war rather than peace. In many cases "they were not willing to accept peace unless their appetites were in some way gratified". But in his view this was only because there was no other means open to them for securing justice. Nothing was more important than to create a more peaceful world. And the best way to reduce the tendency of humans to seek their ends through war would be by establishing some means for securing justice between states comparable to the system of justice which already existed within them.

These Christian thinkers therefore attribute the fact that men make war against each other to a variety of causes: the sinful nature of man; his desire to usurp God's role as the righter of wrongs and the avenger of injustice; their demand to have peace only "as they like" (in the words of Augustine); "anger, ambition and folly" (in the words of Erasmus); "ambition, pride of conquest and greatness of dominion" (in the words of Penn). Sometimes the writers demand, as a condition for creating a more peaceful world, a change in the conduct of rulers (like Erasmus), sometimes new institutions among rulers and states for resolving their disputes (like Penn). But above all they seek a reform in the nature of man himself. It is man's imperfect nature that makes war such a widespread feature of human existence. But if only men would reform their conduct and listen to God's word, it was not necessarily an inescapable fact of human life.

* * *

Augustine – The Universal Love of Peace*

"Joy and peace are desired alike of all men. The warrior would but conquer, and war's aim is nothing but glorious peace. For what is victory but a suppression of resistance, which being done, peace follows? And so peace is war's purpose, the scope of all military discipline, and the limit at which all just contentions aim.

"All men seek peace by war, but none seek war by peace. For they that perturb the peace they live in, do it not for hate of it, but to show their power in alteration of it. They would not disannul it, but they would have it as they like; and though they break into seditions against the rest, yet must they hold a peaceful show with their fellows that are engaged with them, or else they shall never effect what they intend. Even the thieves themselves that molest all the world besides them, are at peace amongst themselves. Admit one be so strong or subtle that he will have no fellow, but plays all his parts of roguery alone, yet with such as he can neither kill, and to whom he does not care to make known his deeds, he must needs maintain a kind of peace. And at home, with his wife and family, must he needs observe quietness; and without question he delights in their obedience unto him, which if they fail in, he chases and chides and strikes, setting all in order by force if need be, or by cruelty: which he sees he cannot do, unless all the rest be subjected under one head, which is himself. And might he have the sway of a city or province in such sort as he has that of his house, he would put off his thievish nature, and put on a king's, albeit his covetousness and malice would remain unchanged.

"Thus then you see that all men desire to have peace with such as they would have live according to their liking. For those against whom they wage war, they would make their own if they could; and if they conquer them they give them such laws as they like.

"But let us imagine some such unsociable fellow as the poet's fable records, calling him 'half-man', for his inhuman barbarism.

"Now although his kingdom lay in a lightless cave, and his villainies were so singular that they gave him that name of Cacus, which is,

---

* From St Augustine (354–430). Father of the Christian church, bishop of Hippo in North Africa for over 30 years. Most systematic Christian thinker of ancient times, who sought to reconcile New Testament religion with the Platonic tradition. A believer in predestination, he attacked the doctrine of free will and the Pelagian heresy. Because he wrote frequently of peace and war he was widely quoted by mediaeval theologians, such as Aquinas, and early international lawyers, many of them theologians themselves, when writing on that subject. Quoted from *The City of God*, trs. J. Healey (London: Dent, 1945).

evil; though his wife never had good word for him, and he never played with his children, nor ruled them in their manlier age, and though he never spoke with friend, not so much as with his father Vulcan (than whom he was far more happy in that he begat no such monster as Vulcan had in begetting him); though he never gave to any, but robbed and spoiled all that he could take from all manner of persons, and even the persons themselves, yet in that horrid dungeon of his, whose floor and walls were always dank with the blood of new slaughters, he desired nothing but to rest in peace therein, without molestation.

"He desired also to be at peace with himself; and what he had, he enjoyed; he ruled over his own body, and to satisfy his own hungry nature that menaced the separation of soul and body, he fell to his robberies with celerity; and though he were barbarous and bloody, yet in all that, he had a care to provide for his life and safety. And therefore if he would have had that peace with others, which he had in the cave with himself alone, he would neither have been called half-man nor monster. . . .

"The worst men of all do fight for their fellows' quietness, and would (if it lay in their power) reduce all into a distinct form of state, drawn by themselves, whereof they would be the heads, which could never be, but by a coherence either through fear or love. For herein is perverse pride an imitator of the goodness of God, hating equality of others with itself under Him, and laying a yoke of obedience upon its fellows, under itself instead of Him. Thus hates it the just peace of God, and builds an unjust one for itself. Yet can it not but love peace, for no vice, however unnatural, can pull nature up by the roots."

Thomas Aquinas – The Duty of Rulers in Peace and War*

"Just as the good life of men on this earth is directed, as to its end, to the blessed life which is promised us in heaven, so also all those

---

* From St Thomas Aquinas (1224–74). Philosopher, theologian and systematiser of Roman Catholic thought. In his youth joined the Dominicans and finally became a teacher at the Jacobin College in Paris. As a scholar of classical philosophy,

particular benefits which men can procure for themselves, such as riches, or gain, or health, or skill, or learning, must be directed to the good of the community. But, as we have said, he who has charge of supreme ends must take precedence over those who are concerned with aims subordinate to these ends, and must guide them by his authority; it follows, therefore, that a king, though subject to that power and authority must, nevertheless, preside over all human activities, and direct them in virtue of his own power and authority. Now, whoever has a duty of completing some task, which is itself connected with some higher aim, must satisfy himself that his action is rightly directed towards that aim. Thus the smith forges a sword which is fit to fight with; and the builder must construct a house so that it is habitable. And because the aim of a good life on this earth is blessedness in heaven, it is the king's duty to promote the welfare of the community in such a way that it leads fittingly to the happiness of heaven; insisting upon the performance of all that leads thereto, and forbidding, as far as is possible, whatever is inconsistent with this end. The road to true blessedness and the obstacles which may be found along it, are learnt through the medium of the divine law; to teach which is the duty of priests, as we read in Malachy (2:34): 'The lips of the priest shall keep knowledge, and they shall seek the law at his mouth.' So the Lord commands (Deuteronomy 17:18): 'But after he is raised to the throne of his kingdom, he shall copy out to himself the Deuteronomy of this law in a volume, taking the copy of the priests of the Levitical tribe, and he shall have it with him and shall read it all the days of his life, that he may learn to fear the Lord his God, and keep his words and ceremonies, that are commanded in the law.' A king then, being instructed in the divine law, must occupy himself particularly with directing the community subject to him to the good life. In this connection he has three tasks. He must first establish the welfare of the community he rules; secondly, he must ensure that nothing undermines the well-being thus established; and thirdly he must be at pains continually to extend this welfare.

"For the well-being of the individual two things are necessary: the

especially that of Aristotle, he adopted the scientific method in defending traditional Christian beliefs. Sought to reconcile faith with reason and traditional Christian doctrine with the scholastic ideas of humanism and rationalism. His doctrine of the just war, an elaboration of Augustine's writings on the subject, was widely quoted by writers on international law in subsequent centuries. Quoted from *De Regimine Principum*, xv, and *Summa Theologica*, xv, trs. J. G. Dawson (Oxford: Basil Blackwell, 1978).

first and most essential is to act virtuously (it is through virtue, in fact, that we live a good life); the other, and secondary requirement, is rather a means, and lies in a sufficiency of material goods, such as are necessary to virtuous action. Now man is a natural unit, but the unity of a community, which is peace, must be brought into being by the skill of the ruler. To ensure the well-being of a community, therefore, three things are necessary. In the first place the community must be united in peaceful unity. In the second place the community, thus united, must be directed towards well-doing. For just as a man could do no good if he were not an integral whole, so also a community of men which is disunited and at strife within itself, is hampered in well-doing. Thirdly and finally, it is necessary that there be, through the ruler's sagacity, a sufficiency of those material goods which are indispensable to well-being. Once the welfare of the community is thus ensured, it remains for the king to consider its preservation. . . .

The Conditions of a Just War
"For a war to be just three conditions are necessary. First, the authority of the ruler within whose competence it lies to declare war. A private individual may not declare war; for he can have recourse to the judgement of a superior to safeguard his rights. Nor has he the right to mobilise the people, which is necessary in war. But since responsibility for public affairs is entrusted to the rulers, it is they who are charged with the defence of the city, realm, or province, subject to them. And just as in the punishment of criminals they rightly defend the state against all internal disturbance with the civil arm; as the Apostle says (Romans 13:4): 'He beareth not the sword in vain. For he is God's minister: an avenger to execute wrath upon him that doth evil.' So also they have the duty of defending the state, with the weapons of war, against external enemies. For this reason rulers are told in Psalm 81 to 'Rescue the poor; and deliver the needy out of the hand of the sinner.' And St Augustine says in his book, *Contra Faustum* (XXIII, 73): 'The natural order of men, to be peacefully disposed, requires that the power and decision to declare war should lie with the rulers.'

"Secondly, there is required a just cause: that is that those who are attacked for some offence merit such treatment. St Augustine says (Book LXXXIII q.; *Super Josue*, qu. X): 'Those wars are generally defined as just which avenge some wrong, when a nation or a state is to be punished for having failed to make amends for the wrong done, or to restore what has been taken unjustly.'

"Thirdly, there is required a right intention on the part of the belligerents: either of achieving some good object or of avoiding some evil. So St Augustine says in the book *De Verbis Domini*: 'For the true followers of God even wars are peaceful, not being made for greed or out of cruelty, but from desire of peace, to restrain the evil and assist the good.' So it can happen that even when war is declared by legitimate authority and there is just cause, it is, nevertheless, made unjust through evil intention. St Augustine says in *Contra Faustum* (LXXIV): 'The desire to hurt, the cruelty of vendetta, the stern and implacable spirit, arrogance in victory, the thirst for power, and all that is similar, all these are justly condemned in war.'"

Erasmus – Man's Natural Inclination to Peace*

"From Nature man receives a mild and gentle disposition. He delights to be loved for the pleasure of being loved, without any view to interest, and feels a satisfaction in doing good without a wish or prospect of remuneration. This disposition to do disinterested good is natural to man. Hence even the People, in the ordinary language of daily conversation, denominate whatever is connected with mutual goodwill, humane; so that the word humanity no longer describes man's nature merely in a physical sense, but signifies humane manners, or a behaviour worthy the nature of man, acting his proper part in civil Society.

• • •

"After all, then, what infernal being, all-powerful in mischief, bursting every bond of Nature asunder, fills the human bosom with an insatiable rage for war? Robbery, blood, butchery, desolation, confound without distinction everything sacred and profane! The most hallowed treaties, mutually confirmed by the strongest sanctions, cannot stop the enraged parties from rushing on to mutual

---

* From Desiderius Erasmus (*c.* 1466–1536). Scholar, humanist and theologian. Born in the Low Countries, probably in Rotterdam, became a priest and later secretary to the bishop of Cambrai. From 1499 spent much time in England, as a teacher and scholar, and became a friend of Sir Thomas More. As a renowned humanist scholar his writing was widely quoted in his own day, both by the reformers and their opponents. Quoted from *The Complaint of Peace*, 1517 (Boston, Mass., 1813), unnamed translator.

destruction, whenever passion or mistaken interest urges them to the irrational decision of battle.

"But be it granted that Nature has no effect on men as men, yet must not Christ therefore avail with Christians? The suggestions of the Christian religion are far more excellent than those of Nature. Why does not the Christian religion persuade those who profess it of a truth which it recommends above all others; that is, the expediency and necessity of peace on earth and goodwill towards men. Or at least why does it fail of effectually dissuading from the unnatural, and more than brutal, madness of waging war?

• • •

"God made man unarmed. But anger and revenge have mended the work of God and furnished his hands with weapons invented in hell. Christians attack Christians with engines of destruction, fabricated by the Devil.

"All wars are carried on with infinite harm to the people; while in most cases, the people had not the smallest concern either in their origin or their issue. Then as to the young men being mainly concerned in this mischief of exciting war; so far from it, that you old men hide your grey hairs with a helmet, and you deem it an honour to the hoary head of a Christian to encourage or even take active part in war; though Ovid says: 'that an old man, a warrior, is a loathsome object!' and Ovid's countrymen considered a man of seventy who set others on to fight was a monster of wickedness and folly.

"As to the laity being only concerned in this mischief of war, it is so far from true that priests, that professors of the purest divinity do not blush; that neither bishops, cardinals, nor Christ's own vicars blush to become the instigators, the very fire-brands of war, against which Christ, from whom they all pretend to derive the only authority they can have, expressed His utter detestation.

• • •

"Among Christians, as if shame had fled from the earth, clergymen, solemnly consecrated to God, are often among the first to inflame the minds both of Rulers and people, to blood and devastation. They convert the gentle accents of the gospel to the trumpet of Mars; and, forgetting the dignity of their profession, run about making proselytes to their opinion, ready to do or suffer anything so long as they can but succeed in kindling the flames of War. A few years ago, when the world, labouring under a deadly fever, was running headlong to arms, the Gospel trumpeters blew a blast from the pulpit, and inflamed the wretched Kings of Europe into a paroxysm, into a state of downright insanity. Among the English, the clergy from the pulpits spoke evil against the French; and among the French, against the English. They all united in urging to war. Not one man amongst the clergy exhorted to peace, or at least not above one or two whose lives would perhaps be in danger if I were even now to name them.

•   •   •

"The absurdest circumstance of all respecting the use of the Cross as a standard is that you see it glittering and waving high in the air in both contending armies. Divine service is also performed to the same Christ in both armies at the same time. Even from the Holy Sacrament itself the warriors who have just received it, rush to arms and endeavour to plunge the dreadful steel into each other's vitals. Let us hear the fighters pray: 'Forgive us our trespasses as we forgive them that trespass against us', and then with all haste they rush to murder their brother Christians for an alleged trespass that after all is but imaginary.

"And yet the Christians will call it a war and a just and necessary war too, which on the most trifling occasion they wage with another people holding the same faith in the same Christ. Wretched is the alternative forced upon us by war. He who conquers is a murderer of his brother and he who is conquered dies equally guilty of fratricide because he did his best to commit it.

"I am well aware of the excuse which men, ever ingenious in devising mischief to themselves as well as others, offer in extenuation of their conduct in going to war. They allege that they are compelled to it; that they are dragged against their will to war. I answer them: deal fairly, pull off the mask, throw away all false colours, consult your own heart, and you will find that anger, ambition and folly are the compulsory force that has dragged you into war, and not any necessity – unless indeed you call the insatiable cravings of a covetous mind, necessity."

Penn – Justice as the Means to Peace*

I. OF PEACE AND ITS ADVANTAGES

"He must not be a man but a statue of brass or stone whose bowels do not melt when he beholds the bloody tragedies of this war, in Hungary, Germany, Flanders, Ireland and at sea, the mortality of sickly and languishing camps and navies, and the mighty prey the devouring winds and waves have made upon ships and men since '88. And as this with reason ought to affect human nature, and deeply kindred, so there is something very moving that becomes prudent men to consider, and that is the vast charge that has accompanied that blood, and which makes no mean part of these tragedies; especially if they deliberate upon the uncertainty of the war, that they know not how or when it will end, and that the expense cannot be less, and the hazard is as great as before. So that in the contraries of peace we see the beauties and benefits of it; which under it, such is the unhappiness of mankind, we are too apt to nauseate, as the full stomach loathes the honeycomb; and like that unfortunate gentleman, that having a fine and a good woman to his wife, and searching his pleasure in forbidden and less agreeable company, said, when reproached with his neglect of better enjoyments, that he could love his wife of all women if she were not his wife, though that increased his obligation to prefer her. It is a great mark of the corruption of our natures, and what ought to humble us extremely, and excite the exercise of our reason to a nobler and juster sense, that we cannot see the use and pleasure of our comforts but by the want of them. As if we could not taste the benefit of health but by the help of sickness; nor understand the satisfaction of fullness without the instruction of want; nor, finally, know the comfort of peace but by the smart and penance of the vices of war: and without dispute that is not the least reason that God is pleased to chastise us so frequently with it. What can we desire better than peace but the grace to use it? Peace

---

* From William Penn (1644–1718). English Quaker and strong advocate of religious toleration. Sent down from Oxford for non-conformist beliefs. Became a Quaker in 1667. Author of pamphlets and books attacking Catholic and Anglican beliefs impartially, for which he was imprisoned. On his father's death became a substantial land-owner and frequented the court of Charles II. Became active in the colonisation of North America, acquiring the land which later became Pennsylvania (named after his father, not himself). Other works include *Some Fruits of Solitude* (1693) and *The Rise and Progress of the People called Quakers* (1694). Quoted from *An Essay Towards the Present and Future Peace of Europe* (1693).

preserves our possessions; we are in no danger of invasions: our trade is free and safe, and we rise and lie down without anxiety. The rich bring out their hoards, and employ the poor manufacturers; buildings and divers projections for profit and pleasure go on: it excites industry, which brings wealth, as that gives the means of charity and hospitality, not the lowest ornaments of a kingdom or common-wealth. But war, like the frost of '83, seizes all these comforts at once, and stops the civil channel of society. The rich draw in their stock, the poor turn soldiers, or thieves, or starve: no industry, no building, no manufactory, little hospitality or charity; but what the peace gave, the war devours. I need say no more upon this head, when the advantages of peace, and mischiefs of war, are so many and sensible to every capacity under all governments, as either of them prevails. I shall proceed to the next point. What is the best means of Peace? which will conduce much to open my way to what I have to propose.

II. OF THE MEANS OF PEACE, WHICH IS JUSTICE RATHER THAN WAR

"As justice is a preserver, so it is a better procurer of peace than war. Though *Pax quaeritur bello* be a usual saying, *Peace is the end of war*, and as such it was taken up by O. C. for his motto; yet the use generally made of that expression shows us that, properly and truly speaking, men seek their wills by war rather than peace, and that as they will violate it to obtain them, so they will hardly be brought to think of peace unless their appetites be some way gratified. If we look over the stories of all times, we shall find the aggressors generally moved by ambition; the pride of conquest and greatness of dominion more than right. But as those leviathans appear rarely in the world, so I shall anon endeavour to make it evident they had never been able to devour the peace of the world, and ingross whole countries as they have done, if the proposal I have to make for the benefit of our present age had been then in practice. The advantage that justice has upon war is seen by the success of embassies, that so often prevent war by hearing the pleas and memorials of justice in the hands and mouths of the wronged party. Perhaps it may be in a good degree owing to reputation or poverty, or some particular interest or con-veniency of princes and states, as much as justice; but it is certain that, as war cannot in any sense be justified, but upon wrongs received and right, upon complaint refused; so the generality of wars have their rise from some such pretension. This is better seen and understood at home; for that which prevents a civil war in a nation is that which may prevent it abroad, viz., justice; and we see where that is notably obstructed, war is kindled between the magistrates and people in particular kingdoms and states; which, however it may be unlawful on the side of the people, we see never fails to follow, and ought to give the same caution to princes as if it were the right of the people to do it: Though I must needs say the remedy is almost ever worse than the disease: the aggressors seldom getting what they seek, or performing, if they prevail, what they promised: and the blood and poverty that usually attend the enterprise weigh more on earth, as well as in heaven, than what they lost or suffered, or what they get by endeavouring to mend their condition, comes to: which disappointment seems to be the voice of heaven and judgment of God against those violent attempts. But to return, I say, justice is the means of peace, betwixt the government and the people, and one man and company and another. It prevents strife, and at last ends it: for besides shame or fear, to contend longer, he or they being under government, are constrained to bound their desires and resentment with the satisfaction the law gives. Thus peace is maintained by justice, which is a fruit of government, as government is from society, and society from consent."

4 The Philosophers' View

The philosophers found different explanations for the prevalence of war. They too saw this tendency as rooted in human nature. But they found other reasons for it than those of the theologians.

The view they took depended partly on their view of the role of the state. The principal feature of this post-mediaeval age in Europe was the development of state power. This was welcomed by some and feared by others: it could be used to protect the citizen against foreign enemies and civil unrest or to threaten his freedom. While the power of the state might reduce conflict within societies it could also increase the prevalence and destructiveness of warfare among states. Differing opinions about which of these dangers was most to be feared affected the views expressed about human nature and the causes of conflict.

Thomas Hobbes, the English political philosopher, in the age of the Thirty Years' War and the English revolution was faced with the spectacle of conflict both abroad and at home: he was thus impressed above all with the insecurity of humans, living in constant fear of one another. In his *Leviathan* he suggested that this insecurity caused them to seek, above all, self-preservation. Competition made them fight for gain, "diffidence" made them fight for security, and desire for glory for reputation. There was thus, in the state of nature, a war of all against all, in which notions of right and wrong, justice and injustice, had no place. Within a single national territory the all-powerful authority of the state, enjoying absolute sovereignty, might be able to contain such conflicts: this was the main reason to support its claim to obedience. But *between* states an equally ruthless struggle was likely to continue, because the rulers were "in continual jealousies and in the state and posture of gladiators". Among them there was no sovereign power to maintain law and order, as the sovereign power within the state was able to do.

Rousseau, writing a century later, held an exactly opposite view. He shared Hobbes's belief in man's natural timidity. But he drew totally different conclusions about it. Far from believing that in a state of nature humans were certain to fight each other for their own safety or to acquire the assets controlled by others, he held that, on the contrary, their natural tendency was to flee. Individuals could have no interest in conquest or war, since this would restrict rather than enlarge their own potential happiness. It was only when they entered into society that they engaged in war: man "only becomes a soldier after he has become a citizen". Though there were conflicts between individuals these were only transitory and never had the lasting form taken by warfare between states. It is not therefore, in his view, the nature of humans that causes war but the nature of states.

David Hume held a different view again. He rejected any broad generalisations about human nature. He held that most men were mixtures: of "ambition, avarice, self-love, vanity, friendship, generosity and public spirit". These contradictory qualities, "mixed in various degree", were to be found everywhere. Nor was there much difference between peoples of different races and countries. Within societies, because of the conflicts that took place and because generally people were not wise enough to recognise that they had a mutual interest in preserving a just order, they had created laws to restrain each other, and magistrates to enforce them, for their mutual advantage. Between societies, too, the law of nations had been established to regulate their conduct towards each other. But states did not recognise the same obligations to observe these restraints as individuals within states. On the contrary, it was generally accepted – by "all politicians" and "most philosophers" – that those rules, and even the rules of justice, might sometimes be overridden and treaties violated if reasons of state demanded it. It was for this reason, Hume believed, that wars between states continued to occur.

Each of these writers, therefore, drew their conclusions about relations among states partly from their views about human nature. Hobbes believed that men were naturally timid and insecure. In seeking their own security against others, they were obliged to try to "master the persons of all men" until there existed "no other power great enough to endanger him"; a characteristic shared also by the states they formed. Rousseau believed that by nature men were peaceful and only fought "through force of habit and experience". But within organised states they were sometimes called on to fight for the artificial society into which they had been conscripted; and this led them into actions – the killing of fellow human-beings – which they would never otherwise have contemplated. Hume saw human nature as neutral in its effect. People were a mixture of qualities and defects who were able, in their own societies, to maintain a peaceful existence through the agency of various laws and institutions. But between states, though there were rules of a kind, they were frequently violated, bringing about a degree of disorder which would not be tolerated within individual nation states. While Hobbes attributes war to the nature of man, therefore, and Rousseau to the nature of states, Hume attributes it to the disordered character of the society of states, which has not yet established the kind of institutions and authorities which had succeeded in establishing peace within smaller societies.

*   *   *

Hobbes – Human Nature and Conflict*

"Nature hath made men so equal, in the faculties of the body and mind; as that though there be found one man sometimes manifestly stronger in body, or of quicker mind than another; yet when all is reckoned together, the difference between man and man is not so considerable as that one man can thereupon claim to himself any benefit, to which another may not pretend as well as he. For as to the strength of body, the weakest has strength enough to kill the strongest, either by secret machination, or by confederacy with others, that are in the same danger with himself.

"And as to the faculties of the mind, setting aside the arts grounded upon words, and especially that skill of proceeding upon general and infallible rules, called science; which very few have, and but in few things; as being not a native faculty, born with us; nor attained, as prudence, while we look after somewhat else, I find yet a greater equality amongst men than that of strength. For prudence is but experience; which equal time equally bestows on all men, in those things they equally apply themselves unto. That which may perhaps make such equality incredible is but a vain conceit of one's own wisdom, which almost all men think they have in a greater

* From Thomas Hobbes (1588–1679). English political philosopher. After studying classics, the physical sciences and geometry became increasingly interested in political theory. An ardent supporter of royal authority and opponent of parliamentary power. Best known for his *Leviathan* in which he suggested that, to safeguard their security, citizens of a state engaged themselves in an implied contract with the sovereign, in whom they vested absolute power to maintain order within the state and its defence from other states. Other writings include *The Elements of Law, Natural and Politic* (1640) and *De Cive* (1642). Quoted from *Leviathan* (1651).

degree than the vulgar; that is, than all men but themselves, and a few others, whom by fame, or for concurring with themselves, they approve. For such is the nature of men, that howsoever they may acknowledge many others to be more witty, or more eloquent, or more learned; yet they will hardly believe there be many so wise as themselves; for they see their own wit at hand and other men's at a distance. But this proveth rather that men are in that point equal than unequal. For there is not ordinarily a greater sign of the equal distribution of any thing than that every man is contented with his share.

"From this equality of ability ariseth equality of hope in the attaining of our ends. And therefore if any two men desire the same thing, which nevertheless they cannot both enjoy, they become enemies; and in the way to their end, which is principally their own conservation, and sometimes their delectation only, endeavour to destroy, or subdue one another. And from hence it comes to pass, that where an invader hath no more to fear, than another man's single power; if one plant, sow, build, or possess a convenient seat, others may probably be expected to come prepared with forces united, to dispossess, and deprive him, not only of the fruit of his labour, but also of his life, or liberty. And the invader again is in the like danger of another.

"And from this diffidence of one another, there is no way for any man to secure himself, so reasonable, as anticipation; that is, by force, or wiles, to master the persons of all men he can, so long, till he see no other power great enough to endanger him: and this is no more than his own conservation requireth, and is generally allowed. Also because there be some, that taking pleasure in contemplating their own power in the acts of conquest, which they pursue farther than their security requires; if others, that otherwise would be glad to be at ease within modest bounds, should not by invasion increase their power, they would not be able, long time, by standing only on their defence, to subsist. And by consequence, such augmentation of dominion over men being necessary to a man's conservation, it ought to be allowed him.

"Again, men have no pleasure, but on the contrary a great deal of grief, in keeping company, where there is no power able to over-awe them all. For every man looketh that his companion should value him, at the same rate he sets upon himself: and upon all signs of contempt, or undervaluing, naturally endeavours, as far as he dares, (which amongst them that have no common power to keep them in quiet, is far enough to make them destroy each other), to extort a greater value from his contemners, by damage; and from others, by the example.

"So that in the nature of man, we find three principal causes of quarrel. First, competition; secondly, diffidence; thirdly, glory.

"The first, maketh men invade for gain; the second, for safety; and the third, for reputation. The first use violence, to make themselves masters of other men's persons, wives, children, and cattle; the second, to defend them; the third, for trifles, as a word, a smile, a different opinion, and any other sign of undervalue, either direct in their persons, or by reflection in their kindred, their friends, their nation, their profession, or their name.

"Hereby it is manifest, that during the time men live without a common power to keep them all in awe, they are in that condition which is called war; and such a war, as is of every man, against every man. For WAR, consisteth not in battle only, or the act of fighting; but in a tract of time, wherein the will to contend by battle is sufficiently known: and therefore the notion of *time* is to be considered in the nature of war; as it is in the nature of weather. For as the nature of foul weather lieth not in a shower or two of rain; but in an inclination thereto of many days together: so the nature of war consisteth not in actual fighting; but in the known disposition thereto, during all the time there is no assurance to the contrary. All other time is PEACE.

"Whatsoever therefore is consequent to a time of war, where every man is enemy to every man; the same is consequent to the time, wherein men live without other security, than what their own strength and their own invention shall furnish them withal. In such condition, there is no place for industry; because the fruit thereof is uncertain: and consequently no culture of the earth; no navigation, nor use of the commodities that may be imported by sea; no commodious building; no instruments of moving, and removing, such things as require much force; no knowledge of the face of the earth; no account of time; no arts; no letters; no society; and which is worst of all, continual fear and danger of violent death; and the life of man, solitary, poor, nasty, brutish and short.

"It may seem strange to some man, that has not well weighed these things; that nature should thus dissociate, and render men apt to invade, and destroy one another: and he may therefore, not trusting to this inference, made from the passions, desire perhaps to have the same confirmed by experience. Let him therefore consider with himself, when taking a journey, he arms himself, and seeks to go well accompanied; when going to sleep, he locks his doors; when even in his house he locks his chests; and this when he knows there be laws, and public officers, armed, to revenge all injuries shall be done him; what opinion he has of his fellow-subjects, when he rides armed; of his fellow citizens, when he locks his doors; and of his children, and servants, when he locks his chests. Does he not there as much accuse mankind by his actions, as I do by my words? But neither of us accuse man's nature in it. The desires, and other passions of man, are in themselves no sin. No more are the actions, that proceed from those passions, till they know a law that forbids them: which till laws be made they cannot know: nor can any law be made, till they have agreed upon the person that shall make it.

"It may peradventure be thought, there was never such a time, nor condition of war as this; and I believe it was never generally so, over all the world: but there are many places, where they live so now. For the savage people in many places of America, except the government of small families, the concord whereof dependeth on natural lust, have no government at all; and live at this day in that brutish manner, as I said before. Howsoever, it may be perceived what manner of life there would be, where there were no common power to fear, by the manner of life, which men that have formerly lived under a peaceful government, use to degenerate into, in a civil war.

"But though there had never been any time, wherein particular men were in a condition of war one against another; yet in all times, kings, and persons of sovereign authority, because of their independency, are in continual jealousies, and in the state and posture of gladiators; having their weapons pointing, and their eyes fixed on one another; that is, their forts, garrisons, and guns upon the frontiers of their kingdoms; and continual spies upon their neighbours; which is a posture of war. But because they uphold thereby, the industry of their subjects; there does not follow from it, that misery, which accompanies the liberty of particular men.

"To this war of every man, against every man, this also is consequent; that nothing can be unjust. The notions of right and wrong, justice and injustice have there no place. Where there is no common power, there is no law: where no law, no injustice. Force, and fraud, are in war the two cardinal virtues. Justice and injustice are none of the faculties neither of the body nor mind. If they were, they might be in a man that were alone in the world, as well as his senses and passions. They are qualities, that relate to men in society, not in solitude. It is consequent also to the same condition, that there be no propriety, no dominion, no *mine* and *thine* distinct; but only that to be every man's, that he can get: and for so long as he can keep it. And thus much for the ill condition, which man by mere nature is actually placed in; though with a possibility to come out of it, consisting partly in the passions, partly in his reason."

Rousseau – Human Nature and War*

"But even if it were true that this boundless and uncontrollable greed had developed in all men to the extent which our sophist imagines, it still would not produce that state of universal war between everyone which Hobbes dares to depict in all its repulsiveness. The frantic desire to possess everything is incompatible with the desire to destroy all one's fellow men; and the conqueror who had the misfortune to remain alone in the world, having killed everyone else, would not thereby enjoy anything for the very reason that he would possess all. What are riches themselves good for if not to be imparted to others? What would be the use of possessing the whole universe, if he was its sole inhabitant? What! Would his stomach devour all the fruits of the earth? Who would gather the produce of the world's climates for him? Who would witness his empire in the vast solitudes where he did not live? What would he do with his treasures? Who would eat his food? For whose eyes would he display his power? I see. Instead of massacring everyone, he would put them all in irons, so that at least he would have slaves. This immediately changes the whole nature of the question; since it is no longer a question of destroying, the state of war is abolished. The reader may here suspend judgement. I shall not omit to discuss this point.

* From Jean-Jacques Rousseau (1712–78). Born in Geneva, he travelled later to Savoy and France, where he won fame for a prize-winning essay, *Discours sur les sciences et les arts* (1750). He believed that in complex, highly organised political systems humans lost their liberty and he therefore advocated the creation of small, simple societies in which the citizens would be "forced to be free" by voluntarily submitting to the general will. Put forward these ideas above all in *The Social Contract* (1762). His other works include a novel, *La Nouvelle Heloïse* (1761) and *Emile* (1762) in which he put forward his ideas about education. (See also the final extract of Chapter 11.) Quoted from *The State of War*, trs. M. G. Forsyth, in M. G. Forsyth, H. M. A. Keens-Soper and P. Savigen, *The Theory of International Relations* (London: George Allen and Unwin, 1970).

"Man is naturally peaceful and timid; at the least danger, his first action is to flee; he only fights through the force of habit and experience. Honour, interest, prejudices, vengeance, all those passions which make him brave danger and death, are remote from him in the state of nature. It is only when he has entered into society with other men that he decides to attack another, and he only becomes a soldier after he has become a citizen. There are no strong natural dispositions to make war on all one's fellow men. But I am lingering too long over a system both revolting and absurd, which has already been refuted a hundred times.

"There is then no general war between men; and the human species has not been created solely in order to engage in mutual destruction. It remains to consider war of an accidental and exceptional nature which can arise between two or more individuals.

"If natural law were inscribed solely in human reason, it would scarcely be capable of guiding the bulk of our actions. But it is also indelibly engraved in the human heart; and it is there that it speaks to man more powerfully than all the precepts of philosophers; it is there that it tells him that he is not permitted to sacrifice the life of his fellow man except in order to preserve his own, and it is there that it gives him a horror of killing in cold blood, even when he is obliged to do so.

"I can conceive that in the unarbitrated quarrels which can arise in the state of nature, a man whose anger has been roused can sometimes kill another, either by open force or by surprise. But if a real war were to take place, imagine the strange position which this same man would have to be in if he could only preserve his life at the expense of that of another, and if an established relationship between them required that one died so that the other could live. War is a permanent state which presupposes constant relations; and these relations are a rare occurrence between men, for between individuals there is a continual flux which constantly changes relationships and interests. Thus a matter of dispute rises and disappears almost at the same moment; a quarrel begins and ends within a day; and one can have fights and murders, but never, or very rarely, long enmities and wars.

• • •

"It may still be asked whether Kings, who are in fact independent of all human power, can establish personal and private wars between themselves, separate from those of the State. This is surely a trifling question; for as one knows it is not the custom of Princes to spare others in order to expose themselves personally. Moreover, this question depends on another which it is not incumbent upon me to decide; that is whether the Prince is himself subject to the State's laws or not; for if he is subject to them, his person is bound and his life belongs to the State, like that of the lowest citizen. But if the Prince is above the laws, he lives in the pure state of nature and is accountable neither to his subjects nor to anyone for any of his actions.

The Social State

"We now enter a new order of things. We are about to see men, united in artificial harmony, band together to cut each other's throats, and to see all the horrors of war arise from the very efforts which have been taken to prevent them. But first it is crucial to formulate a more exact idea of the essence of the body politic than has been done so far. The reader must realise that it is here less a question of history and facts than of right and justice, and that I wish to examine things according to their nature rather than according to our prejudices.

"As soon as the first society is formed the formation of all the others necessarily follows. One has either to join it or to unite to resist it; to imitate it or let oneself be swallowed up by it. Thus the whole face of the earth is changed; everywhere nature has disappeared; everywhere human artifice takes its place; independence and natural liberty give way to laws and slavery; free beings no longer exist; the philosopher searches for man and no longer finds him. But it is fruitless to expect the annihilation of nature; it springs to life again and reveals itself where one least expects it. The independence which is removed from men takes refuge in societies; and these great bodies, left to their own impulses, produce collisions which grow more terrible the more their weight takes a precedence over that of individuals."

Hume – Human Nature and the Relations of States*

"It is universally acknowledged that there is a great uniformity among the actions of men, in all nations and ages, and that human

* From David Hume (1711–66). British philosopher. Believed that philosophy

nature remains still the same in its principles and operations. The same motives always produce the same actions: the same events follow from the same causes. Ambition, avarice, self-love, vanity, friendship, generosity, public spirit; these passions, mixed in various degrees and distributed through society, have been, from the beginning of the world, and still are, the source of all the actions and enterprises, which have ever been observed among mankind. Would you know the sentiments, inclinations, and course of life of the Greeks and Romans? Study well the temper and actions of the French and English: you cannot be much mistaken in transferring to the former *most* of the observations, which you have made with regard to the latter. Mankind are so much the same, in all times and places, that history informs us of nothing new or strange in this particular. Its chief use is only to discover the constant and universal principles of human nature, by shewing men in all varieties of circumstances and situations, and furnishing us with materials, from which we may form our observations, and become acquainted with the regular springs of human action and behaviour. These records of wars, intrigues, factions and revolutions are so many collections of experiments, by which the politician or moral philosopher fixes the principles of his science; in the same manner as the physician or natural philosopher becomes acquainted with the nature of plants, minerals and other external objects, by the experiments which he forms concerning them. Nor are the earth, water and other elements, examined by Aristotle and Hippocrates, more like to those, which at present lie under our observation, than the men, described by Polybius and Tacitus, are to those who now govern the world.

"Should a traveller, returning from a far country, bring us an account of men, wholly different from any with whom we were ever acquainted; men, who were entirely divested of avarice, ambition or revenge; who knew no pleasure but friendship, generosity and public spirit; we should immediately, from these circumstances, detect the falsehood, and prove him a liar with the same certainty as if he had stuffed his narration with stories of centaurs and dragons, miracles and prodigies. . . . So readily and universally do we acknowledge a

should be concerned above all with the inductive study of human nature. He demonstrated this view in his *Treatise on Human Nature* (1739–40) and his *Enquiry Concerning Human Understanding* (1748). Also wrote widely on other subjects, including a history of England and many essays on political and other themes. (See also a further extract on pp. 386–9.) Quoted from *Concerning Human Understanding* (1739–40) and *Concerning the Principles of Morals* (1748).

uniformity in human motives and actions as well as in the operations of body.

      •   •   •

"Had every man sufficient *sagacity* to perceive, at all times, the strong interest, which binds him to the observance of justice and equity, and *strength of mind* sufficient to persevere in a steady adherence to a general and a distant interest, in opposition to the allurements of present pleasure and advantage; there had never, in that case, been any such thing as government or political society, but each man, following his natural liberty, had lived in entire peace and harmony with all others. What need of positive law where natural justice is, itself, a sufficient restraint? Why create magistrates, where there never arises any disorder or iniquity? Why abridge our native freedom, when, in every instance, the utmost exertion of it is found innocent and beneficial? It is evident that, if government were totally useless, it never could have place, and that the SOLE foundation of the duty of ALLEGIANCE is the *advantage* which it procures to society by preserving peace and order among mankind.

"When a number of political societies are erected, and maintain a great intercourse together, a new set of rules are immediately discovered to be *useful* in that particular situation; and accordingly take place under the title of LAWS of NATIONS. Of this kind are the sacredness of the person of ambassadors, abstaining from poisoned arms, quarter in war, with others of that kind which are plainly calculated for the *advantage* of states and kingdoms in their intercourse with each other.

"The rules of justice, such as prevail among individuals, are not entirely suspended among political societies. All princes pretend a regard to the rights of other princes; and some, no doubt, without hypocrisy. Alliances and treaties are every day made between independent states, which would only be so much waste of parchment, if they were not found, by experience, to have *some* influence and authority. But here is the difference between kingdoms and individuals. Human nature cannot, by any means, subsist without the association of individuals; and that association never could have place, were no regard paid to the laws of equity and justice. Disorder, confusion, the war of all against all are the necessary consequences of such a licentious conduct. But nations can subsist without intercourse. They may even subsist, in some degree, under a general war. The observance of justice, though useful among them, is not guarded by so strong a necessity as among individuals; and the *moral obligation* holds proportion with the *usefulness*. All politicians will allow, and most philosophers, that REASONS of STATE may, in particular emergencies, dispense with the rules of justice and invalidate any treaty or alliance, where the strict observance of it would be prejudicial, in a considerable degree, to either of the contracting parties. But nothing less than the most extreme necessity, it is confessed, can justify individuals in a breach of promise, or an invasion of the properties of others."

5 The Citizen as a Restraint on War

Rousseau's belief, increasingly widely shared, that most humans naturally wanted peace and that it was only governments which desired war, led to an obvious conclusion: the greater the influence which ordinary people could secure over their governments – in other words, the more "democratic" governments became – the more likely it was that peace would be secured.

Those who believed, usually for quite other reasons, in the need for a more democratic system of government inevitably also argued that states established on this basis would be less likely to make war against each other. For only in such states, they held, would the desire of ordinary people for peace be expressed in government policy. The Anglo-American radical, Tom Paine, put this point of view in his book, *The Rights of Man*. In denouncing the political systems of his day he sought to show that war comes about because existing governments had an interest, often a direct financial interest, in war, even though their peoples suffered from it. Only the creation of more representative governments all over the world, therefore, reflecting the peaceful intentions of their citizens, was likely to abolish warfare from the earth.

Writing fifty years later, of a state that had implemented for a time, at least partially, Tom Paine's beliefs, de Tocqueville was not so much an advocate of democracy as an observer of it. But he too, in his *Democracy in America*, took the view that countries that were more democratic, where there was a more equal condition among their citizens, would be less inclined to war. Yet, paradoxically, their armies might be more warlike. Because rank would not depend on birth or status, there would be a greater desire for promotion, which was usually the only route towards advancement in such a society. But promotion would be slow except in conditions of war. The result was that, though democratic nations were "naturally prone to peace from their interests and propensities", they were "constantly drawn to war and revolution by their armies".

Cobden, the English radical politician, writing at about the same time as de Tocqueville but from a far more committed viewpoint, also believed that states with parliamentary constitutions and more representative governments were less likely to engage in warfare. In his own day, he declared, the principal threat of war came from the "despotic" states of the north of the continent, Russia, Austria and Prussia, where there were no parliamentary systems. War was less likely to come from those states having more representative institutions, such as England, France or the US, "where, even if governments were to desire war, the people would put a check upon it". This view, in other words, like Paine's, reflected a striking faith (not always justified by subsequent events), in the ability of citizens, through parliamentary institutions, to prevent their governments from making war.

In an age when most governments were undemocratic and warfare common, it was understandable that some sought to establish a correlation between the two facts. Wars resulted, such observers believed, from the decisions of unrepresentative oligarchies who might themselves benefit from war but paid little of the price for it. If the ordinary citizens acquired more effective control of their governments, wars were likely to cease. But such a view depended on the assumption that the ordinary citizen did not desire war. That was an assumption that was not self-evident. And it was to be increasingly subject to challenge in the age to come.

* * *

Paine – Wars are Made by Governments, not Peoples*

"It is attributed to Henry the Fourth of France, a man of enlarged and benevolent heart, that he proposed, about the year 1610, a plan for abolishing war in Europe: the plan consisted in constituting an European Congress, or as the French authors stile it, a Pacific

---

* From Tom Paine (1737–1809). English-American political writer. A passionate believer in republicanism and a supporter of the American cause in the American War of Independence. Author of a number of tracts on political themes. *The Rights of Man* was written as a direct response to Burke's *Letters on a Regicide Peace* (see pp. 175–80), which had denounced the French Revolution and advocated intervention against it. Quoted from *The Rights of Man*, 1791 (London: Dent, 1915).

Republic, by appointing delegates from the several Nations who were to act as a Court of Arbitration in any disputes that might arise between Nation and Nation.

"Had such a plan been adopted at the time it was proposed, the taxes of England and France, as two of the parties, would have been at least ten millions sterling annually to each nation less than they were at the commencement of the French Revolution.

"To conceive a cause why such a plan has not been adopted (and that instead of a Congress for the purpose of *preventing* war, it has been called only to *terminate* a war, after a fruitless expense of several years), it will be necessary to consider the interest of Governments as a distinct interest to that of Nations.

"Whatever is the cause of taxes to a Nation, becomes also the means of revenue to a Government. Every war terminates with an addition of taxes, and consequently with an addition of revenue; and in any event of war, in the manner they are now commenced and concluded, the power and interest of Governments are increased. War, therefore, from its productiveness, as it easily furnishes the pretence of necessity for taxes and appointments to places and offices, becomes a principal part of the system of old Governments; and to establish any mode to abolish war, however advantageous it might be to Nations, would be to take from such Government the most lucrative of its branches. The frivolous matters upon which war is made shew the disposition and avidity of Governments to uphold the system of war, and betray the motives upon which they act.

"Why are not Republics plunged into war, but because the nature of their Government does not admit of an interest distinct from that of the Nation? Even Holland, though an ill-constructed Republic, and with a commerce extending over the world, existed nearly a century without war; and the instant the form of Government was changed in France the republican principles of peace and domestic prosperity and economy arose with the new Government; and the same consequences would follow the same causes in other Nations.

"As war is the system of Government on the old construction, the animosity which Nations reciprocally entertain is nothing more than what the policy of their Governments excites to keep up the spirit of the system. Each Government accuses the other of perfidy, intrigue and ambition, as a means of heating the imagination of their respective Nations and incensing them to hostilities. Man is not the enemy of Man, but through the medium of a false system of Government. Instead, therefore, of exclaiming against the ambition of Kings, the exclamation should be directed against the principle of such Governments; and instead of seeking to reform the individual, the wisdom of a Nation should apply itself to reform the system.

"Whether the forms and maxims of Governments which are still in practice were adapted to the condition of the world at the period they were established is not in this case the question. The older they are the less correspondence can they have with the present state of things.

"Time, and change of circumstances and opinions, have the same progressive effect in rendering modes of Government obsolete as they have upon customs and manners. Agriculture, commerce, manufactures and the tranquil arts, by which the prosperity of Nations is best promoted, require a different system of Government, and a different species of knowledge to direct its operations, than what might have been required in the former condition of the world.

"As it is not difficult to perceive, from the enlightened state of mankind, that hereditary Governments are verging to their decline, and that Revolutions on the broad basis of national sovereignty and Government by representation are making their way in Europe, it would be an act of wisdom to anticipate their approach, and produce Revolutions by reason and accommodation, rather than commit them to the issue of convulsions.

"From what we now see, nothing of reform in the political world ought to be held improbable. It is an age of Revolutions, in which everything may be looked for.

"The intrigue of Courts, by which the system of war is kept up, may provoke a confederation of Nations to abolish it; and an European Congress to patronise the progress of free Government, and promote the civilisation of Nations with each other, is an event nearer in probability than once were the Revolutions and Alliance of France and America."

de Tocqueville – Citizens Love Peace but Soldiers Love War*

"The same interests, the same fears, the same passions which deter democratic nations from revolutions, deter them also from war; the

* From Alexis de Tocqueville (1805–59). French political writer, best known for his wide-ranging analysis of the US political system *Democracy in America*

spirit of military glory and the spirit of revolution are weakened at the same time and by the same causes. The ever-increasing numbers of men of property – lovers of peace, the growth of personal wealth which war so rapidly consumes, the mildness of manners, the gentleness of heart, those tendencies to pity which are engendered by the equality of conditions, that coolness of understanding which renders men comparatively insensible to the violent and poetical excitement of arms – all these causes concur to quench the military spirit. I think it may be admitted as a general and constant rule that, among civilised nations, the warlike passions will become more rare and less intense in proportion as social conditions shall be more equal. War is nevertheless an occurrence to which all nations are subject, democratic nations as well as others. Whatever taste they may have for peace, they must hold themselves in readiness to repel aggression, or, in other words, they must have an army.

"Fortune, which has conferred so many peculiar benefits upon the inhabitants of the United States, has placed them in the midst of a wilderness, where they have, so to speak, no neighbours: a few thousand soldiers are sufficient for their wants; but this is peculiar to America, not to democracy. The equality of conditions, and the manners as well as the institutions resulting from it, do not exempt a democratic people from the necessity of standing armies, and their armies always exercise a powerful influence over their fate. It is therefore of singular importance to inquire what are the natural propensities of the men of whom these armies are composed.

"Among aristocratic nations, especially among those in which birth is the only source of rank, the same inequality exists in the army as in the nation; the officer is noble, the soldier is a serf; the one is naturally called upon to command, the other to obey. In aristocratic armies, the private soldier's ambition is therefore circumscribed within very narrow limits. Nor has the ambition of the officer an unlimited range. An aristocratic body not only forms a part of the scale of ranks in the nation, but it contains a scale of ranks within itself: the members of whom it is composed are placed one above

(1835–40), based on extensive travel in the United States. Soon after writing this he entered French politics as an independent deputy and was frequently critical of government policy during the July Monarchy. After the 1848 revolution, he was briefly Minister of Foreign Affairs but withdrew from public life after Napoleon III's coup in 1851. In 1856 published the first volume of his much-admired *The Ancien Regime and the Revolution*, which he was still engaged in writing on his death in 1859. Quoted from *Democracy in America*, 1840, trs. Henry Reeve (London: Longmans, 1889).

another, in a particular and unvarying manner. Thus one man is born to the command of a regiment, another to that of a company; when once they have reached the utmost object of their hopes, they stop of their own accord, and remain contented with their lot. There is, besides, a strong cause, which, in aristocracies, weakens the officer's desire of promotion. Among aristocratic nations, an officer, independently of his rank in the army, also occupies an elevated rank in society; the former is almost always in his eyes only an appendage to the latter. A nobleman who embraces the profession of arms follows it less from motives of ambition than from a sense of the duties imposed on him by his birth. He enters the army in order to find an honourable employment for the idle years of his youth, and to be able to bring back to his home and his peers some honourable recollections of military life; but his principal object is not to obtain by that profession either property, distinction, or power, for he possesses these advantages in his own right, and enjoys them without leaving his home.

"In democratic armies all the soldiers may become officers, which makes the desire of promotion general, and immeasurably extends the bounds of military ambition. The officer, on his part, sees nothing which naturally and necessarily stops him at one grade more than at another; and each grade has immense importance in his eyes, because his rank in society almost always depends on his rank in the army. . . . In democratic armies the desire of advancement is almost universal: it is ardent, tenacious, perpetual; it is strengthened by all other desires, and only extinguished with life itself.

"But it is easy to see that, of all armies in the world, those in which advancement must be slowest in time of peace are the armies of democratic countries. As the number of commissions is naturally limited, while the number of competitors is almost unlimited, and as the strict law of equality is over all alike, none can make rapid progress – many can make no progress at all. Thus the desire of advancement is greater, and the opportunities of advancement fewer, there than elsewhere. All the ambitious spirits of a democratic army are consequently ardently desirous of war, because war makes vacancies, and warrants the violation of that law of seniority which is the sole privilege natural to democracy.

"We thus arrive at this singular consequence, that of all armies those most ardently desirous of war are democratic armies, and of all nations those most fond of peace are democratic nations: and, what makes these facts still more extraordinary, is that these contrary effects are produced at the same time by the principle of equality.

"All the members of the community, being alike, constantly harbour the wish, and discover the possibility, of changing their condition and improving their welfare: this makes them fond of peace, which is favourable to industry, and allows every man to pursue his own little undertakings to their completion. On the other hand, this same equality makes soldiers dream of fields of battle, by increasing the value of military honours in the eyes of those who follow the profession of arms, and by rendering those honours accessible to all. In either case the inquietude of the heart is the same, the taste for enjoyment as insatiable, the ambition of success as great – the means of gratifying it are alone different.

• • •

"It may, therefore, be asserted, generally speaking, that if democratic nations are naturally prone to peace from their interests and their propensities, they are constantly drawn to war and revolutions by their armies. Military revolutions, which are scarcely ever to be apprehended in aristocracies, are always to be dreaded among democratic nations. These perils must be reckoned among the most formidable which beset their future fate, and the attention of statesmen should be sedulously applied to find a remedy for the evil.

"When a nation perceives that it is inwardly affected by the restless ambition of its army, the first thought which occurs is to give this inconvenient ambition an object by going to war. I speak no ill of war: war almost always enlarges the mind of a people, and raises their character. In some cases it is the only check to the excessive growth of certain propensities which naturally spring out of the equality of conditions, and it must be considered as a necessary corrective to certain inveterate diseases to which democratic communities are liable. War has great advantages, but we must not flatter ourselves that it can diminish the danger I have just pointed out. That peril is only suspended by it, to return more fiercely when the war is over; for armies are much more impatient of peace after having tasted military exploits. War could only be a remedy for a people which should always be athirst for military glory. I foresee that all the military rulers who may rise up in great democratic nations will find it easier to conquer with their armies than to make their armies live at peace after conquest. There are two things which a democratic people will always find very difficult – to begin a war, and to end it."

Cobden – War Will Be Prevented by Giving Citizens the Vote*

"I am anxious to see this extension of the suffrage accelerated in every possible way: and I think I have always given every possible evidence of my sincerity by direct votes in the House of Commons, and outside the House by urging men to qualify themselves, and use every means to get a vote. I do it, because I believe the extension of the franchise gives us a better guarantee not only for the safety of our institutions, but for the just administration of our public affairs; and I have latterly felt another motive for wishing for an extension of the franchise, in what I have seen going on upon the Continent within the last eighteen months, which has convinced me that the great masses of mankind are disposed for peace between nations. You have the fact brought out in strong relief that the people themselves, however they may be troubled with internal convulsions, have no desire to go abroad and molest their neighbours. You have seen Louis Philippe driven from the throne. We were told that he kept the French nation at peace; but we find the masses of the people of France only anxious to remain at home, and diminish, if possible, the pressure of taxation.

"Where do we look for the black gathering cloud of war? Where do we see it rising? Why, from the despotism of the North, where one man wields the destinies of 40,000,000 of serfs. If we want to know where is the second danger of war and disturbance, it is in that province of Russia – that miserable and degraded country, Austria – next in the stage of despotism and barbarism, and there you see again the greatest danger of war; but in proportion as you find the population governing themselves – as in England, in France, or in America – there you will find that war is not the disposition of the people, and that if Government desire it, the people would put a check upon it. Therefore, for the security of liberty, and also, as I believe, that the

---

* From Richard Cobden (1804–65). English radical politician and free-trader. Principal organiser, with John Bright (see p. 443) of the Anti-Corn Law League, which campaigned for the abolition of the corn laws and a liberalisation of trade. Entered Parliament in 1847 and became the president of the Board of Trade under his old opponent, Palmerston. Had the satisfaction of negotiating the so-called Cobden treaty with France in 1860, providing for a substantial abolition of tariffs between the two countries and the establishment of the most-favoured nation principle. Quoted from his speech to the House of Commons, 18 December 1849.

people of every country, as they acquire political power, will cultivate the arts of peace, and check the desire of their governments to go to war – it is on these grounds that I wish to see a wide extension of the suffrage, and liberty prevail over despotism throughout the world."

6 The Citizen as a Stimulus to War

The view that the more ordinary people could control the actions of states the more peaceful they would become was not self-evident. For it was not certain that ordinary people were always peacefully inclined. Even a state having parliamentary institutions might be aggressive in its conduct if its peoples were inspired by strongly nationalistic sentiments.

During the nineteenth century the ideas put forward about relations among states began to reflect the rapid growth in national consciousness and nationalist rivalry. Some saw national sentiment as the essential ingredient of statehood. Others held that such sentiment would justify peoples having a common linguistic, ethnic, historical or cultural identity in establishing national states, even if this required acts of force to liberate them from the existing multi-national empires. Others again believed that increasingly powerful national feeling within states would, and would legitimately, be expressed in warfare against *other* states.

The three passages below exemplify each of these beliefs. Fichte was a teacher of philosophy at the University of Jena. In his *Addresses to the German Nation*, written at the time of the challenge to Germany's nationhood posed by the Napoleonic conquests, he set out the conditions under which a nation might become a state, and a people fulfil its national destiny. The spirit which might achieve this was not the peaceful citizen's love for the constitution and laws but "the devouring flame of higher patriotism . . . for which the noble-minded man joyfully sacrificed himself". So the German peoples in ancient times had resisted the attempts of the Romans to secure world dominion, despite all the blessings which Roman civilisation had to offer them, just as they were in Fichte's day resisting the attempts of Napoleon to secure a similar dominion. They had done so because they took it as a matter of course that they would rather live and remain true Germans than submit to becoming "half Roman".

Less than twenty years later Mazzini, the acknowledged intellectual leader of the Italian *risorgimento*, issued a similar challenge. He called on young Italy to "enter upon an irrevocable and irreconcilable war with the principle governing all the actual governments of

Europe". It was necessary now to reconstruct the map of Europe so that the boundaries of states corresponded more closely with those of nations. Revolution was necessary for this purpose and revolutions "are only to be ratified at the bayonet point". War was thus accepted by Mazzini as the necessary instrument of national liberation, and the means of securing justice among states. It was justified by the imperative of nationalism.

Some writers of the age found another reason to justify the continued prevalence of war: it brought important human advances which could not be secured in any other way. The practice of war promoted the development of courage, intelligence and ingenuity. It promoted technological advance and large-scale industrialisation. It brought increased social solidarity and the development of more large-scale societies (still seen – in that age – as a form of progress). It encouraged the division of labour, the "habit of subordination" and discipline, and a strong government. These are some of the claims for war made by the Social Darwinists, as in the passage quoted below from Herbert Spencer's *The Study of Sociology*. There was also, it is true (as in this passage), a recognition that not all its effects were favourable. War promoted aggressiveness and repressed human sympathies and fellow-feeling. The citizen, "made callous by the killing and wounding of enemies, inevitably brings his callousness home with him". Giving pain to others, which became a habit during war, might remain a habit during peace. Social Darwinists, therefore, who found an evolutionary purpose in warfare among states, were at least willing to recognise that the progress it might bring to humanity was to be had only at a price.

Throughout this age, therefore, the prevailing nationalist sentiment produced a new vision of the nature of mankind and the duty of individuals towards each other. These writers, like those quoted in the preceding section, saw man above all as a citizen; but not, as they had, as the peace-loving citizen urging his government to restraint, but as the patriotic citizen urging it to war. The supreme aim to which citizens should devote themselves was the national destiny. That destiny could be achieved only in competition with other states, and often only through war. War was not therefore a disagreeable burden imposed on the individual by tyrannical governments. It could often be the instrument willingly adopted for securing one of man's highest aspirations: the creation of a national state.

*   *   *

Fichte – Love of Fatherland Entails a Willingness to Fight for It*

" . . . [I]t must be love of fatherland that governs the state by placing before it a higher object than the usual one of maintaining internal peace, property, personal freedom, and the life and well-being of all. For this higher object alone, and with no other intention, does the state assemble an armed force. When the question arises of making use of this, when the call comes to stake everything that the state, in the narrow conception of the word, sets before itself as object, viz., property, personal freedom, life and well-being, nay, even the continued existence of the state itself; when the call comes to make an original decision with responsibility to God alone, and without a clear and reasonable idea that what is intended will surely be attained – for this is never possible in such matters – then, and then only, does there live at the helm of the state a truly original and primary life, and at this point, and not before, the true sovereign rights of government enter, like God, to hazard the lower life for the sake of the higher. In the maintenance of the traditional constitution, the laws and civil prosperity there is absolutely no real true life and no original decision. Conditions and circumstances, and legislators perhaps long since dead, have created these things; succeeding ages go on faithfully in the paths marked out, and so in fact they have no public life of their own; they merely repeat a life that once existed. In such times there is no need of any real government. But when this regular course is endangered, and it is a question of making decisions in new and unprecedented cases, then there is need of a life that lives of itself. What spirit is it that in such cases may place itself at the helm, that can make its own decisions with sureness and certainty, untroubled by any hesitation? What spirit has an undisputed right to summon and to order everyone concerned, whether he himself be willing or not, and to compel anyone who resists, to risk everything including his life? Not the spirit of the peaceful citizen's love for the constitution and the laws, but the devouring flame of higher patriotism,

---

* From J. G. Fichte (1762–1814). Influenced in his youth by Kant, became a teacher of philosophy and author of many philosophical works. Having lost his post of professor of philosophy at Jena he moved to Berlin but was driven from there in 1806 by Napoleon's victory against Prussia. Became increasingly interested in Germany's national struggle and in 1807 delivered the famous *Addresses to the German Nation*. Six years later, when Prussia became engaged in war against Napoleon, he lectured on the *Idea of a True War*. Quoted from *Addresses to the German Nation* (1807–8), trs. R. F. Jones and G. H. Turnbull (New York: Harper and Row, 1968).

which embraces the nation as the vesture of the eternal, for which the noble-minded man joyfully sacrifices himself, and the ignoble man, who only exists for the sake of the other, must likewise sacrifice himself. It is not that love of the citizen for the constitution; that love is quite unable to achieve this, so long as it remains on the level of the understanding. Whatever turns events may take, since it pays to govern they will always have a ruler over them. Suppose the new ruler even wants to introduce slavery (and what is slavery if not the disregard for, and suppression of, the characteristic of an original people? – but to that way of thinking such qualities do not exist), suppose he wants to introduce slavery. Then, since it is profitable to preserve the life of slaves, to maintain their numbers and even their well-being, slavery under him will turn out to be bearable if he is anything of a calculator. Their life and their keep, at any rate, they will always find. Then what is there left that they should fight for? After those two things it is peace which they value more than anything. But peace will only be disturbed by the continuance of the struggle. They will, therefore, do anything just to put an end to the fighting, and the sooner the better; they will submit, they will yield; and why should they not? All they have ever been concerned about, and all they have ever hoped from life, has been the continuation of the habit of existing under tolerable conditions. The promise of a life here on earth extending beyond the period of life here on earth – that alone it is which can inspire men even unto death for the fatherland.

• • •

"In this belief our earliest common forefathers, the original stock of the new culture, the Germans, as the Romans called them, bravely resisted the on-coming world dominion of the Romans.[1] Did they not have before their eyes the greater brilliance of the Roman provinces next to them and the more refined enjoyments in those provinces, to say nothing of laws and judges' seats and lictors' axes and rods in superfluity? Were not the Romans willing enough to let them share in all these blessings? In the case of several of their own princes, who did no more than intimate that war against such benefactors of mankind was rebellion, did they not experience proofs of the be-lauded Roman clemency? To those who submitted the Romans gave marks of distinction in the form of kingly titles, high commands in their armies, and Roman fillets; and if they were driven out by their countrymen, did not the Romans provide for them a place of refuge and a means of subsistence in their colonies? Had they no appreciation of the advantages of Roman civilisation, e.g., of the superior organisation of their armies, in which even an Arminius did not disdain to learn the trade of war? They cannot be charged with ignorance or lack of consideration of any one of these things. Their descendants, as soon as they could do so without losing their freedom, even assimilated Roman culture, so far as this was possible without losing their individuality. Why, then, did they fight for several generations in bloody wars, that broke out again and again with ever-renewed force? A Roman writer puts the following expression into the mouth of their leaders: 'What was left for them to do, except to maintain their freedom or else to die before they became slaves.'[2] Freedom to them meant just this: remaining Germans and continuing to settle their own affairs independently and in accordance with the original spirit of their race, going on with their development in accordance with the same spirit, and propagating this independence in their posterity. All those blessings which the Romans offered them meant slavery to them, because then they would have to become something that was not German, they would have to become half Roman. They assumed as a matter of course that every man would rather die than become half a Roman, and that a true German could only want to live in order to be, and to remain, just a German and to bring up his children as Germans.

"They did not all die; they did not see slavery; they bequeathed freedom to their children. It is their unyielding resistance which the whole modern world has to thank for being what it now is. Had the Romans succeeded in bringing them also under the yoke and in destroying them as a nation, which the Roman did in every case, the whole development of the human race would have taken a different course, a course that one cannot think would have been more satisfactory. It is they whom we must thank – we, the immediate heirs of their soil, their language and their way of thinking – for being Germans still, for being still borne along on the stream of original and independent life. It is they whom we must thank for everything that we have been as a nation since those days, and to them we shall be indebted for everything that we shall be in the future, unless things have come to an end with us now and the last drop of blood inherited from them has dried up in our veins. To them the other branches of the race, whom we now look upon as foreigners, but who by descent from them are our brothers, are indebted for their very existence. When our ancestors triumphed over Roma the eternal, not one of all these peoples was in existence, but the possibility of their existence in the future was won for them in the same fight.

"These men, and all others of like mind in the history of the world, won the victory because eternity inspired them, and this inspiration always does, and always must, defeat him who is not so inspired. It is neither the strong right arm nor the efficient weapon that wins victories, but only the power of the soul. He who sets a limit to his sacrifices, and has no wish to venture beyond a certain point, ceases to resist as soon as he finds himself in danger at this point, even though it be one which is vital to him and which ought not to be surrendered. He who sets no limit whatever for himself, but on the contrary stakes everything he has, including the most precious possession granted to dwellers here below, namely, life itself, never ceases to resist, and will undoubtedly win the victory over an opponent whose goal is more limited."

Notes
1. The parallel between the republican and imperial stages of Rome and France had become a commonplace. The Romans were also accounted by "Hellenizing" Germany as voluptuaries and bellicose thieves of a higher culture.
2. Fichte reread Tacitus prior to preparing the *Addresses*.

Mazzini – National Sentiment Gives the Right to Make War*

"While raising on high the banner of the people, we shall repose our best hopes in them. We shall teach them their rights. We shall oppose no barrier to their action, but endeavour to direct it for good; and use our every effort to promote a truly popular, national, guerrilla war, against which, when universal and determined, no enemy can long resist.

* From Guiseppe Mazzini (1805–72). Acknowledged intellectual leader of the Italian *risorgimento*. Born in Genoa, he joined the revolutionary *carbonari* in his youth and later founded the *Young Italy* organisation, devoted to securing the liberation of Italy by education and insurrection. From 1837, exiled from Piedmont and other European states, he settled in London where he lived most of the rest of his life. Wrote voluminously, mainly on the subject of nationalism and European federation. Organised successive revolts in the Italian states, took an active part in the 1848 revolution in Milan and Rome, but was distrusted by the new leaders of Italy after its unification and died as a fugitive, living under a false name in his own country. Quoted from *The Writers of Young Italy to their Countrymen* (1832), English trs. (London: Smith, Elder, 1864).

"Therefore we shall do everything in our power to destroy privilege, to teach the dogma of equality as a religion, and to fuse and confound the various existing classes into a great national unity."

"Therefore we shall not seek the alliance of kings, nor delude ourselves with any idea of maintaining our liberty by diplomatic arts or treaties: we shall not ask our salvation as an alms from the protocols of conferences, or promises of cabinets; for we well know that by arising in the name of the republic, we are entering upon an irrevocable and irreconcilable war with the principle dominating all the actual governments of Europe. . . . We know that revolutions are only to be ratified at the bayonet's point. We are of the people, and we will treat with the peoples. They will understand us.

• • •

"We have inscribed the device '*Young Italy*' upon our tricoloured banner, because it is in fact the banner of rising and regenerate Italy. . . ."

"If any should now ask of us whence we derive our mandate, we will answer in the words of men bound to us by the double bond of similarity of aim, and of misfortune.[1]

"We derive our mandate from the purity of our convictions, from the faith and moral force we feel within us, in thus constituting ourselves the defenders of the rights and liberties of the immense majority. Whosoever speaks in the name of the rights of man, derives his authority and mandate from the eternal rights of nature. . . .

"We will receive the confirmation of our mandate from those peoples who have done the most to harmonise the progress of their own country with that of humanity; who combine sanctity of principle and respect for the rights of man with the love they bear to their own country, and seek to regain her national existence by these means alone."

Note
1. Manifesto of the Polish Democratic Society, May 1832.

Spencer – War Secures the Survival of the Fittest*

"Warfare among men, like warfare among animals, has had a large share in raising their organisations to a higher stage. The following are some of the various ways in which it has worked.

"In the first place, it has had the effect of continually extirpating races which, for some reason or other, were least fitted to cope with the conditions of existence they were subject to. The killing-off of relatively feeble tribes, or tribes relatively wanting in endurance, or courage, or sagacity, or power of co-operation, must have tended ever to maintain, and occasionally to increase, the amounts of life-preserving powers possessed by men.

"Beyond this average advance caused by destruction of the least-developed races and the least-developed individuals, there has been an average advance caused by inheritance of those further developments due to functional activity. Remember the skill of the Indian in following a trail, and remember that under kindred stimuli many of his perceptions and feelings and bodily powers have been habitually taxed to the uttermost, and it becomes clear that the struggle for existence between neighbouring tribes has had an important effect in cultivating faculties of various kinds. Just as, to take an illustration from among ourselves, the skill of the police cultivates cunning among burglars, which, again, leading to further precautions generates further devices to evade them; so, by the unceasing antagonisms between human societies, small and large, there has been a mutual culture of an adapted intelligence, a mutual culture of certain traits of character not to be undervalued, and a mutual culture of bodily powers.

"A large effect, too, has been produced upon the development of the arts. In responding to the imperative demands of war, industry made important advances and gained much of its skill. Indeed, it may be questioned whether, in the absence of that exercise of manipulat-

---

* From Herbert Spencer (1820–1903). English writer on sociology. Strong advocate of individualism and *laissez-faire*, arguing that human progress depended on the maximum scope for individual inventiveness and self-assertion. Influenced by Darwin's idea on evolution, which he sought to apply to social progress. Asserted the need for scientific, rather than metaphysical, approach to social and historical questions. Principal works include: *The Principles of Psychology* (1855), *The Principles of Biology* (1864–7) and *The Principles of Sociology* (1876–96). Quoted from *The Study of Sociology* (London: Williams and Norgate, 1873).

ive faculty which the making of weapons originally gave, there would ever have been produced the tools required for developed industry. If we go back to the Stone Age, we see that implements of the chase and implements of war are those showing most labour and dexterity. If we take still-existing human races which were without metals when we found them, we see in their skilfully wrought stone clubs, as well as in their large war-canoes, that the needs of defence and attack were the chief stimuli to the cultivation of arts afterwards available for productive purposes. Passing over intermediate stages, we may note in comparatively recent stages the same relation. Observe a coat of mail, or one of the more highly-finished suits of armour – compare it with articles of iron and steel of the same date; and there is evidence that these desires to kill enemies and escape being killed, more extreme than any other, have had great effects on those arts of working in metal to which most other arts owe their progress. The like relation is shown us in the uses made of gunpowder. At first a destructive agent, it has become an agent of immense service in quarrying, mining, railway-making, &c.

"A no less important benefit bequeathed by war, has been the formation of large societies. By force alone were small nomadic hordes welded into large tribes; by force alone were large tribes welded into small nations; by force alone have small nations been welded into large nations. While the fighting of societies usually maintains separateness, or by conquest produces only temporary unions, it produces, from time to time, permanent unions; and as fast as there are formed permanent unions of small into large, and then of large into still larger, industrial progress is furthered in three ways. Hostilities, instead of being perpetual, are broken by intervals of peace. When they occur, hostilities do not so profoundly derange the industrial activities. And there arises the possibility of carrying out the division of labour much more effectually. War, in short, in the slow course of things, brings about a social aggregation which furthers that industrial state at variance with war; and yet nothing but war could bring about this social aggregation.

"These truths, that without war large aggregates of men cannot be formed, and that without large aggregates of men there cannot be a developed industrial state, are illustrated in all places and times among existing uncivilised and semi-civilised races, we everywhere find that union of small societies by a conquering society is a step in civilisation. The records of peoples now extinct show us this with equal clearness. On looking back into our own history, and into the histories of neighbouring nations, we similarly see that only by coercion were the smaller feudal governments so subordinated as to secure internal peace. And even lately, the long-desired consolidation of Germany, if not directly effected by 'blood and iron', as Bismarck said it must be, has been indirectly effected by them. . . .

"Though, during barbarism and the earlier stages of civilisation, war has the effect of exterminating the weaker societies, and of weeding out the weaker members of the stronger societies, and thus in both ways furthering the development of those valuable powers, bodily and mental, which war brings into play; yet during the later stages of civilisation, the second of these actions is reversed. So long as all adult males have to bear arms, the average result is that those of most strength and quickness survive, while the feebler and slower are slain; but when the industrial development has become such that only some of the adult males are drafted into the army, the tendency is to pick out and expose to slaughter the best-grown and healthiest: leaving behind the physically inferior to propagate the race. The fact that among ourselves, though the number of soldiers raised is not relatively large, many recruits are rejected by the examining surgeons, shows that the process inevitably works towards deterioration. Where, as in France, conscriptions have gone on taking away the finest men, generation after generation, the needful lowering of the standard proves how disastrous is the effect on those animal qualities of a race which form a necessary basis for all higher qualities. If the depletion is indirect also – if there is such an overdraw on the energies of the industrial population that a large share of heavy labour is thrown on the women, whose systems are taxed simultaneously by hard working and child-bearing, a further cause of physical degeneracy comes into play: France again supplying an example. War, therefore, after a certain stage of progress, instead of furthering bodily development and the development of certain mental powers, becomes a cause of retrogression.

"In like manner, though war, by bringing about social consolidations, indirectly favours industrial progress and all its civilising consequences, yet the direct effect of war on industrial progress is repressive. It is repressive as necessitating the abstraction of men and materials that would otherwise go to industrial growth; it is repressive as deranging the complex inter-dependencies among the many productive and distributive agencies; it is repressive as drafting off much administrative and constructive ability, which would else have gone to improve the industrial arts and the industrial organisation. And if we contrast the absolutely military Spartans with the partially military Athenians, in their respective attitudes towards culture of every kind, or call to mind the contempt shown for the pursuit of knowledge in purely military times like those of feudalism; we cannot fail to see that persistent war is at variance not only with industrial development, but also with the higher intellectual developments that aid industry and are aided by it.

"So, too, with the effects wrought on the moral nature. While war, by the discipline it gives soldiers, directly cultivates the habit of subordination, and does the like indirectly by establishing strong and permanent governments; and while in so far it cultivates attributes that are not only temporarily essential, but are steps towards attributes that are permanently essential; yet it does this at the cost of maintaining, and sometimes increasing, detrimental attributes – attributes intrinsically anti-social. The aggressions which selfishness prompts (aggressions which, in a society, have to be restrained by some power that is strong in proportion as the selfishness is intense) can diminish only as fast as selfishness is held in check by sympathy; and perpetual warlike activities repress sympathy: nay, they do worse – they cultivate aggressiveness to the extent of making it a pleasure to inflict injury. The citizen made callous by the killing and wounding of enemies inevitably brings his callousness home with him. Fellow-feeling, habitually trampled down in military conflicts, cannot at the same time be active in the relations of civil life. In proportion as giving pain to others is made a habit during war, it will remain a habit during peace: inevitably producing in the behaviour of citizens to one another, antagonisms, crimes of violence, and multitudinous aggressions of minor kinds, tending towards a disorder that calls for coercive government. Nothing like a high type of social life is possible without a type of human character in which the promptings of egoism are duly restrained by regard for others. The necessities of war imply absolute self-regard, and absolute disregard of certain others. Inevitably, therefore, the civilising discipline of social life is antagonised by the uncivilising discipline of the life war involves. So that beyond the direct mortality and miseries entailed by war, it entails other mortality and miseries by maintaining anti-social sentiments in citizens."

7 Class Consciousness as a Restraint on War

It is not only national sentiment that may affect the attitude of individuals towards other states. This may be affected also, some suggested, by class consciousness. If attitudes and actions were influenced not by national sentiment but only by class loyalty, as some of these writers appeared to hope, wars between states might cease to occur and a new type of international society come into being.

This was roughly what was proclaimed by Marx and Engels in the *Communist Manifesto*. They suggested (after more than thirty years of peace among the major states of Europe) that, with the growing network of relationships, commercial and financial, then being established across national boundaries, war was becoming increasingly rare even among bourgeois states. After the revolution the proletariats of Europe would show themselves to be, to a still greater extent, stateless. Once they had acquired power, therefore, they would cease to have any interest in a war against any other state where the people had taken power. War would then, like the state itself, wither away.

This was a faith to be widely expressed by subsequent socialist writers. Fifty years later Karl Kautsky expressed a similar optimism about the ability of the workers of the world to cast off their national allegiances and to create the beginnings of a genuinely international society. He compares different types of patriotism. He believed that the patriotism of the proletariat differed fundamentally from the patriotism of other classes because it recognised that the well-being of their own state could flourish only if it went hand in hand with the well-being of other nations as well. It was more far-sighted than the patriotism of craftsmen and peasants, who in other ways were allies, because the latter had no need of a world economy to increase their productivity; and much more so than that of the petty bourgeoisie which, because they were property-owners, might sympathise with capitalist exploiters from their own nation when they came into conflict with those they exploited in other countries. But it differed above all from the patriotism of the capitalists themselves, who identified the benefit of their nation with their own profits and would willingly allow the masses to suffer in a war to protect those profits. Only the complete victory of socialism could bring that kind of mentality to an end and usher in an age of concord and happiness, when all exploitation of one people by another would cease, and every danger of war would disappear.

Hopes that "socialist internationalism" would inhibit war were to be dashed at the outbreak of the First World War. Social democratic parties within each state, and their associated union movements, then promptly gave full support to their bourgeois governments, and so became engaged in a ruthless conflict against their opposite numbers in other states. This is the situation deplored by Lenin in the last of the passages reproduced below: a war made by the bourgeoisie is supported by social democrats who, as he put it, in that way "substitute nationalism for socialism".

So the idea that "workers" were, in their attitude to those who lived in other states, in some way different from other sections of the population and that, if only they understood their interests correctly, they would cast aside patriotism and renounce war, was proved false. The nature of humans, which led them to war, was not, it seemed, fundamentally altered by a change in political consciousness. National sentiment was still more powerful than class sentiment. And the mentality that led to war was too deeply instilled to be affected by political ideas alone.

*   *   *

Marx and Engels – The Victory of the Proletariat Will End National Differences*

"The Communists are further reproached with desiring to abolish countries and nationality.

---

* Karl Marx (1818–83). Born in Trier in the Rhineland, studied in Bonn and Berlin, but spent most of his life in England. Opposed "Utopian" socialism which he sought to replace with "scientific" socialism, based on the study of the inevitable forces of history. Held that social and political change resulted from technological changes transforming the "forces of production", leading in turn to changes in the "relations of production" and the transformation of society generally. Thus the bourgeois revolution, which had produced capitalism, would in turn be replaced by the

"The working men have no country. We cannot take from them what they have not got. Since the proletariat must first of all acquire political supremacy, must rise to be the leading class of the nation, must constitute itself *the* nation, it is, so far, itself national, though not in the bourgeois sense of the word.

"National differences and antagonisms between peoples are daily more and more vanishing, owing to the development of the bourgeoisie, to freedom of commerce, to the world market, to uniformity in the mode of production and in the conditions of life corresponding thereto.

"The supremacy of the proletariat will cause them to vanish still faster. United action of the leading civilised countries at least is one of the first conditions for the emancipation of the proletariat.

"In proportion as the exploitation of one individual by another is put an end to, the exploitation of one nation by another will also be put an end to. In proportion as the antagonism between classes within the nation vanishes, the hostility of one nation to another will come to an end."

Kautsky – Capitalist Patriotism and Proletarian Patriotism*

"The proletariat is at one with craftsmen and peasants in the struggle to live from their own labour rather than from exploitation. That

proletarian revolution which would establish the socialist society. The *Communist Manifesto*, from which this extract is taken, was written with Engels and appeared in 1848, on the eve of the revolutions which took place all over Europe in that year.
    Friedrich Engels (1820–95). Born, like Marx, in the Rhineland. He inherited his father's Manchester textile firm and lived much of the time in England. Began co-operating with Marx in 1844, having met him in Paris. Especially concerned with the relationship between scientific, historical and social development. Author of *Anti-Duhring*, in which he defended the idea of scientific socialism, based on the study of historic forces, from its non-Marxist critics.
    Quoted from *The Communist Manifesto* (1848), English trs. (London: International Publishing Co., 1888).

* From Karl Kautsky (1854–1938). Born in Prague and studied in Vienna. Became an ardent Marxist and the author of a number of works, including *Karl Marx's Economic Doctrine*, which was widely read. As a pure Marxist he believed, like the Mensheviks in Russia, that the socialist revolution would come about automatically as a result of economic forces and did not therefore require revolutionary political

struggle entails the renunciation of any policy of conquest and a deep concern for peace. In this these democratic classes are alike. But the proletariat differs from craftsmen and peasants in striving for higher productivity, which alone makes it possible for the mass of the population to free themselves from the oppressive burden of work and provides the leisure for culture, science and art. . . .

"The patriotism of the proletariat is not limited to a concern for peace, which it shares with the petty bourgeoisie. It goes beyond that. Higher productivity of labour, which is a condition of liberation, cannot be achieved in an economy limited to a single national state. In the conditions of contemporary technology it demands a world economy: the co-operation of all the workers of the world. That is why the patriotism of the proletariat embraces the idea of international solidarity: the idea that the well-being and civilisation of their own nation can flourish only if they go hand in hand with the well-being and civilisation of other nations.

"This idea corresponds with the final goal of the proletarian class struggle. But it attains its practical power already in the class struggle of today. Already the rise and strengthening of the proletariat of each nation is closely bound up with the rise of the proletariat of other nations. The solidarity of the proletariats of all nations is thus a practical necessity for the present-day proletarian class struggle; and it is this which prepares the way for the solidarity of all nations in socialist society.

"International solidarity is the essential characteristic which distinguishes proletarian patriotism from the patriotism of other classes. Even petty bourgeois democracy has a general desire for peace, but only the proletariat feel the need for the closest co-operation of all nations for their common welfare and common civilisation. And only the proletariat feels the resulting duty to come to the aid of the oppressed and exploited of all nations in their struggle against oppression and exploitation.

"That duty is felt even when the oppressors and exploiters belong to one nation and their victims to another. The proletariat feels itself

action: the German Social Democratic Party should thus in his view be a "revolutionary party", not "a party which makes revolutions". In conformity with the views expressed in this extract he joined the minority of the Social Democratic Party who opposed the voting of credits for the First World War, but after the war helped to bring about the reunification of the party. Quoted from *Patriotismus und Sozialdemokratie* (Leipzig: Leipziger Buchhandler Aktien-gesellschaft, 1907) extract trs. Evan Luard.

closely bound with the latter, and hostile to the former. In this it differs from the petty bourgeoisie, which may feel a certain solidarity with the exploiters when they belong to their own nation, since it feels bound to them by their possession of the means of production.

"The same thing appears in attitudes towards colonialism. Bourgeois democracy only opposes this – if it finds the energy to oppose it at all – because it is costly to the state and brings in little return. Only the politically independent proletariat opposes colonialism on the grounds that it is a policy of aggression and exploitation, and is bound to be this if it is to be profitable for the capitalists (whether or not it is profitable for the state).

"The patriotism of the proletariat and of the petty bourgeoisie are thus very different in nature, and this difference from time to time becomes a significant contradiction. Still more stark is the contradiction between the patriotism of the proletariat and that of the capitalists. At every step these two kinds of patriotism come into total conflict with each other.

"Like every class the capitalist class presents its own interests as those of the whole nation. But its interest rests on surplus value: the greater the surplus value won by one nation's capitalists, in their view, the more the nation itself will flourish. So patriotism means for them the promotion of the interests of surplus value, which the exploiters then pocket on behalf of their own nation.

"However surplus value – that is profit, interest, rent – becomes bigger the greater the exploitation of the working classes: the lower their wages, the longer their working hours, the more a low-paid and compliant work-force – women, children and backward foreign labour – can be substituted for more expensive and rebellious workers. The immiseration of the mass of the people – not just relative immiseration as a result of a slower increase in living standards to that of the capitalist classes, but their absolute immiseration, the physical and spiritual degradation of the mass of the people – is not always the result, but it is always the goal of the capitalist classes. The patriotism of the capitalist class is thus to deliver the nation to ruin. And if the nation is not in fact ruined, this is due to the energetic resistance of the international "unpatriotic" proletariat, not to those circles of society which claim a copyright in patriotism. . . .

"The productivity of labour in a capitalist nation increases faster than the purchasing power of the masses, bringing a constant need for the capitalists to increase their exports, to find new markets and new capital investments abroad, which will become new areas of exploitation. This pressure for expansion brings the capitalists of different nations into conflict, stimulating their patriotism to a new peak. This patriotism means for them not devotion to the fatherland but the exploitation of the fatherland, which will give up the blood and treasure of the masses in order to protect the profits of the capitalists abroad. The fatherland is not there for the people but the people for the fatherland, and the fatherland for the great exploiters: that is the quintessence of capitalist patriotism.

"The same masses whose immiseration the capitalists have sought to bring about through industrial exploitation are, over and above, compelled by the capitalist state to offer up the blood of their sons, and to accept a lowering of already low living-standards, in order to pay the costs of a vast army. This is allegedly required for the defence of the fatherland; but in fact in contemporary conditions it serves nothing else but the defence of profit, and all it does is to strengthen the tendency of capitalism to bring about the immiseration of the masses.

"For the more the productivity of labour grows, the more the technology of war also grows and the greater is the struggle of capitalist nations for expansion, the greater their contradictions on land and sea, and the greater the cost of their armaments. So all the available forces of the nation are devoted to militarism. States become continually less capable of any cultural or social policy which costs money, or of healing the wounds which capitalism creates – even to the extent that living conditions of bourgeois society might allow it.

"Thus capitalist patriotism means not only a growing sharpening of the contradictions among the nations, increasing danger of world war, and the growing devastation which results from the development of military technology; it also means bringing about the ruin of the capitalists' own nation.

"The petty bourgeoisie, which were never capable of an independent policy, may allow themselves to be deceived by this patriotic clap-trap into believing that it is not their own capitalists but foreign nations which threaten the people. But the class-conscious proletariat knows what this kind of patriotism means: that it stands in irreconcilable contradiction with its own patriotism, directed at assuring the well-being and civilisation of the entire mass of the people. That goal will be attained, not through the unleashing of colonial wars or the planning of world wars, but through the struggle against capitalist militarism and expansionist policies. That struggle is undertaken through the class war of the world's proletariat, bound closely together in international solidarity. . . .

"Thus it is understandable that agitation and action against militarists must be undertaken internationally, yet at the same time can only be national. Every population can really only struggle against its own militarism; but it is also only possible to undertake that struggle effectively if it is undertaken with equal energy among all the principal civilised peoples. And the more energetic the opposition it mounts in one land, the greater the resistance it will encounter in others. So the national and the international struggles against militarism are closely interwoven.

• • •

"But if social democracy were to secure a complete victory, it will tear down all the divisions which at present divide nations. Then an era of totally free intercourse among states will open, an era in which peaceful co-operation will assure welfare and civilisation to all nations. All exploitation will be ended, not only of the proletariat by capitalists, but also of poor agricultural people by the richer and more industrialised. All contradictions between social classes and nations will cease. Thus every cause of war will disappear, every danger of war, and every need for weapons of war. Then proletarian patriotism will celebrate its finest triumph in the joy and prosperity of the people. Conversely, that accursed bourgeois patriotism will be brought to an end; a patriotism which does not struggle for the welfare of the peoples, of which the ruling passion is the desire for profit, and which sees its historic mission as to bring misery for the masses of the people and to lead them to the slaughterhouse for the sake of profit. There will be no happiness and no prosperity for the peoples until that kind of patriotism is eliminated for ever."

Lenin – A War Made by the Bourgeoisie Should Not Be Supported by Social Democrats*

"The European war, for which the governments and the bourgeois parties of all countries have been making preparations for decades,

---

* From V. I. Lenin (1870–1924). Principal organiser of the Russian Revolution of 1917. Became a Marxist in his youth and therefore, in the conditions of Tsarist Russia, a

has broken out. The growth of armaments, the extreme sharpening of the struggle for markets in the epoch of the latest, the imperialist, stage of capitalist development in the advanced countries, and the dynastic interests of the most backward East European monarchies were inevitably bound to lead, and have led, to this war. The seizure of territory and the subjugation of foreign nations, the ruin of a competing nation and the plunder of its wealth, the diversion of the attention of the working masses from the internal political crises in Russia, Germany, England and other countries, the division of the workers, fooling them by nationalism, and the extermination of their vanguard with the object of weakening the revolutionary movement of the proletariat – such is the only real meaning, substance and significance of the present war.

"The first duty of the Social Democrats is to disclose this true meaning of the war and ruthlessly to expose the falsehood, sophistry and 'patriotic' phrasemongering spread by the ruling classes, the landlords and the bourgeoisie, in defence of the war.

"The German bourgeoisie heads one group of belligerent nations. It is fooling the working class and the labouring masses by asserting that it is waging war in defence of the fatherland, freedom and civilisation, for the liberation of the peoples oppressed by tsardom, for the destruction of reactionary tsardom. But, as a matter of fact, this bourgeoisie, which servilely grovels before the Prussian Junkers, headed by Wilhelm II, has always been a most faithful ally of tsardom and an enemy of the revolutionary movement of the workers and peasants of Russia. In reality, whatever the outcome of the war may be, this bourgeoisie will, together with the Junkers, exert every effort to support the tsarist monarchy against a revolution in Russia.

"The German bourgeoisie has in reality launched a predatory campaign against Serbia with the object of subjugating her and throttling the national revolution of the Southern Slavs, at the same

revolutionary (his brother had taken part in an assassination attempt against Tsar Alexander II). Believed that only the working class could be an effective revolutionary force and that, properly organised, it could take control even of a revolution in which the bourgeoisie also took part: it was not therefore necessary to wait for a separate bourgeois revolution to take place before a proletarian revolution could succeed. Sought to create a party of professional revolutionaries, directed from the centre, which would then seek the alliance of the peasantry. Deeply shocked, as this extract demonstrates, by the readiness of most social democrats in 1914 to come to terms with their bourgeois governments in order to defend national interests. (See also a further extract on pp. 216–19.) Quoted from *The Russian Social-Democrats and the War* (1914), English trs. (Moscow: Marx–Engels–Lenin Institute, 1947).

time directing the bulk of its military forces against the freer countries, Belgium and France, in order to plunder its richer competitors. Although it is spreading the fable that it is waging a defensive war, the German bourgeoisie, in reality, chose the moment which in its opinion was most propitious for war, taking advantage of its latest improvements in military technique and forestalling the new armaments that had already been planned and decided upon by Russia and France.

"The other group of belligerent nations is headed by the British and French bourgeoisie, which is fooling the working class and the labouring masses by asserting that it is waging a war for the defence of their native lands, freedom and civilisation from the militarism and despotism of Germany. But, as a matter of fact, this bourgeoisie has long been using its billions to hire the armies of Russian tsardom, the most reactionary and barbarous monarchy in Europe, and to prepare them for an attack on Germany.

"In reality, the object of the struggle of the British and French bourgeoisie is to seize the German colonies and to ruin a competing nation which is distinguished for its more rapid economic development. And, in pursuit of this noble aim, the 'advanced' democratic nations are helping the savage tsarist regime to strangle Poland, the Ukraine, etc., and to throttle the revolution in Russia more thoroughly.

"Neither of the two groups of belligerent countries lags behind the other in robbery, atrocities and the infinite brutalities of war; but in order to fool the proletariat and distract its attention from the only real war of liberation, namely, a civil war against the bourgeoisie both of 'its own' and of 'foreign' countries, in order to further this lofty aim, the bourgeoisie of each country is trying with the help of lying talk about patriotism to extol the significance of its 'own' national war and to assert that it is not striving to vanquish the enemy for the sake of plunder and the seizure of territory, but for the sake of 'liberating' all other peoples, except its own.

"But the more zealously the governments and the bourgeoisie of all countries strive to divide the workers and to pit them against each other, and the more ferociously they employ martial law and military censorship (which even now, in time of war, are applied more stringently against the 'internal' than against the foreign enemy) for this lofty purpose, the more urgently is it the duty of the class-conscious proletariat to preserve its class solidarity, its internationalism, its Socialist convictions from the orgy of the chauvinism of the 'patriotic' bourgeois cliques of all countries. The renunciation of this task would mean the renunciation by the class-conscious workers of all their emancipatory and democratic, not to mention Socialist, aspirations.

"It is with a feeling of deepest chagrin that we have to record that the Socialist parties of the leading European countries have not discharged this duty, while the behaviour of the leaders of these parties – particularly of the German – borders on the downright betrayal of the cause of Socialism. At this moment of supreme historical importance to the world, the majority of the leaders of the present, the Second (1889–1914), Socialist International are trying to substitute nationalism for Socialism. Owing to their behaviour, the workers' parties of these countries did not oppose the criminal conduct of the governments but called upon the working class to *identify* its position with that of the imperialist governments. The leaders of the International committed an act of treachery towards Socialism when they voted for war credits, when they seconded the chauvinist ('patriotic') slogans of the bourgeoisie of their 'own' countries, when they justified and defended the war, when they entered the bourgeois Cabinets of belligerent countries, etc., etc. The most influential Socialist leaders, and the most influential organs of the Socialist press of present-day Europe, hold chauvinistic bourgeois and liberal views, and not Socialist views. The responsibility for disgracing Socialism in this way rests primarily on the German Social Democrats, who were the strongest and most influential party in the Second International. But neither can one justify the French Socialists, who accepted ministerial posts in the government of the very bourgeoisie which betrayed its country and allied itself with Bismarck to crush the Commune.

"The German and Austrian Social Democrats try to justify their support of the war by arguing that they are thereby fighting Russian tsardom. We, the Russian Social Democrats, declare that we consider such a justification sheer sophistry. During the past few years, the revolutionary movement against tsardom in our country has again assumed tremendous proportions. This movement has always been led by the Russian working class. In the past few years, political strikes involving millions of workers were held, demanding the overthrow of tsardom and a democratic republic. On the very eve of the war, Poincaré, the President of the French Republic, while on his visit to Nicholas II, had the opportunity to see barricades in the streets of St Petersburg built by the hands of Russian workers. The

Russian proletariat has not shrunk from any sacrifice to rid humanity of the disgrace of the tsarist monarchy. But we must say that if anything can, under certain conditions, delay the fall of tsardom, if anything can help tsardom in its struggle against the whole democracy of Russia, it is the present war, which has placed the moneybags of the British, French and Russian bourgeoisie at the disposal of tsardom for its reactionary aims. And if anything can hinder the revolutionary struggle of the Russian working class against tsardom, it is the behaviour of the German and Austrian Social Democratic leaders, which the chauvinist press of Russia is continually holding up to us as an example.

"Even if we assume that German Social Democracy was so weak that it was compelled to refrain from all revolutionary action, even then it should not have joined the chauvinist camp, it should not have taken steps which caused the Italian Socialists to declare with justice that the leaders of the German Social Democrats were dishonouring the banner of the proletarian International.

"Our Party, the Russian Social Democratic Labour Party, has borne, and will yet bear, great sacrifices in connection with the war. The whole of our legal labour press has been suppressed. The majority of the labour unions have been closed, a large number of our comrades have been arrested and exiled. But our parliamentary representatives – the Russian Social Democratic Labour Group in the State Duma – considered it to be their imperative Socialist duty not to vote for the war credits and even to walk out of the Duma, in order the more energetically to express their protest; they considered it their duty to brand the policy of the European governments as an imperialist one. And notwithstanding the fact that the oppression of the tsar's government has increased tenfold, our comrades, the workers in Russia, are already publishing their first illegal manifestos against the war and thus doing their duty to democracy and the International.

"While the representatives of revolutionary Social Democracy, in the person of the minority of the German Social Democrats and the best Social Democrats in the neutral countries, are experiencing a burning sense of shame over this collapse of the Second International;[1] while voices of Socialists are being raised both in England and in France against the chauvinism of the majority of the Social Democratic parties; while the opportunists, as represented, for instance, by the German *Socialist Monthly* (*Sozialistische Monatshefte*), which has long held a national-liberal position, are justly

celebrating their victory over European Socialism – the worst possible service to the proletariat is being rendered by those who vacillate
between opportunism and revolutionary Social Democracy (like the
'Centre' in the German Social Democratic Party), by those who
attempt to ignore the collapse of the Second International or to cover
it up with diplomatic talk.

"Quite the contrary, this collapse must be frankly admitted and its
causes understood in order to be able to build a new and more lasting
Socialist unity of the workers of all countries.

"The opportunists have nullified the decisions of the Stuttgart,
Copenhagen and Basle Congresses, which made it binding on the
Socialists of all countries to fight chauvinism under all conditions,
which made it binding on Socialists to retort to every war begun by
the bourgeoisie and the governments by intense propaganda for civil
war and for social revolution. The collapse of the Second International is the collapse of opportunism, which grew out of the
peculiarities of a now past (the so-called 'peaceful') historical epoch,
and which in recent years has practically come to dominate the
International. The opportunists have long been preparing the ground
for this collapse by rejecting Socialist revolution and substituting for
it bourgeois reformism; by repudiating the class struggle with its
inevitable transformation into civil war at certain moments, and by
preaching class collaboration; by preaching bourgeois chauvinism
under the guise of patriotism and defence of the fatherland, and
ignoring or repudiating the fundamental truth of Socialism, long ago
expressed in *The Communist Manifesto*, namely, that the working-
men have no country. . . ."

Note
1. Lenin has in mind the declaration of 10 September 1914 made by Karl
   Liebknecht, Franz Mehring, Rosa Luxemburg and Clara Zetkin which
   was published on 30 and 31 October in the Swiss press.

8 Personal Aggressiveness as a Source of War

The unprecedented slaughter of the First World War, and the fear, in the following two decades, that a further, still more murderous conflict might follow, brought new attempts to assess how far war resulted from ineradicable facets of human nature. This question was now increasingly considered, not in the general speculations of philosophers and political writers, but in the pronouncements of psychologists claiming to base their findings on a more scientific foundation.

Among such writers there was growing preoccupation with the idea of "aggression". This was seen as a powerful and universal attribute of the human personality. It was widely suggested that ordinary citizens in modern industrial states, finding few outlets for aggression in their normal everyday lives, were led to project it on to the outside world, and in particular on to rival states and their inhabitants. This, it was proposed by some, was the underlying cause of war in the modern world.

Such theories encountered the same difficulties as comparable ideas expressed by political philosophers in earlier times. Since ordinary citizens were usually unable to declare war on a foreign state, or even to exercise significant influence on the policies of their own government, it was not clear how "aggressive" tendencies among them, even if present, could be the cause of war.

There were two possible ways this could be explained. In the first place, even if the ordinary citizen had no direct influence on decisions to declare war in a particular situation, they could *indirectly* influence them by helping to create a climate of hostility and anger; this would affect the attitudes and actions of the statesmen who reached decisions on peace and war, and so make war more likely. Secondly, the findings of the psychologists might be relevant not so much for the ordinary citizens but for the statesmen themselves. These would share the aggressive tendencies of mankind as a whole, and might even, if they were dictators manifesting the "authoritarian personality", display them in a more extreme form than the mass of ordinary, relatively well-balanced citizens.

The following extracts represent a small sample of the vast literature of this period devoted to analysing those factors in the human personality which, it was believed, might contribute to the warlike behaviour of states. Sigmund Freud, the most influential psychologist of the day, traces warlike feelings to the instinct of destructiveness, or hate, which coexists with the instinct to conserve, or love, in the human mind, and can take the form of a death-instinct. If not turned inward in self-destruction, it must be turned outward, often in the form of war and other types of violence. This aggressive tendency of humans cannot be suppressed, but it can be counteracted if its opposite, Eros or love, can be sufficiently nurtured and developed.

All the other writings quoted show the influence of these ideas. The British psychoanalyst, Edward Glover, saw the causes of war in aggressive impulses which are unsuccessfully repressed, leading to unconscious sadism. Harold Lasswell, the US political scientist, finds them in the anxieties and insecurities which result from threats to parts of the personality, of which nations and classes were the collective symbols. Durbin and Bowlby, writing in Britain at about the same time, find them in the attempts to suppress natural aggressive instincts, love–hate, and the displacement or projection of the repressed aggression.

Most of the writing of this period, therefore, reflects the psychological notions that were common at the time. They provided plausible explanations of the aggressive feelings of individuals towards other individuals, and even towards other states. Whether, in doing so, they explained the aggressive actions of states in making war on other states was less self-evident. Whatever aggressive sentiments ordinary citizens harboured, they had little opportunity to express them in the form of war against other states. It seemed by no means sure, therefore, that individual psychology could provide an adequate explanation of the behaviour of states or of conflict among states.

*   *   *

Freud – The Urge to Destruction as the Source of War*

"You are amazed that it is so easy to infect men with the war-fever, and you surmise that man has in him an active instinct for hatred and destruction, amenable to such stimulations. I entirely agree with you. I believe in the existence of this instinct and have been recently at pains to study its manifestations. In this connection may I set out a fragment of that knowledge of the instincts, which we psycho-analysts, after so many tentative essays and gropings in the dark, have compassed? We assume that human instincts are of two kinds: those that conserve and unify, which we call 'erotic' (in the meaning Plato gives to *Eros* in his *Symposium*), or else 'sexual' (explicitly extending the popular connotation of 'sex'), and, secondly, the instincts to destroy and kill, which we assimilate as the aggressive or destructive instincts. These are, as you perceive, the well-known opposites, Love and Hate, transformed into theoretical entities; they are, perhaps, another aspect of those eternal polarities, attraction and repulsion, which fall within your province. But we must be chary of passing over-hastily to the notions of good and evil. Each of these instincts is every whit as indispensable as its opposite and all the phenomena of life derive from their activity, whether they work in concert or in opposition. It seems that an instinct of either category can operate but rarely in isolation; it is always blended ('alloyed', as we say) with a certain dosage of its opposite, which modifies its aim or even, in certain circumstances, is a prime condition of its attainment. Thus the instinct of self-preservation is certainly of an erotic nature, but to gain its ends this very instinct necessitates aggressive action. In the same way the love-instinct, when directed to a specific object, calls for an admixture of the acquisitive instinct if it is to enter into effective possession of that object. It is the difficulty of isolating the two kinds of instinct in their manifestations that has so long prevented us from recognising them.

---

* From Sigmund Freud (1856–1939). Founder of psychoanalysis, based on the study of subconscious impulses, especially sexual impulses, derived from the study of dreams and clinical evidence. Lived most of his life in Vienna but forced by the anti-Jewish policies of the Nazis to move to London in 1938 where he died a year later. Became during the 1930s deeply concerned about the war psychosis of the period and its causes, which he discussed in a correspondence with Albert Einstein that was subsequently published. Quoted from *Open Letter to Albert Einstein*, in *Why War?* (London: New Commonwealth, 1933).

"If you will travel with me a little further on this road, you will find that human affairs are complicated in yet another way. Only exceptionally does an action follow on the stimulus of a single instinct, which is *per se* a blend of Eros and destructiveness. As a rule several motives of similar composition concur to bring about the act. . . . . Thus, when a nation is summoned to engage in war, a whole gamut of human motives may respond to this appeal; high and low motives, some openly avowed, others slurred over. The lust for aggression and destruction is certainly included; the innumerable cruelties of history and man's daily life confirm its prevalence and strength. The stimulation of these destructive impulses by appeals to idealism and the erotic instinct naturally facilitates their release. Musing on the atrocities recorded on history's page, we feel that the ideal motive has often served as a camouflage for the lust of destruction; sometimes, as with the cruelties of the Inquisition, it seems that, while the ideal motives occupied the foreground of consciousness, they drew their strength from the destructive instincts submerged in the unconscious. Both interpretations are feasible.

"You are interested, I know, in the prevention of war, not in our theories, and I keep this fact in mind. Yet I would like to dwell a little longer on this destructive instinct, which is seldom given the attention that its importance warrants. With the least of speculative efforts we are led to conclude that this instinct functions in every living being, striving to work its ruin and reduce life to its primal state of inert matter. Indeed, it might well be called the 'death-instinct'; whereas the erotic instincts vouch for the struggle to live on. The death instinct becomes an impulse to destruction when, with the aid of certain organs, it directs its action outwards, against external objects. The living being, that is to say, defends its own existence by destroying foreign bodies. But, in one of its activities, the death instinct is operative *within* the living being and we have sought to trace back a number of normal and pathological phenomena to this *introversion* of the destructive instinct. We have even committed the heresy of explaining the origin of human conscience by some such 'turning inward' of the aggressive impulse. Obviously, when this internal tendency operates on too large a scale, it is no trivial matter, rather a positively morbid state of things; whereas the diversion of the destructive impulse towards the external world must have beneficial effects. Here is, then, the biological justification for all those vile, pernicious propensities which we now are combating. We can but own that they are really more akin to nature than this our stand against them, which, in fact, remains to be accounted for.

"All this may give you the impression that our theories amount to a species of mythology and a gloomy one at that! But does not every natural science lead ultimately to this – a sort of mythology? Is it otherwise today with your physical science?

"The upshot of these observations, as bearing on the subject in hand, is that there is no likelihood of our being able to suppress humanity's aggressive tendencies. In some happy corners of the earth, they say, where nature brings forth abundantly whatever man desires, there flourish races whose lives go gently by, unknowing of aggression or constraint. This I can hardly credit; I would like further details about these happy folk. The Bolshevists, too, aspire to do away with human aggressiveness by ensuring the satisfaction of material needs and enforcing equality between man and man. To me this hope seems vain. Meanwhile, they busily perfect their armaments, and their hatred of outsiders is not the least of the factors of cohesion amongst themselves. In any case, as you, too, have observed, complete suppression of man's aggressive tendencies is not in issue; what we may try is to divert it into a channel other than that of warfare.

"From our 'mythology' of the instincts we may easily deduce a formula for an indirect method of eliminating war. If the propensity for war be due to the destructive instinct, we have always its counter-agent, Eros, to our hand. All that produces ties of sentiment between man and man must serve us as war's antidote. These ties are of two kinds. First, such relations as those towards a beloved object, void though they be of sexual intent. The psychoanalyst need feel no compunction in mentioning 'love' in this connection; religion uses the same language: Love thy neighbour as thyself. A pious injunction easy to enounce, but hard to carry out! The other bond of sentiment is by way of identification. All that brings out the significant resemblances between men calls into play this feeling of community, identification, whereon is founded, in large measure, the whole edifice of human society."

Glover – Repression and Unconscious Sadism as the Source of War*

"The first systematic step in investigating the relations of war and peace is to make a list of the instincts or impulses concerned. Here we encounter two difficulties, first, that there are differences of opinion regarding the classification of human impulses, and second, that the collection of available material has so far been carried out in a very perfunctory way. Now whatever classification you adopt, whether you accept the common tripartite grouping, viz., sexual, self-preservatory and group instincts, or prefer the more elaborate groupings of descriptive psychology in which a dozen or more instincts may be specified, there is one practical test by means of which all classifications can be valued. It is a sound principle that any impulse, disturbance of which causes mental conflict or disorder, is of extreme significance to the individual. And investigations carried out by psychoanalysts on neuroses and several forms of insanity have shown that behind these illnesses are to be discovered serious disorders of the sexual impulse (taken in the broadest sense) and serious disturbances of the mechanisms controlling aggressive or destructive impulses. These facts correspond with a classification of instincts into two main groups, viz., appetitive and reactive. Broadly speaking, the human mind begins to crack when it is unable in some way or another to master its destructive impulses, its sexual impulses or any important fusion of destructive and sexual impulses.

"Adopting this classification, the first step in investigation is comparatively simple: it is obvious that war impulses can be identified with the impulses of destruction. This is, however, a very inadequate view. Study of the history of war necessitates a more comprehensive grouping: according to this the impulses concerned in war are those of destruction (of animate and inanimate objects), acquisitiveness (mostly but not exclusively directed towards inanimate objects) and sexual aggression (chiefly directed towards animate objects), Murder, Rapine or Pillage, Lust. This too is inadequate. Together with the loosening of primitive impulse goes a heightening of certain

---

* From E. Glover. Psychoanalyst, once director of scientific research at the London Institute of Psychoanalysis. A devoted follower of Freud (his book *Freud or Jung* (1950) leaves no doubt of his preferences between the two). Also author of *The Technique of Psychoanalysis* (1928), *Psychoanalysis* (1939) and *The Roots of Crime* (1960). Quoted from *War, Sadism and Pacifism* (London: George Allen and Unwin, 1933).

counter-reactions, usually extolled as amongst the noble virtues – devotion to ideals, courageous self-sacrifice and comradeship, strenuous feats of intellectual and physical prowess and endurance. And so on. This is better but it is still utterly inadequate. *The fact is that no serious attempt has been made to catalogue and classify the instinctual phenomena of war.* Gifted amateurs have attempted the task but as a rule they start their war novels or autobiography with strong subjective bias, never with completely objective psychological criteria. And here one feels tempted to anticipate a later discussion of practical measures by putting a test question: How many millions are spent by the League of Nations or at the instigation of the League on psychological research into the nature of war impulses? How many psychological institutions are working day and night in different countries to fathom the riddles of human conflict either individual or social?

•   •   •

"Here we approach the second line of investigation. If you ask why it is that any individual can be unaware of the existence of powerful impulses, the answer is surely that this must be due to an even more powerful controlling mechanism. Repression, to use the technical term, is the greatest and in a limited sense the most secure of all the mechanisms that inhibit instinct. The result of successful repression is that we have not the slightest *idea* of the existence of an impulse and no physical discomfort or mental tension (i.e., *affect*), owing to frustration of the unknown impulse. The description of this mechanism is a highly technical matter into which I cannot hope to enter here, except to say that it involves withdrawal of psychic energy from a subterranean overcharged psychic circuit together with reinforcement of energy in any circuit of ideas which insulates the danger zone. I will only add that although essentially a system of flight, repression has justified itself biologically as much as, if not more than, any other form of flight from danger. By its help primitive impulse has been sufficiently weakened to permit of the residue being dealt with by what we called civilised reactions. Repression is a gigantic self-deception of which the self is unaware. Biologically speaking, as an analyst once put it, it is the father of lies. But like all mechanisms it is justified only by success. *The dangers of repression are the dangers of unsuccessful repression.* Should the idea representing the impulse *threaten* to break through into consciousness any disaster may follow: the mind, shying from the scent of danger like a frightened horse may stampede or kick the shafts to pieces. Even if the idea is safely locked away, should the tension of àn unknown but frustrated impulse be experienced, any disaster may follow, e.g., a vicarious object may be made to function as a lightning conductor. But if the repressed idea can be made conscious and if at the same time the emotional tension can be traced to its source, the individual and society are safe. For the moment at any rate a breathing-space has been gained and in that breathing-space the processes of conscious reflection and judgement have time to operate.

"The phenomena of 'war-mongering' provide an apt illustration of the dangers and uncertainties of faulty repression. In its most official form war-mongering is simply the aggressive aspect of international diplomacy but, of course, it is concealed to a large extent by the manifestly pacific nature of much diplomatic activity. The man in the street has not the same reason to cover his bellicose imaginings. And in the ordinary way preoccupation with international rights and wrongs is a useful substitute activity, a vicarious discharge of emotional tension, the original source of which is infantile sadism. *During actual crises, however, this vicarious discharge may bias the person towards war or peace.* You will observe that we cannot immediately predict in what direction the balance will swing. Knowledge of many other factors is necessary for any such prognostication. The fact remains, however, that the bias is dictated by individual unconscious needs and not by rational considerations of social necessity.

"But the danger of unsuccessful repression is not simply that primitive sadism is liable to be loosened in inappropriate directions. *Faulty repression can itself engender irrational hate.* Experimental proof of this fact can be obtained from the analysis of neurotic individuals. Analyse a neurotic symptom and you discover that huge quantities of anxiety and guilt must be discharged before the symptom disappears. Soon you begin to realise that the symptom represents a spontaneous attempt to master anxiety. In most cases, of course, an unsuccessful attempt. Many neurotic symptoms are in fact called 'anxiety states'. Others again are called 'phobias', implying that excessive fear has been displaced from an unknown to a known idea or situation (fears of domestic animals, of knives, of being buried alive, of closed spaces, of thunder, and so forth). In both cases repression has been faulty, an effect due to unconscious impulses has penetrated to consciousness, the original idea alone remaining repressed. The most significant observation is however that prior to the discharge of anxiety of unknown origin, an otherwise amiable patient not only develops attitudes of intense hostility and dislike, but *hastens to direct this hostility at the nearest available object.* In most cases it is directed at the analyst, who, whatever his failings, has done nothing to justify this sudden change in personal feeling. Anxiety breeds hate; hate arouses anxiety; both together portend destruction."

Lasswell – Anxiety and Insecurity as the Source of War*

"Owing to the assumption of violence in international and interclass relations, collective symbols are presented at the focus of attention under circumstances which are particularly prone to precipitate all manner of anxiety reactions. The meaning of these symbols is a function of the total personalities in which they occur, and they necessarily derive much of their significance from deeper and earlier sources than those connected with the immediate political situation.

"Insecurities which are induced by threats of loss may be abated by direct acts of counterassertion. But in a world of limited opportunities the impulses toward boundless counter-aggression which are elicited under such circumstances must submit to incessant chastening. Impulsive counter-assertions are rarely consummated, and the most direct means by which the underlying anxieties may be removed are therefore unavailable. The continuing necessity of suppressing hostility, or of giving it indirect expression, means that a substantial measure of anxiety remains related to the secondary symbols. There are many ways of disposing of accumulated insecurities in relation to political symbols without directly implicating political symbols. Hence anxieties which arise from the rumours of foreign conspiracies may be effectively abolished by displacing hostilities upon wives, secretaries or chauffeurs; or by orgiastic and diffuse release in orgasm, alcoholism or pugilism. The routes to release are very numerous; they may be classified into acts which involve object orientations, reflective thinking, autism (moods and irrelevant fantasies) and somatic reactions (headaches and other bodily changes in

* From Harold Lasswell (1902–60). American political scientist. Studied and taught at Chicago University and other institutions. Especially interested in the borderland between psychology and politics. Other well-known books include *Psychopathology and Politics* (1930) and *The Analysis of Political Behaviour* (1947). Quoted from *Word Politics and Personal Insecurity* (New York: McGraw-Hill, 1935).

which functional factors are important). Despite the rich variety of insecurity-abolishing alternatives, several circumstances conspire to connect world political symbols with anxiety reactions. The expectation of violence sustains an organisation of communication which pays attention to what the various key participants in the balancing process are doing. Their names are continually before the population as targets for affective displacements of all kinds, and they are reported in connection with many events which directly expose the local symbol to the possibility of losing its independence, its material claims, or its prestige. Vested interests arise in connection with the special function of transmitting symbols in the press and elsewhere; and many of these vested interests extract direct advantages from emphasising the threatening aspects of the world situation.

"Although insecurities arising within the personality in its political aspects may be removed by nonpolitical acts, many of the reactions to insecurity are immediately relevant to politics. We have seen how the suppression of vigorous counter-assertion in a world of many limitations sustains insecurities arising from the balancing process. Some of the aggressions which are mobilised and denied direct expression against the foreign environment are directed against the self. This is one of the most important dynamisms of our intrapsychic life, displaying itself in extreme form as suicide.

"One of the chief immediate results of subjecting an ego symbol to external danger and of inhibiting counter-aggression is thus the preoccupation of the ego with its own relations to the world. This represents a partial withdrawal of libido (affective interest) from the symbols of the surrounding environment. This growing absorption in the more central self-symbols reactivates the earlier, more primitive, less disciplined attitudes of the personality. The result is the elaboration of narcissistically gratifying fantasies of the self. A personality so reacting may create symbols to which he exposes others, boasting of the high moral worth and ultimate omnipotence of the collective symbol; or in the absence of autonomous elaboration, he may respond positively to such symbols when they are supplied by others in conversation or in print. A particular value is attached to acts of ceremonial deference to the collective emblem, since to personalities in such a condition each small detail seems to involve the fate of the whole collective symbol, and of national or class or race 'honour'.

• • •

"That part of the ego symbol which is organised in relation to the ambiguous 'we', called our nation, or class or race, is in most instances but slightly modified by knowledge. In view of the undeveloped character of such a 'we' symbol, it may properly be called a *rudimentary* sentiment or symbol. The ambiguity of reference of these secondary terms and the residues of early emotional attachments and aversions combine to minimise the 'reality critique'. The resulting instability of judgement is displayed in the ease with which uncorrected swings occur between extremes of hostility and of admiration in relation to secondary symbols. . . .

"It should be explicitly stated that persons who are well integrated in their immediate personal relationships may be poorly developed toward remote objects and, reversely, that people who are poorly organised toward primary situations may have acquired the special knowledge which chastens reactions in dealing with remote objects. Indeed one of the principal functions of symbols of remote objects, like nations and classes, is to serve as targets for the relief of many of the tensions which might discharge disastrously in face-to-face relations. The hatred of the physical father may be displaced upon the symbol of the monarch, enabling the person to keep on good terms with the person toward whom the early animosities were mainly directed.

"From this analysis it follows that the rudimentary self-symbols which are related to world politics may function in loose association with other aspects of the personality and, like all partly dissociated systems, may predominate in shaping overt conduct in situations which call them up.

"The elaboration of regressive and fantastic processes in connection with the rudimentary self-symbols of world politics is favoured by the weak superego formations which arise in consequence of the comparative absence of world mores. The assumption that the resort to violence is the ultimate appeal in world politics indicates the weakness of moral imperatives in this sphere of human relations. Impulses are permitted to discharge in elementary form owing to the fragmentary nature of world culture.

"Strictly speaking, it is not legitimate to refer to rudimentary self-symbols as pathological expressions of the individual. Nor is it correct to oppose a sick society to a basically healthy person. Pathology is neither social in contrast with individual, nor individual in contrast with social; pathology is configurational. If the word is used at all, it may be defined as referring to events destructive of certain patterns defined as 'normal' or 'supernormal'.

"We have seen that one of the principal consequences of the expectation of violence in world politics is to build up insecurities which arise from the curbing of counter-aggressive tendencies which are initially elicited by the dangers connected with the we-symbol in the balancing process. This prolonged indulgence of the reality-testing, cautious, self-controlling features of culture and personality favours the drastic redefinition of the situation in directions gratifying to the underindulged, unreflecting, incautious and spontaneous patterns of culture and personality."

Durbin and Bowlby – Aggression, Love–Hate, Displacement and Projection as the Source of War*

"We suggest . . . that the evidence of psychoanalysis justifies the following conclusions:

"1. That the *primary* causes of aggression (and of peaceful co-operation) are identical with those of children and apes. The character of the *id* – or complex of instinctive impulses – does not change materially as the individual grows older. The same sources of satisfaction – food, warmth, love, society – are desired and the same sources of conflict – desire for exclusive possession of the sources of satisfaction, or aggression arising from a sense of frustration – are present. But in the life of most children there is a controlling or warping influence present in a varying degree, that of *authority*. The child is denied for various reasons – good or bad – an open and uninterrupted

---

* E. F. M. Durbin (1906–48). Economist and politician. Teacher at London School of Economics and author of a number of works on economic and political questions. In 1945 became a Labour MP but died prematurely as a result of a bathing accident. Works include *Purchasing Power and Trade Depression* (1933) and *The Problem of Credit Policy* (1935).

John Bowlby (1907–90). Consultant psychiatrist at the Tavistock Clinic in London, now known especially for his work on child care and family bonds. The book from which this extract was taken was written in his youth, when he specialised in psychoanalysis. His other works include: *Child Care and the Growth of Love* (1953), a simplified version of a report for the World Health Organisation, published two years earlier; *Separation, Anxiety and Anger* (1973); *The Making and Breaking of Affectional Bonds* (1979).

Quoted from *Personal Aggressiveness and War* (London: Routledge and Kegan Paul, 1939).

access to the means of its satisfaction. It is denied the breast or bottle, the toy or the company of adults at the time or to the extent that it wishes. The evidence seems overwhelming that such frustration leads to a violent reaction of fear, hatred and aggression. The child cries or screams or bites or kicks. We are not for the moment concerned with the question whether this frustration is desirable or not. We are simply concerned with its results. The result is 'bad temper' or 'naughtiness' – a resentment of frustration. This original resentment and the aggression to which it leads we would call *simple aggression*.

"Further development turns, in our view, upon the way in which this simple aggression is treated. The statistically normal method of treatment is, we suggest, further frustration or *punishment*. The child is slapped or beaten or subjected to moral instruction – taught that its behaviour is wrong or wicked. Again we are not concerned with the question of the rightness or wrongness of this procedure, but only with its consequences. We suggest that the result of punishment is to present the child with a radical conflict – either he must control the expression of his simple aggression or suffer the punishment and the loss of love that simple aggression in a regime of discipline necessarily entails.

"This conflict in the child is in our view an important source of aggressiveness in the adult. The conflict itself is a conflict between a fundamental tendency to resent frustration and the fear of punishment or, what is just as important, the fear of the loss of love. To the child the parent[1] is both the source of satisfactions and the source of frustration. To express aggression is to endanger the life of the goose that lays the golden eggs. Not to express simple aggression towards original objects is the task that faces the child. Now one result of the child's attempt to resolve the conflict is called *repression*.[2] Much has been written about the nature and consequences of repression. The hypothesis of the existence and independent functioning of an unconscious mind has been elaborated to explain the analytical evidence, and a whole literature of theory has been built upon this idea. We are not here primarily concerned with psychoanalytic theory and we feel that the main contributions of the evidence to an understanding of the sources of aggressiveness can be explained quite simply. The overwhelming fact established by the evidence is that aggression, however deeply hidden or disguised, does not disappear. It appears later and in other forms. It is not destroyed. It is safe to conclude from the evidence that it cannot be destroyed. Whether we conceive simple aggression stimulated by frustration as a quantity of energy that has to be released somewhere, or whether we imagine that a secret and unconscious character is formed that is aggressive although the superficial character is peaceful, or whether we simply suppose that a certain kind of character is formed, peaceful in certain directions and aggressive in others – is a matter of comparative indifference and mainly of terminology. The fundamental fact is that the punishment of simple aggression results in the appearance of aggression in other forms. The boy, instead of striking his father whom he fears, strikes a smaller boy whom he does not fear. Disguised aggression has made the boy into a bully. The girl who dares not scream at her mother grows up to hate other women. Again a character has been formed by a simple aggressiveness that has been controlled but not destroyed. And in the same way revolutionaries who hate ordered government, nationalists who hate foreign peoples, individuals who hate bankers, Jews, or their political opponents, may be exhibiting characteristics that have been formed by the suppression of simple aggression in their childhood education.[3] These aggressive aspects of adult character and the aggressiveness to which they lead we call *transformed aggression*. It is the displaced and unrecognised fruit of suppressed simple aggression.

"2. The second great contribution of psychoanalytical evidence is to show the kind of transformations that simple aggression undergoes as the adult faculties develop. The fundamental problem of the child is, as we have seen, a double one: that of self-control and of *ambivalence*. In order to escape punishment the child ·must prevent its aggressive impulses from appearing – it must control its natural aggression. But this is not the whole of the problem. The parent has become for the child the object of two incompatible emotions – love and hatred. As a source of satisfaction and companionship the parent is greatly beloved. As a source of frustration and punishment the parent is greatly feared and hated. The evidence demonstrates overwhelmingly that such a double attitude to one person puts a terrible emotional strain upon the child. In the growth and development of character a number of imaginative and intellectual efforts are made to alleviate or avoid the severity of this internal conflict.

• • •

"It is to reduce anxiety and guilt to a minimum and to resolve the conflict of ambivalence that the major psychological mechanisms are developed. These are of two kinds – *displacement* and *projection*: both of them are frequently used for the expression of transformed aggression.

1. *Displacement.* This is perhaps the simplest mechanism of all. Several examples of it have already been cited. It is extremely common in political and social affairs. It consists in the transference of fear or hatred or love from the true historical object to a secondary object. The secondary object may be loved or hated for its own sake, but to the sensible degree of feeling is added an intensity derived from the transference to it of irrelevant passion. The child is thwarted by its father and then bullies a smaller child. The father is reprimanded by his employer of whom he is afraid and then is angry with his son. A girl both loves and feels jealous of her mother. To deal with this situation she may direct her loving feelings towards her school-mistress and feel free to hate her mother more completely. A boy may hate his father through familial discipline and grow up to hate all authority and government. He would be a revolutionary under any regime. Children who both love and hate their parents grow up to love their own country blindly and uncritically and to hate foreign countries with equal blindness and unreason. They have succeeded in displacing their opposite emotions to different objects.

"The tendency to identify the self with the community is so common as to be obvious.[4] The transference of the predominant feelings of childhood from parents to the organs of political life – to the State and the parties in it – is almost universal. Hence the importance of symbolical figureheads and governors, Kings and Führers. Hence the fanaticism and violence of political life. Hence the comparative weakness of reason and moderation in political affairs.

• • •

"From our present point of view the importance of this mechanism can scarcely be exaggerated. Adult aggression, as we have seen, is normally carried out in group activity. Political parties make civil war. Churches make religious war. States make international war. These various kinds of groups can attract absolute loyalty and canalise torrents of hatred and murder – through the mechanism of displacement. Individuals can throw themselves into the life and work of groups because they find a solution to their own conflicts in them. The stores of explosive violence in the human atom are released by and expressed in group organisation. The power of the group for aggression is derived partly from the sensible and objective judgements of men, but chiefly, in our view, by their power to attract to themselves the displaced hatred and destructiveness of their members. Displacement, though not the ultimate cause, is a direct channel of the ultimate causes of war.

2. *Projection*. A second group of mechanisms that are of the greatest importance in understanding individual and social behaviour are those of projection. It is not so simple a mechanism as that of displacement, but the psychoanalytic evidence demonstrates that it is of frequent occurrence in social life. The mechanism consists in imagining that other individuals are really like our own unrecognised and unaccepted selves. It is the projection of our own characters upon others.

●   ●   ●

"We have now completed our survey of the causes of aggression in human beings. We have suggested that there is no substantial difference in behaviour, that adults are just as cruel – or more so – just as aggressive, just as destructive as any group of animals or monkeys. The only difference in our view is one of psychological and intellectual mechanism. The causes of simple aggression – possessiveness, strangeness, frustration – are common to adults and simpler creatures. But a repressive discipline drives the simple aggression underground – to speak in metaphors – and it appears in disguised forms. These transformations are chiefly those of displacement and projection. These mechanisms have as their immediate motive the reduction of anxiety and the resolution of the conflicts of ambivalence and guilt. They result in the typical form of adult aggressiveness – aggressive personal relations of all kinds – but above all in group aggression: party conflict, civil war, wars of religion, and international war. The group life gives sanction to personal aggressiveness. The mobilisation of transformed aggression gives destructive power to groups. Aggression takes on its social form. And to justify it – to explain the group aggression to the outside world and to the group itself in terms that make it morally acceptable to the members of the group – great structures of intellectual reasoning – theories of history and religion and race – are built up. The impulses are rationalised. The hatred is justified."

Notes
1. Throughout this article we use the term "parent" to refer to the person or persons, whoever they may be, who are responsible for looking after the child – whether they are in fact parents or nurses or aunts or teachers.
2. The tendency to aggression is not the only thing that may be repressed.

Certain other impulses that are punished or condemned by adults or repudiated by the child himself may also be repressed. Much psychoanalytic evidence and theory is concerned with the repression of these other impulses – particularly the sexual impulses.

3. We are not for a moment suggesting either (a) that logical and objective cases cannot be argued in favour of revolutions, wars and persecutions, or (b) that the positive valuation of such things as justice, liberty and other social values may not reasonably involve a hatred of their opposites. We are only suggesting that the repression of simple aggression may result in these forms of hatred. The objective cases of these schools of thought are in every case different in kind from the personal and subjective elements in their supporters' view of them.

4. Nor is such an identification by any means wholly unreasonable. After all, the communities in which we are brought up have entered into us and made us what we are. It is natural that we should feel that what happens to them happens also to us more personally than they really do.

9 Social Influences Affecting the Disposition to War

After the Second World War discussion of the effects of the character and attitudes of individuals on the way in which international relations were conducted took a new turn. Group psychology began to appear more relevant than individual psychology. The development of attitude-testing and opinion-polling made it possible to examine and compare, on a genuinely scientific basis, the sentiments of particular national groups, particular occupation groups (such as the military, civil servants or politicians), or particular age-groups, towards other countries. Many studies of this kind were undertaken in this period. The first extract reproduced below, comparing the attitudes of nationals of particular countries, demonstrate some of the conclusions drawn from studies of this kind.

Some writers in seeking to discover the cause of hostile attitudes to foreign states, attempted to draw analogies with the animal world. The observations of ethologists about aggression among animals led some to conclude that humans inherited similar tendencies from their primeval past. Konrad Lorenz, in his celebrated study of animal aggression, went on to consider (as in the passage reproduced below) reasons for group hostility and war among humans. But he was careful not to draw any direct inference from one to the other. Indeed he discovers quite different factors at work among human beings: factors that had their basis in social organisation rather than individual psychology. He drew attention particularly to a phenomenon he calls "militant enthusiasm", whether for a nation or a cause, and the role this can play in directing aggression to external objects.

Others were less cautious. One conclusion drawn by some from animal behaviour studies was that humans shared with animals a "territorial instinct", which led them to defend with special tenacity the homeland which they saw as their own. This thesis was put forward in disregard of the fact that the primates, the animals closest to the human species, show little evidence of any such "territorial imperative"; or that, among humans, immigrants often fight for their adopted country at least as tenaciously as native-born residents and sometimes more so. These and other factors led many to doubt the thesis that humans share the instinct of some animals and birds to defend a territory. That thesis is however presented here in the extract from Robert Ardrey's book, *The Territorial Imperative*, which won widespread attention at the time it appeared.

More persuasive were the writings of social psychologists. Decisions about peace and war are reached in an institutional setting and there was increasing scepticism about the relevance of conclusions reached on the basis of the individual psychology of citizens (except, perhaps, that of their leaders). Doubts of this kind are expressed in the passage quoted below from Herbert Kelman's book *International Behaviour*. He questions the degree of attention so widely given to the role of "aggression" in personal motivation, suggesting that in modern conditions motives of fear and mistrust may be more significant. But he is particularly concerned to show that in international relationships, individuals, including key decision-makers, are operating always within a particular social and political environment. Only a multidisciplinary approach, therefore, which takes account of all the various sources of influence, is likely to increase our understanding of the attitudes and actions which affect their decisions.

* * *

Buchanan and Cantril – The Individual's Attitude to International Society*

"The individual's assumptions concerning the nature of the world, of which ideas concerning men and nations and war and peace are fragments, form the intellectual framework within which he considers proposals for change. The four questions which deal with these more

* William Buchanan (1918–). Studied at Washington and Lee University and Princeton and has taught in the University of Southern California, Tennessee and Washington and Lee Universities. Interested in public opinion, political parties and the electoral process. Works include *An International Police Force and Public Opinion* (1954), and *Legislative Partisanship: the Deviant Case of California* (1963).

Hedley Cantril (1940–). Specialist in research on public opinion and author of many studies based on the findings of opinion pollsters. Formerly directed the Office or less abstract ideas differ from the other questions in that the 'you' element is subordinated. They demand that the respondent exercise logic, pass on matters of fact or probability, and judge proposals rather than merely describe his position in life or his subjective relations to others.

"Since they demand more of an 'intellectual' than an 'emotional' reaction, these questions were not intended to get at the 'real' reasons for the individual's view of international affairs but rather to get at his rationalisations and assumptions. This should not imply that these opinions are any less firmly held, or necessarily less important to the individual.

"These questions test the prevalence of the sort of thinking embodied in the phrase 'War is inevitable because you can't change human nature'. While this sort of reasoning may not itself motivate people to resist proposals for change, it does supply them with a satisfying rationale, and if it goes unchallenged, presents a stumbling block to any efforts of those who seek to re-order the world along more amicable lines.

"One set of data may be anticipated from this block of results to illustrate the importance of these ideas and how they are believed to function. In Germany 59 per cent, and in Italy 51 per cent, of respondents said their national characteristics were 'born in us'. In the United States, 15 per cent gave this response, in Norway 23 per cent. Nazi–Fascist teachings unquestionably account for the large difference, but they cannot be considered the sole cause, for the figures in the Netherlands (44 per cent) and Britain (39 per cent) are almost as high. The difference is that in Germany these beliefs supported a programme of policy, and for the individual rationalised actions on the part of his government against 'non-Aryans', which he could not otherwise have justified. What were the 'real' motives behind these national acts is far more important, but there are no data on them here. The important point is that this belief sanctioned actions, just as the belief in the inevitability of war may support those who for other reasons oppose international government and hinder those who want to work toward it.

•   •   •

"Neither the sex nor the age of respondents seemed to have a

of Public Opinion Research at Princeton University. Works include *The Psychology of Social Movements* (1941) and *Gauging Public Opinion* (1947).
Quoted from *How Nations See Each Other* (Urbana, Ill.: University of Illinois ·Press, 1953).

'consistent' or 'significant' effect on the answers to any of the questions. . . . Socio-economic status was not related in any way that could not be accounted for by its connection with education.

• • •

"When divided by political views, the results are less equivocal. *'Rightists' tend to believe human nature cannot be changed and that national characteristics are inborn.* This is evident in most countries, but the percentages are only occasionally 'significant'. 'Leftists' do not consistently take the opposite view, a fairly high proportion of them falling in the 'Don't know' category.

"On the possibility of peace, 'Leftists' in every country tend to be optimistic; 'Rightists', pessimistic. The differences are 'significant' in six of the nine countries. The 'Leftists' favour a world government, and the 'Rightists' oppose it in eight of the nine countries, and by significant margins in four of the nine.

"To summarise: of the four clearly independent variables, three (sex, age, and socio-economic status) show no relationship, while the fourth (education) seems to have some effect, but not always in the same direction. The fifth background variable (political predisposition) is in itself a matter of opinion and cannot be considered independent. It is clearly related to views on international affairs and somewhat less clearly to views of human nature and national characteristics.

• • •

"*In every country those who believe human nature can be changed are more likely to believe their national characteristics result from upbringing, and those who believe human nature inflexible are more likely to attribute national characteristics to heredity.* These differences are 'significant' in seven of the nine countries.

"The two questions on international relations were also closely related. *In every country those who thought peace possible were more likely to want world government than those who thought it impossible.* The differences were 'significant' in all nine countries, ranging from 9 per cent to 41 per cent.

"*In every country those who thought· human nature could be changed were more likely to be hopeful of peace than those who said it could not be.* The differences ran from 10 per cent to 34 per cent, all 'significant'. More in the former group also thought peace likely, though by considerably smaller and only occasionally 'significant' margins. *Those who thought human nature could change tended to accept world government in eight of the nine countries*, by 'significant' margins in six of them.

"Whether respondents thought national characteristics were inherited or acquired had no strong relation to their views on peace or world government. There was a slight tendency in seven countries for those who thought their national characteristics due to upbringing to say peace was possible, but this was 'significant' in only two. . . .

Conclusions and suggestions

"Throughout the areas surveyed, opinions on the possibility of peace and world government are closely related to each other, and to views of human nature and politics as well. It is not apparent that these constellations of opinion conform to the age, sex or status reference groups of their holders.

"Opinion divides into two patterns somewhat as follows: on one hand there are the *'optimists' – those who believe human nature perfectible, national character pliable, world peace attainable, and world organisation advisable*; on the other hand are the *'fatalists' – those who believe that 'you'll always have wars because you can't change human nature', and that change is hardly worth trying.* Along the continuum between them stands the bulk of the population, choosing among these various beliefs with magnificent disregard for consistency.

" . . . What purpose does the 'fatalistic' view of the world serve for those who hold it? Age, sex and status give no clue. Politics suggest that this may be part of a philosophy of ultraconservatism in which those who see their own government, regardless of its actual complexion, as 'too much to the left' also derive some grim satisfaction from believing that all these efforts toward change will come to nothing, while only human obstinacy and national bloodlines remain constant. If this is actually the case, the prospect for shaking these beliefs is hardly bright. However, the presence of a considerable body of Communists among the group finding these same governments 'Too right' puts an entirely different connotation on the questions. Then the issue becomes: Are these changes to be achieved gradually or by revolution?

"A third possibility is that the key phrase may be 'human nature' – a phrase which translates with ease from language to language (*la nature humaine, das Wesen des Menschen, la natura umana, naturaleza humana, manselijke natuur, menneskenaturen*), which provokes about the same patterns of response in every country and which perhaps has no really specific meaning anywhere.

"If the 'fatalist's' glib generality about human nature were no more than a useful cracker-barrel debater's point, one would not expect to find it so well integrated in his outlook on politics, heredity, peace and internationalism. It would be naive to expect a campaign designed to deny the aphorism that 'wars are inevitable because of human nature' would by itself improve international understanding.

"The contemporary studies of anthropologists, biologists, psychologists and sociologists demonstrate the infinite variety of cultures and the flexibility of human behaviour. Wider dissemination of these findings through schools and universities should (aside from its intrinsic worth as enlightenment) have a beneficial effect on ideas about peace and international co-operation. 'To the best of our knowledge, there is no evidence to indicate that wars are necessary and inevitable consequences of "human nature" as such' was the first point in a statement issued by eight social scientists at a Unesco conference.

"The comparative strength of the relationships suggests that perhaps hope for peace is the central attitude and that the others are part of a supporting rationale – the whole constellation being provoked by shock at the possibility of another war."

Lorenz – Social Restraints on Aggressiveness[*]

"Norms of social behaviour developed by cultural ritualisation play at least as important a part in the context of human society as instinctive motivation and the control exerted by responsible morality. . . . Customs and taboos may acquire the power to motivate behaviour in a way comparable to that of autonomous instincts. Not only highly developed rites or ceremonies but also simpler and less conspicuous norms of social behaviour may attain, after a number of generations, the character of sacred customs which are loved and considered as values whose infringement is severely frowned upon by public opinion. . . . Sacred custom owes its motivating force to phylogenetically evolved behaviour patterns of which two are of

---

[*] From Konrad Lorenz (1903–). Zoologist and pioneer in the study of animal behaviour. Austrian-born, taught at Vienna University and after the war in Attenburg in Austria and Konigsberg in West Germany. Has sought to show that animal behaviour is the product of adaptive evolution. Best known for his book *On Aggression* (1966). Also author of *Evolution and Modification of Behaviour* (1966) and *The Foundations of Ecology* (1981). Quoted from *On Aggression* (London: Methuen, 1963).

particular importance. One is the response of militant enthusiasm by which any group defends its own social norms and rites against another group not possessing them; the other is the group's cruel taunting of any of its members who fail to conform with the accepted 'good form' of behaviour. Without the phylogenetically programmed love for traditional custom human society would lack the supporting apparatus to which it owes its indispensable structure. Yet, like any phylogenetically programmed behaviour mechanism, the one under discussion can miscarry. School classes or companies of soldiers, which can both be regarded as models of primitive group structure, can be very cruel indeed in their ganging up against an outsider. The purely instinctive response to a physically abnormal individual, for instance the jeering at a fat boy, is absolutely indentical, as far as overt behaviour is concerned, with discrimination against a person who differs from the group in culturally developed social norms – for instance a child who speaks a different dialect.

"The ganging up against an individual diverging from the social norms characteristic of a group, and the group's enthusiastic readiness to defend these social norms and rites, are both good illustrations of the way in which culturally determined conditioned stimulus situations release activities which are fundamentally instinctive. They are also excellent examples of typical compound behaviour patterns whose primary survival value is as obvious as the danger of their misfiring under the conditions of the modern social order. . . .

"A simple and effective way of discharging aggression in an innocuous manner is to redirect it at a substitute object. . . . This method has been employed extensively by the great constructors of evolution to prevent combat between members of a group. It is sound reason for optimism that aggression, more easily than most other instincts, can find complete satisfaction with substitute objects. Even without insight into the consequences of dammed-up drives, the choice of object is directed by reasonable considerations. I have found that even highly irascible people who, in a rage, seem to lose all control of their actions, still refrain from smashing really valuable objects, preferring cheaper crockery. Yet it would be a complete error to suspect that they could, if they only tried hard enough, keep from smashing things altogether! Insight into the physiology of dammed-up drive and its redirected discharge is, of course, a great help in governing aggression. . . .

"Redirection as a means of controlling the functions of aggression and other undischarged drives has been known to humanity for a long time. The ancient Greeks were familiar with the conception of catharsis, of purifying discharge, and psychoanalysis has shown very convincingly that many patterns of altogether laudable behaviour derive their impulses from the 'sublimation' of aggressive or sexual drives. Sublimation, however, must not be confounded with simple redirection of an instinctive activity towards a substitute object. There is a substantial difference between the man who bangs the table instead of hitting his antagonist, and the man who discharges the aggression aroused by an irritating family life by writing an enthusiastic pamphlet serving an altogether unconnected cause.

"One of the many instances in which phylogenetic and cultural ritualisation have hit on very similar solutions of the same problem, concerns the method by which both have achieved the difficult task of avoiding killing without destroying the important functions per-formed by fighting in the interest of the species. All the culturally evolved norms of 'fair fighting', from primitive chivalry to the Geneva Convention, are functionally analogous to phylogenetically ritualised combat in animals. . . .

"What is needed is the arousal of enthusiasm for causes which are commonly recognised as values of the highest order by all human beings, irrespective of their national, cultural or political allegiances. I have already called attention to the danger of defining a value by begging the question. A value is emphatically not just the object to which the instinctive response of militant enthusiasm becomes fixated by imprinting and early conditioning, even if, conversely, militant enthusiasm can become fixated on practically any institutionalised social norm or rite and make it appear as a value. . . .

"We must face the fact that militant enthusiasm has evolved from the hackle-raising and chin-protruding communal defence instinct of our pre-human ancestors and that the key stimulus situations which release it still bear all the earmarks of this origin. Among them, the existence of an enemy, against whom to defend cultural values, is still one of the most effective. Militant enthusiasm, in one particular respect, is dangerously akin to the triumph ceremony of geese and to analogous instinctive behaviour patterns of other animals. The social bond embracing a group is closely connected with aggression directed against outsiders. In human beings, too, the feeling of togetherness which is so essential to the serving of a common cause is greatly enhanced by the presence of a definite, threatening enemy whom it is possible to hate. Also, it is much easier to make people identify with a simple and concrete common cause than with an abstract idea. For all these reasons, the teachers of militant ideologies have an enviably easy job in converting young people. We must face the fact that in Russia as well as in China the younger generation knows perfectly well what it is fighting for, while in our culture it is casting about in vain for causes worth embracing. The way in which huge numbers of young Americans have recently identified themselves with the rights of the American Negro is a glorious exception, though the fervour with which they have done so tends to accentuate the prevalent lack of militant enthusiasm for other equally just and equally important causes – such as the prevention of war in general. The actual war-monger, of course, has the best chances of arousing militant enthusiasm because he can always work his dummy or fiction of an enemy for all it is worth.

"In all these respects the defender of peace is at a decided disadvantage. Everything he lives and works for, all the high goals at which he aims are, or should be, determined by moral responsibility which presupposes quite a lot of knowledge and real insight. Nobody can get really enthusiastic about them without considerable erudition. The one and only unquestionable value that can be appreciated independently of rational morality or education is the bond of human love and friendship from which all kindness and charity springs, and which represents the great antithesis to aggression. In fact, love and friendship come far nearer to typifying all that is good, than aggression, which is only mistakenly identified with a destructive death drive, comes to exemplifying all that is evil."

Ardrey – Man as a Territorial Animal*

"Man, I shall attempt to demonstrate in this inquiry, is as much a territorial animal as is a mockingbird singing in the clear California night. We act as we do for reasons of our evolutionary past, not our cultural present, and our behaviour is as much a mark of our species

* From Robert Ardrey (1908–80). Born and brought up in Chicago and mainly known as a playwright and novelist. In his later years became interested in the relationship of human conflict and conflict among animals. Works include *African Genesis*, a personal investigation into the animal origins and nature of man (1963) and *The Hunting Hypothesis* (1956), a personal conclusion concerning the evolutionary nature of man. Quoted from *The Territorial Imperative* (London: Collins, 1967).

as is the shape of a human thigh bone or the configuration of nerves in a corner of the human brain. If we defend the title to our land or the sovereignty of our country, we do it for reasons no different, no less innate, no less ineradicable, than do lower animals. The dog barking at you from behind his master's fence acts for a motive indistinguishable from that of his master when the fence was built.

"Neither are men and dogs and mockingbirds uncommon creatures in the natural world. Ring-tailed lemurs and great-crested grebes, prairie dogs, robins, tigers, muskrats, meadow warblers and Atlantic salmon, fence lizards, flat lizards, three-spined sticklebacks, nightingales and Norway rats, herring gulls and callicebus monkeys – all of us will give everything we are for a place of our own. Territory, in the evolving world of animals, is a force perhaps older than sex.

"The survival value that territory brings to a species varies as widely as do the opportunities of species themselves. In some it offers security from the predator, in others security of food supply. In some its chief value seems the selection of worthy males for reproduction, in some the welding together of a group, and in many, like sea birds, the prime value seems simply the excitement and stimulation of border quarrels. And there are many species, of course, for which the territorial tie would be a handicap to survival. Grazing animals for the most part must move with the season's grass. Elephant herds acknowledge no territorial bond, but move like fleets of old gray galleons across the measureless African space. The gorilla, too, is a wanderer within a limited range who every night must build a new nest wherever his search for food may take him.

"In those countless species, however, which through long evolutionary trial and error have come to incorporate a territorial pattern into their whole behaviour complex, we shall find a remarkable uniformity. Widely unrelated though the species may be, a few distinct patterns are endlessly repeated. In the next chapter, for example, we shall examine arena behaviour, in which solitary males defend mating stations to which females come solely for copulation. It makes little difference whether the species be antelope or sage grouse, the pattern will be almost the same. And in the chapter after that we shall consider the pair territory, that portion of space occupied and defended by a breeding couple, as in robins and beavers and men. So we shall move along surveying the territorial experience in the world of the animal as it has been observed by science in our generation.

"If, as I believe, man's innumerable territorial expressions are human responses to an imperative lying with equal force on mockingbirds and men, then human self-estimate is due for radical revision. We acknowledge a few such almighty forces, but very few: the will to survive, the sexual impulse, the tie, perhaps, between mother and infant. It has been our inadequate knowledge of the natural world, I suggest, that has led us to look no further. And it may come to us as the strangest of thoughts that the bond between a man and the soil he walks on should be more powerful than his bond with the woman he sleeps with. Even so, in a rough, preliminary way we may test the supposition with a single question: How many men have you known of, in your lifetime, who die for their country? And how many for a woman?

"Any force which may command us to act in opposition to the will to survive is a force to be inspected, at such a moment of history as ours, with the benefit of other than obsolete information. That I believe this force to be a portion of our evolutionary nature, a behaviour pattern of such survival value to the emerging human being that it became fixed in our genetic endowment, just as the shape of our feet and the musculature of our buttocks became fixed, is the premise of this inquiry. Even as that behaviour pattern called sex evolved in many organisms as nature's most effective answer to the problem of reproduction, so that behaviour pattern called territory evolved in many organisms as a kind of defence mechanism, as nature's most effective answer to a variety of problems of survival.

"I regard the territorial imperative as no less essential to the existence of contemporary man than it was to those bands of small-brained proto-men on the high African savannah millions of years ago. I see it as a force shaping our lives in countless unexpected ways, threatening our existence only to the degree that we fail to understand it."

Kelman – The Effect of Social Factors on International Relations*

"Any attempt . . . to conceptualise the causes of war and the conditions for peace that starts from individual psychology rather than from

---

* From H. C. Kelman (1927–). Austrian-born but educated in the US and has taught for many years at Harvard. Interested in social influences on attitude changes,

an analysis of the relations between nation-states is of questionable relevance.

"Thus, some psychological writers, starting from individual be-haviour, have tended to overemphasise the role of aggression. They seemed to reason that, since war represents aggressive behaviour on the part of nation-states, one can understand its causes by examining the determinants of aggressive behaviour in individuals. Occasionally this reasoning was by analogy, but most commonly it was based on the assumption that the behaviour of states consists, after all, of the behaviours of individuals. This assumption, however, ignores the fact that the behaviour of nations is the aggregation of a variety of behaviours on the part of many individuals, representing different roles, different interests, different degrees of influence on final de-cisions, and contributing in very different ways to the complex social processes that eventuate in a final outcome such as war. One cannot, therefore, expect that the behaviour of a nation will be a direct reflection of the motives of its citizens or even of its leaders. While war does involve aggressive behaviour on the part of many individ-uals, this behaviour is not necessarily at the service of aggressive motives. Leaders may engage in aggressive behaviour for strategic reasons, for example, and the population at large for reasons of social conformity. Even where aggressive motives are involved in pre-disposing national leaders to precipitate war and segments of the population to support it enthusiastically,[1] their role in the causation of war cannot be understood without an examination of the societal (and intersocietal) processes that are involved in the decision to engage in war, and of the way in which different elements of the society enter into these processes. There are certainly things to be learned from the psychology of aggression that are relevant to inter-national relations, but they cannot be applied automatically; only by starting from an analysis of international relations at their own level can one identify the points at which such application becomes relevant.

"The personal motivations that play a part in people's preference for war or willingness to accept it are manifold. The motivations of fear and distrust, for example, are likely to be far more relevant to

nationalism and the effects of international contact on conceptions of international society. Editor, *International Behaviour: A Sociopsychological Analysis* (1965), and author of many articles in the field of social psychology. Quoted from "Social-Psychological Approaches to the Study of International Relations", in H. C. Kelman (ed.), *International Behaviour* (New York: Holt, Rinehart and Winston, 1965).

modern warfare than is personal aggression. Even a more complex analysis of the motivational patterns of individuals, however, which takes the entire range of motives into account, is not a proper starting-point for the study of war. War is a societal and intersocietal action carried out in a national and international political context. What has to be explained is the way in which nations, given various societal and political conditions, arrive at various international policies, including war. Part of this explanation involves the motivations and perceptions of different individuals – both decision-makers and various publics – who play different roles in the larger societal process. But only if we know where and how these individuals fit into the larger process, and under what constraints they operate, are we able to offer a relevant psychological analysis. Thus, the study of psychological processes is highly relevant to a full understanding of the causation of war, *if* it recognises that societal and political conditions provide the framework within which the motivations and perceptions of individuals can function.

"Some of the conceptualisations of war and peace that take individual psychology as their point of departure have been marked by another characteristic, related to the emphasis on aggression and other personal motives. This is the tendency to use the language of psychopathology, and to treat war as a form of deviation comparable to psychotic behaviour in individuals. Now, war may be an extremely irrational form of societal behaviour, in terms of the balance between costs and gains; certainly very few observers today would regard *nuclear* war as an instrument of policy that one would deliberately choose on the basis of rational considerations. But this does not mean that the causes of war are in any way comparable to the etiology of pathological behavior in individuals. Such an analogy is likely to obscure the societal and intersocietal dynamics that generate conflicts between nations and that favour particular mechanisms for their resolution.

"Insights derived from the study of behaviour pathology are certainly relevant to the way in which individuals – decision-makers and members of the population at large – react to other nations and to foreign policy issues. Thus, for example, projection and other forms of perceptual distortion, denial in the face of threat, or rigidity in a situation of stress, are behaviour mechanisms that often occur in response to international situations. But – in line with our discussion of psychological processes in general – whether and how these mechanisms contribute to the causation of war can only be understood in terms of the larger societal processes that serve as their context.

"A clear implication of the preceding observations is that it makes little sense to speak of *a* psychological theory of war or of international relations. There cannot be a psychological theory that is complete and self-contained and can in any way be proposed as an alternative to other theories, such as economic or political. There can only be a general theory of international relations in which psychological factors play a part, once the points in the process at which they are applicable have been properly identified. Within such a framework, however, psychological – and, particularly, social-psychological – analyses can potentially make a considerable contribution to the study of international politics, and of international behaviour in general. This is the conviction on which the present volume is based.

"The tendency, particularly in some of the earlier psychological and psychoanalytic writings on war and peace, to focus on aggression and other motives of individuals and to emphasise irrational and pathological processes, without taking the societal and political context into account, has caused some specialists in international relations to question the relevance of psychological contributions. There is no inherent reason, however, why psychological analyses must ignore the environmental context within which behaviour occurs, or must focus on irrational processes at the expense of rational ones. In recent years, the trend in psychology in general has been to move away from this kind of orientation. Psychological analyses of international relations, in particular, have tended increasingly to start at the level of international relations itself and to observe behaviour within the context thus provided. Similarly, they have increasingly tended to use conceptual approaches in which neither rationality nor irrationality is a built-in assumption, but in which, instead, both cognitive and effective factors are integral parts of a common explanatory scheme.

Recent developments

"The social-psychological study of international relations in recent years certainly has not overcome all the shortcomings of earlier work in this area. In absolute terms, the amount of research on these problems is still very small, and the amount of dependable evidence that has been amassed is smaller yet. . . . We have to consider seriously the possibilities – raised by some critics – that some of the

current research and conceptualisation may have only limited relevance to international politics, and especially to the issues of war
and peace; that they may pay insufficient attention to the political
realities that set constraints on psychological processes; that they may
overemphasise the role of attitudinal and personal factors in national
behaviour; and that they may not focus their analysis on the right
people and the right settings. . . .

"Nevertheless, there has been a change of such proportions in the
social-psychological study of international relations during recent
years that one is justified in describing this area as having reached a
new stage in its development. The volume of work has greatly
increased and there has been a concomitant growth in quality and
sophistication. The earlier work on international attitudes and public
opinion has continued, at a greater rate and with greater methodological refinement, and with increasing attempts to link it more
closely to the foreign policy process. There have been quite a number
of studies focusing directly on cross-national contact and interaction.
There have been various attempts to study international conflict and
its resolution experimentally and thus to deal more concretely with
issues of foreign policy-making. Many of the investigators in this area
are acutely aware of the problems of generalisation that this kind of
research entails, and make serious attempts to grapple with them: to
explore the international situation to which they hope to be able to
generalise, and the conditions that would have to be met in order to
permit such generalisation.

"There is, in general, a concern with the theoretical and methodological issues involved in the psychological analysis of international
relations, including the questions of what role psychological variables
play in internation behaviour and what constitutes a proper unit of
analysis. In recent theoretical formulations, there is a greater tendency to start with questions derived from an analysis of international
conflict and the interaction between nations, and to introduce psychological concepts whenever they can contribute to answering these
questions. This has meant a decline in global approaches to the
psychology of war and peace, with greater attention to the psychological analysis of specific subproblems. Similarly, psychological contributions to policy questions have tended to be more specific and
more directly related to concrete issues in foreign affairs.

"All these activities have taken place within a climate that has
become increasingly favourable to research on problems of war and
peace. Until recently, war and peace has not been a respectable,

meaningful target of rigorous inquiry for most students of human behaviour. But the situation has changed, probably due to a combination of forces within and outside the social-science community. The external forces no doubt include the advent of nuclear weapons and the consequent change in the meaning of war; the occurrence of various crises engendered by the Cold War; and the gradual relaxation of Cold-War tensions and, in the United States, of the pressures of the McCarthy era. The internal forces probably include the steady growth of behavioural approaches in political science; the development of more complex theoretical models in psychology; and the emergence of an interdisciplinary behavioural science."

Note

1. It is interesting that most of the psychological analyses of war that stress the role of aggression were written with an eye to Nazi Germany, where the assumption about aggressive motives in many leaders and perhaps large segments of the population may have been more justified than is usually the case.

Part Two
The Nature of States

Introduction

Not all writers have looked to human nature as the explanation of conflict among states. They have recognised that most humans are both competitive and co-operative; have social as well as aggressive impulses; and that those impulses anyway have many outlets that are unrelated to war or to relations among states. Above all, most individuals have little or no influence on the way their states behave; and the few who do act in a collective rather than a personal role.

For these reasons most writers, especially in recent times, have been inclined to attribute the character of international conflict to the nature of *states* rather than to that of individual human beings. International relations, by definition, are conducted by states, not by individuals. Thus a considerable amount of the writing undertaken on the subject has been devoted to analysing the character and motives of states. Just as political philosophers, seeking to consider the nature of the political institutions required to establish a viable social and political order, have traditionally begun by examining the nature of "man", so students of international relations have begun by examining the nature of states.

There are a number of obvious questions to be asked. Do all states respond in similar ways to similar challenges or threats, or are there marked variations? If so, what are the reasons for these variations? Do the policies pursued by states depend on their geographical situation, their historical experience, or their relative size and power? Do they depend on the nature of the domestic political system: how far they are autocratic or democratic, whether many or few have influence on the decisions that are reached? Or are the character and motives of the decision-makers themselves the paramount influence or the national interests of the state? More generally, are the actions of states dependent mainly on the *internal* character of states, or do they depend primarily on the character of the international system as a whole? These are only a few of the questions that have been asked by writers on this subject through the ages.

10 The Interests of States

Some reflections on the essential character of states can be found even in ancient writers.

In his *Peleponnesian War*, for example, Thucydides describes and contrasts the observations of some of the participants in that war on the nature of state interests and the kinds of actions by states they regarded as justifiable to promote those interests. An example is his account of the discussions supposed to have taken place after Athenian forces landed on the island of Melos to persuade, or, if necessary, compel, the latter to join the war against Sparta. Melos, though a colony of Sparta, had so far remained neutral. But this was insufficient to satisfy Athens. She demanded that all the islands should join her in the war, regardless of their prior commitments, and she sent a force to Melos to bring that state to her side.

The discussion, as described by Thucydides, touches on some of the most fundamental questions of international relations. In the first place he presents a dialogue which typifies the relationship between strong and weak: between the representatives of a powerful state, capable of imposing its will by force, presenting the cynical arguments of *realpolitik* and *raison d'état*, against those of a weak state, unable to defend itself, placing its reliance on principles of decency, reason and friendly relations among states. Secondly, the discussion concerns the nature of state interests: short-term and long-term, tangible and intangible. The Athenian delegates are concerned only with the *immediate* interests of their state – the necessity of bringing Melos into her alliance against Sparta; while the Melians urge them to pay regard to Athens' *long-term* interests, including her good name and the disadvantages of becoming known as a tyrannical aggressor, so arousing other states against her. Finally, the discussion is an argument about justice: whether it is the case, as the Athenians state, that justice only means the will of the powerful: or, as the Melians argue, that it must involve "fair play and just dealing".

The whole discussion constitutes a bitter comment on the reality of international relations. At the end of the day, as Thucydides makes clear with brutal simplicity, naked force prevails: the men of Melos are killed, their wives and children enslaved. The message seems to be that in international relations morality and principle count for little and only the will of the powerful finally matters. As the Athenian delegates assert, the "strong do what they have the power to do and the weak accept what they have to accept". On this interpretation the state has no choice but to promote its own interests by whatever means it can.

The ancient Indian writer, Kautilya, also discussed state interests. In his book *Arthasastra* he advises rulers about the best strategy to employ in a competitive struggle with other rulers. Warfare is an essential and inevitable feature of that struggle. The advice given mainly concerns when to make war and against whom. Generally war should be made against weaker rulers or against rulers weakened by internal disorders. If a state is subject to national disasters, such as fire, flood and pestilence, or if its subjects are disaffected and impoverished, it is also suitable to be attacked. If two enemy states in alliance cannot be overcome together, it is wise to make peace with one and war with the other. To make war on another state allies may be sought; but if an ally in turn needs help, he can be provided with a weak or treacherous army; or peace can be made with his enemy and the ally therefore betrayed. Like Machiavelli, therefore, Kautilya does not hesitate to advocate deceit if this is the best way for a king to promote his own interests. The rules he lays down are presented somewhat like the rules of a game of chess. And he depicts an international society in which war is seen as something of a game, a game in which the rulers who control the fortunes of states use every possible ingenuity to overcome their opponents by any means they can.

Both these writers therefore (or those they describe) see the promotion of the state's interests as the highest goal of policy. In an ultra-competitive international environment each regards warfare as an inevitable feature of international society and is concerned with the policies that will enable the individual state to survive in that struggle. Because the character of the wider environment is taken for granted, attention is focused narrowly on the individual unit and its means of self-preservation within that environment. The possibility of changing the environment as a whole, and so directing attention to the wider society of states, is not considered.

*   *   *

Thucydides – The Nature of State Interest*

"The Athenians also made an expedition against the island of Melos. They had thirty of their own ships, six from Chios, and two from Lesbos; 1200 hoplites, 300 archers, and twenty mounted archers, all from Athens; and about 1500 hoplites from the allies and the islanders.

"The Melians are a colony of Sparta. They had refused to join the Athenian empire like the other islanders, and at first had remained neutral without helping either side; but afterwards, when the Athenians had brought force to bear on them by laying waste their land, they had become open enemies of Athens.

"Now the generals Cleomedes, the son of Lycomedes, and Tisias, the son of Tisimachus, encamped with the above force in Melian territory and, before doing any harm to the land, first of all sent representatives to negotiate. The Melians did not invite these representatives to speak before the people, but asked them to make the statement for which they had come in front of the governing body and the few. The Athenian representatives then spoke as follows. . . .

"*Athenians:* We on our side will use no fine phrases saying, for example, that we have a right to our empire because we defeated the Persians, or that we have come against you now because of the injuries you have done us – a great mass of words that nobody would believe. And we ask you on your side not to imagine that you will influence us by saying that you, though a colony of Sparta, have not joined Sparta in the war, or that you have never done us any harm. Instead we recommend that you should try to get what it is possible for you to get, taking into consideration what we both really do think; since you know as well as we do that, when these matters are discussed by practical people, the standard of justice depends on the equality of power to compel and that in fact the strong do what they have the power to do and the weak accept what they have to accept.

"*Melians:* Then in our view (since you force us to leave justice out of

---

* From Thucydides (*c.* 455–400 BC). Athenian historian and author of *The Peloponnesian War*. A contemporary witness of the war, he was at one time given command of an Athenian fleet but, because of his failure to prevent the capture of Amphipolis, was sentenced and exiled until the end of the war. His history provides an objective account of the war, including vivid accounts of many of the main personalities involved and the motives for their actions. Found the ultimate cause of the war in the rise of Athenian power and the threat that this represented to Sparta. In this passage he illustrates the ruthlessness with which the war was sometimes conducted. Quoted from *The Peloponnesian War*, Book 5, Chapter 7, trs. Rex Warner (London: Penguin, 1955).

account and to confine ourselves to self-interest) – in our view it is at any rate useful that you should not destroy a principle that is to the general good of all men – namely, that in the case of all who fall into danger there should be such a thing as fair play and just dealing, and that such people should be allowed to use and to profit by arguments that fall short of a mathematical accuracy. And this is a principle which affects you as much as anybody, since your own fall would be visited by the most terrible vengeance and would be an example to the world.

"*Athenians:* As for us, even assuming that our empire does come to an end, we are not despondent about what would happen next. One is not so much frightened of being conquered by a power which rules over others, as Sparta does (not that we are concerned with Sparta now), as of what would happen if a ruling power is attacked and defeated by its own subjects. So far as this point is concerned, you can leave it to us to face the risks involved. What we shall do now is to show you that it is for the good of our own empire that we are here and that it is for the preservation of your city that we shall say what we are going to say. We do not want any trouble in bringing you into our empire, and we want you to be spared for the good both of yourselves and of ourselves.

"*Melians:* And how could it be just as good for us to be the slaves as for you to be the masters?

"*Athenians:* You, by giving in, would save yourselves from disaster; we, by not destroying you, would be able to profit from you.

"*Melians:* So you would not agree to our being neutral, friends instead of enemies, but allies of neither side?

"*Athenians:* No, because it is not so much your hostility that injures us; it is rather the case that, if we were on friendly terms with you, our subjects would regard that as a sign of weakness in us, whereas your hatred is evidence of our power.

"*Melians:* Is that your subjects' idea of fair play – that no distinction should be made between people who are quite unconnected with you and people who are mostly your own colonists or else rebels whom you have conquered?

"*Athenians:* So far as right and wrong are concerned they think that there is no difference between the two, that those who still preserve their independence do so because they are strong, and that if we fail to attack them it is because we are afraid. So that by conquering you we shall increase not only the size but the security of our empire. We rule the sea and you are islanders, and weaker islanders too than the others; it is therefore particularly important that you should not escape.

"*Melians:* But do you think there is no security for you in what we suggest? For here again, since you will not let us mention justice, but tell us to give in to your interests, we, too, must tell you what our interests are and, if yours and ours happen to coincide, we must try to persuade you of the fact. Is it not certain that you will make enemies of all states who are at present neutral, when they see what is happening here and naturally conclude that in course of time you will attack them too? Does not this mean that you are strengthening the enemies you have already and are forcing others to become your enemies even against their intentions and their inclinations?

"*Athenians:* As a matter of fact we are not so much frightened of states on the continent. They have their liberty, and this means that it will be a long time before they begin to take precautions against us. We are more concerned about islanders like yourselves, who are still unsubdued, or subjects who have already become embittered by the constraint which our empire imposes on them. These are the people who are most likely to act in a reckless manner and to bring themselves and us, too, into the most obvious danger.

"*Melians:* Then surely, if such hazards are taken by you to keep your empire and by your subjects to escape from it, we who are still free would show ourselves great cowards and weaklings if we failed to face everything that comes rather than submit to slavery.

"*Athenians:* No, not if you are sensible. This is no fair fight, with honour on one side and shame on the other. It is rather a question of saving your lives and not resisting those who are far too strong for you.

"*Melians:* Yet we know that in war fortune sometimes makes the odds more level than could be expected from the difference in numbers of the two sides. And if we surrender, then all our hope is lost at once, whereas, so long as we remain in action, there is still a hope that we may yet stand upright.

"*Athenians:* Hope, that comforter in danger! If one already has solid advantages to fall back upon, one can indulge in hope. It may do harm, but will not destroy one. But hope is by nature an expensive commodity, and those who are risking their all on one cast find out what it means only when they are already ruined; it never fails them in the period when such a knowledge would enable them to take precautions. Do not let this happen to you, you who are weak and whose fate depends on a single movement of the scale. And do not be like those people who, as so commonly happens, miss the chance of saving themselves in a human and practical way, and, when every clear and distinct hope has left them in their adversity, turn to what is blind and vague, to prophecies and oracles and such things which by encouraging hope lead men to ruin.

"*Melians:* It is difficult, and you may be sure that we know it, for us to oppose your power and fortune, unless the terms be equal. Nevertheless we trust that the gods will give us fortune as good as yours, because we are standing for what is right against what is wrong; and as for what we lack in power, we trust that it will be made up for by our alliance with the Spartans, who are bound, if for no other reason, then for honour's sake, and because we are their kinsmen, to come to our help. Our confidence, therefore, is not so entirely irrational as you think.

"*Athenians:* So far as the favour of the gods is concerned, we think we have as much right to that as you have. Our aims and our actions are perfectly consistent with the beliefs men hold about the gods and with the principles which govern their own conduct. Our opinion of the gods and our knowledge of men lead us to conclude that it is a general and necessary law of nature to rule wherever one can. This is not a law that we made ourselves, nor were we the first to act upon it when it was made. We found it already in existence, and we shall leave it to exist for ever among those who come after us. We are merely acting in accordance with it, and we know that you or anybody else with the same power as ours would be acting in precisely the same way. And therefore, so far as the gods are concerned, we see no good reason why we should fear to be at a disadvantage. But with regard to your views about Sparta and your confidence that she, out of a sense of honour, will come to your aid, we must say that we congratulate you on your simplicity but do not envy you your folly. In matters that concern themselves or their own constitution the Spartans are quite remarkably good; as for their relations with others, that is a long story, but it can be expressed shortly and clearly by saying that of all people we know the Spartans are most conspicuous for believing that what they like doing is honourable and what suits their interests is just. And this kind of attitude is not going to be of much help to you in your absurd quest for safety at the moment.

"*Melians:* But this is the very point where we can feel most sure. Their own self-interest will make them refuse to betray their own colonists, the Melians, for that would mean losing the confidence of their friends among the Hellenes and doing good to their enemies.

"*Athenians:* You seem to forget that if one follows one's self-interest one wants to be safe, whereas the path of justice and honour involves one in danger. And, where danger is concerned, the Spartans are not, as a rule, very venturesome.

"*Melians:* But we think that they would even endanger themselves for our sake and count the risk more worth taking than in the case of others, because we are so close to the Peloponnese that they could operate more easily, and because they can depend on us more than on others, since we are of the same race and share the same feelings.

"*Athenians:* Goodwill shown by the party that is asking for help does not mean security for the prospective ally. What is looked for is a positive preponderance of power in action. And the Spartans pay attention to this point even more than others do. Certainly they distrust their own native resources so much that when they attack a neighbour they bring a great army of allies with them. It is hardly likely therefore that, while we are in control of the sea, they will cross over to an island.

"*Melians:* But they still might send others. The Cretan sea is a wide one, and it is harder for those who control it to intercept others than for those who want to slip through to do so safely. And even if they were to fail in this, they would turn against your own land and against those of your allies left unvisited by Brasidas. So, instead of troubling about a country which has nothing to do with you, you will find trouble nearer home, among your allies, and in your own country.

"*Athenians:* It is a possibility, something that has in fact happened before. It may happen in your case, but you are well aware that the Athenians have never yet relinquished a single siege operation through fear of others. But we are somewhat shocked to find that, though you announced your intention of discussing how you could preserve yourselves, in all this talk you have said absolutely nothing which could justify a man in thinking that he could be preserved. Your chief points are concerned with what you hope may happen in the future, while your actual resources are too scanty to give you a chance of survival against the forces that are opposed to you at this moment. You will therefore be showing an extraordinary lack of common sense if, after you have asked us to retire from this meeting, you still fail to reach a conclusion wiser than anything you have mentioned so far. Do not be led astray by a false sense of honour – a thing which often brings men to ruin when they are faced with an obvious danger that somehow affects their pride. For in many cases men have still been able to see the dangers ahead of them, but this thing called dishonour, this word, by its own force of seduction, has drawn them into a state where they have surrendered to an idea, while in fact they have fallen voluntarily into irrevocable disaster, in dishonour that is all the more dishonourable because it has come to them from their own folly rather than their misfortune. You, if you take the right view, will be careful to avoid this. You will see that there is nothing disgraceful in giving way to the greatest city in Hellas when she is offering you such reasonable terms – alliance on a tribute-paying basis and liberty to enjoy your own property. And, when you are allowed to choose between war and safety, you will not be so insensitively arrogant as to make the wrong choice. This is the safe rule – to stand up to one's equals, to behave with deference towards one's superiors, and to treat one's inferiors with moderation. Think it over again, then, when we have withdrawn from the meeting, and let this be a point that constantly recurs to your minds – that you are discussing the fate of your country, that you have only one country, and that its future for good or ill depends on this one single decision which you are going to make.

"The Athenians then withdrew from the discussion. The Melians, left to themselves, reached a conclusion which was much the same as they had indicated in their previous replies. Their answer was as follows:

"*Melians:* Our decision, Athenians, is just the same as it was at first. We are not prepared to give up in a short moment the liberty which our city has enjoyed from its foundation for 700 years. We put our trust in the fortune that the gods will send and which has saved us up to now, and in the help of men – that is, of the Spartans; and so we shall try to save ourselves. But we invite you to allow us to be friends of yours and enemies to neither side, to make a treaty which shall be agreeable to both you and us, and so to leave our country.

"The Melians made this reply, and the Athenians, just as they were breaking off the discussion, said:

"*Athenians:* Well, at any rate, judging from this decision of yours, you seem to us quite unique in your ability to consider the future as something more certain than what is before your eyes, and to see uncertainties as realities, simply because you would like them to be so. As you have staked most on and trusted most in Spartans, luck, and hopes, so in all these you will find yourselves most completely deluded.

"The Athenian representatives then went back to the army, and the Athenian generals, finding that the Melians would not submit, immediately commenced hostilities and built a wall completely round the city of Melos, dividing the work out among the various states. Later they left behind a garrison of some of their own and some allied troops to blockade the place by land and sea, and with the greater part of their army returned home. The force left behind stayed on and continued with the siege. . . .

". . . The Melians made a night attack and captured the part of the Athenian lines opposite the market-place. They killed some of the troops, and then, after bringing in corn and everything else useful that they could lay their hands.on, retired again and made no further move, while the Athenians took measures to make their blockade more efficient. . . .

". . . Another force came out afterwards from Athens under the command of Philocrates, the son of Demeas. Siege operations were now carried on vigorously and, as there was also some treachery from inside, the Melians surrendered unconditionally. The Athenians put to death all the men of military age whom they took, and sold the women and children as slaves. Melos itself they took over for themselves, sending out later a colony of 500 men."

Kautilya – The Strategy by which Rulers Should Protect their Interests*

"A king desirous of expanding his own power shall make use of the six-fold policy.

---

* From Kautilya (*c.* 360–280 BC). Born a brahmin, he was educated at Taxila, where he acquired a knowledge of medicine and astrology, and probably of Greek and Persian writing. Became an adviser to the Mauryan emperor, Chandragupta, helping him to overthrow the Nanda dynasty of Pataliputra. His *Arthasastra* gave advice to rulers on the way to govern efficiently (and, if necessary, ruthlessly), including the way they should act to conquer foreign rivals. Quoted from *Arthasastra*, trs. R. Shamasastry (Mysore: Wesleyan Mission Press, 1923) Book VII, chs 3, 6 and 7.

"Agreements of peace shall be made with equal and superior kings; and an inferior king shall be attacked.

"Whoever goes to wage war with a superior king will be reduced to the same condition as that of a foot-soldier opposing an elephant.

"269 War with an equal king brings ruin to both as the collision of an unbaked mud-vessel with a similar vessel is destructive to both. But a superior king attains decisive victory over an inferior king like a stone striking an earthen pot. . . .

"When a king in peace with another finds that greedy, impoverished and oppressed as are the subjects of his ally, they do not yet immigrate into his own territory lest they might be called back by their master, then he should, though of inferior power, proclaim war against his ally.

"When a king at war with another finds that greedy, impoverished and oppressed as are the subjects of his enemy, still they do not come to his side in consequence of the troubles of war, then he should, though of superior power, make peace with his enemy or remove the troubles of war as far as possible.

"When one of the two kings at war with each other and equally involved in trouble finds his own troubles to be greater than his enemy's, and thinks that by getting rid of his (enemy's) trouble his enemy can successfully wage war with him, then he should, though possessing greater resources, sue for peace. . . .

"270 When a king finds the troubles of his enemy irremediable, he should, though of inferior power, march against the enemy.

"When a king finds himself threatened by imminent danger or troubles, he should, though superior, seek the protection of another.

"When a king is sure to achieve his desired ends by making peace with one and waging war with another, he should, though superior, adopt the double policy.

•   •   •

"273 When a king finds that as his enemy's subjects are ill-treated, impoverished and greedy, and are ever being oppressed by the inroads of the army, thieves and wild tribes, they can be made through intrigue to join his side; or that his own agriculture and commerce are flourishing while those of his enemy are waning; or that as the subjects of his enemy are suffering from famine, they will immigrate into his own territory; or that, though his own returns of agriculture and commerce are falling and those of his enemy increasing, his own subjects will never desert him in favour of his enemy; or that by proclaiming war, he can carry off, by force, the grains, cattle and gold of his enemy; or that he can prevent the import of his enemy's merchandise, which was destructive of his own commerce; or that valuable merchandise would come to his own territory, leaving that of his enemy; or that war being proclaimed, his enemy would be unable to put down traitors, enemies and wild tribes and other rebels, and would be involved in war with them; or that his own friend would in a very short time accumulate wealth without much loss and would not fail to follow him in his march, since no friend would neglect the opportunity of acquiring a fertile land and a prosperous friend like himself – then in view of inflicting injuries on his enemy and of exhibiting his own power, he may keep quiet after proclaiming war. . . .

• • •

"When the policy of keeping quiet after proclaiming war is found productive of unfavourable results, then one shall keep quiet after making peace.

"Whoever has grown in strength in consequence of keeping quiet after proclaiming war should proceed to attack his helpless enemy.

"When a king finds that his enemy has fallen into troubles; that the troubles of his enemy's subjects can by no means be remedied; that as his enemy's subjects are oppressed, ill-treated, disaffected, impoverished, become effeminate and disunited among themselves, they can be prevailed upon to desert their master; that his enemy's country has fallen a victim to the inroads of such calamities as fire, floods, pestilence, epidemics (maraka) and famine and is therefore losing the flower of its youth and its defensive power – then he should march after proclaiming war.

"*274* When a king is so fortunate as to have a powerful friend in front and a powerful ally (ākranda) in the rear, both with brave and loyal subjects, while the reverse is the case with his enemies both in front and in the rear, and when he finds it possible for his friend to hold his frontal enemy in check, and for his rear-ally to keep his rear-enemy (pārshnigrāha) at bay, then he may march after proclaiming war against his frontal enemy. . . .

• • •

"Having combined with a neighbouring king, the conqueror may march against another neighbouring king. Or if he thinks that '(my enemy) will neither capture my rear nor make an alliance with my assailable enemy against whom I am going to march; I shall have double the strength with him, i.e., the enemy suing peace; (my ally) will not only facilitate the collection of my revenue and supplies and put down the internal enemies who are causing me immense trouble, but also punish wild tribes and their followers entrenched in their strongholds, reduce my assailable enemy to a precarious condition or compel him to accept the proffered peace, and having received as much profit as he desires, he will endeavour to endear my other enemies to me', then the conqueror may proclaim war against one and make peace with another, and endeavour to get an army for money or money for the supply of an army from among his neighbouring kings. . . .

• • •

"When the king of superior power and free from all troubles is desirous of causing to his enemy loss of men and money in the latter's ill-considered undertaking, or of sending his own treacherous army abroad, or bringing his enemy under the clutches of an inimical army, or of causing trouble to a reducible and tottering enemy by setting an inferior king against that enemy, or is desirous of having peace for the sake of peace itself and is possessed of good intentions, he may accept a less share in the profit (promised for the army supplied to another), and endeavour to make wealth by combining with an ally if the latter is equally of good intentions; otherwise he may declare war (against that ally).

"A king may deceive or help his equal as follows:

"When a king proposes peace to another king of equal power on the condition of receiving the help of the latter's army strong enough to oppose an enemy's army, or to guard the front, centre and rear of his territory, or to help his friend, or to protect any other wild tracts of his territory, in return for the payment of a share in the profit proportionally equal to the strength of the army supplied, the latter may accept the terms if the proposer is of good intentions; otherwise he may declare war."

11 The Competitiveness of States

In late mediaeval Europe, in another international society beset with conflict, similar discussions took place about the policies which states and their rulers should pursue. There too a contrast was sometimes made between the dictates of morality and the necessities of state interest. And there too there was often an assumption that egoism and ruthlessness were an inevitable feature of relations between states, so that even those which may have wished otherwise were obliged to adopt self-seeking tactics in order to protect themselves from others.

A number of the writings of the day, like Kautilya's book and the ancient Chinese writings, took the form of advice to rulers about the way they should conduct their affairs. Though most of this advice related to internal matters, some concerned the relationships which should be adopted with other states. It was generally taken for granted that war was an inevitable feature of international life. It might be desirable for purely domestic reasons: the Italian writer Giovanni Botero, for example, argued that "military enterprises are the most effective means of keeping a people occupied. . . . A wise prince can placate an enraged people by leading it to war against an external enemy." But it could be even more necessary for external purposes. The prudent ruler, therefore, had no option but to enhance the military capacity of his own state if he was to succeed in the ceaseless competition among states.

In Renaissance Italy the competition was particularly fierce. The rulers were concerned to devise policies that might best enable them, even if not militarily powerful, to prevail in this struggle. Machiavelli, who had held responsible positions relating to the conduct of Florence's foreign relations, both as an ambassador and as an official in the responsible department at home, wrote later, when no longer in office, of the policies that he believed were most likely to enable a ruler to succeed in the competition with other states. He believed that the chief foundation of all states should be "good laws and good arms" (so exactly echoing the view of the Legalists in China, see p. 6 above). Because of the frequency of warfare, a good ruler should have "no other aims or thoughts" than "war and its organisation".

For this purpose he should guard against the treachery of others (and of mercenaries, who for this reason should not be employed). But he need not hesitate himself to deceive other rulers if he found this was required in the interests of his own state, for if he did not they would use similar methods against him.

Bodin, the French legal writer, who had also held a minor post within his own country, like Machiavelli presented advice to rulers about the way they should run their affairs. He too was concerned mainly with the internal organisation of the state: how the ruler should assert his rule and own "sovereignty" within his territory. But this purpose could sometimes require action against other states. A good way to maintain unity among the population, he suggested, was to find an enemy against whom they could make common cause. Especially if his own people were naturally warlike ("as are northern peoples") it was expedient to keep them frequently engaged in war and only make peace on very advantageous terms. Like Machiavelli he believed that the ruler should not rely on mercenaries: his army should be a professional force, carefully trained for the purpose and enjoying special privileges, while the carrying of arms should be forbidden to the rest of the population. But he differed from Machiavelli in one important respect. He called on the ruler always to maintain good faith with other rulers, and went so far as to suggest that good faith should be maintained even with enemies and infidels: a position which Machiavelli would certainly not have endorsed.

Here too there is a contrast between two conflicting views of state interest. Machiavelli takes a position closer to that of the Athenians in the Melian dialogue: the interests of the state (or its ruler) are paramount, and if this makes a breach of faith or fair dealing necessary then this must be undertaken. Bodin takes a longer view, recognising that, in the long run, good faith is in the interests of both parties since it is "the sole foundation and prop of that justice on which all commonwealths, alliances and associations of men whatsoever are based": similar, therefore, to the view put by the Melians. In other words, he holds that in the society of states, as in other societies, the basis of a stable coexistence depends upon each member being able to rely on the undertakings of others.

Rousseau, two or three centuries later, resembled Machiavelli and Bodin in believing that states were bound to live in constant fear of their neighbours and must therefore take steps to safeguard their own interests. There was no limit to the power and size which a state could claim, so that each must live in fear that its neighbours would entertain claims at its own expense. For this reason all must seek to increase their own power, if only in self-defence, each feeling that "its safety and preservation demands that it makes itself stronger than its neighbours". And because all rulers demanded absolute independence for their own states, it was possible for them to commit violence against each other, and even against their own citizens, in the "empty name of justice". Thus, while Hobbes had seen *individuals* in incessant conflict and competition, compelling them to seek their security in the state (p. 40 above), Rousseau finds this competitiveness among the states within which they are joined: a competition which compels them to see themselves in conflict with their fellow men, with whom individually they have no quarrel, in other states. The citizen is therefore made into a savage, "continually ready to torment his fellow-men because of passions of which he knows nothing". It is the rivalry among states, not that among people, therefore, that brings about war.

All of these writers, therefore, see competition among states as the essential cause of warfare. All are inclined to see war as an inevitable feature of the state's existence. But while Machiavelli and Bodin are each concerned to examine how the power of their own states (or that of which they write) can be increased, to enable it to compete more successfully in that struggle, Rousseau is concerned to see the power of the state – or at least of the traditional state – destroyed. When that occurs a new type of state may be created, in which power is vested in the people as a whole: if all states were formed on that basis the general will of the people, who have no desire to fight each other, would ensure that no more wars occurred.

* * *

Machiavelli – The Means by which Rulers can Increase their States' Power*

A prince should therefore have no other aim or thought, nor take up any other thing for his study, but war and its organisation and

---

* From Niccolo Machiavelli (1469–1527). As secretary of the magistracy in the Florentine Republic had responsibility for foreign affairs and defence matters; also discipline, for that is the only art that is necessary to one who commands, and it is of such virtue that it not only maintains those who are born princes, but often enables men of private fortune to attain to that rank. And one sees, on the other hand, that when princes think more of luxury than of arms, they lose their state. The chief cause of the loss of states, is the contempt of this art, and the way to acquire them is to be well versed in the same.

"Francesco Sforza, through being well armed, became, from private status, Duke of Milan; his sons, through wishing to avoid the fatigue and hardship of war, from dukes became private persons. For among other evils caused by being disarmed, it renders you contemptible; which is one of those disgraceful things which a prince must guard against, as will be explained later. Because there is no comparison whatever between an armed and a disarmed man; it is not reasonable to suppose that one who is armed will obey willingly one who is unarmed; or that any unarmed man will remain safe among armed servants. For one being disdainful and the other suspicious, it is not possible for them to act well together. And therefore a prince who is ignorant of military matters, besides the other misfortunes already mentioned, cannot be esteemed by his soldiers, nor have confidence in them.

"He ought, therefore, never to let his thoughts stray from the exercise of war; and in peace he ought to practise it more than in war, which he can do in two ways: by action and by study. As to action, he must, besides keeping his men well disciplined and exercised, engaged continually in hunting, and thus accustom his body to hardships; and meanwhile learn the nature of the land, how steep the mountains are, how the valleys debouch, where the plains lie, and understand the nature of rivers and swamps. To all this he should devote great attention. This knowledge is useful in two ways. In the first place, one learns to know one's country, and can the better see how to defend it. Then by means of the knowledge and experience gained in one locality, one can easily understand any other that it may be necessary to observe; for the hills and valleys, plains and rivers of Tuscany, for instance, have a certain resemblance to those

served as ambassador abroad in Spain and directed Florence's forces during the long siege of Pisa. Lost office after the overthrow of his patron Soterini and proceeded to write *The Prince*, dedicated to Lorenzo Medici, then restored to power in Florence. Also wrote (besides poetry and plays) *Discourses on Livy* (1514) and *A History of Florence* (1525). Quoted from *The Prince* (1513), trs. L. Ricci and E. R. P. Vincent (Oxford: Oxford University Press, 1934).

of other provinces, so that from a knowledge of the country in one province one can easily arrive at a knowledge of others. And that prince who is lacking in this skill is wanting in the first essentials of a leader; for it is this which teaches how to find the enemy, take up quarters, lead armies, plan battles and lay siege to towns with advantage.

"Philopoemen, prince of the Achaei, among other praises bestowed on him by writers, is lauded because in times of peace he thought of nothing but the methods of warfare, and when he was in the country with his friends, he often stopped and asked them: If the enemy were on that hill and we found ourselves here with our army, which of us would have the advantage? How could we safely approach him maintaining our order? If we wished to retire, what ought we to do? If they retired, how should we follow them? And he put before them as they went along all the contingencies that might happen to an army, heard their opinion, gave his own, fortifying it by argument; so that thanks to these constant reflections there could never happen any incident when actually leading his armies for which he was not prepared.

"But as to exercise for the mind, the prince ought to read history and study the actions of eminent men, see how they acted in warfare, examine the causes of their victories and defeats in order to imitate the former and avoid the latter, and above all, do as some men have done in the past, who have imitated some one, who has been much praised and glorified, and have always kept his deeds and actions before them, as they say Alexander the Great imitated Achilles, Caesar Alexander, and Scipio Cyrus. And whoever reads the life of Cyrus written by Xenophon, will perceive in the life of Scipio how gloriously he imitated the former, and how, in chastity, affability, humanity, and liberality Scipio conformed to those qualities of Cyrus as described by Xenophon.

A wise prince should follow similar methods and never remain idle in peaceful times, but industriously make good use of them, so that when fortune changes she may find him prepared to resist her blows, and to prevail in adversity. . . .

IN WHAT WAY PRINCES MUST KEEP FAITH

"You must know, then, that there are two methods of fighting, the one by law, the other by force: the first method is that of men, the second of beasts; but as the first method is often insufficient, one must have recourse to the second. It is therefore necessary for a prince to know well how to use both the beast and the man. . . .

"A prince being thus obliged to know well how to act as a beast must imitate the fox and the lion, for the lion cannot protect himself from traps, and the fox cannot defend himself from wolves. One must therefore be a fox to recognise traps, and a lion to frighten wolves. Those that wish to be only lions do not understand this. Therefore, a prudent ruler ought not to keep faith when by so doing it would be against his interest, and when the reasons which made him bind himself no longer exist. If men were all good, this precept would not be a good one; but as they are bad, and would not observe their faith with you, so you are not bound to keep faith with them. Nor have legitimate grounds ever failed a prince who wished to show colourable excuse for the non-fulfilment of his promise. Of this one could furnish an infinite number of modern examples, and show how many times peace has been broken, and how many promises rendered worthless, by the faithlessness of princes, and those that have been best able to imitate the fox have succeeded best. But it is necessary to be able to disguise this character well, and to be a great feigner and dissembler; and men are so simple and so ready to obey present necessities, that one who deceives will always find those who allow themselves to be deceived. . . .

"It is not, therefore, necessary for a prince to have all the above-named qualities, but it is very necessary to seem to have them. I would even be bold to say that to possess them and always to observe them is dangerous, but to appear to possess them is useful. Thus it is well to seem merciful, faithful, humane, sincere, religious, and also to be so; but you must have the mind so disposed that when it is needful to be otherwise you may be able to change to the opposite qualities. And it must be understood that a prince, and especially a new prince, cannot observe all those things which are considered good in men, being often obliged, in order to maintain the state, to act against faith, against charity, against humanity and against religion. And, therefore, he must have a mind disposed to adapt itself according to the wind, and as the variations of fortune dictate, and, as I said before, not deviate from what is good, if possible, but be able to do evil if constrained."

Bodin – The State's Need of Armed Force to Protect its Interests*

"[T]he best way of preserving a state, and guaranteeing it against sedition, rebellion and civil war is to keep the subjects in amity one with another, and to this end, to find an enemy against whom they can make common cause. Examples of this can be found in all commonwealths. The Romans are a specially good illustration. They could find no better antidote to civil war, nor one more certain in its effects, than to oppose an enemy to the citizens. On one occasion, when they were engaged in bitter mutual strife, the enemy found his way into the city and seized the Capitol. The citizens instantly composed their differences, and united to expel the enemy. . . I hold that in a popular state it is expedient to train the subjects to arms because of the weaknesses to which I infer popular states are prone by their very nature. If the subjects are naturally warlike and intractable, as are northern peoples, once they are trained in the art of war and in military discipline, it is expedient to keep them frequently engaged against an enemy, and only make peace, a condition not adapted to a warlike people, on very advantageous terms. Even when peace is concluded, an army must be maintained and kept on the frontiers. This was Augustus' policy after he had converted a popular state into a monarchy. The alternative is to hire them out to allied princes, as the governments of the [Swiss] Confederates very wisely do, to keep them practised in the military art. They have to deal with a mountain population, apt for war and difficult to keep at peace, and used to the enjoyment of popular liberty. By this policy they are always provided with experienced soldiers, maintained at the expense of others, who at the same time earn considerable subsidies for the state, and pensions for individuals. Added to which their safety is assured by the alliances thus formed with some puissant king. . . .

A wise prince should never permit the enemy to invade his king-

---

* From Jean Bodin (1530–96). Lawyer and minor courtier, in the service of the brother of the French king. Deputy for the Third Estate in the Estates-General, where he opposed the resumption of war against the Huguenots. Concerned, like Hobbes, with the means of establishing a stable order within the state under the absolute sovereignty of the ruler. Best known for the *Six Books of the Republic*, from which this extract is taken, in which he examined the conditions under which order might be maintained within the state and concluded that this necessitated recognition of the absolute sovereignty of the state, whether monarchical, aristocratic or democratic. Quoted from *Six Books of the Republic* (1576), trs. M. J. Tooley (Oxford: Basil Blackwell, 1955) Books V and VI.

dom if he can by any means scatter their forces or check their advance before they can cross the frontier, or at any rate unless he has a second army, and some impregnable base to which he can retreat. Otherwise he risks all on a single battle. This was the error of Antiochus, Perseus and Ptolemy, the last King of Egypt, in the war with the Romans; of Darius in the war with Alexander, and the French time and time again in the wars with England. . . . But Francis I took his army across the Alps in order to keep his country free from war, and attacked the enemy in laying siege to Pavia. Apart from the devastation which two powerful armies would have caused in France, the capture of the King would have exposed the kingdom to great danger. But happening, as it did, in Italy, and the victors being at first content with their success, time was given to the King's subjects to rally their forces and secure the frontiers. . . . I do not wish to enter into any discussion of the art of war, for others have treated of this subject.[1] I am only concerned with what touches the state. I hold that the prince should provide for the thorough fortification of his frontiers, and if he suspects that any enemy contemplates invading his territory, he ought to anticipate him and wage war as far from his own frontiers as possible. . . .

THE KEEPING OF TREATIES AND ALLIANCES BETWEEN PRINCES

"[T]here is no matter of state that more exercises the minds of princes and rulers than the securing of treaties, whether with friends, enemies, neutrals, or their own subjects. Some rely on mutual good faith simply. Others demand hostages. Many add the surrender of fortified places. Others cannot feel safe unless they totally disarm the conquered. It has always been considered that the best guarantee of a treaty is ratification by a marriage alliance. But just as there is a difference between friends and enemies, victors and vanquished, equals in power and the weak, princes and subjects, so also must the forms of treaties and their appropriate guarantees be diversified. But there is one general and indisputable principle to be observed, and that is that in all treaties there is no better guarantee of its observation than that the clauses and conditions included in it should be suitable to the parties concerned, and conformable to the matters in dispute. . . .

"Treaties of protection expose the protected party to much greater risks than any other kind of alliance, and therefore it is important that the guarantees should be most carefully considered. For lack of such, how often has one not seen an obligation to protect transformed into sovereign rights. He feels safe indeed who commits the sheep to the care of the wolf. It is therefore in the first instance important that treaties of protection should be limited in time, even in the case of aristocracies and popular states where the ruler never dies. For this reason when Geneva put itself under the protection of Berne, the citizens did not wish to bind themselves for more than thirty years. . . . But the best guarantee for the protected party is to prevent, if possible, the seizure of the fortresses of their towns by the troops of the protector and the introduction of his garrisons into them. The words of the Tribune Brutus to the nobles and people of Rome should never be forgotten, that the only protection that the weak have against the strong whom they fear, is that the latter should not be able to harm them even if they wish to, for the desire to do harm is never lacking in ambitious men who have power to inflict it. On these grounds the Scots were wise when in the treaty which they made in 1559 with the Queen of England, to secure her protection, they stipulated that the hostages surrendered should be changed every six months, and that no fortress should be constructed in Scotland without the consent of the Scots themselves. . . .[2]

"Many think that it is safest for a prince to adopt a policy of neutrality, and so keep out of other people's wars. The principal argument in support of this view is that whereas loss and expense is shared in common, the fruits of victory all accrue to the ruler on whose behalf the quarrel is sustained, added to which one must declare oneself the enemy of princes who have in no way offended one's interests. But he who remains neutral often finds means to reconcile enemies, and so remains himself everyone's friend, and receives honours and rewards at the hands of both parties. If all princes were aligned against one another in hostile camps, who could compose their differences? And again, what better way is there of maintaining one's state in all its strength than to stand aside while one's neighbours ruin one another? In truth, the greatness of a prince largely depends on the decline and fall of his neighbours, and his strength is measured by other people's weakness. . . .

"Since faith is the sole foundation and prop of that justice on which all commonwealths, alliances, and associations of men whatsoever, is founded, it should be preserved sacred and inviolable in all cases where no injustice is contemplated. This applies most particularly to the relations between princes, for seeing that they are the guarantors of good faith and sworn engagements, what assurance will those subject to them have of their own mutual undertakings if the rulers themselves are the principal breakers and violators of good faith? I have added, 'in all cases where no injustice is contemplated', for it is a double sin to engage one's faith to do an evil act. In such a case he who fails of his promise, so far from being perfidious, is to be commended. In like case, if the prince promises not to do something permitted by natural law, he is not perjured if he breaks his oath. Even the subject is not foresworn who breaks his oath regarding any action permitted by the law. But wise princes should never bind themselves by oath to other princes to do anything forbidden by natural law, or the law of nations, nor should they ever compel princes weaker than themselves to swear to an agreement quite unreasonable in terms."

Notes
1. This chapter is largely based on Machiavelli's *Arte della guerra*, published in 1521, though characteristically adapted to Bodin's political views.
2. A reference to the agreement made by the Duke of Norfolk on behalf of the Queen with the Scots Lords in rebellion against the regent, Mary of Guise, and in alliance with Knox. It was concluded in February 1560.

Rousseau – The Reasons for Mutual Competition between States*

"Let us consider closely the formation of political bodies, and we will find that, although each of them has, if need be, enough for its own preservation, their mutual relations are none the less far more intimate that those of individuals. For basically man has no necessary connection with his fellow men; he can maintain his full strength without their help; his need is not so much for men's care as for the earth's produce; and the earth produces more than enough to feed its inhabitants. Also the strength and size of man has a limit set by nature which he cannot go beyond. Whichever way he looks at himself, he finds all his faculties are limited. His life is short, his years

* From Jean-Jacques Rousseau (1712–78). (For biographical details see p. 44.) Quoted from *The State of War* (1753–8), trs. M. Forsyth, in M. Forsyth, H. M. A. Keens-Soper and P. Savigen (eds), *The Theory of International Relations* (London: George Allen and Unwin, 1970).

are numbered. His stomach does not grow with his riches; his passions increase in vain, his pleasures are bounded; his heart is confined, like all the rest; his capacity for enjoyment is always the same. He can rise up in his imagination, he always remains small.

"The State on the other hand, being an artificial body, has no fixed measure; its proper size is undefined; it can always grow bigger; it feels weak so long as there are others stronger than itself. Its safety and preservation demand that it makes itself stronger than its neighbours. It cannot increase, foster, or exercise its strength except at their expense; and even if it has no need to seek for provisions beyond its borders, it searches ceaselessly for new members to give itself a more unshakeable position. For the inequality of men has its limits set by nature, but the inequality of societies can grow incessantly, until one of them absorbs all the others.

"Thus the size of the body politic being purely relative, it is forced to compare itself in order to know itself; it depends on its whole environment and has to take an interest in all that happens. In vain it wishes to stay within its own bounds, neither gaining nor losing; it becomes big or small, strong or weak according to the extent that its neighbour expands or contracts, grows stronger or weaker. Finally its very consolidation, by making its relations more constant, gives greater sureness to all its actions and makes all its quarrels more dangerous.

"It looks as if one has set out to turn every true idea of things upside down. Everything inclines natural man to peace; the sole needs he knows are eating and sleeping, and only hunger drags him from idleness. He is made into a savage continually ready to torment his fellow men because of passions of which he knows nothing. On the contrary, these passions, aroused in the bosom of society by everything that can inflame them, are considered not to exist there at all. A thousand writers have dared to say that the body politic is passionless, and that there is no other *raison d'état* than reason itself. As if no one saw that, on the contrary, the essence of society consists in the activity of its members, and that a state without movement would be nothing but a corpse. As if all the world's histories do not show us that the best constituted societies are also the most active and that the continual action and reaction of all their members, whether within or without, bear witness to the vigour of the whole body.

•   •   •

"For the State to survive then, it is necessary for the intensity of its passions to compensate for that of its movements and for its will to quicken as its power slackens. This is the law of preservation that nature herself establishes between the species, and which maintains them all, despite their inequality. It is also, one may note in passing, the reason why small states have proportionately more vigour than big ones. Public feeling does not grow with territory; the more the latter extends, the more the will relaxes and movements grow weaker, until finally the huge body, overloaded with its own weight, caves in, and falls into listlessness and decay.

"These examples suffice to give an idea of the various methods whereby a state can be weakened, and of those which war seems to sanction in order to harm its enemy. As for treaties in which some of these means are incorporated, what basically is a peace of this sort except a war continued with all the more cruelty in that the enemy no longer has the right to defend himself? . . .

"Add to this the visible signs of ill will, which indicate the intention to do harm; such as refusing to accord a Power the status due to it, or ignoring its rights, rejecting its claims, refusing its subjects freedom to trade, rousing enemies against it, or finally breaking international law towards it, under some pretext or other. These various ways of offending a body politic are neither equally practicable nor equally useful to the state that uses them, and those which result simultaneously in our own advantage and the enemy's disadvantage are naturally preferred. Land, money, men, all the booty that one can carry off thus become the principal object of reciprocal hostilities. As this base greed imperceptibly changes people's ideas about things, war finally degenerates into brigandage, and little by little enemies and warriors become tyrants and thieves.

"From fear of thoughtlessly adopting this change of ideas ourselves, let us fix our own thoughts by a definition, and try to make it so simple that it cannot be abused.

"I call then war between Power and Power the effect of a constant, overt, mutual disposition to destroy the enemy State, or at least to weaken it by all the means one can. When this disposition is transformed into action it is war properly called; in so far as it remains untransformed it is only the state of war.

•　　•　　•

"If there has never been, and if it is impossible to have, a true war between individuals, between whom then does it take place, and who can really call themselves enemies? I reply that they are public persons. And what is a public person? I reply that it is the moral being which one calls sovereign, which has been brought into existence by the social pact, and whose will always carries the name of law. Let us apply here the distinctions made earlier; one can say that, in considering the effects of war, the Sovereign inflicts the injury and the State receives it.

"If war only takes place between moral beings, it is not intended to be between men, and one can conduct a war without depriving anyone of their life. But this requires an explanation.

"If one looks at things solely and strictly in the light of the social pact, land, money, men, and everything contained within the boundary of the State, belongs unreservedly to it. But as the rights of society, founded on those of nature, cannot abolish the latter, all these objects must be considered in a double context: that is, the earth must be seen both as public land and as the patrimony of individuals; goods belong in one sense to the Sovereign, and in another to their owners; people are both citizens and men. Basically the body politic, in so far as it is only a moral being, is merely a thing of reason. Remove the public convention and immediately the State is destroyed, without the least change in all that composes it; for all man's conventions are unable to change anything in the nature of things. What then does it mean to wage war on a Sovereign? It means an attack on the public convention and all that results from it; for the essence of the State consists solely in that. If the social pact could be sundered with one blow, immediately there would be no more war; and by this one blow the State would be killed, without the death of one man. . . .

"The first thing I notice, in considering the condition of the human species, is an open contradiction in its constitution which causes it to vacillate incessantly. As individual men we live in a civil state subject to laws; as peoples we each enjoy a natural liberty: this makes our position fundamentally worse than if these distinctions were unknown. For living simultaneously in the social order and in the state of nature we are subjected to the inconveniences of both, without finding security in either. The perfection of the social order consists, it is true, in the conjunction of force and law. But this demands that law guides the use of force; whereas according to the ideas of absolute independence held by Princes, force alone, speaking to the citizens under the name of law and to foreigners under the name of *raison d'état*, removes from the latter the power, and from the former the will to resist, in such a way that everywhere the empty name of justice serves only as a safeguard for violence."

12 The Duties of States

Side by side with these emerging ideas as to how states in fact behave, a body of doctrine emerged about how they *should* behave.

Already during the Middle Ages conventions had emerged about some aspects of state conduct: for example, the treatment of heralds, declarations of war, diplomatic practice and similar matters. The rules of chivalry established a code governing the behaviour which knights should adopt towards each other on the battlefield (though they were under no obligation to apply the rules to those who were not of knightly rank). Canon law established rules about the conduct of war and other aspects of state conduct. In particular the doctrine of "just war" laid down for what purposes war was justifiable and rules about the ways in which wars should be conducted. Finally, there was a widespread belief that the actions of states, like all other behaviour, were subject to a "natural law", a law of reason, which dictated certain principles of conduct, including the circumstances in which war was justified.

From the sixteenth century there emerged a class of theologians and lawyers who wrote extensively about the obligations which should bind rulers in their dealings with other states. One question that arose concerned the extent of their obligations: the area and peoples to which it applied. The Spanish theologian, Vitoria, for example, was insistent that the rights enjoyed by all humans, under natural law, applied equally to the Indians in the territories conquered by Spain in South America. He was on those grounds deeply critical of the policies pursued in that area by local settlers, by local officials, and even by the Spanish government itself (a criticism which brought on his head a rebuke from the Spanish king, the emperor Charles V himself). Vitoria argued that the emperor was not emperor of all the world; and, even if he had been, was not entitled to seize the land and property of the Indians. These remained the owners of their land and could not be deprived of their rights because of their lack of faith. Nor could even the pope claim temporal powers over them. In the passage below he refutes the argument that it was legitimate to make war with the Indians because of their heresy. He points out that they could not be blamed for being heretics before the Spaniards came, when they knew nothing of Christianity. They had therefore done no wrong and, as Augustine and Aquinas had taught, for a war to be just a wrong must have been committed. Nor was the fact that they had now heard the teaching of Christian missionaries and not been converted a reason for making war on them, or for depriving them of their property. Nor could a war be justified as a punishment for other mortal sins, since the pope had no jurisdiction over them, and had not the right to make war even against Christians for that reason. This was a challenging and highly courageous statement on the limits to the justified power of princes, and even of popes. It represented one of the earliest assertions that there exist fundamental human rights which are independent of the power of states.

Those who wrote on international law were naturally particularly concerned about the duties of states in questions of peace and war. None claimed that it was always wrong to make war; and they frequently quoted earlier authorities who had held that wars were justified if undertaken for just purposes. But they were concerned to delimit more clearly which laws were "just" and which were not. Thus even Vitoria defended the right of a state to make war to recover its own property, for vengeance, for the punishment of enemies, and to defend subjects of another state who were suffering unjustly, or who were in rebellion against their king; but he equally held that a war to seize the territory of another state was not just, and that the subjects of the attacking ruler were justified in refusing to fight such a war even if ordered to do so. In the same way Grotius, a century later, upheld the right of states to make war for defence, for the recovery of property or punishment, or even to prevent "an injury which, though not yet done, threatens either our persons or property". He too believed, like Vitoria, that it was legitimate for a state to make war to protect the people of another state from the oppression of its ruler. On the other hand he does not accept the right of a state to make war for balance of power reasons: that is, to "enfeeble a rising power which, if too much augmented, may become dangerous to it", differing in this from the position which was to be taken by some international lawyers a century later. Only if such a power had the clear intention of injuring another state was the latter justified in taking up arms against it. Though, therefore, Grotius conceded a large number of legitimate reasons for war, he was concerned to define those reasons more clearly and limit the ability of states to justify their actions by unwarranted rationalisations.

Writers on international law began to emphasise a whole range of other duties which states and their rulers should recognise. These related to the conduct of their relations with other states, the right of travel and trade, recognition of foreign rulers, observance of treaties and so on. Thus Christian Wolff, the German mathematician, scientist and philosopher (as well as international lawyer), included in his *Law of Nations*, after a chapter relating to the duty of states towards themselves (such as the obligation to "perfect themselves", to be "cultured and civilised" and even to "strive as far as they are able to be powerful"), an even more lengthy chapter on the "duties of nations towards each other". Some of these duties are similar to those which individuals have towards each other, for example to "love and cherish" each other, to "preserve and foster" each other, to contribute to mutual tranquillity and security. But he also emphasises the right of each state "not to allow some other nation to take away any of its rights"; to secure their rights against others, by force if necessary; and "to punish another nation which has injured it". And he reflects the growing concern in this age with the concept of sovereignty by emphasising the right of every state not to allow any other nation to "interfere in any way in its government".

The growing body of writings of this sort, therefore, did not place any very onerous burdens on states. No writer claimed that they never had the right to make war, even offensive war, for certain purposes. But the writing did reflect a growing belief that no state was altogether self-sufficient and a law unto itself, and that all were bound by the body of rules which "natural law" demanded. There was by no means unanimity as to what these rules were. But the belief that such rules existed at all represented some kind of recognition that states were members of a common international society, having its own conventions of intercourse.

*   *   *

de Vitoria – The Duty to Respect the Rights of Indigenous Peoples*

"[L]et my first proposition be: Before the barbarians heard anything about Christianity, they did not commit the sin of unbelief by not

---

* From F. de Vitoria (*c.* 1483–1546). Spanish theologian. After having studied at Burgos and taught at the University of Valladolid, he became professor of theology

believing in Christ. This proposition is precisely that of St Thomas in *Secunda Secundae*, qu. 10, art. 1, where he says that in those who have not heard of Christ unbelief does not wear the guise of sin, but rather of punishment, such ignorance of things divine being a consequence of the sin of our first parent. . . . Such as have never heard anything, however much they may be sinners in other respects, are under an invincible ignorance; therefore, their ignorance is not sin. The antecedent is evident from the passage (Romans 10): 'How shall they believe in him of whom they have not heard, and how shall they hear without a preacher?' Therefore, if the faith has not been preached to them, their ignorance is invincible, for it was impossible for them to know. . . .

"10. Second proposition: The Indians in question are not bound, directly the Christian faith is announced to them, to believe it, in such a way that they commit mortal sin by not believing it, merely because it has been declared and announced to them that Christianity is the true religion and that Christ is the Saviour and Redeemer of the world, without miracle or any other proof or persuasion. This proposition is proved by the first: For if before hearing anything of the Christian religion they were excused, they are put under no fresh obligation by a simple declaration and announcement of this kind, for such announcement is no proof or incentive to belief. . . .

"11. From this proposition it follows that, if the faith be presented to the Indians in the way named only and they do not receive it, the Spaniards can not make this a reason for waging war on them or for proceeding against them under the law of war. This is manifest, because they are innocent in this respect and have done no wrong to the Spaniards. And this corollary receives confirmation from the fact that, as St Thomas lays it down (*Secunda Secundae*, qu. 40, art. 1), for a just war 'there must be a just cause, namely, they who are attacked for some fault must deserve the attack'. Accordingly, St Augustine says (*Liber 83 Quaestionum*): 'It is involved in the definition of a just war that some wrong is being avenged, as where a people or state is to be punished for neglect to exact amends from its citizens for their wrongdoing or to restore what has been wrongfully

---

at Salamanca where he remained until his death. His principal writings consist of the lectures he undertook there on the rights of the Indians and on the law of war. In these he taught, among other things, that the ultimate power of government rests with the people, and that the natural law which applies to relations among individuals applies also to relations among states. Quoted from *On the Indians* (1532, publ. 1557), trs. J. P. Bare (Washington, D.C.: Carnegie Institution, 1917).

taken away.' Where, then, no wrong has previously been committed by the Indians, there is no cause of just war. . . .

"12. Third proposition: If the Indians, after being asked and admonished to hear the peaceful preachers of religion, refused, they would not be excused of mortal sin. The proof lies in the supposition that they have very grave errors for which they have no probable or demonstrable reasons. Therefore, if any one admonishes them to hear and deliberate upon religious matters, they are bound at least to hear and to enter into consultation. . . .

"13. Fourth proposition: If the Christian faith be put before the oborigines with demonstration, that is, with demonstrable and reasonable arguments, and this be accompanied by an upright life, well-ordered according to the law of nature (an argument which weighs much in confirmation of the truth), and this be done not once only and perfunctorily, but diligently and zealously, the aborigines are bound to receive the faith of Christ under penalty of mortal sin. This is proved by our third proposition, for, if they are bound to hear, they are in consequence bound also to acquiesce in what they hear, if it be reasonable. . . .

"14. Fifth proposition: It is not sufficiently clear to me that the Christian faith has yet been so put before the aborigines and announced to them that they are bound to believe it or commit fresh sin. I say this because (as appears from my second proposition) they are not bound to believe unless the faith be put before them with persuasive demonstration. Now, I hear of no miracles or signs or religious patterns of life; nay, on the other hand, I hear of many scandals and cruel crimes and acts of impiety. Hence it does not appear that the Christian religion has been preached to them with such sufficient propriety and piety that they are bound to acquiesce in it, although many religious and other ecclesiastics seem both by their lives and example and their diligent preaching to have bestowed sufficient pains and industry in this business, had they not been hindered therein by others who had other matters in their charge.

"15. Sixth proposition: Although the Christian faith may have been announced to the Indians with adequate demonstration and they have refused to receive it, yet this is not a reason which justifies making war on them and depriving them of their property. This conclusion is definitely stated by St Thomas (*Secunda Secundae*, qu. 10, art. 8), where he says that unbelievers who have never received the faith, like Gentiles and Jews, are in no wise to be compelled to do so. This is the received conclusion of the doctors alike in the canon law and the civil law. The proof lies in the fact that belief is an operation of the will. Now, fear detracts greatly from the voluntary (*Ethics*, bk. 3), and it is a sacrilege to approach under the influence of servile fear as far as the mysteries and sacraments of Christ. Our conclusion is also proved by the canon *de Judaeis* (can. 5, Dist. 45), which says: 'The holy synod also enjoins concerning the Jews that thenceforth force be not applied to any of them to make him believe; "for God has compassion on whom He wills, and whom He wills He hardens".'[1] There is no doubt about the doctrine of the Council of Toledo, that threats and fears should not be employed against the Jews in order to make them receive the faith. And Gregory expressly says the same in the canon *qui sincera* (can. 3, Dist. 45): 'Who with sincerity of purpose', says he, 'desires to bring into the perfect faith those who are outside the Christian religion should labor in a manner that will attract and not with severity; . . . for whosoever does otherwise and under cover of the latter would turn them from their accustomed worship and ritual is demonstrably furthering his own end thereby and not God's end.'

"Our proposition receives further proof from the use and custom of the Church. For never have Christian Emperors, who had as advisors the most holy and wise Pontiffs, made war on unbelievers for their refusal to accept the Christian religion. Further, war is no argument for the truth of the Christian faith. Therefore the Indians can not be induced by war to believe, but rather to feign belief and reception of the Christian faith, which is monstrous and a sacrilege. . . .

"Another, and a fifth, title is seriously put forward, namely, the sins of these Indian aborigines. For it is alleged that, though their unbelief or their rejection of the Christian faith is not a good reason for making war on them, yet they may be attacked for other mortal sins which (so it is said) they have in numbers, and those very heinous. A distinction is here drawn with regard to mortal sins, it being asserted that there are some sins, which are not against the law of nature, but only against positive divine law, and for these the aborigines can not be attacked in war, while there are other sins against nature, such as cannibalism, and promiscuous intercourse with mother or sisters and with males, and for these they can be attacked in war and so compelled to desist therefrom. The principle in each case is that, in the case of sins which are against positive law, it can not be clearly shown to the Indians that they are doing wrong, whereas in the case of the sins which are against the law of nature, it can be shown to them that they are offending God, and they may consequently be prevented from continuing to offend Him. Further they can be compelled to keep the law which they themselves profess. . . .

"16. I, however, assert the following proposition: Christian princes cannot, even by the authorisation of the Pope, restrain the Indians from sins against the law of nature or punish them because of those sins. My first proof is that the writers in question build on a false hypothesis, namely, that the Pope has jurisdiction over the Indian aborigines, as said above. . . . Further, the Pope can not make war on Christians on the ground of their being fornicators or thieves or, indeed, because they are sodomites; nor can he on that ground confiscate their land and give it to other princes; were that so, there would be daily changes of kingdoms, seeing that there are many sinners in every realm. And this is confirmed by the consideration that these sins are more heinous in Christians, who are aware that they are sins, than in barbarians, who have not that knowledge. Further, it would be a strange thing that the Pope, who can not make laws for unbelievers, can yet sit in judgement and visit punishment upon them."

Note

1. Romans 9:18.

Grotius – The Duty to Make Only Just Wars*

"Having seen what are the sources of law, let us now come to the first and most general question, which is this: Can any war be just, or, in other words, is war ever lawful?

"I. (1) This question itself, as well as others which follow, must be

---

* From Hugo Grotius (1583–1645). Dutch theologian, jurist, philosopher and historian. Sometimes regarded as the father of international law (though a number of predecessors, especially Vitoria, equally deserve that honour). Adviser to moderate Netherlands leader, Oldenbarnevelt, he was captured and imprisoned by militant Calvinists, but was able to escape with the assistance of his wife. Because of his reputation was welcomed in France and later given a position of honour by the Swedish government and made Swedish ambassador to France. Wrote widely on theology and Dutch jurisprudence as well as international law. Quoted from *The Law of War and Peace* (1625), trs. F. W. Kelsey *et al.* (Oxford: Clarendon Press, 1925) Book I.ii, and Book II.i, xxii, xxv.

first examined by reference to Natural Law. . . . It is man's first duty to preserve himself in the state of nature, his next being to retain what is in conformity with nature and reject all that is opposed to it. . . . (3) . . . But, as we have already said, that which is to be discovered when Natural Law is in question, is whether a particular thing can be done without injustice. And what is necessarily repugnant to a rational and social nature is to be regarded as unjust. (4) There is nothing in the first principles of nature that is repugnant to war. On the contrary, everything rather favours it. For the object of war, which is the preservation of life and limb, and the retention or acquisition of things useful to life, is very agreeable to those first principles. And so, if to attain this object it is necessary to use force, those principles will offer no opposition, for nature has given strength to every living creature in order to defend and help itself. . . . (5) But right reason and the nature of society, which must be examined in the next and chief place, do not prohibit all force, but only that which is repugnant to society, namely, that which invades the right of another. For society, by its general strength and agreement assures to each the safe possession of that which is his own. . . . (6) It is therefore not against the nature of society to provide for, and to take care of, one's self, provided the right of another is not infringed. And so that force which does not violate another's right is not unjust . . .

"IV. (1) Therefore, it is quite clear that by Natural Law, which may also be called the Law of Nations, all warfare is not to be condemned. (2) And history and the laws and customs of all peoples teach us quite plainly that war is not condemned by the voluntary Law of Nations. . . . [A] certain mode of warfare was introduced by the Law of Nations, so that wars that conform to that mode have, by the rules of war, certain well-defined incidents. Whence arises a distinction, of which we shall presently make use, between 'solemn' wars, also called just or full or complete wars, and 'non-solemn' wars which yet, on that account, do not cease to be just, that is, to conform to law and justice. For, as will hereafter appear, the Law of Nations neither allows nor condemns 'non-solemn' or informal wars, provided the cause be just. . . .

BOOK II

Chapter I. Of the Causes of War; and First, of Self-Defence and the Defence of Our Property

• • •

". . . (2) Most writers assign three just causes of war – defence, recovery of property, and punishment. . . . (3) . . . The first cause, therefore, of a just war is an injury which, though not yet done, threatens either our person or property.

"III. We have already said that if a man is menaced by a present force so that his life is in inevitable danger, then he may not only attack but even destroy his aggressor; and from this premise, which all must allow, we have proved that private war may, in some cases, be lawful. And it must be noted that this right of self-defence is inherent and fundamental and depends not at all upon the injustice or wrong-doing of the aggressor. So, I do not lose my right of self-defence even if he has no intention to do wrong, as when, for instance, he is performing his duty as a soldier, or mistakes me for someone else, or acts as one insane or in a dream – all of which we have read of. It is sufficient that I am not bound to suffer the wrong he threatens any more than any injury with which I might be threatened by a wild beast.

"IV. (1) It is a disputed question, however, whether we may kill or trample down innocent persons who, interposing, hinder a defence or escape by which alone we can avoid death. There are some, even divines, who think it lawful. . . .

"V. (1) It is necessary that the danger should be present, and, as it were, immediate. But I have no doubt that if a man is actually taking up weapons, obviously with the intent to kill another, the latter may anticipate and prevent his intention; and this is so because in the moral code, as in the laws of nature, there is no rule which does not admit of some latitude in application. Yet they are greatly in error, and deceive others, who presume that a bare apprehension of danger would justify a precautionary homicide. . . . (2) . . . If a danger can be otherwise avoided, or if it is not quite certain that it cannot be otherwise avoided, delay gives opportunity for many remedies and many chances, or, as the ancient saw has it, many things may intervene between the mouth and the morsel. Nor are there wanting divines and jurists who extend this indulgence even farther.

"XI. We now come to those injuries that affect our property. And here, if we have regard to corrective justice, I shall not deny that it is lawful to slay a robber if it be necessary for the preservation of our goods. . . .

"XVI. What we have so far said of the right of defending one's person and one's property belongs properly to private war, but, subject to difference of circumstances, it is also applicable to public war. In private war the right of defence is, as it were, a momentary and temporary one, disappearing as soon as the tribunal is available for the settlement of the matter in dispute. But in public war, since it arises only because there is no such tribunal or that tribunal has ceased to function, that right has permanency and continually develops with the occurrence of new wrongs and injuries. Moreover, in private war the right is limited to mere defence, while public authorities exact satisfaction as well. Hence, a danger which is not present but threatens from afar may be warded off by such authorities, though not directly (for, as we have above shown, that would be unjust), but indirectly, that is to say, by exacting satisfaction for a wrong already begun but not completed. . . .

"XVII. But I can hardly approve the doctrine of some writers, that by the Law of Nations we may rightly take up arms to enfeeble a rising power which, if too much augmented, may become dangerous to us. Undoubtedly, in arriving at a decision about a proposed war, these things may be taken into calculation, though not as a matter of justice but as a matter of interest, so that, if the war be just on other grounds it may, on this account, be prudent to declare it. And not any of the authorities cited say anything else. But it is a doctrine contrary to every principle of equity that justice allows us to resort to force in order to injure another merely because there is a possibility that he may injure us. Indeed, human life is such that we can never enjoy a condition of complete security. Against uncertain fears protection must be sought in divine providence and innocent precaution, and not in the exercise of our strength."

Wolff – The Duties of States Towards Each Other*

"Every nation owes to every other nation that which it owes to itself, in so far as the other does not have that in its own power, while the first nation without neglect of duty toward itself can perform this for

---

* From Christian Wolff (1679–1754). German philosopher, mathematician and scientist. Forced to leave the University of Halle, where he was teaching, because of his rationalist views but recalled by Frederick the Great when the latter came to the throne. A polymath, like Grotius, he published works on a wide range of subjects,

the other. For the law of nations is originally nothing else than the law of nature applied to nations, which are considered as individual persons living in a state of nature. Therefore, since every man owes to every other man that which he owes himself, in so far as the other does not have it in his power, while he without neglect of duty to himself can perform this for the other, every nation also owes toward every other nation that which it owes to itself, in so far as the other does not have that in its own power, while the first nation without neglect of duty toward itself can perform this for the other. . . .

§ 161. *Of mutual love of nations*
"Every nation ought to love and cherish every other nation as itself, even though it be an enemy. For every man ought to love and cherish every other man as himself. Therefore, since the law of nations is originally nothing else than the law of nature applied to nations, every nation too ought to love and care for every other nation as for itself. Which was the first point.

"And since we ought to love and cherish even an enemy as ourselves, it is evident in like manner that every nation ought to love and cherish another nation as itself, even though it be an enemy. Which was the second point. . . .

§ 162. *Of consideration for the happiness of other nations*
"Since he who cherishes another has the fixed and lasting desire to promote the happiness of the other and does all he can to make the other happy and avoids making him unhappy, since, moreover, every nation ought to cherish every other nation; every nation ought to have the fixed and lasting desire to promote the happiness of other nations and to do all it can to make them happy and avoid making them unhappy.

• • •

"Every ruler of a state ought to consider the ruler of another state as his equal by nature. For by nature all nations are equal. Therefore, since the ruler of a state represents his nation, when he is dealing with others, all rulers of states also are by nature equal. Therefore every one ought to consider the other as his equal by nature.

• • •

including philosophy, science and mathematics, but is best known today probably for his *Law of Nations* from which this extract is taken. Quoted from *The Law of Nations* (1749), trs. T. J. Hemelt (Oxford: Clarendon Press, 1934).

"Since every ruler of a state ought to look at the ruler of another state as equal to himself, all acts are illegal by which any ruler of a state indicates that he does not look upon another as equal by nature to himself, that is, as equally a ruler of a state, consequently much more illegal are the acts by which he shows that he judges another unworthy to be considered as ruler of a state and therefore as one to whom the duties are owed which a ruler of a state owes to a ruler of a state. But since acts of this sort verge on contempt and scorn of another, all acts are illegal which verge on contempt and scorn of the ruler of another state, and consequently since contempt and scorn are wrong, he who is guilty of acts of that sort does a wrong to another.

• • •

"The right belongs to every nation not to allow that it should be injured by another, and that is a perfect right. For no nation ought to injure another. Since, therefore, from a passive obligation on one party a right arises for the other party, and since, of course, if one party is bound not to do a thing, the other has the right not to allow it to be done; the right belongs to every nation also not to allow itself to be injured by another. Which was the first point.

"For nations are regarded as individual persons living in a state of nature, consequently just as a right belongs to every man by nature not to allow himself to be injured by another, so also a right belongs to every nation not to allow itself to be injured by another nation. Since, therefore, the right not to allow himself to be injured by another is a perfect right belonging by nature to every man, the right also, which belongs to every nation, not to allow itself to be injured by another nation, is a perfect right. Which was the second point.

• • •

"The right belongs to every nation not to allow some other nation to take away from it any of its rights. For every nation ought to allow its own right to another, consequently ought by no means to take it away. Since, therefore, from this obligation of the one party the right of one comes into existence to a negative act of the other, that right can be nothing else than that of not allowing your right to be taken away from you. Therefore the right belongs to every nation not to allow some other nation to take any right away from it.

• • •

"From the obligation of one party, which is established by a prohibitive law, the right arises for the other party not to allow the first party to do that which it is bound not to do, and that is a perfect right. For from the obligation of one party a certain right is brought into existence for the other party. Therefore, since a prohibitive law binds one not to do, since it is to the advantage of the other party that he should not do, the right which arises from the obligation established by this law can be nothing else than the right not to allow the party obligated to do what he is bound not to do. . . .

"Since the right belongs to you not to allow the other party to do what he is bound to you not to do (as proved above); and the means are also permitted, without which the other party could not be prevented from doing what he is bound to you not to do, consequently the right belongs to you to compel that party not to do. Therefore, since a right which is bound up with the right to coerce another, if he is unwilling to perform his obligation, is a perfect right, the right, established by a prohibitive law, which arises from the obligation of one party to the other, is a perfect right. . . .

"A perfect right belongs to every nation not to allow any other nation to interfere in any way in its government. For if any nation interferes with the government of another, it does this in contravention of the other's right. Therefore, since no one ought to do anything which is contrary to the right of another, since, moreover, from the obligation of one party, which is established by a prohibitive law, the right comes into existence for the other party not to allow the first party to do that which he is bound not to do, and that is a perfect right; a perfect right belongs to every nation not to allow any other nation to interfere in any way with its government. . . .

"The right belongs to every nation to obtain its right against another nation by force, if the other is unwilling to allow that right. For the right belongs to every nation not to permit any other nation to take away its right, consequently also not to permit it not to allow that right. Therefore it is necessary, when one does not wish to allow a right, that the other compel it by force to allow it. Therefore the right belongs to the one nation against the other nation to obtain its right by force, if the other does not wish to allow it.

"The right belongs to every nation to punish another nation which has injured it. For by nature the right belongs to every man to punish the one who has injured him. Therefore, since the same right must be applied to nations also, the right belongs to every nation to punish another which has injured it.

"This is likewise proved in this way. The right belongs to every nation not to allow that it be injured by another. Therefore, since we bind others by penalties to omit actions, the right belongs to every nation to punish another which has injured it."

13 Reasons of State

If theologians and lawyers put forward views concerning the *duties* of rulers and states, other writers were more concerned to assert their *rights*.

States, it was believed, could take actions which were prohibited to individuals. The morality that was supposed to govern the actions of men and women did not apply, under this view, to the behaviour of states. States might be compelled to undertake actions which would be condemned if undertaken in the everyday life of individual human beings: for example, deceit, betrayal, the making of war and the violation of treaties. These acts were forced on rulers by the necessities of state interest: *raison d'état*.

This view was widely shared by the principal rulers of the day. From the seventeenth century onwards the actions of rulers were directed not so much to the advancement of themselves and their houses as to that of the state which they ruled. In declaring himself to *be* the state Louis XIV demonstrated how far he identified his own interests with those of the state he embodied. In demanding glory for himself he demanded it likewise for his state. And in his aggressive foreign policies he showed only too clearly how he believed his duty to his country should be fulfilled. In the *Memoires* he wrote for his son in the 1660s he described how he believed a ruler should conduct himself in order to promote the interests of his country. In the passage quoted below he describes the reasons which caused him to decide in favour of war against Spain in 1666 – the so-called War of Devolution, in which he sought to promote bogus claims on behalf of his Spanish wife to territory in the Low Countries – and almost decided in favour of launching a separate war against England at the same time. Such enterprises, he believed, would provide the opportunity for him to "fulfil the great expectations that I had for some time inspired in the public", since, in his view, war was undoubtedly "the most brilliant way to acquire glory". And he describes with pride how skilfully he lulled the representatives of Franche Comté, the duchy he coveted, still under Spanish control, into believing that his intentions were peaceful before he ordered the invasion of that territory.

Frederick the Great equally identified his own interests and that of his house with those of his state. He not only declared himself to be the "first servant" of the state he ruled, but asserted that "state

interest is the only motive that should govern the councils of princes".
When he too, exactly a century after Louis XIV, wrote instructions
for his successor on how the affairs of the state should best be guided,
he made no attempt to conceal the designs he had on the territory of
other states. He openly listed those territories which he believed
Prussia should acquire to advance her interests. He made clear that,
given the self-interested and unscrupulous conduct to be expected
from other rulers, the head of a state could not afford always to be
too straightforward in his dealings with other countries; writing that it
was sometimes necessary for a ruler to conceal his true intentions
until he could see the opportune moment for action (as he himself
had seized the opportune moment, on the death of the Emperor
Charles VI, to invade Silesia in 1740). And he declared roundly that
the chief aim of a ruler in his dealings with other states must be
"self-preservation" and "aggrandisement".

Lord Palmerston, 80 years later, though he would never have
admitted such crude ambitions as these, also had no doubt that his
own duty, in guiding the policies of his country, was above all to
promote Britain's interests. It was right to seek peace and friendly
understanding with other states; but only so long as it was possible to
do so "consistently with a due regard to the interests, the honour and
dignity of this country". He himself had done everything possible to
uphold British interests in other parts of the world. He did not accept
that it was necessary for Britain, for this purpose, to inhibit her
freedom of action by alliances with other states since, so long as she
continued to "sympathise with right and justice" and "countenance
no wrong", she would never find herself alone. Britain's interests, he
believed, were "eternal and perpetual". And in conducting Britain's
affairs he followed Canning's watchword that "the interests of England ought to be the shibboleth of his policy".

Another 80 years later the German historian and philosopher von
Meinecke sought to describe the philosophy of *raison d'état*. He did
this in no critical spirit. *Raison d'état* was in his view a fundamental
law of state behaviour. Being a disciple of Ranke (and so of Hegel
before him) he saw "the State" as a mystical entity, with a life and
purpose of its own. It was, he declared, "an organic structure whose
full power can only be maintained by allowing it in some way to
continue growing, and *raison d'état* indicates both the path and the
goal for such a growth". The path and goal were not the same for all
states, but had to be judged by each according to its own situation
and environment. For each state at each particular moment there

existed an ideal course of action, an ideal *raison d'état*. This involved
it sometimes in courses of action outside normal law and morality.
The state, more than any other type of community, depended on
power, and found it "fundamentally difficult" to use this power in a
normal way. Observation showed that in practice always "some
pressure of obligation carries a State beyond justice and morality".
Nor did he believe that this situation could be improved. Attempts to
develop a law and morality to govern states, or to build the recently
established League of Nations into an effective institution, were
bound to fail. It only needed one state to diverge from the principles
laid down to cause all others to do so. Thus historical experience
showed that "it is not possible to improve the character of state
activity" because the necessities of state stripped away the "fetters of
justice and morality".

All these writers share the view that states have no choice but to
promote their own interests, even if this sometimes involves them in
actions which transgress traditional morality. Even if one state were
to wish to pursue a more principled course of conduct it would not be
able to do so, because of the ruthless and self-interested conduct of
others. Even Palmerston, who among these writers is the most
inclined to attribute moral purposes to a state (at least to his own), is
obliged to accept that it must sometimes be willing to use force to
secure the "justice" which it claims to uphold (see also pp. 186–8).
The kind of moral rules which, it was universally accepted, should
govern the conduct of individual humans in their relations with each
other, could not, under this view, be expected to prevail in the relations
of states, since states are by their nature self-seeking and amoral.

* * *

Louis XIV – The State's Need for Military Triumphs*

"The death of the King of Spain and the war between the English and
the United Provinces occurring at almost the same time, offered me

---

* From Louis XIV (1638–1715). Ruler of France for over 60 years from 1643 to 1715.
  His aggressive foreign policy, pursued in the name of "glory" and French national

two important opportunities at once for exerting my arms: one against the Spanish, in pursuit of the rights inherited by the Queen through the death of the King her father;[1] and the other against the English in defence of the States of Holland, according to our recent treaty. The King of England, of course, did furnish me with a rather plausible pretext for disengaging myself from this last quarrel, maintaining that the Dutch were the aggressors and that I had promised to aid them only if they were attacked. But even though it may have been in my interest to accept such a fine opportunity for remaining neutral, I could not refrain from acting in good faith, knowing that the English were the aggressors.

"I postponed declaring myself, however, in the hope of reconciling them. But seeing that my intercession was not succeeding and fearing that they might reach an agreement between themselves to my prejudice, I finally openly took the stand that I should. But it remained for me to decide if it was in my interest as well as that of my allies to go to war against both England and Spain, or if I should merely assume the quarrel of the Dutch and wait for a better time to settle my own, undoubtedly an important deliberation, owing to the importance and the weight of the arguments on both sides.

"On the one hand, I envisaged with pleasure the prospect of these two wars as a vast field that could create great opportunities for me to distinguish myself and to fulfil the great expectations that I had for some time inspired in the public. So many fine men whom I saw enthusiastic for my service seemed to be constantly urging me to furnish some scope for their valour, and it would not have been satisfied through a maritime war in which the most valiant hardly ever have the opportunity to distinguish themselves. But thinking of my own interest, I considered that the good of the kingdom not permitting me to expose myself to the caprices of the sea, I would be obliged to commit everything to my lieutenants without ever being able to act in person; that, moreover, my various ideas always obliging me to maintain a great number of troops, it would be more convenient for me to thrust them upon the domains of the King of Spain than to feed them constantly at the expense of my subjects; that besides, the entire house of Austria, convinced of my intentions, would not fail to

interests, united most of Europe against him. Wrote his *Memoire for the Instruction of the Dauphin* early in his reign as a guide to statecraft and a justification for the policies he had pursued in the previous decade. Quoted from *Memoire for the Instruction of the Dauphin* (1668), trs. P. Sonnino (New York: Free Press, 1970).

harm me indirectly with all its power; that if there was to be a war, it was better to fight it for some apparent profit than to direct all my efforts against islanders, from whom I could hardly conquer anything without it being burdensome to me; that if I undertook the two wars at once, the States would serve me better against Spain in order to have my support against England, whereas if they were entirely out of danger they would perhaps fear the increase of my power instead of recalling my favours; that, finally, many of my predecessors had been confronted with equally great affairs and that if I refused to expose myself to similar difficulties, I was in danger of not meriting similar praises.

• • •

"[D]uring all these preparations for war, there was still talk of peace. The Dutch, inspired by their own fear, were constantly pressing me to consent to it. While I was in Avesnes, Van Beuningen had arrived there for this purpose and even requested to accompany me to my camp, but I did not feel that I should permit this, because with so many people, there would hardly fail to be someone with a real or imaginary cause for complaint, and I did not want this to be observed unsympathetically.

• • •

"I received some very courteous offers from the King of Denmark, but as he did not seem to be in a position to do anything of importance for me, I merely replied with equal courtesy.

"I was more careful to maintain the good will of the Duke of Savoy, whom I had initially informed of my plan; and because he could be useful to me in Italy, I tried to attach him to my interests by making him whatever proposals I believed might please him.

"The Dutch, who did not think, perhaps, that I knew of their intrigues against me, still spoke freely with me about their interests and tried to commit me not to conquer anything near their frontiers, but this is precisely what I refused them. And when the three months of grace that I had given to the Spanish at their intercession had expired around the end of December, I announced that I did not intend to extend it.

"And indeed, already tired of remaining idle, I had everyone look around for something that could be executed suddenly. Among others, when the Prince de Condé went to hold the Estates of Burgundy, I charged him with looking into what might be done in Franche-Comté.

• • •

"It just so happened that the Francs-Comtois, alarmed by the previous campaign, had recently made a request for the renewal of their neutrality, which they had often obtained, and I believed that this negotiation would be good for keeping them occupied while I made my preparations. But in order to derive the full benefit from it, I transferred it from Mouslier, my resident in Switzerland, who had begun it, to the Prince de Condé, who could in this way innocently send back and forth into the country as often as was necessary for our plans; which was so well handled that between the Francs-Comtois coming to see him and he in turn sending off to them, he learned and arranged all that was necessary, always making it seem as if the conclusion of the negotiation was entirely up to them, so that they were not merely not alarmed, but even when they heard the truth in those vague rumours that cannot be prevented from preceding the most secret things, they took them as an artifice specifically intended to make them increase their offers. Such was their assurance, that the Swiss, who had already become suspicious of these moves, were reassured by the tranquillity of those who should have been most concerned by them.

"Even Castel-Rodrigo, whom they kept informed of their negotiation, was for a long while fooled by it like them, along with all my other neighbours, although these could observe my conduct more closely through their ministers at my court. For even though it was impossible to prevent someone from guessing the truth, I gave so many indications to the contrary that even those who had been the first to suspect it sometimes had their doubts, and those who had been told of it could not believe it.

"But finally, as I was about to depart, I wanted to inform the states of Europe myself of what I could no longer hide from them; and lest the most malicious take advantage of this undertaking to bring the others around to their sentiments, I declared that whatever its success, I would still keep my word.

"I left accompanied by the entire nobility of my court. Only then were the Francs-Comtois finally aroused from their stupor, whether by the rumours of my voyage, or by the warnings of Castel-Rodrigo, or even by the declaration of the Prince de Condé, who, taking the opportunity of some difficulty that they were raising, suddenly broke with them.

"They immediately asked for help from Flanders, offered great sums to the Swiss for troops, and mustered their own militia for February 8; but it was all too late, for I had ordered the Prince de

Condé to invade the country on the fourteenth of the same month and to seize certain posts that would prevent both the junction of the militia and communication between the principal cities."

Note
1. Louis now claimed that certain territories in the Spanish Low Countries were subject to a law of devolution, by which a daughter of the first marriage (Maria Theresa) succeeded prior to a son by a second marriage (Charles II).

Frederick the Great – The State's Need for Territory*

"In international politics you should have no special predilections for one people, nor aversion to another. You must follow the interests of the state blindly, allying yourself with the power whose interests at the time match the interests of Prussia. . . .

"The wisest policy is to wait for the right moment, to see what is the situation in which you find yourself and then to profit from it so far as you can. Those who hope to lead events in their own direction nearly always prove mistaken and see their plans fail. What policies were not pursued to determine in advance the succession in Spain; yet all those plans made by ministers finally came to grief. Or, to take an even more striking example, consider the projects made by so many powers against us during the last war [the Seven Years War] and see what became of them! The safest way, therefore, is to seize events and profit from them as they happen.

"The greatest error one can fall into is to believe that kings and ministers are interested in our fate. These people only love themselves; their own self-interest is their god. Their manner becomes flattering and insinuating only in so far as they have need of you. They will swear, with shameless falsehood, that your interests are as

* From Frederick the Great (1712–86). Became King of Prussia in 1740 at the age of 28 and ruled for nearly fifty years. Immediately after his accession took advantage of the death of Emperor Charles VI to seize Silesia from Austria and subsequently retained it in the Seven Years War (1756–63) in which Prussia fought, almost single-handed, against most of the other powers of the continent. Author of two "political testaments", intended for his successor, setting out his views of European politics and the way in which Prussia's national interests could best be promoted. Quoted from *Politisches Testament* (1768), extract trs. Evan Luard.

dear to them as their own. But do not believe them: block your ears to their siren calls.

"One knows pretty well what to expect of the great powers with which one deals. The English will pay you subsidies but will treat you as a paid hand, to be shown the door as soon as they have no more need of your services. The French will be hard put to give you any subsidies at all, or will give only miserable ones, because they are heavily burdened themselves. They will offer you the moon to secure your attention, if you will only take the trouble to conquer it. The Austrians are slow in their deliberations, and regard their allies as their subjects, rather than independent powers joined to them for common advantage. The Russians demand that their allies do more for them than they have any intention of doing in return.

"Such are the great powers of Europe. You will need cleverness, flexibility, a capacity for intrigue and substantial expenditure to take advantage of them, and to get them to assist (without noticing it) in the achievement of your goals. You can engage the French quite easily in a war by flattering their vanity and representing to them that it will be demeaning to their dignity not to be mixed up in everything that is happening in Europe. Their setbacks in war have been a grave embarrassment to their allies: having started with some brilliant coup, you will see them beaten and in flight, however short a time the war may last. . . .

"The first concern of a prince must be self-preservation, the second aggrandisement. To achieve this demands suppleness and a willingness to be ready for anything. At times one sails close to the wind, at others with a full sail; but never lose your main objective from sight. What does not succeed the first day may come to maturity in time. The way to conceal your secret ambitions is to affect peaceful sentiments until the favourable moment when you can deploy your true aims. This is how all the great politicians have behaved. It is a principle that cannot be abandoned without provoking the jealousy of other nations and giving them time to preempt your plans. . . .

"It is necessary to be prepared for every eventuality. Thus, having calculated in advance the measures that can be taken against the powers with which you may come into conflict, you can foresee and prevent the dangers they can cause, and make yourself aware of the advantages you can gain, whether by their friendship or their hostility. For example, it is much better to have Russia as ally than as enemy because she can do us a great deal of harm which we cannot repay to them.[1]

"Prussia's claims on different provinces
"The margravates of Bayreuth and Ansbach should revert to the ruling house after the extinction of their present ruling princes. But we should not flatter ourselves that this acquisition can be made without spilling blood – not unless the great powers happen to be preoccupied elsewhere at the time. I think we should take possession of them by sending in a single regiment of hussars, so as not to weaken the army by detaching forces unnecessarily and so as to remain in a position to bring force to bear on Saxony and on the frontiers of the queen-empress [Maria Theresa of Austria]. The Viennese court envies us this acquisition . . . but I believe it might be possible to come to an arrangement by swapping the margravates for territories that immediately adjoin our frontiers, either Lusatia or the duchy of Mecklenburg. By this change the queen-empress would be spared the chagrin of having us as her neighbour on other frontiers and such an arrangement would spare us a war. . . .

"A neighbouring country of ours, one that rounds out our frontiers, is a hundred times more important than one that is distant and separated from our frontiers. Considered only in terms of suitability I would say the country that would best meet our needs is Saxony: it would round our frontiers and would cover the capital against Austrian incursion. It is already linked with us commercially and, if it was joined to us, it would bring the greatest advantages to our State. After Saxony, Polish Prussia and Danzig would be the most favourable possessions to acquire: by fortifying several places on the Vistula, we could then defend Royal Prussia against Russian attacks. Finally, Mecklenburg, and the city of Hamburg joining it, would put us in a position to increase our trade, and to do so on a far more favourable basis than before."

Note
1. This is the same view that Bismarck was to hold about friendship with Russia a century later.

Palmerston – The Promotion of the State's Interest the Chief Aim of Policy*

"The principle on which I have thought the foreign affairs of this country ought to be conducted is the principle of maintaining peace and friendly understanding with all nations, as long as it was possible to do so consistently with a due regard to the interests, the honour and the dignity of this country. My endeavours have been to preserve peace. All the Governments of which I have had the honour to be a Member have succeeded in accomplishing that object. The main charges brought against me are that I did not involve this country in perpetual quarrels from one end of the globe to the other. There is no country that has been named, from the United States to the empire of China, with respect to which part of the hon. Member's charge has not been that we have refrained from taking steps that might have plunged us into conflict with one or more of these Powers. On these occasions we have been supported by the opinion and approbation of Parliament and the public. We have endeavoured to extend the commercial relations of the country, or to place them where extension was not required, on a firmer basis, and upon a footing of greater security. Surely in that respect we have not judged amiss, nor deserved the censure of the country; on the contrary, I think we have done good service.

"I hold with respect to alliances, that England is a Power sufficiently strong, sufficiently powerful, to steer her own course, and not to tie herself as an unnecessary appendage to the policy of any other Government. I hold that the real policy of England – apart from questions which involve her own particular interests, political or commercial – is to be the champion of justice and right; pursuing that course with moderation and prudence, not becoming the Quixote of the world, but giving the weight of her moral sanction and support wherever she thinks that justice is, and wherever she thinks that wrong has been done. Sir, in pursuing that course, and in pursuing

* From Lord Palmerston (1784–1865). British statesman, Foreign Secretary for 16 years between 1830 and 1851, Prime Minister in 1855–8 and again in 1859–65. In his public statements upheld the need for a vigorous foreign policy to promote British interests, but also recognised the necessity of frequent consultation with foreign powers to arrive at understandings concerning crisis situations when they arose. Concerned to promote liberal and constitutional systems of government abroad and to abolish the slave trade. Quoted from his reply to debate in the House of Commons, 1 March 1848.

the more limited direction of our own particular interests, my conviction is, that as long as England keeps herself in the right – as long as she wishes to permit no injustice – as long as she wishes to countenance no wrong – as long as she labours at legislative interests of her own – and as long as she sympathises with right and justice, she never will find herself altogether alone. She is sure to find some other State, of sufficient power, influence, and weight to support and aid her in the course she may think fit to pursue.

"Therefore I say that it is a narrow policy to suppose that this country or that is to be marked out as the eternal ally or the perpetual enemy of England. We have no eternal allies, and we have no perpetual enemies. Our interests are eternal and perpetual, and those interests it is our duty to follow. When we find other countries marching in the same course, and pursuing the same objects as ourselves, we consider them as our friends, and we think for the moment that we are on the most cordial footing; when we find other countries that take a different view, and thwart us in the object we pursue, it is our duty to make allowance for the different manner in which they may follow out the same objects. It is our duty not to pass too harsh a judgement upon others, because they do not exactly see things in the same light as we see; and it is our duty not lightly to engage this country in the frightful responsibilities of war, because from time to time we may find this or that Power disinclined to concur with us in matters where their opinion and ours may fairly differ. That has been, as far as my faculties have allowed me to act upon it, the guiding principle of my conduct. And if I might be allowed to express in one sentence the principle which I think ought to guide an English Minister, I would adopt the expression of Canning, and say that with every British Minister the interests of England ought to be the shibboleth of his policy."

Meinecke – *Raison d'État**

"*Raison d'état* is the fundamental principle of national conduct, the State's first Law of Motion. It tells the statesman what he must do to

* From Friedrich Meinecke (1862–1954). German historian, concerned especially with the history of ideas. In his first book, *Weltburgertum und Nationalstaat* (1908), he

preserve the health and strength of the State. The State is an organic structure whose full power can only be maintained by allowing it in some way to continue growing; and *raison d'état* indicates both the path and the goal for such a growth. This path and this goal cannot be chosen quite at random; but neither can exactly the same ones be prescribed for all States. For the State is also an individual structure with its own characteristic way of life; and the laws general to the species are modified by a particular structural pattern and a particular environment. So the 'intelligence' of the State consists in arriving at a proper understanding both of itself and its environment, and afterwards in using this understanding to decide the principles which are to guide its behaviour. These principles are always bound to be at the same time both individual and general, both constant and changeable. They will change subtly as alterations take place in the State itself and in its environment. But they must also tally with what is lasting in the structure of the individual State, as well as with that which is permanent in the laws governing the life of all States. Thus from the realm of what is and what will be, there constantly emerges, through the medium of understanding, a notion of what ought to be and what must be. The statesman *must*, if he is convinced of the accuracy of his understanding of the situation, act in accordance with it in order to reach his goal. The choice of path to the goal is restricted by the particular nature of the State and its environment. Strictly speaking, only *one* path to the goal (i.e., the best possible one at the moment) has to be considered at any one time. For each State at each particular moment there exists one ideal course of action, one ideal *raison d'état*. The statesman in power tries hard to discern this course, and so too does the historian surveying the past in retrospect. Any historical evaluations of national conduct are simply attempts to discover the true *raison d'état* of the States in question. . . .

"It is worth while then to try . . . and see clearly why it is that the State – although it is the very guardian of law, and although it is just as dependent as any other kind of community on an absolute validity of ethics and law, is yet unable to abide by these in its own behaviour. Power belongs to the essence of the State; without it the

presented the national state as the ideal form of political organisation. Best known for his *Die Idee der Staatsräson* he traced the history of the concept of *raison d'état* and concluded (like Niebuhr, pp. 274–6) that states were sometimes obliged to act in ways that were contrary to individual morality. Quoted from *The Idea of "Raison d'État"* (1924), in *Modern History*, trs. Douglas Scott (London: Routledge and Kegan Paul, 1957).

State cannot carry out its task of upholding justice and protecting the community. All the other communities need its power, in order to develop without hindrance, and in order to keep under control the bestial element in Man. Only the State possesses this power in a full degree which embraces both physical and spiritual means. All other communities, although dependent on the use of power, are nevertheless not required to have their own physical power, and are thus freer from the temptations of power. Power is not indeed 'evil in itself' . . .; on the contrary it is naturally indifferent both towards good and evil. But whoever holds power in his hands is continuously subject to a moral temptation to misuse it, and to overstep the boundaries of justice and morality. We saw this clearly enough when we analysed action prompted by *raison d'état*. One can describe it as a curse that lies on power – it cannot be withstood. Thus for the very reason that the State needs more elemental and natural power-means than any other community, the State also finds it more fundamentally difficult to keep these power-means moral.

"But this radical moralisation of the other communities does not in any way signify that their practice is spotlessly pure, but solely that their norms and principles of conduct are pure. Why cannot the State, too, achieve at least this purity of its standards and laws of movement? Why is there not at least a pure theory of State life, even if the practice has to remain impure? Time and again the attempt has been made to set up just such a pure theory, which would bring the State consistently within the rule of the law of morality and the command of justice; but, as has already been remarked, this was never historically successful. Whoever attempts to derive the theory of State conduct from the historical essence of the State (something which must certainly happen of necessity) is always bound to come up against that stumbling-block in action prompted by *raison d'état*, where apparently some pressure of obligation carries the State beyond justice and morality. It lies in the State's action towards the outside, not towards the inside. Within the State it is possible for *raison d'état* to remain in harmony with justice and morality, because no other power hinders that of the State. This was not always so; it is only a result of historical development. So long as the State authority did not hold all the domestic means of physical power concentrated in its own hand, so long as it still had to struggle in domestic affairs with rival or opposing power, then it was always being tempted (indeed, in its own view it was frequently obliged) to combat these forces by unjust and immoral means. And even today every revolution which it has to repress still renews the temptation, with just this difference: that a finer moral feeling is working against it, and the form of exceptional legislation makes it possible to legalise the unusual power-means which the State, in such situations, requires. But in any case it is also in the essential interest of the State that it should obey the law which it itself promulgates, and thus foster civil morality in domestic affairs by its own example. It is thus possible for morality, justice and power to work together in harmony with each other within the State.

"Yet they are not capable of doing this in their relationship to other States. Justice can only be upheld, if a power exists which is able and ready to uphold it. Otherwise the natural situation arises, where each tries to fight for the right he believes in, with whatever power-means he has at his disposal. States (says Hegel) are not subject to any Praetor, who could give just decisions and uphold them by might. Nor would he know which set of laws he ought to be guided by in his decisions; for the mutually conflicting vital interests of the States generally take advantage of the disorder that exists amongst the recognised legal principles. This makes it possible for the States to pour out all kinds of elemental power against one another, and gives free play to all the moral temptations of the power-impulse. But in this situation *raison d'état* now exhibits once again its inner duplicity and duality, for it also fears these elemental forces which it unleashes. Freely released power shall (when *raison d'état* is properly exercised) really only constitute the means of implementing by force those vital necessities of the State, which are not to be secured by legal methods. But this means, once freed from legal fetters, threatens to set itself up as an end-in-itself, and to carry the State beyond the frontier of which it stands in real need. Then the excesses of power politics set in; the irrational outruns the rational. That mere technical utility, which (as we observed) forms as it were the kernel of *raison d'état*, does not indeed always possess enough strength to hem in effectively the elemental impulses of force. But perhaps it always does have more strength for this purpose than the ethical ideas have, which grow up around *raison d'état*, when it reaches its highest form. Motives of utility and morality, working together in the life of States, have not in any case been able to produce hitherto more than the precarious pattern of International Law, and the modern League of Nations which is at least equally precarious. And despite International Law and the League of Nations we continue, up to the present minute, to observe excesses of power politics on the part of those States who do not have to fear any Forum or any more powerful adversary.

"It is certainly also true that, in the course of centuries, further changes have taken place in the nature and character of power politics – changes which can be traced back (though not perhaps exclusively) to the influence of moral ideas. But it may well be asked whether it is not the case that everything that has been accomplished in the way of ennobling and humanising power politics (and its most important instrument – war) is compensated for by other fateful effects of civilisation, that is to say, of the progressive rationalisation and technicalisation of life. The answer to this question belongs – as does everything which can only be stated after an elucidation of the developmental process of the idea of *raison d'état* – to the close of our treatise.

"But now we must certainly look more closely at that constraining force which, in the corporate life of States together, carries *raison d'état* beyond the bounds of law and morality. The State (we have said) must create for itself its own imaginary right and necessity for existence, because no other authority can create this on its behalf; and because there does not exist any directive and arbitrative State-authority over all States. But why is it not possible then for the properly understood interest of the States themselves, co-operating by reason of ethical motives, to induce them to unite and freely restrict the methods of their power politics, to abide by Law and Morality, and to develop the institutions of International Law and the League of Nations to a full and satisfactory efficiency? Because no one of them will trust another round the corner. Because no one of them believes for certain about any of the others, that it would abide by the agreed limitations in absolutely every instance and without any exception; but on the contrary suspects that in certain instances that other would once again lapse into following his own natural egoism. The first lapse back into evil ways on the part of one State (out of anxiety for its own welfare) and attended by success, would be sufficient to shatter the whole undertaking once again, and destroy the credit of ethical policy. Even if one wished to conduct the foreign policy of one's own State by methods which were not ethically objectionable, one would nevertheless always have to be on one's guard in case one's opponent failed to do so too; and in such a case (according to the principle *à corsaire corsaire et demi*) one would feel oneself released from the moral imperative – whereupon the old, age-old game would then start again from the beginning.

"Thus what makes any reform apparently impossible is the profound and pessimistic conviction (rooted in the instincts, and borne out by historical experience) to the effect that it is not possible to improve the character of State activity. The Idealist will always be repeating his demand for such a reform, and will always be declaring it to be possible. The responsible and executive statesman (even if fundamentally an Idealist himself) will always find himself constrained by the pressure of the responsibility he bears for the whole, to doubt the possibility of it, and to take up a line of conduct that is in accordance with this doubt. Once again we recognise that this 'necessity of State', which strips away the fetters of justice and morality, simultaneously possesses an ethical and an elemental aspect; and that the State is an amphibious creature, which simultaneously inhabits the ethical and the natural worlds. In like manner, every man and every human association is an amphibian of this kind. But they are subject to the constraining force of the State, which exacts retribution for every misuse of natural impulses – at least in so far as such a misuse offends against the laws. Nevertheless the State itself is now once more under an obligation, whereby it must both use and misuse a natural impulse in one and the same breath."

14 The State's Right to Intervene

The most clear-cut affirmation of the rights of states was the assertion of the principle of sovereignty. In defending this claim such writers as Bodin and Hobbes (pp. 136 and 40 above) had in effect declared that the ruler could do as he pleased within his own lands; and that those who had previously enjoyed rights independent of the prince – feudal lords, municipalities and the church – were subject to his sovereign power. The most fundamental right of rulers, and therefore of states, was to order the lives of those within their borders according to their own discretion.

But the idea of sovereignty also had important implications for relations with other states. The independence of each state within its own borders implied that it had the right to be free of interference from others. If each was content to exercise sovereignty within its own borders, and to allow other states to do the same within theirs (assuming that there was no conflict about where those borders lay), then all should in theory be able to live in peace together.

In practice states were not always willing to accept that self-denying ordinance. Especially after the French Revolution and the national uprisings of the following century, intervention – for or against such revolutions – became increasingly frequent. As a result the right of a state to intervene in other states was discussed almost as intensely in this age as it was to be debated 150 years later, after the Second World War, in another revolutionary age, among statesmen, lawyers and commentators. Many of the same arguments, on the same points of principle, were employed in both periods.

The first question to be debated (in both ages) concerned what gave the right to intervene? Could it be justified only if the state against which action was envisaged was itself guilty of offensive action elsewhere? Or could it be undertaken even if the offence was less overt and less immediate? Some argued, especially the more conservative commentators (in both ages), that a country might represent a dangerous threat even though it had undertaken no overt offensive action against other states in the region. This was the view that, in a later age, was to be taken by some in Stalin's Russia, Nasser's Egypt and Qadaffi's Libya in the period after 1945 – sources of infection that might need to be neutralised. At this time it was put forward by Edmund Burke in his *Letters on a Regicide Peace* reproduced below. He claimed that the regime then established in France represented a form of public nuisance, which was a standing threat to the established governments throughout the continent. On these grounds outside states had the right to take action to suppress the nuisance. The states of Europe, he argued, formed a kind of commonwealth, sharing a similar culture and tradition, and no single state could be allowed to remain in exile from that tradition. The other states thus had the right to prevent any "innovation" which might, like the new regime in France, amount to a dangerous threat: what in civil society was a ground for a legal action was in international society a ground for war, which remained the only ultimate means of securing justice among nations. This was the argument of a conservative observer, disturbed both at the illegitimacy of the regime established in France and its consequences for the rest of the continent.

This kind of argument – that states had the right to intervene against a revolutionary regime elsewhere (closely parallel to the arguments to be used 150 years later to justify US intervention against Cuba, the Dominican Republic and Nicaragua) – was widely used by conservative statesmen after 1815 to justify intervention, unilateral or collective, to put down revolution in other states. But the right of states to use force elsewhere could be put forward on quite other grounds. While Metternich (like Burke) had wanted intervention to suppress revolution, others wanted intervention to support it. J. S. Mill, for example, as a liberal observer of the international scene, defended the right of a state to intervene in the affairs of another to prevent tyrannical or alien government. According to him the legitimacy of a government and its right to rule could be challenged because of its non-representative character: because it was imposed rather than willingly accepted. He refused to accept that this argument could be used to challenge the right of the British to rule in India or France in Algeria, since he held that in those cases they had substituted good government for "barbaric" systems. On the other hand Austria's attempt to reassert her power in Hungary in 1849 against the will of most Hungarians could not be so justified; and there was thus no reason for Britain to decline assistance to the revolutionaries there (or presumably in Poland, Italy and other countries seeking national independence at the time) on the basis of the same general principle of "non-intervention". But this right of states to intervene to overthrow an unjust government was not unlimited: only in so far as an oppressed people were themselves willing to fight for their own freedom, he believed, did outside states enjoy the right to take up arms to help them.

Burke and Mill were concerned with different kinds of revolution: one ideological, the other national. One supported intervention to overcome revolution, the other to support it. But the arguments they put forward touched on fundamental issues in international relations. What was at issue in their arguments was the balance between two rights: the right of one state to settle its internal conflicts free of interference from without on the basis of its "sovereignty", and the right of others to intervene to affect the outcome, whether to protect their own security (as Burke argues) or to protect fundamental human rights (as Mill suggests). This conflict has continued to pre-occupy observers of international relations ever since; and both grounds have been put forward many times to justify the use of force over the years.

A similar dispute arose over the right of states to intervene to protect their own nationals in other states. This too was a justification many times asserted (then as now) for the use of force by one state against another. It is the issue discussed in the speech of Lord Palmerston quoted below. The issue had arisen over the affair of Don Pacifico, which nearly cost Palmerston his job. Don Pacifico, a British subject of Maltese origin, had suffered damage to his property as a result of a riot in Greece. When the Greek government refused to compensate him Palmerston sent British warships to extract the necessary undertakings. That action shocked a large section of the British public, and when the affair was debated in Parliament Palmerston spoke to defend his political life. He argued that a government was entitled to intervene abroad to defend the rights of its own nationals when they were threatened. He saw no reason why British subjects (such as Don Pacifico), if they could not secure justice in the country in which they found themselves, should not look to their own country for protection. Especially where despotic governments were in power, or where no fair legal system operated, this might be the only way of ensuring that their rights were respected. He accepted that British subjects should be willing to seek redress in local courts in the first place. But if they encountered a "denial" of justice, or "decisions manifestly unjust", they were entitled to appeal to their own government for assistance. The British government was then entitled to afford them necessary protection, including the mobilisation of armed forces for that purpose.

An almost exactly opposite view was taken by Gladstone in the same debate. Like liberals in the US a century later, accusing interventionist administrations of seeking to make their country the "world's policeman", he deplored the tendency he saw in Palmerston to interfere in all parts of the world to promote British interests. It was legitimate for any government to seek to influence other governments elsewhere, even in their internal affairs, if the latter themselves were willing to accept that influence. What they should not do was to "make occasions" for *imposing* the kind of settlements they desired. If Britain undertook such actions, she could hardly complain if other countries tried to do the same. This would create a system of competitive interference, which was not only inimical to the freedom of other countries, but could finally destroy the peace of the world (again exactly paralleling the arguments to be used against interventionism – for example by Senator Fulbright and others of like mind – a century or so later).

There were few writers in this age, therefore, whether among statesmen or international lawyers, who did not (despite the doctrine of sovereignty) uphold the right of states to intervene against other states in particular circumstances. They differed only in their judgements of what those circumstances were. Some believed that an act of war was permissible to maintain the existing international order and the balance of power; others believed that force could and should be used to help oppressed people in their own countries. Almost nowhere was it believed that intervention as such, even by armed force, was always an illegitimate use of state power.

*   *   *

Burke – The Right to Intervene against a Public Menace*

"In the intercourse between nations, we are apt to rely too much on the instrumental part. We lay too much weight upon the formality of treaties and compacts. We do not act much more wisely when we

---

* From Edmund Burke (1729–97). British politician and political writer. Born in Ireland, he studied law in Dublin and soon became associated with Whig politicians, becoming a Member of Parliament in 1774. Asserted the power of parliament

trust to the interests of men as guarantees of their engagements. The interests frequently tear to pieces the engagements; and the passions trample upon both. Entirely to trust to either, is to disregard our own safety, or not to know mankind. Men are not tied to one another by papers and seals. They are led to associate by resemblances, by conformities, by sympathies. It is with nations as with individuals. Nothing is so strong a tie of amity between nation and nation as correspondence in laws, customs, manners, and habits of life. They have more than the force of treaties in themselves. They are obligations written in the heart. They approximate men to men, without their knowledge, and sometimes against their intentions. The secret, unseen, but irrefragable bond of habitual intercourse holds them together, even when their perverse and litigious nature sets them to equivocate, scuffle, and fight, about the terms of their written obligations.

"As to war, if it be the means of wrong and violence, it is the sole means of justice amongst nations. Nothing can banish it from the world. They who say otherwise, intending to impose upon us, do not impose upon themselves. But it is one of the greatest objects of human wisdom to mitigate those evils which we are unable to remove. The conformity and analogy of which I speak, incapable, like everything else, of preserving perfect trust and tranquillity among men, has a strong tendency to facilitate accommodation, and to produce a generous oblivion of the rancour of their quarrels. With this similitude, peace is more of peace, and war is less of war. I will go further. There have been periods of time in which communities, apparently in peace with each other, have been more perfectly separated than, in latter times, many nations in Europe have been in the course of long and bloody wars. The cause must be sought in the similitude throughout Europe of religion, laws and manners. At bottom, these are all the same.

"The writers on public law have often called this *aggregate* of nations a commonwealth. They had reason. It is virtually one great state having the same basis of general law, with some diversity of provincial customs and local establishments. The nations of Europe

---

against the king and defended the rights of the American colonies to a say in their future. Played a prominent part in the unsuccessful impeachment of Warren Hastings. Unlike many Englishmen was from the beginning deeply hostile to the French revolution, as to democracy in general, as a threat to traditional European values. Quoted from *Letters on the Proposals for Peace with the Regicide Directory of France* (London, 1796).

have had the very same Christian religion, agreeing in the fundamental parts, varying a little in the ceremonies and in the subordinate doctrines. The whole of the polity and economy of every country in Europe has been derived from the same sources. It was drawn from the old Germanic or Gothic customary, from the feudal institutions which must be considered as an emanation from that customary; and the whole has been improved and digested into system and discipline by the Roman law.

"From hence arose the several orders, with or without a monarch (which are called states), in every European country; the strong traces of which, where monarchy predominated, were never wholly extinguished or merged in despotism. In the few places where monarchy was cast off, the spirit of European monarchy was still left. Those countries still continued countries of states; that is, of classes, orders, and distinctions such as had before subsisted, or nearly so. Indeed the force and form of the institution called states continued in greater perfection in those republican communities than under monarchies. From all those sources arose a system of manners and of education which was nearly similar in all this quarter of the globe; and which softened, blended, and harmonised the colours of the whole. There was little difference in the form of the universities for the education of their youth, whether with regard to faculties, to sciences, or to the more liberal and elegant kinds of erudition.

"From this resemblance in the modes of intercourse, and in the whole form and fashion of life, no citizen of Europe could be altogether an exile in any part of it. There was nothing more than a pleasing variety to recreate and instruct the mind, to enrich the imagination, and to meliorate the heart. When a man travelled or resided for health, pleasure, business or necessity, from his own country, he never felt himself quite abroad.

"The whole body of this new scheme of manners, in support of the new scheme of politics, I consider as a strong and decisive proof of determined ambition and systematic hostility. I defy the most refining ingenuity to invent any other cause for the total departure of the Jacobin republic from every one of the ideas and usages, religious, legal, moral, or social, of this civilised world, and for her tearing herself from its communion with such studied violence, but from a formed resolution of keeping no terms with that world. It has not been, as has been falsely and insidiously represented, that these miscreants had only broke with their old government. They made a schism with the whole universe, and that schism extended to almost everything great and small. For one, I wish, since it is gone thus far, that the breach had been so complete, as to make all intercourse impracticable: but partly by accident, partly by design, partly from the resistance of the matter, enough is left to preserve intercourse, whilst amity is destroyed or corrupted in its principle.

"This violent breach of the community of Europe we must conclude to have been made (even if they had not expressly declared it over and over again) either to force mankind into an adoption of their system, or to live in perpetual enmity with a community the most potent we have ever known. Can any person imagine that, in offering to mankind this desperate alternative, there is no indication of a hostile mind, because men in possession of the ruling authority are supposed to have a right to act without coercion in their own territories? As to the right of men to act anywhere according to their pleasure, without any moral tie, no such right exists. Men are never in a state of *total* independence of each other. It is not the condition of our nature: nor is it conceivable how any man can pursue a considerable course of action without its having some effect upon others; or, of course, without producing some degree of responsibility for his conduct. The *situations* in which men relatively stand produce the rules and principles of that responsibility, and afford directions to prudence in exacting it.

"Distance of place does not extinguish the duties of the rights of men; but it often renders their exercise impracticable. The same circumstance of distance renders the noxious effects of an evil system in any community less pernicious. But there are situations where this difficulty does not occur; and in which, therefore, these duties are obligatory, and these rights are to be asserted. It has ever been the method of public jurists to draw a great part of the analogies, on which they form the law of nations, from the principles of law which prevail in civil community. Civil laws are not all of them merely positive. Those, which are rather conclusions of legal reason than matters of statutable provision, belong to universal equity, and are universally applicable. Almost the whole praetorian law is such. There is a *law of neighbourhood* which does not leave a man perfectly master on his own ground. When a neighbour sees a *new erection*, in the nature of a nuisance, set up at his door, he has a right to represent it to the judge; who, on his part, has a right to order the work to be stayed; or, if established, to be removed. On this head the parent law is express and clear, and has made many wise provisions, which, without destroying, regulate and restrain the right of *ownership*, by the right of *vicinage*. No *innovation* is permitted that may redound, even secondarily, to the prejudice of a neighbour. The whole doctrine of that important head of praetorian law, '*De novi operis nunciatione*', is founded on the principle that no *new* use should be made of a man's private liberty of operating upon his private property, from whence a detriment may be justly apprehended by his neighbour. This law of denunciation is prospective. It is to anticipate what is called *damnum infectum*, or *damnum nondum factum*, that is a damage justly apprehended, but not actually done. Even before it is clearly known, whether the innovation be damageable or not, the judge is competent to issue a prohibition to innovate, until the point can be determined. This prompt interference is grounded on principles favourable to both parties. It is preventive of mischief difficult to be repaired, and of ill blood difficult to be softened. The rule of law, therefore, which comes before the evil, is amongst the very best parts of equity, and justifies the promptness of the remedy; because, as it is well observed, *Res damni infecti celeritatem desiderat, et periculosa est dilatio*. This right of denunciation does not hold, when things continue, however inconveniently to the neighbourhood, according to the *ancient* mode. For there is a sort of presumption against novelty, drawn out of a deep consideration of human nature and human affairs; and the maxim of jurisprudence is well laid down, *Vetustas pro lege semper habetur*.

"Such is the law of civil vicinity. Now where there is no constituted judge, as between independent states there is not, the vicinage itself is the natural judge. It is, preventively, the assertor of its own rights, or, remedially, their avenger. Neighbours are presumed to take cognizance of each other's acts. '*Vicini vicinorum facta praesumuntur scire*'. This principle, which, like the rest, is as true of nations, as of individual men, has bestowed on the grand vicinage of Europe a duty to know, and a right to prevent, any capital innovation which may amount to the erection of a dangerous nuisance.[1] Of the importance of that innovation, and the mischief of that nuisance, they are, to be sure, bound to judge not litigiously: but it is in their competence to judge. They have uniformly acted on this right. What in civil society is a ground of action, in politic society is a ground of war. But the exercise of that competent jurisdiction is a matter of moral prudence. As suits in civil society, so war in the political, must ever be a matter of great deliberation. It is not this or that particular proceeding, picked out here and there, as a subject of quarrel, that will do. There must be an aggregate of mischief. There must be marks of deliberation, there must be traces of design, there must be indications of malice, there must be tokens of ambition. There must be force in the body where they exist, there must be energy in the mind. When all these circumstances are combined, or the important parts of them, the duty of the vicinity calls for the exercise of its competence: and the rules of prudence do not restrain, but demand it."

Note

1. "This state of things cannot exist in France without involving all the surrounding powers in one common danger, without giving them the right, without imposing it on them as a duty, to stop the progress of an evil which attacks the fundamental principles by which mankind is united in civil society" (Declaration, 29 October 1793).

Mill – The Right to Intervene against an Oppressive Alien Government*

"There seems to be no little need that the whole doctrine of non-interference with foreign nations should be reconsidered, if it can be said to have as yet been considered as a really moral question at all. We have heard something lately about being willing to go to war for an idea. To go to war for an idea, if the war is aggressive, not defensive, is as criminal as to go to war for territory or revenue; for it is as little justifiable to force our ideas on other people, as to compel them to submit to our will in any other respect.

"But there assuredly are cases in which it is allowable to go to war, without having been ourselves attacked, or threatened with attack; and it is very important that nations should make up their minds in time, as to what these cases are. There are few questions which more require to be taken in hand by ethical and political philosophers, with a view to establish some rule or criterion whereby the justifiableness of intervening in the affairs of other countries, and (what is some-

---

* From John Stuart Mill (1806–73). Philosopher, economist and political thinker who worked for 20 years for the East India Company, overseeing its relations with the native states of India. Wrote prolifically on literature, logic and economics, but became increasingly concerned with ethical and political questions. This extract is from one of his only writings on international affairs. Principal works include *On Liberty* (1859), *Considerations on Representative Government* (1861), and *Utilitarianism* (1863). Quoted from *A Few Words on Non-Intervention* (London, 1859).

times fully as questionable) the justifiableness of refraining from intervention, may be brought to a definite and rational test. Whoever attempts this, will be led to recognise more than one fundamental distinction, not yet by any means familiar to the public mind, and in general quite lost sight of by those who write in strains of indignant morality on the subject. There is a great difference (for example) between the case in which the nations concerned are of the same, or something like the same, degree of civilisation, and that in which one of the parties to the situation is of a high, and the other of a very low, grade of social improvement.

"To suppose that the same international customs, and the same rules of international morality, can obtain between one civilised nation and another, and between civilised nations and barbarians, is a grave error, and one which no statesman can fall into, however it may be with those who, from a safe and unresponsible position, criticise statesmen. Among many reasons why the same rules cannot be applicable to situations so different, the two following are among the most important. In the first place, the rules of ordinary international morality imply reciprocity. But barbarians will not reciprocate. They cannot be depended on for observing any rules. Their minds are not capable of so great an effort, nor their will sufficiently under the influence of distant motives. In the next place, nations which are still barbarous have not got beyond the period during which it is likely to be for their benefit that they should be conquered and held in subjection by foreigners. Independence and nationality, so essential to the due growth and development of a people further advanced in improvement, are generally impediments to theirs. The sacred duties which civilised nations owe to the independence and nationality of each other, are not binding towards those to whom nationality and independence are either a certain evil, or at best a questionable good. The Romans were not the most clean-handed of conquerors, yet would it have been better for Gaul and Spain, Numidia and Dacia, never to have formed part of the Roman Empire? To characterise any conduct whatever towards a barbarous people as a violation of the law of nations, only shows that he who so speaks has never considered the subject. A violation of great principles of morality it may easily be: but barbarians have no rights as a *nation*, except a right to such treatment as may, at the earliest possible period, fit them for becoming one. The only moral laws for the relation between a civilised and a barbarous government, are the universal rules of morality between man and man.

"The criticisms, therefore, which are so often made upon the conduct of the French in Algeria, or of the English in India, proceed, it would seem, mostly on a wrong principle. . . .

"But among civilised peoples, members of an equal community of nations, like Christian Europe, the question assumes another aspect, and must be decided on totally different principles. It would be an affront to the reader to discuss the immorality of wars of conquest, or of conquest even as the consequence of lawful war; the annexation of any civilised people to the dominion of another, unless by their own spontaneous election. Up to this point, there is no difference of opinion among honest people; nor on the wickedness of commencing an aggressive war for any interest of our own, except when necessary to avert from ourselves an obviously impending wrong. The disputed question is that of interfering in the regulation of another country's internal concerns; the question whether a nation is justified in taking part, on either side, in the civil wars or party contests of another; and chiefly, whether it may justifiably aid the people of another country in struggling for liberty; or may impose on a country any particular government or institutions, either as being best for the country itself, or as necessary for the security of its neighbours.

"Of these cases, that of a people in arms for liberty is the only one of any nicety, or which, theoretically at least, is likely to present conflicting moral considerations. The other cases which have been mentioned hardly admit of discussion. Assistance to the government of a country in keeping down the people, unhappily by far the most frequent case of foreign intervention, no one writing in a free country needs take the trouble of stigmatising. A government which needs foreign support to enforce obedience from its own citizens, is one which ought not to exist; and the assistance given to it by foreigners is hardly ever anything but the sympathy of one despotism with another. A case requiring consideration is that of a protracted civil war, in which the contending parties are so equally balanced that there is no probability of a speedy issue; or if there is, the victorious side cannot hope to keep down the vanquished but by severities repugnant to humanity, and injurious to the permanent welfare of the country. In this exceptional case it seems now to be an admitted doctrine, that the neighbouring nations, or one powerful neighbour with the acquiescence of the rest, are warranted in demanding that the contest shall cease, and a reconciliation take place on equitable terms of compromise. Intervention of this description has been repeatedly practised during the present generation, with such general approval, that its legitimacy may be considered to have passed into a maxim of what is called international law. The interference of the European Powers between Greece and Turkey, and between Turkey and Egypt, were cases in point. That between Holland and Belgium was still more so. The intervention of England in Portugal, a few years ago, which is probably less remembered than the others, because it took effect without the employment of actual force, belongs to the same category. At the time, this interposition had the appearance of a bad and dishonest backing of the government against the people, being so timed as to hit the exact moment when the popular party had obtained a marked advantage, and seemed on the eve of overthrowing the government, or reducing it to terms. But if ever a political act which looked ill in the commencement could be justified by the event, this was; for, as the fact turned out, instead of giving ascendancy to a party, it proved a really healing measure; and the chiefs of the so-called rebellion were, within a few years, the honoured and successful ministers of the throne against which they had so lately fought.[1]

"With respect to the question, whether one country is justified in helping the people of another in a struggle against their government for free institutions, the answer will be different, according as the yoke which the people are attempting to throw off is that of a purely native government, or of foreigners; considering as one of foreigners, every government which maintains itself by foreign support. When the contest is only with native rulers, and with such native strength as those rulers can enlist in their defence, the answer I should give to the question of the legitimacy of intervention is, as a general rule, No. The reason is, that there can seldom be anything approaching to assurance that intervention, even if successful, would be for the good of the people themselves. The only test possessing any real value, of a people's having become fit for popular institutions, is that they, or a sufficient portion of them to prevail in the contest, are willing to brave labour and danger for their liberation. I know all that may be said. I know it may be urged that the virtues of freemen cannot be learnt in the school of slavery, and that if a people are not fit for freedom, to have any chance of becoming so they must first be free. And this would be conclusive, if the intervention recommended would really give them freedom. But the evil is, that if they have not sufficient love of liberty to be able to wrest it from merely domestic oppressors, the liberty which is bestowed on them by other hands than their own, will have nothing real, nothing permanent. No people ever was and remained free, but because it was determined to be so; because neither its rulers nor any other party in the nation could compel it to be otherwise. If a people – especially one whose freedom has not yet become prescriptive – does not value it sufficiently to fight for it, and maintain it against any force which can be mustered *within* the country, even by those who have the command of the public revenue, it is only a question in how few years or months that people will be enslaved. Either the government which it has given to itself, or some military leader or knot of conspirators who contrive to subvert the government, will speedily put an end to all popular institutions: unless indeed it suits their convenience better to leave them standing, and be content with reducing them to mere forms; for, unless the spirit of liberty is strong in a people, those who have the executive in their hands easily work any institutions to the purposes of despotism. There is no sure guarantee against this deplorable issue, even in a country which has achieved its own freedom; as may be seen in the present day by striking examples both in the Old and New Worlds: but when freedom has been achieved *for* them, they have little prospect indeed of escaping this fate. When a people has had the misfortune to be ruled by a government under which the feelings and the virtues needful for maintaining freedom could not develop themselves, it is during an arduous struggle to become free by their own efforts that these feelings and virtues have the best chance of springing up. Men become attached to that which they have long fought for and made sacrifices for; they learn to appreciate that on which their thoughts have been much engaged; and a contest in which many have been called on to devote themselves for their country, is a school in which they learn to value their country's interest above their own. . . .

"But the case of a people struggling against a foreign yoke, or against a native tyranny upheld by foreign arms, illustrates the reasons for non-intervention in an opposite way; for in this case the reasons themselves do not exist. A people the most attached to freedom, the most capable of defending and of making a good use of free institutions, may be unable to contend successfully for them against the military strength of another nation much more powerful. To assist a people thus kept down, is not to disturb the balance of forces on which the permanent maintenance of freedom in a country depends, but to redress that balance when it is already unfairly and violently disturbed. The doctrine of non-intervention, to be a legitimate principle of morality, must be accepted by all governments. The despots must consent to be bound by it as well as the free States. Unless they do, the profession of it by free countries comes but to this miserable issue, that the wrong side may help the wrong, but the right must not help the right. Intervention to enforce non-intervention is always rightful, always moral, if not always prudent. Though it may be a mistake to *give* freedom to a people who do not value the boon, it cannot but be right to insist that if they do value it, they shall not be hindered from the pursuit of it by foreign coercion. It might not have been right for England (even apart from the question of prudence) to have taken part with Hungary in its noble struggle against Austria; although the Austrian Government in Hungary was in some sense a foreign yoke. But when, the Hungarians having shown themselves likely to prevail in this struggle, the Russian despot interposed, and joining his force to that of Austria, delivered back the Hungarians, bound hand and foot, to their exasperated oppressors, it would have been an honourable and virtuous act on the part of England to have declared that this should not be, and that if Russia gave assistance to the wrong side, England would aid the right. It might not have been consistent with the regard which every nation is bound to pay to its own safety, for England to have taken up this position single-handed. But England and France together could have done it; and if they had, the Russian armed intervention would never have taken place, or would have been disastrous to Russia alone: while all that those Powers gained by not doing it, was that they had to fight Russia five years afterwards, under more difficult circumstances, and without Hungary for an ally. The first nation which, being powerful enough to make its voice effectual, has the spirit and courage to say that not a gun shall be fired in Europe by the soldiers of one Power against the revolted subjects of another, will be the idol of the friends of freedom throughout Europe. That declaration alone will ensure the almost immediate emancipation of every people which desires liberty sufficiently to be capable of maintaining it: and the nation which gives the word will soon find itself at the head of an alliance of free peoples, so strong as to defy the efforts of any number of confederated despots to bring it down. The prize is too glorious not to be snatched sooner or later by some free country; and the time may not be distant when England, if she does not take this heroic part because of its heroism, will be compelled to take it from consideration for her own safety."

Note
1. Nuño José de Mendonça Rolim de Moura Barreto, Duke of Loulé, and Bernardo Sá de Bandeira.

Palmerston – The Right to Intervene to Secure Justice for a National*

"[T]he resolution of the House of Lords . . . lays down for the future a principle of national policy, which I consider totally incompatible with the interests, with the rights, with the honour, and with the dignity of the country; and at variance with the practice, not only of this, but of all other civilised countries in the world. . . . The country is told that British subjects in foreign lands are entitled – for that is the meaning of the resolution – to nothing but the protection of the laws and the tribunals of the land in which they happen to reside. The country is told that British subjects abroad must not look to their own country for protection, but must trust to that indifferent justice which they may happen to receive at the hands of the government and tribunals of the country in which they may be.

•   •   •

"Now, I deny that proposition; and I say it is a doctrine on which no British minister ever yet has acted, and on which the people of England never will suffer any British minister to act. Do I mean to say that British subjects abroad are to be above the law, or are to be taken out of the scope of the laws of the land in which they live? I mean no such thing; I contend for no such principle. Undoubtedly, in the first instance, British subjects are bound to have recourse for redress to the means which the law of the land affords them, when that law is available for such purpose. That is the opinion which the legal advisers of the Crown have given in numerous cases; and it is the opinion on which we have founded our replies to many applications for our interposition in favour of British subjects abroad. . . .

"I say then, that if our subjects abroad have complaints against individuals, or against the government of a foreign country, if the courts of law of that country can afford them redress, then, no doubt, to those courts of justice the British subject ought in the first instance to apply; and it is only on a denial of justice, or upon decisions manifestly unjust, that the British government should be called upon to interfere. But there may be cases in which no confidence can be placed in the tribunals, those tribunals being, from their composition and nature, not of a character to inspire any hope of obtaining justice

---

* From Lord Palmerston (1784–1865). (For biographical details see p. 165.) Quoted from speech in House of Commons, 25 June 1850.

from them. It has been said, 'We do not apply this rule to countries whose governments are arbitrary or despotic, because there the tribunals are under the control of the government, and justice cannot be had; and, moreover, it is not meant to be applied to nominal constitutional governments, where the tribunals are corrupt.' But who is to be the judge in such a case, whether the tribunals are corrupt or not? The British government, or the government of the State from which you demand justice?

• • •

"I say, then, that our doctrine is, that, in the first instance, redress should be sought from the law courts of the country; but that in cases where redress cannot be so had – and those cases are many – to confine a British subject to that remedy only, would be to deprive him of the protection which he is entitled to receive.

• • •

"I do not complain of the conduct of those who have made these matters the means of attack upon her Majesty's Ministers. The government of a great country like this is undoubtedly an object of fair and legitimate ambition to men of all shades of opinion. It is a noble thing to be allowed to guide the policy and to influence the destinies of such a country; and, if ever it was an object of honourable ambition, more than ever must it be so at the moment at which I am speaking. For while we have seen, . . . the political earthquake rocking Europe from side to side – while we have seen thrones shaken, shattered, levelled; institutions overthrown and destroyed – while in almost every country of Europe the conflict of civil war has deluged the land with blood, from the Atlantic to the Black Sea, from the Baltic to the Mediterranean, this country has presented a spectacle honourable to the people of England, and worthy of the admiration of mankind.

"We have shown that liberty is compatible with order; that individual freedom is reconcilable with obedience to the law. We have shown the example of a nation, in which every class of society accepts with cheerfulness the lot which Providence has assigned to it; while at the same time every individual of each class is constantly striving to raise himself in the social scale – not by injustice and wrong, not by violence and illegality but by persevering good conduct, and by the steady and energetic exertion of the moral and intellectual faculties with which his Creator has endowed him. To govern such a people as this is indeed an object worthy of the ambition of the noblest man who lives in the land; and therefore I find no fault with those who may think any opportunity a fair one, for endeavouring to place themselves in so distinguished and honourable a position. But I contend that we have not in our foreign policy done anything to forfeit the confidence of the country. We may not, perhaps, in this matter or in that, have acted precisely up to the opinions of one person or of another – and hard indeed it is, as we all know by our individual and private experience, to find any number of men agreeing entirely in any matter, on which they may not be equally possessed of the details of the facts, and circumstances, and reasons, and conditions which led them to action. But, making allowance for those differences of opinion which may fairly and honourably arise among those who concur in general views, I maintain that the principles which can be traced through all our foreign transactions, as the guiding rule and directing spirit of our proceedings, are such as deserve approbation. I therefore fearlessly challenge the verdict which this House, as representing a political, a commercial, a constitutional country, is to give on the question now brought before it; whether the principles on which the foreign policy of Her Majesty's government has been conducted, and the sense of duty which has led us to think ourselves bound to afford protection to our fellow-subjects abroad, are proper and fitting guides for those who are charged with the government of England; and whether, as the Roman, in days of old, held himself free from indignity, when he could say *Civis Romanus sum*; so also a British subject, in whatever land he may be, shall feel confident that the watchful eye and the strong arm of England will protect him against injustice and wrong."

Gladstone – The Principle of Non-Intervention*

"[T]here is plainly a great question of principle at issue between us, to which I cannot hesitate to advert. This is a matter in which mere

* From William Ewart Gladstone (1809–98). British prime minister 1868–74, 1880–5, and 1890–4. Although he never held the office of Foreign Secretary, throughout his career he took a close interest in foreign affairs (for example he spoke against the Opium War with China in 1839, the continuation of the Crimean war in 1855, Palmerston's war with China in 1857 and Disraeli's support for Turkey in 1877–8). His thoughts on foreign affairs were most clearly expressed during his Midlothian campaign of 1879, during which he set out explicitly his ideas about the aims of British foreign policy. Quoted from his speech to the House of Commons, 27 June 1850.

words and mere definitions convey little meaning; but the idea which
I have in my mind is that commonly expressed by the word non-
interference or non-intervention. Such a word, apart from all cavils,
as to exact definition, does convey a principle, a temper, a course of
policy, which is practically understood and practically approved by
the people of England. Sir, so strong is this House, with a strength
founded both in its nature as a representative body and in its general
conduct, that it can sometimes even afford to deviate a little from the
true line of action; its credit with the people may suffer some
deduction, and yet remain in great vigour. You may, I say, afford the
loss, but certain I am that you will incur such a loss, if you pass any
vote which shall seem to disparage that principle and policy which
shall be calculated to impress the people with the belief that you are
infected with a mania and an itch for managing the affairs of other
nations, and that you are not contented with your own weighty and
honourable charge. . . .

"What is the antagonistic principle which we advance? . . . it is the
principle of non-intervention in the domestic affairs of other
countries. . . . Greatly as I respect in general the courage, the
energy, the undoubted patriotism of the noble Lord, I accuse him of
this, that his policy is marked and characterised by what I must call a
spirit of interference. I hold that this is a fundamental fault: a fault
not to be excused. The noble Lord tells us, indeed, that he does not
go abroad to propagate extreme opinions in other countries; and that
I do not for a moment doubt. I do not doubt that he has the feeling –
which must, indeed, be the feeling of every Englishman, and especially of every Secretary of State in England for Foreign Affairs –
which has been the feeling, I am convinced, of the various distinguished persons who have held that office since the Peace – of the
Earl of Aberdeen, of Mr Canning, and of the Marquess of London-
derry likewise; I mean a sincere desire that when a legitimate opportunity creates itself, and makes it our duty, in conformity with the
principles of public law, to exercise a British influence in the regulation of the internal affairs of other countries, that influence should be
exercised in the spirit which we derive from our own free and stable
form of government, and in the sense of extending to such countries,
as far as they are able and desirous to receive them, institutions akin
to those of which we know from experience the inestimable blessings.
Upon this there can be no difference of opinion among us; no man
who sits here can be the friend of absolute power any more than of
licence and disorder.

"There can be no difference upon the proposition that, considering how the nations of Europe are associated together, and, in some sense, organised as a whole, such occasions will of necessity from time to time arise; but the difference among us arises upon this question: Are we, or are we not, to go abroad and make occasions for the propagation even of the political opinions which we consider to be sound? I say we are not. I complain of the noble Lord that he is disposed to make these occasions: nay, he boasts that he makes them. He refers back to his early policy in Spain and Portugal, and he says it was to us a matter of very small moment whether Portugal were ruled by Dom Miguel or Donna Maria; whether the Crown of Spain went to Don Carlos or to Donna Isabella; but then, he says, there were opportunities of propagating the political sentiments which we think sound, and therefore we did what otherwise it might not have been wise to do. This doctrine, Sir, of the noble Lord is, I admit, a most alluring doctrine. We are soothed and pleased with denunciations the most impartial alike of tyranny and of anarchy; and assured, I doubt not with truth, that the only part played by the noble Lord is that of the moderate reformer. Sir, I object to the propagandism even of moderate reform. In proportion as the representation is alluring, let us be on our guard. The noble Lord lays a snare for us, into which, as Englishmen, glorying in our country and its laws, we are but too likely to fall. We must remember that if we claim the right not only to accept, where they come spontaneously and by no act of ours, but to create and to catch at, opportunities for spreading in other countries the opinions of our own meridian, we must allow to every other nation, every other Government, a similar licence both of judgement and of action. What is to be the result? That if in every country the name of England is to be the symbol and the nucleus of a party, the name of France, of Russia, or of Austria, may and will be the same. And are you not, then, laying the foundation of a system hostile to the real interests of freedom, and destructive of the peace of the world?

"Sir, we hear something in this debate of success as not being the true test of the excellence of public measures. And God forbid that I should say it is their true test, when you are in your own sphere, minding your own affairs. But when you think fit to go out of that sphere and to manage those of other people for them, then do I think success throws much light upon the examination of the question whether your intervention was wise and just. Interference in foreign countries, Sir, according to my mind, should be rare, deliberate, decisive in character, and effectual for its end. Success will usually show that you saw your way, and that the means you used were adapted and adequate to their purpose. Such, if I read them aright, were the acts done by Mr Canning in the nature of intervention: they were few, and they were effectual – effectual whether when, in his own noble language, he 'called the new world into existence to redress the balance of the old', or when, founding himself on the obligations of public law, he despatched the troops of England to prevent the march of a Spanish force into Portugal. I do not find the same character in the interventions of the noble Lord opposite. I cannot look upon all that has taken place during the four years which are the subject-matter of this Motion, without seeing a rash desire, an habitual desire, of interference – a disposition to make the occasions of it, and, that which will always follow, a disposition, in making them, to look too slightly at the restraints imposed by the letter and spirit of the law of nations. . . .

"Sir, great as is the influence and power of Britain, she cannot afford to follow, for any length of time, a self-isolating policy. It would be a contravention of the law of nature and of God, if it were possible for any single nation of Christendom to emancipate itself from the obligations which bind all other nations, and to arrogate, in the face of mankind, a position of peculiar privilege. And now I will grapple with the noble Lord on the ground which he selected for himself, in the most triumphant portion of his speech, by his reference to those emphatic words, *Civis Romanus sum*. He vaunted, amidst the cheers of his supporters, that under his administration an Englishman should be, throughout the world, what the citizen of Rome had been. What then, Sir, was a Roman citizen? He was the member of a privileged caste; he belonged to a conquering race, to a nation that held all others bound down by the strong arm of power. For him there was to be an exceptional system of law; for him principles were to be asserted, and by him rights were to be enjoyed, that were denied to the rest of the world. In such, then the view of the noble Lord, as to the relation that is to subsist between England and other countries? Does he make the claim for us, that we are to be uplifted upon a platform high above the standing-ground of all other nations? It is, indeed, too clear, not only from expressions, but from the whole spirit of the speech of the noble Viscount, that too much of this notion is lurking in his mind; that he adopts in part that vain conception, that we, forsooth, have a mission to be the censors of vice and folly, of abuse and imperfection, among the other countries of the world; that we are to be the universal schoolmasters; and that all those who hesitate to recognise our office, can be governed only by prejudice or personal animosity, and should have the blind war of diplomacy forthwith declared against them. And certainly if the business of a Foreign Secretary properly were to carry on such diplomatic wars, all must admit that the noble Lord is a master in the discharge of his functions.

"What, Sir, ought a Foreign Secretary to be? Is he to be like some gallant knight at a tournament of old, pricking forth into the lists, armed at all points, confiding in his sinews and his skill, challenging all comers for the sake of honour, and having no other duty than to lay as many as possible of his adversaries sprawling in the dust? If such is the idea of a good Foreign Secretary, I, for one, would vote to the noble Lord his present appointment for his life. But, Sir, I do not understand the duty of a Secretary for Foreign Affairs to be of such a character. I understand it to be his duty to conciliate peace with dignity. I think it to be the very first of all his duties studiously to observe, and to exalt in honour among mankind, that great code of principles which is termed the law of nations, which the hon. and learned Member for Sheffield has found, indeed, to be very vague in their nature, and greatly dependent on the discretion of each particular country; but in which I find, on the contrary, a great and noble monument of human wisdom, founded on the combined dictates of reason and experience – a precious inheritance bequeathed to us by the generations that have gone/before us, and a firm foundation on which we must take care to build whatever it may be our part to add to their acquisitions, if, indeed, we wish to maintain and to consolidate the brotherhood of nations, and to promote the peace and welfare of the world."

15 The Nationhood of States

With the rise of nationalism in the early nineteenth century the state was increasingly identified with the nation; or, more accurately, it was increasingly asserted that it should be conterminous with the nation. Those people sharing a similar race, language, culture and history, it came to be widely asserted, should be united within the same state. So a new conception of the state emerged.

The most extreme manifestation of this feeling was the idea of the national state as a semi-spiritual entity, which had a special role to play in the unfolding of the process of history. This was the belief of Hegel, who saw the state as a manifestation of the Idea; and the Prussian state in particular as the supreme embodiment of the evolving human spirit, "God walking on earth". In his *Philosophy of Right* he expressed the belief that the nation-state represented a form of "mind" and the "absolute power on earth". One characteristic of such states was that they were totally sovereign and "in a state of nature" – that is, subject to no superior authority in their relation with other states. Even the general principle that treaties should be observed, which otherwise applied in inter-state relations, was not unconditional, since it depended upon the will of the parties: relations within the terms of such undertakings, therefore, alternated with relations outside their terms. When the particular wills of states could not be harmonised the questions in dispute could only be settled by war. Thus new relationships were created among states, which reflected the dialectic of history. In this way the universal mind was reflected in "the history of the world, which is the world's court of judgement".

These philosophical speculations reflected a more mundane reality: the growth of the concept of nationhood throughout Europe during this period. The increasingly widespread identification of the state with the nation had important effects on the view taken of international relations and the way they should be conducted. The boundaries of many states in Europe bore no relationship to those of national entities. In some cases existing states, by enclosing a number of ethnic and cultural groups, directly negated their aspirations to nationhood. As we have seen in the last section, one conclusion was

193

an assertion of the right of other states to give armed support to peoples seeking to establish their nationhood by revolution. More significant was the effect it had on those peoples themselves. Increasingly it was asserted that national feeling should be expressed in the establishment of a national state. Mazzini, asserting this view in the passage below, presented a new conception of the state as a fellowship of free and equal people sharing a national consciousness, an "association" not an aggregation: a "country of the people". Such states would arise on the ruin of the countries of kings and privileged ruling classes. Divisions of class, privilege and inequality would be cast aside within them. They would be based on democratic, or at least on parliamentary, systems. And international relationships would be transformed, since between such "countries of the people", according to Mazzini, there would be "only harmony and brotherhood".

The difficulty with this view was that the same national spirit which inspired the demand for the creation of new "countries of the people" also inspired nationalist competition *among* such states once they were founded. The newly created state which Mazzini helped to bring about in Italy was itself to engage in several foreign wars in the first 50 years of its life; as did, with equal enthusiasm, the new states established on the national principle in the Balkans. Wars could be initiated not only to create national states but to express national identity and consolidate national unity. So Bismarck in his memoirs, of which an extract is reproduced below, justified the three wars for which he was responsible on the grounds that they had made good "the claim of the German people to lead an autonomous political life" on the basis of their peculiar national capacity. He felt that it was the "national sense of honour" which had compelled Germany to go to war in 1870: in particular the need to keep alive the "German national feeling" which had been aroused in the South German states after the war against Austria four years earlier. But though war was sometimes seen as the legitimate means by which national states were created or consolidated, it was not to be undertaken frivolously. Bismarck felt that, once a new nation-state had been successfully established, it should not lightly decide to go to war, like a duellist reacting indignantly to every pinprick. War should be undertaken only for a goal that was genuinely worthy of the sacrifices it entailed.

The powerful national feeling of the day contributed to the belief that war was the instrument by which, in the final resort, conflicts between nations had to be resolved. This is what Bismarck's compatriot, von Treischke, argued in his book *Politics*, which appeared at the close of the nineteenth century. War was, from time to time, Treischke argued, a necessity, enabling a state to fulfil essential national goals. If existing treaties no longer expressed current conditions, and other states were not prepared to make concessions in negotiations, nations would inevitably "proceed to ordeal by battle". Warfare, he believed, was "part of the divinely appointed order" for settling the great issues which arose between them. The ideal of perpetual peace – such as Kant had proclaimed (see pp. 417–23) – was therefore not only impossible but "immoral".

The emergence of powerful national sentiments did not, therefore, as Mazzini had hoped, usher in a new age of peace and brotherhood. The belief persisted that states – even national states – were engaged in a constant competition, and that this must result sometimes in war. But these wars were now justified in a new cause: not the cause of a dynasty, or even of a state, but that of the nation.

* * *

Hegel – The Absolute Power of the Nation-State*

"**331.** The nation state is mind in its substantive rationality and immediate actuality and is therefore the absolute power on earth. It follows that every state is sovereign and autonomous against its neighbours. It is entitled in the first place and without qualification to be sovereign from their point of view, i.e., to be recognised by them as sovereign. At the same time, however, this title is purely formal, and the demand for this recognition of the state, merely on the ground that it is a state, is abstract. Whether a state is in fact

---

* From Friedrich Hegel (1770–1831). German philosopher, affirming a belief in history as a dialectical process, in which contradictions between the ideal and the real, spirit and nature, universal and particular, social harmony and individual freedom, are progressively resolved, so bringing into being higher forms of social and political organisation and a progressive extension of human freedom. Unlike his early master, Kant (see Chapter 26), he did not believe that war between nations could be abolished since states were absolutely sovereign and war was the only means by which conflict between them could be resolved. Quoted from *The Philosophy of Right* (1821), trs. T. M. Knox (Oxford: Oxford University Press, 1942).

something absolute depends on its content, i.e., on its constitution and general situation; and recognition, implying as it does an identity of both form and content, is conditional on the neighbouring state's judgement and will.

"332. The immediate actuality which any state possesses from the point of view of other states is particularised into a multiplicity of relations which are determined by the arbitrary will of both autonomous parties and which therefore possess the formal nature of contracts pure and simple. The subject-matter of these contracts, however, is infinitely less varied than it is in civil society, because in civil society individuals are reciprocally interdependent in the most numerous respects, while autonomous states are principally wholes whose needs are met within their own borders.

"333. The fundamental proposition of international law (i.e., the universal law which ought to be absolutely valid between states, as distinguished from the particular content of positive treaties) is that treaties, as the ground of obligations between states, ought to be kept. But since the sovereignty of a state is the principle of its relations to others, states are to that extent in a state of nature in relation to each other. Their rights are actualised only in their particular wills and not in a universal will with constitutional powers over them. This universal proviso of international law therefore does not go beyond an ought-to-be, and what really happens is that international relations in accordance with treaty alternate with the severance of these relations.

"334. It follows that if states disagree and their particular wills cannot be harmonised, the matter can only be settled by war. A state through its subjects has widespread connections and many-sided interests, and these may be readily and considerably injured; but it remains inherently indeterminable which of these injuries is to be regarded as a specific breach of treaty or as an injury to the honour and autonomy of the state. The reason for this is that a state may regard its infinity and honour as at stake in each of its concerns, however minute, and it is all the more inclined to susceptibility to injury the more its strong individuality is impelled as a result of long domestic peace to seek and create a sphere of activity abroad.

"335. Apart from this, the state is in essence mind and therefore cannot be prepared to stop at just taking notice of an injury *after* it has actually occurred. On the contrary, there arises in addition as a cause of strife the *idea* of such an injury as the idea of a danger *threatening* from another state, together with calculations of degrees of probability on this side and that, guessing at intentions, &c., &c.

"**336**. Since states are related to one another as autonomous entities and so as particular wills on which the very validity of treaties depends, and since the particular will of the whole is in content a will for its own welfare pure and simple, it follows that welfare is the highest law governing the relation of one state to another. This is all the more the case since the Idea of the state is precisely the supersession of the clash between right (i.e., empty abstract freedom) and welfare (i.e., the particular content which fills that void), and it is when states become *concrete* wholes that they first attain recognition (see Paragraph 331).

"**337**. The substantial welfare of the state is its welfare as a particular state in its specific interest and situation and its no less special foreign affairs, including its particular treaty relations. Its government therefore is a matter of particular wisdom, not of universal Providence. Similarly, its aim in relation to other states and its principle for justifying wars and treaties is not a universal thought (the thought of philanthropy) but only its actually injured or threatened welfare as something specific and peculiar to itself.

"At one time the opposition between morals and politics, and the demand that the latter should conform to the former, were much canvassed. On this point only a general remark is required here. The welfare of a state has claims to recognition totally different from those of the welfare of the individual. The ethical substance, the state, has its determinate being, i.e., its right, directly embodied in something existent, something not abstract but concrete, and the principle of its conduct and behaviour can only be this concrete existent and not one of the many universal thoughts supposed to be moral commands. When politics is alleged to clash with morals and so to be always wrong, the doctrine propounded rests on superficial ideas about morality, the nature of the state, and the state's relation to the moral point of view.

"**338**. The fact that states reciprocally recognise each other as states remains, even in war – the state of affairs when rights disappear and force and chance hold sway – a bond wherein each counts to the rest as something absolute. Hence in war, war itself is characterised as something which ought to pass away. It implies therefore the proviso of the *jus gentium* that the possibility of peace be retained (and so, for example, that envoys must be respected), and, in general, that war be not waged against domestic institutions, against the peace of family and private life, or against persons in their private capacity.

"**339**. Apart from this, relations between states (e.g., in war-time, reciprocal agreements about taking prisoners; in peace-time, concessions of rights to subjects of other states for the purpose of private trade and intercourse, &c.) depend principally upon the customs of nations, custom being the inner universality of behaviour maintained in all circumstances.

"**340**. It is as particular entities that states enter into relations with one another. Hence their relations are on the largest scale a maelstrom of external contingency and the inner particularity of passions, private interests and selfish ends, abilities and virtues, vices, force and wrong. All these whirl together, and in their vortex the ethical whole itself, the autonomy of the state, is exposed to contingency. The principles of the national minds are wholly restricted on account of their particularity, for it is in this particularity that, as existent individuals, they have their objective actuality and their self-consciousness. Their deeds and destinies in their reciprocal relations to one another are the dialectic of the finitude of these minds, and out of it arises the universal mind, the mind of the world, free from all restriction, producing itself as that which exercises its right – and its right is the highest right of all – over these finite minds in the 'history of the world which is the world's court of judgement'."

Mazzini – The Idea of Nationhood*

"Bad governments have disfigured the design of God, which you may see clearly marked out, as far, at least, as regards Europe, by the courses of the great rivers, by the lines of the lofty mountains, and by other geographical conditions; they have disfigured it by conquest, by greed, by jealousy of the just sovereignty of others; disfigured it so much that today there is perhaps no nation except England and France whose confines correspond to this design. They did not, and they do not, recognise any country except their own families and dynasties, the egoism of caste. But the divine design will infallibly be fulfilled. Natural divisions, the innate spontaneous tendencies of the peoples will replace the arbitrary divisions sanctioned by bad govern-

* From J. Mazzini (1805–72). (For biographical details see p. 64.) Quoted from *The Duties of Man* (1858). trs. Ella Noyes (London: J. M. Dent, 1907).

ments. The map of Europe will be remade. The Countries of the People will rise, defined by the voice of the free, upon the ruins of the Countries of Kings and privileged castes. Between these Countries there will be harmony and brotherhood. And then the work of Humanity for the general amelioration, for the discovery and application of the real law of life, carried on in association and distributed according to local capacities, will be accomplished by peaceful and progressive development; then each of you, strong in the affections and in the aid of many millions of men speaking the same language, endowed with the same tendencies, and educated by the same historic tradition, may hope by your personal effort to benefit the whole of Humanity.

"To you, who have been born in Italy, God has allotted, as if favouring you specially, the best-defined country in Europe. In other lands, marked by more uncertain or more interrupted limits, questions may arise which the pacific vote of all will one day solve, but which have cost, and will yet perhaps cost, tears and blood; in yours, no. God has stretched round you sublime and indisputable boundaries; on one side the highest mountains of Europe, the Alps; on the other the sea, the immeasurable sea. Take a map of Europe and place one point of a pair of compasses in the north of Italy on Parma; point the other to the mouth of the Var, and describe a semicircle with it in the direction of the Alps; this point, which will fall, when the semicircle is completed, upon the mouth of the Isonzo, will have marked the frontier which God has given you. As far as this frontier your language is spoken and understood; beyond this you have no rights. Sicily, Sardinia, Corsica, and the smaller islands between them and the mainland of Italy. Brute force may for a little while contest these frontiers with you, but they have been recognised from of old by the tacit general consent of the peoples; and the day when, rising with one accord for the final trial, you plant your tricoloured flag upon that frontier, the whole of Europe will acclaim re-risen Italy, and receive her into the community of the nations. To this final trial all your efforts must be directed.

"Without Country you have neither name, token, voice, nor rights, no admission as brothers into the fellowship of the Peoples. You are the bastards of Humanity. Soldiers without a banner, Israelites among the nations, you will find neither faith nor protection; none will be sureties for you. Do not beguile yourselves with the hope of emancipation from unjust social conditions if you do not first conquer a Country for yourselves; where there is no Country there is no common agreement to which you can appeal; the egoism of self-interest rules alone, and he who has the upper hand keeps it, since there is no common safeguard for the interests of all. Do not be led away by the idea of improving your material conditions without first solving the national question. You cannot do it. Your industrial associations and mutual help societies are useful as a means of educating and disciplining yourselves; as an economic fact they will remain barren until you have an Italy. The economic problem demands, first and foremost, an increase of capital and production; and while your Country is dismembered into separate fragments – while shut off by the barrier of customs and artificial difficulties of every sort, you have only restricted markets open to you – you cannot hope for this increase. Today – do not delude yourselves – you are not the working-class of Italy; you are only fractions of that class; powerless, unequal to the great task which you propose to yourselves. Your emancipation can have no practical beginning until a National Government, understanding the signs of the times, shall, seated in Rome, formulate a Declaration of Principles to be the guide for Italian progress, and shall insert into it these words, *Labour is sacred, and is the source of the wealth of Italy*.

"Do not be led astray, then, by hopes of material progress which in your present conditions can only be illusions. Your Country alone, the vast and rich Italian Country, which stretches from the Alps to the farthest limit of Sicily, can fulfil these hopes. You cannot obtain your *rights* except by obeying the commands of *Duty*. Be worthy of them, and you will have them. O my Brothers! love your Country. Our Country is our home, the home which God has given us, placing therein a numerous family which we love and are loved by, and with which we have a more intimate and quicker communion of feeling and thought than with others; a family which by its concentration upon a given spot, and by the homogeneous nature of its elements, is destined for a special kind of activity. Our Country is our field of labour; the products of our activity must go forth from it for the benefit of the whole earth; but the instruments of labour which we can use best and most effectively exist in it, and we may not reject them without being unfaithful to God's purpose and diminishing our own strength. In labouring according to true principles for our Country we are labouring for Humanity; our Country is the fulcrum of the lever which we have to wield for the common good. If we give up this fulcrum we run the risk of becoming useless to our Country and to Humanity. Before *associating* ourselves with the Nations which compose Humanity we must exist as a Nation. There can be no association except among equals; and you have no recognised collective existence.

"Humanity is a great army moving to the conquest of unknown lands, against powerful and wary enemies. The Peoples are the different corps and divisions of that army. Each has a post entrusted to it; each a special operation to perform; and the common victory depends on the exactness with which the different operations are carried out. Do not disturb the order of the battle. Do not abandon the banner which God has given you. Wherever you may be, into the midst of whatever people circumstances may have driven you, fight for the liberty of that people if the moment calls for it; but fight as Italians, so that the blood which you shed may win honour and love, not for you only, but for your Country. And may the constant thought of your soul be for Italy, may all the acts of your life be worthy of her, and may the standard beneath which you range yourselves to work for Humanity be Italy's. Do not say *I*; say *we*. Be every one of you an incarnation of your Country, and feel himself and make himself responsible for his fellow-countrymen; let each one of you learn to act in such a way that in him men shall respect and love his Country.

• • •

" . . . A Country must have, then, a single government. The politicians who call themselves federalists, and who would make Italy into a brotherhood of different states, would dismember the Country, not understanding the idea of Unity. The States into which Italy is divided today are not the creation of our own people; they are the result of the ambitions and calculations of princes or of foreign conquerors, and serve no purpose but to flatter the vanity of local aristocracies for which a narrower sphere than a great Country is necessary. What you, the people, have created, beautified, and consecrated with your affections, with your joys, with your sorrows, and with your blood, is the City and the Commune, not the Province or the State. In the City, in the Commune, where your fathers sleep and where your children will live, where you exercise your faculties and your personal rights, you live out your lives as *individuals*. It is of your City that each of you can say what the Venetians say of theirs: *Venezia la xe nostra: l'avemo fatta nu.*[1] In your City you have need of *liberty* as in your Country you have need of *association*. The Liberty of the Commune and the Unity of the Country – let that, then, be your faith. Do not say Rome and Tuscany, Rome and Lombardy,

Rome and Sicily; say Rome and Florence, Rome and Siena, Rome and Leghorn, and so through all the Communes of Italy. Rome for all that represents Italian life; your Commune for whatever represents the *individual* life. All the other divisions are artificial, and are not confirmed by your national tradition.

"A Country is a fellowship of free and equal men bound together in a brotherly concord of labour towards a single end. You must make it and maintain it such. A Country is not an aggregation, it is an *association*. There is no true Country without a uniform right. There is no true Country where the uniformity of that right is violated by the existence of caste, privilege, and inequality – where the powers and faculties of a large number of individuals are suppressed or dormant – where there is no common principle accepted, recognised and developed by all. In such a state of things there can be no Nation, no People, but only a multitude, a fortuitous agglomeration of men whom circumstances have brought together and different circumstances will separate. In the name of your love for your Country you must combat without truce the existence of every privilege, every inequality, upon the soil which has given you birth. One privilege only is lawful – the privilege of Genius when Genius reveals itself in brotherhood with Virtue; but it is a privilege conceded by God and not by men, and when you acknowledge it and follow its inspirations, you acknowledge it freely by the exercise of your own reason and your own choice. Whatever privilege claims your submission in virtue of force or heredity, or any right which is not a common right, is a usurpation and a tyranny, and you ought to combat it and annihilate it. Your Country should be your Temple. God at the summit, a People of equals at the base. Do not accept any other formula, any other moral law, if you do not want to dishonour your Country and yourselves. Let the secondary laws for the gradual regulation of your existence be the progressive application of this supreme law.

"And in order that they should be so, it is necessary that *all* should contribute to the making of them. The laws made by one fraction of the citizens only can never by the nature of things and men do otherwise than reflect the thoughts and aspirations and desires of that fraction; they represent, not the whole country, but a third, a fourth part, a class, a zone of the country. The law must express the general aspiration, promote the good of all, respond to a beat of the nation's heart. The whole nation therefore should be, directly or indirectly, the legislator. By yielding this mission to a few men, you put the egoism of one class in the place of the Country, which is the union of *all* the classes.

"A Country is not a mere territory; the particular territory is only its foundation. The Country is the idea which rises upon that foundation; it is the sentiment of love, the sense of fellowship which binds together all the sons of that territory. So long as a single one of your brothers is not represented by his own vote in the development of the national life – so long as a single one vegetates uneducated among the educated – so long as a single one able and willing to work languishes in poverty for want of work – you have not got a Country such as it ought to be, the Country of all and for all. *Votes, education, work* are the three main pillars of the nation; do not rest until your hands have solidly erected them."

Note
1. "Venice is our own: we have made her."

Bismarck – National Honour as a Justification for War*

"I put a few questions to Moltke as to the extent of his confidence in the state of our preparations, especially as to the time they would still require in order to meet this sudden risk of war. He answered that if there was to be war he expected no advantage to us by deferring its outbreak; and even if we should not be strong enough at first to protect all the territories on the left bank of the Rhine against French invasion, our preparations would nevertheless soon overtake those of the French, while at a later period this advantage would be diminished; he regarded a rapid outbreak as, on the whole, more favourable to us than delay.

"In view of the attitude of France, our national sense of honour compelled us, in my opinion, to go to war; and if we did not act according to the demands of this feeling, we should lose, when on the

---

* From Otto von Bismarck (1815–98). Prime minister of Prussia from 1862, Chancellor of the North German Federation from 1866 and of united Germany from 1870 until 1890. Played a leading part in European politics for over 30 years during which time, through Prussia's wars against Denmark (1864), Austria (1866) and France (1870–1) he brought about the reunification of Germany and helped establish it as the most powerful state of the continent. In his *Memoirs*, from which this extract is taken, written after his dismissal from office, he reflected on the lessons he had learnt during his years of power. Quoted from *Memoirs* (1896), trs. A. Butler (1898) (New York: Howard Fertig, 1966).

way to its completion, the entire impetus towards our national development won in 1866, while the German national feeling south of the Main, aroused by our military successes in 1866, and shown by the readiness of the southern states to enter the alliances, would have to grow cold again. The German feeling, which in the southern states lived long with the individual and dynastic state feeling, had, up to 1866, silenced its political conscience to a certain degree with the fiction of a collective Germany under the leadership of Austria, partly from South German preference for the old imperial state, partly in the belief of her military superiority to Prussia. After events had shown the incorrectness of that calculation, the very helplessness in which the South German states had been left by Austria at the conclusion of peace was a motive for the political Damascus that lay between Varnbüler's 'Væ victis' and the willing conclusion of the offensive and defensive alliance with Prussia. It was confidence in the Germanic power developed by means of Prussia, and the attraction which is inherent in a brave and resolute policy if it is successful, and then proceeds within reasonable and honourable limits. This nimbus had been won by Prussia; it would have been lost irrevocably, or at all events for a long time, if in a question of national honour the opinion gained ground among the people that the French insult, *La Prusse cane*, had a foundation in fact.

• • •

"[I]n the future not only military equipment but also a correct political eye will be required to guide the German ship of state through the currents of coalitions to which we are exposed in consequence of our geographical position and our previous history. We shall not avoid the dangers which lie in the bosom of the future by amiability and commercial *pourboires* to friendly Powers. We should only increase the greed of our former friends and teach them to reckon on our anxieties and necessities. What I fear is, that by following the road in which we have started our future will be sacrificed to small and temporary feelings of the present. Former rulers looked more to the capacity than the obedience of their advisers; if obedience alone is the criterion, then demands will be made on the general ability of the monarch, which even Frederick the Great himself would not satisfy, although in his time politics, both in war and peace, were less difficult than they are today.

"Our reputation and our security will develop all the more permanently, the more, in all conflicts which do not immediately touch us, we hold ourselves in reserve and do not show ourselves sensitive to every attempt to stir up and utilise our *vanity*. Attempts of this kind were made during the Crimean war by the English press and the English Court, and the men who tried to push themselves forward at our own Court by depending on England; we were then so successfully threatened with the loss of the title of a Great Power, that Herr von Manteuffel at Paris exposed us to great humiliations in order that we might be admitted to take part in signing a treaty, which it would have been useful to us not to be bound by. Now also Germany would be guilty of a great folly if in Eastern struggles which did not affect her interests she were to take a side sooner than the other Powers who were more directly concerned.

• • •

"If Germany has the advantage that her policy is free from direct interests in the East, on the other side is the disadvantage of the central and exposed position of the German Empire, with its extended frontier which has to be defended on every side, and the ease with which anti-German coalitions are made. At the same time Germany is perhaps the single Great Power in Europe which is not tempted by any objects which can only be attained by a successful war. It is our interest to maintain peace, while without exception our continental neighbours have wishes, either secret or officially avowed, which cannot be fulfilled except by war. We must direct our policy in accordance with these facts – that is, we must do our best to prevent war or limit it. We must reserve our hand, and not allow ourselves before the proper time to be pushed out of a waiting into an active attitude by any impatience, by the desire to oblige others at the expense of the country, by vanity or other provocation of this kind; otherwise *plectuntur Achivi*.

"Our non-interference cannot reasonably be directed to sparing our forces so as, after the others have weakened themselves, to fall upon any of our neighbours or a possible opponent. On the contrary, we ought to do all we can to weaken the bad feeling which has been called out through our growth to the position of a real Great Power, by honourable and peaceful use of our influence, and so convince the world that a German hegemony in Europe is more useful and less partisan and also less harmful for the freedom of others than that of France, Russia, or England. That respect for the rights of other states in which France especially has always been so wanting at the time of her supremacy, and which in England lasts only so long as English interests are not touched, is made easy for the German Empire and its policy, on one side owing to the practicality of the German character, on the other by the fact (which has nothing to do with our deserts) that we do not require an increase of our immediate territory, and also that we could not attain it without strengthening the centrifugal elements in our own territory. It has always been my ideal aim, after we had established our unity within the possible limits, to win the confidence not only of the smaller European states, but also of the Great Powers, and to convince them that German policy will be just and peaceful, now that it has repaired the *injuria temporum*, the disintegration of the nation. . . .

"During the time that I was in office I advised three wars, the Danish, the Bohemian and the French; but every time I first made myself clear whether the war, if it were successful, would bring a prize of victory worth the sacrifices which every war requires, and which now are so much greater than in the last century. Had I had to say to myself that after one of these wars we should find some difficulty in discovering conditions of peace which were desirable, I should scarcely have convinced myself of the necessity for these sacrifices as long as we were not actually attacked. I have never looked at international quarrels which can only be settled by a national war from the point of view of the Göttingen student code or the honour which governs a private duel, but I have always considered simply their reaction on the claim of the German people, in equality with the other great states and Powers of Europe, to lead an autonomous political life, so far as is possible on the basis of our peculiar national capacity."

von Treitschke – War as the Foundation of the State*

"Without war no state could be. All those we know of arose through war, and the protection of their members by armed force remains their primary and essential task. War, therefore, will endure to the

---

* From Heinrich von Treitschke (1834–96). German nationalist historian and political writer. Member of the Reichstag, where he was a supporter of Bismarck and an advocate of colonial expansion for Germany. His *Politics* was published in England during the First World War (with an introduction by Arthur Balfour) as a demonstration of the chauvinist views held by some prominent Germans. Quoted from *Politics* (1899), trs. B. Dugdale and T. de Bille (London: Macmillan, 1916).

end of history, as long as there is multiplicity of states. The laws of human thought and of human nature forbid any alternative, neither is one to be wished for. The blind worshipper of an eternal peace falls into the error of isolating the state, or dreams of one which is universal, which we have already seen to be at variance with reason.

"Even as it is impossible to conceive of a tribunal above the state, which we have recognised as sovereign in its very essence, so it is likewise impossible to banish the idea of war from the world. It is a favourite fashion of our time to instance England as particularly ready for peace. But England is perpetually at war; there is hardly an instant in her recent history in which she has not been obliged to be fighting somewhere. The great strides which civilisation makes against barbarism and unreason are only made actual by the sword. Between civilised nations also war is the form of litigation by which states make their claims valid. The arguments brought forward in these terrible law suits of the nations compel as to argument in civil suits can ever do. Often as we have tried by theory to convince the small states that Prussia alone can be the leader in Germany, we had to produce the final proof upon the battlefields of Bohemia and the Main.

"Moreover war is a uniting as well as a dividing element among nations; it does not draw them together in enmity only, for through its means they learn to know and to respect each other's peculiar qualities.

"It is important not to look upon war always as a judgement from God. Its consequences are evanescent; but the life of a nation is reckoned by centuries, and the final verdict can only be pronounced after the survey of whole epochs.

"Such a state as Prussia might indeed be brought near to destruction by a passing phase of degeneracy; but being by the character of its people more reasonable and more free than the French, it retained the power to call up the moral force within itself, and so to regain its ascendancy. Most undoubtedly war is the one remedy for an ailing nation. Social selfishness and party hatreds must be dumb before the call of the state when its existence is at stake. Forgetting himself, the individual must only remember that he is a part of the whole, and realise the unimportance of his own life compared with the common weal.

"The grandeur of war lies in the utter annihilation of puny man in the great conception of the state, and it brings out the full magnificence of the sacrifice of fellow-countrymen for one another. In war the chaff is winnowed from the wheat. Those who have lived through 1870 cannot fail to understand Niebuhr's description of his feelings in 1813, when he speaks of how no one who has entered into the joy of being bound by a common tie to all his compatriots, gentle and simple alike, can ever forget how he was uplifted by the love, the friendliness and the strength of that mutual sentiment.

"It is war which fosters the political idealism which the materialist rejects. What a disaster for civilisation it would be if mankind blotted its heroes from memory. The heroes of a nation are the figures which rejoice and inspire the spirit of its youth, and the writers whose words ring like trumpet blasts become the idols of our boyhood and our early manhood. He who feels no answering thrill is unworthy to bear arms for his country. To appeal from his judgement to Christianity would be sheer perversity, for does not the Bible distinctly say that the ruler shall rule by the sword, and again that greater love hath no man than to lay down his life for his friend? To Aryan races, who are before all things courageous, the foolish preaching of everlasting peace has always been vain. They have always been men enough to maintain with the sword what they have attained through the spirit.

"Goethe once said that the north Germans were always more civilised than the south Germans. No doubt they were, and a glance at the history of the princes of Lower Saxony shows that they were for ever either attacking or defending themselves. One-sided as Goethe's verdict is, it contains a core of truth. Our ancient empire was great under the Saxons; under the Swabian and the Salic emperors it declined. Heroism, bodily strength, and chivalrous spirit is essential to the character of a noble people.

"Such matters must not be examined only by the light of the student's lamp. The historian who moves in the world of the real will sees at once that the demand for eternal peace is purely reactionary. He sees that all movement and all growth would disappear with war, and that only the exhausted, spiritless, degenerate periods of history have toyed with the idea. . . .

"When a state recognises that existing treaties no longer express the actual political conditions, and when it cannot persuade the other powers to give way by peaceful negotiation, the moment has come when the nations proceed to the ordeal by battle. A state thus situated is conscious when it declares war that it is performing an inevitable duty. The combatant countries are moved by no incentives of personal greed, but they feel that the real position of power is not expressed by existing treaties and that they must be determined afresh by the judgement of the nations, since no peaceful agreement can be reached. The righteousness of war depends simply and solely upon the consciousness of a moral necessity. War is justified because the great national personalities can suffer no compelling force superior to themselves, and because history must always be in constant flux; war therefore must be taken as part of the divinely appointed order. . . .

"War is both justifiable and moral, and . . . the ideal of perpetual peace is not only impossible but immoral as well. It is unworthy of man's reason to regard the impracticable as feasible, but a life of pure intellect is all too often enervating to the reasoning faculty. War cannot vanish from the earth as long as human sins and passions remain what they are. It is delightful to observe how the feeling of patriotism breaks involuntarily through the cosmopolitan phrases even of the apostles of perpetual peace. The prophet Joel prayed that before its day should dawn Israel might call all the heathen to a bloody reckoning in the valley of Jehoshaphat, and Victor Hugo likewise demanded that the Germans should get their drubbing first. Yet again we must repeat – the arbitrament of force is the logical outcome of the nature of the state. The mere fact of the existence of many states involves the necessity of war. The dream of eternal peace – said Frederick the Great – is a phantom, which each man rejects when the call of war rings in his own ears. It is impossible to imagine – he went on to say – any balance of power which can last."

16 The Imperialism of States

The growth of nationalist sentiment and the increasing identification of the state with the nation was not the only development during the nineteenth century which altered the views that were generally held about the role of the state and of relations between states. Another was the acquisition, or extension, by many European states of substantial overseas empires. This not only created a new kind of international relationship between the colonial powers and the peoples they had mastered, but substantially influenced relations among the colonial powers themselves.

Different analyses were made about the cause and significance of this development. In the early part of the century colonies were widely seen as a burden rather than an asset. Disraeli saw them as a "mill-stone round the neck" of the colonial powers. Bismarck was (before 1885) "never a man for colonies". But towards the end of the century, with depression in Europe, the advantages which colonies could bring began to be more widely recognised. Some Europeans began to see colonial empires above all as the source of new markets. So Jules Ferry, prime minister of France, declared that "the colonial question is for countries like ours, which are, by the very character of their industry, tied to large exports, vital to the question of markets . . . the foundation of a colony is the creation of a market".

Those of liberal sentiment did not share this enthusiasm. They had always had doubts about the urge to acquire overseas possessions. Bentham had called on the imperial powers to "emancipate your colonies". At the turn of the century, when most of the globe had been partitioned among the colonial powers and become subject to increasing financial as well as commercial penetration, these doubts began to be expressed more forcefully. In Britain J. A. Hobson, in his famous book *Imperialism,* denounced the parasitism of West European States on the peoples of Asia and Africa. He suggested that the main instigators of imperialism were the "world-wide forces of international finance", which increasingly demanded political and military intervention by their own governments to create conditions favourable for their investments overseas. Imperialism, he believed, promoted the direct material interests of investors and traders, who

210

won the protection of their governments for their activities abroad. For the governments themselves it provided increased economic activity at home, and so diverted the energies of their population from "domestic agitation". An unholy alliance developed, through which private interests were able to mobilise state power on their own behalf.

Lenin, who knew and admired Hobson's book, used essentially similar arguments, though now decked out in Marxist terminology. Writing during the First World War, he traced the roots of imperialism to the increasing concentration of production and the emergence of large monopolistic combines, often in alliance with big banking houses. Together these sought to win control of sources of raw materials elsewhere and to find markets for manufactured products. The new colonialism of the last part of the nineteenth century therefore was essentially inspired by the competitive struggle for raw materials, for opportunities for investment and for monopolistic or semi-monopolistic conditions of trade: in other words, the search for "economic territories in general". This competitive struggle would lead, however, not only to conflict between the colonial powers and the people they ruled, but to war among those powers themselves.

There were, however, problems about this analysis. Why had there been in practice, throughout the nineteenth century, so *little* conflict among the colonial powers in acquiring their overseas possessions? If imperialism was an expression of capitalism, why had some relatively advanced capitalist states acquired none at all? Was the motivation for colonialism purely economic, as this analysis suggested, or rather strategic and political, as the historical record seemed to indicate? Were the material benefits to be acquired as great as was sometimes alleged, when administrative and military costs were taken into account? Were there not indeed many in the metropolitan countries who gained little or even lost?

Because of doubts of this kind some were unwilling to accept the simple Leninist analysis of the forces behind imperialism. Some believed that interests within capitalist states were more complex. Thus J. A. Schumpeter, writing at exactly the same time as Lenin, but apparently without knowledge of his books (he replied to the arguments of other Marxists, especially his fellow-Austrian, Hilferding, rather than to Lenin), put forward a more penetrating and subtle analysis of the conflicting interests of different social classes than those of Hobson and Lenin. Capitalism in general seemed to flourish best in conditions where there was minimum interference in the free flow of trade and capital; and some successful capitalist economies had been built up without the benefit of colonial territories elsewhere. Only particular sections of the population – the arms industry, industrial profiteers, and above all monopolies and cartels which became increasingly dependent on export markets and foreign contracts – were likely to benefit from war and foreign conquest. For the latter the use of force, and the conquest of foreign territory, could be valuable instruments for ensuring the level of sales and production needed to justify a high volume of investment. But the importance of this interest should not, in Schumpeter's view, be overestimated. In the modern world, there was increasing interdependence and community of interests among states. "Export monopolism" was thus not a necessary stage in capitalist development; nor was imperialism, therefore, a necessary phase of capitalism.

So the development of colonial empires, which by the turn of the century covered much of the globe, brought new ideas about the legitimate uses of state power. There were many in Europe and North America who took pride in the conquest of weaker and poorer peoples in other parts of the world, declaring that it represented a "civilising mission", which brought order and progress to formerly benighted areas; or represented the "white man's burden", a sacred duty which had to be undertaken whatever the cost. There were others who attributed their acquisition to commercial and financial greed, and foresaw that increasing competition among the colonial powers themselves might eventually lead to widespread international conflict. Others again believed that interests were mixed, even among the population of the colonising state, and rejected the view that any universal law of capitalist development was at work.

Whatever the motives attributed to those who undertook it, colonialism changed the character of international society and of the states within it. The new empires and all who lived in them were generally accepted as existing under the "sovereignty" of the colonial powers, and so beyond the sphere of international relations in the strict sense. The concept of the state was thus extended to comprehend vast assemblages of territories of diverse culture, race, religion and loyalty.

*   *   *

Hobson – The Use of State Power to Sustain Imperialism*

If Imperialism may no longer be regarded as a blind inevitable destiny, is it certain that imperial expansion as a deliberately chosen line of public policy can be stopped?

"We have seen that it is motived, not by the interests of the nation as a whole, but by those of certain classes, who impose the policy upon the nation for their own advantage. The amalgam of economic and political forces which exercises this pressure has been submitted to close analysis. But will the detection of this confederacy of vicious forces destroy or any wise abate their operative power? For this power is a natural outcome of an unsound theory in our foreign policy. Put into plain language, the theory is this, that any British subject choosing, for his own private pleasure or profit, to venture his person or his property in the territory of a foreign State can call upon this nation to protect or avenge him in case he or his property is injured either by the Government or by any inhabitant of this foreign State. Now this is a perilous doctrine. It places the entire military, political, and financial resources of this nation at the beck and call of any missionary society which considers it has a peculiar duty to attack the religious sentiments or observances of some savage people, or of some reckless explorer who chooses just those spots of earth known to be inhabited by hostile peoples ignorant of British power; the speculative trader or the mining prospector gravitates naturally towards dangerous and unexplored countries, where the gains of a successful venture will be quick and large. All these men, missionaries, travellers, sportsmen, scientists, traders, in no proper sense the accredited representatives of this country, but actuated by private personal motives, are at liberty to call upon the British nation to spend millions of money and thousands of lives to defend them against risks which the nation has not sanctioned. It is only right to add that unscrupulous statesmen have deliberately utilised these

---

* From J. A. Hobson (1858–1940). English economist and radical political writer. After a short period teaching and lecturing he travelled widely in North America and South Africa. In his economic writing he anticipated by several decades the theories of Keynes on under-consumption and the need for a correct balance between expenditure on consumption and capital goods (a debt which Keynes, writing in another age of depression, recognised when his own work was published 45 years later). Best known today for his *Imperialism*, which is known to have influenced Lenin. Quoted from *Imperialism* (London: George Allen and Unwin, 1902).

insidious methods of encroachment, seizing upon every alleged outrage inflicted on these private adventurers or marauders as a pretext
for a punitive expedition which results in the British flag waving over
some new tract of territory. Thus the most reckless and irresponsible
individual members of our nation are permitted to direct our foreign
policy. Now that we have some four hundred million British subjects,
any one of whom in theory or in practice may call upon the British
arms to extricate him from the results of his private folly, the
prospects of a genuine *pax Britannica* are not particularly bright.

But these sporadic risks, grave though they have sometimes
proved, are insignificant when compared with the dangers associated
with modern methods of international capitalism and finance. It is
not long since industry was virtually restricted by political boundaries, the economic intercourse of nations being almost wholly confined to commercial exchanges of goods. The recent habit of
investing capital in a foreign country has now grown to such an extent
that the well-to-do and politically powerful classes in Great Britain
today derive a large and ever larger proportion of their incomes from
capital invested outside the British Empire. This growing stake of our
wealthy classes in countries over which they have no political control
is a revolutionary force in modern politics; it means a constantly
growing tendency to use their political power as citizens of this State
to interfere with the political condition of those States where they
have an industrial stake.

"The essentially illicit nature of this use of the public resources of
the nation to safeguard and improve private investments should be
clearly recognised. If I put my savings in a home investment, I take
into consideration all the chances and changes to which the business
is liable, including the possibilities of political changes of tariff,
taxation, or industrial legislation which may affect its profits. In the
case of such investment, I am quite aware that I have no right to call
upon the public to protect me from loss or depreciation of my capital
due to any of these causes. The political conditions of my country are
taken into calculation at the time of my investment. If I invest in
consols, I fully recognise that 'no right of political interference with
foreign policy affecting my investment is accorded to me in virtue of
my interest as a fund-holder. But, if I invest either in the public funds
or in some private industrial venture in a foreign country for the
benefit of my private purse, getting specially favourable terms to
cover risks arising from the political insecurity of the country or the
deficiencies of its Government, I am entitled to call upon my Govern-

ment to use its political and military force to secure me against those very risks which I have already discounted in the terms of my investment. Can anything be more palpably unfair?

• • •

"As these forms of international investment and finance are wider spread and better organised for economic and political purposes, these demands for political and military interference with foreign countries, on the ground of protecting the property of British subjects, will be more frequent and more effective; the demands of investors will commonly be backed by personal grievances of British outlanders, and we shall be drawn into a series of interferences with foreign Governments, which, if we can conduct them successfully, will lead to annexation of territory as the only security for the lives and property of our subjects. . . .

"The chief economic source of Imperialism has been found in the inequality of industrial opportunities by which a favoured class accumulates superfluous elements of income which, in their search for profitable investments, press ever farther afield: the influence on State policy of these investors and their financial managers secures a national alliance of other vested interests which are threatened by movements of social reform: the adoption of Imperialism thus serves the double purpose of securing private material benefits for favoured classes of investors and traders at the public cost, while sustaining the general cause of conservatism by diverting public energy and interest from domestic agitation to external employment.

"The ability of a nation to shake off this dangerous usurpation of its power, and to employ the national resources in the national interest, depends upon the education of a national intelligence and a national will, which shall make democracy a political and economic reality. To term Imperialism a national policy is an impudent falsehood: the interests of the nation are opposed to every act of this expansive policy. Every enlargement of Great Britain in the tropics is a distinct enfeeblement of true British nationalism. Indeed, Imperialism is commended in some quarters for this very reason, that by breaking the narrow bounds of nationalities it facilitates and forwards internationalism. There are even those who favour or condone the forcible suppression of small nationalities by larger ones under the impulse of Imperialism, because they imagine that this is the natural approach to a world-federation and eternal peace. A falser view of political evolution it is difficult to conceive. If there is one condition precedent to effective internationalism or to the establishment of any reliable relations between States, it is the existence of strong, secure, well-developed, and responsible nations. Internationalism can never be subserved by the suppression or forcible absorption of nations; for these practices react disastrously upon the springs of international- ism, on the one hand setting nations on their armed defence and stifling the amicable approaches between them, on the other debili- tating the larger nations through excessive corpulence and indiges- tion. The hope of a coming internationalism enjoins above all else the maintenance and natural growth of independent nationalities, for without such there could be no gradual evolution of internationalism, but only a series of unsuccessful attempts at a chaotic and unstable cosmopolitanism. As individualism is essential to any sane form of national socialism, so nationalism is essential to internationalism: no organic conception of world politics can be framed on any other supposition."

Lenin – Monopoly Capitalism the Basis of the Imperialist State*

"We have seen that by its economic essence imperialism is monopol- ist capitalism. This fact alone determines the place of imperialism in history, for monopoly growing up on the basis of free competition, and precisely out of free competition, is the transition from the capitalist to a higher social economic order. We must take special note of four main aspects of monopolies, or principal manifestations of monopoly capitalism, which are characteristic of the period under discussion.

"First, monopoly arose out of the concentration of production at a very high stage of development. This refers to the monopolist capi- talist combines: cartels, syndicates and trusts. We have seen the important part they play in modern economic life. Towards the beginning of the twentieth century, they acquired complete su- premacy in the advanced countries, and although the initial steps towards the formation of combines were first taken by countries with

---

* From V. I. Lenin (1870–1924). (For biographical details see p. 76.) Quoted from *Imperialism: The Highest Stage of Capitalism* (1916), English trs. (Moscow: Martin Lawrence, 1933).

high protective tariffs (Germany, America), Great Britain, with her system of free trade, was not far behind in revealing the same fundamental fact, namely, the birth of monopolies out of the concentration of production.

"Second, monopolies have accelerated seizure of the most important sources of raw materials, especially for the coal and iron industry, which is the basic and most highly trustified industry in capitalist society. The monopolistic control of the most important sources of raw materials has enormously increased the power of big capital, and has sharpened the antagonism between trustified and non-trustified industry.

"Third, monopoly arose out of the banks. The banks changed from modest intermediary enterprises into the monopolists of finance capital. Some three or five of the biggest banks in any of the most advanced capitalist countries have achieved a 'personal union' of industrial and banking capital, and have concentrated in their hands the control of billions upon billions, which form the greatest part of the capital and revenue of an entire country. A financial oligarchy, creating a close network of ties of dependence upon all the economic and political institutions of contemporary bourgeois society without exception – this is the most striking manifestation of this monopoly.

"Fourth monopoly arose out of colonial policy. To the numerous 'old' motives of colonial policy finance capital has added the struggle for sources of raw materials, for the export of capital, for 'spheres of influence', i.e., spheres of good business, concessions, monopolist profits, and so on; in fine, for economic territory in general. When the colonies of the European powers in Africa comprised only one-tenth of that territory, as was still the case in 1876, colonial policy was able to develop in a non-monopolist manner, like 'freebooters' taking land, so to speak. But when nine-tenths of Africa had been seized (by 1900); when the whole world had been divided up, there was inevitably ushered in a period of monopolist possession of colonies, and, consequently, of particularly intense struggle for the partition and for the re-partition of the world.

"The extent to which monopolist capital has intensified all the contradictions of capitalism is generally known. It is sufficient to mention the high cost of living and the heavy hand of the cartels. This intensification of contradictions constitutes the most powerful driving force in the transitional period of history, which began at the time of the final victory of world finance capital.

"Monopolies, oligarchy, striving for domination instead of striving for liberty, exploitation of an increasing number of small or weak nations by an extremely small group of the richest or most powerful nations – all these have given birth to those distinctive characteristics of imperialism which compel us to define it as parasitic or decaying capitalism. More and more prominently there appears, as one of the tendencies of imperialism, the creation of the 'rentier-state', the usurer state, whose bourgeoisie lives more and more on capital exports and by 'clipping coupons'. It would be a mistake to believe that this tendency to decay precludes a rapid growth of capitalism. It does not; in the epoch of imperialism, now one, now another of these tendencies is displayed, to greater or less degree by certain branches of industry, by certain strata of the bourgeoisie, and by individual countries. As a whole, capitalism is growing far more rapidly than before, but not only is this growth becoming more and more uneven, but also this unevenness is showing itself in particular in the decay of the countries which are richest in capital (such as England).

•   •   •

"In its turn, this finance capital, which has grown so extraordinarily rapidly, is not unwilling (precisely because it has grown so quickly) to pass on to a more 'peaceful' possession of colonies available for seizure – and not only by peaceful methods – from richer nations. In the United States, economic development during the last decades has been still more rapid than in Germany, and precisely *for this reason* the parasitic character of modern American capitalism has stood out so prominently. On the other hand, a comparison between, say, the republican American bourgeoisie with the monarchist Japanese or German bourgeoisie shows that the greatest political differences become very much toned down during the imperialist period – not because they are unimportant in themselves, but because throughout it is a case of a bourgeoisie showing definite traits of parasitism.

"The receipt of monopolistically high profits by the capitalists of one of numerous branches of industry, of one of numerous countries, etc., makes it economically possible for them to bribe individual strata of the workers, and sometimes also a fairly considerable minority of them, and win them to the side of the bourgeoisie of an industry or nation, against all the others. The intensification of antagonisms between imperialist nations for the partition of the world increases this tendency. And so there is created that bond between imperialism and opportunism, which revealed itself first and most clearly in England, owing to the fact that certain features of imperialist development were apparent there much earlier than in other countries.

• • •

"From all that has been said above on the economic essence of imperialism, it follows that it must be characterised as capitalism in transition, or, more precisely, as dying capitalism. . . .

"What, then, is the meaning of this little word 'interlocking'? It applies only to the most striking aspect of the process going on before our eyes. It shows that the observer cannot see the forest for the trees. It slavishly copies the external, the fortuitous, the chaotic. It reveals him as a man overwhelmed by the mass of material and wholly incapable of appreciating its meaning and importance. Ownership of shares of stock and relations between owners of private property 'interlock accidentally'. But the foundation of this interlocking, that which constitutes its base, is the changing social relations in production. When a big enterprise becomes a gigantic one and, working on the basis of exactly computed mass data, systematically organises the supply of primary raw materials to the extent of two-thirds or three-fourths of all that is necessary for tens of millions of people; when these raw materials are transported to the most suitable places of production, sometimes hundreds or thousands of miles from each other, in a systematic and organised manner; when one centre controls all the successive stages of working up the raw materials right up to the manufacture of numerous varieties of finished articles; when these products are distributed according to a single plan among tens and hundreds of millions of consumers (the marketing of oil in America and Germany by the American Oil Trust), then it becomes evident that we have socialisation of production going on right before our eyes, and not mere 'interlocking'; that private business relations, and private property relations, constitute a shell which is no longer suitable to its contents, a shell which must inevitably begin to decay if its removal is postponed by artificial means; a shell which may continue in a state of decay for a comparatively long period (particularly if the cure of the opportunist abscess is protracted), but which will inevitably be removed."

Schumpeter – Conflicting Interests in Imperialism*

"A purely capitalist world . . . can offer no fertile soil to imperialist impulses. . . . [I]ts people*are likely to be essentially of an unwarlike disposition. Hence we must expect that anti-imperialist tendencies will show themselves wherever capitalism penetrates the economy and, through the economy, the mind of modern nations – most strongly, of course, where capitalism itself is strongest, where it has advanced furthest, encountered the least resistance, and preeminently where its types and hence democracy – in the 'bourgeois' sense – come closest to political dominion. We must further expect that the types formed by capitalism will actually be the carriers of these tendencies. Is such the case? The facts that follow are cited to show that this expectation, which flows from our theory, is in fact justified.

"1. Throughout the world of capitalism, and specifically among the elements formed by capitalism in modern social life, there has arisen a fundamental opposition to war, expansion, cabinet diplomacy, armaments, and socially-entrenched professional armies. This opposition had its origin in the country that first turned capitalist – England – and arose coincidentally with that country's capitalist development. 'Philosophical radicalism' was the first politically influential intellectual movement to represent this trend successfully, linking it up, as was to be expected, with economic freedom in general and free trade in particular. Molesworth became a cabinet member, even though he had publicly declared – on the occasion of the Canadian revolution – that he prayed for the defeat of his country's arms. In step with the advance of capitalism, the movement also gained adherents elsewhere – though at first only adherents without influence. It found support in Paris – indeed, in a circle oriented toward capitalist enterprise (for example, Frédéric Passy). True, pacifism as a matter of principle had existed before, though only among a few small religious sects. But modern pacifism, in its political foundations if not its derivation, is unquestionably a phenomenon of the capitalist world.

---

* From J. A. Schumpeter (1883–1950). Austrian economist who spent much of his career in the US. Interested above all in the role of innovation and technological development in promoting economic change. Other principal works are *The Theory of Economic Development* (1911) and *Capitalism, Socialism and Democracy* (1943). Quoted from *The Sociology of Imperialisms* (1919), trs. H. Nordern (New York: Augustus M. Kelley, 1951).

"2. Wherever capitalism penetrated, peace parties of such strength arose that virtually every war meant a political struggle on the domestic scene. . . . No people and no ruling class today can openly afford to regard war as a normal state of affairs or a normal element in the life of nations. No one doubts that today it must be characterised as an abnormality and a disaster. True, war is still glorified. But glorification in the style of King Tuglâtî-palisharra is rare and unleashes such a storm of indignation that every practical politician carefully dissociates himself from such things. Everywhere there is official acknowledgment that peace is an end in itself – though not necessarily an end overshadowing all purposes that can be realised by means of war. Every expansionist urge must be carefully related to a concrete goal. All this is primarily a matter of political phraseology, to be sure. But the necessity for this phraseology is a symptom of the popular attitude. And that attitude makes a policy of imperialism more and more difficult – indeed, the very word imperialism is applied only to the enemy, in a reproachful sense, being carefully avoided with reference to the speaker's own policies.

"3. The type of industrial worker created by capitalism is always vigorously anti-imperialist. In the individual case, skilful agitation may persuade the working masses to approve or remain neutral – a concrete goal or interest in self-defence always playing the main part – but no initiative for a forcible policy of expansion ever emanates from this quarter. On this point official socialism unquestionably formulates not merely the interests but also the conscious will of the workers. Even less than peasant imperialism is there any such thing as socialist or other working-class imperialism.

"4. Despite manifest resistance on the part of powerful elements, the capitalist age has seen the development of methods for preventing war, for the peaceful settlement of disputes among states. The very fact of resistance means that the trend can be explained only from the mentality of capitalism as a mode of life. It definitely limits the opportunities imperialism needs if it is to be a powerful force. True, the methods in question often fail, but even more often they are successful. I am thinking not merely of the Hague Court of Arbitration but of the practice of submitting controversial issues to conferences of the major powers or at least those powers directly concerned – a course of action that has become less and less avoidable. True, here too the individual case may become a farce. But the serious setbacks of today must not blind us to the real importance or sociological significance of these things.

"5. Among all capitalist economies, that of the United States is least burdened with precapitalist elements, survivals, reminiscences and power factors. Certainly we cannot expect to find imperialist tendencies altogether lacking even in the United States, for the immigrants came from Europe with their convictions fully formed, and the environment certainly favoured the revival of instincts of pugnacity. But we can conjecture that among all countries the United States is likely to exhibit the weakest imperialist trend. This turns out to be the truth. The case is particularly instructive, because the United States has seen a particularly strong emergence of capitalist interests in an imperialist direction – those very interests to which the phenomenon of imperialism has so often been reduced, a subject we shall yet touch on. Nevertheless the United States was the first advocate of disarmament and arbitration. It was the first to conclude treaties concerning arms limitations (1817) and arbitral courts (first attempt in 1797) – doing so most zealously, by the way, when economic interest in expansion was at its greatest. . . .

"These facts are scarcely in dispute. And since they fit into the picture of the mode of life which we have recognised to be the necessary product of capitalism, since we can grasp them adequately from the necessities of that mode of life and industry, it follows that capitalism is by nature anti-imperialist. Hence we cannot readily derive from it such imperialist tendencies as actually exist, but must evidently see them only as alien elements, carried into the world of capitalism from the outside, supported by non-capitalist factors in modern life. The survival of interest in a policy of forcible expansion does not, by itself, alter these facts – not even, it must be steadily emphasised, from the viewpoint of the economic interpretation of history. For objective interests become effective – and, what is important, become powerful political factors – only when they correspond to attitudes of the people or of sufficiently powerful strata. Otherwise they remain without effect, are not even conceived of as interests. The economic interest in the forcible conquest of India had to await free-booter personalities, in order to be followed up. In ancient Rome the domestic class interest in an expansive policy had to be seized upon by a vigorous, idle aristocracy, otherwise it would have been ruled out on internal political grounds. Even the purely commercial imperialism of Venice – assuming that we can speak of such a thing, and not merely of a policy of securing trade routes in a military sense, which was then necessary – even such a policy needed to have examples of a policy of conquest at hand on every side, needed mercenary groups and bellicose adventurers among the *nobili* in order to become true imperialism. The capitalist world, however, suppresses rather than creates such attitudes. Certainly, all expansive interests within it are likely to ally themselves with imperialist tendencies flowing from non-capitalist sources, to use them, to make them serve as pretexts, to rationalise them, to point the way toward action on account of them. And from this union the picture of modern imperialism is put together; but for that very reason it is not a matter of capitalist factors alone. . . .

"It is in the nature of a capitalist economy – and of an exchange economy generally – that many people stand to gain economically in any war. Here the situation is fundamentally much as it is with the familiar subject of luxury. War means increased demand at panic prices, hence high profits and also high wages in many parts of the national economy. This is primarily a matter of money incomes, but as a rule (though to a lesser extent) real incomes are also affected. There are, for example, the special war interests, such as the arms industry. If the war lasts long enough, the circle of money profiteers naturally expands more and more – quite apart from a possible paper-money economy. It may extend to every economic field, but just as naturally the commodity content of money profits drops more and more, indeed, quite rapidly, to the point where actual losses are incurred. The national economy as a whole, of course, is impoverished by the tremendous excess in consumption brought on by war. It is, to be sure, conceivable that either the capitalists or the workers might make certain gains as a class, namely, if the volume either of capital or of labour should decline in such a way that the remainder receives a greater share in the social product and that, even from the absolute viewpoint, the total sum of interest or wages becomes greater than it was before. But these advantages cannot be considerable. They are probably, for the most part, more than outweighed by the burdens imposed by war and by losses sustained abroad. Thus the gain of the capitalists as a class cannot be a motive for war – and it is this gain that counts, for any advantage to the working class would be contingent on a large number of workers falling in action or otherwise perishing. There remain the entrepreneurs in the war industries, in the broader sense, possibly also the large landowner – a small but powerful minority. Their war profits are always sure to be an important supporting element. But few will go so far as to assert that this element alone is sufficient to orient the people of the capitalist world along imperialist lines. At most, an interest in expansion may make the capitalists allies of those who stand for imperialist trends."

17 Geographical Influences on States

One of the main concerns of writers on international relations at all times has been to define what are the main influences on state actions: what causes some states to behave in a particular way and others quite differently.

One theory that has been put forward from early times is that the policies of states are influenced by their geographical situation. It has seemed reasonable to suppose that a state surrounded by mountains, and so easily defensible (such as Switzerland), might adopt a different policy from one that was more vulnerable but controlled strategic positions valuable to other powers (such as Savoy); that states bordering the sea, such as England and the Netherlands, were likely to pursue different and more outward-looking policies than those that were land-based, such as Austria and Saxony.

A thesis on these lines was first put forward by Montesquieu in *L'Esprit des lois*. Though primarily concerned with the relative merits of different legal and constitutional systems, he also considered the reason why laws and institutions varied from one state to another. He drew the conclusion that, in this and other respects, including their foreign policies, nations were much influenced by climatic conditions. Southern peoples, enervated by warm climates, were less vigorous than the peoples of the north and were less likely to engage in foreign adventures, and more willing to submit to oppressive conquerors. Between the countries of Europe and of Asia there was another contrast. In the former, strong and vigorous states of the temperate zone lived in close proximity to each other, so that all had to remain capable of competing effectively in a continual struggle for survival. In Asia, on the contrary, the strong countries of the north immediately adjoined weaker, more slothful countries to the south. They were therefore able to conquer them with little effort, so that their warlike capabilities were eroded and weakened. Thus it was that in Asia and Africa there were large empires, which suited peoples of "servile spirit"; while the Europeans, each developing their own states according to their own laws, had acquired a "genius for liberty" which made every country of the continent difficult for another to subdue.

224

Later writers, such as Buckle in England, shared Montesquieu's view that climate had a major influence on national behaviour. Others presented a variant of this thesis. Writers on military strategy suggested that, apart from climatic influences on character, there were *strategic* reasons why states in different geographical situations pursued different policies. Mahan, the US naval historian, presented an interpretation of international history in these terms. As a naval officer himself, he was profoundly convinced of the importance of sea-power, and he saw Britain's supremacy at sea in the eighteenth and nineteenth centuries as primarily responsible for the dominant position which she had acquired. That sea-power in turn had derived from her geographical situation, which had compelled her to develop a powerful navy to defend her territory and safeguard her interests beyond the seas. In the passage below, from his book *The Influence of Sea Power on History*, he reviews the result of the Seven Years War and the decisive effect which British naval strength had on the course of that war. Because of her sea-power Britain had been in a position to expand into weak and previously unoccupied parts of the earth. A similar vacuum of power would, he believed, soon need to be filled among the unstable and sometimes under-populated countries of Latin America. He made no secret of his hope that the US, if she could build up her sea-power, as Britain had done in earlier years, might find herself in a position to intervene effectively in these areas and so "incline the balance of power in some future sea war".

During the early years of the twentieth century, there was increasing interest in "geopolitical" concepts of this kind. It came to be suggested that particular states were constrained to pursue particular kinds of policies because of their geographical situation. There was increasing interest in the distribution of raw material resources, the importance of river frontiers, effective railway networks and the vulnerability of wide flat plains. One of the better-known exponents of these ideas was the British geographer, Mackinder. They were expounded most explicitly in his book, *Democratic Ideals and Reality*. There he suggested that the world was divided naturally into a "heartland" of Eurasia, a "world-island" consisting of the main mass of Asia, Europe and Africa, dominated by the chief European powers, and the wider seas beyond, dominated by sea powers such as Britain. The passage quoted below demonstrates his somewhat simple-minded view (highly inaccurate, incidentally, in his account of the events of 1839–40) of world history over the previous century, which he sees mainly as a struggle by Russia to extend her power outside the "heartland" which she already controlled, and of Britain and France to resist that effort. The powers of the West, he believed, "must necessarily be opposed to whatever Power attempts to organise the resources of east Europe and the Heartland", and were thus obliged to come together, as during the Crimean war and on other occasions, to oppose Russia. But as the centre of gravity in Europe had moved from Russia to Germany, the latter had become in time the major threat to the Heartland. The western powers had therefore later been obliged to make common cause with Russia to resist German ambitions there. Nothing could prevent a similar struggle for these strategic areas from continuing until the end of time.

Over the last 50 years interest in theories of this sort have somewhat declined. Geographical factors have usually been seen as only one among many others; and of far less importance, for example, than power balances and ideological objectives as an influence on international politics. But there has continued to be some interest in the general question of the relation of states to their geographical environment. Harold and Margaret Sprout, for example, originally mainly interested in strategic problems, especially in naval power, later increasingly devoted themselves to the study of "man–milieu" relationships. Individuals and groups, they believed, responded to their environment according to their conception of it. They were thus influenced by their knowledge of the constraints which it imposed and the opportunities which it offered. In the passage quoted here they point out that, whatever importance was attributed to geographical factors by earlier writers, this always derived ultimately from their effect on a state's general capabilities. But the capabilities of states depended not only on physical factors of this kind but on non-physical elements, including operational capacities, such as the ability to provide and use information; in other words, on the utilisation as well as the possession of resources. The international significance of geographical location and the distribution of resources and population, was therefore not absolute but relative. It depended on what type of contest was being undertaken, and against what adversaries. Thus their importance varied in different periods, and their significance could not be assessed without regard to the way they were seen by the individual human beings of which "states" were composed. More accurate explanation and prediction of human behaviour would require the adoption of an "ecological perspective", which continually took account of the relationships of humans to their total environment, human and material.

The importance accorded to geographical factors by writers on international relations has inevitably varied according to their real significance at different times in history. It can reasonably be argued that, with the rapid shrinkage of the world which improved communications has brought, and the general increase in capabilities that are unrelated to situation or resources (for example the development of modern weaponry, aircraft, missiles, electronics and high technology generally), purely geographical factors have had progressively less influence on the relationships among states. The theories that attributed great importance to these factors have therefore had a declining influence among those who have thought about such questions.

* * *

Montesquieu – The Effect of Climate on National Policies*

HOW THE LAWS OF POLITICAL SERVITUDE BEAR A RELATION TO THE NATURE OF THE CLIMATE

1. *Of political servitude*
"Political servitude does not less depend on the nature of the climate than that which is civil and domestic; and this we shall now demonstrate.

2. *The difference between nations in point of courage*
"We have already observed that great heat enervates the strength and courage of men, and that in cold climates they have a certain vigor of body and mind, which renders them patient and intrepid, and qualifies them for arduous enterprises. This remark holds good,

---

* From Charles de Montesquieu (1689–1755). French philosopher and political writer. Best known for his *Lettres persanes* (1721) presenting a satirical picture of French life and civilisation as seen by two imaginary Persian travellers; and *L'Esprit des lois*, a large-scale work in which he undertook a comparison of different systems of government and the varying principles on which they were based. Besides asserting the influence of climate on social and political organisation, this work first declared the need for a separation of powers between legislature, executive and judicature. Quoted from *The Spirit of the Laws* (1748), trs. T. Nugent (London: George Bell, 1878) Book XVII.

not only between different nations, but even in the different parts of the same country. In the north of China people are more courageous than those in the south; and those in the south of Korea have less bravery than those in the north.

"We ought not, then, to be astonished that the effeminacy of the people in hot climates has almost always rendered them slaves; and that the bravery of those in cold climates has enabled them to maintain their liberties. This is an effect which springs from a natural cause.

"This has also been found true in America; the despotic empires of Mexico and Peru were near the Line, and almost all the little free nations were, and are still, near the Poles.

3. *Of the climate of Asia*
•   •   •

"Asia has properly no temperate zone, as the places situated in a very cold climate immediately touch upon those which are exceedingly hot, that is, Turkey, Persia, India, China, Korea and Japan.

"In Europe, on the contrary, the temperate zone is very extensive, though situated in climates widely different from each other; there being no affinity between the climates of Spain and Italy and those of Norway and Sweden. But as the climate grows insensibly cold upon our advancing from south to north, nearly in proportion to the latitude of each country, it thence follows that each resembles the country joining it; that there is no very extraordinary difference between them, and that, as I have just said, the temperate zone is very extensive.

"Hence it comes that in Asia the strong nations are opposed to the weak; the warlike, brave, and active people touch immediately upon those who are indolent, effeminate, and timorous; the one must, therefore, conquer, and the other be conquered. In Europe, on the contrary, strong nations are opposed to the strong; and those who join each other have nearly the same courage. This is the grand reason of the weakness of Asia, and of the strength of Europe; of the liberty of Europe, and of the slavery of Asia: a cause that I do not recollect ever to have seen remarked. Hence it proceeds that liberty in Asia never increases; whilst in Europe it is enlarged or diminished, according to particular circumstances. . . .

4. *The consequences resulting from this*
"What we have now said is perfectly conformable to history. Asia has

been subdued thirteen times; eleven by the northern nations, and twice by those of the south. In the early ages it was conquered three times by the Scythians; afterwards it was subdued once by the Medes, and once by the Persians; again by the Greeks, the Arabs, the Moguls, the Turks, the Tartars, the Persians and the Afghans. I mention only the Upper Asia, and say nothing of the invasions made in the rest of the south of that part of the world which has most frequently suffered prodigious revolutions.

"In Europe, on the contrary, since the establishment of the Greek and Phœnician colonies, we know but of four great changes; the first caused by the conquest of the Romans; the second by the inundation of barbarians, who destroyed those very Romans; the third by the victories of Charlemagne; and the last by the invasions of the Normans. And if this be rightly examined, we shall find, even in these changes, a general strength diffused through all the parts of Europe. We know the difficulty which the Romans met with in conquering Europe, and the ease and facility with which they invaded Asia. We are sensible of the difficulties the northern nations had to encounter in overturning the Roman empire; of the wars and labours of Charlemagne; and of the several enterprises of the Normans. The destroyers were incessantly destroyed.

5. *That when the people in the North of Asia and those of the North of Europe made conquests, the effects of the conquest were not the same*

"The nations in the north of Europe conquered as freemen; the people in the north of Asia conquered as slaves, and subdued others only to gratify the ambition of a master.

"The reason is, that the people of Tartary, the natural conquerors of Asia, are themselves enslaved. They are incessantly making conquests in the south of Asia, where they form empires: but that part of the nation which continues in the country finds that it is subject to a great master, who, being despotic in the South, will likewise be so in the North, and exercising an arbitrary power over the vanquished subjects, pretends to the same over the conquerors. This is at present most conspicuous in that vast country called Chinese Tartary, which is governed by the emperor, with a power almost as despotic as that of China itself, and which he every day extends by his conquests.

"We may likewise see in the history of China that the emperors[1] sent Chinese colonies into Tartary. These Chinese have become Tartars, and the mortal enemies of China; but this does not prevent their carrying into Tartary the spirit of the Chinese government.

"A part of the Tartars who were conquerors have very often been themselves expelled; when they have carried into their deserts that servile spirit which they had acquired in the climate of slavery. The history of China furnishes us with strong proofs of this assertion, as does also our ancient history.[2]

"Hence it follows that the genius of the Getic or Tartarian nation has always resembled that of the empires of Asia. The people in these are governed by the cudgel; the inhabitants of Tartary by whips. The spirit of Europe has ever been contrary to these manners; and in all ages, what the people of Asia have called punishment those of Europe have deemed the most outrageous abuse.[3]

"The Tartars who destroyed the Grecian Empire established in the conquered countries slavery and despotic power: the Goths, after subduing the Roman Empire, founded monarchy and liberty.

" . . . In the North were formed those valiant people who sallied forth and deserted their countries to destroy tyrants and slaves, and to teach men that, nature having made them equal, reason could not render them dependent, except where it was necessary to their happiness.

6. *A new physical cause of the slavery of Asia, and of the liberty of Europe*

"In Asia they have always had great empires; in Europe these could never subsist. Asia has larger plains; it is cut out into much more extensive divisions by mountains and seas; and as it lies more to the south, its springs are more easily dried up; the mountains are less covered with snow; and the rivers being not so large form more contracted barriers.

"Power in Asia ought, then, to be always despotic: for if their slavery was not severe they would make a division inconsistent with the nature of the country.

"In Europe the natural division forms many nations of a moderate extent, in which the ruling by laws is not incompatible with the maintenance of the state: on the contrary, it is so favorable to it, that without this the state would fall into decay, and become a prey to its neighbours.

"It is this which has formed a genius for liberty that renders every part extremely difficult to be subdued and subjected to a foreign power, otherwise than by the laws and the advantage of commerce.

"On the contrary, there reigns in Asia a servile spirit, which they have never been able to shake off, and it is impossible to find in all the histories of that country a single passage which discovers a freedom of spirit; we shall never see anything there but the excess of slavery."

Notes
1. As Vouty V, Emperor of the fifth dynasty.
2. The Scythians thrice conquered Asia, and thrice were driven thence. (Justin, lib. II).
3. This is in no way contrary to what I shall say in book XXVIII, ch. XX, concerning the manner of thinking among German nations in respect to the cudgel; let the instrument be what it will, the power or action of beating was always considered by them as an affront.

Mahan – The Benefits of Sea Power*

"[T]he gains of England [from the Seven Years War] were very great, not only in territorial increase, nor yet in maritime preponderance, but in the prestige and position achieved in the eyes of the nations, now fully opened to her great resources and mighty power. To these results, won by the sea, the issue of the continental war offered a singular and suggestive contrast. France had already withdrawn, along with England, from all share in that strife, and peace between the other parties to it was signed five days after the Peace of Paris. The terms of the peace were simply the *status quo ante bellum*. By the estimate of the King of Prussia, one hundred and eighty thousand of his soldiers had fallen or died in this war, out of a kingdom of five million souls; while the losses of Russia, Austria and France aggregated four hundred and sixty thousand men. The result was simply that things remained as they were.[1] To attribute this only to a difference between the possibilities of land and sea war is of course absurd. The genius of Frederick, backed by the money of England, had proved an equal match for the mismanaged and not always hearty efforts of a coalition numerically overwhelming.

"What does seem a fair conclusion is, that States having a good seaboard, or even ready access to the ocean by one or two outlets,

---

* From A. T. Mahan (1840–1914). US admiral and naval writer. Served for 40 years in the US navy, becoming the president of the US Naval War College in 1886 and subsequently holding senior commands. Wrote widely on naval history and strategy. Saw Anglo-US naval supremacy as the surest safeguard of world peace. Books include *The Influence of Sea Power on the French Revolution and Empire* (1892) and *The Life of Nelson* (1897). Quoted from *The Influence of Sea Power upon History* (London: Sampson Low, Marston, 1890).

will find it to their advantage to seek prosperity and extension by the way of the sea and of commerce, rather than in attempts to unsettle and modify existing political arrangements in countries where a more or less long possession of power has conferred acknowledged rights, and created national allegiance or political ties. Since the Treaty of Paris in 1763, the waste places of the world have been rapidly filled; witness our own continent, Australia and even South America. A nominal and more or less clearly defined political possession now generally exists in the most forsaken regions, though to this statement there are some marked exceptions; but in many places this political possession is little more than nominal, and in others of a character so feeble that it cannot rely upon itself alone for support or protection. The familiar and notorious example of the Turkish Empire, kept erect only by the forces pressing upon it from opposing sides, by the mutual jealousies of powers that have no sympathy with it, is an instance of such weak political tenure; and though the question is wholly European, all know enough of it to be aware that the interest and control of the sea powers is among the chief, if not the first, of the elements that now fix the situation; and that they, if intelligently used, will direct the future inevitable changes.

"Upon the western continents the political condition of the Central American and tropical South American States is so unstable as to cause constant anxiety about the maintenance of internal order, and seriously to interfere with commerce and with the peaceful development of their resources. So long as – to use a familiar expression – they hurt no one but themselves, this may go on; but for a long time the citizens of more stable governments have been seeking to exploit their resources, and have borne the losses arising from their distracted condition. North America and Australia still offer large openings to immigration and enterprise; but they are filling up rapidly, and as the opportunities there diminish, the demand must arise for a more settled government in those disordered States, for security to life and for reasonable stability of institutions enabling merchants and others to count upon the future. There is certainly no present hope that such a demand can be fulfilled from the existing native materials; if the same be true when the demand arises, no theoretical positions, like the Monroe doctrine, will prevent interested nations from attempting to remedy the evil by some measure, which, whatever it may be called, will be a political interference.

"Such interferences must produce collisions, which may be at times settled by arbitration, but can scarcely fail at other times to cause war. Even for a peaceful solution, that nation will have the strongest arguments which has the strongest organised force. It need scarcely be said that the successful piercing of the Central American Isthmus at any point may precipitate the moment that is sure to come sooner or later. The profound modification of commercial routes expected from this enterprise, the political importance to the United States of such a channel of communication between her Atlantic and Pacific seaboards, are not, however, the whole nor even the principal part of the question. As far as can be seen, the time will come when stable governments for the American tropical States must be assured by the now existing powerful and stable States of America or Europe.

"The geographical position of those States, the climatic conditions, make it plain at once that sea power will there, even more than in the case of Turkey, determine what foreign State shall predominate – if not by actual possession, by its influence over the native governments. The geographical position of the United States and her intrinsic power give her an undeniable advantage; but that advantage will not avail if there is a great inferiority of organised brute-force, which still remains the last argument of republics as of kings. Herein lies to us the great and still living interest of the Seven Years War. In it we have seen and followed England, with an army small as compared with other States, as is still her case today, first successfully defending her own shores, then carrying her arms in every direction, spreading her rule and influence over remote regions, and not only binding them to her obedience, but making them tributary to her wealth, her strength and her reputation. As she loosens the grasp and neutralises the influence of France and Spain in regions beyond the sea, there is perhaps seen the prophecy of some other great nation in days yet to come, that will incline the balance of power in some future sea war, whose scope will be recognised afterward, if not by contemporaries, to have been the political future and the economical development of regions before lost to civilisation; but that nation will not be the United States if the moment find her indifferent, as now, to the empire of the seas."

Note
1. See *Annual Register, 1762*, p. 63.

Mackinder – The Struggle for Control of the Heartland*

"The map reveals at once the essential strategic aspects of the rivalry between Russia and Britain during the nineteenth century. Russia, in command of nearly the whole of the Heartland, was knocking at the landward gates of the Indies. Britain, on the other hand, was knocking at the sea gates of China, and advancing inland from the sea gates of India to meet the menace from the north-west. Russian rule in the Heartland was based on her man-power in East Europe, and was carried to the gates of the Indies by the mobility of the Cossack cavalry. British power along the sea frontage of the Indies was based on the man-power of the distant islands in West Europe, and was made available in the East by the mobility of British ships. Obviously there were two critical points in the alternative voyages round from West to East; those points ·we know today as the 'Cape' and the 'Canal'. The Cape lay far removed from all overland threat throughout the nineteenth century; practically South Africa was an island. The Canal was not opened until 1869, but its construction was an event which cast its shadow before. It was the Frenchman, Napoleon, who gave to Egypt, and therefore also to Palestine, its modern importance, just as it was the Frenchman Dupleix, who, in the eighteenth century, showed that it was possible to build an empire in India from the coast inward, on the ruins of the Mogul Empire which had been built from Delhi outward. Both ideas, that of Napoleon and that of Dupleix, were essentially ideas of sea-power, and sprang not unnaturally from France in the Peninsula of West Europe. By his expedition to Egypt Napoleon drew the British Fleet to the battle of the Nile in the Mediterranean, and also drew the British Army from India, for the first time, overseas to the Nile Valley. When, therefore, Russian power in the Heartland increased, the eyes both of Britain and France were necessarily directed towards Suez, those of Britain for obvious practical reasons, and those of France partly for the sentimental reason of the great Napoleonic tradition, but also

---

* From H. J. Mackinder (1861–1947). Geographer and exponent of geopolitics. His ideas about the importance of control of the "heartland" were first put forward in a paper read to the Royal Geographical Society in London 1904. He later reiterated them in this extract and in his book *The Real World and the Winning of the Peace*, published in 1942 during the Second World War. Quoted from *Democratic Ideals and Reality* (London: Constable, 1919).

because the freedom of the Mediterranean was essential to her comfort in the Western Peninsula.

But Russian land-power did not reach, in the eyes of people of that time, as far as to threaten Arabia. The natural European exit from the Heartland was by the sea-way through the Straits of Constantinople. We have seen how Rome drew her frontier through the Black Sea, and made Constantinople a local base of her Mediterranean sea-power against the Scythians of the steppes. Russia, under Tsar Nicholas, sought to invert this policy, and, by commanding the Black Sea and its southward exit, aimed at extending her land-power to the Dardanelles. The effect was inevitably to unite West Europe against her. So it happened that when Russian intrigue had involved Britain in the First Afghan War in 1839, Britain could not view with equanimity the encampment of a Russian Army on the Bosporus in order to defend the Sultan from the attack, through Syria, of Mehemet Ali, the insurgent Khedive of Egypt. Therefore Britain and France dealt with Mehemet themselves, by attacking him in Syria in 1840.

"In 1854 Britain and France were again involved in action against Russia. France had assumed the protectorate of the Christians in the Near East, and her prestige in that respect was being damaged by Russian intrigue in regard to the Holy Places at Jerusalem. So France and Britain found themselves involved in support of the Turks when the Russian armies came against them on the Danube. Lord Salisbury, shortly before his death, declared that in supporting Turkey we had backed the wrong horse. Is that so certain in regard to the middle of last century? Time is of the essence of International Policy; there is an opportunism which is the tact of politics. In regard to things which are not fundamental, is it not recognised that in ordinary social intercourse it is possible to say the right thing at the wrong time? In 1854 it was Russian power, and not yet German power, which was the centre of organisation in East Europe, and Russia was pressing through the Heartland against the Indies, and by the Straits of Constantinople was seeking to issue from the Heartland into the west, and Prussia was supporting Russia.

"In 1876 Turkey was again in trouble and was again backed by Britain, though necessarily without the support of France. The result was to head off Russian power from Constantinople, but at the cost of giving to the Germans their first step towards the Balkan Corridor by handing over to Austrian keeping the Slav Provinces, hitherto Turkish, of Bosnia and Herzegovina. On that occasion the British Fleet, by Turkish sufferance, steamed through the Dardanelles to within sight of the minarets of Constantinople. The great change in the orientation of Russian policy had not yet occurred, and neither Russia nor Britain yet foresaw the economic methods of amassing man-power to which Berlin was about to resort.

• • •

"In 1870 Britain did not support France against Prussia. With the after-wisdom of events should we not, perhaps, be justified in asking whether we did not in this instance fail to back the right horse? But the eyes of the islanders were still blinded by the victory of Trafalgar. They knew what it was to enjoy sea-power, the freedom of the ocean, but they forgot that sea-power is, in large measure, dependent on the productivity of the bases on which it rests, and that East Europe and the Heartland would make a mighty sea-base. In the Bismarckian period, moreover, when the centre of gravity in East Europe was being shifted from Petrograd to Berlin, it was perhaps not unnatural that contemporaries should fail to realise the subordinate character of the quarrels between the three autocracies, and the fundamental character of the war between Prussia and France.

"The recent Great War arose in Europe from the revolt of the Slavs against the Germans. The events which led up to it began with the Austrian occupation of the Slav provinces of Bosnia and Herzegovina in 1878, and the alliance of Russia with France in 1895. The Entente of 1904 between Britain and France was not an event of the same significance; our two countries had co-operated more often than not in the nineteenth century, but France had been the quicker to perceive that Berlin had supplanted Petrograd as the centre of danger in East Europe, and our two policies had, in consequence, been shaped from different angles for a few years. West Europe, both insular and peninsular, must necessarily be opposed to whatever Power attempts to organise the resources of East Europe and the Heartland. Viewed in the light of that conception, both British and French policy for a hundred years past takes on a large consistency. We were opposed to the half-German Russian tsardom because Russia was the dominating, threatening force both in East Europe and the Heartland for half a century. We were opposed to the wholly German Kaiserdom, because Germany took the lead in East Europe from the tsardom, and would then have crushed the revolting Slavs, and dominated East Europe and the Heartland. German *Kultur*, and all that it means in the way of organisation, would have made that German domination a chastisement of scorpions as compared with the whips of Russia."

Sprout and Sprout – The Influence of the Environment on Decision-Makers*

"Many geopolitical hypotheses have been propounded: hypotheses that purport to identify those factors, the uneven distribution of which over the face of the earth has determined (or presumably will determine) the major patterns of international politics. For Mahan, Mackinder and others, the determinative set of environing factors was mainly, though never exclusively, the layout and configuration of the lands and seas of the globe. For Ellsworth Huntington, and others before and after him, the strategic political variable has been climate. Still others have discovered the key to the rise and decline of nations, and the geographical patterns of international politics, in the uneven distribution of 'natural resources', or in the uneven distribution and differential growth-rates of national populations, or in national differences in economic development and technological proficiency, or in some other set of variables. So far as we can ascertain, all such geopolitical hypotheses represent estimations of the relative capabilities of nations, derived by possibilistic reasoning, within a policy-contingency framework of competitive expansion and periodic payoffs by means of large-scale military war.

"Until quite recently nearly all students of international politics would have accepted this 'realist' frame of expansion and recurrent military war as the basis for analysing the relative capabilities and achievements from which international patterns are deduced. It admittedly was difficult to compare and rank states in a hierarchy of power even in the days when periodic major wars provided a crude sort of objective testing of assumptions and judgements. Even then, as indicated above, there was always disagreement as to which variables were most significant. The development of weapons systems that cast doubt on the possibility of meaningful victory for anyone in the contingency of World War III adds further complicating dimensions to the concept of international capabilities. It is manifestly more difficult to rank states according to their total im-

* From Harold Sprout (1901–) and Margaret Sprout (1903–). Husband and wife team, teachers at Stanford and Princeton Universities. Authors of many books on the bases of national power, ecology and international politics. Principal works include *The Foundations of International Politics* (1962) and *The Ecological Perspective in Human Affairs, with special reference to international politics* (1965). Quoted from *The Ecological Perspective of World Affairs* (Princeton, N.J.: Princeton University Press, 1965).

pacts on other nations when many nonmilitary and paramilitary variables have to be given more weight, and when all the variables are changing more rapidly than formerly, and at different rates in different countries.

•   •   •

"Numerous frames of analysis have been offered for estimating and comparing the capabilities of states under various policy-contingency assumptions. In another place we have suggested one possible approach to this complex set of issues. The essence of our suggestion was to compare national capabilities under the functional categories of: (1) information-providing functions, (2) information-utilising functions, (3) means-providing functions, (4) means-utilising functions, and (5) resistance functions, to the extent that these last are not covered in the preceding four categories.

"This may or may not prove to be an especially fruitful approach. We cite it here chiefly because it directs attention once again to the essential difference between a policy analysis and a capabilities analysis. Categories (1) and (2) represent aspects of decision-making. But these and other aspects of decision-making enter into the estimation of capabilities in a context wholly different from the context of explanation or prediction of particular decisions. In the latter type of analysis, one endeavours to ascertain how those who make decisions in the name of the state envisage the opportunities and limitations implicit in their milieu. Such an inquiry is *not* capability analysis, but is rather an aspect of policy analysis.

•   •   •

"Putting a capabilities problem into some policy-contingency frame of reference, and setting up a scheme for breaking down the problem into some set of functions to be evaluated, constitute only the initial steps in the estimation of political capabilities. Given the most explicit assumptions (as to what is to be undertaken, by what means, against what adversaries, when and where, etc.) and given the most elegant conceptual scheme for analytically differentiating significant functional aspects of a state's capabilities, one still has to establish criteria for judging the significance of variables: for example, the international significance, if any, of geographic location, distance, space and configuration, the uneven distribution of natural resources and population, variations in economic development, political organisation, and other social phenomena. In short, one learns nothing about the relative capabilities of nations merely by collecting, sorting and comparing raw data. Such data acquire political significance, we repeat, in one way, and one way only: by application of suitable explanatory hypotheses. . . .

"As emphasised from the outset, a necessary first step towards clearer understanding of man–milieu relationships is to distinguish relationships derived via psychological processes from those derived otherwise. With respect to the former, the thesis is that . . . values and preferences, moods and attitudes, choices and decisions are relateable to the milieu only via the environed individual's selective perception and his psychological reactions to what is perceived. From the perspective of decisions and decision-making, what matters is how the individual or group imagines the milieu to be, *not* how it actually is. A corollary of this thesis is that *only* psycho-ecological concepts and theories are relevant to descriptions and explanations of decisions (policies, strategies, undertakings), but that psychological concepts and theories are appropriately applicable *only* to environed units capable of psychological behaviour.

"In the context of human affairs, this corollary confines the relevance of psycho-ecological concepts and theories to human individuals, concrete human groups, and to more formal organisations *in their concrete human aspect*. We have argued, and we reiterate again, that *psycho*-ecological terms and modes of expression cannot be sensibly employed with reference to high-level abstractions such as the state and the international system, *unless* it is made explicitly clear that the reference is not to the system, *qua* system, but *only* to the human agents of the system. Avoidance of words and sentences that attribute human-like characters to the state, *qua* state, and to the international system, *qua* system, is, in our view, a long overdue step towards combating the tendency to reification that, paradoxically, dehumanises politics, a tendency that also fosters deterministic thinking about political institutions and relationships. Alternative vocabularies are needed and are readily available.

"With respect to the operational results of decisions, our thesis is that what matters is how the milieu actually is, *not* how the environed individual or group imagines it to be. In every instance, the structures of the environed unit and the factors of the milieu set limits to that unit's achievement, with reference to whatever task or strategy is undertaken. From the standpoint of achievement, at least some of these limiting factors may be effective, irrespective of whether or how the environed individual or group perceived and took them into account in defining the undertaking and setting the course of action.

"A corollary of this thesis is that explanations of achievement and estimations of capabilities for achievement invariably and necessarily presuppose antecedent undertakings or assumptions regarding undertakings. Unless there is an undertaking, there can be no achievement – and nothing to explain or to estimate. This requirement is implicit in all possibilistic analyses, of which estimation of the capabilities of states and explanation of international political patterns are simply special cases.

"We say special cases because, as previously emphasised, the ecological perspective permeates every sector of human activity. More general awareness of the intellectual, and also the moral and civic, consequences of ecological terms, modes of expression and theories of man–milieu relationships should contribute to more precise and enlightening explanations and predictions of human behaviour and achievement.

18 The Strategic Interests of States

The insistence of politicians on the right of states to intervene by force where necessary was matched by the increasing concern of soldiers to devise the means by which that force could best be applied. Though there had for many years been some writing about the arts of generalship, fortification and military strategy, this had taken the form mainly of technical manuals, of interest to the military alone. But from the time of Napoleon, and of the French revolutionary strategist Jomini, there was increasing recognition of the political factors which influenced military outcomes.

The relationship between military means and political ends was a major preoccupation of the most famous military writer of all time, von Clausewitz, and it is the theme of the first of the pieces reproduced below. While von Clausewitz was convinced of the necessity, when force was required, of applying it with the maximum rigour and decisive effect, he was equally clear that warfare could not be effectively undertaken without a clear appreciation of the political purposes which underlay it. The character of the military strategy applied depended crucially on the character of the political strategy which it implemented. It was useless for civilian leaders to summon generals to their side and ask for their advice about the way a war should be fought, since this would depend on what the politicians themselves wished the war to achieve. Thus the closest collaboration was required from the beginning between military and political leaders; and the military should be directly represented in political decision-making. Warfare merely added a new dimension to a political process that was continuous. The early successes of the French revolution, for example, were due to political as much as to military causes: the effect of the revolution within France and on her capacity to win hearts and minds among foreign peoples. It was only when political circumstances changed, especially in the countries opposed to France, that the tide of war could finally be turned.

The importance of political factors was recognised by other military writers. Increasingly the most important of these was seen to be the national sentiment which influenced the way states and their peoples behaved. The significance of this was recognised by the elder

241

von Moltke in his reflections about the Rhine frontier. In this passage, written only ten years after von Clausewitz's famous book appeared, and nearly 30 years before Germany and France were to go to war, in part at least over that frontier, he expresses his concern about the powerful national sentiment in France in favour of recovering the Rhineland. The arguments he puts forward for the existing frontier are not strategic. France, in von Moltke's view, had no moral claim to the Rhine frontier and should, on the contrary, be grateful for the generous way in which she was treated by Germany at the end of the Napoleonic wars. But the French rejected reason and, driven by passion, believed the issue could only be determined by force. If France were to reject the Treaty of Vienna as the basis of peace in Europe, Germany should reserve the right to abandon it too and to claim provinces now ruled by France, such as Alsace-Lorraine, which had once been part of the German empire. Thus it was necessary to arouse the entire German nation in defence of the existing frontier: the peoples of Germany must overcome their internal divisions and make themselves into "a great armed camp in sight of a powerful enemy".

Forty-five years later, after the two countries had fought out that decisive battle, another German military writer, von der Goltz, considered a possible renewal of the struggle. He examined the changes which had altered the character of war over the previous decades. He is impressed above all by the increased scale of war, the increased size of armies, the increased levels of fire-power and the increasing intensity of military preparation. This meant that war from now on was to be a national enterprise, a war of the masses, in which the glory accorded to the great commanders must equally be shared by the common soldier. For this reason it was necessary for the whole nation to be educated in the arts of war, since it was certain that war would remain a fact of life "for as long as earthly nations strive after earthly goods". The final struggle for the existence and greatness of Germany was yet to come; but it must come one day, with full fury. When it came the German army, which was the "German nation in arms", could enter on that struggle with the full assurance of ultimate victory.

Twenty years later another German army officer, imbued with strong national feelings, von Bernhardi, expressed similar sentiments. He too declared himself the heir of von Clausewitz and, like von Clausewitz, was particularly concerned to examine the relationship of war to politics. The unification of Germany had made her one of the most powerful and successful states of Europe, but her successes in industry and the humanities needed, he believed, to be matched by an increase in her political power: as measured for example in colonies, trade and the influence of "Teutonic culture". But any such growth of German power and influence was certain to be resisted by other European states. Germany should not be deceived by the growing propaganda in other countries in favour of the peaceful settlement of disputes, for example by arbitration and other means. This was an attempt by those states which benefited from the status quo to prevent a rising state, such as Germany, from gaining "the position in the world that is due to us". Germany would therefore need to rely on her sword and should renounce all debilitating visions of peace. The German armed forces should be built up and the public generally educated about military affairs, so that doctrines of war were made the common property of the German people. Here too strategic notions are closely intertwined with political – in this case nationalist – concepts.

Strategic writers, therefore, in this age, were increasingly conscious of the political factors which influenced military success. They were themselves in many cases influenced by the nationalist sentiment which affected so many of their compatriots. They no longer saw the military as a specialised profession or a privileged caste. War was seen as a national enterprise which should engage the people as a whole. Since they themselves shared the prevailing nationalist sentiment, and since they, not unnaturally, believed that their own profession was one that should be given employment from time to time, their writing did not generally incline governments always to seek for peaceful settlements of their disputes.

*   *   *

von Clausewitz – The Political Purposes of War*

"Up to now we have considered the difference that distinguishes war from every other human interest, individual or social – a difference

---

* From C. von Clausewitz (1780–1831). Leading German military theorist. Took part in Napoleonic wars as officer in the Prussian, and for a time the Russian, armies.

that derives from human nature, and that therefore no philosophy can resolve. We have examined this incompatibility from various angles so that none of its conflicting elements should be missed. Now we must seek out the unity into which these contradictory elements combine in real life, which they do by partly neutralising one another. We might have posited that unity to begin with, if it had not been necessary to emphasise the contradictions with all possible clarity and to consider the different elements separately. This unity lies in *the concept that war is only a branch of political activity; that it is in no sense autonomous.*

"It is, of course, well known that the only source of war is politics – the intercourse of governments and peoples; but it is apt to be assumed that war suspends that intercourse and replaces it by a wholly different condition, ruled by no law but its own.

"We maintain, on the contrary, that war is simply a continuation of political intercourse, with the addition of other means. We deliberately use the phrase 'with the addition of other means' because we also want to make it clear that war in itself does not suspend political intercourse or change it into something entirely different. In essentials that intercourse continues, irrespective of the means it employs. The main lines along which military events progress, and to which they are restricted, are political lines that continue throughout the war into the subsequent peace. How could it be otherwise? Do political relations between peoples and between their governments stop when diplomatic notes are no longer exchanged? Is war not just another expression of their thoughts, another form of speech or writing? Its grammar, indeed, may be its own, but not its logic.

"If that is so, then war cannot be divorced from political life; and whenever this occurs in our thinking about war, the many links that connect the two elements are destroyed and we are left with something pointless and devoid of sense.

"This conception would be ineluctable even if war were total war, the pure element of enmity unleashed. All the factors that go to make up war and determine its salient features – the strength and allies of each antagonist, the character of the peoples and their governments, and so forth, all the elements listed in the first chapter of Book I – are

Principally known for his magisterial work, *On War* (published in 1858 but written 20 years earlier). Asserted that strategy should be directed at the enemy's forces, his resources and his will to fight, and believed that military strategy should be closely related to political objectives. Quoted from *On War* (1832), trs. Michael Howard and P. Paret (Princeton, N.J.: Princeton University Press, 1976) Book 8.

these not all political, so closely connected with political activity that it is impossible to separate the two? But it is yet more vital to bear all this in mind when studying actual practice. We will then find that war does not advance relentlessly toward the absolute, as theory would demand. Being incomplete and self-contradictory, it cannot follow its own laws, but has to be treated as a part of some other whole; the name of which is policy.

"In making use of war, policy evades all rigorous conclusions proceeding from the nature of war, bothers little about ultimate possibilities, and concerns itself only with immediate probabilities. Although this introduces a high degree of uncertainty into the whole business, turning it into a kind of game, each government is confident that it can outdo its opponent in skill and acumen.

"Thus policy converts the overwhelmingly destructive element of war into a mere instrument. The terrible two-handed sword that should be used with total strength to strike once and no more, becomes the lightest rapier – sometimes even a harmless foil fit only for thrusts and feints and parries.

"Thus the contradictions in which war involves that naturally timid creature, man, are resolved; if this is the solution we choose to accept.

"If war is part of policy, policy will determine its character. As policy becomes more ambitious and vigorous, so will war, and this may reach the point where war attains its absolute form. If we look at war in this light, we do not need to lose sight of this absolute: on the contrary, we must constantly bear it in mind.

"Only if war is looked at in this way does its unity reappear; only then can we see that all wars are things of the *same* nature; and this alone will provide the right criteria for conceiving and judging great designs.

"Policy, of course, will not extend its influence to operational details. Political considerations do not determine the posting of guards or the employment of patrols. But they are the more influential in the planning of war, of the campaign, and often even of the battle.

"That is why we felt no urge to introduce this point of view at the start. At the stage of detailed study it would not have been much help and might have been distracting. But when plans for a war or a campaign are under study, this point of view is indispensable.

"Nothing is more important in life than finding the right standpoint for seeing and judging events, and then adhering to it. One point and *one only* yields an integrated view of all phenomena; and only by holding to that point of view can one avoid inconsistency.

"If planning a war precludes adopting a dual or multiple point of view – that is, applying first a military, then an administrative eye, then a political, and so on – the question arises whether *policy* is bound to be given precedence over everything.

"It can be taken as agreed that the aim of policy is to unify and reconcile all aspects of internal administration as well as of spiritual values, and whatever else the moral philosopher may care to add. Policy, of course, is nothing in itself; it is simply the trustee for all these interests against the outside world. That it can err, subserve the ambitions, private interests, and vanity of those in power, is neither here nor there. In no sense can the art of war ever be regarded as the preceptor of policy, and here we can only treat policy as representative of all interests of the community.

"The only question, therefore, is whether, when war is being planned, the political point of view should give way to the purely military (if a purely military point of view is conceivable at all): that is, should it disappear completely or subordinate itself, or should the political point of view remain dominant and the military be subordinated to it?

"That the political view should wholly cease to count on the outbreak of war is hardly conceivable unless pure hatred made all wars a struggle for life and death. In fact, as we have said, they are nothing but expressions of policy itself. Subordinating the political point of view to the military would be absurd, for it is policy that creates war. Policy is the guiding intelligence and war only the instrument, not vice versa. No other possibility exists, then, than to subordinate the military point of view to the political. . . .

"In short, at the highest level the art of war turns into policy – but a policy conducted by fighting battles rather than by sending diplomatic notes.

"We can now see that the assertion that a major military development, or the plan for one, should be a matter for *purely military* opinion is unacceptable and can be damaging. Nor indeed is it sensible to summon soldiers, as many governments do when they are planning a war, and ask them for *purely military advice*. But it makes even less sense for theoreticians to assert that all available military resources should be put at the disposal of the commander so that on their basis he can draw up purely military plans for a war or a campaign. It is in any case a matter of common experience that despite the great variety and development of modern war its major lines are still laid down by governments; in other words, if we are to be technical about it, by a purely political and not a military body.

"This is as it should be. No major proposal required for war can be worked out in ignorance of political factors; and when people talk, as they often do, about harmful political influence on the management of war, they are not really saying what they mean. Their quarrel should be with the policy itself, not with its influence. If the policy is right – that is, successful – any intentional effect it has on the conduct of the war can only be to the good. If it has the opposite effect the policy itself is wrong.

"Only if statesmen look to certain military moves and actions to produce effects that are foreign to their nature do political decisions influence operations for the worse. In the same way as a man who has not fully mastered a foreign language sometimes fails to express himself correctly, so statesmen often issue orders that defeat the purpose they are meant to serve. Time and again that has happened, which demonstrates that a certain grasp of military affairs is vital for those in charge of general policy.

"Before continuing, we must guard against a likely misinterpretation. We are far from believing that a minister of war immersed in his files, an erudite engineer or even an experienced soldier would, simply on the basis of their particular experience, make the best director of policy – always assuming that the prince himself is not in control. Far from it. What is needed in the post is distinguished intellect and strength of character. He can always get the necessary military information somehow or other. The military and political affairs of France were never in worse hands than when the brothers Belle-Isle and the Duc de Choiseul were responsible – good soldiers though they all were.

"If war is to be fully consonant with political objectives, and policy suited to the means available for war, then unless statesman and soldier are combined in one person, the only sound expedient is to make the commander-in-chief a member of the cabinet, so that the cabinet can share in the major aspects of his activities.[1] But that, in turn, is only feasible if the cabinet – that is, the government – is near the theatre of operations, so that decisions can be taken without serious loss of time. That is what the Austrian Emperor did in 1809, and the allied sovereigns in 1813–15. The practice justified itself perfectly.

• • •

"Clearly the tremendous effects of the French Revolution abroad were caused not so much by new military methods and concepts as by radical changes in policies and administration, by the new character of government, altered conditions of the French people, and the like. That other governments did not understand these changes, that they wished to oppose new and overwhelming forces with customary means: all these were political errors. Would a purely military view of war have enabled anyone to detect these faults and cure them? It would not. Even if there really had existed a thoughtful strategist capable of deducing the whole range of consequences simply from the nature of the hostile elements, and on the strength of these of prophesying their ultimate effects, it would have been quite impossible to act on his speculations.

"Not until statesmen had at last perceived the nature of the forces that had emerged in France, and had grasped that new political conditions now obtained in Europe, could they foresee the broad effect all this would have on war; and only in that way could they appreciate the scale of the means that would have to be employed, and how best to apply them.

"In short, we can say that twenty years of revolutionary triumph were mainly due to the mistaken policies of France's enemies.

"It is true that these mistakes became apparent only in the course of the wars, which thoroughly disappointed all political expectations that had been placed on them. But the trouble was not that the statesmen had ignored the soldiers' views. The military art on which the politicians relied was part of a world they thought was real – a branch of current statecraft, a familiar tool that had been in use for many years. But *that* form of war naturally shared in the errors of policy, and therefore could provide no corrective. It is true that war itself has undergone significant changes in character and methods, changes that have brought it closer to its absolute form. But these changes did not come about because the French government freed itself, so to speak, from the harness of policy; they were caused by the new political conditions which the French Revolution created both in France and in Europe as a whole, conditions that set in motion new means and new forces, and have thus made possible a degree of energy in war that otherwise would have been inconceivable.

"It follows that the transformation of the art of war resulted from the transformation of politics. So far from suggesting that the two could be disassociated from each other, these changes are a strong proof of their indissoluble connection.

"Once again: war is an instrument of policy. It must necessarily bear the character of policy and measure by its standards. The conduct of war, in its great outlines, is therefore policy itself, which takes up the sword in place of the pen, but does not on that account cease to think according to its own laws."

Note

1. The first edition has: "*so bleibt . . . nur ein gutes Mittel übrig, nämlich den obersten Feldherrn zum Mitglied des Kabinets zu machen, damit dasselbe Theil an den Hauptmomenten seines Handelns nehme*". In the second edition, which appeared in 1853, the last part of the sentence was changed to: "*damit er in den wichtigsten Momenten an dessen Beratungen und Beschlüssen teilnehme*". In his 1943 translation, based on the second or on a still later edition, O. J. M. Jolles rendered this alteration correctly as: "that he may take part in its councils and decisions on important occasions". That, of course, is a reversal of Clausewitz's original sense. By writing that the commander-in-chief must become a member of the cabinet so that the cabinet can share in the major aspects of his activities, Clausewitz emphasises the cabinet's participation in military decisions, not the soldier's participation in political decisions.

Of the several hundred alterations of the text that were introduced in the second edition of *On War*, and became generally accepted, this is probably the most significant change.

von Moltke the Elder – Germany's Western Frontier*

"Even though peace is continued, the younger generation in France is bred to believe that it has a sacred right to the Rhine, and its mission is to make it, at the first opportunity, the boundary of France. 'The Rhine boundary must be a reality', that is the theme for the future of France.

"We think that we have sufficiently proved in the preceding historical discussion that France has not the slightest legal claim to the

---

* From H. von Moltke (1800–91). Chief of Staff of Prussian, and later German, army for over 30 years, including the period of the Prussian wars of 1864, 1866 and 1870. Served for a time also in the Danish and Turkish armies. Strong believer in the necessity of German unification and held that the army had a vital role to play in achieving this. Recognised from an early time the important role which the railways could play in improving mobility and the need for good staff work and the maximum delegation to local commanders. Closely associated in all his three successful wars with von Roon, the minister of war, and Bismarck, the chancellor. Quoted from "The Western Boundary", in *Essays, Speeches and Memoirs*, trs. C. F. McClumpha (London: James Osgood, 1893).

Rhine boundary. But we also know very well that all that has been said to the French about it has been like talking to the wind. They will not hear. The more plainly all the proofs of history and nature and all the arguments of reason and morals speak against them, the less are they willing to hear of them.

"So it only remains to be seen whether Germany is strong enough, and will remain so, to reject by force the illegal claims of France under all circumstances. It is truly lamentable that after we have been neighbours of two thousand years standing, after we have received so many blows from the French and given them so many back in turn, they, notwithstanding, have not yet been able to bring themselves to understand their true position to us. The study of history flourishes in France as with us, a thousand means and avenues to intelligence are open, and yet such a blinded passionateness prevails among the French that they intentionally deceive themselves with an illusion and disdain to see the truth, even in its brightest daylight.

"Thoughtful reflection, reason, justice, and fairness, which ought to be present in the intercourse of two such old and powerful neighbours, and which we are always ready to keep, are despised by the French. Only might shall decide; whenever they differ with us, they seize the sword. History must vanish in all directions before the passion of the moment. Future dangers are despised just as past experiences are trampled under foot. Desire rushes upon its object in spite of everything, indifferent as to who will perish thereby.

"Even though we are strong enough to drive away might with might, yet it is sad to see the darkness of rude, barbarous passion, and the domain of unreasonable force again impend threateningly over us, after so many experiences and in the century of the greatest enlightenment. But who warrants us that some weakness will not sometime come upon us, that we shall not be involved in some conflict of internal or external policy wherein our vigilance and our strength will be relaxed? What have we then to fear from a neighbour who knows no right but might, and who is not ashamed openly to confess that he, today even, as in the centuries of fist-combats, is only on the watch to find us once weak, disunited or unguarded, in order to fall upon us again and rob us?

"Therefore it is our task, if we cannot instruct the old wicked neighbour, to make our good right perfectly clear to ourselves at least, to bring the whole body of the German nation to conscious-ness. To no German must it be hidden or remain indifferent that if France and Germany ever come to settle with each other all debit is on his side and all credit on ours. We have to demand of France only what it has wrongfully torn from us. France, on the other hand, has nothing to demand of us, not a hamlet, not a tree. The Rhine is, as Arndt has said briefly and well, Germany's river, not Germany's boundary. If we argue from historical right, then everything that France has gained on its eastern frontier since the thirteenth century, has been robbed from Germany, then all Burgundian and Lorrainian lands are our old property wrongfully seized upon, and we should have accordingly still more to reclaim than the boundary fixed by the language. If we argue from the national point of view and make the language the national boundary of the nations, then the entire Rhine belongs to us, its whole bank on the left and right, for German has been spoken in the whole river-district of the Rhine for fourteen centuries; accordingly, France would not have to claim the left bank of the Rhine from us, but we should have to claim Alsace and Lorraine from it. If, finally, we argue from positive right as it has been fixed by the last treaties, then France has sanctioned indeed its unjust possession of Lorraine and Alsace by means of these, but these treaties exclude France from every claim to the other parts of the left bank of the Rhine. But if France no longer recognises the treaties of 1814 and 1815, the only legal titles that have secured to it its old theft from Germany, and which we have always honestly recognised, though they were very detrimental to us, if France itself breaks these treaties and begins war, then we ought to unite with the firm determination, as God wills and as He grants victory to the righteous cause, never again to make those treaties the basis of a new peace, and not to sheathe the sword until our whole right has become ours, until France has paid its whole debt to us.

"Our task is further to educate more intelligently and more thoroughly the political sense which seems to return gradually among us, after that we have lost it for centuries, that is, to view all the questions of the day, be it the discussion of a principle or of some particular point of interest, from a higher national point of view, and never to forget the external policy because of internal differences. This forgetfulness alone has been the source of all our misfortune. Only because we Germans were quarrelling among ourselves about opinions, or about provincial interests and thereby forgot to protect our frontiers against external foes, could neighbours have robbed us and weakened us. Much has happened to prevent the return of such unfortunate quarrels in Germany for the future. The German peoples no longer cherish that former unreasonable jealousy towards one another, or by no means to such a degree as formerly. The dynasties also are more closely connected, and they find their interest is much better protected in a policy of agreement than formerly in one of separation. Only the strife over opinions and convictions, over constitutional and religious questions, is still rife and has not yet reached a satisfactory solution. But has too much been asked of a nation so great, so ancient, so experienced, and thoroughly educated as the German, if one begs of it not to hostilise itself within itself so long as so many foes threaten it from without? Whatever be the object about which we hostilise ourselves, the result will always be that each of our inner quarrels will be used from the outside for our ruin. We must ever regard ourselves, even in the midst of peace, as a great army in camp and in sight of a powerful foe. In such a condition it does not become us to take our stand hostilely against one another, however natural and right may apparently be the occasion for it. We must always stand with our face towards the enemy without."

von der Goltz – The Growing Scale of Warfare*

"Although the leading principles of warfare are said to be eternal, yet the phenomena which have to be dealt and reckoned with are liable to continuous change. War, as an act of human intercourse, is, in its external form, subject to all the same changes which affect the latter. Railways and telegraphs, which show new ways to trade, have also opened hitherto closed paths to military science. Technical skill, which supplied industry with improved machinery, has also placed into the soldier's hands new weapons, which enable him to produce effects never dreamt of by his forebears. Military precepts are thus continually changing in their application, and it may rightly be said, that every age has its own peculiar mode of warfare. Hence, the methods which, in 1870, led to triumph, cannot now be regarded as the absolute standard for the future; new conditions, ushered in by

---

* From K, von der Goltz (1843–1916). German field marshal. Besides long service in the German army he was seconded to the Turkish army in 1883–95 and deputy chief of the Turkish General Staff in 1909–13. Sharing the nationalist attitude of many of his countrymen, and especially of his fellow-officers at this period, he wrote extensively on military affairs. In 1911 he founded the Young German League to instil patriotism into German youth. Quoted from *The Nation in Arms* (1883), trs. P. A. Ashworth (London: Hugh Rees, 1906).

the present, compel us to devise fresh ways and means.

"All the great Continental Powers have, during the last few years, made strenuous efforts to increase their fighting strength. There has either taken place, as in France and Russia, a complete reorganisation of the military system, or, as in Germany, Austria, and Italy, steps have been taken to develop the existing institutions so as to increase the forces available for the defence of the country to the utmost limit, and, more particularly, to provide greater numbers for employment in the field. Not a single State in Europe could afford to hold aloof from the general tendency.

"Our last wars included five great battles, viz.: Königgrätz, Wörth, Vionville, St Privat and Sedan. Even what we beheld there, will be repeated in the future on a vastly greater scale. At Königgrätz almost the entire army present in the theatre of war where the final issue was decided was engaged in a single locality; at St Privat rather more than one-half. Applying the same to present conditions, it will be seen that gigantic struggles between forces composed of from ten to fifteen army corps, under a single commander, will not be beyond the bounds of probability. Such are, however, proportions which have not yet been realised in modern times; and it is easily conceivable how greatly the questions of feeding and mobility will be affected, no less than the tactical leading.

"Since the last war, France has supplied the first example of artificial preparation of a possible theatre of war, and is by no means any longer unique in that respect. Germany has witnessed the creation of practically one vast entrenched camp on the eastern frontier of Poland and Lithuania. Austria, Italy, Switzerland, Belgium and Roumania have methodically prepared the defence of their dominions by means of fortification, and the movement shows as yet no signs of arrest. In proportion as the material wealth of nations increases, the greater becomes their striving to ensure themselves against the fateful consequences of invasion, for which purposes increased opulence supplies ever growing financial means.

• • •

"The moral effects of wars will differ according to the form which they take, according to their final issue, and according to the times in which they fall. We must accept what the gods send. What is, however, absolutely certain, is that *wars are the fate of mankind, the inevitable destiny of nations; and that eternal peace is not the lot of mortals in this world.*

"Today, then, it is not sufficient, as Machiavelli proposes, that rulers alone should know war, the nations themselves do no less need this knowledge. They should know to forge them weapons, to cultivate strength to wield them, and to steel their hearts so as to be prepared to endure the trials imposed by a struggle for the Fatherland.

"The question then arises: Is a knowledge of war valuable to the ordinary mortal, when it may only tempt him to dare difficulties and dangers, perhaps to his own undoing? Certainly!

"What true soldierly nature would hesitate long to brush aside all scruples, and seize the opportunity, when offered, of wielding the baton of a field-marshal? The prize is a great one; it is that which beckons the poet and the artist onward on a thorny path – Immortality. This word has an irresistible charm. The fortunate warrior rescues his name from oblivion. The names of Frederick and Napoleon will ring as long as the world lasts.

"But is it worth while to impose such heavy trials upon the masses, in order that a single man may be immortalised? The thousands that have fallen for the glory of the great commander are not mentioned. They go without reward. This may be the opinion of short-sighted wisdom, but we regard things in a different light. Even the greatest captain needs many capable, faithful, and bold assistants, and *these share in his glory*.

"We Germans today are in a happy position. The star of the young Empire has only just risen on the horizon; its full course lies still before it. The upward course to the zenith is more pleasant than that down the incline. And if ever a rising State held a guarantee of long existence, it is a strong, united and military Germany in the midst of the Great Powers of Europe. Such a position is rightly called perilous, but it is the consciousness of danger which keeps energy alive. Certainly, if our Fatherland was to rest upon laurels won, and surrender itself to the pleasant dream that its existence, its prestige, and its security had been gained once for all, and that its neighbours were not, after all, ill-disposed, it would perforce soon become their prize. Accessible to all, in the way of all who hanker after expansion, its frontier districts, inhabited by people who, either from tradition, or from restlessness and love of change, conceive their centre of gravity to lie beyond, nowhere barred by natural obstructions, it would have to bear the cost of every revulsion in our part of the world. But so far as human foresight can conceive and provide, it will not come to this. A strong arm and a sharp sword will protect the heart of Europe.

"But we must ever bear in mind that we have yet to climb the height. Ever upward is our watchword. Unceasing effort to perfect our national military system will, for a long time to come, be our highest political wisdom. Hand in hand with it must go the *increase* of our moral forces, which decide everything in war; *increase*, not mere conservation; for 'never are moral forces at rest; they decline as soon as they cease to mount upwards'.[1]

"First of all, then, it is necessary to make it clear to ourselves and to the children growing up about us, and whom we have to train, that a time of rest has not yet come, that the prediction of a final struggle for the existence and greatness of Germany is not a mere fancy of ambitious fools, but that it will come one day, inevitably, with full fury, and with the seriousness which every struggle deciding the fate of a nation entails ere a new political system receives unreserved recognition. Bearing this constantly in mind, we must work incessantly, by example, by word, and by our writings towards this end, that loyalty towards the Emperor, passionate love for the Fatherland, determination not to shrink from hard trials, self-denial, and cheerful sacrifice may wax ever stronger in our hearts and in those of our children. Then will the German army, which must be, and shall ever remain, the German nation in arms, enter upon the coming conflict with full assurance of ultimate victory."

Note
1. Scharnhorst in 1806.

von Bernhardi – The Need to Expand Germany's Power*

"Germany supports today 65,000,000 inhabitants on an area about equal the size of France, whilst only 40,000,000 live in France. Germany's enormous population increases annually by about

* From F. von Bernhardi (1849–1930). German general. Served as section chief of the German General Staff from 1898 to 1901, and was later commanding general of VII Army Corps. Frequent writer on military affairs and seen as leading expert in Germany on the eve of the First World War. Besides the book quoted here, he was

1,000,000. There is no question, agriculture and industry of the home country cannot give permanently sufficient employment to such a steadily increasing mass of human beings. We therefore need to enlarge our colonial possessions so as to afford a home and work to our surplus population, unless we wish to run the risk of seeing again the strength and productive power of our rivals increased by German emigration as in former days. Partitioned as the surface of the globe is among the nations at the present time, such territorial acquisitions we can only realise at the cost of other States or in conjunction with them; and both are only possible if we succeed, above all, in securing our power in the centre of Europe better than hitherto.

"With every move of our foreign policy today we have to face a European war against superior enemies. This sort of thing is becoming intolerable. The freedom of action of our people is thereby hampered to an extraordinary degree. Such a state of affairs is highly dangerous, not only for the peace of Europe, which, after all, is only a secondary matter for us, but, above all, is most dangerous to ourselves. It is we, whose economical, national and political development is being obstructed and injured; it is we, whose position in the world is being threatened after we have purchased it so dearly with the blood of our best. We must therefore strive to find out by all means who is for or who is against us. On this depends not only the possibility of carrying into execution the political aims befitting the greatness and the wants of our country, but also the very existence of our people as a civilised nation.

"Hand in hand with the increase of population and the growth of political power, resulting from our struggles for a united Germany, trade and industry rose to an extent hardly experienced by any nation before. Germany's output in brain work is at the same time greater than that of any other people. Our prominent importance as a civilising nation is plain to everybody after the German clans have joined hands to form one powerful State. We ourselves have become conscious of being a powerful, as well as a necessary, factor in the development of mankind. This knowledge imposes upon us the obligation of asserting our mental and moral influence as much as possible, and of paving the way everywhere in the world for German

the author of *Germany and the Next War*, which went through nine editions between 1912 and 1914. This made clear his belief that Germany needed a war to establish itself as a world power and must make sure she was in a position to win that war. Quoted from *On War of Today* (1911), trs. K. von Donat (London: Hugh Rees, 1912).

labour and German idealism. But we can only carry out successfully these supreme civilising tasks if our humanising efforts are accompanied and supported by increasing *political* power, as evinced by enlarged colonial possessions, extended international commerce, increased influence of Teutonic culture in all parts of the globe, and, above all, by a perfect safeguarding of our political power in Europe.

"Opposed to these efforts are the most powerful States of Europe. . . .

"It is possible that in case of war we will have to face all these enemies single-handed. At least, we must be prepared for this. The Triple Alliance is purely defensive. Neither Austria nor Italy are bound by treaty to support us in all cases of war or under all circumstances. In so far as their own advantage is not touched, they take no interest in Germany's world-politics; and it must at any rate be left an open question whether their statesmen will always be far-sighted enough to make the lasting advantage of their States the pole of their policy even at the risk of a war. We are thus, in all that is essential, dependent on our own strength, and must plainly see that on the power of our defensive forces alone depends, not only our future development, but our very existence as one of the great Powers of Europe.

"It is true the world is dominated today by the idea of war being an antiquated means of policy, unworthy of a civilised nation. The dream of eternal peace has got a hold on vast sections of the community in the Old and particularly in the New World. Whereas, formerly, in addition to Emmanuel Kant, only enthusiasts and visionaries were the champions of universal brotherhood, the Governments of great and powerful States have now seized this idea as well, and are cloaking themselves with the mantle of a superior humanity. The arbitration courts, which the contracting Powers engage to obey, are meant not only to lessen the dangers of war, but to remove them altogether. This is the publicly avowed object of such politics. In reality, it is hardly caused by an ideal love of peace, but is evidently meant to serve quite different political purposes.

"It is obvious that, above all, all *those* States are interested in such treaties, who wish to cover their rear so as to be able to pursue the more undisturbed and ruthlessly their advantages on other parts of the world's stage; and from this argument at once follows that such treaties, where not confined to some distinctly limited spheres of right, are only a disguise for covering other political aims, and are apt to promote just that war, perhaps, which they pretend is their intention to remove.

"We Germans, therefore, must not be deceived by such official efforts to maintain the peace. Arbitration courts must evidently always consider the existing judicial and territorial rights. For a rising State, which has not yet attained the position due to it, which is in urgent need of colonial expansion, and can only accomplish it chiefly at the cost of others, these treaties therefore augur ill at once as being apt to prevent a rearrangement of power. In the face of this widespread peace propaganda, and in opposition to it, *we* must firmly keep in view the fact that no arbitration court in the world can remove and settle any real great tension that exists and is due to a deep-seated national, economical and political antagonism; and that, on the other hand, it is impossible to change the partition of the earth as it now exists in our favour by diplomatic artifices. If we wish to gain the position in the world that is due to us, we must rely on our sword, renounce all weakly visions of peace, and eye the dangers surrounding us with resolute and unflinching courage.

"In the situation we are in, absolutely necessitating an extension of power, and requiring us to force our claims in the face of superior enemies, I think the law of self-preservation ought to have dictated to us an increase of our defensive forces by all means available, so as to throw into the scale at the decisive moment the full strength of our 60,000,000 populace. This we have not considered necessary. Universal service, which formed the basis for our military and political greatness, is the law with us it is true, but we have not enforced it as a matter of fact for a long time, because we shirk the sacrifice we ought to make in the interest of our armed forces and of our future. The further development of our army in proportion with the growth of our population is completely paralysed for the next five years by a law of the Empire. We seem to have forgotten that a policy to be successful must be backed by force, and that on the other hand the physical and moral health of a nation depends on its martial spirit. We have accustomed ourselves to looking upon our armaments as a heavy burden, borne unwillingly, forgetting thereby that the army is the well from which our people constantly draws afresh strength, self-sacrificing spirit and patriotism. In the hour of danger we shall have to pay in blood for what we have neglected in peace, from want of willingness to make some sacrifice.

"But we have to reckon with all these circumstances as given factors. The enmities surrounding us cannot be exercised by diplomacy. Armaments, under modern conditions, cannot be improvised at will the moment they are wanted. It seems impossible to get ahead of our rivals in matters technical. So much more, therefore, must we take care of maintaining spiritual superiority in case of war, and of making good, by will-power on the one hand, and by the skill of our operations on the other, the superiority in material and personnel possessed by our likely adversaries.

"The more we study the nature of the art of war, and the more fully the army is alive to what is essential in war in general, and in the conduct of modern war in particular, the more uniformly and to the point will every portion of our army co-operate in war, and the greater will be the mental and moral superiority we shall gain over our enemies."

19 The State's Search for Peace

But while many observers of international relations in the nineteenth century saw war as a legitimate instrument of state policy – for promoting national interests or winning national independence, for acquiring colonies or for freeing colonies – by the end of the century there was also increasing recognition of its heavy cost, both in blood and treasure. Were the wars which the nationalist writers demanded likely to prove worthwhile? The view came to be expressed by some that their costs outweighed any gains that could conceivably be won. Modern armaments were increasingly complex and expensive. Casualty figures in recent wars had become heavier and heavier. No advantage that could be gained from any future war, it was widely asserted, could conceivably match the price that would have to be paid.

This view was powerfully put forward by Jean Bloch in his book, *The Future of War*, which appeared in 1897. The book won widespread interest and was rapidly translated into other languages. It is thought by some to have inspired the proposal of the Tsar Nicholas II to convene the first Hague Conference two years later. Its six volumes provided a wide-ranging survey of developments in military technology and methods of war and of its human and social consequences. Based largely on an examination of earlier wars of the century, especially those of 1870–1 and 1877–8, it forecast, with considerable accuracy, the form which a future world war might take. Bloch recognised that future wars would be total wars which would involve the entire population, and that the heavy fire-power of highly trained professional forces might increasingly be challenged and counteracted by well-motivated guerrilla forces operating within their home territory (a forecast which the Boer War immediately afterwards seemed to bear out). And he predicted that advances in military technology would involve a huge increase in the cost of armaments, a burden which populations would become less willing to bear at a time when there were so many other urgent tasks requiring government expenditure. Thus the social order in many states could be threatened by the mere cost of preparing for war; and far more by the disruption brought about by war itself. For this reason war could not in practice bring the advantages which those who planned it expected.

A similar message was expressed 15 years later by Norman Angell in his book, *The Great Illusion*, published on the eve of the First World War. The benefits which war had traditionally been thought to procure were in his view illusory. One state could not win the wealth or trade of another as a result of defeating it in war. An acquisition of territory did not increase the industrial production or the standard of living of a people. When Germany had won Alsace-Lorraine, individual Germans had not been made any the richer. Still less could one state, by taking possession of foreign territory, impose its own culture, social institutions, moral conceptions or way of life on another people. If only governments could be made to understand how illusory were the benefits to be had by war, therefore, a radical transformation of international relationships might be brought about.

There was another reason why some believed that war might become less frequent, or even be abolished altogether. This was the idea that governments were becoming everywhere more democratic, and that democratic governments would be more peace-loving than the autocratic and militaristic governments which they replaced. This was a view especially associated with Woodrow Wilson. It was expressed in the brief concluding chapter which he added, at the close of the First World War in 1918, to his book, *The State*, previously published several years earlier. In this brief chapter Wilson (referring to himself in the third person) encapsulates many of the ideas for which he is famous. In his view the most fundamental change taking place as a result of the war was the democratic revolution occurring all over the world, even among the belligerent states. This would reduce the danger of war. Dynastic rivalries would be eliminated, and it would no longer be possible for autocratic rulers to plunge their countries into wars for personal ends. Secret treaties and alliances would be forbidden and disarmament would be brought about. Arbitration would increasingly be used in place of war as a means of resolving differences between states. And the new league of states to enforce peace, shortly to be established, should make war unnecessary or impossible in future. The US itself must support this transformation of international relations, and never again remain neutral in a major European war.

Writings of this character were of course designed to persuade rather than describe. Bloch and Angell genuinely believed that the benefits to be won by war could never match its costs and hoped that by preaching that message to a sufficiently wide audience they would make war less likely to occur. In the same way Wilson genuinely believed that democratic governments were less likely to engage in war than autocratic ones; and perhaps hoped that his writing might make both democracy and peace more probable. In neither case were the injunctions accompanied by any serious study of the way contemporary states in fact behaved or of the motives that led them to seek war – or at least to undertake actions which they knew must risk war. The rationality to be expected of governments is exaggerated by all three writers; the power of nationalist sentiment underestimated. Neither the growing costs of war, in blood even more than in treasure, nor the development of more democratic systems in some European states, were to prove sufficient, whatever they might hope, to abolish warfare from the behaviour pattern of contemporary states.

*   *   *

Bloch – The Costs of War in the Modern Age*

"In recent times war has become even more terrible than before in consequence of perfected weapons of destruction and systems of equipment and training utterly unknown in the past. What is graver still, the immensity of armies and the training of soldiers in entrenchment must call forth difficulties in provisioning and defence from climatic conditions.

•   •   •

"The thought of those convulsions which will be called forth by a war, and of the terrible means prepared for it, will hinder military enterprise, notwithstanding the passionate relations of the people to some of the questions in dispute among them. But on the other hand, the present conditions cannot continue to exist for ever. The peoples groan under the burdens of militarism. Europe is ever confronted

* From Jean Bloch (1836–1902). Polish writer. A railway magnate who only turned his attention to international affairs in later life. Known almost entirely for this influential book, a vast six-volume survey of war over the previous decades. Was convinced that the destructiveness of any future war would be such that there could be no victors. Only the last volume of the book has been translated into English. Quoted from *The Future of War in its Technical, Economic and Political Relations* (1897), trs. R. C. Long (London: Grant Richards, 1899).

with the necessity of drawing from the productive forces of the peoples new and new millions for military purposes. Hardly was the small-calibre rifle adopted when invention made a new advance, and there can be no doubt that soon the Great Powers will be compelled to adopt a weapon of still smaller calibre with double the present energy, allowing soldiers to carry a greater number of cartridges. At the same time we see in France and Germany preparation of new artillery to turn to the best advantage the new smokeless powder. Millions are expended on the construction of new battleships and cruisers. But every year brings such radical improvements in guns, in speed and in coal-carrying capacity that vessels hardly launched are obsolete, and others must be built to replace them. In view of what we see in Germany, Italy and Austria, we are compelled to ask, Can the present incessant demands for money from Parliament for armaments continue for ever without social outbreaks? And will not the present difficulty of carrying on war at last be replaced by an absolute impossibility, at least in those countries where high culture has increased the value of the life of every citizen? Thus, in the war of the future will appear not only quantitative differences in the number of armies but also qualitative differences which may have immense importance.

"But what is still graver are the economic and social convulsions which war will call forth in consequence of the summons under the flag of almost the whole male population, the interruption of maritime communications, the stagnation in industry and trade, the increase in the price of the necessaries of life, and the destruction of credit. Will these convulsions not be so great that governments will find it impossible in the course of time indicated by military specialists as the probable duration of war to acquire means for maintaining their armies, satisfy the requirements of budgets, and at the same time feed the destitute remainder of the civil population?

"Within the last twenty-five years such changes have taken place in the very nature of military operations that the future war will in no way be like its predecessors. In consequence of the adoption of improved artillery, explosive shells and small-arms which allow the soldier to carry an immense number of cartridges, in consequence of the absence of concealing smoke, in consequence of the immense proportions which military operations must take as a result of the vastness of armies, such unquestioned authorities on military affairs as Moltke and Leer and many other eminent military writers declare that a future war will last many years. . . .

"Without acquaintance with the technicalities of warfare it is impossible to understand what will be its precise conditions, or to define the limits where the operation of defined laws will cease and accidental phenomena appear. A result could only be obtained by careful study of the very nature of war in all its phenomena. Twenty years ago such a task would have been comparatively easy. But the last two decades have witnessed immense changes equal to revolutions. First of all a fundamental change has taken place in the very elements which take part in war and from which its course depends. In a future war on the field of battle, instead of professional soldiers, will appear whole peoples with all their peculiar virtues and failings.

"A full appreciation of the conditions of a future war is all the more difficult since on the one hand new methods of attack and defence, as yet insufficiently tested, will be employed, and, on the other hand, because former wars were carried on by means of long-service professional soldiers. But not only will a future war take the character of a struggle of whole nations living a wide and complex life, with military problems corresponding in complexity, but the arms and apparatus of destruction are the very finest result of the inventiveness and creative activity of mankind.

• • •

"That war will become impossible in time – this is indicated by all. Its apparatus grows more rapidly than the productiveness of European states, and preparations will continue to swallow more and more of the income of peoples. Meantime the relations of the nations become closer and closer, their interdependence more plain, and their solidarity in any great convulsion will constantly grow.

"That war will finally become impracticable is apparent. The question is more apposite – when will the recognition of this inevitable truth be spread among European governments and peoples? When the impossibility of resorting to war for the decision of international quarrels is apparent to all, other means will be devised."

Angell – The Illusory Benefits of Military Victory*

"What are the fundamental motives that explain the present rivalry of armaments in Europe, notably the Anglo-German? Each nation

* From Norman Angell (1872–1967). English political writer and politician. Travelled in the US for several years before settling in Paris as a journalist. This experience

pleads the need for defence; but this implies that someone is likely to attack, and has therefore a presumed interest in so doing. What are the motives which each State thus fears its neighbours may obey?

"They are based on the universal assumption that a nation, in order to find outlets for expanding population and increasing industry, or simply to ensure the best conditions possible for its people, is necessarily pushed to territorial expansion and the exercise of political force against others (German naval competition is assumed to be the expression of the growing need of an expanding population for a larger place in the world, a need which will find a realization in the conquest of English Colonies or trade, unless these were defended); it is assumed, therefore, that a nation's relative prosperity is broadly determined by its political power; that nations being competing units, advantage, in the last resort, goes to the possessor of preponderant military force, the weaker going to the wall, as in the other forms of the struggle for life.

The author challenges this whole doctrine. He attempts to show that it belongs to a stage of development out of which we have passed; that the commerce and industry of a people no longer depend upon the expansion of its political frontiers; that a nation's political and economic frontiers do not now necessarily coincide; that military power is socially and economically futile, and can have no relation to the prosperity of the people exercising it; that it is impossible for one nation to seize by force the wealth or trade of another – to enrich itself by subjugating, or imposing its will by force on another; that, in short, war, even when victorious, can no longer achieve those aims for which peoples strive.

"He establishes this apparent paradox, in so far as the economic problem is concerned, by showing that wealth in the economically civilised world is founded upon credit and commercial contract (these being the outgrowth of an economic interdependence due to the increasing division of labour and greatly developed communication). If credit and commercial contract are tampered with in an attempt of confiscation, the credit-dependent wealth is undermined, and its collapse involves that of the conqueror; so that if conquest is not to

encouraged a cosmopolitan approach set out in his first work *Patriotism Under Three Flags* (1903). *The Great Illusion* was rejected by many publishers and was originally published privately (under the title *Europe's Optical Illusion*). However it soon caught the attention of the public, was translated into many languages and sold over a million copies. A strong supporter of the League of Nations, he was for a short time a Labour Member of Parliament. Awarded the Nobel Peace Prize in 1933. Quoted from *The Great Illusion* (London: Heinemann, 1909).

be self-injurious it must respect the enemy's property, in which case it becomes economically futile. Thus the wealth of conquered territory remains in the hands of the population of such territory. When Germany annexed Alsatia, no individual German secured a single mark's worth of Alsatian property as the spoils of war. Conquest in the modern world is a process of multiplying by x, and then obtaining the original result by dividing by x. For a modern nation to add to its territory no more adds to the wealth of the people of such nation than it would add to the wealth of Londoners if the City of London were to annex the county of Hertford.

"The author also shows that international finance has become so interdependent and so interwoven with trade and industry that the intangibility of an enemy's property extends to his trade. It results that political and military power can in reality do nothing for trade; the individual merchants and manufacturers of small nations, exercising no such power, compete successfully with those of the great. Swiss and Belgian merchants drive English from the British Colonial market; Norway has, relatively to population, a greater mercantile marine than Great Britain; the public credit (as a rough-and-ready indication, among others, of security and wealth) of small States possessing no political power often stands higher than that of the Great Powers of Europe, Belgian Three per Cents standing at 96, and German at 82; Norwegian Three and a Half per Cents at 102, and Russian Three and a Half per Cents at 81."

"The forces which have brought about the economic futility of military power have also rendered it futile as a means of enforcing a nation's moral ideals or imposing social institutions upon a conquered people. Germany could not turn Canada or Australia into German colonies – i.e., stamp out their language, law, literature, traditions, etc. – by 'capturing' them. The necessary security in their material possessions enjoyed by the inhabitants of such conquered provinces, quick inter-communication by a cheap press, widely-read literature, enable even small communities to become articulate and effectively defend their special social or moral possessions, even when military conquest has been complete. The fight for ideals can no longer take the form of fight between nations, because the lines of division on moral questions are within the nations themselves and intersect the political frontiers. There is no modern State which is completely Catholic or Protestant, or liberal or autocratic, or aristocratic or democratic, or socialist or individualist; the moral and spiritual struggles of the modern world go on as between citizens of the same State in unconscious intellectual co-operation with corresponding groups in other States, not as between the public powers of rival States.

"This classification by strata involves necessarily a redirection of human pugnacity, based rather on the rivalry of classes and interests than on State divisions. War has no longer the justification that it makes for the survival of the fittest; it involves the survival of the less fit. The idea that the struggle between nations is a part of the evolutionary law of man's advance involves a profound misreading of the biological analogy.

"The warlike nations do not inherit the earth; they represent the decaying human element. The diminishing role of physical force in all spheres of human activity carries with it profound psychological modifications.

"These tendencies, mainly the outcome of purely modern conditions (rapidity of communication), have rendered the problems of modern international politics profoundly and essentially different from the ancient; yet our ideas are still dominated by the principles and axioms, images and terminology of the old.

"The author urges that these little-recognised facts may be utilised for the solution of the armament difficulty on at present untried lines – by such modification of opinion in Europe that much of the present motive to aggression will cease to be operative, and by thus diminishing the risk of attack, diminish by that much the need for defence. He shows how such a political reformation is within the scope of practical politics, and the methods which should be employed to bring it about."

Wilson – The Coming Age of Peace*

"The governments of all the powers actively participating in the war have experienced important changes. Germany, Austria-Hungary

---

* From Woodrow Wilson (1856–1924). President of the United States from 1916 to 1920. The 14 points which he proposed as the principles which should underlie a peace settlement after the First World War were largely implemented in the Treaty of Versailles. Strongly supported US membership of the League of Nations, which was however rejected by the US Senate. The approach to foreign affairs with which he is mainly associated is summarised in the passage quoted here. Quoted from *The State*, special rev. edn (New York: D. C. Heath, 1918).

and Russia are in the midst of revolution; in place of kingdoms and empires, republics have been proclaimed; in place of autocracy, democracy has been enthroned. The governments of the other belligerent countries have not escaped the growing sense of popular supremacy, but have everywhere been brought into closer contact with the people.

"An important result of these changes will be a greater unity among the states of the world; competing forms of government, with their different ideals, will, we believe, be replaced by governments organised on the common basis of popular representation and control: dynastic rivalries will no longer vex the world with wars nor will it be possible again for ambitious rulers to plunge the world into warfare for the accomplishment of their personal ends. A surer basis for peace has been laid in the common and universal control of governments by their peoples.

"Though it be true that democratic government will make wars less likely, it will not eliminate all causes of conflict between nations, and if the enormous sacrifices of this war are not to be made in vain, not merely must democracy triumph in the individual states, but in the society of states as well.

"The development of modern democracy has meant two things: equality of rights and the assurance of those rights through popular control of government. Within the individual states special privilege has steadily been replaced by equality of all men before the law, and the right of a few to administer government as their private possession has made way for the conception that the whole people has the right to direct government for the welfare of all. To put it in another way, democracy may be regarded as the realisation of human rights through the agency of government in channels determined by the popular will.

"In the field of international relations all states have been regarded theoretically as equal; this has been the basis upon which international law has rested, yet outside the realm of theory this equality has been confronted by a doctrine of state action directly in conflict with it. The modern state is a territorial state and in the realm of international politics the possession or lack of territory has largely determined the influence and importance of states. Consequently the acquisition of territory came to be regarded as a necessity in the expansion of national life. But new territory could be acquired only at the expense of some other power. Here was a frequent source of animosities and wars. In this struggle for territory no small state could successfully compete, but worse still no small state could feel itself safe from the menace of imperialism. Moreover every large state was jealous of the extension of the power of every other and each bit of territory brought within the control of one, excited both the antagonism and the greed of every other whose relative position of power and influence was thereby affected. The logical result was deep-seated distrust and a fear of being overreached, accompanied by standing armies and powerful navies on whose existence the peace of Europe was said to depend. Over against this whole conception of armed imperialism there arose the movement to do away with armies and navies and the oppressive tax burdens which they uselessly imposed. Many different motives animated the people who sympathised with this idea; some adhered to it out of antagonism to war as in itself a brutal and unreasonable thing; some because they desired to see the expenditures hitherto directed to preparation for war diverted to improving the social well-being of humanity.

"The stages in the development of this idea are clearly marked by the means which were to replace war in the settlement of international difficulties. Following the adjustment of the Alabama claims by arbitration at Geneva in 1871, this method of settlement was eagerly taken up and pressed upon the attention of the world. The First Hague Conference in 1899, summoned to consider the question of disarmament and heralded as a Peace Conference, was unable to agree upon any measures whatever looking toward disarmament, but in behalf of peace it adopted a plan providing a general scheme of arbitration and a so-called permanent court of arbitration available for any states desiring to make use of it. The establishment of the permanent court of arbitration was received as a great achievement and stimulated to renewed activity those who looked upon arbitration as the means by which peace could be maintained. Numerous arbitration treaties were concluded but as they almost universally excluded questions touching national honour and interests, little was accomplished by them.

"Arbitration, moreover, did not seem adequate to many who were seeking a peaceful settlement of international disputes and the judicial settlement of such disputes was advocated by individuals and societies. At the Second Hague Conference in 1907 an international prize court was provided but due to a failure to agree upon the law which this court should enforce, it remained a dead letter. Finally in 1914 the great European conflict, so long anticipated, became a reality through the wanton aggression of Germany and Austria. The doctrine of imperialism became in the hands of Germany a demand for 'a place in the sun', a demand for a conquest as the right of the strong over the weak, as the supremacy of might over right, and a determination to extend her boundaries and acquire territory at the expense of her neighbours and in utter disregard of international law, of right, and of humanity. The sentiment aroused in the United States by Germany's violation of the neutrality of Belgium in complete disregard of solemn treaty obligations, the terrible atrocities committed by her armed forces upon the civilian population of Belgium and northern France, her defiance and disregard of neutral rights, and the menace of her conduct to the existence of the society of states led to the establishment of a society for the advocacy of a League to Enforce Peace. The fundamental principle of the society was to secure the establishment among the nations of a League, the members of which would bind themselves to use economic pressure or military force against any state which should go to war without first resorting to peaceful means, including arbitration, for the settlement of the difficulty. It was the application to the society of nations of the principle in force in every individual state. The law-breaker who violates the rights of another finds the combined force of the society arrayed against him.

"The success of such a League must depend upon the whole-hearted acceptance by its members of the obligations it imposes. The small states will find in it a source of protection that will free them from the fear of aggression and conquest and their acceptance of it may naturally be anticipated; but the large and powerful states will be equally benefited through the prevention of a repetition of another world war. It will mean, however, a certain limitation upon their freedom of action; they must renounce any claim to overcome the weaker by their superior strength, and they must forgo the right in any dispute to resort straightway to force; they must be prepared to use their power in behalf of the established law though their own rights be not immediately endangered. Secret treaties and alliances must be forbidden, and disarmament be brought about.

"President Wilson has declared that the United States can never again be a neutral in a great European war. The world has become too closely knit together for us to pursue in the future the policy of isolation.

"The hope of such a League and the possibility of its realisation have been immeasurably advanced by the destruction of autocracy and the universal establishment of democracy."

20 The State's Search for Power

The world that came into being after the end of the First World War seemed to belie Woodrow Wilson's optimistic forecast. The majority of governments were not democratic. The intentions of many appeared far from peaceful. And as a result, in the years between the wars there was a reaction away from the idealistic viewpoint which Wilson had propounded among students of international relations.

Especially after the rise of the dictators in Europe most of the writing which appeared on the subject was sceptical about the chances of establishing a more co-operative international system. Writers of the period saw little evidence that most governments had a natural inclination towards peace. They were especially concerned that a failure to recognise the motives underlying states' actions could induce the false responses of isolationism or appeasement. These writers were therefore concerned to quench the romantic idea that, if only states became more democratic, or if only alliances and secret diplomacy could be abolished, war could quickly be banished from the earth. They placed heavy emphasis on the self-interested, power-seeking and sometimes aggressive character of state action. And they thus became increasingly inclined to identify international relations with "power politics" (as the title of many of the best-known books of the period bears witness).

The most prominent feature of all these writings is the bald assertion that the search for "power" is the dominant motive influencing state actions. This is a contention which is to be found, in only slightly varying forms, among all of these writers. So, for example, among the extracts given below, Schuman holds that all foreign policy is "an expression of the state's will for power"; Schwarzenberger calls power "the overriding consideration in international relations"; Morgenthau believes that "statesmen think and act in terms of interest defined as power"; and even Carr (who only by virtue of his firm rejection of utopianism can be said to belong to this group) believes that "the attempt to ignore power as a decisive factor in every political situation is purely utopian".

What exactly did such writers understand by "power"? Given the importance they attributed to the concept there is surprisingly little

271

agreement among them about its meaning. Often there is little attempt to define it at all. Some imply that it is *armed* power which is meant; others a general capacity to coerce or exert influence on other states. Nor is it always clear if power is important to states as a means, or desired as an end in itself. Even when it is recognised that it is usually a means to other ends, it is held to be so overwhelmingly the most important means that it becomes the overriding aim of state policy.

But are states all alike in this respect? One of the somewhat surprising features of these writings is that there is little attempt to distinguish, either between particular states or between groups or types of states. Statements are made in highly generalised terms and without qualifications. Writing, as they were, in the 1930s and 1940s they might, one could have supposed, have noted that some states of the time – Germany, Italy and Japan, for example – appeared particularly determined to increase their own power and to resolve disputes on that basis, while others (for example those pursuing policies of appeasement or isolationism) showed little inclination of that kind, and appeared on the contrary to downplay the power factor to the maximum extent possible in their international relationships. Sometimes indeed, it would appear it was precisely the failure of those countries to recognise the importance of power which stimulated these writers to emphasise their importance. In other words, such writings were, in their own way, as much influenced by normative intentions as those which they denounced. The emphasis on power was not so much descriptive as prescriptive: it contained an implied rebuke to those statesmen who had underestimated its role in the past and so allowed other states which had not done so to secure their ends by the use of threat or force.

A second feature of this kind of writing is that, in a warlike era, it concentrated on one particular feature of international relationships and ignored all others. It took little account of the fact that in the greater part of international relations – political, cultural and economic – the power balance is largely irrelevant. It was not the case, for example, that when the Canadian government discussed matters of national interest with the US, or France with Britain, or Denmark with Sweden, the outcome of their discussions was mainly determined by the power relationship between the two. Between those countries, and indeed the great majority of states, power factors rarely came into account. And even among potentially hostile states it was only on particular issues – though admittedly highly important ones – that the power-balance became of substantial importance. Yet these writers were insistent on describing international relationships in terms of a "universal quest for power" or the "universality of violence in international politics" (in the words of Schuman), or of the invariable desire to promote "interests defined in terms of power" (in the words of Morgenthau).

Another implication of most of these writings is that "morality" has little or no part to play in international relations. This is stated most categorically by Niebuhr, who suggests in the passage below that state action is by its nature self-interested action and that it is wrong-headed to apply to it the moral standards that are applied to relations among individuals. Schuman equally contrasts relationships within the state, where there is a "constitutional consensus", and where therefore differences can be resolved by peaceful, consti- tutional means, and those *between* states for which, he holds, co- ercion is the accepted means of resolving disputes. In the same way Schwarzenberger maintains that in international societies the "law of the lowest level" operates, so that all must be in a position to protect themselves against the most aggressive and anti-social of their mem- bers. Morgenthau, while recognising that political action can have moral significance, holds that there is an "ineluctable tension" be- tween moral commands and the requirements of successful political action. Only Carr explicitly asserts the need to establish a "new morality" in international behaviour (which he sees in the develop- ment of international co-operation for economic purposes). This is an excessively cynical approach and it is a reasonable criticism of these writers that, rather than present a positive international morality to replace the immorality which they perceive in traditional state action, they are inclined to suggest that the aggressive and self-interested behaviour they describe can never be changed: and, even more, that any attempt to apply moral considerations to the action of states is itself wrong-headed.

All these writers, therefore, bear the marks of the age in which they lived. Seeing the devastating effects of power politics as prac- tised in their own day, and concerned at the folly of those who underestimated its consequences, they tended to see that phenom- enon as the essential and universal reality of international relations, and the search for power as the characteristic feature of all state action. Since their writing became highly influential in the world that emerged after 1945 they stamped this particular belief about the nature of states on to the minds of many who exercised power in the postwar age.

* * *

Niebuhr – The Amorality of States*

"The selfishness of nations is proverbial. It was a dictum of George Washington that nations were not to be trusted beyond their own interest. 'No state', declares a German author, 'has ever entered a treaty for any other reason than self interest', and adds: 'A statesman who has any other motive would deserve to be hung.' 'In every part of the world', said Professor Edward Dicey, 'where British interests are at stake, I am in favour of advancing these interests even at the cost of war. The only qualification I admit is that the country we desire to annex or take under our protection should be calculated to confer a tangible advantage upon the British Empire.' National ambitions are not always avowed as honestly as this, as we shall see later, but that is a fair statement of the actual facts, which need hardly to be elaborated for any student of history.

"What is the basis and reason for the selfishness of nations? If we begin with what is least important or least distinctive of national attitudes, it must be noted that nations do not have direct contact with other national communities, with which they must form some kind of international community. They know the problems of other peoples only indirectly and at second hand. Since both sympathy and justice depend to a large degree upon the perception of need, which makes sympathy flow, and upon the understanding of competing interests, which must be resolved, it is obvious that human communities have greater difficulty than individuals in achieving ethical relationships. While rapid means of communication have increased the

---

* From R. Niebuhr (1892–1962). US protestant theologian. Exponent of the "new theology" which sought to restate Christian teaching in a form relevant to contemporary concerns. Although his humanism dictated a relatively liberal approach to social problems at home, this was combined with an ultra-cynical view of international affairs. Other principal works are *The Nature and Destiny of Man* (1941–3) and *Faith and History* (1949). Quoted from *Moral Man and Immoral Society* (New York: Charles Scribner's Sons, 1932).

breadth of knowledge about world affairs among citizens of various nations, and the general advance of education has ostensibly promoted the capacity to think rationally and justly upon the inevitable conflicts of interest between nations, there is nevertheless little hope of arriving at a perceptible increase of international morality through the growth of intelligence and the perfection of means of communication. The development of international commerce, the increased economic interdependence among the nations, and the whole apparatus of a technological civilisation, increase the problems and issues between nations much more rapidly than the intelligence to solve them can be created. . . .

" . . . There is an ethical paradox in patriotism which defies every but the most astute and sophisticated analysis. The paradox is that patriotism transmutes individual unselfishness into national egoism. Loyalty to the nation is a high form of altruism when compared with lesser loyalties and more parochial interests. It therefore becomes the vehicle of all the altruistic impulses and expresses itself, on occasion, with such fervour that the critical attitude of the individual toward the nation and its enterprises is almost completely destroyed.

"The unqualified character of this devotion is the very basis of the nation's power and of the freedom to use the power without moral restraint. Thus the unselfishness of individuals makes for the selfishness of nations. That is why the hope of solving the larger social problems of mankind, merely by extending the social sympathies of individuals, is so vain. Altruistic passion is sluiced into the reservoirs of nationalism with great ease, and is made to flow beyond them with great difficulty. What lies beyond the nation, the community of mankind, is too vague to inspire devotion. The lesser communities within the nation, religious, economic, racial and cultural, have equal difficulty in competing with the nation for the loyalty of its citizens. The church was able to do so when it had the prestige of a universality it no longer possesses. Future developments may make the class rather than the nation the community of primary loyalty. But for the present the nation is still supreme. It not only possesses a police power, which other communities lack, but it is able to avail itself of the most potent and vivid symbols to impress its claims upon the consciousness of the individual. Since it is impossible to become conscious of a large social group without adequate symbolism this factor is extremely important. The nation possesses in its organs of government, in the panoply and ritual of the state, in the impressive display of its fighting services, and, very frequently, in the splendours of a royal house, the symbols of unity and greatness, which inspire awe and reverence in the citizen. Furthermore the love and pious attachment of a man to his countryside, to familiar scenes, sights and experiences, around which the memories of youth have cast a halo of sanctity, all this flows into the sentiment of patriotism; for a simple imagination transmutes the universal beneficences of nature into symbols of the peculiar blessings which a benevolent nation bestows upon its citizens. Thus the sentiment of patriotism achieves a potency in the modern soul, so unqualified, that the nation is given *carte blanche* to use the power, compounded of the devotion of individuals, for any purpose it desires. Thus, to choose an example among hundreds, Mr Lloyd George during the famous Agadir Crisis in 1911 in which a European war became imminent, because marauding nations would not allow a new robber to touch their spoils in Africa, could declare in his Mansion House speech: 'If a situation were to be forced upon us in which peace could only be preserved by the surrender of the great and beneficent position Britain has won by centuries of heroism and achievement, by allowing Britain to be treated, when her interests were vitally affected, as if she were of no account in the cabinet of nations, then I say emphatically that peace at that price would be a humiliation intolerable for a great country like ours to endure.' The very sensitive 'honour' of nations can always be appeased by the blood of its citizens and no national ambition seems too base or petty to claim and to receive the support of a majority of its patriots.

"Unquestionably there is an alloy of projected self-interest in patriotic altruism. The man in the street, with his lust for power and prestige thwarted by his own limitations and the necessities of social life, projects his *ego* upon his nation and indulges his anarchic lusts vicariously. So the nation is at one and the same time a check upon, and a final vent for, the expression of individual egoism."

Schuman – The State's Will to Power*

"Foreign policy is an expression of a State's will-to-power. States consist of sundry millions of patriots who obey the leaders who

---

* From F. L. Schuman (1904–   ). Teacher of international relations in Chicago University and Williams College. Interested in comparative government, diplomacy

decide how and when and where power is to be pursued and against whom and with whom. Leaders in democracies are elected representatives answerable to their followers and periodically subject to reelection or retirement. They therefore find it difficult to practise *Realpolitik*, for they are impeded not only by the stubborn facts of the international environment to which they must adapt their ends and means, but also by the desires and hopes and illusions of masses of voters who know little of the subtleties of diplomacy. Leaders in autocracies are more free because their followers are less free. They may often say, with Louis XIV, '*L'État, c'est moi!*' ('The State? That's me!'). They may play the game of power abroad with no checks at home so long as they win successes or at least avoid disasters.

• • •

"This universal quest for power goes on under the conditions imposed by the nature of the State system and by the technological differentials between its members. Each State left to itself tends to extend its power over as wide a sphere as possible. Its power flows outward from a central nucleus in all directions. It is directed toward control of territory and people. If the ruling class of the State is an agrarian aristocracy, as in most of the States of the ancient world, control over territory and people is sought in order that the agricultural resources of the territory may be utilised to the profit of the conquerors, and the labour power of the people may be exploited through slavery or serfdom. If the ruling class is a commercial bourgeoisie, as in Western Europe between the sixteenth and nineteenth centuries, conquests are sought in order that the import and export trade of the region conquered may be monopolised. If it is an industrial and financial bourgeoisie, as in the twentieth century Western world, commodity and investment markets are sought – and they may be obtained by methods of control more subtle and indirect than open conquest and annexation. If the revolutionary proletariat is in power, as in the Soviet Union, it may seek conquests in order to extend the scope of the revolution and weaken the power of its enemies. If the élite, as in the Fascist States, is a war-driven and power-hungry brotherhood, recruited from middle-class outcasts, the objective of action is glory and conquest as ends which justify all means thereto. These purposes are rationalised, disguised, modified

and political psychology. Known mainly for his *International Politics* (1934) which was influential in the interwar period. Quoted from *International Politics* (1934), 3rd edn (New York: McGraw-Hill, 1941).

and supplemented by others, in accordance with the attitudes and sentiments of the ruling group. But the enhancement of State power is always the goal. The will-to-power necessarily expresses itself in economic terms, both because political control is often sought as a means of economic exploitation and because territories and populations are useful for the further enhancement of power only when their resources and energies are harnessed to the victor's chariot.

"In a State system in which the sovereign units are engaged in a constant competitive struggle, power is at all times a relative quantity. In a world of one State, power considerations would disappear unless that State were threatened by internal revolution or barbarian incursions. A State existing in complete isolation from all other States would have no 'power interests', for such interests grow out of contact, competition, and conflict among States. The 'power' of a State is a meaningless concept except in relation to the power of other States. The power of each State, moreover, is significant only in relation to the other Powers with which it is in geographical proximity. The power of Italy is important as compared with the power of Germany, Spain or Great Britain, but not of much importance as compared with the power of Japan, Bolivia or Afghanistan, for normally Italian power will not come into contact with Powers so far away. The power of the United States is important in relation to the power of Cuba, Nicaragua, Mexico and Great Britain, but not important ordinarily in relation to the Soviet Union, Nepal or Iraq, for it cannot be exercised effectively in such remote places. The power of lesser States has meaning only in relation to their immediate neighbors. Power has meaning only as against other Powers which can be reached by it.

• • •

"The Western State system has developed in such fashion that no one of its members possesses at any time sufficient power to extend its control over all the others. In the interests of self-defence, the members tend to combine against any one which is a potential menace to all. Invariably the pretender to world power is repressed by a coalition of the prospective victims. Each Power thus retains its independence, and the State System is preserved. Under these circumstances, an equilibrium or balance of power results. Any enhancement of the power of one State is a disturbance of the equilibrium and a potential threat to the others. At times this equilibrium is intangible, imponderable and in the background of diplomatic action. At other times, and more frequently, it is clearly and sharply defined in alliances and coalitions. Each member of an alliance has an interest in forestalling any enhancement of the power of some member of the opposing alliance. The two coalitions or groupings of Powers are thus held together by common power interests, and conflicts for power become issues between the alliances as a whole. This pattern of power relationships has characterised the Western State system from its earliest beginnings.

"The role of small States in this system of relationships is a peculiar one. The very minute States of Europe are historical curiosities and play no part in Power relationships. But such States as Portugal, Belgium, the Netherlands, Denmark, Switzerland, Albania and the like, are all adjacent to infinitely more powerful States which could easily impose their will upon them and extinguish their independence if granted a free hand. In some cases, this has happened: Ireland was conquered by England in the middle ages; Poland was partitioned among her great neighbours at the end of the eighteenth century; the Low Countries, Poland and two of the Scandinavian Kingdoms are at the time of writing under the conqueror's heel. But usually this result is rendered impossible by the conflicting power interests of the great States themselves. The small States, being impotent, have no power interests of their own save the preservation of their independence; and this they are able to protect, not by their own power, but by fitting themselves into the power relations of their mighty neighbours. The small States are often 'buffers'. They stand at the focal points of tension between the Great Powers, with the result that each Power prefers the maintenance of the independence of the small State to the extinction of that independence at the hands of a rival Power.

• • •

"That the assumption of violence lies behind all diplomacy is a truism which would be too obvious to dwell upon, were it not so frequently forgotten, often with disastrous results, in piping times of peace. Diplomatic bargaining and armed coercion are complementary weapons in the struggle for power among the nation-states. In the Western State system, as in all the state systems which have preceded it, military force has ever been the decisive means by which State power has been created, increased, reduced, or destroyed. The competitive struggle for hegemony and survival in which States have always engaged has been carried on from time immemorial through the clash of fighting soldiery and ships of war. The 'Gallery of Battles' in the great palace at Versailles, depicting the combats by which the

French nation was created and its power enhanced, could be duplicated for every sovereign State of the world. The world historical drama of international politics is a pageant of strife. Assyrians descend like the wolf on the fold. Hittite and Egyptian war chariots clash on the Mediterranean shore. Greek triremes ram Persian fighting ships at Salamis. Macedonian phalanxes conquer a world empire. The war elephants of Hannibal charge the legions of Rome. The hosts of the Caesars conquer a vast realm embracing all of Classical civilisation. Barbarian hordes overwhelm the Roman world State. Feudal knights and barons fight one another and battle the infidels. Mercenary armies of ambitious monarchs carve out nations. Popular armies of the nation-states engage in intermittent conflicts for power. The mechanised war monsters of the machine age ride roughshod over Africa and Asia and cover with blood and destruction the fields of Flanders and Galicia, Picardy and Lombardy, Manchuria and Ethiopia.

"This universality of violence in international politics has been explained by numberless commentators in terms of original sin, the punishments of Providence, the machinations of the devil, the 'fighting instinct' of man, the cry for bread, the periodical reversion of *homo sapiens* to savagery, etc. Though certain of these explanations have suggestive value, it is perhaps more relevant to recall that international politics is essentially a competitive struggle for power among sovereign members of State systems. War is an incident of this struggle. Military violence is the ultimate means resorted to by States in their pursuit of power. The present problem is not that of explaining why men fight in general, but why States habitually resort to force in their differences with one another. All politics is a struggle for power, but in the domestic or national arenas recourse is had to violence only rarely. In international politics, on the contrary, violence or threatened violence is customary. War is to international politics what revolution is to national politics: a resort to physical coercion to achieve political objectives, i.e., to preserve the power of the user against attack, to enhance that power at the expense of a rival, to upset an established equilibrium of power, or to prevent it from being upset."

Schwarzenberger – The State's Pursuit of Power*

" . . . [P]ower politics may be defined as a system of international relations in which groups consider themselves as ultimate ends; use, at least for vital purposes, the most effective means at their disposal and are graded according to their weight in case of conflict. If a system of power politics is not actually replaced by an international community proper but continues on the same basis as before in the cloak of a community, such a state of affairs may be described as a system of *power politics in disguise.*

"So far, power has been the overriding consideration in international relations. *Power* is the mean between influence and force. All three are different ways of establishing a social nexus on a footing regarded as desirable by the active agent in such relations. Power distinguishes itself, however, from *influence* by reliance on external pressure as a background threat, and from *force* by preference for achieving its ends without the actual use of physical pressure. Thus, *power* may be defined as capacity to impose one's will on others by reliance on effective sanctions in case of non-compliance.

"It follows that power is both a subjective and relative phenomenon. The exercise of power may be tempered by reason. Yet this is accidental. The essence of power is the ability to exercise compelling pressure irrespective of its reasonableness. If the group or individual passively involved in the power nexus submits to pressure, this is due to a desire to avoid disagreeable consequences of resistance. The presence, if only in the background, of the means to give effect to demands, possibly including the application of physical force, is the silent threat and sanction behind power politics. It explains situations in which, irrespective of the rights or wrongs of a case, one side obtains what it wants and the other accepts what it must. It is irrelevant whether a State uses power for its own sectional ends or for purposes it believes to be in the interest of international society. So long as States insist on being judges in their own cause, the borderline between power and law, too, must remain fluid. Nor does power

---

* From G. Schwarzenberger (1908–). Educated at Heidelberg, Berlin and other universities. Became Reader in international law at London University and, from 1962, Professor. Author of a number of books on international law and international affairs, including *A Manual of International Law* (1947), *The Fundamental Principles of International Law* (1955) and *The Legality of Nuclear Weapons* (1958). Quoted from *Power Politics* (London: Stevens, 1941).

politics necessarily cease to be such because it happens to be institutionalised. Each individual case must be separately examined to
discover whether an international institution is merely an organ in a
system of power politics in disguise, or exercises controlled power
freely delegated by its members.

"In this context, it is also appropriate to explain the terminology in
which the hierarchies of international society are expressed. The
international aristocracy stands for the sum total of sovereign States,
big and small alike. The *international oligarchy* is limited to the inner
ring of the great Powers inside the international aristocracy, and the
rest of the players are viewed as minor members of the international
cast.

• • •

"Is it implied in speaking of a system of power politics, that the
courses of action in such an environment are rigidly determined? This
question can be answered adequately only on the basis of a full
analysis of the mechanics of power politics. Yet some preliminary
guidance may be ventured on the scope for individual personality in
such an environment. Some historians tend to convey that personality is the most important single factor in international affairs. Others
consider that men in governmental positions as elsewhere are so
conditioned by their surroundings and the functions they are called
upon to fulfil that personality matters relatively little.

"It appears to be impossible to answer the question one way or the
other without far-reaching qualifications. It is arguable that, without
Napoleon and Lenin, the French and Russian Revolutions would
have taken entirely different courses. It may be thought that, without
Hitler, there would never have been a Second World War; that,
without Churchill and Roosevelt, Germany might have achieved
world domination. Equally tenable propositions are that, without
Napoleon and Lenin, the social forces of which these men were the
spearheads would have thrown up other leaders, and that these
would have worked with more or less success towards the same ends;
that, in the social and mental state pervading post-1919 Germany, the
German people would have been equally mesmerised by any other
demagogue of a sufficiently demoniac character, or that Churchill
and Roosevelt were as successful as they were because they had the
vision to make actual the potential world balance of power and acted
with truer insight into the workings of world power politics.

• • •

"Such an approach to international relations is supported by the experience that, in a system of power politics, the permanent interests of Powers, and especially of great Powers, are remarkably stable. Leaders such as Napoleon or Hitler may fly in their face and even be temporarily successful in doing so. They may choose to make use of their freedom of action and lead their nations into the abyss. Yet whatever misery such extravagances may bring to millions, their long-range significance is limited. In the end, with a great deal of unnecessary sacrifice, France achieved in nineteenth-century Europe a position which, without Napoleon, she could have had for the asking at any time. Hitler may have succeeded in undoing Bismarck's work for generations, but he has merely thrust on the world Powers the responsibility to find a substitute, which, in the heart of Europe, can fulfil the functions formerly fulfilled by Germany. On the surface, no greater contrast exists than between tsarist Russia and the Soviet Union. Yet it is possible to see in Stalin and Khrushchev the executors of Peter the Great's political testament. Thus, as long as nations are aware of their permanent interests, and their rulers act in accordance with them, it is probably wise for purposes of a sociological interpretation of international relations not to overestimate the role of personality in international affairs.

"Reflections of this kind may also put us on guard against attempts to explain international affairs in terms of the good and bad motives, or the greater or lesser wisdom, of the chief actors on the international scene. It is hard for any observer to judge motives with any degree of accuracy. How many stupidities have been committed for the best of motives, and how often has vice engendered virtuous deeds. Similarly, what does it matter if a foreign minister does the right thing for his country for a silly reason? Erasmus may have been right when he thought that the whole proceedings of the world were but a continuous scene of folly. But it appears to make little difference whether we proceed on this or the opposite assumption and grant to all concerned the benefit of the best intentions and the maximum of intelligence. There is eternal truth in the advice: 'You shall know them by their fruits.' Let men be judged by their actions rather than by their words and let results speak for themselves.

"Power politics has been a constant feature of international relations throughout the ages. It appears therefore prima facie justifiable to work on the assumption *plus ça change, plus c'est la même chose*. This is not meant to imply that because international relations have been – and are – conducted on this footing, they must always remain in undeviating grooves. Men are free to organise any type of relations, whether they be personal or of a group character, on a society or community basis. Yet even in smaller communities, such as clubs, churches or universities, some are in key positions and have greater freedom than others of influencing the community or society character of relations in their group. Thus, in international society the willingness of small States or middle Powers to raise international society to a community level counts for little if the world Powers are not able or willing to change their approach to international relations."

Wight – Power Politics*

"Power politics is a colloquial phrase for international politics. . . . It has the merit of pointing to a central truth about international relations, even if it gets certain other things out of focus. For, whatever else it may suggest, 'power politics' suggests the relationship between independent powers, and we take such a state of affairs for granted. It implies two conditions. First, there are independent political units acknowledging no political superior, and claiming to be 'sovereign'; and secondly, there are continuous and organised relations between them. This is the modern states-system. We have the independent units, which we call states, nations, countries or *powers*, and we have a highly organised system of continuous relationships between them, political and economic, diplomacy and commerce, now peace, now war.

• • •

"The power that makes a 'power' is composed of many elements. Its basic components are size of population, strategic position and geographical extent, and economic resources and industrial production. To these must be added less tangible elements like administrative and financial efficiency, education and technological skill, and above all moral cohesion. Powers which have declined from former

* From Martin Wight (1913–72). On the staff of the Royal Institute of International Affairs for a number of years between 1936 and 1949; Reader in International Relations at London University from 1949 to 1961; Professor of International Relations at Sussex University from 1961 to 1972. Author of studies of colonial government and of *Systems of States* (1977). Joint editor (with H. Butterfield) of *Diplomatic Investigations* (1966). Quoted from *Power Politics* (London: Royal Institute of International Affairs, 1946).

greatness, like Britain or France, or which have not attained great power, like India, naturally emphasise the value of political maturity and moral leadership, though these phrases are more likely to carry weight within their own frontiers than beyond. In times of international tranquillity these imponderables can have great influence. Nevertheless, just as in domestic politics influence is not government, so in international politics influence is not power. It is concrete power in the end that settles great international issues.

'When men dislike Bismarck for his realism, what they really dislike is reality. Take his most famous sentence: "The great questions of our time will not be settled by resolutions and majority votes – that was the mistake of the men of 1848 and 1849 – but by blood and iron." Who can deny that this is true as a statement of fact? What settled the question of Nazi domination of Europe – resolutions or the allied armies? What will settle the question of Korea – majority votes at Lake Success or American strength? This is a very different matter from saying that principles and beliefs are ineffective. They can be extremely effective if translated into blood and iron and not simply into resolutions and majority votes.'[1]

"The moral cohesion of powers is often spoken of in terms of nationality or nationalism. But this can cause confusion, since these words have several meanings. First, in its oldest sense, a nation means a people supposed to have a common descent and organised under a common government. Here the word nation is almost interchangeable with the words state or power; it was formerly possible to speak of the republic of Venice or the kingdom of Prussia as nations. The sense is illustrated by the phrase 'the law of nations', and survives in the adjective 'international'. Secondly, after the French Revolution the word nation came to mean in Europe a *nationality*, a people with a consciousness of historic identity expressed in a distinct language. Italy or Germany or Poland were nations in this sense, though each was divided among many states, and the Habsburg and Russian Empires were 'multinational' powers. The principle of national self-determination asserts the right of every nationality to form a state and become a power, and the peace settlement of 1919 attempted to reorganise Europe in accordance with it. Thirdly, in Asia and Africa, since the First World War, the word nation has come to mean a political unit asserting its right of independent statehood against European domination. Some of these units are ancient civilisations, like India and China; some are historic kingdoms, like Ethiopia and Persia; some, like the Arab states, are fragments of a wider linguistic group and most perhaps have been created by European colonial administrators, like Indonesia and Ghana. But in terms of nationality more of them resemble the Habsburg Empire than Ireland or Denmark. They combine the passions of the second kind of nation with the social diversity of the first kind. Of the five surviving nominal great powers today, France alone comes near to being a homogeneous nationality. The Soviet Union and China are multinational states; the United Kingdom is the political union of the English, Welsh, Scottish and Northern Irish nations; and the United States is a unique attempt to create a new nation from immigrants of all European nationalities.

"The word 'nationalism' describes the collective self-assertion of a nation in any of these three senses, but especially in the second and third. This compels us to speak of conflicting nationalisms within a single state: there is both a Scottish nationalism and a British, a Sikh nationalism and an Indian, a Ukrainian and a Soviet nationalism. (The word 'patriotism' is generally reserved by the ruling class for the larger and inclusive loyalty.) The student of power politics will not be misled by nationalist claims, and will remember that in most cases the freedom or rights of one nation or nationality have been purchased only by the oppression of another nation or nationality. Every power that is a going concern will in course of time generate loyalties which it will be proper to call nationalist, but powers are less the embodiment of national right than the product of historical accident.

"It is a consequence of nineteenth-century nationalism that we personify a power, calling it 'she', and saying that *Britain* does this, *America* demands that, and the *Soviet Union*'s policy is something else. This is mythological language, as much as if we speak of John Bull, Uncle Sam or the Russian Bear. 'Britain' in such a context is a symbol for an immensely complex political agent, formed by the permanent officials of the Foreign Office, the Foreign Service, the Foreign Secretary, the Prime Minister, the Cabinet, the House of Commons, the living electorate, and the dead generations who have made the national tradition, combining and interacting in an infinitude of variations of mutual influence. These shorthand terms are of course unavoidable in political writing, but they are dangerous if they lead us into thinking that powers are inscrutable and awesome monsters following predestined laws of their own. A power is simply a collection of human beings following certain traditional ways of action, and it is possible that if enough of them chose to alter their collective behaviour they might succeed in doing so. There is reason to suppose, however, that the deeper changes in political behaviour can only be produced by a concern for non-political ends.

"We must note in conclusion that the phrase 'power politics' in common usage means, not only the relations between independent powers, but something more sinister. Indeed, it is a translation of the German word *Machtpolitik*, which means the politics of force – the conduct of international relations by force or the threat of force, without consideration of right and justice. (About the time of the First World War, 'power politics' in this sense superseded an older and more elegant phrase, *raison d'état*, which implied that statesmen cannot be bound in public affairs by the morality they would respect in private life, that there is a 'reason of state' justifying unscrupulous action in defence of the public interest.) As Franklin Roosevelt said in his last Annual Message to Congress, 'In the future world the misuse of power as implied in the term "power politics" must not be the controlling factor in international relations.' It would be foolish to suppose that statesmen are not moved by considerations of right and justice, and that international relations are governed exclusively by force. But it is wisest to start from the recognition that power politics as we defined them at the outset are always inexorably approximating to 'power politics' in the immoral sense, and to analyse them in this light. When we have done this we can more usefully assess the moral problem."

Note
1. A. J. P. Taylor, *Rumours of War* (London: Hamish Hamilton, 1952) p. 44.

Morgenthau – State Interest Defined in Terms of Power*

" . . . The history of modern political thought is the story of a contest between two schools that differ fundamentally in their conceptions of

* From Hans Morgenthau (1904–80). German-born, studied at Frankfurt University but later taught at a variety of US institutions before becoming Professor at Chicago University. His *Politics among Nations* was for many years the most widely used textbook on international relations in the US. Criticism of his basic thesis concerning the role of power (which Morgenthau somewhat modified in his later years) has tended to obscure the many valuable insights contained in this wide-ranging book. Quoted from *Politics among Nations* (New York: Alfred A. Knopf, 1948).

the nature of man, society and politics. One believes that a rational and moral political order, derived from universally valid abstract principles, can be achieved here and now. It assumes the essential goodness and infinite malleability of human nature, and blames the failure of the social order to measure up to the rational standards on lack of knowledge and understanding, obsolescent social institutions, or the depravity of certain isolated individuals or groups. It trusts in education, reform and the sporadic use of force to remedy these defects.

"The other school believes that the world, imperfect as it is from the rational point of view, is the result of forces inherent in human nature. To improve the world one must work with those forces, not against them. This being inherently a world of opposing interests and of conflict among them, moral principles can never be fully realised, but must at best be approximated through the ever-temporary balancing of interests and the ever-precarious settlement of conflicts. This school, then, sees in a system of checks and balances a universal principle for all pluralist societies. It appeals to historic precedent rather than to abstract principles, and aims at the realisation of the lesser evil rather than of the absolute good.

"This theoretical concern with human nature as it actually is, and with the historic processes as they actually take place, has earned for the theory presented here the name of realism. What are the tenets of political realism? No systematic exposition of the philosophy of political realism can be attempted here; it will suffice to single out six fundamental principles, which have frequently been misunderstood.

1. SIX PRINCIPLES OF POLITICAL REALISM

1. *Political realism* believes that politics, like society in general, is governed by objective laws that have their roots in human nature. In order to improve society it is first necessary to understand the laws by which society lives. The operation of these laws being impervious to our preferences, men will challenge them only at the risk of failure.

"Realism, believing as it does in the objectivity of the laws of politics, must also believe in the possibility of developing a rational theory that reflects, however imperfectly and onesidedly, these objective laws. It believes also, then, in the possibility of distinguishing in politics between truth and opinion – between what is true objectively and rationally, supported by evidence and illuminated by reason, and what is only a subjective judgement, divorced from the facts as they are and informed by prejudice and wishful thinking.

"Human nature, in which the laws of politics have their roots, has not changed since the classical philosophies of China, India and Greece endeavoured to discover these laws. Hence, novelty is not necessarily a virtue in political theory, nor is old age a defect. The fact that a theory of politics, if there be such a theory, has never been heard of before tends to create a presumption against, rather than in favour of, its soundness. Conversely, the fact that a theory of politics was developed hundreds or even thousands of years ago – as was the theory of the balance of power – does not create a presumption that it must be outmoded and obsolete. A theory of politics must be subjected to the dual test of reason and experience. To dismiss such a theory because it had its flowering in centuries past is to present not a rational argument but a modernistic prejudice that takes for granted the superiority of the present over the past. To dispose of the revival of such a theory as a 'fashion' or 'fad' is tantamount to assuming that in matters political we can have opinions but no truths.

"For realism, theory consists in ascertaining facts and giving them meaning through reason. It assumes that the character of a foreign policy can be ascertained only through the examination of the political acts performed and of the foreseeable consequences of these acts. Thus, we can find out what statesmen have actually done, and from the foreseeable consequences of their acts we can surmise what their objectives might have been.

"Yet examination of the facts is not enough. To give meaning to the factual raw material of foreign policy, we must approach political reality with a kind of rational outline, a map that suggests to us the possible meanings of foreign policy. In other words, we put ourselves in the position of a statesman who must meet a certain problem of foreign policy under certain circumstances, and we ask ourselves what the rational alternatives are from which a statesman may choose who must meet this problem under these circumstances (presuming always that he acts in a rational manner), and which of these rational alternatives this particular statesman, acting under these circumstances, is likely to choose. It is the testing of this rational hypothesis against the actual facts and their consequences that gives meaning to the facts of international politics and makes a theory of politics possible.

2. The main signpost that helps political realism to find its way through the landscape of international politics is the concept of interest defined in terms of power. This concept provides the link

between reason trying to understand international politics and the facts to be understood. It sets politics as an independent sphere of action and understanding apart from other spheres, such as economics, ethics, aesthetics, or religion. Without such a concept a theory of politics, international or domestic, would be altogether impossible, for without it we could not distinguish between political and nonpolitical facts, nor could we bring at least a measure of systematic order to the political sphere.

"We assume that statesmen think and act in terms of interest defined as power, and the evidence of history bears that assumption out. That assumption allows us to retrace and anticipate, as it were, the steps a statesman – past, present or future – has taken or will take on the political scene. We look over his shoulder when he writes his dispatches: we listen in on his conversation with other statesmen: we read and anticipate his very thoughts. Thinking in terms of interest defined as power, we think as he does, and as disinterested observers we understand his thoughts and actions perhaps better than he, the actor on the political scene, does himself.

"The concept of interest defined as power imposes intellectual discipline upon the observer, infuses rational order into the subject matter of politics, and thus makes the theoretical understanding of politics possible. On the side of the actor, it provides for rational discipline in action and creates that astounding continuity in foreign policy which makes American, British or Russian foreign policy appear as an intelligible, rational continuum, by and large consistent within itself, regardless of the different motives, preferences, and intellectual and moral qualities of successive statesmen. A realist theory of international politics, then, will guard against two popular fallacies: the concern with motives and the concern with ideological preferences.

"To search for the clue to foreign policy exclusively in the motives of statesmen is both futile and deceptive. It is futile because motives are the most illusive of psychological data, distorted as they are, frequently beyond recognition, by the interests and emotions of actor and observer alike. Do we really know what our own motives are? And what do we know of the motives of others?

"Yet even if we had access to the real motives of statesmen, that knowledge would help us little in understanding foreign policies and might well lead us astray. It is true that the knowledge of the statesman's motives may give us one among many clues as to what the direction of his foreign policy might be. It cannot give us, however, the one clue by which to predict his foreign policies. History shows no exact and necessary correlation between the quality of motives and the quality of foreign policy. This is true both of moral and of political qualities.

"We cannot conclude from the good intentions of a statesman that his foreign policies will be either morally praiseworthy or politically successful. Judging his motives, we can say that he will not intentionally pursue policies that are morally wrong, but we can say nothing about the probability of their success. If we want to know the moral and political qualities of his actions, we must know them, not his motives. How often have statesmen been motivated by the desire to improve the world, and ended by making it worse? And how often have they sought one goal, and ended by achieving something they neither expected nor desired?

• • •

"A realist theory of international politics will also avoid the other popular fallacy of equating the foreign policies of a statesman with his philosophic or political sympathies, and of deducing the former from the latter. Statesmen, especially under contemporary conditions, may well make it a habit of presenting their foreign policies in terms of their philosophic and political sympathies in order to gain popular support for them. Yet they will distinguish with Lincoln between their '*official* duty', which is to think and act in terms of the national interest and their '*personal* wish', which is to see their own moral values and political principles realised throughout the world. Political realism does not require, nor does it condone, indifference to political ideals and moral principles, but it requires indeed a sharp distinction between the desirable and the possible, between what is desirable everywhere and at all times and what is possible under the concrete circumstances of time and place.

"It stands to reason that not all foreign policies have always followed so rational, objective and unemotional a course. The contingent elements of personality, prejudice and subjective preference, and of all the weaknesses of intellect and will which flesh is heir to, are bound to deflect foreign policies from their rational course. Especially where foreign policy is conducted under the conditions of democratic control, the need to marshal popular emotions to the support of foreign policy cannot fail to impair the rationality of foreign policy itself. Yet a theory of foreign policy which aims at rationality must for the time being, as it were, abstract from these irrational elements and seek to paint a picture of foreign policy which presents the rational essence to be found in experience, without the contingent deviations from rationality which are also found in experience."

Carr – Power and Morality in International Relations*

" . . . To attempt to ignore power as a decisive factor in every political situation is purely utopian. It is scarcely less utopian to imagine an international order built on a coalition of states, each striving to defend and assert its own interests. The new international order can be built only on a unit of power sufficiently coherent and sufficiently strong to maintain its ascendancy without being itself compelled to take sides in the rivalries of lesser units. Whatever moral issues may be involved, there is an issue of power which cannot be expressed in terms of morality.

MORALITY IN THE NEW INTERNATIONAL ORDER

"If, however, it is utopian to ignore the element of power, it is an unreal kind of realism which ignores the element of morality in any world order. Just as within the state every government, though it needs power as a basis of its authority, also needs the moral basis of the consent of the governed, so an international order cannot be based on power alone, for the simple reason that mankind will in the long run always revolt against naked power. Any international order presupposes a substantial measure of general consent. We shall, indeed, condemn ourselves to disappointment if we exaggerate the role which morality is likely to play. The fatal dualism of politics will always keep considerations of morality entangled with considerations of power. We shall never arrive at a political order in which the grievances of the weak and the few receive the same prompt atten-

---

* From E. H. Carr (1892–1982). Worked for 15 years in the British foreign office, attending the Versailles Peace Conference in this capacity. Became Professor of International Politics at Aberystwyth University and was the author of several works on international affairs of which *The Twenty-Years Crisis* is best known. Devoted the last 30 years of his life to writing a mammoth history of the Russian revolution and the early years of Soviet power in Russia. Quoted from *The Twenty-Years Crisis (1919–39)* (London: Macmillan, 1949).

tion as the grievances of the strong and the many. Power goes far to create the morality convenient to itself, and coercion is a fruitful source of consent. But when all these reserves have been made, it remains true that a new international order and a new international harmony can be built up only on the basis of an ascendancy which is generally accepted as tolerant and unoppressive or, at any rate, as preferable to any practicable alternative. To create these conditions is the moral task of the ascendant Power or Powers. The most effective moral argument which could be used in favour of a British or American, rather than a German or Japanese, hegemony of the world was that Great Britain and the United States, profiting by a long tradition and by some hard lessons in the past, have on the whole learned more successfully than Germany and Japan the capital importance of this task. Belief in the desirability of seeking the consent of the governed by methods other than those of coercion has in fact played a larger part in the British and American than in the German or Japanese administration of subject territories. Belief in the uses of conciliation even in dealing with those against whom it would have been easy to use force has in the past played a larger part in British and American than in German and Japanese foreign policy. That any moral superiority which this may betoken is mainly the product of long and secure enjoyment of superior power does not alter the fact, though this consideration may well affect the appeal of the argument to Germans and Japanese and expose British and Americans to the charge of self-righteousness when they invoke it.

• • • •

" . . . Responsible British and American statesmen still commonly speak as if there were a natural harmony of interests between the nations of the world which requires only good-will and common sense for its maintenance, and which is being wilfully disturbed by wicked dictators. British and American economists still commonly assume that what is economically good for Great Britain or the United States is economically good for other countries and therefore morally desirable. Few people are yet willing to recognise that the conflict between nations like the conflict between classes cannot be resolved without real sacrifices, involving in all probability a substantial reduction of consumption by privileged groups and in privileged countries. There may be other obstacles to the establishment of a new international order. But failure to recognise the fundamental character of the conflict, and the radical nature or the measures necessary to meet it, is certainly one of them.

"Ultimately the best hope of progress towards international

conciliation seems to lie along the path of economic reconstruction. Within the national community, necessity has carried us far towards the abandonment of economic advantage as the test of what is desirable. In nearly every country (and not least in the United States), large capital investments have been made in recent years, not for the economic purpose of earning profits, but for the social purpose of creating employment. For some time the prejudice of orthodox economists against this policy was strong enough to restrict it to half measures. In Soviet Russia, such prejudice was non-existent from the outset. In the other totalitarian states, it rapidly disappeared. But elsewhere rearmament and war provided the first substantial cure for unemployment. The lesson will not be overlooked. A repetition of the crisis of 1930–3 will not be tolerated anywhere, for the simple reason that workers have learned that unemployment can be cured by a gigantic programme of economically unremunerative expenditure on armaments; and such expenditure would be equally effective from the standpoint of employment if it were devoted to some other economically unremunerative purpose such as the provision of free housing, free motor cars or free clothing. In the meanwhile we are moving rapidly everywhere towards the abolition or restriction of industrial profits. In the totalitarian countries this has now been virtually accomplished. In Great Britain, the assumption has long been made that to earn more than a limited rate of profit on the provision of essential public services is immoral. This assumption has now been extended to the armaments industry. Its extension to other industries is only a matter of time, and will be hastened by any crisis. The rearmament crisis of 1939, even if it had passed without war, would have produced everywhere changes in the social and industrial structure less revolutionary only than those produced by war itself. And the essence of this revolution is the abandonment of economic advantage as the test of policy. Employment has become more important than profit, social stability than increased consumption, equitable distribution than maximum production.

"Internationally, this revolution complicates some problems and may help to solve others. So long as power wholly dominates international relations, the subordination of every other advantage to military necessity intensifies the crisis, and gives a foretaste of the totalitarian character of war itself. But once the issue of power is settled, and morality resumes its role, the situation is not without hope. Internationally as nationally, we cannot return to the pre-1939 world any more than we could return to the pre-war world in 1919.

Frank acceptance of the subordination of economic advantage to social ends, and the recognition that what is economically good is not always morally good, must be extended from the national to the international sphere. The increasing elimination of the profit motive from the national economy should facilitate at any rate its partial elimination from foreign policy. After 1918, both the British and United States Governments granted to certain distressed countries 'relief credits', from which no economic return was ever seriously expected. Foreign loans for the purpose of stimulating production in export trades have been a familiar feature of post-war policy in many countries. Later extensions of this policy were dictated mainly by military considerations. But if the power crisis can be overcome, there can be no reason why it should not be extended for other purposes. The more we subsidise unproductive industries for political reasons, the more the provision of a rational employment supplants maximum profit as an aim of economic policy, the more we recognise the need of sacrificing economic advantage for social ends, the less difficult will it seem to realise that these social ends cannot be limited by a national frontier, and that British policy may have to take into account the welfare of Lille or Düsseldorf or Lodz as well as the welfare of Oldham or Jarrow. The broadening of our view of national policy should help to broaden our view of international policy; and . . . it is by no means certain that a direct appeal to the motive of sacrifice would always fail.

"This, too, is a Utopia. But it stands more directly in the line of recent advance than visions of a world federation or blue-prints of a more perfect League of Nations. Those elegant superstructures must wait until some progress has been made in digging the foundations."

21 The Motives of States

In the years after the Second World War the study of international relations was dominated for a time by the writings of the realist school. In the US Hans Morgenthau's *Politics among Nations* was the most widely used textbook in universities and colleges. Its hard-headed approach perhaps made a special appeal in the years of the Cold War when, in the eyes of some, the actions of Stalin's Russia seemed to justify, as clearly as had the behaviour of Hitler's Germany in the previous decade, the analysis he put forward.

From the middle 1950s, however, there was an increasing willingness to challenge the assumptions of this school. On the one hand the political climate had changed. The intensity of the cold war relaxed somewhat. The struggle for power was no longer, in a period of *détente*, so visibly the chief manifestation of state activity. Just as the foreign policy of John Foster Dulles was, in such a political climate, criticised by some for its inflexibility, so the apparent hawkishness of realist writings began to be criticised by some students of international relations.

More important, however, was the fact that the academic climate changed. International relations was emerging as a recognised academic discipline, and there was a demand for more rigorous analysis and careful enquiry than most writers of the realist school had thought to employ. There was increasing impatience with broad generalisations and bald assertions. The emergence of the "behavioural" movement, which was affecting all the social sciences in the US at this time, demanded a more "scientific" approach to the study of international relations.

For all these reasons, over the following decade or two the realists' pessimistic view of the nature of states, and the sweeping generalisations by which they were supported, were increasingly disputed. Not all accepted so readily that the maximisation of "power" was always the overriding objective of states: certainly not of all states. Many challenged the ambiguous definition of "power" the realist writers had used and showed that such writers had used that word in a variety of meanings often inadequately defined.

This led to an attempt to undertake a somewhat more realistic analysis of the motives which inspired state action. It was increasingly doubted whether any single overriding aim could be said to deter-

296

mine all such actions. It came to be recognised that the motives of states, like those of individuals, were highly various; and that even a particular action might be influenced by a number of different motives. Moreover, motives might differ widely from one state to another, so that generalisations intended to apply to all states were not necessarily helpful. A distinction began to be made between the short-term goals of states, which were the most inclined to vary significantly from one state to another, and their long-term goals which were more widely shared, which remained relatively stable over considerable periods, and which might remain unchanged even when there was a change of government or a revolution. Finally, within each state, motives, it was recognised, varied among different individuals and groups, each of which might attribute more importance to some goals than to others.

The first two extracts below are specifically directed to criticism of the realist writings of the period before. Stanley Hoffmann and Inis Claude each point to various weaknesses of their thesis. They criticise first the excessive emphasis on power as the overriding concern of political activity. The confusion of power as an end and power as a means is noted by Hoffmann. This in turn involves a failure to analyse what are the real ends of policy: although the way power is used is determined by human purposes, realist theory, Hoffmann observes, "neglects all the factors which influence or define purposes". Overemphasis of a single factor, or more accurately, a single word called on to embrace a number of different concepts, leads to distortion. There is a failure to take into account different historical contexts, so that a theory which may fit the eighteenth and nineteenth centuries reasonably well will not necessarily provide a helpful analysis for the twentieth. The concept of national interests is shown to be a subjective one which cannot be clearly defined; and this difficulty is particularly great in a period of ideological conflicts when ends themselves are disputed. Finally, because of the narrowness of the definition of state motives, and especially because of its failure to take into account any non-state relationships and activities, the thesis cannot make any claim to put forward a general theory of international relations.

Claude demonstrates other inadequacies in the realist thesis. He challenges in particular the attempt of Morgenthau, the best-known exponent of the realist thesis, to establish, as an "iron law of politics", that states are bound to pursue the "national interest conceived in terms of power". In many passages of his writing Morgenthau himself, Claude points out, had recognised that states in fact faced clear choices between different courses of policy, and could not therefore be bound by any "law". What he described as a scientific law was in fact, therefore, more in the nature of a normative injunction: his own prescription of the type of policy which a prudent state should pursue. On the basis of this finding Claude is able to show that, redefined in this way (as in the penultimate paragraph quoted here), the Morgenthau thesis said little more than would be accepted by most observers of the international scene.

Other writers presented alternative formulations of the role of power in international relationships. Deutsch, following Talcott Parsons, compares power with a currency which can be called on, when required, to achieve particular purposes. International statesmen spent their power on other values, which would in turn bring further power, which could then be invested again. But just as economics had advanced beyond a crude "bullion theory" of money, identifying economic power with the possession of the precious metals, to theories emphasising organisation for productive purposes, so a new theory of international politics would place emphasis on co-operative efforts among states to enhance political growth and development rather than the traditional crude competition on the basis of power alone.

Other writers of the period sought to provide a broader definition of the motives of states than had been offered by the realist school. K. J. Holsti, in his widely-used textbook *International Politics; A Framework for Analysis*, suggested a wide range of objectives pursued by states in their foreign policies. No such list is exclusive, since the total number of motives which can influence the behaviour of states are as infinite as those that can influence the actions of individuals. Some are general, some particular; some enduring, some fleeting. Motives which are important to some states may be insignificant for others. Any attempt to describe the motives of states, therefore, is necessarily oversimplified. But those that began to be given during this period were at least rather more comprehensive and more realistic than those which had been provided by the "realists" – by no means realistic in this respect – a decade or two earlier.

Nor was it always accepted that states are governed entirely by self-interested motives. The last of the extracts below suggests that the state actions are influenced also by various kinds of rules of conduct, derived from the wider society of states. These become incorporated in state motivations and may alter state behaviour.

* * *

Hoffmann – The Search for Power not the Sole End of States*

"The theory which has occupied the centre of the scene in this country during the last ten years is Professor Morgenthau's 'realist' theory of power politics. It is an attempt at providing us with a reliable 'map' of the landscape of world affairs; an effort at catching the essence of world politics. The master key is the concept of interest defined in terms of power. To what extent does the theory accomplish its mission? It succeeds in focusing attention on the units which remain the principal actors in world affairs: the States. The theory also stresses the factors that account for the large degree of autonomy of international relations: the differences between domestic and world politics which thwart the operation in the latter of ideas and institutions that flourish in the former, the drastic imperatives of survival, self-preservation and self-help which are both the causes and the products of such differences.

"However, as a general theory, the 'realist' analysis fails because it sees the world as a static field in which power relations reproduce themselves in timeless monotony. . . .

"Now, the decision to equate politics and power would be acceptable only if power were analysed, not as a limited and specific set of variables, but as a complex and diffuse balance between all the variables with which the social sciences are concerned. Political man should properly be seen as the 'integrator' of moral man, economic man, religious man, and so on – not as a creature reduced to one special facet of human nature. Unfortunately such an Aristotelian position is not adopted here: the decision to equate politics and the effects of man's 'lust for power' is combined with a tendency to

---

* From Stanley Hoffmann (1928–). Born in France but has spent most of his working life at Harvard University. Prolific bilingual author of works on international relations, US policy and French politics. Incisive critic of the ultra-theoretical approach of much US writing on international affairs. Works include *The State of War* (1965), *Gullivers Troubles* (1968) and *Primacy or World Order* (1978). Quoted from *Contemporary Theory in International Relations* (Englewood Cliffs, .N.J.: Prentice-Hall, 1960).

equate power and evil or violence – a combination which mutilates reality. A 'power monism' does not account for all politics, when power is so sombrely defined; even in world affairs, the drive for participation and community plays a part, and the image of political man interested exclusively in the control of the actions of others for the sake of control, is simply not acceptable as a basis for theory.

"Furthermore, the extent to which power as a carrier of evil and violence expresses a basic human instinct is questionable. Much of the international (or domestic) evil of power is rooted not in the sinfulness of man but in a context, a constellation, a situation, in which even good men are forced to act selfishly or immorally. Discrimination between the inherent or instinctive aspects of the 'power drive', and the situational or accidental ones, is an important task. However, reactions to shifting situations are scarcely considered by the theory.

"Also, it is dangerous to put in a key position a concept which is merely instrumental. Power is a means toward any of a large number of ends (including power itself). The quality and quantity of power used by men are determined by men's purposes. It would have been more logical to begin with a theory of ends rather than with the notion of power, which is here both ambiguous and abstracted from its ends. The 'realist' theory neglects all the factors that influence or define purposes. Why statesmen choose at times to use national power in a certain way (say a policy of 'imperialism') rather than in another is not made clear. The domestic considerations that affect national power: the nature of the regime, the structure of power, beliefs and values which account in great measure for the nation's goals and for the statesmen's motivations, are either left out or brushed aside. For instance it is not enough to say that 'the political cohesion of a federal system is the result of superior power located in some part of it', for what remains to be explained is how such superior power got to be located there, what convergence of interests or what community of values led to its establishment and underlies its authority. Similarly, internationally shared beliefs and purposes are left out. Reality comes out oversimplified, for we get a somewhat mechanistic view of international affairs in which the statesmen's role consists of adjusting national power to an almost immutable set of external 'givens'. Professor Morgenthau's metaphor about theory which, like a portrait, and unlike a photograph, should try to show 'one thing that the naked eye cannot see: the human essence of the person portrayed' is most revealing. It is quite possible that there is a human essence of the person; but even if we had been able to discover it, we would still have to account for all the twists and vagaries of the person's existence and we cannot assume that they would be easily deducible from the 'human essence' discovered. The same is true in world politics. Unfortunately, the 'realist' world is a frozen universe of separate essences.

"Even if the role of power were as determining as the theory postulates, the question arises whether any scheme can put so much methodological weight upon one concept, even a crucial one; for it seems to me that the concept of power collapses under the burden. It is impossible to subsume under one word variables as different as: power as a condition of policy and power as a criterion of policy; power as a potential and power in use; power as a sum of resources and power as a set of processes. Power is a most complex product of other variables, which should be allowed to see the light of the theory instead of remaining hidden in the shadow of power. Otherwise the theory is bound either to mean different things at different steps of the analysis (or when dealing with different periods), or else to end by selecting for emphasis only one aspect of power: either military force or economic strength. Thus, instead of a map which simplifies the landscape so that we can understand it, we are left with a distortion.

"There is a second reason for the inadequacy of the map. The rigidity that comes from the timeless concept of power is compounded by the confusing use of other concepts that are dated in more ways than one, and which the theory applies to situations in which they do not fit. The model of the 'realists' is a highly embellished ideal-type of eighteenth and nineteenth century international relations. This vision of the golden age is taken as a norm, both for empirical analysis and for evaluation. A number of oddities of the theory are explained thereby. First, the lack of an adequate discussion of ends; for when all the actors have almost the same credo, as they did during most of that period, it becomes easy to forget the effects of the common credo on the actors' behaviour, and to omit from among the main variables of the theory a factor whose role seems constant. It is nevertheless an optical illusion to mistake a particular historical pattern for the norm of a scientific system. When we deal with a period such as twentieth century world politics, whose main characteristic may well be the division of an international society which had previously been rather coherent into rival groups devoted to mutually exclusive purposes and values, the neglect of ends is a fatal mistake.

"Second, the analysis of power apart from the processes and pressures of domestic politics follows from the same optical illusion. It is easy to understand why public philosophers should bemoan the days when no visible and organised groups challenged the primacy of foreign affairs, the continuity of diplomatic action, unsentimental equilibrium calculations, and privacy. But these principles are not eternal; the Greek city-states did not observe them – at their own peril, of course, but then the world restored in 1815 balanced its power and played its cards into the abyss of 1914; and no one has yet found a way of reversing the trend and of insulating the experts on Olympus from the germs carried by the common men in the swamps below.

"Third, the conception of an objective and easily recognisable national interest, the reliable guide and criterion of rational policy, is one which makes sense only in a stable period in which the participants play for limited ends, with limited means, and without domestic kibitzers to disrupt the players' moves. In such a period, the survival of the main units is rarely at stake in the game, and a hierarchy can rather easily be established among the other more stable and far less vital interests that are at stake. In such a period, the influence on foreign policies of factors such as geography, natural resources, industrial capacity, and inherited traditions of national principles is particularly strong and relatively constant. Today, however, survival is almost always at stake, and technological leaps have upset the hierarchy of 'stable' factors. The most divergent courses of action can be recommended as valid choices for survival. Ordinarily less compelling objectives, such as prestige, or an increment of power in a limited area, or the protection of private citizens abroad, all become tied up with the issue of survival, and the most frequent argument against even attempting to redefine a hierarchy of national objectives so as to separate at least some of them from survival, is the familiar fear of a 'chain of events' or a 'row of dominoes falling'. In such circumstances of mutual fear and technological turmoil, interpretations of the national interest become almost totally subjective and the relative weight of 'objective' factors which affect the states' capabilities and thereby influence state policies is almost impossible to evaluate. Consequently, a scholar attempting to use the theory as a key to the understanding of, or successful influence upon, contemporary realities risks being in the unhappy position of a Tiresias who recognises interests which the parties concerned refuse to see, who diagnoses permanence where the parties find confusing change and whose *ex post facto* omniscience is both irritating and irrelevant.

"Fourth, the idea that the national interest carries its own morality is also one which makes sense almost only in a stable period. For it is a period in which an international consensus assures at least the possibility of accommodation of national objectives; the conflicts of interests which are involved are not struggles between competing international moralities. The philosophical pluralism implicit in the 'realist' theory (which purports to be both normative and empirical) is not sufficiently thought through. For in periods of stability and moderation, which bloom only because of a basic agreement on values, the national interest can be said to be moral and legitimate only because it expresses aspirations of a community which do not rule out those of another group. What is moral is not the national interest as such but its reasonableness, which insures its compatibility with the interests of other states and with the common values of international society; and what is legitimate is the possibility for each group to have such temperate aspirations recognised. This is, at best, the kind of pluralism which is implied by *one* particular set of values – those of liberalism. As for periods of 'nationalistic universalism', of secular religions and incompatible ideologies – here the tolerance characteristic of liberal pluralism makes no sense whatsoever. It is one thing to say that ideological differences do not justify crusades which would push the world into the chaos of total war; it is quite another to suggest that *all* national interests (as they are defined by statesmen) are to be given free play and recognition, in a period when one state's interest all too often resides in eliminating another state. A difference must be made between the pluralism of harmony, and the pluralism of the jungle.

"Fifth, the emphasis on the 'rationality' of foreign policy and the desire to brush aside the irrational elements as irrelevant intrusions or pathological deviations are understandable only in terms of cabinet diplomacy, where such deviations appear (especially with the benefit of hindsight) to have been rare. There, rationality seemed like the simple adjustment of means to stable and generally recognised ends. These concepts are far less applicable to a period in which the political struggles involve primarily the determination of ends. In such a period, a conception of rationality adequate only for the selection of means cannot help us evaluate and classify the ends of states (the narrowness of the theory's conception of rationality makes it even more easy to understand why ends are insufficiently examined). Also, revolutionary periods are often characterised by the selection of means which are perfectly irrational from any point of view, *including* that of the adequacy of those means to the previously selected ends. Forgetting these two facts can entail serious mistakes. Thus, on the one hand, to apply a rationality of means to the selection of ends can have disastrous consequences in areas such as contemporary strategic doctrines. For instance, it can lead us to advocate limited nuclear war as the most rational way of employing the military resources of the West in the case of a conflict, without however having faced the previous question: whether such a strategy fits entirely the purposes the West has set for its relations both with the Communist camp and with the uncommitted nations, or, to put it somewhat differently, whether the purpose of this strategy – economy of force – is the highest end the West pursues. On the other hand, to forget that a nation might at some point select totally irrational means and be pushed by the dark logic of mutual fears into the very abyss of war that it wanted to avoid, is to assume too lightly that cool calculations of interest necessarily guide a nation's policy, or that mistaken calculations do not occur. Now, as the reader will see, debates among sociologists about the nature of war are not conclusive enough to allow us to assume that nations make war only because, and when, their leaders see in war a rational instrument of policy. In other words, a theory of world politics should certainly be rational but there is no need to suppose that reality is generally rational too.

"Finally, the exclusion from the pale of world politics of those activities which were not undertaken by the states as such (i.e., by their governments), or which do not represent an obvious attempt to gain control over other nations (such as the signing of extradition treaties, or exchanges of goods and services, to use Mr Morgenthau's own examples), is also understandable in certain periods only. It makes sense when a considerable range of activities which do, if only indirectly, affect the political power of the state, is left to private citizens (as was the case in the century of the liberal states). It makes sense when these activities are carried out unobtrusively within the common framework in which 'power politics' operate, instead of serving as counters in the struggle for the establishment of a new framework. Nevertheless, even in the study of stable periods, the total exclusion of these acts is a mistake, because their temporary removal from the range of issues that involve directly the states' power is precisely the underpinning and one of the defining features of international relations in these periods – the submerged part of the iceberg. Behind the claim to realism, we thus find a reactionary Utopia."

Claude – Is there an Iron Law that States Pursue Power?*

"An incident which has a bearing on this question arises out of Morgenthau's discovery of an 'iron law of politics which requires that states pursue the national interest conceived in terms of power. This position is fundamentally rooted in his general theory of 'political realism', with its premise that 'politics, like society in general, is governed by objective laws that have their roots in human nature'. Morgenthau assumes 'that statesmen think and act in terms of interest defined as power', and asserts that 'the evidence of history bears that assumption out' (p. 5). Over and over in his writing, this proposition is presented as a law of politics, grounded in a necessity which denies choice to the managers of the affairs of states. Thus, referring to the United States, he says: 'We have acted on the international scene, *as all nations must*, in power-political terms.' He regards the subordination by a state of its legal obligations to its national interests as an 'iron law of international politics', or 'a general law of international politics, applicable to all nations at all times' (pp. 144, 147). It should be noted that he establishes a close connection between this proposition and his doctrine concerning balance of power; power politics is lumped with 'its necessary outgrowth, the balance of power', in a passage in which he denounces the 'misconception' that 'men have a choice' regarding them.

"Having established this objective law of politics, Morgenthau does some curious things with it. He accuses various American statesmen of having violated it – of having disregarded or even

* From Inis Claude (1922–   ). Teacher of International Relations in Harvard, Ann Arbor and the University of Virginia. Author of two masterly and influential works on international relations: *Swords into Ploughshares* (an analysis of the United Nations and its role) and *Power and International Relations* (1962). Quoted from *Power and International Relations* (New York: Random House, 1962).

explicitly rejected the national interest as the foundation of policy, substituting moral principles for national interest. He shatters his assertion that no choice exists by commenting that the débâcle of collective security in the Italo-Ethiopian case of 1935 demonstrated the dire results of statesmen's incapacity to decide 'whether to be guided by the national interest'. He writes one remarkable sentence in which he describes as an 'iron law' a precept from which, he thinks, 'no nation has ever been completely immune' – which implies that some nations have sometimes been somewhat immune from its operation. Ultimately, he finds it desirable to conclude the volume in which he most often asserts that the pursuit of the national interest defined in power terms is an iron law, with an eloquent sermon exhorting American statesmen to obey that law.

"The revelation comes when Morgenthau responds to the obvious criticism of his position. Having been subjected by Robert W. Tucker to the charge that he was inconsistent in regard to his iron laws, Morgenthau retorts that 'It ought not to need special emphasis that a principle of social conduct, in contrast to a law of nature, allows of, and even presupposes, conduct in violation of the principle', and accuses his critic of 'zeal to find contradictions where there are none'.

"The cat, so to speak, is out of the bag. Morgenthau does not wish to be interpreted as meaning what he seems to say when he speaks of iron laws and inevitability. Even though he may invoke the analogy of the law of gravity, he wants to be understood as advocating adherence to wise and prudent principles of social conduct. In the happy world of academic freedom, Morgenthau has the right to use words as he pleases, but the reader of his works must be cautiously aware that when Morgenthau asserts that 'it is an iron law of politics that states must . . .', he probably means to convey the idea that 'it is a basic rule of wise policy that a state ought to . . .'. Nature's laws of iron turn out to be Morgenthau's rules of prudence. Inevitable means desirable. The proposition that it is inherent in the nature of things that a state can only act in a certain fashion should be translated 'Morgenthau believes that it would be stupid for a state not to act in that way'.

"The justification for this interpretation of Morgenthau is indicated by a passage, introducing a section entitled 'The Balance of Power – the Fundamental Law of International Politics', in which balance of power is described as 'a universal instrument of foreign policy used at all times by all nations *who wanted to preserve their independence*'; the idea 'that a nation has a choice between a balance-of-power policy and some other kind of foreign policy' is labelled a 'misconception', and Hume's essay on the balance of power is cited as showing 'that no such choice exists for *a rationally conducted foreign policy* and that a nation which *disregarded* the requirements of the balance of power would either have to conquer the world or perish'. The import of the italicised words is that a choice does exist, but that Morgenthau and Thompson believe that a statesman would be *unwise* to choose any policy other than the balance of power.

"Further insight into Morgenthau's version of inevitability may be gained from analysis of the opening page of a chapter on 'The Disparagement of Diplomacy', in which he notes that traditional diplomatic methods have been largely abandoned since World War II, argues that these methods 'have grown ineluctably from the objective nature of things political' and can be disregarded only at great risk, and then asserts that autonomous entities which are intent upon preserving their status 'cannot but resort to what we call the traditional methods of diplomacy'. States *cannot* fail to use these methods, but they *are* failing to do so; clearly, what Morgenthau is really saying is that states *should not* abandon the methods which he believes to be so fundamentally appropriate to the conduct of international relations.

"With this revised understanding of the concept of inevitability, we can return to the problem of interpreting Morgenthau's doctrine concerning the necessity of the balance of power. He has said that 'the balance of power . . . is the very law of life for independent units dealing with other independent units – domestic or international – that want to preserve their independence. Independent power, in order to be kept in check, must be met by independent power of approximately equal strength.' More frequently, he has stated the power objective as either equality or superiority, with the latter regarded as preferable. Perhaps the point comes to this: In a world of multistate power struggle, a state should be basically concerned about its power situation, and do what it can to develop and maintain its power. Its power must be adequate to protect its interests and promote its purposes. Its policy can succeed only if backed by power, and policy aims should be kept in balance with the power resources available or likely to become available to support them. The power of competitors is mortally dangerous to the state; a state can be secure only if it can mobilise, unilaterally or in combination with others, power equal or superior to that which might be exercised against it.

States may fail to recognise these truths, or they may not be able to meet these requirements successfully, but prudent men will recognise the validity of this analysis of international reality and try to conform to the requirements which it poses.

"If this is what Morgenthau means, then it should be noted that the concept of the balance of power is essentially a redundancy in his theory of international politics. It really says that in a power struggle, states must and do struggle for power. A reasonable and dutiful statesman can be expected to recognise that his state must have at least as much power as its probable enemy, or be conquered, and to act accordingly. Conceivably the notion of balance adds one idea: that the statesman should be moderate in his quest for power, lest in trying for too much he precipitate a reaction of fear and hostility, thus defeating his own purposes."

Deutsch – Power as a Means and Power as an End*

"Power can be thought of as a means of getting other things that men value. In this sense, the concept of power seems almost self-implied or tautological. To desire any value – wealth, wellbeing, respect, affection or any other – necessarily implies desiring the power to get it, somewhat as in much of economic life to desire any good or service is to desire the ability to buy it. As men spend money in economic life to buy what they want, so in politics men spend their power to get what they desire.

"But if men only *spend* their money, they end up penniless, and if politicians only *spend* their power, they end up powerless. The thrifty businessman is an *investor*. He spends his money on those goods and services (such as valued commodities or capital goods) which eventually will bring him more money than he spent on them. For instance, an investor may buy a factory to produce goods which he will then

---

* From K. W. Deutsch (1912–   ). Born in Prague, but has taught international relations at Yale and Harvard Universities. Interested in political integration and communication, and the use of quantitative measures in the study of international relations. His many publications include *Nationalism and Social Communication* (1953) and, from which this extract is quoted, *The Analysis of International Relations* (Englewood Cliffs, N.J.: Prentice-Hall, 1968).

sell for more money than he had to spend on getting them produced. Thus, to *invest* is to *spend* money to *get more* money, in cycle after cycle, again and again.

"In politics some men invest in power. They spend their power on other values in such a manner that these values in turn will bring more power back to them. They are driven, as Thomas Hobbes suggested more than 300 years ago, by 'a thirst for power after power which only ceases in death'. In order to invest thus, they must use the political support which they have at one time, so as to make more-or-less enforceable decisions of such a kind as to get more support; and then they must use this increased support for new decisions that will produce still more support for further decisions, in an expanding feedback cycle, as far as they can carry it.

"In essence it was this that Machiavelli urged his prince to do. A prince who did not wish to lose his realm, he suggested, always had to think and act in terms of power. He had to hoard and increase his resources, not dissipate them; to strive to enhance his own power and prestige and to diminish those of his competitors; to keep the common people passive and content, but willing to fight loyally at his command; to rule by force and fraud, being admired and feared but not hated; and to keep or break his word in quick accordance with whether loyalty or perfidy at any moment would more enhance his power. A prudent prince, Machiavelli thought, should never be neutral in a war among his neighbours, for if he let his weaker neighbour be defeated by some other prince, the strengthened victor would then turn on him. If he helped his weaker neighbour, however, they might jointly defeat the stronger neighbour who was the greater threat to both of them. Or thus allied, even if defeated, the two weaker princes might at least be allies in misfortune. Generally, however, today's ally was tomorrow's enemy, and one's strongest ally was one's greatest threat, for a prince promoting another's power, Machiavelli said, ruins his own.

"In theory, this calculus of power politics was impersonal and inexorable. Every prince and would-be prince – that is, every political actor – had to act out of necessity, since every other prince would do the same harsh things to him; and those who failed to do so would soon cease to be princes and would lose all their domains. Much as businessmen eventually will be pushed out of the market if they cannot meet their expenses and make their capital grow at least as fast as the prevailing rate of interest, so governments and rulers eventually will be eliminated from the political arena if they cannot make their power grow at least as fast as that of their competitors. Power politics, in short, appeared to Machiavelli as the characteristic of the large political system which in turn determined the character- istics of all competitors surviving in it.

"Clearly, Machiavelli's model of an extremely competitive system is one of the great achievements of the human mind. His political man is an intellectual ancestor (or at least a close relative) of the equally competitive 'economic man' of Adam Smith and his fol- lowers, and of the almost no less competitive animals and plants produced by Charles Darwin's process of 'natural selection'.

"Yet all these models, fruitful as they were in their own day, are only partly true at best. In politics, Machiavelli's model in important aspects is quite false. It is inadequate in a way similar to that in which a mere model of extreme competition would miss the essential core of economics. It is true in economics that buying power for the individual means his power to appropriate goods and services for himself, usually in competition against sellers and against other buyers. But for society as a whole the heart of economics, as Adam Smith already had made clear, is not the power of individuals to appropriate, but the ability of a country or nation to produce goods and services, and in particular the enhancement of this productive capacity through the division of labour, increased and speeded through the ability to exchange such goods and services with the aid of money.

"Something similar holds for political power. For the individual, it means his ability to command and be obeyed, in competition with rival commands by other contenders, and in competition with the autonomous desires of his audience. For society as a whole, however, politics in any country – and among any group of countries – means the ability of the whole political community to co-ordinate the efforts of its members, to mobilise their support, and to redirect their patterns of cooperation; and, in particular, to do all this more quickly, more widely, and more accurately through the manipulation of power in the interplay of the probabilities of enforcement, com- pliance, and support.

"If this is true, we can already now foresee a coming change in much of our political thinking. Economics has shifted from a 'bullion theory' that identified wealth with gold, to more sophisticated theories of capital investment and the division of labour, and to theories of economic growth and industrial development. Somewhat similarly, our political theory in time may come to shift from a theory of power to a theory of the interplay of spontaneity and sanctions in the steering and coordination of men's efforts, and in the processes of autonomy and social learning – that is, toward a theory of the politics of growth. Such a theory of political growth and development will be needed for every level of human organisation, from the politics of small groups and local communities all the way to the politics of nations at all levels of economic advancement, and even to the politics of all mankind. Such a theory will necessarily direct our attention to the limits of power. It will make us look to the limits of the scope of power – the things power can and cannot do – and to the limits of its domain, the boundaries where power cannot be relied on to prevail and where the breakdown of political control explodes into war."

Holsti – The Objectives of States*

"[P]olitical units seek to achieve a complete range of private and collective, concrete and value objectives. In some areas, state interests are still indistinguishable from dynastic interests. It is questionable, for example, whether the former King of Saudi Arabia or some recently bygone Latin American dictators perceived that the interests of their country might be distinct from their private family interests. To them, the primary objectives of foreign policy were to protect their ruling position and secure quantities of personal wealth and prestige. On the other extreme we find governments which commit national resources to the expansion of messianic philosophies, regardless of what the effects will be on the personal lives, prestige, and fortunes of those who formulate these objectives. Between these extremes exist the vast majority of modern states which seek to achieve collective objectives and national security, welfare of citizens, access to trade routes, markets and vital resources, and some-

* From K. J. Holsti (1935–   ). Born in Switzerland but educated in the US; has taught mainly at Stanford and the University of British Columbia, Vancouver. Interested in the study of foreign policy and conflict resolution. His book *International Politics: A Framework for Analysis* (1967), from which this extract is taken, is one of the most widely used textbooks in the US today. Other works include *Why Nations Realign* (ed., 1982); and *The Dividing Discipline; Hegemony and Diversity in International Theory* (1985). Quoted from *International Politics: A Framework for Analysis* (Englewood Cliffs, N. J.: Prentice-Hall, 1967).

times the territory of their neighbours. Given the wide range of objectives that exist today, then, how can they be classified?

"One method might be to distinguish among military, economic, political and ideological objectives, but divisions between such categories are not at all clear and it is doubtful whether policy-makers operate in terms of these criteria – even if most governments contain separate departments dealing with the military, economic, political and ideological aspects of foreign policy. A second scheme might classify objectives according to geographic area: what are a particular state's objectives toward its immediate neighbours? the states in a neighbouring continent? or areas on the other side of the world? This scheme would correspond to actual government organisation, since most foreign offices are subdivided into geographic bureaux and sections. But if we wish to make general statements about *types* of objectives, then the nation-by-nation description of policies would be largely repetitive. Instead, we will employ a combination of three criteria: (1) the *value* placed on the objective, or the extent to which policy-makers commit themselves and their countries' resources to achieving a particular objective; (2) the *time element* placed on its achievement; and (3) the kinds of *demands* the objective imposes on other states in the system. From these we can construct categories of objectives such as the following: (1) 'core' values and interests, to which governments and nations commit their very existence and which must be preserved or extended at all times (achievement of these values or interests may or may not impose demands on others); (2) middle-range goals which normally impose demands on several other states (commitments to their achievement are serious and some time limits are usually attached to them); and (3) universal long-range goals, which seldom have definite time limits.[1] In practice statesmen rarely place the highest value on long-range goals and do not, consequently, commit many national capabilities or policies to their achievement – unless the goals are central to a political philosophy or ideology, in which case they may be considered 'core' or middle-range interests. Those states which work actively toward achieving universal long-range goals usually make radical demands on *all* other units in the system and thus create great instability.

'CORE' INTERESTS AND VALUES

"'Core' values and interests can be described as those kinds of goals for which most people are willing to make ultimate sacrifices. They are usually stated in the form of basic 'principles' of foreign policy and become the articles of faith which a society accepts uncritically.[2] Such terms as 'command of the sea', a 'frontier on the Rhine', and the 'Monroe Doctrine' suggest basic foreign policy orientations, attitudes towards others, or goals which at one time were held sacrosanct by entire communities.

"'Core' interests and values are most frequently related to the self-preservation of a political unit. These are short-range objectives because other goals obviously cannot be achieved unless the political units pursuing them maintain their own existence. The exact definition of a 'core' value or interest in any given country depends on the attitudes of those who make policy. There are, for example, many different interpretations of self-preservation. Some disagree over definitions of self – that is, what constitutes an integrated polity. Others will disagree equally on what policies contribute best to preservation. Some colonial regimes have been willing to grant independence to indigenous peoples voluntarily, while others have considered that overseas holdings constitute an integral part of the nation which must be defended at all costs. Nevertheless, most policy-makers in our era assume that the most essential objective of any foreign policy is to ensure defence of the *home* territory and perpetuate a particular political, social and economic system based on that territory.

• • •

"After self-preservation and defence of strategically vital areas, another prominent 'core' value or interest is ethnic, religious or linguistic unity. Today, no less than in the great era of nationalism in the nineteenth century, the most legitimate bases of frontiers correspond to ethnic, linguistic or religious divisions. Territories carved up according to historical or strategic criteria, where ethnic groups are arbitrarily divided between sovereignties, are likely to become areas of conflict as neighbouring states attempt to 'liberate' their own kin from foreign rule. Irredentist movements, subversion, and sometimes racial warfare are often the products of frontiers which divide ethnic, linguistic or religious groups. In almost all areas where such arbitrary divisions occur, governments make reunification a major objective of foreign policies, and sometimes place such a high value upon it that they are willing to employ large-scale force to achieve it. The Aaland Island dispute between Finland and Sweden, the Karelian war of 1921–2 between Finland and the Soviet Union, several conflicts in central Europe and the Balkans in the interwar period, the Sudetenland crisis of 1937–8, as well as the serious problem between the Netherlands and Indonesia over West Irian, the Kashmir wars, intermittent crises in Germany, arguments between Austria and Italy over the Tyrol, and tensions between Kenya and Somaliland, and Somaliland and Ethiopia have arisen since World War II essentially because one government attempted through threats, subversion or outright military attack to incorporate into its own territory ethnically related people living in neighbouring states.

"The kinds of demands that pursuit of these 'core' values or interests require of other actors in the system vary. States with well-established frontiers corresponding to ethnic divisions, which protect their territories and social orders through ordinary defence policies, are not likely to disturb even their immediate neighbours. Those which seek more favourable strategic frontiers or ethnic unity normally do so at the expense of the 'core' values and interests of their neighbours, and thus create dangerous conflicts.

"Such conflicts may not always lead to violence or war because interpretations of 'core' values or 'vital interests' may change under different circumstances. The British were willing for decades to fight against any internal or external assaults on their empire as if they were fighting for the city of London. But in 1945 the economic and military strains of maintaining the empire were so great that many British leaders recognised they could no longer consider the colonies as 'core' interests to be preserved at all costs. A bizarre interpretation of 'core' values and interests was the view propounded by Lenin that the development of world revolution was more important than saving either his Bolshevik regime or the independence of the Russian nation.[3] It was partly because of his exceptional commitment to world revolution that he was willing to concede to Germany in the Brest-Litovsk treaty almost one-quarter of Russia's traditional territory and one-half of its population. In this case, although the objective of world revolution was a middle-range goal if we are using the criterion of time, in terms of the value Lenin placed on its achievement it was 'core' interest. Lenin's successors have displayed quite different – and more traditional – attitudes, however, through their claims that the defence of Russian territory and the Soviet state, rather than promotion of revolution, is the first foreign policy priority.[4] Lenin's priorities were exceptional; in most cases, policy-makers explicitly state or reveal through their actions that the basic objective, to which any degree of sacrifice may be required, is defence of the home territory plus any other territory deemed necessary to self-preservation, and perpetuation of a particular political, social, and economic order, or as some call it, a "way of life".

MIDDLE-RANGE OBJECTIVES

"Since there is such a variety of middle-range objectives, it would be useful to divide this category into four further types and illustrate each with contemporary examples. The first type of middle-range objective would include the attempts of governments to meet public and private demands and needs through international action. Social welfare and economic development – a primary goal of all governments in our era – cannot be achieved through self-help, as most states have only limited resources, administrative services and technical skills. Interdependence means that to satisfy domestic needs and aspirations, states have to interact with others. Trade, foreign aid, access to communications facilities, sources of supply and foreign markets are for most states absolutely necessary to enable them to provide for increasing social welfare.

"A variation of this type of objective occurs when governments commit themselves to promote private citizens' interests abroad, whether or not these relate to broad social needs. Instead of encouraging general expansion of trade or access to foreign markets, they might, under pressure from specific domestic groups or economic interests, undertake certain foreign policy initiatives that have little connection with the interests of society in general. The American government in the early twentieth century, for instance, committed its power and resources to protect the foreign investments of private firms operating in Latin America. It intervened frequently, sometimes with force, in the internal affairs of Caribbean and Central American states essentially to guarantee the profits of these firms. It was thus translating private business interests into middle-range government objectives, even though the interests had little to do with the general level of social welfare in the United States.

• • •

"A second type of middle-range objective is to increase a state's prestige in the system. In the past, as today, this was done primarily through diplomatic ceremonial and displays of military capabilities, but increasingly in our era prestige is measured by levels of industrial development and scientific and technological skills. In addition to responding to domestic pressures for higher living standards, political élites of underdeveloped states who are acutely sensitive to their material poverty may undertake massive development programme primarily to raise international prestige. Development has become one of the great national goals of our times and is sought with almost as much commitment of resources as the securing of some 'core' values and interests. This middle-range goal has no particular time element, but most of today's leaders in underdeveloped countries hope that they can begin to catch up with more economically advanced countries within their own lifetimes.

•   •   •

LONG-RANGE GOALS

"Long-range goals are those plans, dreams and visions concerning the ultimate political and/or ideological organisation of the international system, rules governing relations in that system and the role of particular nations within it. The difference between middle-range and long-range goals relates not only to different time elements inherent in them; there is also a significant difference in scope. In pressing for middle-range goals, states make *particular* demands against *particular* states; in pursuing long-range goals, states normally make *universal* demands, for their purpose is no less than to reconstruct an entire international system according to a universally applicable plan or vision. As Lenin, one of the great modern visionaries, wrote in 1920:

"We have always known, and shall never forget, that our task is an international one, and that our victory [in Russia] is only half a victory, perhaps less, until an upheaval takes place in all states, including the wealthiest and most civilized.'[5]

"Since destruction and reconstitution of an established international order obviously conflicts with the middle-range and 'core' objectives of its members, any system which contains one or more actors committed to such plans will be unstable and typified by violent international conflict."

Notes
1. Arnold Wolfers has outlined an alternative scheme for classifying goals. He distinguishes between *aspirations* and genuine *policy goals*, which correspond roughly to the distinction between long-range goals and others of more immediate importance. *Possession goals* refer to the achievement of national values and needs, while *milieu goals* are those conditions

outside of the nation state itself which a state seeks to change. Wolfers also distinguishes between *national goals* and *indirect goals* which correspond roughly to my concepts of "collective interests" and "private interests". See Arnold Wolfers, "The Goals of Foreign Policy", in his *Discord and Collaboration: Essays in International Politics* (Baltimore, Md: The Johns Hopkins Press, 1962) ch. 5.

2. Modelski, *A Theory of Foreign Policy*, p. 86.
3. Lenin's priority on the "world revolution" is illustrated by comments he made shortly after the Bolshevik revolution to a group of his friends: "We are creating a socialist state. From now on Russia will be the first state in which a socialist regime has been established. Ah, you are shrugging your shoulders. Well, you have still more surprises coming! It isn't a question of Russia. No, gentlemen, I spit on Russia! That's only one stage we have to pass through on our way to world revolution!" Quoted in Robert S. Payne, *The Life and Death of Lenin* (New York: Simon and Schuster, 1964) p. 418.
4. As, for example, when former Premier Khrushchev, in reply to Chinese claims to certain Soviet territory, announced: "Our borders are sacred and inviolable and any attempt to change them by force means war." UPI release from Moscow, 13 September 1964.
5. V. I. Lenin, *Collected Works* (Moscow: Foreign Languages Publishing House, 1961) vol. XXXI, p. 371.

Luard – Motivations and Norms among States*

"The first of the sources from which national motivations are derived are the innate drives of individuals within states. These include aggressive drives, fear, demands for security, and perhaps some gregarious instincts. Individual drives are channelled by the culture into specific directions. Some (the aggressive drives) may find expression mainly in collective forms; others (the sexual drive) can be satisfied only in personal forms. Acquired characteristics also affect international attitudes. Those who have had an authoritarian upbringing are often especially nationalistic in outlook. The collective drives that result, such as aggression, may be relatively stable in disposition (against all foreigners or all Russians), as an individual's

* From Evan Luard (1926–91). Has been diplomat and politician, twice serving as junior minister in the British Foreign Office, as well as writer on international relations. He writes mainly on international conflict and international institutions. His books include a trilogy on "international sociology" (see pp. 584–90) and a *History of the United Nations*. Quoted from *Conflict and Peace in the Modern International System* (Boston, Mass.: Little, Brown, 1968).

might be habitually directed against wife or employer. But they will usually, like personal drives, be aroused especially by particular situations (such as those causing frustration or anger).

"Second, desires (as the desire for national status) and activities (say, collective aggression or national philanthropy), which are not necessarily related to innate drives, may be learned from the international culture. They may be acquired principally by imitation and suggestion, as are the corresponding individual desires and activities. And they are reinforced by the rewards and punishments that are experienced in gains or losses in national power, prestige, popularity and good name. By this procedure nations learn, just as individuals do, the most effective means of securing objectives and values within the limitations set by the environment and the range of choice available. Something like what psychologists call 'operant conditioning' and the 'law of effect' may take place, so that by trial and error relatively stable attitudes and tendencies to action result.

"Conversely, certain activities are inhibited or redirected by social taboos, different types of communal norm. . . . Sometimes the assessment of rewards and punishments will depend on the direction of attention. Action that brings punishment in the form of disapproval from the international community may bring rewards in approval of the home electorate (just as, for the individual, action that brings punishment in the form of social censure may bring rewards in personal drive-satisfaction). Which is most valued will depend on education and the degree of socialisation in each case.

"The cultural environment will channel and direct individual drives and desires in different ways at different times. For example, it may in one age direct individual aggression against other nations, while in another it directs it against other classes, and in a third, against opposing ideologies and political creeds. The actors involved will vary at different times. Besides nations there are regional organisations (such as the Arab League or the Organisation of American States), economic unions and free trade areas, international organisations, international political parties, ideological groupings and others. But because nations exercise a command over loyalties and over armed force far more direct than do these groupings, and become engaged in armed conflict in a way that the others do not, it is with nations and their motives that any study of international relations must be mainly concerned. And even if, in time, they come to be replaced by continents, exercising a corresponding command over loyalties and armed power, similar considerations are likely to apply to these as to nations today.

"The communal drives that result are clearly not strictly analogous to individual drives. Because the innate element is small and divided among numerous individuals, the cultural influence on them is more important. The drives are thus less constant in their effect on national conduct. But the common national situations which individuals often share, and the powerful conditioning established by traditional responses to particular situations, may mean that, unless new conditioning and expectations are set up, nations will respond in similar and to some extent predictable ways to similar stimuli.

"The stimulus involved may be, as for individuals, either internal or external. Just as the drives of individuals may be set in motion either by purely internal changes (such as hunger or thirst) or by external perceptions (such as the aggressive response of a robin to a bunch of red feathers, or the maternal activity aroused in a mother by any threat to her own offspring), so communal drives may be stimulated by purely internal changes (such as the rise of a nationalist government or widespread unemployment) or by external ones (such as threats from a neighbour or humiliations from a rival.

•   •   •

"Cultural influences will determine not only the type of response chosen for particular situations, but the entire range of situations demanding a response. The situations calling for armed retaliation bear little relation to their intrinsic importance to the nation. Nations today, for example, continue to respond with great violence to the occupation of small and totally valueless strips of border territory, or to insults to national prestige. But even the most bitter dispute about trade terms, tariff regulations, immigration laws, investment and aid, the functioning of the UN system or the powers of the Secretary General will not lead to warlike responses though they may be of much greater long-term importance to the state concerned. The culture pattern does not tolerate war on these grounds. And it is this which finally determines national behaviour and motivations.

•   •   •

"Over relationships *between* communities there is as yet no such consistent pattern of expectations. Yet relationships between communities – large and small, national and subnational, economic or social – may be as important to their members as are those within them. With extended communications, increased contacts, and the more and more complex organisation of modern societies, individuals today increasingly belong to a large number of disparate groups, entering into complicated relationships with each other. Individuals may undertake personal relationships with individuals in other communities elsewhere. But those relationships themselves are more than ever conditioned politically, economically, even socially, by the relations of the larger communities to which they belong. *Communal relationships* become as important to man's welfare as individual relationships. *Communal drives*, the desires and aspirations of the group, become as powerful in influence, and more dangerous in effect, than the drives of individuals and may equally lead them into violent conflict. And *communal expectations*, the assumptions shared within each group on relations between them, become the main factor influencing relationships and drives alike.

• • •

"Between communities, as within them, the absence of any commonly expected structure of relationships will give rise to an interaction regulated by vagary and violence. Here too, relationships may come to be ruled by a system of competition and conflict, providing insecurity for the weak, and instability for all. Here, too, aggressive drives and self-seeking instincts will set up a mode of existence governed by brute force alone. Here, too, therefore, only socialising agencies to inculcate a commonly expected pattern of relations, comparable to those which already govern relationships within communities, could create the basis for a harmonious interaction.

"Within societies there is a wide spectrum of such agencies. These vary in their working from unconscious conditioning through explicit persuasion to physical coercion. Their effect is to bring individualistic drives and impulses into sufficient reconciliation to make possible a stable and harmonious existence for all. The most satisfactory forms of control will seek to create the basis for a mutually compatible intercourse without destroying the capacity for individual spontaneity; to instil a modicum of restraint with the minimum of constraint.

• • •

"The problem of establishing norms among a society of sovereign and conflicting national states clearly differs significantly from that which arises within other societies. The first and fundamental difference lies in the fact that, although within national societies ultimate power, in the shape of armed force, is concentrated at the centre, so that principles of interaction may be partly *imposed* on its members, in the international community both power and loyalties remain dispersed. One of the most important agents of social order within states is here, therefore, lacking. . . .

"This does not, however, as it is often suggested, mean that there can be no basis of order.

• • •

"The international community today appears to have more in common with a primitive community than with any more developed society. Its individual members exist, more perhaps than in any other society, in that state of mutual suspicion and fear sometimes held to be the natural condition of man himself. But the *voluntary* submission to a central authority that might provide security for all, such as has been imagined taking place within human societies, is as improbable in this case as in the other. For in each case mutual suspicion, and the consequent difficulty of agreeing on the ways in which authority may be used, is likely to mean that greater security will be found in known methods of private defence than in imaginary systems of public enforcement. As in other primitive communities in which the individualistic urges of their members have not yet been strongly restrained by social pressures, *coercive* power therefore remains unavailable within the foreseeable future. But this does not exclude the other possible agencies of social control. Each of these has been employed effectively in many societies in which centralised force was not available (including some national states, until relatively recent times). And each may have its application within the international community today.

"In the international community there may exist *communal practices*: agreed forms of interaction between two or more communities to serve their mutual interests as similar practices serve those of individuals. In the relations of states, as in those of individuals, there is often a need merely for standardised forms, set procedures on which each party is able to rely. A common interest in these may be held where little else is held in common. To some extent such communal practices already exist in the international field in elementary form, in bilateral or multilateral agreements or understandings on trade and navigation, customs procedures, diplomatic practice, or even more crucial aspects of their mutual relations, such as respect for frontiers, notification of troop movements, and other usages.

"The international community also makes use of *communal conventions*, to establish more general and more formal understandings concerning national conduct. These may create common expectations more dependable, permanent and universal in application than those which exist between individual nations. They enjoy the more effective sanctions exerted by common international opinion, instead of remaining dependent on that of individual aggrieved parties. These are to be seen in international conventions that have received widespread ratification, in those international customs which have come to have the force of international law, and in some other provisions of current international law which are generally recognised.

"Finally, communities may be restrained by *communal morality*, the provisions of which are more compulsive and inward than other principles governing their behaviour. Certain antisocial activities of communities, it can be argued, are as fundamental in their effect on common order and individual welfare, and may be as much an affront to deeply rooted convictions, as the actions that have become subject to individual moral codes. They may equally be made the subject of the most binding and fervently revered proscriptions and injunctions. The sentiments that have grown up within the international community concerning acts of aggression, genocide, threats and bullying, war crimes and certain other forms of national conduct, already have something of the quality that colours moral revulsion in other spheres. Any other provision of international law that was as universally and profoundly revered by the members of the international community could equally come to perform the function of communal morality. So far such a code is only embryonic, both in the scope of its provisions, and in the degree of respect accorded it. And even the provisions generally accepted are, as will be seen later, so ill-defined that it is, even more than in cases of individual morality, made easy to find convincing rationalisations to justify exceptions.

•   •   •

"[I]n the international community . . . the tradition of independence and autonomy among nations is such that it may seem impossible, in default of powerful sanctions, that they will ever be bound by a commonly accepted code. The diversity of values and preconceptions among their leaders is such as to make it seem unlikely that any common code could emerge as within narrower communities, where other members appear of like kind and hold similar values. But in fact even the premise here cannot be fully sustained. Among many communities, obligations will be acknowledged to those who are by no means regarded as like, and whose views on most topics are wholly divergent. Codes of interaction may themselves create common values. And it is arguable that, with modern communication of persons and ideas, the sense of essential likeness – even the community of values – among members of different nations today is at least as great as existed between the disparate elements and classes of many well-ordered societies until the most recent times.

"For different types and levels of authority different degrees of consensus are required. Within the international community there is no necessity, nor desire, for any all-comprehensive authority or law to regulate detailed aspects of its members' conduct as do legal codes within states. All that is required are principles of interaction sufficient to create the conditions for a peaceful coexistence between them. These need not condition the way of life *within* the communities to which they are applied. Nor do they demand common attitudes on those questions which most give rise to diverging valuations within states: political principles and moral codes. The only element of community required is the common interest in security among states."

22 The Decisions of States

Another result of the desire to undertake a more scientific study of the behaviour of states was increasing interest among students of international affairs in the way the decisions of government about relations with other states are reached. Since the actions of states represent the basic raw material of international relations study, it was important to know how those actions originated: how the decisions to undertake them were arrived at.

Political and social studies at this time were dominated, especially in the US, by the so-called "behavioural" approach. This had been affected by earlier developments in the field of psychology: that study, once based largely on speculative hypotheses about internal mental processes, had come to be devoted to systematic, *empirical* study of human behaviour. In time the "behaviourism" of psychology became the "behavioural" approach of the social sciences generally: sociology, politics and international relations.

There were obvious problems about trying to apply the methods of the physical sciences to the study of social phenomena. These applied particularly in the field of international relations where systematic experiment was impossible. But there was at least one area which could be examined in a fairly systematic way. This was the study of decision-making in foreign policy, including especially the way important decisions on peace and war, which could have a decisive effect on the pattern of international relationships, were made. In the mid-1950s a new approach to the study of international relations on these lines was proposed. An article by Snyder, Brock and Sapin which appeared in 1955 set out a framework for examining the various influences which had an effect on those decisions. The article was later expanded and incorporated in a book entitled *Foreign Policy Decision-Making*. The first of the extracts below presents a passage from that book describing some of the factors which the authors believed to be important in analysing the decision-making process.

The importance of the approach clearly depended on the effectiveness by which it could be applied to the decisions reached in particular cases. It would have been particularly valuable if applied, on a comparative basis, to a number of different decisions by the same government, or by the governments of different states. No such ambitious undertaking was attempted either by the original authors or by others working in the field. There were, however, a number of books written over the next decade or two devoted to the examination of particular important foreign policy decisions: for example those relating to the Korean War, the Cuban missile crisis and various stages of the Vietnam War. The best known of these is the study of the Cuban missile crisis by G. P. Allison. In this the author proposed three alternative ways of examining foreign policy decisions: as the purposive acts of unified national governments; as the output of a particular organisational structure, integrated for the purpose of securing rational decisions; and as the result of a complex play of forces among different organisational units with varying perceptions and motivations. In the passage below he describes and compares these three possible methods of approach.

Parallel with these studies of particular decisions, or of the decision-making process generally, were broader examinations of the foreign policy process as a whole. Studies of the foreign policy of particular states had been undertaken for many years. There was now increasing interest in a comparative analysis of the way foreign policy was formulated in different countries and of the various kinds of influence which affected these policies. A number of important questions arose which were significant for the study of international relations generally. What is the effect of different kinds of political system and social structures on the policy process? To what extent do abstract formulations of long-term policy influence short-term decisions in immediate situations? How far does the policy of a state remain consistent, as is often suggested, even after changes of government or changes in the entire political system (does, for example, the US government pursue broadly similar policies under Republican and Democratic administrations; does the Soviet government pursue essentially similar aims to its tsarist predecessors?). What is the relative influence which particular groups – foreign office officials, the military, Members of Parliament, the press or public opinion as a whole – exert over policy? These are the kinds of questions which were increasingly studied in many examinations of foreign policy which were undertaken during this period. The third extract below reproduces a passage from a book on the way such questions should be studied by one of the better-known students of foreign policy, J. N. Rosenau.

* * *

Snyder, Bruck and Sapin – The Decision-Making Process in International Politics*

"Existing treatises on international politics seem to ignore or assume the fact that decision-makers operate in a highly particular and specific context. To ignore this context omits a range of factors which significantly influence the behaviour of decision-makers (and therefore state behaviour), including not only the critical problem of *how* choices are made but also the *conditions under which* choices are made.

"To assume the organisational factors is perfectly permissible if one is interested only in *what* was decided and in interaction patterns among states. But for purposes of analysing state behaviour in general such assumptions beg most of the crucial questions. We are convinced that many of the abortive attempts to apply personality theory, culture theory and small group theory to the analysis of foreign policy have been due to a failure to consider the peculiar social system in which decision-makers function. Often, as remarked earlier, the individual policy-makers are treated as though they performed their duties in a vacuum.

•   •   •

"[I]t may be helpful to list some of the features of the organisational structure we shall assume:

1. The *personnel* of formal organisations gain their livelihood from membership, have a limited working life and differ in skills;

---

* From R. C. Snyder, H. W. Bruck and Burton Sapin. Colleagues at Princeton during the 1950s and authors of a short monograph, *Decisionmaking as an Approach to International Politics* (1954). This was later published in an extended form as a book, from which this extract is taken. Richard Snyder, who later taught at North Western University and the University of California, Irvine, was also joint author of *American Foreign Policy: Formulation, Principles and Programmes* (1955), and edited *Foreign Policy Decision-making* (1962). H. W. Bruck is a political scientist, chiefly known for his contribution to *Foreign Policy Decision-Making*. Burton Sapin is professor at George Washington University and author of *The Making of US Foreign Policy*. Quoted from *Foreign Policy Decision-Making* (New York: Macmillan, 1962).

2. Specific, limited, hierarchised *objectives* – either given or decided by the organisation;

3. *Internal specialisation or division of labour*, which implies:
   (a) recruitment and training (including in-service);
   (b) universalistic standards of placement;
   (c) functionally specific role relationships among members based on organisationally defined patterns of behaviour;
   (d) two kinds of specialisation – vertical (delegation to levels of authority) and horizontal (boundaries of co-ordinate units and roles);

4. *Authority and control*, which imply:
   (a) normatively sanctioned power distributed unequally throughout the organisation
   (b) superior–subordinate relationships to insure co-ordination of specialised activities;
   (c) motivation for exercise and acceptance of authority;
   (d) pyramidal structure of power;

5. *Motivation* – members are moved to participate in co-operative pursuit of organisational objectives or activities related to such objectives;

6. *Communication* – circulation of orders, directions, information;

7. *Relationships are formalised and routinised*, serving to:
   (a) insure predictability of behaviour;
   (b) allocate roles according to competence;
   (c) depersonalise relationships and insure continuity with personnel turnover;

8. *Positions and careers 'professionalised'* in terms of operating codes and procedures, lines of career development, criteria of advancement.

"This check-list of structural specifications to be taken for granted does not mean that we are consciously begging any vital questions having to do with organisational behaviour as we will define it below. Indeed, the list is a reminder that the actors who participate in decision-making are members of a certain type of social structure (not society in the more general sense), and that when we come to discuss spheres of competence, internal specialisation is relevant, or when we come to discuss motivation, recruitment and training are relevant.

•   •   •

DEFINITION OF THE DECISIONAL UNIT AND OF THE DECISION-MAKERS

"We have decided to build our analysis around the concept of decisional unit for a very practical reason. Ordinarily, when we think of foreign policy-making in the United States, for example, we think of the sixty-odd concrete agencies – such as the State Department, Defense Department, the National Security Council and so on – which may be involved in the conduct of foreign affairs. It is tempting, and somewhat logical, to consider these common-sense units as the decisional units we must analyse. But it becomes obvious at once that there are several difficulties in this 'self-evident' approach. First, not all members (or employees) of these common-sense units are responsible decision-makers under all circumstances. It would be manifestly absurd to include every last file clerk in, say, the State Department. So, in any case, we have a selection problem on our hands. Second, not all the sixty-odd agencies are involved the *same way in all* decisions. Each may have several different kinds of potential roles it can play in various problems or situations. Third, not all these agencies are equally important. The State Department has, obviously, a larger over-all role than the Department of Agriculture. Fourth, when these agencies do participate, they are not necessarily related to each other in the same way. Sometimes they are equals, sometimes not. Fifth, for different problems, different members of the concrete agencies may actually participate. For these reasons we have found it impossible to attempt to relate concrete units *as such* in the decision-making process. Rather we insist that it is necessary to abstract from these, so to speak, those decision-makers who participate in reaching a decision.

"The problem here is to establish the boundaries which will encompass the actors and activities to be observed and explained. We have stated above that the focus of attention is the analytical concept of an event, that is, decision-making. Moreover, we have said that the type of decision-making event in which we are interested is one that takes place in an organisational context. The organisational system within which the decision-making event takes place is the *unit* of observation. The question now is, by what criteria is the decisional unit to be isolated and differentiated from the setting?

"The criterion that seems most useful at this time is the objective or mission.

"Before we can discuss the nature of the decisional unit, it is necessary to say something further about objectives. We have already spoken of some of the basic characteristics of the concept of the objective. As already noted, the objective is taken as being a particular desired future state of affairs having a specific referent. The aspect upon which we must insist is the specificity, whether this is the production of ten thousand maroon convertibles, a peace treaty with Japan or any other objective for which it is possible to designate a period of time, a place and a system of activities.

• • •

"It is immediately apparent that there is a very large number of different kinds of foreign policy objectives. Seemingly one of the great needs in foreign policy analysis is a typology of these different kinds of objectives. These objectives might be classified on the basis of whether they are political, economic, military or some other or a combination. The degree of urgency attached to them must be considered. Furthermore, it would be of considerable importance to take into account the time element, that is, whether the objective is considered to long-term or short-term and what substantive meaning is given to these time spans. This is not to indicate that many treatments of foreign policy-making do not speak of, for example, 'short-term military objectives' or 'long-term political objectives'. What is needed, however, is a systematic classification with clearly stated and easily applicable criteria.

"For purposes of an historical study of a foreign policy decision such a typology would be useful but not essential. The student would still be able to isolate the unit which made a particular decision and to analyse the factors influencing the actions of the decision-makers, provided the necessary information is available and accessible. If, however, it is the intent of the observer to predict the kinds of decisions which will emerge from various units, then the typology of objectives becomes essential. That is, the typology will tell the observer something about the kinds of systems that would be involved in these types of decision. And prediction can only be predicated on knowledge of how these types of unit act.

The organisational unit
"Since the *organisational or decisional unit* is at the very heart of the kind of analysis we are suggesting, its constituent elements will be discussed at length below. Here we shall confine ourselves to some fairly general observations. The unit, as we have indicated above, is an observer's analytical device to allow identification and isolation of

those actions and activities which are of concern to him. We are assuming that all units will be 'organisational' in the sense discussed in a previous section. In our view all decisional units are organisational systems, and by organisation we mean the system of activities and the structure of relationships. That is, the activities and relationships will be the outcome of the operation of formal rules governing the allocation of power and responsibility, motivation, communication, performance of functions, problem-solving and so on. Each unit will have its own organisation in this sense. Naturally the particular organisational form which a unit takes will depend on how and why the unit was established, who the members are, and what its specific task is.

"It should be apparent that for the observer one and only one organisational unit can act with respect to any one objective. That is, for example, there can be only one set of American decision-makers who were concerned with the Japanese Peace Treaty, since the Japanese Peace Treaty was a unique historical event. This holds true whether the primary institutional affiliation of these decision-makers was the Department of State, the Department of Defense, the Congress or whatever. Here we must once again point to the importance of typification of objectives and units. An initial and tentative listing of some of the criteria by which units may be typified is the following:

1. *Size*   The number of participants may range from a single member to large bodies such as legislatures. In addition to sheer size the number of participants at any one level would have to be considered;
2. *Structure*   Some of the factors that may be relevant here are whether or not the unit is hierarchical, whether the relationships of authority and the communications net are clearly defined or are ambiguous, and the degree of explicitness and conventionalisation of the competences;
3. *Location in the institutional setting*   Two factors are pointed to here: first, the primary institutional affiliation of the members; second, the level in the institutional setting at which the unit operates;
4. *Relation to other organisational units*   Here the relative dependence of independence, isolation or involvement, would be indicated;
5. *Duration of the unit*   The relative permanence or impermanence of units would be the guiding consideration here;

6. *Type of objective* This is probably one of the most important criteria, and further exposition of the factors involved will have to await the development of a typology of objectives."

Allison – The Analysis of Foreign Policy Decision-Making*

"In thinking about problems of foreign affairs, professional analysts as well as ordinary laymen proceed in a straightforward, informal nontheoretical fashion. Careful examination of explanations of events like the Soviet installation of missiles in Cuba, however, reveals a more complex theoretical substructure. Explanations by particular analysts show regular and predictable characteristics, which reflect unrecognised assumptions about the character of puzzles, the categories in which problems should be considered, the types of evidence that are relevant and the determinants of occurrences. The first proposition is that bundles of such related assumptions constitute basic frames of reference or conceptual models in terms of which analysts and ordinary laymen ask and answer the questions: What happened? Why did it happen? What will happen?[1] Assumptions like these are central to the activities of explanation and prediction. In attempting to explain a particular event, the analyst cannot simply describe the full state of the world leading up to that event. The logic of explanation requires that he single out the relevant, important determinants of the occurrence. Moreover, as the logic of prediction underscores, he must summarise the various factors as they bear on the occurrence. Conceptual models not only fix the mesh of the nets that the analyst drags through the material in order to explain a particular action; they also direct him to cast his nets in select ponds, at certain depths, in order to catch the fish he is after.

"Most analysts explain (and predict) the behaviour of national

---

* From G. T. Allison (1940–). US political scientist. Studied in Oxford and Harvard, now professor at Harvard. Interested in foreign policy and the way it is made. Works include (as joint author) *Remaking Foreign Policy: The Organisational Connection* (1976) and (as editor) *Hawks, Doves and Owls* (1985), an analysis of differing attitudes and approaches to foreign policy questions. Quoted from *The Essence of Decision: Explaining the Cuban Missile Crisis* (Boston, Mass.: Little, Brown, 1971).

governments in terms of one basic conceptual model, here entitled Rational Actor or 'Classical' Model (Model I).
"In spite of significant differences in interest and focus, most analysts and ordinary laymen attempt to understand happenings in foreign affairs as the more or less purposive acts of unified national governments. Laymen personify rational actors and speak of their aims and choices. Theorists of international relations focus on problems between nations in accounting for the choices of unitary rational actors. Strategic analysts concentrate on the logic of action in the absence of an actor. For each of these groups, the point of an explanation is to show how the nation of government could have chosen to act as it did, given the strategic problems it faced. For example, in confronting the problem posed by the Soviet installation of strategic missiles in Cuba, the Model I analyst frames the puzzle: Why did the Soviet Union decide to install missiles in Cuba? He then fixes the unit of analysis: governmental choice. Next, he focuses attention on certain concepts: goals and objectives of the nation or government. And finally, he invokes certain patterns of inference: if the nation performed an action of this sort, it must have had a goal of this type. The analyst has 'explained' this event when he can show how placing missiles in Cuba was a reasonable action, given Soviet strategic objectives. Predictions about what a nation will do or would have done are generated by calculating the rational thing to do in a certain situation, given specified objectives.

"Two alternative conceptual models, here labelled an Organisational Process Model (Model II) and a Governmental (Bureaucratic) Politics Model (Model III),[2] provide a base for improved explanations and predictions
"Although the Rational Actor Model has proved useful for many purposes, there is powerful evidence that it must be supplemented, if not supplanted, by frames of reference that focus on the governmental machine – the organisations and political actors involved in the policy process. Model I's implication that important events have important causes, i.e., that monoliths perform large actions for large reasons, must be balanced by the appreciation that (1) monoliths are black boxes covering various gears and levers in a highly differentiated decision-making structure, and (2) large acts result from innumerable and often conflicting smaller actions by individuals at various levels of bureaucratic organisations in the service of a variety of only partially compatible conceptions of national goals, organisational goals and political objectives. Model I's grasp of national

purposes and of the pressures created by problems in *inter*national relations must confront the *intra*national mechanisms from which governmental actions emerge.

"Recent developments in organisation theory provide the foundation for the second model, which emphasises the processes and procedures of the large organisations that constitute a government. According to this Organisational Process Model, what Model I analysts characterise as 'acts' and 'choices' are thought of instead as *outputs* of large organisations functioning according to regular patterns of behaviour. Faced with the problem of Soviet missiles in Cuba, a Model II analyst frames the puzzle: From what organisational context and pressures did this decision emerge? He then fixes the unit of analysis: organisational output. Next, he focuses attention on certain concepts: the strength, standard operating procedures and repertoires of organisations. And finally, he invokes certain patterns of inference: if organisations produced an output of this kind today, that behaviour resulted from existing organisational features, procedures and repertoires. A Model II analyst has 'explained' the event when he has identified the relevant Soviet organisations and displayed the patterns of organisational behaviour from which the action emerged. Predictions identify trends that reflect established organisations and their fixed procedures and programmes.

"The third model focuses on the politics of a government. Events in foreign affairs are understood, according to this model, neither as choices nor as outputs. Rather, what happens is characterised as a *resultant* of various bargaining games among players in the national government. In confronting the problem posed by Soviet missiles in Cuba, a Model III analyst frames the puzzle: Which results of what kinds of bargaining among which players yielded the critical decisions and actions? He then fixes the unit of analysis: political resultant. Next, he focuses attention on certain concepts: the perceptions, motivations, positions, power and manoeuvres of the players. And finally, he invokes certain patterns of inference: if a government performed an action, that action was the resultant of bargaining among players in games. A Model III analyst has 'explained' this event when he has discovered who did what to whom that yielded the action in question. Predictions are generated by identifying the game in which an issue will arise, the relevant players and their relative power and skill.

"A central metaphor illuminates the differences among these models. Foreign policy has often been compared to moves and sequences of moves in the game of chess. Imagine a chess game in which the observer could see only a screen upon which moves in the game were projected, with no information about how the pieces came to be moved. Initially, most observers would assume – as Model I does – that an individual chess player was moving the pieces with reference to plans and tactics toward the goal of winning the game. But a pattern of moves can be imagined that would lead some observers, after watching several games, to consider a Model II assumption: the chess player might not be a single individual but rather a loose alliance of semi-independent organisations, each of which moved its set of pieces according to standard operating procedures. For example, movement of separate sets of pieces might proceed in turn, each according to a routine, the king's rook, bishop and their pawns repeatedly attacking the opponent according to a fixed plan. It is conceivable, furthermore, that the pattern of play might suggest to an observer a Model III assumption: a number of distinct players, with distinct objectives but shared power over the pieces, could be determining the moves as the resultant of collegial bargaining. For example, the black rook's move might contribute to the loss of a black knight with no comparable gains for the black team, but with the black rook becoming the principal guardian of the palace on that side of the board."

Notes
1. In arguing that explanations proceed in terms of implicit conceptual models, this essay makes no claim that foreign policy analysts have developed any satisfactory, empirically tested theory. In this study the term *model* without qualifiers should be read "conceptual scheme or framework".
2. Earlier drafts of this argument have generated heated discussion about proper names for the models. To choose names from ordinary language is to promote familiarity and to court confusion. Perhaps it is best to think of these models simply as Model I, Model II and Model III.

Rosenau – The Analysis of Foreign Policy*

"Not being able to draw on general theories, work in the foreign policy field has been largely historical and single-country oriented.

* From J. N. Rosenau (1924–). Educated at Johns Hopkins and Princeton, later professor at the University of Southern California. Has written especially on

An overwhelming preponderance of the inquiries into foreign policy is confined either to analysing the external behaviour of a specific country at a specific moment in time or to identifying the patterns which mark its external behaviour over a period of time. Indeed, so pronounced is this orientation that most, if not all, American universities offer courses which are exclusively devoted to depicting and analysing the patterned external behaviour of various countries. Courses in American foreign policy and in Soviet foreign policy abound, and those on the external behaviour of India, England, Japan, France and other leading nations are hardly less numerous. The evolution of such a curriculum has spurred the creation of a vast textbook literature, which in turn has reinforced the tendency to approach the field from a historical, single-country perspective. A measure of the spiralling process is provided by the fact that in 1958 a text containing a separate treatment of the foreign policies of ten different nations was published and that 1963 saw the publication of a similar book covering the external behaviour of twenty-four different nations.[1]

"It might be argued that this single-country orientation is the first step in a slow progression toward general theory, that analyses of the external behaviour of many countries constitute bases for the construction of systems of testable generalisations about the foreign policies of general classes of countries, thus leading to the eventual development of if–then models accounting for the behaviour of any country. Unfortunately, however, this line of reasoning is refuted by the unsystematic and uneven nature of the single-country research that has been and is being done. In the first place, the premises underlying the work on each country are so varied that comparative analysis is almost, if not entirely, impossible. It is difficult to find two analyses of two different countries that consider the same variables, ask the same questions and gather comparable data. Even the aforementioned compilations of ten and twenty-four foreign policies do not make comparative analysis possible. In both instances the editors presented an introductory chapter suggesting certain common characteristics of the external behaviour of all nations, but in neither case did the contributors adhere to the outline. In one case, more-

comparative foreign policy and transnational relations. Books include *Domestic Sources of Foreign Policy* (1967), *Linkage Politics* (1969) and, from which this extract is quoted, *The Scientific Study of Foreign Policy* (New York: Free Press, 1971).

over, the editor himself lost interest in developing his model and instead devoted the last half of his introduction to a discussion of 'three obstacles that confound American policy-makers and that must at least be mitigated if the struggle is to be won'.[2]

"In addition to precluding comparison, the single-country analyses are themselves theoretically deficient. By placing a society's foreign policies in a historical and problem-solving context, analysts tend to treat each international situation in which the society participates as unique and, consequently, to view its external behaviour with respect to each situation as stemming from immediate and particular antecedents. This approach does not prevent the derivation of generalisations about the goals and character of the society's behaviour in many situations, but it does inhibit the construction of if–then models which link the behaviour patterns to a systematic set of stimuli. Rather the stimuli, being comprised of unique historical circumstances, are conceived to vary from one situation to the next, and rarely is a construct offered to account for the variations. Consider, for example, how numerous are the analyses of the Soviet foreign policy which attribute causation to a Khrushchev in one situation, to a pent-up consumer demand in another, to a conflict within the leadership structure in a third, to a reality of Russian geography in a fourth and to an aspect of the Sino-Soviet struggle in a fifth situation. Or reflect on the differential explanations of why the United States entered a war in Korea in 1950, avoided one in Indo-China in 1954, fomented one in Cuba in 1961 and enlarged one in Vietnam in 1965. Undoubtedly each of these actions was a response to a different combination of external and internal stimuli; and no doubt, too, there is considerable variability in the complex of factors which determine Soviet policies. But at the same time it is also true that the variability is patterned. The stimuli which produce external behaviour must be processed by the value and decision-making systems of a society, so that it ought to be possible, as with rats in a maze, to link up varying types of responses with varying types of stimuli. To repeat, however, few foreign policy researchers structure their materials in such a way as to allow for this kind of analysis. Just as it is difficult to compare the external behaviour of different countries in the same international situation, so it is often next to impossible to engage in comparative analysis of the actions of the same country in different situations. One is reminded of the state that the field of political theory was in not so long ago: We have many histories of American foreign policy but very few theories of American foreign policy, and much the same can be said about research on every country presently attracting the attention of foreign policy analysts.

A PRE-THEORY OF FOREIGN POLICY

"The resolution of ambivalence is never easy. A residue of unease always seems to remain, especially if the resolution is in a negative direction. Having resolved initial ambivalence with the conclusion that the endless piling up of historical case materials is leading foreign policy research down to a dead end, one is inclined to pause and wonder whether extenuating circumstances have been overlooked or, indeed, whether one's focus is so narrow as to distort perception and exaggerate defect. There must be good reasons why the lack of theory has not aroused researchers to undertake corrective measures. Could it be that the author and not the field has gone astray?

"The answer, of course, is that each has special needs – the field for solutions to urgent policy problems and the author for accretions to an evergrowing science of politics. The satisfaction of these needs leads down two different paths, neither better than the other.

"But one wonders, too, whether the paths need be so divergent. Is a problem-solving orientation necessarily incompatible with the development of empirical materials that lend themselves to an if–then kind of analysis? Cannot historical investigation be carried out in such a way as to facilitate meaningful comparisons and generalisations that are not bound by time and place? An affirmative response to these questions is not unreasonable. Economic theory has been helped, not hindered, by work done in applied economics. Sociological theory has been spurred, not stifled, by empirical inquiries into social processes. Of late, political theory, as distinguished from the history of political thought, has been enriched and enlivened by research into the development of non-Western polities. Surely there is nothing inherent in the nature of foreign policy phenomena which renders them more resistant to theoretical treatment than the gross data that comprise these other applied fields.

"The non-theoretical state of foreign policy research is all the more perplexing when it is contrasted with developments elsewhere in American political science. In recent years the discipline has been transformed from an intuitive to a scientific enterprise, and consequently the inclination to develop models and test theories has become second nature to most political scientists. Each day – or at least each new publication – brings into the field fresh concepts, propositions and theories about local, national and international political systems. New models of the processes of political development abound. And so do conceptualisations of how party, legislative, bureaucratic and judicial systems function. In each of these areas, moreover, political scientists are beginning to build on one another's work (the surest sign of a maturing discipline), and thus innovative theorising is being accompanied by a healthy convergence on similar models of the political process.

"In short, the lack of theory in foreign policy research cannot be readily justified or easily explained. Clearly it cannot be dismissed as a mere reflection of general tendencies in the discipline. Nor can it be attributed to the requirements of problem-solving and the precedents of history. Researchers in other areas of the discipline also engage in historical analysis and expend energy seeking solutions to immediate and practical problems, yet this does not inhibit their inclination to press ahead in the development of general theories. Nor, obviously, is it sufficient to speculate that in foreign policy research the 'avoidance of the general in preference to the individual unique and empirical may be a reflection of the very recent and chiefly American origins of this field of study'. Other more basic obstacles must be blocking the road to general theory, else long ago foreign policy researchers would have begun to move down it alongside economists, sociologists and other political scientists."

Notes
1. Roy C. Macridis (ed.), *Foreign Policy in World Politics* (Englewood Cliffs, N.J.: Prentice-Hall, 1958); and Joseph E. Black and Kenneth W. Thompson (eds), *Foreign Policies in a World of Change* (New York: Harper and Row, 1963).
2. Macridis, *Foreign Policy in World Politics*, p. 22.

23 The Defence of the State

Another feature of writing on international relations in the 1950s and 1960s was the proliferation of writing on strategic questions. The cold war confrontation, the increasing concern about the threat of nuclear weapons, and the danger of war generally, stimulated a huge debate on strategic policy. Whatever views they took about the motives of states and their search for power, most writers on international relations accepted that states in the modern world were bound to seek the capability to defend themselves from other states. Whether adversaries were believed to be actively or only potentially threatening, prudence was seen to demand a level of military capability that would deter attack from elsewhere, and defend effectively if that deterrent failed. Most of this literature, rather than attempting a study of the behaviour of states in general, was concerned with desirable policies for *particular* states or alliances (normally their own): what was the most rational strategic policy for them to pursue?

The two objectives of deterrence and defence came to be seen in this writing as distinct objectives which were not always easy to reconcile. The emergence of nuclear weapons placed this dilemma in a new light. The policy that was most likely to deter – for example, to threaten the maximum response even to minimum provocation – might represent a foolish, or suicidal, policy in terms of defence; while, conversely, the most prudent policy for defence might be the least likely to deter. The new dilemmas of this kind created by the emergence of nuclear weapons stimulated a vast outpouring of writing on strategic questions. These writings were inevitably dominated by the problem posed for policy-makers by the appearance of nuclear weapons, especially when, from the late 1950s onwards, the capacity to threaten a nuclear attack had become mutual. The passages presented below, taken from the works of four of the most distinguished of the innumerable writers in this field, are all concerned with different aspects of this dilemma.

Writings on this theme in this age differed in significant ways from those of earlier times. In earlier ages most strategic writing was concerned as much with offensive as defensive war. They assumed, as von Clausewitz had done, that it was for the politicians to decide what sort of war they wanted and for the military then to tell them how it should be fought. After 1945 strategic writings was concerned mainly with defence. It was indeed concerned more with how war could be *avoided* (given the power available to other states) than with how it should be conducted once started.

This led to the stress on deterrence. Thus in the first of the extracts below Bernard Brodie emphasises that, once the idea of preventive (that is, offensive) war is abandoned (as he believed it had been by the US), the main object of strategic policy was to find the most effective means to deter. This must involve creating the capacity to withstand any first strike by a potential opponent. He therefore points to the importance of ensuring the survivability of retaliatory weapons: for example by the hardening and dispersion of missiles, by developing mobile missiles and by creating submarine- and air-based missile strength (all policies which have remained essential elements of US defence strategy until today). Kissinger likewise, in the works he wrote at this period, examined the problem of establishing a credible deterrent power: for example, the psychological factors which can influence deterrence; the differing interests which super-powers have in different geographical areas; the special difficulty for democratic societies, where any use of force may prove controversial, in maintaining the credibility of their posture; the unpredictable influence of allies having divergent interests. He shows the instability that could be created by the development of invulnerable deterrent forces, which might lead to an unwarranted recklessness on the part of one side or another.

The second effect of the development of nuclear weapons on strategic thinking was a redefinition of the concept of national self-interest. In previous ages any increase in relative power was believed to promote the interest of the state, and such an increase was seen as the main purpose of strategic policy. In this age there is increasing recognition that too sudden and steep an accretion of power may be *contrary* to the interest of a state, since it may frighten opponents into an excessive reaction, whether in the form of new defence expenditures, which in turn will need to be met, or even of some type of pre-emptive strike. So Brodie points out that though a state can hardly be too strong for its own security, it can easily be too "forward and menacing" in the use which it makes of that strength: for example, by emplacing missiles (as US missiles then were) too close to the borders of another state. Thomas Schelling also sought to demonstrate that the value of power was maximised when not actually employed. The degree to which one party could gain its ends, depended on choices by the other, who might in turn be influenced by the first, whether by inducements or threats: when there was a conflict of interest, therefore – which was most of the time – it might be possible to reach an accommodation by an exchange of signals, indicating the maximum concessions either is prepared to make. Michael Howard too shows that in modern conditions the ultimate self-interest of a state may be to avoid the use of force altogether; and he sees the capacity to live with disagreement as the basis of international order. This *mutual* interest which adversaries share in avoiding nuclear war, and even in avoiding the confrontations that may lead to such a war, is one of the almost universal assumptions of writing of this type.

Thirdly, recognition of this fact leads to an increased interest in the possibility of *limited* war, deliberately restricted in scope in order to avoid these dangers. It is increasingly accepted that a capability which will deter nuclear war (by threatening a retaliation in kind) will not necessarily deter war on a lesser scale. So Howard stresses that the wars of the future may become quite different from those of the past, being undeclared, untidy, irregular affairs, probably localised and almost certainly non-nuclear (like all the many wars since 1945). In the same way Kissinger recognises that the strategic superiority of the US had not been able to deter a whole range of Soviet challenges in different parts of the world, even at the time when the former possessed a nuclear monopoly. It comes therefore to be generally accepted in the writings of the age that it is necessary to distinguish carefully between different types of war, at different levels of intensity, and to consider the different postures and capabilities necessary to deter each.

The development of the capacity for mutual annihilation, together perhaps with a moderation in the ambition of states towards other states – especially of territorial ambitions – thus influenced the nature of the ideas that were now held concerning the mobilisation and use of military power. Since total war was increasingly seen as an unusable option, limited war, in limited areas and for limited purposes, was increasingly seen, by writers and statesmen alike, as the only military option which remained.

*   *   *

Brodie – The Principles of Defence in the Nuclear Age*

"Thus it seems inescapable that the first and most basic principle of action for the United States in the thermonuclear age is the following: a great nation which has forsworn preventive war *must* devote much of its military energies to cutting down drastically the advantage that the enemy can derive from hitting first by surprise attack. This entails doing a number of things, but it means above all guaranteeing through various forms of protection the survival of the retaliatory force under attack.

"The last statement naturally assumes that various things *can* be done, that these will make a large and even a critical difference, and that their cost is well within reason. The criterion of costs being 'within reason' invokes a subjective judgement, but the requirement to reduce the vulnerability of the retaliatory force deserves such priority that if necessary certain other kinds of military expenditure should be sacrificed to it; secondly, there is no question that this country can afford, if it must, a much larger military budget than it has become accustomed to at this writing. . . .

"We have . . . noted that studies made of the subject have established that a critical change can be accomplished from a potentially high vulnerability to a very much lower one at a relatively modest cost (i.e., something like 10 per cent of what we are already spending on equipping and maintaining our bomber forces). The first requirement is that we adopt a reasonable and objective attitude about 'hardening' and its utility, one which rejects as irrelevant the usual references to 'Maginot Line complex'. Dispersion in itself is not a substitute for hardening; neither, certainly, is the accumulation of more unprotected aircraft and missiles. And although warning, whether strategic or tactical, is decidedly worth buying in so far as it can be bought, we should never depend upon it as a justification for

* From Bernard Brodie (1909–). US writer on strategic questions. Worked at Dartmouth College, Yale and the Rand Corporation before becoming Emeritus Professor of Political Science at the University of California, Los Angeles. Has written widely on defence matters including *Sea Power in the Machine Age* (1941), *A Guide to Naval Strategy* (1958), *Escalation and the Nuclear Option* (1966) and *War and Politics* (1974). Quoted from *Strategy in the Missile Age* (Princeton, N.J.: Princeton University Press, 1959).

neglecting passive defences. That will be especially true for the missile age now dawning.

"All this applies to land bases only. The aircraft carrier cannot be suitably hardened against nuclear weapons, and the Polaris-type submarine is intrinsically a well-concealed and protected missile base – though obviously it is not without flaws in its armour. The development of a submarine fleet capable of launching missiles like Polaris and its successors will with time provide a retaliatory force of low vulnerability though probably also of limited capabilities. This development, however, does nothing to solve the vulnerability problem of the land-based missiles and aircraft. In view of what we know about relevant costs and also about the hazards involved, the conclusion seems inescapable that a bomber should be bought together with a strong shelter, because it is hardly worth buying without one. Much the same is true of missiles, though the idea of shelter protection for missiles seems to be much more acceptable than the idea of shelters for aircraft, probably because a missile cannot take to the air subject to recall. How strong the shelters should be is a matter for the specialist, but we have to bear in mind that we are talking primarily about protection from thermonuclear weapons aimed with the accuracy that long-range guided missiles are expected to reach by the middle or late 'sixties.

"In the not so distant future, mobility may have to replace hardening as the main prop of security to the retaliatory force. That will surely happen if the accuracies which some predict for the long-range missiles of the future are realised. All sorts of ways are conceivable for making retaliatory missiles mobile. There is, for example, the American railway system with its enormous length of trackage, much of it little used. There is also the inland waterway system. On the high seas, not all missile launchers have to take the form of submarines or large aircraft carriers. The USAF also has its *Bold Orion* project, designed to investigate the possibilities of using bombers as missile-launching platforms.

"The second basic principle of action for the United States is to provide a real and substantial capability for coping with limited and local aggression by local application of force. This is to avoid our finding ourselves some day in a dilemma where we must either accept defeat on a local issue of great importance, or else resort to a kind of force which may be intrinsically inappropriate and which may critically increase the risk of total war.

"In view of the danger that limited war can erupt into total war, especially under the great incentive-to-strike-first circumstances now prevailing, we also have to accept the idea that the methods of limiting the use of force cannot be dictated by us according to our conceptions of our own convenience. Among the compromises with our presumed convenience which we have to be prepared to consider is the possible abjuration of nuclear weapons in limited war. Obviously we have to be prepared also to fight with them, but that is very different from not being prepared to fight without them. There will be time enough to readjust our conception of what is permissible in limited war when incentives to strategic attack have been markedly reduced.

The third principle follows simply from taking *seriously* the fact that the danger of total war is real and finite. Provision must be made for the saving of life on a vast scale. There is room for earnest debate on how big a programme is necessary and on what kinds of shelters are worth their cost, but little room for the assumption that *no* shelters are needed. At minimum there is need for a considerable programme of fallout shelters outside cities. The present neglect of a shelter programme of any dimensions bears no perceptible relation to the military risks we seem daily willing to take.

THE PROBLEM OF STABILITY

"The three points made in the foregoing paragraphs are so elemental in their importance that one hesitates to place any other proposition on a level with them. However, the inexorable progress of weapons towards ever more immediate and even automatic response and towards ever more overwhelming power underlines the importance of still another idea, the need to limit or control the unsettling effects of our deterrent posture.

"Deterrence after all depends on a subjective feeling which we are trying to create in the opponent's mind, a feeling compounded of respect and fear, and we have to ask ourselves whether it is not possible to overshoot the mark. It is possible to make him fear us too much, especially if what we make him fear is our over-readiness to react, whether or not he translates it into clear evidence of our aggressive intent. The effective operation of deterrence over the long term requires that the other party be willing to live with our possession of the capability upon which it rests.

•   •   •

"In general terms, we can hardly be too strong for our security, but we can easily be too forward and menacing in our manipulation of that strength. For example, it may be true that an ICBM deep in our own country menaces the Soviet Union as much as a shorter-range missile pointed at her from just outside her frontiers, but the chances are that the Soviet leaders will be more disturbed by the latter. Unlike the ICBM, the nearby missile seems to denote arrogance as well as strength, and perhaps also a wider dispersal of the authority to fire it. If it is left unprotected, it trumpets the fact that it is intended for a strike-first attack, not retaliation. No one policy of this kind will precipitate a total war, and if there are overriding reasons for that or comparable policies the provocative aspects have to be accepted. On the other hand, over a broad range of policies one sometimes senses an attitude which seems to be somewhat lacking in awareness that deterrence is supposed to last a very long time.

• • •

"It is trite to say that our foreign policy has to be in harmony with our military policy, and vice versa. In itself the statement offers little or no operational guidance. It is as preposterous to assume that there is some mathematical equivalence or correspondence between military power and negotiatory strength on any international issue as to assume that the latter is unrelated to the former. The slogan used to explain our rearmament programme in 1952 – that we must be able 'to negotiate from strength' – supposed that there was some marvellously effective mode of negotiation which we thoroughly understood and which we were quite ready to use for clearly-conceived goals but which was currently denied us because of marginal inadequacies in our military strength. This supposition was in no wise correct and, in addition, the power advantage moved over the succeeding years in the opposite direction from what our slogan seemed to suggest – for reasons, incidentally, for which we can hold ourselves only partly accountable. The complex relationships between military power and foreign policy have by no means been adequately explored, and what we have learned or could learn from history on the subject needs to be reappraised in the light of the totally new circumstances produced by the new armaments."

Kissinger – The Dilemmas of Deterrence*

"Complex as the strategic problem is, the psychological difficulty of balancing penalties and benefits is more complicated still. For if the benefits of aggression seem to outweigh the penalties only once, deterrence will fail. And this could come about simply because the two sides interpret the nature of benefits and penalties differently. In any given situation a number of psychological asymmetries are likely to prevail as between us and the Communist countries. These are only indirectly related to the strategic balance. They involve such factors as the importance of the objective, the willingness of the contenders to run risks, their reputation and their political relationship to the threatened territory. These asymmetries will be discussed in turn.

"1. *Importance of the objective.* Only on the most fundamental questions of national survival will both sides feel equally committed. In almost every conceivable crisis, one side or the other is likely to have a psychological advantage. Hungary seemed more important to the Soviet Union than to us. Though we were still significantly stronger, the Soviets, in repressing the Hungarian revolution, substituted the importance they attached to maintaining their position in the satellite orbit for real strength. Though we could still have won an all-out war at tolerable cost, we were deterred from intervening by the fear that the Soviet leaders were prepared to run all risks in order to prevail. In some circumstances, an area may be protected by the importance that it has or which it is thought to have. Our threat of all-out war is more effective in protecting Europe than in protecting countries like Laos or Burma or Iran because it is more credible: Europe 'matters' more to us – it is therefore credible that we may pay a higher price in its defence.

"Theoretically, the psychological balance should favour the defender. The aggressor can gain only what he has never possessed; the defender stands to lose something heretofore identified with his world position. That the Communist bloc has managed to press on all peripheral areas none the less is due to two factors: (a) the Commu-

---

* From Henry Kissinger (1923–). US statesman and writer on international affairs. Professor at Harvard before becoming national security adviser, and later Secretary of State, to Presidents Nixon and Ford in 1968–76. His principal works include *A World Restored* (1957), a study of the Congress of Vienna and the settlement it achieved, *The Necessity for Choice* (1960) and *The Troubled Partnership* (1965). Quoted from *The Necessity for Choice* (New York: Harper and Row, 1960).

nist ability to bring to bear forces graduated to the nature of the issue. This has shifted the onus and the risk of initiating all-out war on us. In effect, we have paralysed ourselves by the alternatives which our own doctrine and military establishment have presented; (b) superior Communist will power or at least the reputation for it. The Soviet leaders have managed to convince many in the West that their desire to prevail is stronger than the West's interest in the *status quo*.

"The side which is willing to run greater risks – or which can make its opponent believe that it is prepared to do so – gains a psychological advantage. During the Suez crisis, the Soviet Union threatened obliquely to launch rocket attacks against London and Paris – despite the fact that it would almost certainly have lost an all-out war. During the Hungarian revolution the West, though it was far stronger, was not willing to make similar threats against the USSR. This trend has continued at an accelerated pace. In every crisis, from Berlin to the Congo to Cuba, the Soviet Union has threatened missile attacks often in a fashion which has made subsequent actions seem to have been the result of Soviet missile blackmail. The diplomatic position of the Soviet Union has been greatly enhanced by its ability to shift to its opponents the risks and uncertainties of countermoves.

"2. *Reputation*. Since deterrence depends not only on the magnitude but also on the credibility of a threat, the side which has a greater reputation for ruthlessness or for a greater willingness to run risks gains a diplomatic advantage. This reputation is importantly affected by what may perhaps be called *the experience of the last use of force*. The Communist leaders have used force to maintain their sphere, as in Hungary and Tibet. They have threatened the use of force to expand their influence, as in the Middle East, Berlin and Cuba. The brutality of the repression in Hungary and Tibet may reflect the conviction that as long as the opprobrium of using force had to be shouldered it may as well be coupled with a reputation for ruthlessness and overwhelming power. By contrast, our last experience in resisting aggression, that of Korea, produced a bitter domestic debate and a seeming resolve never again to engage in what many have described an 'unproductive' war. The decision of a threatened country, allied or neutral, to resist and its resolution in the face of a menace may importantly depend on its assessment of the past actions of the West and Communist countries.

"3. *Political alignment*. A final asymmetry derives from the political context in which deterrence takes place. The threat of all-out war is more credible as a counter to a direct threat to a nation's survival than to a challenge to an ally. A challenge to an ally will call forth a greater willingness to run risks than pressure on a neutral. A psychological imbalance is created by the structure of the free world as against the Communist empire. The Soviet Union or Communist China can threaten all peripheral areas from their own territory. No country around the Communist periphery is capable of resisting alone. The Soviet Union can threaten our allies or neutrals. In order to deter by the threat of all-out war, we must menace metropolitan Russia or China. This alone creates a psychological problem in making the threat of all-out war credible and will do so increasingly as the Soviet nuclear and missile arsenal grows. For however firm allied unity may be, the threat of all-out war in defence of a foreign territory is less plausible than in defence of one's own. At least an aggressor may believe this, and such a conviction, however unjustified, would cause deterrence to fail.

"The imbalance is emphasised also by the structure of alliances in the free world as compared to the Communist bloc. The free-world alliances are composed of *status quo* powers. The Communist world is composed of revolutionary states of varying degrees of fanaticism. To hold the free-world alliances together it is necessary to demonstrate calmness, reasonableness and willingness to settle differences. By contrast within the Communist bloc, whatever the personal convictions of individual leaders, it is necessary to engage in periodic acts of intransigence to prove ideological purity. The pressures within the free world are in the direction of a lowest common denominator. Within the Communist bloc the requirements of alliance policy tend to produce a kind of addition of the different goals.

"These asymmetries explain why our undoubted strategic superiority did not deter a whole range of Soviet challenges even during the period of our atomic monopoly. Our strategic superiority was more than outweighed by the fact that the alternatives posed by our military policy gave the Soviet Union a psychological advantage. From the Berlin blockade to Korea, to Indo-China, to Suez, to Hungary, to the Congo and Cuba, the combination of reputation for ruthlessness, willingness to run risks, and the difficulties of alliance policy enabled the Soviet Union to blackmail the free world. The dilemma of our postwar strategy has been that the power which was available to us has also produced the greatest inhibitions, while we have had no confidence in the kind of forces which might have redressed the psychological balance.

"If deterrence by the threat of all-out war is difficult for us, it is nearly insurmountable for our allies. The retaliatory force on which we rely for deterrence is at least within our own control. We have the possibility of increasing its credibility by a daring diplomacy. But daring, even recklessness, will avail our allies little unless it is backed up by the United States. If the threat of all-out war is the chief counter to Soviet aggression, none of our allies will be able to pose an effective retaliatory threat should they create strategic forces of their own. The result will be either a sense of impotence or irresponsibility, either resignation or a futile attempt to achieve an independent deterrent position.

"Such a situation will expose our allies to the most intractable form of blackmail. Their leaders can be told that unless they accede to Soviet demands it will make little difference whether or not we retaliate against the Soviet Union. Resistance would mean certain devastation, so the Soviet argument may go, even if the United States made good on its promise to retaliate. Indeed, it would give the Soviet Union an added incentive to create a *fait accompli*. The destruction of their country can be prevented only by accommodating themselves to the Soviet Union. This indeed was the theme of Premier Khrushchev's press conference after the collapse of *the* summit conference:

> 'It is said that the United States would discharge their [*sic*] duties to their allies. By doing so they tell those countries where the bases are located, don't be afraid, if the Soviet Union smashes you, strikes a retaliatory blow with rockets, we shall attend your funeral when you have been smashed.'

"If deterrence by the threat of all-out war was difficult when we were strategically superior, it will grow intolerable in the age of mutual invulnerability. It will put a premium on recklessness and thus undermine the psychological basis for our foreign policy. It will lead to a diplomacy of bluff where even success makes for instability. If over a period of years the contenders become convinced that the situations of threat and counterthreat will always be resolved by *somebody* backing down, a showdown may be produced by this very sense of security. After all, the crisis which led to World War I seemed at first no different from innumerable others which had been resolved by the threat of going to the brink of war. And when war finally came, it was fought as a total war over a relatively trivial issue because no other alternative had been considered. It would be tragic

if our generation allowed itself to repeat the errors of its grand-
fathers. The penalty now would be incomparably more severe."

Schelling – The Strategy of Conflict*

"Among diverse theories of conflict – corresponding to the diverse
meanings of the word 'conflict' – a main dividing line is between those
that treat conflict as a pathological state and seek its causes and
treatment, and those that take conflict for granted and study the
behaviour associated with it. Among the latter there is a further
division between those that examine the participants in a conflict in
all their complexity – with regard to both 'rational' and 'irrational'
behaviour, conscious and unconscious, and to motivations as well as
to calculations – and those that focus on the more rational, conscious,
artful kind of behaviour. Crudely speaking, the latter treat conflict as
a kind of contest, in which the participants are trying to 'win'. A
study of conscious, intelligent, sophisticated conflict behaviour – of
successful behaviour – is like a search for rules of 'correct' behaviour
in a contest-winning sense.

"We can call this field of study the *strategy* of conflict.[1] We can be
interested in it for at least three reasons. We may be involved in a
conflict ourselves; we all are, in fact, participants in international
conflict, and we want to 'win' in some proper sense. We may wish to
understand how participants actually do conduct themselves in conflict situations; an understanding of 'correct' play may give us a bench
mark for the study of actual behaviour. We may wish to control or
influence the behaviour of others in conflict, and we want, therefore,
to know how the variables that are subject to our control can affect
their behaviour.

"If we confine our study to the theory of strategy, we seriously
restrict ourselves by the assumption of rational behaviour – not just
of intelligent behaviour, but of behaviour motivated by a conscious

---

* From Thomas Schelling (1921–). Taught economics at Yale for many years.
Leapt to fame in the early 1960s when he turned his attention to arms control
and the bargaining process between major military powers, especially nuclear
powers. Works include *Strategy and Arms Control* (joint author, 1961) and *Arms
and Influence* (1966). Quoted from *The Strategy of Conflict* (Cambridge, Mass.:
Harvard University Press, 1963).

calculation of advantages, a calculation that in turn is based on an explicit and internally consistent value system. We thus limit the applicability of any results we reach. If our interest is the study of actual behaviour, the results we reach under this constraint may prove to be either a good approximation of reality or a caricature. Any abstraction runs a risk of this sort, and we have to be prepared to use judgement with any results we reach.

"The advantage of cultivating the area of 'strategy' for theoretical development is not that, of all possible approaches, it is the one that evidently stays closest to the truth, but that the assumption of rational behaviour is a productive one. It gives a grip on the subject that is peculiarly conducive to the development of theory. It permits us to identify our own analytical processes with those of the hypothetical participants in a conflict; and by demanding certain kinds of consistency in the behaviour of our hypothetical participants, we can examine alternative courses of behaviour according to whether or not they meet those standards of consistency. The premise of 'rational behaviour' is a potent one for the production of theory. Whether the resulting theory provides good or poor insight into actual behaviour is, I repeat, a matter for subsequent judgement.

"But, in taking conflict for granted, and working with an image of participants who try to 'win', a theory of strategy does not deny that there are common as well as conflicting interests among the participants. In fact, the richness of the subject arises from the fact that, in international affairs, there is mutual dependence as well as opposition. Pure conflict, in which the interests of two antagonists are completely opposed, is a special case; it would arise in a war of complete extermination, otherwise not even in war. For this reason, 'winning' in a conflict does not have a strictly competitive meaning; it is not winning relative to one's adversary. It means gaining relative to one's own value system; and this may be done by bargaining, by mutual accommodation, and by the avoidance of mutually damaging behaviour. If war to the finish has become inevitable, there is nothing left but pure conflict; but if there is any possibility of avoiding a mutually damaging war, of conducting warfare in a way that minimises damage, or of coercing an adversary by threatening war rather than waging it, the possibility of mutual accommodation is as important and dramatic as the element of conflict. Concepts like deterrence, limited war and disarmament, as well as negotiation, are concerned with the common interest and mutual dependence that can exist between participants in a conflict.

"Thus, strategy – in the sense in which I am using it here – is not concerned with the efficient *application* of force but with the *exploitation of potential force*. It is concerned not just with enemies who dislike each other but with partners who distrust or disagree with each other. It is concerned not just with the division of gains and losses between two claimants but with the possibility that particular outcomes are worse (better) for *both* claimants than certain other outcomes. In the terminology of game theory, most interesting international conflicts are not 'constant-sum games' but 'variable-sum games': the sum of the gains of the participants involved is not fixed so that more for one inexorably means less for the other. There is a common interest in reaching outcomes that are mutually advantageous.

"To study the strategy of conflict is to take the view that most conflict situations are essentially *bargaining* situations. They are situations in which the ability of one participant to gain his ends is dependent to an important degree on the choices or decisions that the other participant will make. The bargaining may be explicit, as when one offers a concession; or it may be by tacit manoeuvre, as when one occupies or evacuates strategic territory. It may, as in the ordinary haggling of the market-place, take the *status quo* as its zero point and seek arrangements that yield positive gains to both sides; or it may involve threats of damage, including mutual damage, as in a strike, boycott or price war, or in extortion.

"Viewing conflict behaviour as a bargaining process is useful in keeping us from becoming exclusively preoccupied either with the conflict or with the common interest. To characterise the manoeuvres and actions of limited war as a bargaining process is to emphasise that, in addition to the divergence of interest over the variables in dispute, there is a powerful common interest in reaching an outcome that is not enormously destructive of values to both sides. A 'successful' employees' strike is not one that destroys the employer financially, it may even be one that never takes place. Something similar can be true of war.

"The idea of 'deterrence' has had an evolution that is instructive for our purpose. It is a dozen years since deterrence was articulated as the keystone of our national strategy, and during those years the concept has been refined and improved. We have learned that a threat has to be credible to be efficacious, and that its credibility may depend on the costs and risks associated with fulfilment for the party making the threat. We have developed the idea of making a threat credible by getting ourselves committed to its fulfilment, through the stretching of a 'trip wire' across the enemy's path of advance, or by making fulfilment a matter of national honour and prestige – as in the case, say, of the Formosa Resolution. We have recognised that a readiness to fight limited war in particular areas may detract from the threat of massive retaliation, by preserving the choice of a lesser evil if the contingency arises. We have considered the possibility that a retaliatory threat may be more credible if the means of carrying it out and the responsibility for retaliation are placed in the hands of those whose resolution is strongest, as in recent suggestions for 'nuclear sharing'. We have observed that the rationality of the adversary is pertinent to the efficacy of a threat, and that madmen, like small children, can often not be controlled by threats. We have recognised that the efficacy of the threat may depend on what alternatives are available to the potential enemy, who, if he is not to react like a trapped lion, must be left some tolerable recourse. We have come to realise that a threat of all-out retaliation gives the enemy every incentive, in the event he should choose not to heed the threat, to initiate his transgression with an all-out strike at us; it eliminates lesser courses of action and forces him to choose between extremes. We have learned that the threat of massive destruction may deter an enemy only if there is a corresponding implicit promise of non-destruction in the event he complies, so that we must consider whether too great a capacity to strike him by surprise may induce him to strike first to avoid being disarmed by a first strike from us. And recently, in connection with the so-called 'measures to safeguard against surprise attack', we have begun to consider the possibility of improving mutual deterrence through arms control.

• • •

"What would 'theory' in this field of strategy consist of? What questions would it try to answer? What ideas would it try to unify, clarify or communicate more effectively? To begin with, it should define the essentials of the situation and of the behaviour in question. Deterrence – to continue with deterrence as a typical strategic concept – is concerned with influencing the choices that another party will make, and doing it by influencing his expectations of how we will behave. It involves confronting him with evidence for believing that our behaviour will be determined by his behaviour.

"But what configuration of value systems for the two participants – of the 'payoffs', in the language of game theory – makes a deterrent threat credible? How do we measure the mixture of conflict and common interest required to generate a 'deterrence' situation? What communication is required, and what means of authenticating the evidence communicated? What kind of 'rationality' is required of the party to be deterred – a knowledge of his own value system, an ability to perceive alternatives and to calculate with probabilities, an ability to demonstrate (or an inability to conceal) his own rationality?

"What is the need for trust, or enforcement of promises? Specifically, in addition to threatening damage, need one also guarantee to withhold the damage if compliance is forthcoming; or does this depend on the configuration of 'payoffs' involved? What 'legal system', communication system or information structure is needed to make the necessary promises enforceable?

"Can one threaten that he will 'probably' fulfil a threat; or must he threaten that he certainly will? What is the meaning of a threat that one will 'probably' fulfil when it is clear that, if he retained any choice, he'd have no incentive to fulfil it after the act? More generally, what are the devices by which one gets committed to fulfilment that he would otherwise be known to shrink from, considering that if a commitment makes the threat credible enough to be effective it need not be carried out. What is the difference, if any, between a threat that deters action and one that compels action, or a threat designed to safeguard a second party from his own mistakes? Are there any logical differences among deterrent, disciplinary and extortionate threats?

"How is the situation affected by a third participant, who has his own mixture of conflict and common interest with those already present, who has access to or control of the communication system, whose behaviour is rational or irrational in one sense or another, who enjoys trust or some means of contract enforcement with one or another of the two principals? How are these questions affected by the existence of a legal system that permits and prohibits certain actions, that is available to inflict penalty on nonfulfilment of contract, or that can demand authentic information from the participants. To what extent can we rationalise concepts like 'reputation', or 'face' or 'trust', in terms of a real or hypothetical legal system, in terms of modification of the participants' value systems, or in terms of relationships of the players concerned to additional participants, real or hypothetical?

"This brief sample of questions may suggest that there is scope for the creation of 'theory'. There is something here that looks like a mixture of game theory, organisation theory, communication theory,

theory of evidence, theory of choice and theory of collective decision. It is faithful to our definition of 'strategy': it takes conflict for granted, but also assumes common interest between the adversaries; it assumes a 'rational' value-maximising mode of behaviour; and it focuses on the fact that each participant's 'best' choice of action depends on what he expects the other to do, and that 'strategic behaviour' is concerned with influencing another's choice by working on his expectation of how one's own behaviour is related to his."

Note

1. The term "strategy" is taken, here, from the *theory of games*, which distinguishes games of skill, games of chance and games of strategy, the latter being those in which the best course of action for each player depends on what the other players do. The term is intended to focus on the interdependence of the adversaries' decisions and on their expectations about each other's behaviour. This is not the military usage.

Howard – The Special Character of Modern War*

"[T]he inhibitions on the use of violence between states are considerable. They are not grounded simply on humanitarian considerations, or on any formal respect for international law. Fundamentally they rest on the most naked kind of self-interest. The use of violence, between states as between individuals, is seldom the most effective way of settling disputes. It is expensive in its methods and unpredictable in its outcome; and these elements of expense and unpredictability have both grown enormously over the last hundred years. The advent of nuclear weapons has only intensified an aversion to the use of violence in international affairs, which has, with certain rather obvious exceptions, increasingly characterised the conduct of foreign policy by the major powers since the latter part of the nineteenth century.

* From Michael Howard (1922–). British military historian and writer on defence questions. Professor of War Studies at Kings College London and Oxford, before becoming Regius Professor of Modern History in Oxford. Has written widely on military affairs. Principal works include *The Franco-Prussian War* (1961), *The Theory and Practice of War* (1965), *Studies in War and Peace* (1970) and *War in European History* (1976). Quoted from *Studies in War and Peace* (London: Temple Smith, 1970).

"For this aversion there was little historical precedent. In most of the societies known to history, war has been an established and usually rather enjoyable social rite. In western Europe until the first part of the seventeenth century warfare was a way of life for considerable sections of society, its termination was for them a catastrophe, and its prolongation, official or unofficial, was the legitimate objective of every man of spirit. Even in the seventeenth and eighteenth centuries war, elaborate and formal as its conduct had become, was an accepted, almost an indispensable part of the pattern of society, and it was curtailed and intermittent only because of its mounting expense. If war could be made to pay, as it did for the Dutch merchants in the seventeenth century and the English in the eighteenth, then its declaration was as welcome as its termination was deplored. Habits of mind formed in days when war was the main social function of the nobility and a source of profit to the merchants survived into our own century, even though new weapons had rendered aristocratic leadership anachronistic if not positively dangerous, and the City of London confidently predicted ruin and bankruptcy when war threatened in 1914. Such atavistic belligerence was fanned by the jingoistic enthusiasm of the masses in the great cities of western Europe, where gusts of emotion greeted every war from the Crimea to that of 1914.

"But by 1914 governments and peoples were largely at cross-purposes. Since 1870 the size and expense of the war-machines, and the uncertainty of the consequences of war for society as a whole, made violence an increasingly unusable instrument for the conduct of international affairs. Defeat, even at the hands of a moderate and restrained adversary, might mean social revolution, as it nearly had for France in 1870 and Russia in 1905; while even a successful war involved a disturbance of the economic life of the nation whose consequences were quite unforeseeable. Clausewitz in his great work *On War* had suggested that 'policy', the adaptation of military means to political objectives, could convert the heavy battlesword of war into a light, handy rapier for use in limited conflicts; but the mass armies of 1870, of 1914 and of 1939 could not be wielded as rapiers in the cut and thrust of international politics. Indeed, so great was the expense of modern war, so heavy were the sacrifices that it entailed, that it was difficult to conceive of causes warranting having resort to it at all. Could the national resources really be mobilised and the youth of the nation really be sacrificed in hundreds of thousands for anything short of national survival, or some great ideological crusade?

"So at least it appeared to the great western democracies in the
1930s; and it was this sentiment that Hitler exploited with such
superb and sinister skill. Mass war, as Britain and France had learned
to fight it between 1914 and 1918, was not a rational instrument of
foreign policy. French and British statesmen were naturally and
properly unwilling to invoke it for such limited objectives as the
preservation of the Rhineland from re-militarisation; or the prevention of the *Anschluss* of an acquiescent Austria with Germany; or to
prevent the German population of the Sudetenland being accorded
the privileges of self-determination which had been granted to other
peoples in Central Europe; and there appeared to be no other
instruments they could use instead. To suggest that Hitler could not
have been planning for war because in 1939 the German economy
was not fully mobilised nor the armed forces at full battle strength is
to apply the standards of 1914 to a different situation. Hitler had not
armed Germany, as Britain and France had systematically armed
since 1935, for a full-scale, formal Armageddon. He had every hope
that it might be avoided. But he had the means available to use
violence as an instrument of policy in a limited but sufficient degree,
and he had no more inhibitions about using it in foreign than he had
in domestic affairs. The Western democracies, committed to a policy
of total violence in international affairs or none at all, could only
watch him paralysed; until they took up arms on a scale, and with a
crusading purpose, which could result only in the destruction of
Germany or of themselves, and quite conceivably of both.

"We should not, therefore, overestimate the change brought about
in international relations through the introduction of nuclear weapons.
The reluctance to contemplate the use of such weapons, which is
fortunately so characteristic of the powers which at present possess
them, is a continuation, although vastly intensified, of the reluctance
to use the older techniques of mass war. Even as the statesmen of the
1930s found it difficult to conceive of a cause urgent enough to justify
the use of the massive weapons of which they potentially disposed,
so, *a fortiori*, is it still more difficult for us to foresee the political
problem to which the destruction of a score of millions of civilians
will provide the appropriate military solution. It is for this reason that
political influence does not necessarily increase in direct proportion
to the acquisition of nuclear power. Similarly, there is no cause to
suppose that the capacity to use nuclear weapons will be any more
effective as a deterrent to, or even as an agent of, disturbances of the
international order than was, in the 1930s, the ability, given the will,

to wage mass war. Those who wish to use violence as an instrument of policy – and since 1945 they have not been rare – can find, as did Hitler, more limited and effective forms; and those who hope to counter it need equally effective instruments for doing so.

"Perhaps, indeed, it is necessary, in reassessing the place of military force in international affairs, to rid ourselves of the idea that if such force is employed it must necessarily be in a distinct 'war', formally declared, ending in a clear decision embodied in a peace treaty, taking place within a precise interval of time during which diplomatic relations between the belligerents are suspended and military operations proceed according to their own peculiar laws. We reveal the influence of this concept whenever we talk about 'the next war', or 'if war breaks out' or 'the need to deter war'. If an inescapable *casus belli* were to occur between nuclear powers, there *might* follow a spasm of mutual destruction which the survivors, such as they were, would be justified in remembering as the Third World War; but such an outcome is by no means inevitable, and appears to be decreasingly likely. It seems more probable that a *casus belli* would provoke threats and, if necessary, execution of limited acts of violence, probably though not necessarily localised, probably though not necessarily non-nuclear; all accompanied by an intensification rather than a cessation of diplomatic intercourse. Instead of a formal state of war in which diplomacy was subordinated to the requirements of strategy, specific military operations might be carried out under the most rigorous political control. It will certainly no longer be enough for the statesman to give general guidance to a military machine which then proceeds according to its own laws. Politics must now interpenetrate military activity at every level as thoroughly as the nervous system penetrates the tissues of a human body, carrying to the smallest muscle the dictates of a controlling will. The demands on the military for discipline and self-sacrifice will be great beyond all precedent, and the opportunities for traditional honour and glory negligible. Regiments will bear as their battle honours the names, not of the battles they have fought, but those that they have averted.

"The maintenance of armed forces for this role creates many problems. Such conflicts must be waged with forces in being, and the task for which they are recruited is a thankless one. The standard of technical expertise, already high, may become still more exacting; military commanders will need exceptional political wisdom as well as military skill; but they must refrain from attempting to shape the political world to their military image, as the French army tried to do, so tragically, in Algeria. Indeed, the tendency which has been so general during the past fifteen years of regarding all international relations as an extension of warfare, and the description of national policy in such terms as 'national strategy' or 'Cold War' betrays a dangerous confusion of categories and a fundamental misunderstanding of the nature of international affairs, even in an age of bitter ideological conflict.

"On the other hand, statesmen now require a deeper understanding of military matters, of the needs and capabilities and limitations of armed forces, than they have ever needed in the past. Only if there is complete mutual understanding and co-operation between civil and military leaders, only if there is effective functioning of the mechanism of command and control, only if there is entire discipline and obedience in every rank of military hierarchy can military power serve as an instrument of international order at all, rather than one of international anarchy and world destruction.

"The order which exists between sovereign states is very different in kind from that which they maintain within their borders, but it is an order none the less, though precarious in places and everywhere incomplete. There does exist a comity of nations, an international community transcending ideological and other rivalries. Its activities in many fields – those of commerce and communications, of health and diplomatic representation, of use of the high seas and of the air – are regulated by effective and precise provisions of international law, which are for the most part meticulously observed. But even in those aspects of international relations which international law does not regulate, order still obtains. It is preserved by certain conventions of behaviour established and adjusted by a continuing and subtle process of communication and negotiations, with which not even the most revolutionary of states – neither the United States in the eighteenth century nor the Soviet Union in the twentieth – has ever found it possible to dispense for very long. This order is based on no system of positive law, nor of natural justice, nor of clearly defined rights, nor even of agreed values. It has never been very easy for sovereign states to agree about such things. Even if the differing pattern of their international development does not lead them to adopt divergent and conflicting ideologies, states are bound by their very nature to regard the maintenance of their own power as the main criterion of all their actions and to pursue that, whatever their noble professions to the contrary. International order is based rather on recognition of disagreement, and of the limitation on one's own capacity to secure agreement. It is based on the understanding by nations that their capacity to impose and extend their own favoured order is limited by the will and effective ability of other states to impose theirs. The conduct of international relations must therefore always be a delicate adjustment of power to power, a mutual exploration of intentions and capabilities, so as to find and preserve an order which, though fully satisfying to nobody, is just tolerable to all."

24 The State and the Society of States

Students of international relations became, during the 1950s and 1960s, increasingly concerned to discover the best way of studying the behaviour of states in interaction. In particular they debated what should be the main area of attention on which they should concentrate.

Those who study international relationships may focus not only on different areas of subject-matter (foreign policy or international institutions, political or economic relationships, diplomacy or war, conflict or co-operation), but, as the arrangement of this volume implies, on different *levels* of interaction. Thus study can be directed mainly to *individuals*: the way they acquire their foreign policy attitudes, the way they give expression to these attitudes, the way they exercise positions of responsibility. It can be directed at *states*: the way decisions on foreign policy are reached within states, the influences that determine state policies, the motivations of states generally. Or, finally, it may be directed at the system as a whole, the *society of states*: the structure of power within that society, the institutions established for resolving conflicts, the conventions that govern relationships within the society.

The choice of the level to be studied has aroused considerable discussion among scholars. The two extracts presented below are concerned with different aspects of this choice. Kenneth Waltz, in his study *Man, the State and War*, examined three alternative "images" which have been used over the ages in studying the problem of peace and war. The first image concentrated on the individual human being: since some have believed, for example, that the root of all evil is in man, they have held that the problems of war and peace can only be solved by rooting out the evil that is in the human mind. The second image consists of the individual state: so others have believed that it is the state which is good or bad, and that the evil conduct of men, for example in making war, results from the compelling influence of state institutions, whether those of all states or those of some states only. The third image is that of the society of states within which states live: under this view it is the character of the international society which determines the conduct of states rather than the character of the individual state: thus for war to be abolished it will not be sufficient to improve the attitudes of individuals, nor to improve the conduct of individual states (for even the state which wants peace may be forced into war by the threatening behaviour of other states), but only to improve the character of the international society as a whole.

David Singer, in his essay on the "Level-of-Analysis Problem", considers two alternative models for the study of international relations: the international system as a whole and the individual national state. He suggests that a useful analytical model should be able to describe, to explain and to predict (though he believes that the most important of these is explanation). He examines the two different levels and considers the advantage each has for these three purposes. He finds that in terms of description the study of the international system as a whole has both advantages and disadvantages; that in terms of explanation it suffers from serious limitations (since it tends to exaggerate the effect of the system on the state and to downplay the importance of differences between states); but that in terms of prediction it has distinct advantages over the alternative model. Conversely, the study directed at individual states will naturally bring out more clearly the differences between states, but may exaggerate those differences; it has advantages in terms of explanation since it can examine how and why particular policies are chosen by states; and enjoys certain advantages in terms of prediction. Thus both models are useful for different purposes, and both have their contribution to make. They are not exclusive alternatives, since other approaches altogether are possible. The important thing for the scholar is to be aware which approach is being used, not to switch erratically from one to the other; and to remain fully conscious of the descriptive, explanatory and predictive explanations of the choice that is made.

Of the three possible levels of approach it is probably true to say that there is today less interest in that which relates to the individual human being (though there may still be room for fruitful psychological studies of individual decision-makers, or types of decision-maker, and of the influences on their decisions). Of the other two, both are widely used, as this Reader shows. There may today be rather greater interest in the system, or "society", as a whole, relative to the study of individual states: the opposite of the situation described by Singer 30 years ago. But most students of the subject would probably agree that each has a part to play; and that there is a danger in exclusive reliance on one without the corrective influence of the other. In other words the state cannot be understood except in its relationship with the international society of which it is a part; any more than the international society can be studied effectively without attention to the peculiar characteristics of its individual members.

*   *   *

Waltz – Man, the State and the Society of States*

"The root of all evil is man, and thus he is himself the root of the specific evil, war. This estimate of cause, widespread and firmly held by many as an article of faith, has been immensely influential. It is the conviction of St Augustine and Luther, of Malthus and Jonathan Swift, of Dean Inge and Reinhold Niebuhr. In secular terms, with men defined as beings of intermixed reason and passion in whom passion repeatedly triumphs, the belief has informed the philosophy, including the political philosophy, of Spinoza. One might argue that it was as influential in the activities of Bismarck, with his low opinion of his fellow man, as it was in the rigorous and austere writings of Spinoza. If one's beliefs condition his expectations and his expectations condition his acts, acceptance or rejection of Milton's statement becomes important in the affairs of men. And, of course, Milton might be right even if no one believed him. If so, attempts to explain the recurrence of war in terms of, let us say, economic factors, might still be interesting games, but they would be games of little consequence. If it is true, as Dean Swift once said, that 'the very same principle that influences a bully to break the windows of a whore who has jilted him, naturally stirs up a great prince to raise mighty armies, and dream of nothing but sieges, battles, and victories', then the reasons given by princes for the wars they have waged are mere rationalisations covering a motivation they may not themselves have

---

* From Kenneth N. Waltz. Studied at Columbia University and taught at Swarthmore, Brandeis and Berkeley. Interested in political theory, foreign policy and international politics generally. Writings include *Foreign Policy and Domestic Politics* (1957) and *The Theory of International Politics* (1979). Quoted from *Man, the State and War* (New York: Columbia University Press, 1956).

perceived and could not afford to state openly if they had. It would follow as well that the schemes of the statesman Sully, if seriously intended to produce a greater peace in the world, were as idle as the dreams of the French monk Crucé – idle, that is, unless one can strike at the roots, the pride and petulance that have produced the wars as they have the other ills that plague mankind.

•   •   •

"Can man in society best be understood by studying man or by studying society? The most satisfactory reply would seem to be given by striking the word 'or' and answering 'both'. But where one begins his explanation of events makes a difference. The Reverend Thomas Malthus once wrote that, 'though human institutions appear to be the obvious and obtrusive causes of much mischief to mankind; yet, in reality, they are light and superficial, they are mere feathers that float on the surface, in comparison with those deeper seated causes of impurity that corrupt the springs, and render turbid the whole stream of human life'. Rousseau looked at the same world, the same range of events, but found the locus of major causes in a different ambit.

"Following Rousseau's lead in turn raises questions. As men live in states, so states exist in a world of states. If we now confine our attention to the question of why wars occur, shall we emphasise the role of the state, with its social and economic content as well as its political form, or shall we concentrate primarily on what is sometimes called the society of states? Again one may say strike the word 'or' and worry about both, but many have emphasised either the first or the second, which helps to explain the discrepant conclusions reached. Those who emphasise the first in a sense run parallel to Milton. He explains the ills of the world by the evil in man; they explain the great ill of war by the evil qualities of some or of all states. The statement is then often reversed: If bad states make wars, good states would live at peace with one another. With varying degrees of justification this view can be attributed to Plato and Kant, to nineteenth-century liberals and revisionist socialists. They agree on the principle involved, though they differ in their descriptions of good states as well as on the problem of bringing about their existence.

"Where Marxists throw the liberals' picture of the world into partial eclipse, others blot it out entirely. Rousseau himself finds the major causes of war neither in men nor in states but in the state system itself. Of men in a state of nature, he had pointed out that one man cannot begin to behave decently unless he has some assurance that others will not be able to ruin him. This thought Rousseau develops and applies to states existing in a condition of anarchy in his fragmentary essay on 'The State of War' and in his commentaries on the works of the Abbé de Saint-Pierre. Though a state may want to remain at peace, it may have to consider undertaking a preventive war; for if it does not strike when the moment is favourable it may be struck later when the advantage has shifted to the other side. This view forms the analytic basis for many balance-of-power approaches to international relations and for the world-federalist programme as well. Implicit in Thucydides and Alexander Hamilton, made explicit by Machiavelli, Hobbes and Rousseau, it is at once a generalised explanation of states' behaviour and a critical *point d'appui* against those who look to the internal structure of states to explain their external behaviour. While some believe that peace will follow from the improvement of states, others assert that what the state will be like depends on its relation to others. The latter thesis Leopold Ranke derived from, or applied to, the history of the states of modern Europe. It has been used to explain the internal ordering of other states as well.

"Statesmen, as well as philosophers and historians, have attempted to account for the behaviour of states in peace and in war. Woodrow Wilson, in the draft of a note written in November of 1916, remarked that the causes of the war then being fought were obscure, that neutral nations did not know why it had begun and, if drawn in, would not know for what ends they would be fighting. But often to act we must convince ourselves that we do know the answers to such questions. Wilson, to his own satisfaction, soon did. He appears in history as one of the many who, drawing a sharp distinction between peaceful and aggressive states, have assigned to democracies all the attributes of the first, to authoritarian states all the attributes of the second. To an extent that varies with the author considered, the incidence of war is then thought to depend upon the type of national government. Thus Cobden in a speech at Leeds in December of 1849:

'Where do we look for the black gathering cloud of war? Where do we see it rising? Why, from the despotism of the north, where one man wields the destinies of 40,000,000 of serfs. If we want to know where is the second danger of war and disturbance, it is in that province of Russia – that miserable and degraded country, Austria – next in the stage of despotism and barbarism, and there you see again the greatest danger of war; but in proportion as you find the population governing themselves – as in England, in France, or in

America – there you will find that war is not the disposition of the people, and that if Government desire it, the people would put a check upon it.'

"The constant interest of the people is in peace; no government controlled by the people will fight unless set upon. But only a few years later, England, though not set upon, did fight against Russia; and Cobden lost his seat in 1857 as a result of his opposition to the war. The experience is shattering, but not fatal to the belief; for it relives in the words of Wilson, for example, and again in those of the late Senator Robert Taft. In the manner of Cobden but in the year 1951, Taft writes: 'History shows that when the people have the opportunity to speak they as a rule decide for peace if possible. It shows that arbitrary rulers are more inclined to favour war than are the people at any time.' Is it true, one wonders, that there is a uniquely peaceful form of the state? If it were true, how much would it matter? Would it enable some states to know which other states they could trust? Should the states that are already good seek ways of making other states better, and thus make it possible for all men to enjoy the pleasures of peace? Wilson believed it morally imperative to aid in the political regeneration of others; Cobden thought it not even justifiable. Agreeing on where the causes are to be found, they differ in their policy conclusions."

Singer – National State and International System*

"[W]e find in the total international system a partially familiar and highly promising point of focus. First of all, it is the most comprehensive of the levels available, encompassing the totality of interactions which take place within the system and its environment. By focusing on the system, we are enabled to study the patterns of interaction

* From David Singer (1925–). Studied at Duke and New York Universities but has taught now for many years at Ann Arbor, where he also directs a major study on the Correlates of War. Has written widely on international relations, stressing the need for a strictly quantitative approach to the subject. Works include *Deterrence, Arms Control and Disarmament* (1962), *Quantitative International Politics* (1968), *The Study of International Politics* (1976) and *Explaining War* (1979). Quoted from "The Level-of-Analysis Problem", in K. Knorr and S. Verba (eds), *The International System* (Princeton, N.J.: Princeton University Press, 1961).

which the system reveals, and to generalise about such phenomena as the creation and dissolution of coalitions, the frequency and duration of specific power configurations, modifications in its stability, its responsiveness to changes in formal political institutions, and the norms and folklore which it manifests as a societal system. In other words, the systemic level of analysis, and only this level, permits us to examine international relations in the whole, with a comprehensiveness that is of necessity lost when our focus is shifted to a lower, and more partial, level. For descriptive purposes, then, it offers both advantages and disadvantages; the former flow from its comprehensiveness, and the latter from the necessary dearth of detail.

"As to explanatory capability, the system-oriented model poses some genuine difficulties. In the first place, it tends to lead the observer into a position which exaggerates the impact of the system upon the national actors and, conversely, discounts the impact of the actors on the system. This is, of course, by no means inevitable; one could conceivably look upon the system as a rather passive environment in which dynamic states act out their relationships rather than as a socio-political entity with a dynamic of its own. But there is a natural tendency to endow that upon which we focus our attention with somewhat greater potential than it might normally be expected to have. Thus, we tend to move, in a system-oriented model, away from notions implying much national autonomy and independence of choice and toward a more deterministic orientation.

"Secondly, this particular level of analysis almost inevitably requires that we postulate a high degree of uniformity in the foreign policy operational codes of our national actors. By definition, we allow little room for divergence in the behaviour of our parts when we focus upon the whole.

• • •

"[T]hough this may be an inadequate foundation upon which to base any *causal* statements, it offers a reasonably adequate basis for *correlative* statements. More specifically, it permits us to observe and measure correlations between certain forces or stimuli which seem to impinge upon the nation and the behaviour patterns which are the apparent consequence of these stimuli. But one must stress the limitations implied in the word 'apparent'; what is thought to be the consequence of a given stimulus may only be a coincidence or artifact, and until one investigates the major elements in the causal link – no matter how persuasive the deductive logic – one may speak only of correlation, not of consequence.

"Moreover, by avoiding the multitudinous pitfalls of intra-nation observation, one emerges with a singularly manageable model, requiring as it does little of the methodological sophistication or onerous empiricism called for when one probes beneath the behavioural externalities of the actor. Finally, as has already been suggested in the introduction, the systemic orientation should prove to be reasonably satisfactory as a basis for prediction, even if such prediction is to extend beyond the characteristics of the system and attempt anticipatory statements regarding the actors themselves; this assumes, of course, that the actors are characterised and their behaviour predicted in relatively gross and general terms.

"These, then, are some of the more significant implications of a model which focuses upon the international system as a whole. Let us turn now to the more familiar of our two orientations, the national state itself.

THE NATIONAL STATE AS LEVEL OF ANALYSIS

"The other level of analysis to be considered in this paper is the national state – our primary actor in international relations. This is clearly the traditional focus among Western students, and is the one which dominates almost all of the texts employed in English-speaking colleges and universities.

"Its most obvious advantage is that it permits significant differentiation among our actors in the international system. Because it does not require the attribution of great similarity to the national actors, it encourages the observer to examine them in greater detail. The favourable results of such intensive analysis cannot be overlooked, as it is only when the actors are studied in some depth that we are able to make really valid generalisations of a comparative nature. And though the systemic model does not necessarily preclude comparison and contrast among the national sub-systems, it usually eventuates in rather gross comparisons based on relatively crude dimensions and characteristics. . . .

"But just as the nation-as-actor focus permits us to avoid the inaccurate homogenisation which often flows from the systemic focus, it also may lead us into the opposite type of distortion – a marked exaggeration of the differences among our sub-systemic actors. While it is evident that neither of these extremes is conducive to the development of a sophisticated comparison of foreign policies, and such comparison requires a balanced preoccupation with both similarity and difference, the danger seems to be greatest when we succumb to the tendency to overdifferentiate; comparison and contrast can proceed only from observed uniformities.

• • •

"Another and perhaps more subtle implication of selecting the nation as our focus or level of analysis is that it raises the entire question of goals, motivation, and purpose in national policy. Though it may well be a peculiarity of the Western philosophical tradition, we seem to exhibit, when confronted with the need to explain individual or collective behaviour, a strong proclivity for a goal-seeking approach. The question of whether national behaviour is purposive or not seems to require discussion in two distinct (but not always exclusive) dimensions.

"Firstly, there is the more obvious issue of whether those who act on behalf of the nation in formulating and executing foreign policy consciously pursue rather concrete goals. And it would be difficult to deny, for example, that these role-fulfilling individuals envisage certain specific outcomes which they hope to realise by pursuing a particular strategy. In this sense, then, nations may be said to be goal-seeking organisms which exhibit purposive behaviour.

• • •

"Also involved in the goal-seeking problem when we employ the nation-oriented model is the question of how and why certain nations pursue specific sorts of goals. While the question may be ignored in the system-oriented model or resolved by attributing identical goals to all national actors, the nation-as-actor approach demands that we investigate the processes by which national goals are selected, internal and external factors that impinge on those processes, and the institutional framework from which they emerge. It is worthy of note that despite the strong predilection for the nation-oriented model in most of our texts, empirical or even deductive analyses of these processes are conspicuously few. Again, one might attribute these lacunae to the methodological and conceptual inadequacies of the graduate training which international relations specialists traditionally receive. But in any event, goals and motivations are both dependent and independent variables, and if we intend to explain a nation's foreign policy, we cannot settle for the mere postulation of these goals; we are compelled to go back a step and inquire into their genesis and the process by which they become the crucial variables that they seem to be in the behaviour of nations.

• • •

"Having discussed some of the descriptive, explanatory and predictive capabilities of these two possible levels of analysis, it might now be useful to assess the relative utility of the two and attempt some general statement as to their prospective contributions to greater theoretical growth in the study of international relations.

"In terms of description, we find that the systemic level produces a more comprehensive and total picture of international relations than does the national or sub-systemic level. On the other hand, the atomised and less coherent image produced by the lower level of analysis is somewhat balanced by its richer detail, greater depth, and more intensive portrayal. As to explanation, there seems little doubt that the sub-systemic or actor orientation is considerably more fruitful, permitting as it does a more thorough investigation of the processes by which foreign policies are made. Here we are enabled to go beyond the limitations imposed by the systemic level and to replace mere correlation with the more significant causation. And in terms of prediction, both orientations seem to offer a similar degree of promise. Here the issue is a function of what we seek to predict. Thus the policy-maker will tend to prefer predictions about the way in which nation x or y will react to a contemplated move on his own nation's part, while the scholar will probably prefer either generalised predictions regarding the behaviour of a given class of nations or those regarding the system itself.

"Does this summary add up to an overriding case for one or another of the two models? It would seem not. For a staggering variety of reasons the scholar may be more interested in one level than another at any given time and will undoubtedly shift his orientation according to his research needs. So the problem is really not one of deciding which level is most valuable to the discipline as a whole and then demanding that it be adhered to from now unto eternity. Rather, it is one of realising that there *is* this preliminary conceptual issue and that it must be temporarily resolved prior to any given research undertaking. And it must also be stressed that we have dealt here only with two of the more common orientations, and that many others are available and perhaps even more fruitful potentially than either of those selected here. Moreover, the international system gives many indications of prospective change, and it may well be that existing institutional forms will take on new characteristics or that new ones will appear to take their place. As a matter of fact, if incapacity to perform its functions leads to the transformation or decay of an institution, we may expect a steady deterioration and even ultimate disappearance of the national state as a significant actor in the world political system.

"However, even if the case for one or another of the possible levels of analysis cannot be made with any certainty, one must nevertheless maintain a continuing awareness as to their use. We may utilise one level here and another there, but we cannot afford to shift our orientation in the midst of a study. And when we do in fact make an original selection or replace one with another at appropriate times, we must do so with a full awareness of the descriptive, explanatory and predictive implications of such choice."

Part Three
The Nature of the
International System

Introduction

Just as those who have thought and written about relationships among individuals came in time to think increasingly about the nature of the community to which they belonged, which has influenced their relationships with each other, so those who have thought and written about relations among states have in time become increasingly concerned about the wider world beyond the state: the international society to which all states belong.

Most early writing about international relationships, like much of that quoted in Part Two of this collection, was primarily concerned with the needs and interests of *particular* states (those to which the writers themselves belonged) and those in authority within it, rather than with the needs and interests of the entire association of states of which their own was a member. But because that state was in frequent intercourse with other states, and established more or less enduring relationships with them, the idea in time inevitably emerged that there existed a wider society of states, with purposes and interests of its own, beyond those of any individual state. It was this wider society which eventually became the main subject of interest.

Beliefs about the nature of the system of states were inevitably influenced by judgements about the nature of individual states. Just as political philosophers, in considering the type of political system they believed should be established, have begun by considering the nature of "man", so those who have written about the society of states have been influenced by their conception of the nature of states. Observers who have seen the primary characteristic of states as their desire for power have recognised that this implied an international system which would always be rent with conflict. Such writers have tended to be cynical about the hopes of bringing about a more peaceful system of relations among states or a more integrated international society. They have doubted whether these aims were likely to be attainable either by taming the aggressive tendencies of governments or by establishing more effective international institutions that could exercise a restraining influence.

If each state was concerned above all to maximise its own power, as they have believed, the only effective way of reducing conflict, or at least preventing any one state securing total domination, was likely to be by establishing some system through which the self-interest of each state could be mobilised to maintain stability. The principal means by which this might be done, they argued, was for states to adopt policies designed to prevent any particular nation from acquiring a predominance of power. In early discussions of the international system this was usually the approach recommended.

25 The Balance of Power

Whenever a state enters into alliance with another state it is concerned, in a crude sense, with a balancing of power: with establishing a concentration of power which will withstand, or overcome, that of likely opponents. Often the state that pursues that policy is concerned only with its immediate, *short-term* interest; and will see advantage, therefore, in an alliance with the stronger of two neighbours in order to prevail over a third. But it has often been recognised that this could lead, over the long term, to an undue accretion in the power of the new ally. A true "balance of power" policy comes about only when a state looks beyond its short-term advantage to its long-term interest in a stable international environment, and therefore in preventing any particular state acquiring such power as to dominate the system. In this situation, it may be seen as wiser to undertake an alliance, not with the stronger of the two possible partners but with the *weaker*. Where such a judgement is made a true "balance of power" policy results.

Early writers on international affairs rarely thought in terms of a "system", or even of a society of states. Most such writers were advisers to rulers. They were, therefore, concerned about how the interests of *particular* states could best be promoted, and with the policies their rulers should pursue to bring this about. In considering that question they naturally sometimes gave thought to the alliance policy which would best serve the interests of that state. And occasionally the suggestion was made by them that it was wiser to support the weaker of the two neighbouring states than the stronger, so as to prevent the latter from becoming eventually too powerful: in other words to pursue a true balance of power policy.

From time to time states undoubtedly acted in accordance with this principle. In the ancient Chinese system smaller and weaker states joined together to defeat the stronger, as they did during Greek and Roman times in Europe (see, for example, the description of this process in the passage quoted from David Hume below). In the system of states which emerged in Italy in the fourteenth and fifteenth centuries there was a fairly consistent effort, by some states at least, to balance the power of other states. In the first half of the fifteenth century, when Milan, under the Sforzas, was the main expanding city and the main threat to peace, Florence, the principal balancing state, felt it wisest to combine with Venice against her; while in the latter half of the century, when Venice became the greater threat, Florence combined with Milan or Naples against Venice. Guicciardini, writing in the early sixteenth century, noted this tendency. He described it as a deliberate policy of the states of Italy, above all of Florence, to form alliances on this principle. In the passage below, from the early pages of his book, he describes how Lorenzo de Medici, recognising that it would be "most perilous to the Florentine Republic and himself if any of the major powers should extend their area of dominion", carefully saw to it that the Italian situation "should be maintained in a state of balance".

A little later, when Charles V and François I were engaged in their long duel for pre-eminence in Europe, Henry VIII prided himself that, by allying first with one and then with the other, he had kept the "balance of Europe" in England's hands. This was a claim English statesmen were to make many times in the following centuries; and it was, at certain moments at least, a conscious aim of British policy. When Louis XIV's France became an increasing threat to all other states in the second half of the Seventeenth Century the need to create an effective combination against him was recognised all over Europe, and it was then that the idea of the "balance of power" came to be most widely discussed. There were some French writers who (despite the fact that it was their own king who represented the main threat to the peace) recognised the need for other states to combine against the threat if the stability of the continent was to be maintained. Fénelon, the leading French theologian and adviser to Louis XIV, for example, in the passage below, eloquently expressed this view. He explicitly refers to the needs of the European society of states, distinct from that of any individual state. On these grounds he held that where the power of a state had increased "to such a pitch that all its neighbours are hardly a match for it", the latter "have an undoubted right to unite for the restraining of that increase".

The success of such a policy, however, depended on states being willing to put the general interest of the society of states above the immediate interest of their own (which might often be better served by alliance with the most powerful): that is, to prefer a remote long-term interest to a direct short-term interest. Would states always be willing to make that choice? This is the question raised by David Hume in the next passage quoted below. Having attempted to show how widely the principle had been applied in classical times, he asserted its continuing relevance to his own day, founded as it was on "common sense and obvious reasoning". But he roundly condemned the failure of British governments to practise it after recent wars. Often their aim, he believed, had been to seek undue advantage for England, instead of recognising the importance, even in England's own interests, of a genuine balance within the continent.

If balance was the supreme objective, did this justify the use of force against any state believed to threaten it? This question was much debated. Grotius, as we saw above (p. 149), had rejected that view. But now Vattel, in his much-acclaimed and much-quoted treatises on international law, suggested that the need to maintain the balance of power provided a legal justification of the use of force against a state which had become too powerful. He recognised that this principle might be used to justify almost any act of force. But he failed to overcome that danger by defining unmistakably the type of threat which would justify such action: it was sufficient in his eye that there was a "reasonable presumption" that the state concerned was showing signs of "imperious pride and insatiable ambition" to justify joint action against it. Since this was a charge which (if it was found necessary to seek a justification at all) could be raised against almost any state at any time, the rule he advocated hardly provided a firm basis for creating a peaceful international society.

If any kind of international "system" can be said to have been recognised in this period, therefore, it consisted in the systematic use of balance of power policies. By forming themselves into constantly changing alliances against each other, it was believed, the leading states might maintain a rough parity between them and so ensure that none was able to increase its power excessively. But whatever could be claimed for this system in preventing any one power from becoming dominant, it certainly did not succeed in preserving the peace. War was for a century and a half after 1648 endemic: scarcely surprising since war was the main instrument for maintaining – or restoring – the balance. And when Napoleon succeeded in conquering most of the continent in the following years, it was apparent that the system had not even been able to effect its primary purpose: to contain the excessive power of any particular state. It was this situation that was deplored by Friedrich von Gentz, a former Prussian official, in the excerpt below from his *Fragments upon the Present State of the Political Balance of Europe*. Writing in 1806, at the height of Napoleon's power, he looked back nostalgically to the preceding period, when something like a balance had been maintained; a balance he believed had even secured the integrity of smaller states

(though this was conspicuously untrue of Poland which had been
entirely swallowed up by her neighbours, allegedly in the interests of
the "balance of power").

To describe the policies pursued in this period as a "system" is to
do it too much honour. It was usually self-interest, rather than
conformity to a known and recognised system, which caused states to
build mutually hostile alliances. But in so far as the idea of a balance
of power was explicitly pursued, it did begin to establish the conception of an interest that was wider than that of any individual state:
that of Europe as a whole.

*   *   *

Guicciardini – The Balance of Power among the Italian States*

"I have determined to write about those events which have occurred
in Italy within our memory, ever since French troops, summoned by
our own princes, began to stir up very great dissensions here: a most
memorable subject in view of its scope and variety, and full of the
most terrible happenings; since for so many years Italy suffered all
those calamities with which miserable mortals are usually afflicted,
sometimes because of the just anger of God, and sometimes because
of the impiety and wickedness of other men. From a knowledge of
such occurrences, so varied and so grave, everyone may derive many
precedents salutary both for himself and for the public weal. Thus
numerous examples will make it plainly evident how mutable are
human affairs, not unlike a sea whipped by winds; and how
pernicious, almost always to themselves but always to the people, are
those ill-advised measures of rulers who act solely in terms of what is

---

* From Francesco Guicciardini (1483–1540). Florentine historian. After a period as a
successful lawyer, served as Florence's ambassador in Spain during the Florentine
republic. After the return of the Medicis to power, continued to hold official and
military posts in Florence and the papal states. His support for the unsuccessful
alliance with France in 1526–7 caused decline in his influence but he remained active
in Florentine politics as a supporter of the Medicis and an opponent of the emperor
Charles V. However, an accommodation between the Medici ruler Cosimo I and
Charles V caused Guicciardini to retire to write in his last years the famous history
for which he is now mainly known. Quoted from *The History of Italy* (1537–40, publ.
1561–4), trs. S. Alexander (New York: Macmillan, 1969).

in front of their eyes: either foolish errors or shortsighted greed. Thus by failing to take account of the frequent shifts of fortune, and misusing, to the harm of others, the power conceded to them for the common welfare, such rulers become the cause of new perturbations either through lack of prudence or excess of ambition.

"But the misfortunes of Italy (to take account of what its condition was like then, as well as the causes of so many troubles) tended to stir up men's minds with all the more displeasure and dread inasmuch as things in general were at that time most favourable and felicitous. It is obvious that ever since the Roman Empire, more than a thousand years ago, weakened mainly by the corruption of ancient customs, began to decline from that peak which it had achieved as a result of marvellous skill and fortune, Italy had never enjoyed such prosperity, or known so favourable a situation as that in which it found itself so securely at rest in the year of our Christian salvation, 1490, and the years immediately before and after. The greatest peace and tranquillity reigned everywhere; the land under cultivation no less in the most mountainous and arid regions than in the most fertile plains and areas; dominated by no power other than her own, not only did Italy abound in inhabitants, merchandise and riches, but she was also highly renowned for the magnificence of many princes, for the splendour of so many most noble and beautiful cities, as the seat and majesty of religion, and flourishing with men most skilful in the administration of public affairs and most nobly talented in all disciplines and distinguished and industrious in all the arts. Nor was Italy lacking in military glory according to the standards of that time, and adorned with so many gifts that she deservedly held a celebrated name and reputation among all the nations.

"Many factors kept her in that state of felicity which was the consequence of various causes. But it was most commonly agreed that, among these, no small praise should be attributed to the industry and skill of Lorenzo de' Medici, so eminent amongst the ordinary rank of citizens in the city of Florence that the affairs of that republic were governed according to his counsels. Indeed, the power of the Florentine Republic resulted more from its advantageous location, the abilities of its citizens and the availability of its money than from the extent of its domain. And having recently become related by marriage to the Roman Pontiff, Innocent VIII, who was thus induced to lend no little faith in his advice, Lorenzo's name was held in great esteem all over Italy, and his authority influential in deliberations on joint affairs. Realising that it would be most perilous to the Florentine Republic and to himself if any of the major powers should extend their area of dominion, he carefully saw to it that the Italian situation should be maintained in a state of balance, not leaning more toward one side than the other. This could not be achieved without preserving the peace and without being diligently on the watch against every incident, even the slightest.

"Sharing the same desire for the common peace was the King of Naples, Ferdinand of Aragon,[1] undoubtedly a most prudent and highly esteemed prince, despite the fact that quite often in the past he had revealed ambitions not conducive toward maintaining the peace, and at this time he was being greatly instigated by his eldest son Alfonso, Duke of Calabria. For the Duke tolerated with ill grace the fact that his son-in-law, Giovan Galeazzo Sforza, Duke of Milan, already past twenty, although of very limited intellectual capacity, kept his dukedom in name only, having been suppressed and supplanted by Lodovico Sforza, his uncle. More than ten years before, as a result of the reckless and dissolute behaviour of Donna Bona, the young prince's mother, Lodovico Sforza had taken tutelage over his nephew and, using that as an excuse, had little by little gathered into his own hands all the fortresses, men-at-arms, treasury and foundations of the state, and now continued to govern, not as guardian or regent but, except for the title of Duke of Milan, with all the outward trappings and actions of a prince.

"Nevertheless, Ferdinand, more immediately concerned with present benefits than former ambitions, or his son's grievances, however justified, desired that Italy should not change. Perhaps he feared that troubles in Italy would offer the French a chance to assail the kingdom of Naples, since he himself, a few years earlier, had experienced amidst the gravest perils the hatred of his barons and his people, and he knew the affection which many of his subjects held toward the name of the house of France in remembrance of things past. Or perhaps he realised that it was necessary for him to unite with the others, and especially with the states of Milan and Florence, in order to create a counterbalance against the power of the Venetians, who were then formidable in all of Italy.

"Lodovico Sforza, despite the fact that he was restless and ambitious, could not help but incline toward the same policy, since the danger of the Venetian Senate hung over those who ruled Milan as well as over the others, and because it was easier for him to maintain his usurped authority in the tranquillity of peace rather than in the perturbations of war. And although he always suspected the intentions of Ferdinand and Alfonso of Aragon, nevertheless, since he was aware of Lorenzo de' Medici's disposition toward peace, as well as the fear that Lorenzo also had of their grandeur, Sforza persuaded himself that, in view of the diversity of spirit and ancient hatred between Ferdinand and the Venetians, it would be foolish to fear that they might set up an alliance between them, and decided that it was most certain that the Aragonese would not be accompanied by others in attempting against him what they could not achieve by themselves.

"Therefore, since the same desire for peace existed among Ferdinand, Lodovico and Lorenzo, in part for the same reasons and in part for different reasons, it was easy to maintain an alliance contracted in the names of Ferdinand, King of Naples, Giovan Galeazzo, Duke of Milan, and the Republic of Florence, in defence of their states. This alliance, which had been agreed upon many years before and then interrupted as a result of various occurrences, had been adhered to in the year 1480 by practically all the minor Italian powers and renewed for twenty-five years. The principal aim of the pact was to prevent the Venetians from becoming any more powerful since they were undoubtedly stronger than any of the allies alone, but much weaker than all of them together. The Venetians continued to follow their own policies apart from common counsels, and while waiting for the growth of disunion and conflicts among the others, remained on the alert, prepared to take advantage of every mishap that might open the way for them toward ruling all of Italy. The fact that they aspired toward Italian hegemony had been very clearly shown at various times; especially, when taking advantage of the death of Filippo Maria Visconti, Duke of Milan, they had tried to become lords of that state, under the pretext of defending the liberty of the Milanese; and more recently when, in open war, they attempted to occupy the duchy of Ferrara.

"This alliance easily curbed the cupidity of the Venetian Senate, but it did not unite the allies in sincere and faithful friendship, in so far as, full of emulation and jealousy among themselves, they did not cease to assiduously observe what the others were doing, each of them reciprocally aborting all the plans whereby any of the others might become more powerful or renowned. This did not result in rendering the peace less stable; on the contrary, it aroused greater vigilance in all of them to carefully stamp out any sparks which might be the cause of a new conflagration."

Note
1. This Italian prince should not be mistaken for his contemporary, Ferdinand V, the Catholic, 1452–1516, King of Aragon and husband of ‑Isabella I, Queen of Castille and Leon.

Fénelon – The Balance of Power as a Source of Stability*

"We are then to expect, what in reality we see frequently happen, that every nation will seek to prevail over its neighbours; and therefore every nation is obliged, for its proper security, to watch against, and by all means restrain the excessive increase of greatness in any of its neighbours. Nor is this injustice; 'tis to preserve itself and its neighbours from servitude; 'tis to contend for the liberty, tranquillity, and happiness of all in general. For the over-increase of power in any one influences the general system of all the surrounding nations. Thus the successive changes which have happened in the house of Burgundy, and which afterwards raised that of Austria, have altered the face of affairs throughout Europe. All Europe had reason to dread an universal monarchy under Charles V, especially after he had defeated and taken Francis I at Pavia. 'Tis certain that a nation, having no pretence directly to meddle with the affairs of Spain, had at that time a very good right to oppose that formidable power which appeared ready to swallow up all.

"Private men indeed have no right to oppose the increase of their neighbour's wealth, because they cannot pretend it may prove prejudicial or destructive to them. There are laws and magistrates to suppress injustice and violence among families unequal in power.

"But the case of states is different, the overgrowth of one of these may prove the ruin and enslavement of all its neighbours. Here are neither laws nor judges established for a barrier against the invasions of the strongest; they have, therefore, reason to suppose that the strongest will invade their liberties as soon as there is no force sufficient to oppose them. Each of them may and ought to prevent that increase of power which would endanger the liberty of his own people, and that of all his neighbours. For example, Philip II of Spain, after he had conquered Portugal, would have made himself master of England. 'Tis true, he had no right that was well founded; but supposing his right to have been incontestable, it was the interest

* From François Fénelon (1651–1715). French archbishop, theologian and writer. In 1688 he became tutor to the Duke of Burgundy, grandson of Louis XIV and at the time his heir, for whom this work was written. Became archbishop of Cambrai in 1695, but later fell out of favour, coming under attack for his pietist views. At the end of his life his opinions were condemned by the pope and he was exiled to his diocese. Quoted from *L'Examen de la conscience surs les devoirs de la royauré* (1700), trs. William Gaunt (London, 1720).

of all Europe to oppose his establishment in England; because so powerful a kingdom, added to his other dominions of Spain, Italy, Flanders, and the Indies, would have enabled him to subject by his maritime force all the other powers of Christendom. Then *summum jus, summa injuria.* Any particular right of succession or donation, should have given way to the natural law that provides for the security of so many nations. Whatever destroys the balance and tends to set up an universal monarchy, can be no other than unjust; however it may be founded on the written laws of a particular country, which can never prevail over the sovereign and universal law of nature for the common security and liberty, engraven in the hearts of all the nations of the world.

"When a power is grown to such a pitch that all its neighbours are hardly a match for it, they have an undoubted right to unite for the restraining of that increase, which, were it suffered to proceed, would become too great to be opposed in its attempts on the common liberty. But that such confederacies for restraining the growing power of a state may be lawful, the danger from it must be real and pressing; the league defensive, or no further offensive than a just and necessary defence requires; and such bounds must be set to it as it may not entirely destroy that power which it was formed only to limit and moderate.

"This care to maintain a kind of equality and balance among neighbouring nations, is that which secures the common repose; and in this respect such nations, being joined together by commerce, compose, as it were one great body and a kind of community. Christendom, for example, makes a sort of general republic which has its interests, its dangers, and its policy. All the members of this great body owe to one another for the common good, and to themselves for their particular security, that they oppose the progress of any one member, which may destroy the balance, and tend to the inevitable ruin of the other members. Whatever alters the general system of Europe is dangerous, and draws after it many fatal consequences.

"All neighbouring nations are so connected together by their mutual interests, that the least progress of any one is sufficient to alter the general balance, which makes the security of the whole; as when one stone is taken out of an arch, the whole falls to the ground, because all the stones sustain each other in pushing against each other. 'Tis a duty then for neighbouring nations to concur for the common safety against one who grows too powerful, as it is for fellow-citizens to unite against an invader of the liberty of their country. If there is a duty owing by every citizen to his particular society or country, every nation, by the same reason, is obliged to consult the welfare and repose of that universal republic of which it is a member in which are enclosed all the countries composed of private men.

"These defensive alliances are then just and necessary, when they are in reality intended to prevent an exorbitant power, such as might be in a condition to subdue all. Nor can the superior power justly break the peace with the lesser states, merely upon account of their defensive leagues, which it was their right and their duty to enter into. The justice of these leagues depends on their circumstances: They should be founded on some infractions of the peace, or the seizure of some places of the allies, or some certain ground of the like nature: They ought likewise to be limited by such conditions as may prevent (what we have often seen) one nation's pretending a necessity of reducing another which aspires to universal tyranny, only that itself may succeed in the same design.

"The address, as well as justice and faith required in making treaties of alliance, is to frame them as plain as possible, and as remote from an equivocal meaning, and exactly calculated for procuring a certain benefit which you would immediately be possessed of. You must take care that the engagements you lay yourself under, do not reduce your enemy too low, and prove too beneficial to your ally; which may lay you under a necessity either to suffer what may be ruinous to you, or to violate your engagements. And of these, 'tis hard to determine which is more fatal."

Hume – Maintenance of the Balance of Power as a Doctrine of Prudence*

"It is a question whether the *idea* of the balance of power be owing entirely to modern policy, or whether the *phrase* only has been invented in these later ages? It is certain, that Xenophon, in his Institution of Cyrus, represents the combination of the Asiatic

---

* From David Hume (1711–66). (For biographical details see p. 46.) Quoted from *A Treatise of Human Nature* (1742) Essay VII.

powers to have arisen from a jealousy of the increasing force of the Medes and Persians; and though that elegant composition should be supposed altogether a romance, this sentiment, ascribed by the author to the eastern princes, is at least a proof of the prevailing notion of ancient times.

"In all the politics of Greece, the anxiety, with regard to the balance of power, is apparent, and is expressly pointed out to us, even by the ancient historians. Thucydides represents the league, which was formed against Athens, and which produced the Peloponnesian war, as entirely owing to this principle. And after the decline of Athens, when the Thebans and Lacedemonians disputed for sovereignty, we find, that the Athenians (as well as many other republics) always threw themselves into the lighter scale, and endeavoured to preserve the balance. They supported Thebes against Sparta, till the great victory gained by Epaminondas at Leuctra; after which they immediately went over to the conquered, from generosity, as they pretended, but in reality from their jealousy of the conquerors.

"Whoever will read Demosthenes's oration for the Megalopolitans, may see the utmost refinements on this principle, that ever entered into the head of a Venetian or English speculatist. And upon the first rise of the Macedonian power, this orator immediately discovered the danger, sounded the alarm throughout all Greece, and at last assembled that confederacy under the banners of Athens, which fought the great and decisive battle of Chaeronea.

• • •

"The only prince we meet with in the Roman history, who seems to have understood the balance of power, is Hiero king of Syracuse. Though the ally of Rome, he sent assistance to the Carthaginians, during the war of the auxiliaries: 'Esteeming it requisite,' says Polybius, 'both in order to retain his dominions in Sicily, and to preserve the Roman friendship, that Carthage should be safe; lest by its fall the remaining power should be able, without contrast or opposition, to execute every purpose and undertaking. And here he acted with great wisdom and prudence. For that is never, on any account, to be overlooked; nor ought such a force ever to be thrown into one hand, as to incapacitate the neighbouring states from defending their rights against it.' Here is the aim of modern politics pointed out in express terms.

"In short, the maxim of preserving the balance of power is founded so much on common sense and obvious reasoning, that it is impossible it could altogether have escaped antiquity, where we find, in other particulars, so many marks of deep penetration and discernment. If it was not so generally known and acknowledged as at present, it had, at least, an influence on all the wiser and more experienced princes and politicians. And indeed, even at present, however generally known and acknowledged among speculative reasoners, it has not, in practice, an authority much more extensive among those who govern the world.

"After the fall of the Roman empire, the form of government, established by the northern conquerors, incapacitated them, in a great measure, for farther conquests, and long maintained each state in its proper boundaries. But when vassalage and the feudal militia were abolished, mankind were anew alarmed by the danger of universal monarchy, from the union of so many kingdoms and principalities in the person of the emperor Charles. But the power of the house of Austria, founded on extensive but divided dominions, and their riches, derived chiefly from mines of gold and silver, were more likely to decay, of themselves, from internal defects, than to overthrow all the bulwarks raised against them. In less than a century, the force of that violent and haughty race was shattered, their opulence dissipated, their splendour eclipsed. A new power succeeded, more formidable to the liberties of Europe, possessing all the advantages of the former, and labouring under none of its defects; except a share of that spirit of bigotry and persecution, with which the house of Austria was so long, and still is so much infatuated.

"In the general wars, maintained against this ambitious power, Great Britain has stood foremost; and she still maintains her station. Beside her advantages of riches and situation, her people are animated with such a national spirit, and are so fully sensible of the blessings of their government, that we may hope their vigour never will languish in so necessary and so just a cause. On the contrary, if we may judge by the past, their passionate ardour seems rather to require some moderation; and they have oftener erred from a laudable excess than from a blameable deficiency.

"In the *first* place, we seem to have been more possessed with the ancient Greek spirit of jealous emulation, than actuated by the prudent views of modern politics. Our wars with France have been begun with justice, and even, perhaps, from necessity; but have always been too far pushed from obstinacy and passion. The same peace which was afterwards made at Ryswick in 1697, was offered so early as the year ninety-two; that concluded at Utrecht in 1712 might have been finished on as good conditions at Gertruytenberg in the year eight; and we might have given at Frankfort, in 1743, the same terms, which we were glad to accept of at Aix-la-Chapelle in the year forty-eight. Here then we see, that above half of our wars with France, and all our public debts, are owing more to our own imprudent vehemence, than to the ambition of our neighbours.

"In the *second* place, we are so declared in our opposition to French power, and so alert in defence of our allies, that they always reckon upon our force as upon their own; and expecting to carry on war at our expense, refuse all reasonable terms of accommodation. *Habent subjectos, tanquam suos: viles, ut alienos.* All the world knows, that the factious vote of the House of Commons, in the beginning of the last parliament, with the professed humour of the nation, made the queen of Hungary inflexible in her terms, and prevented that agreement with Prussia, which would immediately have restored the general tranquillity of Europe.

"In the *third* place, we are such true combatants, that, when once engaged, we lose all concern for ourselves and our posterity, and consider only how we may best annoy the enemy. To mortgage our revenues at so deep a rate, in wars, where we were only accessories, was surely the most fatal delusion, that a nation, which had any pretension to politics and prudence, has ever yet been guilty of. That remedy of funding, if it be a remedy, and not rather a poison, ought, in all reason, to be reserved to the last extremity; and no evil, but the greatest and most urgent, should ever induce us to embrace so dangerous an expedient."

Vattel – Maintenance of the Balance of Power as a Justification for War*

"The sovereign, who, by inheritance, by free election, or by any other just and honourable means, enlarges his dominions by the

---

* From Emerich de Vattel (1714–67). Swiss jurist, principally known for his treatise on international law, *Le Droit des gens*. This work was closely modelled on Wolff's *Jus Gentium* (see p. 152) but soon became much more famous than the original. In it he rejected Wolff's notion of a commonwealth of nations bound by mutual obligations and emphasised the essential independence of states, which were governed in their relations with each other only by voluntary undertakings and by the principles of the law of nature. He affirmed the "positivist" view that each state was entitled to judge for itself what were the obligations by which it was bound. Quoted from *The Law of Nations* (1758), English trs. (London, 1811) Book III.

addition of new provinces or entire kingdoms, only makes use of his right, without injuring any person. How then should it be lawful to attack a state which, for its aggrandisement, makes use only of lawful means? We must either have actually suffered an injury or be visibly threatened with one, before we are authorised to take up arms, or have just grounds for making war. On the other hand, it is but too well known from sad and uniform experience, that predominating powers seldom fail to molest their neighbours, to oppress them, and even totally subjugate them, whenever an opportunity occurs, and they can do it with impunity. Europe was on the point of falling into servitude for want of a timely opposition to the growing fortune of Charles V. Is the danger to be waited for? Is the storm, which might be dispersed at its rising, to be permitted to increase? Are we to allow of the aggrandisement of a neighbour, and quietly wait till he makes his preparations to enslave us? Will it be a time to defend ourselves when we are deprived of the means? – Prudence is a duty incumbent on all men, and most pointedly so on the heads of nations, as being commissioned to watch over the safety of a whole people. Let us endeavour to solve this momentous question, agreeably to the sacred principles of the law of nature and of nations. We shall find that they do not lead to weak scruples, and that it is an invariable truth that justice is inseparable from sound policy.

"And first, let us observe, that prudence, which is, no doubt, a virtue highly necessary in sovereigns, can never recommend the use of unlawful means for the attainment of a just and laudable end. Let not the safety of the people, that supreme law of the state, be alleged here in objection; for the very safety of the people itself, and the common safety of nations, prohibit the use of means which are repugnant to justice and probity. Why are certain means unlawful? If we closely consider the point, if we trace it to its first principles, we shall see that it is purely because the introduction of them would be pernicious to human society, and productive of fatal consequences to all nations. See particularly what we have said concerning the observance of justice. For the interest, therefore, and even the safety of nations, we ought to hold it as a sacred maxim, that the end does not sanctify the means. And since war is not justifiable on any other ground than that of avenging an injury received, or preserving ourselves from one with which we are threatened, it is a sacred principle of the law of nations, that an increase of power, cannot, alone and of itself, give any one a right to take up arms in order to oppose it.

"No injury has been received from that power (so the question supposes). We must therefore have good grounds to think ourselves threatened by him, before we can lawfully have recourse to arms. Now power alone does not threaten an injury: it must be accompanied by the will. It is indeed very unfortunate for mankind, that the will and inclination to oppress may be almost always supposed, where there is a power of oppressing with impunity. But these two things are not necessarily inseparable: and the only right which we derive from the circumstance of their being generally or frequently united, is that of taking the first appearances for a sufficient indication. When once a state has given proofs of injustice, rapacity, pride, ambition, or an imperious thirst of rule, she becomes an object of suspicion to her neighbours, whose duty it is to stand on their guard against her. They may come upon her at the moment when she is on the point of acquiring a formidable accession of power, – may demand securities, – and, if she hesitates to give them, may prevent her designs by force of arms. The interests of nations are, in point of importance, widely different from those of individuals; the sovereign must not be remiss in his attention to them, nor suffer his generosity and greatness of soul to supersede his suspicions. A nation that has a neighbour at once powerful and ambitious, has her all at stake. As men are under a necessity of regulating their conduct in most cases by probabilities, those probabilities claim their attention in proportion to the importance of the subject: and (to make use of a geometrical expression) their right to obviate a danger is in a compound ratio of the degree of probability, and the greatness of the evil threatened. If the evil in question be of a supportable nature, – if it be only some slight loss, – matters are not to be precipitated: there is no great danger in delaying our opposition to it, till there be a certainty of our being threatened. But if the safety of the state lies at stake, our precaution and foresight cannot be extended too far. Must we delay to avert our ruin till it is become inevitable? If the appearances are so easily credited, it is the fault of that neighbour, who has betrayed his ambition by several indications. If Charles II king of Spain, instead of settling the succession on the duke of Anjou, had appointed for his heir Louis XIV himself, – to have tamely suffered the union of the monarchy of Spain with that of France, would, according to all the rules of human foresight, have been nothing less than delivering up all Europe to servitude, or at least reducing it to the most critical and precarious situation. But, then, if two independent nations think fit to unite, so as afterwards to form one joint empire, have they not a right to do it? And who is authorised to oppose them? I answer, they have a right to form such a union, provided the views by which they are actuated be not prejudicial to other states. Now if each of the two nations in question be, separately and without assistance, able to govern and support herself, and to defend herself from insult and oppression, it may be reasonably presumed that the object of their coalition is to domineer over their neighbours. And on occasions where it is impossible or too dangerous to wait for an absolute certainty, we may justly act on a reasonable presumption. If a stranger levels a musket at me in the middle of a forest, I am not yet certain that he intends to kill me: but shall I, in order to be convinced of his design, allow him time to fire? What reasonable casuist will deny me the right to anticipate him? But presumption becomes nearly equivalent to certainty, if the prince who is on the point of rising to an enormous power, has already given proofs of imperious pride and insatiable ambition. In the preceding supposition, who could have advised the powers of Europe to suffer such a formidable accession to the power of Louis XIV? Too certain of the use he would have made of it, they would have joined in opposing it: and in this their safety warranted them. To say that they should have allowed him time to establish his dominion over Spain, and consolidate the union of the two monarchies, – and that, for fear of doing him an injury, they should have quietly waited till he crushed them all, – would not this be, in fact, depriving mankind of the right to regulate their conduct by the dictates of prudence and to act on the ground of probability. . . .

"But, suppose that powerful state, by the justice and circumspection of her conduct, affords us no room to take exception to her proceedings, are we to view her progress with an eye of indifference? are we to remain quiet spectators of the rapid increase of her power, and imprudently expose ourselves to such designs as it may inspire her with? – No, beyond all doubt. In a matter of so high importance, imprudent supineness would be unpardonable. The example of the Romans is a good lesson for all sovereigns. Had the potentates of those times concerted together to keep a watchful eye on the enterprises of Rome, and to check her encroachments, they would not have successively fallen into servitude. But force of arms is not the only expedient by which we may guard against a formidable power. There are other means, of a gentler nature, and which are at all times lawful. The most effectual is a confederacy of the less powerful sovereigns, who, by this coalition of strength, become able to hold the balance against that potentate whose power excites their alarms. Let them be firm and faithful in their alliance; and their union will prove the safety of each.

"They may also mutually favour each other, to the exclusion of him whom they fear; and by reciprocally allowing various advantages to the subjects of the allies, especially in trade, and refusing them to those of that dangerous potentate, they will augment their own strength, and diminish his, without affording him any just cause of complaint, since every one is at liberty to grant favours and indulgences at his own pleasure.

"Europe forms a political system, an integral body, closely connected by the relations and different interests of the nations inhabiting this part of the world. It is not, as formerly, a confused heap of detached pieces, each of which thought herself very little concerned in the fate of the others, and seldom regarded things which did not immediately concern her. The continual attention of sovereigns to every occurrence, the constant residence of ministers, and the perpetual negotiations, make of modern Europe a kind of republic, of which the members – each independent, but all linked together by the ties of common interest – unite for the maintenance of order and liberty. Hence arose that famous scheme of the political balance, on the equilibrium of power; by which is understood such a disposition of things, as that no one potentate be able absolutely to predominate, and prescribe laws to the others.

"The surest means of preserving that balance would be, that no power should be much superior to the others, that all, or at least the greater part, should be nearly equal in force. Such a project has been attributed to Henry IV: but it would have been impossible to carry it into execution without injustice and violence. Besides, suppose such equality once established, how could it always be maintained by lawful means? Commerce, industry, military pre-eminence, would soon put an end to it. The right of inheritance, vesting even in women and their descendants, – a rule, which it was so absurd to establish in the case of sovereignties, but which nevertheless is established, – would completely overturn the whole system.

"It is a more simple, an easier, and a more equitable plan, to have recourse to the method just mentioned, of forming confederacies in order to oppose the more powerful potentate, and prevent him from giving law to his neighbours. Such is the mode at present pursued by the sovereigns of Europe. They consider the two principal powers, which on that very account are naturally rivals, as destined to be checks on each other; and they unite with the weaker, like so many weights thrown into the lighter scale, in order to keep it in equilibrium with the other. The house of Austria has long been the preponderating power: at present France is so in her turn. England, whose opulence and formidable fleets have a powerful influence, without alarming any state on the score of its liberty, because that nation seems cured of the rage of conquest, – England, I say, has the glory of holding the political balance. She is attentive to preserve it in equilibrium: – a system of policy, which is in itself highly just and wise, and will ever entitle her to praise, as long as she continues to pursue it only be means of alliances, confederacies, and other methods equally lawful.

"Confederacies would be a sure mode of preserving the equilibrium, and thus maintaining the liberty of nations, did all princes thoroughly understand their true interests, and make the welfare of the state serve as the rule in all their proceedings. Great potentates, however, are but too successful in gaining over partisans and allies, who blindly adopt all their views. Dazzled by the glare of a present advantage, seduced by their avarice, deceived by faithless ministers, – how many princes become the tools of a power which will one day swallow up either themselves or their successors! The safest plan, therefore, is to seize the first favourable opportunity when we can, consistently with justice, weaken that potentate who destroys the equilibrium – or to employ every honourable means to prevent his acquiring too formidable a degree of power. For that purpose, all the other nations should be particularly attentive not to suffer him to aggrandise himself by arms: and this they may at all times do with justice. For if this prince makes an unjust war, every one has a right to succour the oppressed party. If he makes a just war, the neutral nations may interfere as mediators for an accommodation, – they may induce the weaker state to propose reasonable terms and offer a fair satisfaction, – and may save her from falling under the yoke of a conqueror! On the offer of equitable conditions to the prince who wages even the most justifiable war, he has all that he can demand. The justice of his cause, as we shall soon see, never gives him a right to subjugate his enemy, unless when that extremity becomes necessary to his own safety, or when he has no other mode of obtaining indemnification for the injury he has received. Now, that is not the case here, as the interposing nations can by other means procure him a just indemnification, and an assurance of safety.

"In fine, there cannot exist a doubt, that, if that formidable potentate certainly entertain designs of oppression and conquest, – if he betray his views by his preparations and other proceedings, – the other states have a right to anticipate him: and if the fate of war declares in their favour, they are justifiable in taking advantage of this happy opportunity to weaken and reduce a power too contrary to the balance, and dangerous to the common liberty."

von Gentz – The Balance of Power a Safeguard of the Independence of States*

"What is usually termed a balance of power, is that constitution subsisting among neighbouring states more or less connected with one another; by virtue of which no one among them can injure the independence or the essential rights of another, without meeting with effectual resistance on some side, and consequently exposing itself to danger.

• • •

"Among independent nations there is neither an executive nor a judicial power; to create the one or the other has been long a fruitless, pious wish, and the object of many a vain, well-meaning effort. But what the nature of these relations prevented from ever being perfectly accomplished was, at least, obtained in approximation; and in the general political system of modern Europe the problem was as happily solved as could be expected from the endeavours of men, and the application of human wisdom.

"There was formed among the states of this quarter of the globe an extensive social commonwealth, of which the characteristic object was the preservation and reciprocal guarantee of the rights of all its

---

* From Friedrich von Gentz (1764–1832). Studied in Berlin and Konigsberg before entering the Prussian civil service. At first welcomed the French revolution, but later became an impassioned opponent of it. On these grounds he published his own translation of Burke's *Reflections on the Revolution in France*, with his own commentary, and it was this which established his reputation. He rejected the principles of popular sovereignty, the rights of man and political equality which inspired the French Revolution, and demanded that Prussia should become more actively engaged in the war against Napoleon. Because of his conservative views, he was opposed to German nationalism and after the war was over co-operated closely with Metternich, at the Vienna and subsequent congresses, in restoring the prewar system in Europe. Quoted from *Fragments upon the Present State of the Political Balance of Europe* (1806), English trs. (London, 1806).

members. From the time that this respectable object came to be distinctly and clearly recognised, the necessary eternal conditions, on which it was attainable, unfolded themselves by degrees. Men were soon aware that there were certain fundamental principles, arising out of the proportional power of each of the component parts to the whole, without the constant influence of which order could not be secured; and the following maxims were gradually set down as a practical basis, which was not to be deviated from;

"That if the states system of Europe is to exist and be maintained by common exertions, no one of its members must ever become so powerful as to be able to coerce all the rest put together;

"That if that system is not merely to exist, but to be maintained without constant perils and violent concussions; each member which infringes it must be in a condition to be coerced, not only by the collective strength of the other members, but by any majority of them, if not by one individual;

"But that to escape the alternate danger of an uninterrupted series of wars, or of an arbitrary oppression of the weaker members in every short interval of peace; *the fear* of awakening common vengeance, must of itself be sufficient to keep every one within the bounds of moderation; and

"That if ever a European state attempted by unlawful enterprises to attain to a degree of power, (or had in fact attained it), which enabled it to defy the danger of a union of several of its neighbours, or even an alliance of the whole, such a state should be treated as a common enemy; and that if, on the other hand, it had acquired that degree of force by an accidental concurrence of circumstances, and without any acts of violence, when ever it appeared upon the public theatre, no means which political wisdom could devise for the purpose of diminishing its power, should be neglected or untried.

"These maxims contain the only intelligible theory of a balance of power in the political world.[1]

"The original equality of the parties in such a union as is here described is not an accidental circumstance, much less a casual evil; but is in a certain degree to be considered as the previous condition and foundation of the whole system.[2] It is not *how much power* one or other possess, but whether he possess it in such a manner that he cannot with impunity encroach upon that of the rest; which is the true question to be answered, in order to enable us to judge at every given moment of the proportion between individual parts and of the general sufficiency of the structure: hence even a subsequent increase of that original necessary inequality, provided it has not sprung from sources, or been introduced by practices, which contravene one of the fundamental maxims above-mentioned, may be in itself blameless.

"It is only when a state with open wantonness, or under fictitious pretences and titles artificially invented, proceeds to such enterprises as immediately, or in their unavoidable consequences, prepare the way for the subjugation of its weaker neighbours, and for perpetual danger to the stronger, that conformably to sound conceptions of the general interest of the commonwealth, a rupture of the balance is to be apprehended; it is only then that several should unite together to prevent the decided preponderance of one individual power.

"By this system, which has been acted upon since the beginning of the sixteenth century, with more or less good fortune, but with great constancy, and often with uncommon prudence; at first more in a practical way, and, as it were from political instinct, afterwards with clear, reflecting, and methodical constancy, two great results were obtained, in the midst of a tumultuous assemblage of the most decisive events. The one was, that no person succeeded in prescribing laws to Europe, and that (till our times), all apprehension, even of the return of a universal dominion, was gradually banished from every mind. The other, that the political constitution, as it was framed in the sixteenth century, remained so entire in all its members till the end of the eighteenth (when all ancient ordinances were abolished), that none of the independent powers, which originally belonged to the confederacy, had lost their political existence.

"How these two important results were obtained, amid cares and dangers of various sorts, amid many storms and tempests, to the credit of the European statemanship, and to the no small advantage of humanity, is to be learnt in the history of that period.[3] It was only at the commencement of this period, before experience and deeper observation had spoiled the phantom of its terrors, that the possibility of an universal monarchy obtained belief.[4] But wiser men afterwards perceived, that though a complete universal dominion, such as the Romans established, might on sufficient grounds be declared impossible in modern Europe, this was by no means the only danger: they perceived that by extraordinary circumstances, and by neglecting to oppose the proper obstacles, one great kingdom or another might attain such a degree of preponderance as might gradually draw upon the whole system, if not immediate sudden destruction, at least the loss of its independence; as might change substantive parts of its territory (under whatever title it might be), into provinces of the principal state; as might convert regents into vassals, and whatever other evils might arise out of such a constitution, they clearly and with utter abhorrence recognised in its eventual establishment, the unavoidable ruin of the smaller, the oppression and degradation of the greater, and the constant peril of the middling states.

"But by the arrangements adopted by the statesmen of better times, and less by individual measures than by the general vigilance, alertness, energy, and true political spirit which guided them at every step, they succeeded in most successfully solving their second problem, in preserving inviolate the whole structure committed to their care, even in its lowest compartments, and in protecting with eminent dexterity those weaker parts which were in danger from time to time of being undermined. It is certainly a remarkable occurrence, that in the course of three most eventful centuries, amid so many bloody wars, so various and decisive negotiations, so frequent changes of power, so great and extended revolutions, amid a general anarchy of all social, civil, religious, and political relations, not one independent state was annihilated by violent means. Neither Switzerland, nor Holland, nor any spiritual nor temporal German prince, nor the most insignificant imperial town, nor Venice, nor Genoa, nor the small Italian republics, though surrounded on all sides by states of gigantic greatness, nor Malta left to itself, nor the weak, though flourishing Geneva pressed by France on one side, and Savoy on the other; nor even the power of Savoy, at one time threatened by Austria, at another by France; nor Portugal, enclosed on all sides by the Spanish territory; nor Sweden, nor Denmark, both endangered by the prodigious extension and aggrandisement of the Russian and Prussian powers; not one of all these states disappeared. Several of them certainly maintained themselves by their own courage and strength, or by superior wisdom, or by the recollection of those achievements by means of which in earlier times they had attained to independence and dignity. But the greater part of them, if not all, would, to the vast prejudice of the whole, have gone to ruin, had they not been supported and protected by the general interest of Europe, and those great enlightened principles, by which that interest was conducted.

"The whole of this excellent system has now at length, like all the works of man, seen the hour of its fall approach; and it has sunk under those maladies which gradually prove fatal to all the productions of the moral world, *abuse of form* on one hand, and *apathy of spirit* on the other."

Notes

1. It perhaps would have been with more propriety called a system of *counterpoise*. For perhaps the highest of its results is not so much a perfect *equipoise* as a constant alternate *vacillation* in the scales of the balance, which, from the application of *counterweights*, is prevented from ever passing certain limits.

2. Had the surface of the globe been divided into equal parts, no such union would ever have taken place; and an eternal war of each against the whole is probably the only event we should have heard of.

3. Few writers have illustrated modern history in this point of view with more learning and ingenuity than Mr Ancillon, in his *Tableau des révolutions du systéme politique de l'Europe.*

4. The extent of the possessions of Charles V had suggested the idea of such an event, and had given it a certain importance; but it has never been made even probable that this monarch entertained this project, or pursued it under any form. Posterior to his time, when the power of the house of Austria was divided into two separate branches, it was indeed attempted to revive the terror, but it was merely an artifice of hostile powers. It is remarkable that Hume, one of the most dispassionate, soberest, and most impartial of our modern historians, pointedly maintains that the house of Austria, particularly from the scattered situation of its provinces, was by no means so well calculated to establish a universal monarchy as France, 'which possessed all the advantages of the Austrian powers, and laboured under none of its defects'. See 'Essay on the Balance of Power' in Hume's *Essays and Treatises*, vol. I.

26 Systems of Universal Peace

Those who advocated balance of power policies as the means of regulating relations among states assumed that the same objective could not be brought about by more radical means: for example by changing state behaviour and inducing governments voluntarily to adopt more co-operative policies. Conflict, they believed, was a natural feature of international existence, and conflict itself was necessary to tame the appetite of any state seeking to acquire excessive power: it was therefore only by mobilising combinations and alliances against the most serious threats to international order that order could be maintained. But there were others who hoped that a better system of international relations could be established by different means: by appealing to rulers and governments to adopt more peaceful policies or by establishing new arrangements having the effect that their disputes would henceforth be resolved only by peaceful means.

Some believed that a change in policies alone was sufficient to create a new international system. Writers of this type were essentially moralists calling (like the advisers to rulers in ancient China) for the adoption of more pacific policies by governments. Thus Erasmus, in his *Complaint of Peace*, not only, as we saw earlier, demanded less warlike attitudes both among rulers and among citizens generally. He also made some practical suggestions to bring this about. He wished to see less use made of flags, trophies and other national emblems, which he denounced as "monuments of human depravity". He called for the clergy to do more to inculcate the desire for peace everywhere, instead of themselves often inciting war in the name of some great cause, as they did at that time. Rulers should cease to rely on peace treaties which so often stored up resentment for the future, as the means of assuring peace, and try instead to undertake acts of friendship and goodwill to other states, acts which those states would be likely to reciprocate in the future. For while each war, by inspiring sentiments of revenge, sowed the seeds of another, each act of kindness and goodwill, on the contrary, stimulated similar sentiments and actions in response.

Other writers placed their main emphasis on the need to create new arrangements among states to bring about a more peaceful international system: usually some form of federation, league or assembly of states, within which disputes could be resolved and war therefore made unnecessary. In Europe, from mediaeval times, a number of writers had proposed some kind of league of states to maintain peace (even if the prime purpose was often to enable them to fight more effectively against another threat, the Turks in the East). So, in the early fourteenth century, the Frenchman Dubois had called for a renunciation of war among Christian states and the establishment among them of a Common Council which would appoint arbitrators to settle disputes; and for its members to bind themselves to use sanctions, including war, against any states which refused to comply with council decisions. George Podiebrad of Bohemia had made a similar proposal in 1458; and Sully's "grand design", which he attributed to Henry IV of France, contained comparable ideas, although (like both the others) it was partly intended to increase the power and influence of the state which proposed it.

A number of similar plans were put forward over the following centuries. Towards the end of the seventeenth century, for example, during the Nine Years' War, in which most of the states of Europe, including his own, were then engaged, William Penn called for the establishment of a general European "Diet" to maintain peace. Deputies representing the rulers of Europe would meet once a year or so to consider the differences between states which could not be resolved by private diplomacy. Decisions of this body would be taken under a system of weighted voting, with the largest and most powerful states wielding 12 votes each and the smallest only one; while a 75 per cent vote would be required for a resolution to carry. If any state refused to accept the decision arrived at, the other states, acting together, would "compel" the performance of that decision. Because no individual states were strong enough to resist the combined power of the others acting together, the system, he argued, would provide for Europe the peace which she so badly needed.

The question which such proposals raised (then as ever since) was: would individual states ever accept such a diminution of their sovereignty as the system demanded? To overcome such apprehensions Penn particularly stressed that his European Diet would be concerned only with external matters, never with the internal affairs of a state: it therefore would not threaten its essential sovereignty. The Abbe de Saint-Pierre, who a little later proposed an essentially similar system, was even more concerned to insist that it would not affect the internal government of each state. Indeed one of the purposes of his system was to protect the sovereignty of each state: it was intended, he said, to secure the suppression of "any Sedition, Revolt, Conspiracy, Suspicion of Poison", or any other violence to the sovereign (especially, for example, during regencies, minorities and other periods of uncertainty). Thus his system could be seen in part as a means for collectively sustaining monarchical power. But it would also maintain the territorial status quo: for each state would undertake to make no claim to the territory of any other, and not to seek any kind of aggrandisement, whether by succession, agreement, election, donation, sale or conquest, or even by the voluntary submission of their subjects (in this way conflicts such as that which had so recently occurred, as the result of the voluntary transfer of the Spanish crown to France, would be avoided). A European Senate would be created within which each of the 24 main European states would be represented, each wielding one vote. This would act as arbitrator of disputes between member-states, and the state which refused to accept its judgement would be declared an enemy of society. Other members would then together make war upon it to enforce its judgements. The sanction relied on in the plan, therefore, was that of armed force, collectively imposed.

But it was also possible, on a more optimistic view, to rely on the sanction of public opinion alone. Such a system was proposed in Jeremy Bentham's *Plan for a Universal and Perpetual Peace*, put forward towards the end of the eighteenth century. This was a judicial rather than a political system (in this sense it anticipated the International Court of Justice rather than the Council and Assembly of the League of Nations and the UN). He proposed the establishment of a "Common Court of Judicature" to settle disputes between states. The Court would not possess any coercive powers. But Bentham hoped that the availability of a legal recourse would none the less prevent war because it would enable states to renounce claims without losing face and so "save the credit, the honour of the contending party". He quoted the US federal system, the German Diet and the Swiss Confederation as examples which showed that, even without enforcement powers, a system of this kind could work reasonably well. In addition to the Court there would be a Congress or Diet, to which each state would send two deputies. The opinion of the Diet on the issues which came before it would be published and circulated to the population of each state. Eventually the state which refused to accept a decision of the Court would be placed under the ban of Europe (comparable to the ban of the German Empire) and the collective forces of the member-states might then be used to enforce a judgement. But Bentham believed that, so long as freedom of the press was established in every state, recourse to force would not be necessary since public opinion would ensure that the Court's authority was respected.

Kant's *Perpetual Peace* presented a more wide-ranging survey of the causes of war and the conditions of peace. He followed the Abbé de Saint-Pierre in demanding that every state should accept that there would never be any further exchange of territory, whether on grounds of conquest, inheritance, exchange, purchase or gift. In this way the most common single motive for war would be eliminated. No treaty of peace should be made with the secret plan of making war, and each state would undertake not to intervene in the internal affairs of other states. At the same time – because in Kant's day wars were nearly always financed by foreign borrowing – each state was to undertake that it would contract no foreign debts, so reducing its capacity to make war. But the most important difference between his plan and the other proposals is that he believed that the establishment of European peace depended not only on arrangements *between* states but on changes in their *internal* structure as well. Thus a major provision of his plan is that each state should become a republic. The reasoning behind this was that since a republic, having the most democratic form of constitution, would be controlled by those who actually took part in war and suffered its hardships, such states would be most likely to ensure the maintenance of a peaceful system. He was contemptuous of the role of international law in reducing war, pointing out (with some reason) that, in going to war, states habitually claimed to be acting within the law and would "cite Hugo Grotius, Pufendorf, Vattel and others" on their own behalf, all of them nothing but "miserable consolers". On these grounds Kant demanded the creation of a federal constitution among the European states which, while falling short of world government, would ensure that they all lived in peace together under a common and mutually accepted law.

The passages below set out the essential provisions of each of these plans. They are only examples of many similar projects of this kind which were published during this period. Though a few became famous – especially the plan of the Abbé de Saint-Pierre – they were none of them taken seriously by any of the governments or rulers of the day. But they remained part of the public consciousness. And, by providing models for an alternative system for undertaking relations among states, they perhaps had some influence on the thinking of statesmen a century or two later, when they did begin to think seriously about the creation of new international institutions which might establish a more peaceful system of relations among states.

* * *

Erasmus – The Way to Secure Peace*

"The causes of war are to be cut up, root and branch, on their first and slightest appearance. Many real injuries and insults must be connived at. Men must not be too zealous about a phantom called national glory, often inconsistent with individual happiness. Gentle behaviour on one side, will tend to secure it on the other, but the insolence of a haughty minister may give offence and be dearly paid for by the nation over which he domineers.

"There are occasions when, if peace can be had in no other way, it must be paid for. It can scarcely be purchased too dearly, if you take into account how much treasure you must expend in war; and what is more precious than treasure, how many of the lives of the people you save by peace. Though the cost of this purchase be great, yet war would certainly cost more. Form but this estimate and you will never repent the highest price paid for peace.

• • •

"Flags, standards, banners and other trophies of war brought from the field of carnage, should not be placed as ornaments in churches and great cathedrals. These trophies, all smeared and stained with the blood of men for whom Christ died, should not be hung among the tombs and images of apostles and martyrs, as if in future it were to be reckoned a mark of sanctity not to suffer martyrdom, but to inflict it; not to lay down one's life for the truth, but to take away the life of others for worldly purposes of vanity and avarice. For these

---

* From Desiderius Erasmus (c. 1466–1536). (For biographical details see p. 32.) Quoted from *The Complaint of Peace* (1517), English trs. (Boston, Mass.: Charles Williams, 1813).

flags and banners are but the disgraceful monuments of human depravity.

"If the clergy were but unanimous in such sentiments, if they would inculcate them everywhere, there is no doubt, notwithstanding the great power of the secular arm, that their authority, personal and professional, would have a preponderance against the influence of courts and ministers of State, and thus prevent war, the calamity of human nature.

"Upon the whole it must be said that *the first and most important step towards peace is sincerely to desire it.* All the obstacles to it the peace-lovers will despise and remove; all hardships and difficulties they will bear with patience so long as they can keep this one great blessing whole and entire.

"On the contrary, there are men who go out of their way to seek occasions of war and what makes for peace they run down in their sophistical speeches, or even basely conceal from the Public. But whatever tends to promote their favourite war system they industriously exaggerate and inflame, not scrupling to propagate lies and false and garbled intelligence and grossest misrepresentation of the enemy. I am ashamed to relate what real and dreadful tragedies in real life they found on these vile despicable trifles; from how small an ember they blow up a flame and set the world on fire. So that an impartial observer would swear that great men love war for its own sake with all their hearts and souls, provided their own persons are safe!

"Kings, Rulers, Statesmen, Commoners: If you detest robbery and pillage, remember these are among the duties of war; and that to learn how to commit them adroitly, is a part of military discipline. Do you shudder at the idea of murder? You cannot require to be told that to commit it with dispatch and by wholesale, constitutes the celebrated 'art of war'. If there cannot be a greater misfortune to the Commonwealth than a general neglect and disobedience of the Laws, let it be considered as a certain truth, that the voice of Law, divine or human, is never heard amidst the clang of arms, and the din of battle. If you deem debauchery, rape, incest and crimes of still greater turpitude than these, foul disgraces to human nature, depend upon it that war leads to all of these, in their most aggravated atrocity. Be assured that religion is always overwhelmed in the storm of war.

"But suppose the cause the justest in the world, the event the most prosperous, yet take into the account all the damages of war of every kind and degree, and weigh them in the balance with all the advantages of Victory, and you will find the most brilliant success not worth the trouble.

"Why should men show more sagacity in creating misery than in securing and increasing the loveliness of life? Why should they be more quicksighted in finding evil than good? All men of sense weigh, consider and use great circumspection before they enter upon any private business of momentous consequences. Yet they throw themselves headlong into war with their eyes shut. And usually war from a little one, becomes a very great one; from a single war, multiplies into a complication and runs from carnage to carnage; and at last rises to a storm which does not overwhelm one or two, the chief instigators of the mischief, but all the unoffending peoples also, confounding the innocent with the guilty.

•   •   •

"In all countries the greater part of the people certainly detest war and most devoutly wish for peace. A very few of them, indeed, whose unnatural happiness depends upon the public misery, may wish for war.

"You plainly see that hitherto nothing has been effectively done towards permanent Peace by treaties, neither by violence, nor by revenge. Now it is time to pursue different measures; to try the experiments of what a kindly disposition and a mutual desire to acts of Friendship and goodwill can accomplish in promoting national Peace.

"IT IS THE NATURE OF WARS, THAT ONE SHOULD SOW THE SEEDS OF ANOTHER; IT IS THE NATURE OF REVENGE TO PRODUCE RECIPROCAL REVENGE.

"Now, let kindness beget kindness, one good turn become productive of another; and let him be considered the greatest and wisest potentate who is ready to concede all exclusive privileges to the happiness of the people.

"The people will possess tranquillity with greater plenty, and plenty with greater tranquillity than they have ever yet known.

"Then the Christian profession will become respectable to the enemies of the Cross."

Penn – A Diet of Europe*

"In my first section, I showed the desirableness of peace; in my next, the truest means of it; to wit, justice not war. And in my last, that this justice was the fruit of government, as government itself was the result of society which first came from a reasonable design in men of peace. Now if the sovereign princes of Europe, who represent that society, or independent state of men that was previous to the obligations of society, would, for the same reason that engaged men first into society, viz., love of peace and order, agree to meet by their stated deputies in a general diet, estates or parliament, and there establish rules of justice for sovereign princes to observe one to another; and thus to meet yearly, or once in two or three years at furthest, or as they shall see cause, and to be styled, the Sovereign or Imperial Diet, Parliament, or State of Europe; before which sovereign assembly should be brought all differences depending between one sovereign and another that cannot be made up by private embassies before the sessions begin; and that if any of the sovereignties that constitute these imperial states shall refuse to submit their claim or pretensions to them, or to abide and perform the judgement thereof, and seek their remedy by arms, or delay their compliance beyond the time prefixed in their resolutions, all the other sovereignties, united as one strength, shall compel the submission and performance of the sentence, with damages to the suffering party, and charges to the sovereignties that obliged their submission. To be sure, Europe would quietly obtain the so much desired and needed peace to her harassed inhabitants; no sovereignty in Europe having the power and therefore cannot show the will to dispute the conclusion; and, consequently, peace would be procured and continued in Europe.

• • •

"The composition and proportion of this Sovereign Part, or Imperial State, does, at the first look, seem to carry with it no small difficulty what votes to allow for the inequality of the princes and states. But with submission to better judgements, I cannot think it invincible; for if it be possible to have an estimate of the yearly value of the several sovereign countries, whose delegates are to make up this august assembly, the determination of the number of persons or votes in the states for every sovereignty will not be impracticable. Now that England, France, Spain, the Empire, etc., may be pretty

* From William Penn (1644–1718). (For biographical details see p. 35.) Quoted from *The Peace of Europe* (1693).

exactly estimated is so plain a case, by considering the revenue of lands, the exports and entries at the custom houses, the books of rates, and surveys that are in all governments, to proportion taxes for the support of them, that the least inclination to the peace of Europe will not stand or halt at this objection. I will, with pardon on all sides, give an instance far from exact; nor do I pretend to it, or offer it for an estimate; for I do it at random: only this, as wide as it is from the just proportion, will give some aim to my judicious reader, what I would be at: Remembering I design not by any computation an estimate from the revenue of the prince, but the value of the territory, the whole being concerned as well as the prince. And a juster measure it is to go by, since one prince may have more revenue than another, who has much a richer country: though in the instance I am now about to make, the caution is not so necessary, because, as I said before, I pretend to no manner of exactness, but go wholly by guess, being but for example's sake. I suppose the Empire of Germany to send twelve; France, ten; Spain, ten; Italy, which comes to France, eight; England, six; Portugal, three; Sweedland, four; Denmark, three; Poland, four; Venice, three; the seven provinces, four; the thirteen cantons and little neighbouring sovereignties, two; dukedoms of Holstein and Courland, one; and if the Turks and Muscovites are taken in, as seems but fit and just, they will make ten apiece more. The whole makes ninety. A great presence when they represent the fourth, and now the best and wealthiest part of the known world; where religion and learning, civility and arts have their seat and empire. But it is not absolutely necessary there should be always so many persons to represent the larger sovereignties; for the votes may be given by one man of any sovereignty as well as by ten or twelve: though the fuller the assembly of states is, the more solemn, effectual, and free the debates will be, and the resolutions must needs come with greater authority. The place of their first session should be central, as much as is possible, afterwards as they agree.

•   •   •

"It seems to me that nothing in this Imperial Parliament should pass but by three quarters of the whole, at least seven above the balance. I am sure it helps to prevent treachery, because if money could ever be a temptation in such a court, it would cost a great deal of money to weigh down the wrong scale. All complaints should be delivered in writing in the nature of memorials and journals kept by a proper person, in a trunk or chest, which should have as many differing locks as there are tens in the states. And if there were a clerk for each ten, and a pew or table for those clerks in the assembly; and at the end of every session one out of each ten were appointed to examine and compare the journals of those clerks, and then lock them up as I have before expressed, it would be clear and satisfactory. And each sovereignty if they please, as is but very fit, may have an exemplification, or copy of the said memorials, and the journals of proceedings upon them. The liberty and rules of speech, to be sure, they cannot fail in, who will be wisest and noblest of each sovereignty, for its own honour and safety. If any difference can arise between those that come from the same sovereignty that then one of the major number do give the balls of that sovereignty. I should think it extremely necessary that every sovereignty should be present under great penalties, and that none leave the session without leave, till all be finished; and that neutralities in debates should by no means be endured: for any such latitude will quickly open a way to unfair proceedings, and be followed by a train, both of seen and unseen inconveniences. I will say little of the language in which the session of the Sovereign Estates should be held, but to be sure it must be in Latin or French; the first would be very well for civilians, but the last most easy for men of quality.

"I will first give an answer to the objections that may be offered against my proposal: and in my next and last section I shall endeavour to show some of the manifold conveniences that would follow this European league or confederacy.

"The first of them is this, that the strongest and richest sovereignty will never agree to it, and if it should, there would be danger of corruption more than of force one time or other. I answer to the first part, he is not stronger than all the rest, and for that reason you should promote this and compel him into it; especially before he be so, for then it will be too late to deal with such a one. To the last part of the objection, I say the way is as open now as then; and it may be the number fewer, and as easily come at. However, if men of sense and honour and substance are chosen, they will either scorn the baseness, or have wherewith to pay for the knavery: at least they may be watched so that one may be a check upon the other, and all prudently limited by the sovereignty they represent. In all great points, especially before a final resolve, they may be obliged to transmit to their principals the merits of such important cases depending, and receive their last instructions: which may be done in four and twenty days at the most, as the place of their session may be appointed.

"The second is that it will endanger an effeminacy by such a disuse of the trade of soldiery; that if there should be any need for it, upon any occasion, we should be at a loss as they were in Holland in '72.

"There can be no danger of effeminacy, because each sovereignty may introduce as temperate or severe a discipline in the education of youth as they please, by low living and due labour. Instruct them in mechanical knowledge and in natural philosophy by operation, which is the honour of the German nobility. This would make them men: neither women nor lions: for soldiers are the other extreme to effeminacy. But the knowledge of nature, and the useful as well as agreeable operations of art, give men an understanding of themselves, of the world they are born into, how to be useful and serviceable, both to themselves and others: and how to save and help, not injure or destroy. The knowledge of government in general; the particular constitutions of Europe; and above all of his own country, are very recommending accomplishments. This fits him for the parliament and council at home, and the courts of princes and services in the imperial states abroad. At least, he is a good commonwealth's man, and can be useful to the public or retire as there may be occasion.

• • •

"I am come now to the last objection, that sovereign princes and states will hereby become not sovereign: a thing they will never endure. But this also, under correction, is a mistake, for they remain as sovereign at home as ever they were. Neither their power over their people, nor the usual revenue they pay them, is diminished: it may be the war establishment may be reduced, which will indeed of course follow, or be better employed to the advantage of the public. So that the sovereignties are as they were, for none of them have now any sovereignty over one another: And if this be called a lessening of their power, it must be only because the great fish can no longer eat up the little ones, and that each sovereignty is equally defended from injuries, and disabled from committing them: *Cedant Arma Togæ* is a glorious sentence; the voice of the dove; the olive branch of peace. A blessing so great, that when it pleases God to chastise us severely for our sins, it is with the rod of war that for the most part He whips us: and experience tells us none leaves deeper marks behind it."

Abbé de Saint-Pierre – A European Union*

A PROJECT FOR SETTLING AN EVERLASTING PEACE IN EUROPE

"First proposed by Henry IV of France, and approved of by Queen Elizabeth, and most of the then Princes of Europe, and now discussed at large and made practicable.

By the Abbé de Saint-Pierre, of the French Academy.

FUNDAMENTAL ARTICLES

"*Article I.* The Present Sovereigns, by their under-written Deputies, have agreed to the following articles: There shall be from this Day following a Society, a permanent and perpetual Union, between the Sovereigns subscribed, and if possible among all the Christian Sovereigns, in the Design to make the Peace unalterable in Europe; and in that view the Union shall make, if possible, with its neighbours the Mahometan Sovereigns, Treaties of Alliance, offensive and defensive, to keep each of them in Peace within the Bounds of his Territory, by taking of them and giving to them, all possible reciprocal Securities. The Sovereigns shall be perpetually represented by their Deputies, in a perpetual Congress or Senate, in a free City.

"*Article II.* The European Society shall not at all concern itself about the Government of any State, unless it be to preserve the Fundamental Form of it, and give speedy and sufficient Assistance to the Princes in Monarchies, and to the Magistrates in Republicks, against any that are Seditious and Rebellious. Thus it will be a Guarantee that the Hereditary Sovereignties shall remain hereditary according to the Manner and Custom of each Nation; that those that are elective shall remain elective in that Country where Election is usual; that among the Nations where there are Capitulations, and Conventions which are called *Pacta Conventa*, those sorts of Treaties shall be exactly observed, and that those who in Monarchies should

---

* From Abbé de Saint-Pierre (1658–1743). Born into the minor aristocracy. Frequented Paris salons and gained a footing at court through the patronage of the Duchess of Orleans (Madame), who also had him made an Abbé. Took part in the congress which led to the peace of Utrecht as member of the French delegation. Wrote prolifically about French politics, law and social institutions, but is today best known for his *Projet de paix perpetuelle*, which was translated into English within two years of its publication in France. Quoted from *Project for Settling an Everlasting Peace in Europe* (1713), English trs. (London, 1714).

have taken up Arms against the Prince, or in Republicks against some of the chief Magistrates shall be punished with Death and Confiscation of Goods.

"*Article III.* The Union shall employ its whole Strength and Care to hinder, during the Regencies, the Minorities, the weak Reigns of each State, any Prejudice from being done to the Sovereign, either in his Person, or in his Prerogatives, either by his Subjects, or by Strangers, and if any Sedition, Revolt, Conspiracy, Suspicion of Poison, or any other Violence should happen to the Prince, or to the Royal Family, the Union, as its Guardian and Protectress born, shall send Commissioners into that State, to look into the Truth of the Facts, and shall at the same time send Troops to punish the guilty according to the Rigour of the Laws.

"*Article IV.* Each Sovereign shall be contented, he and his Successors, with the Territory he actually possesses, or which he is to possess by the Treaty hereunto joyned. All the Sovereignties of Europe shall always remain in the condition they are in, and shall always have the same Limits that they have now. No Territory shall be dismembered from any Sovereignty, nor shall any be added to it by Succession, Agreement between different Houses, Election, Donation, Cession, Sale, Conquest, voluntary Submission of the Subjects or otherwise. No Sovereign, nor Member of a Sovereign Family, can be Sovereign of any State besides that or those which are actually in the possession of his Family. . . . No Sovereign shall assume the Title of Lord of any Country, of which he is not in actual Possession, or the Possession of which shall not be promised him by the Treaty hereunto joyned. The Sovereigns shall not be permitted to make an Exchange of any Territory, nor to sign any Treaty among themselves, but with the Consent and under the Guarantee of the Union by the three-fourths of the four and twenty Voices, and the Union shall remain Guarantee for the execution of reciprocal Promises.

"*Article V.* No Sovereign shall henceforth possess two Sovereignties, either Hereditary or Elective; however the Electors of the Empire may be elected Emperors, so long as there shall be Emperors. If by Right of Succession there should fall to a Sovereign a State more considerable than that which he possesses, he may leave that he possesses, and settle himself in that which is fallen to him.

• • •

"*Article VIII.* No Sovereign shall take up Arms or commit any Hostility, but against him who shall be declared an Enemy to the European Society. But if he has any cause to complain of any of the

Members, or any Demand to make upon them, he shall order his Deputy to give a Memorial to the Senate in the City of Peace, and the Senate shall take care to reconcile the Differences by its mediating Commissioners; or if they cannot be reconciled, the Senate shall judge them by Arbitral Judgement by Plurality of Voices provisionally, and by the three-fourths of the Voices definitely. This Judgement shall not be given till each Senator shall have received the Instructions and Orders of his Master upon the Fact, and till he shall have communicated them to the Senate. The Sovereign who shall take up Arms before the Union has declared War, or who shall refuse to execute a Regulation of the Society, or a Judgement of the Senate, shall be declared an Enemy to the Society, and it shall make War upon him, 'Till he be disarmed, and 'Till the Judgement and Regulations be executed; and he shall even pay the Charges of the War, and the Country that shall be conquered from him at the time of the Suspension of Arms shall be for ever departed from his Dominions. If after the Society is formed to the number of fourteen Voices, a Sovereign shall refuse to enter into it, it shall declare him an enemy to the Repose of Europe, and shall make War upon him 'till he enter into it, or 'till he be entirely dispossessed.

"*Article IX.* There shall be in the Senate of Europe four and twenty Senators, or Deputies of the united Sovereigns, neither more nor less, namely, France, Spain, England, Holland, Savoy, Portugal, Bavaria and Associates, Venice, Genoa and Associates, Florence and Associates, Switzerland and Associates, Lorraine and Associates, Sweden, Denmark, Poland, the Pope, Muscovy, Austria, Courland and Associates, Prussia, Saxony, Palatine and Associates, Hanover and Associates, Ecclesiastical Electors and Associates. Each Deputy shall have but one Vote.

"*Article X.* The Members and Associates of the Union shall contribute to the Expenses of the Society, and to the Subsidies for its Security, each in Proportion to his Revenues, and to the Riches of his People, and every one's Quota shall at first be regulated provisionally by Plurality, and afterwards by the three-fourths of the Voices, when the Commissioners of the Union shall have taken, in each State, what Instructions and Informations shall be necessary thereupon; and if anyone is found to have paid too much provisionally, it shall afterwards be made up to him in Principal and Interest, by those who shall have paid too little. The less powerful Sovereigns and Associates in forming one Voice, shall alternately nominate their Deputy in Proportion to their Quota.

"*Article XI.* When the Senate shall deliberate upon any thing pressing and provisionable for the Security of the Society, either to prevent or quell Sedition, the Question may be decided by plurality of Voices provisionally, and before it is deliberated they shall begin by deciding, by plurality, whether the matter is provisionable.

"*Article XII.* None of the eleven fundamental Articles above named shall be in any point altered without the *unanimous* Consent of All the Members; but as for the other Articles, the Society may always, by the three-fourths of the Voices, add or diminish, for the common Good, whatever it shall think fit.

● ● ●

"The Language of the Senate shall be the Language most in use in Europe.

"The Revenue of the Union shall consist in the ordinary Quota each Sovereign shall pay.

"The Army shall be composed of an equal number of Troops from each State, but the Union can lend Money to the poorer and smaller States, through the most powerful Sovereigns. So the Quota of the international Army can be in Money or in Troops. In Peace, there shall be a reduction of Armaments to six thousand for each State.

"The Sovereigns, Princes, chief Officers, and Ministers shall renew their oaths Annually.

"If the Union enters upon a War it shall appoint a Generalissimo, who shall be elected by a majority of Voices, shall be revocable at pleasure of the Union, and shall not be a member of a Sovereign Family.

"The Union shall appoint Commissioners to settle Limits and Boundaries in America and elsewhere. Nothing in these remote Lands should be left to Sovereigns to seize at their pleasure. These Colonies cost more than they bring in: Colonies are opening a Door for the common People to desert the State. Commerce is not so good when Populations are dispersed, as when People are gathered in a small compass – as in Holland and Zeeland.

"The Union shall endeavour to procure a permanent Society in Asia, that Peace may be maintained there too. If the Union had been established two hundred years ago, Europe would now be four times richer than it is. It will cost very little to establish the Union – chiefly the restitution of unjust Conquests – and will cost almost nothing to maintain it, in comparison with the expense of War. Neither the Balance of Power nor Treaties are sufficient to maintain Peace; the only way is by a European Union."

Bentham – An International Code*

A PLAN FOR A UNIVERSAL AND PERPETUAL PEACE

"An International Code, . . . ought to regulate the conduct of nations in their mutual intercourse. Its objects for any given nation would be: (1) general utility, so far as it consists in doing no injury, and (2) in doing the greatest possible good to other nations, to which two objects, . . . the *duties* which the given nation ought to recognise may be referred; and (3) general utility, in so far as it consists in not receiving injury, or (4) in receiving the greatest possible benefit from other nations, to which the rights it ought to claim may be referred.

"But if these rights be violated there is, at present, no mode of seeking compensation but that of *War*, which is not only an evil, it is the complication of all other evils.

"The fifth object of an International Code would be to make such arrangement that the least possible evil may be produced by War consistently with the acquisition of the good which is sought for.

"'The laws of Peace would be the substantive laws of the International Code; the laws of War would be the adjective laws of the same Code.'

PREVENTION OF WAR

". . . [A] plan for a universal and perpetual Peace . . . grounded upon two fundamental propositions . . . :

"1. The reduction and fixation of the forces of the several nations that compose the European system.

"2. The emancipation of the colonial dependencies of each State.

". . . [There are] fourteen Pacific Propositions, [of] which . . . the thirteenth . . . includes [t]his scheme:

"Proposal XIII. That the maintenance of such a permanent pacifica-

---

* From Jeremy Bentham (1748–1832). English political philosopher, economist and leading exponent of utilitarianism. After brief career as a lawyer, devoted himself to writing on political, economic and philosophical subjects. Made his reputation with *An Introduction to the Principles of Morals and Legislation* (1789) which set out the basis of utilitarian doctrine (influenced by the writings of the French writer, Dumont, on rewards and punishments). Wrote widely thereafter on political and penal reform. Quoted from *A Plan for Universal and Perpetual Peace* (London, 1786–9).

tion might be considerably facilitated by the establishment of a Common Court of Judicature for the decision of differences between the several nations, although such Court were not to be armed with any coercive powers.

"'It is an observation of somebody's, that no nation ought to yield any evident point of justice to another. This must mean, evident in the eyes of the nation that is to judge, evident in the eyes of the nation called upon to yield. What does this amount to? That no nation is to give up anything of what it looks upon as its rights: no nation is to make any concessions. Wherever there is any difference of opinion between the negotiators of the two nations, war is to be the consequence.

"'While here is no common tribunal, something might be said for this. Concession to notorious injustice invites fresh injustice.

"'But, establish a common tribunal, the necessity for war no longer follows from difference of opinion. Just or unjust, the decision of the Arbiters will save the credit, the honour of the contending party.'

"Can the arrangement proposed be justly styled visionary, when it has been proved of it that:

1. It is the interest of the parties concerned.
2. They are already sensible of the interest.
3. The situation it would place them in is no new one, nor any other than the original situation they set out from.

"Difficult and complicated Conventions have been (already) effectuated: e.g., (1) the Armed Neutrality; (2) the American Confederation; (3) the German Diet; (4) the Swiss League. Why should not the European fraternity subsist as well as the German Diet or the Swiss League?

"These latter have no ambitious views. Be it so; but is not this already become the case with the former?

"How then shall we concentrate the approbation of the people, and obviate their prejudices?

"One main object of the plan is to effectuate a reduction, and that a mighty one, in the contributions of the people. The amount of the reduction for each nation should be stipulated in the treaty; and even previous to the signature of it, laws for the purpose might be prepared in each nation, and presented to every other, ready to be enacted, as soon as the treaty should be ratified in each State.

"By these means the mass of people, the part most exposed to be led away by prejudice, would not be sooner apprised of the measure, than they would feel the relief it brought them. They would see it was for their advantage it was calculated, and that it could not be calculated for any other purpose.

"Such a Congress or Diet might be constituted by each Power sending two deputies to the place of meeting; one of these to be the principal, the other to act as an occasional substitute.

"The proceedings of such Congress or Diet should be all public.

"Its power would consist:

1. In reporting its opinion.
2. In causing that opinion to be circulated in the dominion of each State. Manifestos are in the common use. A manifesto is designed to be read either by the subjects of the State complained of, or by other States, or by both. It is an appeal to them. It calls for their opinion. The difference is, that in that case (of a manifesto) nothing of proof is given; no opinion regularly made known.
3. After a certain time, in putting the refractory State under the ban of Europe.

"There might, perhaps, be no harm in regulating as a last resource, the contingent to be furnished by the several States for enforcing the decrees of the Court. But the necessity for the employment of this resource would, in all human probability, be superseded for ever by having recourse to the much more simple and less burdensome expedient of introducing into the instrument by which each Court was instituted a clause, guaranteeing the liberty of the Press in each State, in such sort, that the Diet might find no obstacle to its giving, in every State, to its decrees, and to every paper whatever, which it might think proper to sanction with its signature, the most extensive and unlimited circulation."

Kant – The Conditions of Peace*

"1. 'No treaty of peace shall be regarded as valid, if made with the secret reservation of material for a future war.'

* From Immanuel Kant (1724–1804). German philosopher, exponent of transcendental idealism. Spent much of his life as teacher of logic and metaphysics at Konigsberg University. His most important works are *The Critique of Pure Reason* (1781), *The Critique of Practical Reason* (1788), and the *Critique of Judgement*

"For then it would be a mere truce, a mere suspension of hostilities, not peace. A peace signifies the end of all hostilities and to attach to it the epithet 'eternal' is not only a verbal pleonasm, but matter of suspicion. The causes of a future war existing, although perhaps not yet known to the high contracting parties themselves, are entirely annihilated by the conclusion of peace, however acutely they may be ferreted out of documents in the public archives. There may be a mental reservation of old claims to be thought out at a future time, which are none of them mentioned at this stage, because both parties are too much exhausted to continue the war, while the evil intention remains of using the first favourable opportunity for further hostilities. Diplomacy of this kind only Jesuitical casuistry can justify: it is beneath the dignity of a ruler, just as acquiescence in such processes of reasoning is beneath the dignity of his minister, if one judges the facts as they really are.

"If, however, according to present enlightened ideas of political wisdom, the true glory of a state lies in the uninterrupted development of its power by every possible means, this judgement must certainly strike one as scholastic and pedantic.

"2. 'No state having an independent existence – whether it be great or small – shall be acquired by another through inheritance, exchange, purchase or donation.'

"For a state is not a property, as may be the ground on which its people are settled. It is a society of human beings over whom no one but itself has the right to rule and to dispose. Like the trunk of a tree, it has its own roots, and to graft it on to another state is to do away with its existence as a moral person, and to make of it a thing. Hence it is in contradiction to the idea of the original contract without which no right over a people is thinkable. Everyone knows to what danger the bias in favour of these modes of acquisition has brought Europe (in other parts of the world it has never been known). The custom of marriage between states, as if they were individuals, has survived even up to the most recent times, and is regarded partly as a new kind of industry by which ascendency may be acquired through family alliances, without any expenditure of strength; partly as a device for territorial expansion. Moreover, the hiring out of the troops of one

(1790). His principal work devoted explicitly to international affairs, from which this extract is quoted is *Thoughts on a Perpetual Peace* (1793), trs. M. Campbell Smith (London: Swan Sonnenschein, 1903).

state to another to fight against an enemy not at war with their native country is to be reckoned in this connection; for the subjects are in this way used and abused at will as personal property.

"3. 'Standing armies shall be abolished in course of time.'

"For they are always threatening other states with war by appearing to be in constant readiness to fight. They incite the various states to outrival one another in the number of their soldiers, and to this number no limit can be set. Now, since owing to the sums devoted to this purpose, peace at last becomes even more oppressive than a short war, these standing armies are themselves the cause of wars of aggression, undertaken in order to get rid of this burden. To which we must add that the practice of hiring men to kill or to be killed seems to imply a use of them as mere machines and instruments in the hand of another (namely, the state) which cannot easily be reconciled with the right of humanity in our own person. The matter stands quite differently in the case of voluntary periodical military exercise on the part of citizens of the state, who thereby seek to secure themselves and their country against attack from without.

"The accumulation of treasure in a state would in the same way be regarded by other states as a menace of war, and might compel them to anticipate this by striking the first blow. For of the three forces, the power of arms, the power of alliance and the power of money, the last might well become the most reliable instrument of war, did not the difficulty of ascertaining the amount stand in the way.

"4. 'No national debts shall be contracted in connection with the external affairs of the state.'

"This source of help is above suspicion, where assistance is sought outside or within the state, on behalf of the economic administration of the country (for instance, the improvement of the roads, the settlement and support of new colonies, the establishment of granaries to provide against seasons of scarcity, and so on). But, as a common weapon used by the Powers against one another, a credit system under which debts go on indefinitely increasing and are yet always assured against immediate claims (because all the creditors do not put in their claim at once) is a dangerous money power. This ingenious invention of a commercial people in the present century is, in other words, a treasure for the carrying on of war which may exceed the treasures of all the other states taken together, and can only be exhausted by a threatening deficiency in the taxes – an event, however, which will long be kept off by the very briskness of commerce resulting from the reaction of this system on industry and trade. The ease, then, with which war may be waged, coupled with the inclination of rulers towards it – an inclination which seems to be implanted in human nature – is a great obstacle in the way of perpetual peace. The prohibition of this system must be laid down as a preliminary article of perpetual peace, all the more necessarily because the final inevitable bankruptcy of the state in question must involve in the loss many who are innocent; and this would be a public injury to these states. Therefore other nations are at least justified in uniting themselves against such and its pretensions.

"5. 'No state shall violently interfere with the constitution and administration of another.'

"For what can justify it in so doing? The scandal which is here presented to the subjects of another state? The erring state can much more serve as a warning by exemplifying the great evils which a nation draws down on itself through its own lawlessness. Moreover, the bad example which one free person gives another, (as *scandalum acceptum*) does no injury to the latter. In this connection, it is true, we cannot count the case of a state which has become split up through internal corruption into two parts, each of them representing by itself an individual state which lays claim to the whole. Here the yielding of assistance to one faction could not be reckoned as interference on the part of a foreign state with the constitution of another, for here anarchy prevails. So long, however, as the inner strife has not yet reached this stage the interference of other powers would be a violation of the rights of an independent nation which is only struggling with internal disease. It would therefore itself cause a scandal, and make the autonomy of all states insecure.

"6. 'No state at war with another shall countenance such modes of hostility as would make mutual confidence impossible in a subsequent state of peace: such are the employment of assassins or of poisoners, breaches of capitulation, the instigating and making use of treachery in the hostile state.'

"These are dishonourable stratagems. For some kind of confidence in the disposition of the enemy must exist even in the midst of war, as otherwise peace could not be concluded, and the hostilities would pass into a war of extermination. War, however, is only our wretched expedient of asserting a right by force, an expedient adopted in the state of nature, where no court of justice exists which could settle the matter in dispute. In circumstances like these, neither of the two parties can be called an unjust enemy, because this form of speech presupposes a legal decision: the issue of the conflict – just as in the case of the so-called judgements of God – decides on which side right is. Between states, however, no punitive war is thinkable, because between them a relation of superior and inferior does not exist. Whence it follows that a war of extermination, where the process of annihilation would strike both parties at once and all right as well, would bring about perpetual peace only in the great graveyard of the human race. Such a war then, and therefore also the use of all means which lead to it, must be absolutely forbidden.

● ● ●

FIRST DEFINITIVE ARTICLE OF PERPETUAL PEACE

"I. 'The civil constitution of each state shall be republican.'

"The only constitution which has its origin in the idea of the original contract, upon which the lawful legislation of every nation must be based, is the republican. It is a constitution, in the first place, founded in accordance with the principle of the freedom of the members of society as human beings: secondly, in accordance with the principle of the dependence of all, as subjects, on a common legislation: and, thirdly, in accordance with the law of the equality of the members as citizens. It is then, looking at the question of right, the only constitution whose fundamental principles lie at the basis of every form of civil constitution. And the only question for us now is, whether it is also the one constitution which can lead to perpetual peace.

"Now the republican constitution apart from the soundness of its origin, since it arose from the pure source of the concept of right, has also the prospect of attaining the desired result, namely, perpetual peace. And the reason is this. If, as must be so under this constitution, the consent of the subjects is required to determine whether there shall be war or not, nothing is more natural than that they should weigh the matter well, before undertaking such a bad business. For in decreeing war, they would of necessity be resolving to bring down the miseries of war upon their country. This implies: they must fight themselves; they must hand over the costs of the war out of their own property; they must do their poor best to make good the devastation which it leaves behind; and finally, as a crowning ill, they have to accept a burden of debt which will embitter even peace itself, and which they can never pay off on account of the new wars which are always impending. On the other hand, in a government where the subject is not a citizen holding a vote, (i.e., in a constitution which is not republican), the plunging into war is the least serious thing in the world. For the ruler is not a citizen, but the owner of the state, and does not lose a whit by the war, while he goes on enjoying the delights of his table or sport, or of his pleasure palaces and gala days. He can therefore decide on war for the most trifling reasons, as if it were a kind of pleasure party. Any justification of it that is necessary for the sake of decency he can leave without concern to the diplomatic corps who are always only too ready with their services.

• • •

SECOND DEFINITIVE ARTICLE OF PERPETUAL PEACE

"II. 'The law of nations shall be founded on a federation of free states.'

"Nations, as states, may be judged like individuals who, living in the natural state of society – that is to say, uncontrolled by external law – injure one another through their very proximity.[1] Every state, for the sake of its own security, may – and ought to – demand that its neighbour should submit itself to conditions, similar to those of the civil society where the right of every individual is guaranteed. This would give rise to a federation of nations which, however, would not have to be a State of nations. That would involve a contradiction. For the term 'state' implies the relation of one who rules to those who obey – that is to say, of lawgiver to the subject people: and many nations in one state would constitute only one nation, which contradicts our hypothesis, since here we have to consider the right of one nation against another, in so far as they are so many separate states and are not to be fused into one.

• • •

" . . . Without a compact between the nations, however, this state of peace cannot be established or assured. Hence there must be an alliance of a particular kind which we may call a covenant of peace, which would differ from a treaty of peace in this respect, that the latter merely puts an end to one war, while the former would seek to put an end to war for ever. This alliance does not aim at the gain of any power whatsoever of the state, but merely at the preservation and security of the freedom of the state for itself and of other allied states at the same time.[2] The latter do not, however, require, for this reason, to submit themselves like individuals in the state of nature to public laws and coercion. The practicability or objective reality of this idea of federation which is to extend gradually over all states and so lead to perpetual peace can be shewn. For, if Fortune ordains that a powerful and enlightened people should form a republic, – which by its very nature is inclined to perpetual peace – this would serve as a centre of federal union for other states wishing to join, and thus secure conditions of freedom among the states in accordance with the idea of the law of nations. Gradually, through different unions of this kind, the federation would extend further and further."

Notes

1. 'For as amongst masterless men, there is perpetual war, of every man against his neighbour; no inheritance, to transmit to the son, nor to expect from the father; no propriety of goods, or lands; no security; but a full and absolute liberty in every particular man: so in states, and commonwealths not dependent on one another, every commonwealth, not every man, has an absolute liberty, to do what it shall judge, that is to say, what that man, or assembly that representeth it, shall judge most conducing to their benefit. But withal, they live in the condition of a perpetual war, and upon the confines of battle, with their frontiers armed, and cannons planted against their neighbours round about' (Hobbes, *Leviathan*, II. ch. 21).

2. Cf. Rousseau, *Gouvernement de Pologne*, ch. 5: federate government is the only one which unites in itself all the advantages of great and small states'.

27 A System of Great Power Consultation

None of the proposals of these thinkers, dreaming of a differently structured world that would offer perpetual peace, was put into effect. But at the end of the Napoleonic wars an attempt was made to establish a new system which, if less visionary than some of the schemes proposed over previous years, might, it was hoped, at least do something to reduce confrontation among the major powers and enable them to maintain greater stability in the affairs of the continent.

In 1815, renewing the Treaty of Chaumont, the four main victors of the war against Napoleon agreed to meet together "at fixed intervals" (though the precise intervals were never fixed) "for the purpose of consulting upon their common interests, and for the examination of the measures which . . . should be considered most salutary for the repose and prosperity of the nations and for the maintenance of the peace of Europe". In 1818, France, the indemnity imposed on her having been paid, and the occupation of her territories brought to an end, was invited to join in the new arrangements. Though "Congresses" of the type originally proposed ceased after a few years, regular consultations continued to take place among the powers, not only through normal diplomatic channels but through frequent conferences in a particular capital, at which most of the powers were represented by their ambassadors, called to consider particular problems as they arose. In this way a system of great power consultation was established to maintain the peace of the continent.

The basic principle was multilateralism: all five were to be consulted on every issue that arose and joint decisions, reflecting the common "European" interest, were to be arrived at. As a protocol to the 1831 Treaty of Paris (in which the five had settled the problem of Belgian independence) put it: "Each nation has its rights; but Europe too has its rights, which the social order has created." On these grounds Palmerston declared, in relation to the Egyptian crisis of 1838–40, that Europe would "never endure that the matter should be settled by the independent and self-regulated interference of any one Power. . . . The only way in which it could be resolved, without risking a disturbance of the peace, would be by the establishment of . . . consent between the five powers." In the same way Louis

Philippe demanded that "no change, no alienation of territory should take place without the concurrence of all the Powers" and wished to see an "entente of the five Powers for the solution of all the great political questions". And it was on the same principle that Russia in 1871 even demanded the right to take part in the settlement of the Franco-Prussian war, declaring that "it is impossible that the other great Powers be excluded from the negotiations, even if they did not take part in the war". For some wars that policy was indeed adopted. Austria, which had remained neutral throughout the Crimean war, was allowed to play a prominent part in the Congress of Paris at its end. Britain, France, Austria and Prussia, which had not been involved in the Balkan conflict of 1875–8, were permitted to share in the decisions on its outcome (as well as in the spoils), at the Congress of Berlin at its conclusion. The six "powers" (Italy had now joined them), which had played no part at all in the Balkan wars of 1912–13, insisted on supervising the settlement of those conflicts at the London Conference at their end.

There were, however, many difficulties in putting the new principle into practice. The first concerned the very purpose of the system. Was it designed simply to maintain the *territorial* status quo which had been established at Vienna? Or was it supposed to guarantee the status quo *within* states as well: in other words to preserve them from revolution? Was it only the external order that was to be preserved from change, or did it include the internal order as well? Most of the great powers believed that it should perform both functions; and therefore wanted collective decisions to authorise Austrian action against revolution in Italy in 1820–1, or French action against revolution in Spain in 1822–3. The British government were strongly of the opposite opinion, believing this would involve unwarranted interference in the internal affairs of states. That view is expressed in the first of the extracts reproduced below, the Memorandum which Castlereagh circulated to the other powers in 1818. He pointed out that the fact that the four allies (before the admission of France to the system) had agreed to guarantee the territorial settlement at Vienna did not mean that they had undertaken to give their support everywhere to "established power", no matter how that power was used or abused. So far as Britain was concerned therefore (and the same view was to be expressed still more strongly by Canning in subsequent years) the purpose of the system was not that the "powers" should intervene to prevent political change all over the world: merely that they should "take the initiative in watching over the peace of Europe".

Even a system having this more limited ambition raised problems. What was the authority which the "powers" could claim in seeking to impose settlements on lesser states? What right had they to impose their views on other governments? This is the issue discussed by Palmerston in the second of the extracts quoted below. Sometimes the questions to be discussed were not covered by the terms of the Vienna treaties: or they concerned a state that was not a signatory. In either case the authority of the Concert could be challenged. The situation, he pointed out, was no longer that of 1814–15, when, in the flush of victory, the powers were able to impose their authority on almost every state in Europe. Today (in 1849) the smaller states would not submit to "external dictation without the actual employment of over-ruling force", which the powers at that time were unable or unwilling to employ. In other words, in default of a new "European gendarmerie", the Concert – to use the phrase used of the League of Nations in later years – lacked teeth.

A third difficulty concerned the circumstances which justified the calling of a conference or "Congress". While one or another power might want one, others might not agree. Since the system of regular conferences had never been put into effect, no criteria existed for determining whether or not there was a need for such a meeting. This question too is raised by Palmerston in the other document under his name reproduced below, written 15 years later. He points to the difficulties about proposals for a Congress without a clearly defined purpose. Like a modern statesman refusing a demand for a summit without a specific and agreed agenda, he points to the disadvantages of a meeting that was inadequately prepared. There were now no major territorial conflicts to be settled, as there had been at Vienna. Some changes made since 1815 had been authorised by new treaties; while others ought not to be collectively endorsed at all. The changes that were really required were major alterations to make that settlement conform better with the national principle – for example, in Italy, Poland, Schleswig-Holstein and other places – but there was no chance that other powers would consent to this now. There could also be disputes about which states shall be represented (another difficulty surrounding some modern conferences), and other questions. On these grounds, he believed, a new Congress, while it would not worsen things or lead to war, was unlikely to produce any very fruitful results.

There was a fourth problem. The essence of the new system, as we have seen, was multilateralism: collective decisions were to be made to prevent any one of the powers from securing unilateral advantages for itself. Multilateral settlements of this kind were secured: on the question of Greek and Belgian independence, the neutralisation of Belgium and Luxembourg, the conflict between Mahomet Ali and Turkey, navigation on the Danube, Elbe and Rhine and (temporarily) on the question of Schleswig-Holstein. But there was always a danger that one power would try to go behind the back of the rest to secure unilateral advantages. In this way the benefits of the system would be destroyed. This was the charge made by Gladstone against Disraeli in the next extract printed below (from one of the speeches of his Midlothian campaign). At the Congress of Berlin the powers as a whole had agreed on a settlement of the Russian war with Turkey in 1877–8: as a result the other powers had reduced the gains made by Russia and each managed to secure corresponding advantages for themselves. But, in Gladstone's view, the British government had seriously prejudiced the effect of the settlement by reaching a bilateral agreement with Turkey in violation of the multilateral principle. Though it was important that coercion should be applied against Turkey, as he and his party had consistently demanded, this should have been undertaken by the "united authority of Europe", and not by the "single authority and single hand of England" (again there is a parallel with the demands of many liberals today for multilateral rather than unilateral action). Turkey would more willingly have accepted the authority of six powers than one; the concessions desired could have been obtained far earlier; and much bloodshed would have been avoided.

This raised a final problem: the vital importance of securing consensus among the "powers" as a whole. The need for this was stressed by Lord Salisbury in the last of the extracts reproduced below. The powers had in general been agreed on two vital points in relation to Turkey. They all accepted that she needed to introduce a better system of government, especially for her Christian subjects; and most accepted – most of the time – that she should not be extinguished altogether (though Russia, Austria and Britain all toyed with the idea of partition at one time or another). The problem was that from time to time, especially after particularly gruesome atrocities had been committed by the Ottoman authorities, some powers were doubtful whether both these aims were compatible. Lord Salisbury makes no secret of his preference for reforming rather than dismembering Turkey. But he stresses the need, if reform is to be secured, of maintaining unity among the powers as a whole. Some of

them were already acting together to bring about the partial decolonisation of Crete (they were shortly to send an international force to
control the island). Now he wanted them to agree exactly what
reforms Turkey needed to introduce at home, as well as the way in
which these should be implemented. Their unanimous decision on
these points should be final and should be "executed up to the
measure of such force as the Powers have at their command".

Thus there were varying opinions about the effectiveness of a
system of great power co-operation during this period. Where the
differences of opinion between them were not too great they might be
able (as Gladstone and Salisbury suggested) to exercise a collective
influence which was far greater than any one of them could exert in
isolation. The Concert was less well equipped (as Palmerston pointed
out) to discuss general issues in the continent or for reviewing the
workings of earlier treaties. It could work reasonably well when the
issues in dispute mainly concerned smaller states, scarcely able to
resist the united voice of the great powers together. But when the
differences were between the great powers themselves – for example,
the balance of power and prestige between Prussia and Austria in
Germany, or between Prussia and France on the Rhine or between
Austria and Russia in the Balkans – in other words on the most vital
issues of all, and those most likely to lead to war, the system was
largely without effect. The habit of co-operation was not sufficiently
deeply instilled to operate in the situations where it was most
required.

*   *   *

Castlereagh – The Principles of the Concert*

MEMORANDUM ON THE TREATIES OF 1814 AND 1815, AIX-LA-CHAPELLE, OCTOBER 1818

"The present Diplomatick Position of Europe may be considered
under two distinct Heads: Ist The treaties which may be said to bind

---

* From Lord Castlereagh (1769–1822). British Foreign Minister from 1812 until 1822.
 Played a leading part in the closing stages of the Napoleonic war in negotiating with
 the other principal allied powers on the principles that should govern the peace

its States collectively. 2ly The treaties which are peculiar to particular States.

"Under the first Head, may be enumerated, The Treaty of Peace signed at Paris 30th May 1814, – The Act of the Congress of Vienna, signed June 9th 1815, and the Treaty of Peace, signed at Paris, the 20th of Nov[embe]r 1815.

"These transactions, to which all the States of Europe, (with the exception of the Porte) are at this day either signing or acceding Parties, may be considered as the great Charte, by which the Territorial System of Europe, unhinged by the events of war and Revolution, has been again restored to order. The Consent of all the European States, France included, has not only been given to this settlement, but their Faith has been solemnly pledged to the strict observance of its arrangements.

• • •

"It is further to be observed, that none of these three Treaties contain any express guarantee, general or special, by which their observance is to be enforced, save and except the temporary Guarantee intended to be assured by Article 5 of the Treaty of 1815 which regulates the Army of Occupation to be left in France.

"There is no doubt, that a breach of the Covenant by any one State is an Injury, which all the other States may, if they shall think fit, either separately or collectively resent, but the Treaties do not impose, by express stipulation, the doing so, as matter of positive obligation. So solemn a Pact, on the faithful execution and observance of which all Nations should feel the strongest Interest, may be considered, as under the Protection of a moral guarantee, of the highest Nature, but as those who framed these acts did not probably see how the whole Confederacy could, without the utmost Inconvenience, be made collectively to enforce the observance of these Treaties, the execution of this duty seems to have been deliberately left to arise out of the Circumstances of the Time and of the Case, and the offending State to be brought to reason by such of the injured States, as might, at the moment think fit to charge themselves with the Task of defending their own rights, thus invaded.

"If this Analysis of these Treaties be correct, they cannot be said to

---

settlement. Was concerned that this should establish a reasonable balance of power between the five major states of Europe: and that therefore neither Prussia nor Russia should be unduly strengthened, nor France unduly weakened. Convinced of the need for regular consultations among the powers to maintain this balance. Quoted from *Memorandum on the Treaties of 1814 and 1815* (1818).

form an Alliance, in the strict sense of the Word. They no doubt form the general Pact, by which all is regulated, which, at that moment was open, in Europe to regulation, but they can hardly be stated to give any special or superior security to the parts of the European system thus regulated, as compared with those parts, which were not affected by these Negotiations, upon which consequently those Transactions are wholly silent, and which rest, for their title, upon anterior Treaties, or publick Acts of equal and recognised Authority.

"Under the 2d Head, vizt, that of Treaties which are peculiar to particular States, may be enumerated, the Treaties of Alliance of Chaumont and Paris, as signed by the four great Allied Powers.

• • •

"The Restoration and Conservation of Europe against the Power of France may be stated to be the avowed Principle and object of both Treaties.

• • •

"The Treaty of Chaumont in 1814 aimed at effectuating an Improvement in the State of Europe as the preliminary Condition to a Peace with France, and at defending by the force of the Alliance, the terms of that Peace, if made. The Treaty of Paris in 1815 had only to place the State of Things, as established by the Treaties of Paris and Vienna, under the Protection of the Quadruple Alliance.

"The Treaty of Chaumont gave to this Alliance that Character of Permanence which the deep rooted Nature of the danger against which it was intended to provide, appeared to require, viz., twenty years from March 1814, with an eventual Continuance. This Character of Permanence was additionally recognised by the Language of the Paris Treaty, the whole of the Provisions of which proceed, not only upon the admission of a danger still existing, but upon the necessity of keeping alive the precautionary Arrangements of the Treaty even after the Army of occupation shall have been withdrawn.

• • •

"Having discussed and endeavoured to state with precision what the existing Treaties have really done, there will remain open to fair discussion the question; – Have they done enough, or does not much remain yet to be done? No question can be more proper for examination and no Gov[ernmen]t more disposed to consider it than that of Great Britain, whenever any clear and specifick proposition shall be brought forward, always holding in view the Inconvenience of agitating in time of Peace, Questions that presuppose a state of war or disturbance. The desire of the Prince Regent always is, to act cordially with His Allies, but in doing so, to stand quite clear in the view of his own engagements not to be supposed to have taken engagements beyond the Text and Import of the Treaties signed.

"The problem of an Universal Alliance for the Peace and Happiness of the world has always been one of speculation and of Hope, but it has never yet been reduced to practice, and if an opinion may be hazarded from its difficulty, it never can; but you may in practice approach towards it, and perhaps the design has never been so far realised as in the last four years – during that eventful Period the Quadruple Alliance, formed upon Principles altogether limited has had, from the Presence of the Sovereigns, and the unparalleled unity of design with which their Cabinets have acted, the power of travelling so far out of the sphere of their immediate and primitive obligations, without at the same time, transgressing any of the principles of the law of Nations or failing in the delicacy which they owe to the rights of other States, as to form more extended Alliances such as that of the 25th March 1815 at Vienna, To interpose their good offices for the settlement of differences subsisting between other States, To take the initiative in watching over the Peace of Europe and finally in securing the execution of its Treaties in the mode most consonant to the Convenience of all the Parties.

"The idea of an 'Alliance Solidaire' by which each State shall be bound to support the State of Succession, Government, and Possession, within all other States from violence and attack upon Condition of receiving for itself a similar guarantee must be understood as morally implying the previous establishment of such a System of general Government as may secure and enforce upon all Kings and Nations an internal System of Peace and Justice; till the mode of constructing such a System shall be devised, the Consequence is inadmissible, as nothing would be more immoral or more prejudicial to the Character of Government generally, than the Idea that their force was collectively to be prostituted to the support of established Power without any Consideration of the Extent to which it was abused. Till then a System of administrating Europe by a general Alliance of all its States can be reduced to some practical Form, all Notions of general and unqualified guarantee must be abandoned and States must be left to rely for their Security, upon the Justice and Wisdom of their respective Systems, aided by such support as other States may feel prepared to afford them, and as Circumstances may point out and justify without outstepping those Principles which are to be found in the Law of Nations, as long recognised and practised."

Palmerston – Weaknesses of the Concert System*

"This notion of a European Congress to settle all pending matters and to modify the Treaty of Vienna so as to adapt it to the interests and necessities of the present time sounds well enough to the ear, but would be difficult and somewhat dangerous in its execution. First in regard to pending matters, some of them relate to parties who did not sign the Treaty of Vienna and who perhaps might not choose to submit their affairs to the decision of the new Congress; and the new Congress would not have the power and assumed right which recent conquest vested in the Congress of 1814–15. At that time all Europe may be said to have been occupied by the armies of the allies. Nations counted for nothing, sovereigns submitted to the decisions of the Congress, and its resolves became easily law. But nowadays sovereigns count for little, and nations will submit to no external dictation without the actual employment of overruling force; and a Congress might not find it easy to give effect to its resolutions without establishing a European *gendarmerie*. Then in regard to France, the notion of modifying the Treaty of Vienna implies some intention of asking for cessions to France which the other Powers would not be disposed to consent to. If the modifications in question related to the past only, and were to be stipulations giving a European sanction to violations heretofore committed of the Treaty of Vienna, such as what has been done about Poland and Cracow, neither England nor France would much like to give their sanction to things which they have protested against and condemned. If the proposed modifications relate to future changes of still existing arrangements, it seems to me that such a chapter had better not be opened. On the whole therefore I should be for giving a civil but declining answer, pointing out the many difficulties which would arise in such a course.

"This Proposal of a Congress seems to require very serious Consideration. We might simply accept, or simply refuse or ask what Questions would be considered, and what excluded. At the End of a war when States of Territorial Possession have been forcibly changed, a Congress may be necessary in order to Settle what should thencefor-

---

* From Lord Palmerston (1784–1865). (For biographical details see p. 165.) Quoted from *Letters to Lord John Russell* (6 March 1849 and 8 November 1863).

ward be the Boundaries of States and the Rights of Sovereigns; and so it was in 1815, and to a less Degree in 1856 after the war with Russia. But what are the unsettled Territorial Questions of the present Day? The arrangements of Vienna of 1815 have in many Instances it is true been modified, and in some violently set aside, the modifications were sanctioned at the Time by Treaties, are we prepared now to legalise the violations – to some we should willingly give our Sanction from others we should withhold it. The Separation of Belgium from Holland was a modification regularly Sanctioned at the Time and not requiring any fresh assent. The Elevation of Napoleon to the Throne was a setting aside, not of the general Treaty of 1815, but of a separate Engagement, but it has been sanctioned by the acknowledgement of all civilised Nations and requires no Confirmation. The Transfer of Lombardy to Pie[d]mont was an alteration of the Treaty of Vienna, but was sanctioned by the Treaty of Villa Franca. The Cession of Nice and Savoy to France were alterations of the Vienna Treaty, but were regularised by Treaty, only that in the Case of Savoy the Stipulation of Vienna about the Neutrality of Chablais and Fraucigny has been dropped. The Cession requires no Confirmation, and we should not sanction the leaving out of the neutrality Condition. These are the Changes made by formal Compacts at the Time. There are some made without proper Sanction, some of which we could . . . not sanction. The annexation of Tuscany, Parma Modena Emilia Naples and Sicily to the Kingdom of Italy, were all Breaches of the Treaty of Vienna which have as far as I recollect received no direct European sanction by any formal Treaty. To these Transactions however we should most willingly give our sanction. Cracow has been swallowed up by Austria in violation of the Vienna Treaty, are we prepared to give our formal sanction to that absorption? perhaps it was sure to happen sooner or later, for a little Republic could hardly be long lived between Three military Powers. The Kingdom of Poland has been misgoverned in violation of the Vienna Treaty but Russia does not seem inclined to govern it better.

"Well then there are Two Functions which the Congress would, or might have to perform. The first to make regular, the Changes that have practically been accomplished and those are chiefly what I have just mentioned. The other Function would be to bring about and to sanction changes which are wished for, or which would be desirable. This last Function might range over a wide Field, and would give Rise to more Difference than agreement.

434   *Basic Texts in International Relations*

"Many Sovereigns and States wish to have what belongs to their Neighbours, but are there many of those neighbours who would consent to the Cessions asked of them, and is the Congress to be invested with the Power possessed by that of Vienna in 1815: to compel submission to its Decrees? Does the Emperor conceive that his Congress would give its Seal to his Map of Europe of 1860? If there was any chance that a Congress would give Moldo Wallachia to Austria and Venetia and Rome to Italy and incorporate Sleswig with Denmark, and separate the Poland of 1815 from Russia and make it an independent State not touching the Question of The Rhine as a French Frontier nor the relieving Russia from what was imposed upon her by the Treaty of Paris such a Congress would be a well doer by Europe but such Results can scarcely be expected. The Congress – if it met would probably separate without any important Results. But there would be France and Russia on one side, England and Austria on the other and the other States acting acording to their views of the Questions discussed. What States are to be represented? of Course the 5 who signed the Vienna Treaty, and probably Turkey in addition as well as Italy. But I see the German Confederation, and the Swiss Confederation are to be invited. Switzerland is an independent aggregate, but the German Confederation consists partly of Delegates from Powers who would have Representatives of their own. Would Belgium and Holland be represented. Here would be 13 or 14 States some of them no Doubt with Two Representatives. What a Babel of Tongues and what a Confusion of Interests. It is not likely that war would follow out of it, but there would not be much Chance of any considerable Results. I doubt whether we should even get Spain to give up her Slave Trade, or France to abide [by] and faithfully to execute her abandonment of that Crime."

Gladstone – The Need for Multilateral Action*

"We had never given countenance to single-handed attempts to coerce Turkey. We felt that single-handed attempts to coerce Turkey would probably lead to immediate bloodshed and calamity, with

---

* From William Ewart Gladstone (1809–98). (For biographical details see p. 188.) Quoted from First Speech of Midlothian Campaign, 25 November 1879.

great uncertainty as to the issue. The coercion we recommended was coercion by the united authority of Europe, and we always contended that in the case where the united authority of Europe was brought into action, there was no fear of having to proceed to actual coercion. The Turk knew very well how to measure strength on one side and the other, and he would have yielded to that authority. But no, there must be no coercion under any circumstances. Such was the issue, gentlemen. Well, where do we stand now? We know what has taken place in the interval. We know that a great work of liberation has been done, in which we have had no part whatever. With the traditions of liberty which we think we cherish, with the recollection that you Scotchmen entertain of the struggles in which you have engaged to establish your own liberties here, a great work of emancipation has been going on in the world, and you have been prevented by your Government from any share in it whatever. But bitter as is the mortification with which I for one reflect upon that exclusion, I thank God that the work has been done. It has been done in one sense, perhaps, by the most inappropriate of instruments; but I rejoice in the result, that six or seven millions of people who were in partial subjection have been brought into total independence, and many millions more who were in absolute subjection to the Ottoman rule have been brought into a state which, if not one of total independence, yet is one of practical liberation actually attained, or very shortly to be realised – practical liberation from the worst of the evils which they suffered.

"But what happens now? Why, it appears the Turk is going to be coerced after all. But is not it a most astounding fact that the Government, who said they would on no consideration coerce the Turk, and who said that if Europe attempted to coerce the Turk nothing but misery could result, now expects to coerce the Turk by sending an order to Admiral Hornby at Malta, and desiring him to sail with his fleet into the east of the Mediterranean? Now, gentlemen, neither you nor I are acquainted with the whole of the circumstances attendant upon these measures. We don't know the reasons of State that have brought about this extraordinary result. But what I have pointed out to you is this, that Her Majesty's Government have in matter of fact come round to the very principle upon which they compelled the Liberals to join issue with them two or three years ago – the very principle which they then declared to be totally inadmissible, and for urging which upon them, their agents and organs through the country have been incessantly maintaining that nothing but the spirit of faction could have induced us to do anything so monstrous. That which nothing but the spirit of faction could have induced us to do, is embraced in principle by Her Majesty's Government.

"But is it embraced in the same form? No. We said: Let coercion be applied by the united authority of Europe – that is to say, for it is not an exaggeration so to put it, by the united authority of the civilised world applicable to this case. Our American friends have too remote an interest in it to take part. God forbid I should exclude them from the civilized world; but it was by the united authority of Europe that we demanded it. It is now attempted by the single authority and by the single hand of England. Will it succeed? All I can say is this, if it be directed to good and honest ends, to practical improvement, with all my heart I hope it may; but it may not, and then where is the responsibility? Where is the responsibility of those who refused to allow all Europe to act in unison, and who then took upon themselves this single-handed action? If it fails, they incur an immense responsibility. If it succeeds, it only becomes the more plain that had they but acceded to the advice which was at first so humbly tendered by the Liberal party, and which only after a long time was vigorously pressed – had they then acceded to the view of the Liberal party, and allowed Turkey to be dealt with as she ought to have been dealt with at the close of the Constantinople Conference, Turkey would have given way at once. The Power which yields to one State would still more readily have yielded to the united voice of the six great States. The concessions to be made by her would then have been made, and the horrors and the bloodshed, the loss of life and treasure, the heartburnings, the difficulties, the confusion and the anarchy that have followed, would all of them have been saved."

Salisbury – The Need for Consensus among the Powers*

"It is the common object of the European Powers that the Turkish Empire should be sustained, because no arrangement to replace it

* From Lord Salisbury (1830–1903). British Prime Minister 1885–6, 1886–92 and 1895–1902, and for much of this time also Foreign Secretary. Spent a time as

can be suggested which would not carry with it a serious risk of European conflict. The predominant importance of this considera- tion has led the European Powers to protect the Turkish Empire from dissolution, under the hope that the many evils by which the Ottoman rule was accompanied would be removed or mitigated by the reforming efforts of the Government. Not only has this hope been entirely disappointed, but it has become evident that unless these great evils can be abated, the forbearance of the Powers of Europe will be unable to protract the existence of a dominion which by its own vices is crumbling into ruin. It is difficult to say with confidence that any change that can be made will now prevent the threatened danger; but so long as the possibility of averting it exists, the Powers will feel it to be a matter of duty as well as matter of prudence, after satisfying themselves as to the changes which are the most urgent and best calculated to have a salutary operation, to provide effectively for those changes being carried through. Great authorities have up to this time been strenuously opposed to any measures by which Europe should become in any sense responsible for the internal administra- tion of the Turkish Empire. The arguments against such a policy undoubtedly are very cogent, and nothing but the urgency and the imminence of the dangers which attach to a purely negative policy would justify us in disregarding them. All the Powers of Europe are at one in desiring to maintain the territorial *status quo* of the Turkish Empire, and those Powers whose territories lie nearest to that Em- pire are most strongly impressed with this necessity. Their convic- tions upon this point may be sufficient to guarantee the Empire from any possible shock arising from external aggression, but they will not save it from the effect of misgovernment and internal decay.

"The consultation of the Six Ambassadors at Constantinople ap- pears to have been accompanied with a favourable result in dealing with the disorders of the Island of Crete. Their guidance is probably superior to any other that we can command, and I think we shall do wisely to commit to them the larger problem presented to us by the

Conservative MP in the House of Commons but moved to the House of Lords when he succeeded his father in 1868. Member of Disraeli's government in 1874. In 1878 became Foreign Secretary, immediately demanding a European Congress to discuss the settlement reached between Turkey and Russia of their recent war. Was a firm believer in understandings among the major powers to resolve European disputes and was one of the first British statesmen to show some understanding of Russian concerns in the Balkans. Quoted from "Confidential Circular Dispatch, 20 October 1896", in *Parliamentary Papers 1897*.

general condition of the Turkish Empire, and especially those portions of the Empire which are inhabited in considerable proportion by a Christian population. I propose that the Six Powers should instruct their Representatives to consider and report to their Governments what changes in the Government and administration of the Turkish Empire are, in their judgement, likely to be most effective in maintaining the stability of the Empire, and preventing the recurrence of the frightful cruelties by which the last two years have been lamentably distinguished. But before those instructions are given, Her Majesty's Government are of opinion that provision ought to be made that any resolution to which the Powers may, in consequence, unanimously come should be carried into operation.

"It is an object of primary importance that the concert of Europe should be maintained; and as long as any of the Powers, or any one Power, is not satisfied with the expediency of the recommendations that are put forward, no action in respect to them can be taken. But if any recommendations made by the Ambassadors should approve themselves to all the Powers as measures suitable for adoption, it must not be admitted, at the point which we have at present reached, that the objections of the Turkish Government can be an obstacle to their being carried into effect. I trust that the Powers will, in the first instance, come to a definite understanding, that their unanimous decision in these matters is to be final, and will be executed up to the measure of such force as the Powers have at their command. A preliminary agreement to this effect will greatly facilitate the deliberations of the Ambassadors, and will prevent much of the evasion and delay by which ameliorations in Turkish administration have on former occasions been obstructed."

28 Maintaining the Balance by Diplomacy

The Congress system was not generally thought to have replaced the balance of power. It was seen rather as an institution designed to *maintain* the balance, but to achieve this aim by diplomatic negotiation among the major powers rather than by the use of force against potential threats to the peace.

Different observers placed different weight on the two concepts. Some stressed the continuing importance of maintaining the balance; others that successful diplomacy should make power factors less significant. British statesmen, who were less willing than their continental partners to countenance joint action by the major powers, were inclined to attach greater importance to maintaining the balance in the traditional way. There were even some who thought to extend the idea beyond the continent. Thus Canning, British Foreign Secretary after Castlereagh, in his famous speech of 1826, conceived a wider balance on a global scale. The development of colonial empires beyond the seas had the effect that extra-European commitments and responsibilities had now sometimes to be taken into account. Seeking to justify British inaction against French intervention in Spain three years earlier, he sought to show that any advantage which France had gained there was more than balanced by the expanded influence which Britain had acquired in Latin America. By extending the diplomatic arena to that region Britain had been able, in his words, to call in the new world to redress the balance of the old.

There were others who held a very different opinion of the relative merits of the two approaches. Those of radical temperament frequently denounced the balance of power as a sham. Such observers maintained that the idea of the balance had little objective meaning. It was merely a rationalisation, called in aid by statesmen to justify almost any act of force which they wished to defend. Thus Cobden declared that "the theory of the balance of power is a mere chimera, a creation of the politician's brain – a phantasm, without definite form or tangible existence, a mere conjunction of syllables to convey sound with meaning". A similar view is expressed in the passage below by Cobden's friend and colleague, John Bright. He too declared that the balance of power was a concept without meaning. It had been blindly worshipped for 170 years. But it had led to the deaths of "hundreds of thousands of Englishmen"; and it was now, in his view, "dead and buried".

Palmerston expressed a middle view. He continued to hold that the balance of power was an essential foundation of the European system. In the speech reproduced below (from almost the same time as John Bright's) he rejected the view that the balance of power was an "exploded doctrine belonging to ancient times". On the contrary, he held, it was a doctrine founded "on the nature of man". Under such a view the Concert of Europe could only operate effectively if it took account of the balance, ensuring that the advantages acquired by one power were suitably balanced, or "compensated", by those acquired by its rivals. Thus Palmerston argued that it was not only in the British interests but in the interests "of the community of nations" that no other state should acquire a preponderance of power, and that smaller states should not be "swallowed up by their more powerful neighbours". But he makes it clear that he does not feel it is for Britain alone to maintain the balance: for example by supporting Denmark over Schleswig-Holstein. Only if France and Russia had combined with her, and so made war impossible, could Denmark have been protected. And that would have been a victory by diplomacy rather than by war.

This reflected a general reluctance to go to war to maintain the balance at this time, as states had been willing to do so frequently in the age before. If one state increased its power, even through war, others did not, as before, join together to prevent it. Thus Prussia was able to fight three wars between 1864 and 1870, all against individual opponents, each of which were obliged to fight single-handed, and each of which was in turn defeated, securing a substantial accretion to Prussia's power. Only in the Crimean War, when Britain and France joined to defend Turkey against the pretensions of Russia in 1854–6, can it be said that a war was fought largely for balance of power purposes. In general the balance was maintained more by diplomacy rather than by war. That effort was often successful: for example in the successive conferences in London in 1830–2 and in 1839–40, in Paris in 1856, and in Berlin in 1878. In each of these cases the main objective was to ensure that no single power should extract excessive advantage from the wars and crises which had preceded them. Brougham, in the passage below, foresees this state of affairs. Suggesting that the balance of power had created a new stability in the conduct of international affairs; making Europe into a "great federacy . . . united by certain common principles", and not in watching on the others to prevent any one becoming dominant.

For many, however, the development of the Concert system appeared altogether too unreliable as a means of maintaining stability and balance in the European system. After 1879 reliance was placed rather on the creation of alliances; alliances which, unlike those of the previous era, were now relatively permanent. So the Franco-Russian alliance of 1891–4 was established explicitly to counter that established a dozen years earlier between Germany and Austria, and both remained in existence, each balancing the other, until the First World War. But the fact that, even after Germany had clearly become the most powerful and threatening state of the Continent, Britain at the turn of the century seriously considered entering into alliance with her rather than against her, shows that the policy of major states was still in many cases dictated by immediate interests, or traditional antipathies, rather than by concern to maintain the balance. Only as German power inexorably grew, was Britain compelled to consider joining the opposite camp to restore the balance (see extract on p. 473 below). Thus by the time of the First World War the "balance of power" was now increasingly identified with the alliance system. Both were widely condemned, being held by many as responsible for intensifying rather than deterring conflict. This is the view expressed by Brailsford, radical British political writer, in the last extract reproduced here from a book published on the eve of the First World War. So convinced is he of the iniquity of the alliance system that he is determined that Britain should not join too closely with her partners in the Triple Entente, whatever value that might have as others believed, in improving the European "balance of power". In his view the balance was a euphemism for a confrontation between two rival alliances, and he was determined that Britain should have nothing to do with either of them.

Ideas about the balance of power thus underwent a significant change during this period. There were now some (like Bright and Brailsford) who denounced the whole concept as a convenient rationalisation used by governments to justify efforts to increase their own power at the expense of others. There were others, like Canning and Palmerston, who saw the maintenance of the balance as an essential condition for stabilising the continent. But governments in general were no longer so willing to go to war for the sake of maintaining, or restoring, the balance. The main concern of states now was to assist, or to oppose, aspirations for nationhood, and neither objective was much influenced by considerations of power balance. When rival alliances did finally establish a visible, and apparently almost equal, balance at the period's end, this as was soon to be apparent was not in itself sufficient to deter war.

*   *   *

Canning – A World-Wide Balance*

"Is the balance of power a fixed and unalterable standard? Or is it not a standard perpetually varying, as civilisation advances and as new nations spring up, and take their place among established political communities? The balance of power a century and a half ago was to be adjusted between France and Spain, the Netherlands, Austria and England. Some years afterwards, Russia assumed her high station in European politics. Some years after that again, Prussia became not only a substantive, but a preponderating monarchy. Thus, while the balance of power continued in principle the same, the means of adjusting it became more varied and enlarged. They became enlarged, in proportion to the increased number of considerable states, – in proportion, I may say, to the number of weights which might be shifted into the one or the other scale. To look to the policy of Europe, in the times of William and Anne, for the purpose of regulating the balance of power in Europe at the present day, is to disregard the progress of events, and to confuse dates and facts which throw a reciprocal light upon each other.

"It would be disingenuous, indeed, not to admit that the entry of the French army into Spain, was in a certain sense, a disparagement – an affront to the pride – a blow to the feelings of England: and it can

* From George Canning (1770–1827). British Foreign Secretary 1822–7, and briefly Prime Minister in 1827. He entered Parliament as a protégé of Pitt in 1793 and held several junior offices in his government. Quarrelled with Castlereagh in 1809 and fought a duel with him. Was mainly out of office until Castlereagh's suicide in 1822 when he replaced him as Foreign Secretary. As Foreign Secretary he rejected intervention by the major powers in the internal affairs of smaller states, abandoned the Congress system and defended the independence of the South American colonies: it is this last aim which inspired the famous speech here reproduced. Quoted from his speech in the House of Commons, 12 December 1826.

hardly be supposed that the government did not sympathise, on that occasion, with the feelings of the people. But I deny that, questionable or censurable as the act might be, it was one which necessarily called for our direct and hostile opposition. Was nothing then to be done? Was there no other mode of resistance, than by a direct attack upon France – or by a war to be undertaken on the soil of Spain? What, if the possession of Spain might be rendered harmless in rival hands – harmless as regarded us – and valueless to the possessors? Might not compensation for disparagement be obtained, and the policy of our ancestors vindicated, by means better adapted to the present time? If France occupied Spain, was it necessary, in order to avoid the consequences of that occupation – that we should blockade Cadiz? No. I looked another way – I sought materials of compensation in another hemisphere. Contemplating Spain, such as our ancestors had known her, I resolved that if France had Spain, it should not be Spain 'with the Indies'. I called the New World into existence, to redress the balance of the Old."

Bright – The Myth of the Balance of Power*

"I think I am not much mistaken in pronouncing the theory of the balance of power to be pretty nearly dead and buried. You cannot comprehend at a thought what is meant by that balance of power. If the record could be brought before you – but it is not possible to the eye of humanity to scan the scroll upon which are recorded the sufferings which the theory of the balance of power has entailed upon this country. It rises up before me when I think of it as a ghastly phantom which during one hundred and seventy years, whilst it has been worshipped in this country, has loaded the nation with debt and with taxes, has sacrificed the lives of hundreds of thousands of Englishmen, has desolated the homes of millions of families, and has left us, as the great result of the profligate expenditure which it has

* From John Bright (1811–89). Radical English politician and passionate free-trader. Son of a textile manufacturer, he became, with Richard Cobden (see p. 57), an ardent campaigner against the Corn Laws, which raised the price of bread to consumers in Britain and for free trade generally. After his election to Parliament in 1847, he became an assiduous campaigner for electoral reform and a strong opponent of Palmerston's interventionist policies abroad. Quoted from his speech at Birmingham, 18 January 1865.

caused, a doubled peerage at one end of the social scale, and far more than a doubled pauperism at the other. I am very glad to be here tonight, amongst other things, to be able to say that we may rejoice that this foul idol – fouler than any heathen tribe ever worshipped – has at last been thrown down, and that there is one superstition less which has its hold upon the minds of English statesmen and of the English people."

Palmerston – The Balance of Power Defended*

"[W]e are told that the balance of power is an exploded doctrine belonging to ancient times. Why, it is a doctrine founded on the nature of man. It means that it is to the interest of the community of nations that no nation should acquire such a preponderance as to endanger the security of the rest; and it is for the advantage of all that the smaller Powers should be respected in their independence and not swallowed up by their more powerful neighbours. That is the doctrine of the balance of power, and it is a doctrine worthy of being acted upon. We have done our best to rescue Denmark from the danger to which she was exposed, first by counselling her to put herself right when she was wrong, and next by endeavouring to induce her aggressors to refrain from continuing their aggression; and by inducing the neutral Powers to join us in adopting the same course. And what said the right hon. Gentleman in his opening speech on this subject? He said that if England and France were agreed upon the same policy, war would be difficult; but that if England, France and Russia were agreed, war would be impossible. Well, we tried to make war impossible. But France and Russia would not combine with us, and therefore war became possible, and took place. The right hon. Gentleman has therefore pronounced a panegyric upon our policy, and he ought to vote against his own Resolution. We adopted the best means of rendering war impossible, and the failure was not our fault. . . .

". . . It is a libel on our country to record by a vote of the House what is not the fact – namely, that the influence and position of

* From Lord Palmerston (1784–1865). (For biographical details see p. 165.) Quoted from his speech in the House of Commons, 8 July 1864.

England have been lowered. Sir, the influence of a country depends upon other things than protocols and despatches. It depends on its power to defend itself, on its wealth and prosperity, on its intelligence and cultivation of mind, on the development of the arts and sciences, and on all those things which made a nation truly great and powerful. As long as England retains these conditions, so long shall I deny that her influence has been diminished."

Brougham – Maintaining the Balance among European States*

"It is not, then, in the mere plan of forming offensive or defensive alliances; or in the principle of attacking a neighbour in order to weaken his power, before he has betrayed hostile views; or in the policy of defending a rival, in order to stay, in proper time, the progress of a common enemy: it is not in these simple maxims that the modern system consists. These are, indeed, the elements, the great and leading parts of the theory; they are its most prominent features; they are maxims dictated by the plainest and coarsest views of political expediency: but they do not form the whole system; nor does the knowledge of them (for it cannot be pretended that ancient states were in possession of anything beyond the speculative knowledge of them) comprehend an acquaintance with the profounder and more subtle parts of modern policy. The grand and distinguishing feature of the balancing theory, is the systematic form to which it reduces those plain and obvious principles of national conduct; the perpetual attention to foreign affairs which it inculcates; the constant watchfulness which it prescribes over every movement in all parts of the system; the subjection in which it tends to place all national passions and antipathies to the views of remote expediency; the unceasing care which it dictates of nations most remotely situated, and apparently unconnected with ourselves; the general union, which

---

* From Lord Brougham (1778–1868). British liberal politician, reformer and political writer. Was Lord Chancellor from 1830 to 1834 in the Whig administrations of Grey and Melbourne. Agitated for law reform, the improvement of education, the abolition of slavery and other reforms. *The Balance of Power* is an early book, written when the author was only 25 and little known. Quoted from *The Balance of Power* (1803) (London: Richard Griffin, 1857).

it has effected, of all the European powers in one connecting system – obeying certain laws, and actuated, for the most part, by a common principle; in fine, as a consequence of the whole, the right of mutual inspection, now universally recognised among civilised states, in the appointment of public envoys and residents. This is the balancing theory. It was as much unknown to Athens and Rome, as the Keplerian or Newtonian laws were concealed from Plato and Cicero, who certainly knew the effect of gravitation upon terrestrial bodies. It has arisen, in the progress of science, out of the circumstances of modern Europe – the greater extent and nearer equality of the contiguous states – the more constant intercourse of the different nations with each other. We have been told by historians, that the principle of the balance of power was a discovery made at the end of the fifteenth century by the Italian politicians, in consequence of the invasion of Charles VIII. Against such statements as this, it is perfectly fair to adduce the arguments of Mr Hume and others, who have traced in ancient times, vastly more refined notions of policy than any that dictated the Italian defensive league. It was, in truth, not to any such single event, that the balancing system owed either its origin, or its refinement; but to the progress of society, which placed the whole states of Europe in the same relative situation in which the states of Italy were at that period, and taught them not to wait for an actual invasion, but to see a Charles at all times in every prince or commonwealth that should manifest the least desire of change.

"The circumstances of the European states, by promoting national intercourse, have been singularly favourable to the development of those principles of easy and constant union. Consolidated into one system of provincial government under the empire of Rome, they were separated by the same causes, and nearly at the same time. Reduced by a people whose character and manners were never effaced by the most rapid conquests, or most remote emigrations, they were formed into divisions under constitutions of the same nature, peculiarly calculated to preserve the uniformity of customs, which originally marked the whole. The progress of political government has been similar in all, from the dominion of the nobles to the tyranny of the prince, and, in these latter times, to the freedom of the people. That spirit of commercial intercourse, which produces a perpetual connection, little known in the ancient world, has conspired with the similarity of situation, and the resemblance of manners, to render Europe a united whole within itself, almost separated from the rest of the world; – a great federacy, acknowledging, indeed, no common chief; but united by certain common principles, and obeying one system of international law.

• • •

"The circumstances in the relative situation of the European powers – their proximity, their constant intercourse, their rivalry, and the uniform desire that all princes have to extend their dominions, render it absolutely necessary that no one power should view with indifference the domestic affairs of the rest, more particularly those affairs which have a reference to the increase or consolidation of national resources.

"For the purpose of acquiring such information, the institution of ambassadors has been adopted, or of *privileged spies*, as they have been called by witty men, with much the same propriety of speech as would mark the personage who should be pleased to call Generals master-butchers, or Judges hangmen. From the institution of ambassadors, an essential and peculiar part of the modern system, have resulted the important consequences – a constant intercourse between the two governments; frequent opportunities of detecting and preventing hostile measures or artifices; and still more frequent occasions of avoiding ruptures by timely complaint, and explanation or redress. The natural effects of the system to which this matter has been reduced, are certainly the prevention of wars, and the systematising of the grand art of pacification.

• • •

"It may thus be laid down as a principle, applicable to this extreme case, that, whenever a sudden and great change takes place in the internal structure of a state, dangerous in a high degree to all neighbours, they have a right to attempt, by hostile interference, the restoration of an order of things safe to themselves; or, at least, to counterbalance, by active aggression, the new force suddenly acquired. If a highwayman pulls out a pistol from his bosom, shall we wait till he loads and presents it, before we disarm him? shall we not attack him with like arms, if he displays such weapons, whether he takes them from his own stores, or seizes them from some other person in our sight?[1] We do not attack a neighbouring nation for plundering or conquering a third power, because we wish to avenge or redress the injury; but because we shall be ourselves affected by its consequences. Shall we be less injured by the same consequences, because the dangerous power of doing us mischief is developed from its recesses within, and not forcibly snatched from without?

• • •

"It appears, then, that, by the modern system of foreign policy, the fate of nations has been rendered more certain; and the influence of chance, of the fortune of war, of the caprices of individuals upon the general affairs of men, has been exceedingly diminished. Nations are no longer of transient or durable existence in proportion to their internal resources, but in proportion to the place which they occupy in a vast and regular system; where the most powerful states are, for their own sakes, constantly watching over the safety of the most insignificant. A flourishing commonwealth is not liable to lose its independence or its prosperity by the fate of one battle. Many battles must be lost; many changes must concur: the whole system must be deranged, before such a catastrophe can happen. The appearance of an Epaminondas can no longer raise a petty state to power and influence over its neighbour, suddenly to be lost, with the great man's life, by some defeat at Mantineia, as it had been gained by some unforeseen victory at Leuetra. In the progress of freedom, knowledge, and national intercourse, this great change has been happily effected by slow degrees: it is a change which immediately realises the advantages that every former change has gained to mankind; a step in our progress, which secures the advancement made during all our previous career; and contributes, perhaps more than any other revolution that has happened in common affairs, to the improvement of the species."

Note
1. The doctrine of the balance of power is deduced, by Vattel, from similar grounds. See *Droit des gens*, liv. iii., chap. 3, sec. 44, *et seq.*

Brailsford – The Fallacy of the Balance of Power*

"We have followed for nearly a decade a policy defined as the preservation in Europe of 'a balance of power'. It is a familiar idea,

* From H. N. Brailsford (1873–1958). English radical writer. After a brilliant academic career as a student, fought for the Greeks against Turkey in the war of 1897. He later became a journalist, covering especially Balkan affairs. A friend of J. A. Hobson (see p. 460) he shared his views about the economic causes of war and set out that conclusion most cogently in *The War of Steel and Gold* (1914), which scored

and the words recall some of the most cherished memories in our history. But like all traditional phrases it illustrates the danger of adapting to modern conditions a notion which bore for our ancestors a meaning which we cannot give it today. It arrests thinking, confuses emotion, and covers with its venerable mantle a policy which is in reality entirely new. 'To maintain a balance of power in Europe' is the motive which inspired us to erect the Triple Entente as a barrier against the Triple Alliance, led us into a conscious and habitual rivalry with Germany, made us the ally of France in a quarrel not our own, and set us, after the Manchurian campaign, to restore Russia by financial aid and diplomatic backing to her place among the Great Powers. All metaphors mislead, and this metaphor is peculiarly fallacious. One may doubt whether any statesman in his own inner mind ever desired a balance, if the word means what it conveys – an exact equipoise in force and influence among the Powers of Europe. What every statesman desires is that the scales of power shall be more heavily weighted on his own side. He begins to talk of a balance when the scales descend on the other side. He piles a weight on his own side or snatches a weight from the other, but he never stops at the crucial moment when the scales are even. The balance is a metaphor of venerable hypocrisy which serves only to disguise the perennial struggle for power and predominance.

"When a statesman talks of a balance, he means a balance favourable to himself. Equipoise between two rival groups, if ever it could be attained, would mean a condition intolerable to the normal human mind. It would mean stagnation and stalemate, the throttling and handcuffing, not of one nation, but of all. It is for liberty of movement, for opportunity to carry out their national purposes that all Powers strive. In a Concert that liberty is sought through the amicable adjustment of interests round a Council-Board, and just in so far as Powers form permanent groups which support each other in issue after issue on the principle of 'my ally right or wrong' does any Concert governed by the disinterested opinion of neutrals become impossible. Without a Concert the group system means that all negotiation, even when it is outwardly courteous, is carried on with the knowledge that arguments are weighed by the number of army corps and guns and ships which each combination can muster. The

an immediate success. Joined with Hobson and others in campaigning for a permanent organisation to maintain the peace after the war: it is said that Woodrow Wilson was influenced by his book, *A League of Nations* (1917). Quoted from *The War of Steel and Gold* (London: G. Bell, 1914).

evil reaches its climax when all the Great Powers are regimented, as they are today, in one group or the other, and none of them is free, without some measure of disloyalty to partners, to approach any question with an open mind or to consider any aspect of it save its reaction upon the interests of these partners.

A Balance of Power is not a self-sufficing ideal. Power is sought for certain ends, and that is true whether it is at an equality or at a preponderance of power that one aims. It is here that the real difference emerges between the contemporary struggle to maintain a sort of balance in Europe and the epic wars of the eighteenth and early nineteenth centuries. When our ancestors talked of redressing the balance, and formed coalitions, subsidised allies and landed armies on the Continent, they had something to fear. They were fighting for hearths and homes. They knew that their own liberties, political and religious, were at issue, and if the struggle imposed on them inordinate burdens, the stake was worth the sacrifice. In the former of the two periods dominated by the notion of a balance, Louis XIV had made himself the arbiter of Europe. He gave a king to Spain, a mistress and a pension to Charles II, stood behind a Catholic restoration under his successor, and menaced the Netherlands and the Rhine with unceasing and devastating warfare. When William of Orange taught our ancestors to think in terms of the balance of power, it was because our shores were threatened with an invasion which would have brought back a despotic king. His strategy was a league of the weaker Powers against a nation whose cohesion and superiority in culture and wealth overtopped the liberty of Western Europe. No less elementary, no less monstrous, were the perils which caused Pitt to revive the theory of the balance against Napoleon. Frontiers had become fluid under the tread of his armies, and his will moulded national institutions and made and unmade kings. In both periods the things that were weighed in the balance were the home territories and the domestic liberties of the peoples which sought to adjust it. The stake was their national existence, the fields and the cities which were their home. Our fathers under William of Orange and Pitt did not aspire to a balance as a thing good and necessary in itself, or as a condition of the normal life of European societies. They meant by the balance such a checking of the excessive power of France as would save Devonshire from her fleets, the Palatinate from her armies, their thrones from her nominees and their Parliaments from her dictation. The balance, in short, was the condition of national self-government.

"We must free ourselves from the obsession of this phrase, if we would judge contemporary diplomacy clearly. There is no analogy, there is not even a plausible parallel between our own case and that of our forefathers who coined the phrase. To pursue a balance for its own sake is not an axiom of British policy. What is axiomatic is rather that we must adopt any policy necessary to the preservation of our national liberties. The balance was always a means to that end; it was never an end in itself. We shall not reason honestly about the modern problems of diplomacy, until we have first of all recognised that the dangers which forced our ancestors into European coalitions and Continental wars have gone never to return. We need not argue that human character is absolutely better than it was in earlier centuries, nor even that the predatory instincts of mankind have grown appreciably weaker. Human character, for that matter, is not a fixed or self-subsistent thing; it is the habit which human beings acquire of adjusting themselves to their environment. The environment changes and the character with it. What mainly differentiates our century from those which went before it is that the forms of wealth have changed. Wealth in the days of the wars for a balance of power meant primarily land. Wealth in our day is primarily the opportunity for peculiarly profitable investment. This economic evolution has modified most of our social institutions, and with them our diplomacy. Conquest in the old sense of the world has become obsolete. A predatory Power does not go out with drums and banners to seize estates for its feudal aristocracy. It applies pressure, and pressure which often involves the possession of fleets and armies, to secure concessions for its financiers. There is no advance in morality here, no conscious progress towards a Golden Age. The change cannot be described in phrases from Isaiah or in verses from Vergil [*sic*]. It is a non-moral development, but it has none the less a direct bearing upon our hopes of peace. The instinct to conquer is as sharp and insatiable as ever, but it has found a means of conquering beyond frontiers. Our modern *conquistadores* do not burn their ships when they alight on coveted soil, as though to anchor themselves for ever on its fertile acres. Our bankers will not do in China what Cortes and Pizarro did in the New World. They build a railway or sink a mine. Our Ahabs do not take Naboth's vineyard; they invest money in it. The struggle for a balance of power means today a struggle for liberty and opportunity to use 'places in the sun' across the seas. For the modern world a place in the sun is not a smiling valley, or a rich plain in which a victorious army will settle, and build homes and found families. It is a territory to 'exploit', and the active agents in the process are now the bankers and investors who float loans, and secure concessions. Even where conquest is incidentally necessary, as in Morocco, there is no migration to the new territory and the conquering Power rarely troubles to annex it. It 'occupies' it, only because without occupation it cannot safely employ its capital in building railways or sinking mines. Land-hunger is not the malady of the modern world. In all this we shall not discover the faintest resemblance to the perils and ambitions which roused the passions and stimulated the sacrifices of the earlier struggles for a balance of power."

29 A System of Collective Security

By the beginning of the twentieth century the system of regular conferences among the "powers" was seen as increasingly inadequate as a means of resolving international conflicts. There were demands for a new and better system for maintaining world order. Successive crises, over Fashoda in 1898, Morocco in 1905–6 and 1911 and Bosnia-Herzegovina in 1908, had demonstrated the fragility of the system even before the First World War. After the total breakdown of the existing international order in 1914 calls for a better way of maintaining the peace became more insistent.

There were a number of obvious defects in the old system. First, meetings of the Concert were called only on an *ad hoc* basis. Whether or not a conference was convened to consider a particular crisis depended, not on the severity of the crisis or the likelihood that such a meeting might secure useful results, but on whether it was demanded by a particular power or group of powers. Thus while conferences considered and resolved, reasonably successfully, the crises over Morocco in 1906 and the Balkans in 1913, none took place at the time of the Austrian annexation of Bosnia-Herzegovina in 1908, a far greater threat to the peace of the continent; nor (despite a proposal to the effect by the British Foreign Secretary) in July 1914, though everybody then recognised that war could be imminent. Even before the final breakdown, therefore, many were criticising the way the conference system operated and were calling for reforms. In Britain H. N. Brailsford, writing on the eve of the First World War, while he endorsed the fundamental principle on which the Concert was based – that all major powers had an interest in the settlement of crises all over the world and should therefore be consulted on their resolution – condemned the self-interested and illiberal way in which the powers had operated the system in the past. He therefore wanted it to be made "less restricted in its scope and more permanent in its aims". Several of the major states now had interests that were world-wide and which therefore interacted with those of other states. Even those that were not directly involved in a crisis had a right to a say: indeed precisely because they were disinterested they were better qualified to make a judgement. The most powerful states might act more reasonably if they were members of a Council which claimed to base its decisions on the common good of the continent. If the "supremacy of the Council" in resolving such disputes were generally recognised, an effective system for preventing war could be established and the incentive to compete in the acquisition of arms would be destroyed.

This was essentially a call for a reform of the Concert system to make it more democratic and more predictable. But after the First World War broke out it became evident that the old system could not be re-established and there was increasing interest in the establishment of a totally new method of maintaining the peace. This would have to meet a number of requirements. First, its operation must be made much more automatic than that of the Concert had been. The states participating would have to make a formal commitment to maintain the peace and to submit their disputes to collective decision. Thus J. A. Hobson, in his book *Towards International Government*, written shortly after the war began, proposed that in any new organisation to be established every member should commit itself to submit disputes not resolved by normal diplomatic processes to arbitration or conciliation; to bring pressure on other states to ensure that they would do the same; and if necessary to take joint action with others to defend another member which was under attack and secure redress of an injury done. Leonard Woolf, writing a year later (under the same title of *International Government*) also called for a more automatic procedure for securing the resolution of disputes. He believed it was essential for each state to accept the "right of the nations collectively to settle questions which imperil the peace of the world". This meant abandoning the "popular view of the independence and sovereignty of states": in other words it demanded a revolutionary change in the existing state system.

A second need was for the new system to be made more representative than the Concert had been. The Concert system had been essentially oligarchic: a few powerful states – at first five, later six – came together to agree on settlements which often affected other, weaker states even more than they did the powerful few themselves. Such a system was likely to be increasingly unacceptable to the small states of the world (of which more were to be created at the end of the current conflict). And it was out of accord with increasingly acknowledged principles of "democracy". Thus, it was generally believed, any new organisation had to be made more democratic. J. A. Hobson, for example, in his book held that the usefulness of any new organisation would be limited if a few nations only were willing to join it: it might then not differ substantially from a nominally defensive alliance of several powers. As a minimum, if it was to be effective, any new organisation must win the adherence of the majority of the great powers, and so acquire an absolute preponderance of military and naval strength over potential threats to the peace.

The third requirement for the new organisation was that it should be more institutionalised than the informal and *ad hoc* procedures of the Concert had been. The general expectation was that it would be a formal organisation, with its own constitution and established procedures, such as the Concert had lacked. Leonard Woolf rejected the notion that institutional developments of this kind are of no value unless accompanied by a fundamental change in state motivation. Though such a change was also desirable, institution innovations could be of importance in themselves in determining the response made to a crisis. There was thus need for agreement in advance on what kinds of issue should be submitted for collective decision. But what was needed above all was acceptance of the principle that majority decisions were binding on minorities: a wholly new principle, since in the conferences of the nineteenth century agreement had depended on the unanimous consent of those participating.

The works of Hobson and Woolf are typical of a great deal of writing at this time about the kind of institutional system to be established when the "Great War" was over. The League of Nations, when it was established in 1919, implemented many of the principles which such writers had set out. It was much more comprehensive in membership than the Concert had been (though the US never joined, and other major powers such as Germany, Italy, Japan and the Soviet Union were members for only a period); members committed themselves to abide by certain principles and to settle their disputes peacefully; and regular procedures were established for the consideration of disputes which could not be resolved in traditional ways. Thus it conformed to many of the ideas put forward by the pioneer writers. In theory this was now a genuine collective security system, in which all were expected to join in maintaining the peace by coming to the defence of any state that was under attack. But it was still left to the voluntary decision of each state if and how it would fulfil this commitment; and in practice when the members were finally put to the test (over Manchuria in 1931 and Ethiopia in 1935–6) they failed to respond in the way that a collective security system demanded. Despite these failures, in the final passage quoted below Sir Alfred

Zimmern, writing in the late 1930s, reviews the record of the League till that time and arrives at a surprisingly optimistic judgement. He points out that it had never been expected that the new machinery would in itself solve the world's problems: simply that it might prevent a breakdown in international relations resulting from the lack of such machinery. The important advance was that this now existed and was likely to "become a permanent part of the political arrangements of mankind". The organisation was not designed to remake the world: for example by recreating states on the basis of nations (as its little might have suggested). What it could do was "to provide a more satisfactory means of carrying on some of the business which states conduct between one another".

This was a relatively undemanding test to make of a new international organisation. It is arguable that, even on the basis of that test, the League of Nations was a failure. But the idea that an international organisation was essentially simply an agency through which states could do business with each other more effectively than before increasingly came to rival the earlier, and more widespread, assumption, that it should represent some kind of higher authority imposing its will on the erring states which were its members. As the next great international conflict drew towards its end, and plans were again being drawn up for a new international organisation, it came to be urged in some quarters that the former concept should be at least as influential as the latter in determining the blueprint for any new system to be established.

* * *

Brailsford – A Reformed Concert of Europe*

"Every Power in Europe is a member of a Group, and even if the issue in question does not oblige the others to share in the hostilities to which it may give rise, they cannot afford without an effort to see their partner preoccupied, weakened by a struggle, and perhaps defeated. To that extent the system of alliances, which seems at a first

---

* From H. N. Brailsford (1873–1958). (For biographical details see p. 448.) Quoted from *The War of Steel and Gold* (London: G. Bell, 1914).

glance only to dig a chasm in Europe, does make for a certain perverted and paradoxical solidarity. If the Powers are as yet incapable of a broadly European outlook, if they do not realise the fraternity which in every issue would make them the brother's keeper of any member of the European family, each is of necessity its ally's keeper. Three Powers, at least, are today world-Powers, with interests or ambitions so widespread that nothing which can happen anywhere can find them quite indifferent. The stoic *nil humanum a me alienum puto* is a moral ideal beyond modern diplomacy. But a Power comes near it in effect when it declares that every human issue touches its interests. Our own country, by reason of its trade and its scattered possessions, has been for many generations the type of a world-Power. France by the intricate permeation of her investments is in the same case. Germany has in our day claimed this status, and built a navy to enforce it. If Russia's interests are not world-wide, they do at least cover a vast area. The Moroccan question was the test case which demonstrated that in the modern world it is henceforth impossible for two Powers to settle a considerable issue without considering the views of their neighbours. After that experience the choice is clear. It lies between such perils and confusions as the vain attempt to exclude Germany from the settlement caused in fact, and a frank recognition from the start that 'world-politics' are a matter for the Concert to settle.

"Midway in the Moroccan quarrel, the Kaiser, in one of his more truculent speeches, remarked that nothing must happen in the world 'without Germany'. This claim to be consulted in every world-event may be, and doubtless in the Kaiser's mouth it was, simply an expression of political high spirits. But the maxim is capable, in the Kantian phrase, of being universalised. It lays down the basis on which a real Concert of Europe might be founded. Let us say rather that nothing should happen throughout the world without the consent of all the civilised Powers. We should, perhaps, exclude America, since the Monroe Doctrine makes it a self-contained continent. We may also admit that, for practical purposes, the Concert will not in every instance be the same. Japan has no status in a European, nor Austria and Italy in an Asiatic question.

"But the meaning of our principle is clear. There ought to be no change in the *status quo*, which means the acquisition by any Power of rights over another State, however backward or weak, without the consent of the general body of civilised opinion. It is obvious that this principle, and this principle alone, can set a check upon lawless aggression, appease the rivalries of predatory Powers, and create a tribunal to which the weak may appeal. It will be objected that this means the constant meddling in questions which do not concern them of Powers which have no real 'interest' in some given region of the earth. When Germany claimed a voice in the Moroccan affair, Britain and France retorted that she is not a Mediterranean Power. A like answer would doubtless be returned if she were to obtrude her opinion at some phase of the Persian crisis. But, to our thinking, an opinion gains in value precisely in so far as it is disinterested. What a monstrous theory it is that Britain and Russia, simply because they have considerable material interests, political, strategic and mercantile, in Persia, should have the right to dispose of the destinies of its people. Just because they are bound to think of their own interests, rather than the good of the Persian people, are they incapable of fulfilling their assumed task. British financiers have lent money to Egypt, and therefore British administrators are held to be the proper persons to conduct the education of Egypt. There could be no more immoral or unreasonable proposition than this. John Smith, let us suppose, has been made bankrupt for a debt to some Amalgamated Dynamite Trust, and has gone to the mad-house in despair. Does it follow that the Trust should be made the guardian and tutor of John Smith's children?

"We can usually find in modern diplomacy a precedent for any principle, even for the wider and humaner principles. There was, in 1905, a phase of the Turkish question when the Powers were discussing who should take the initiative or the main responsibility for the reforms in Macedonia, Austria and Russia, because they are the neighbours of Turkey, claimed to be the 'interested' Powers, and demanded the right on that account to carry through a scheme of their own. Lord Lansdowne, in a memorable despatch, challenged this claim, both in theory and in its particular application, and vindicated the right of the disinterested Powers to a parity of control over Macedonia. He was emphatically right. Austria and Russia, because they were interested, were certain to pursue only their own interests. The other Powers have occasionally allowed some fitful regard for the interests of the peoples of Turkey to influence their policy. The Concert of Europe is a very slow and very fallible instrument of justice. It has sanctioned many a wrong, ignored many a misery, and proved itself in crisis after crisis, nerveless, lethargic and unintelligent. But with all its faults it is a check upon the ambitions of any single Power; it cannot be captured by any one national group of financiers, and it has, on occasion, at least affected to listen to the pleas of the subject races or lesser States whose fate hung in the balance.

"The fundamental basis in the theory of a Concert is that interests must not be confused with rights. No Power has any rights over another people. The Moors, the Persians and the Bosnians alone have rights in Morocco, Persia and Bosnia. To an act of barter between interested Powers we must refuse the sanctity of law. If change is inevitable in the status of any people, it is the Common Council of the civilised world which alone can sanction it. We must go on to say that the formation of alliances among the Powers is an act of treason to this ideal of a Concert, because they stand in the way of any decision based upon the merits of the case. The Concert ought to decide what would be best for Morocco, Persia or Bosnia, as the case may be. It cannot do this if Britain is pledged to think only of what will be best for France, and Austria only of what will be best for Germany. Groupings of Powers are, of course, inevitable. But they should resemble rather the coalition of parties in a Parliament than the old-world dynastic alliance. Their basis must be a community of principles and opinions.

"On one condition only should we reluctantly approve of a temporary alliance. If any Power or group of Powers seeks to evade the control of the Concert, refuses to submit common European affairs to its judgement, defies the decisions reached at a Conference, or seeks to impose its will on others without a mandate from the Common Council, it would be legitimate to combine against it, to 'isolate' it, and to make it impotent for evil. Let this principle once be acknowledged and the chief motive for armaments is gone. Armaments are the means by which Powers seek to obtain immunity and opportunity for expansion. But if expansion itself is dependent on the consent of the Concert, armaments have lost half their utility.

"It would, of course, be folly to suppose that the acceptance of this principle of the supremacy of the Concert would at once create harmony, and bring about a reduction of armaments. But it would at once achieve this – it would make a standard for the conscience of the civilised world, it would provide an objective test by which the loyalty of any policy might be tried, and above all it would supply a common ground on which all the parties of peace might take their stand. It would conduce to a gradual slackening of the European tension, a gradual loosening of the existing alliances, and in time create an atmosphere in which a proposal for the reduction of armaments, and eventually some scheme for the creation of a loose Federal Council to decide the common affairs of Europe might at least be considered."

Hobson – The Need for a New League of States*

The general form in which a co-operation of nations for these objects presents itself is that of a League of Confederation. The primary object of such a League is to bind all its members to submit all their serious differences to arbitration or some other mode of peaceful settlement, and to accept the judgement or award thus obtained. Some advocates of a League of Peace think that the sense of moral obligation in each State, fortified by the public opinion of the civilised world, would form a valid sanction for the fulfilment of such undertakings, and would afford a satisfactory measure of security. But most hold that it is advisable or essential that the members of such a League should bind themselves to take joint action against any member who breaks the peace.

"Assuming that a considerable body of nations entered such a League with good and reliable intentions, how far would it be likely to secure the peace of the world and a reduction of armed preparations? The answer to this question would depend mainly upon the number and status of the Powers constituting the League and their relation to outside nations. If, as is not unlikely, at first only a small number of nations were willing to enter such a League, the extent of the pacific achievement would be proportionately circumscribed. If, say, Britain, France, and the United States entered the League, undertaking to settle all their differences by peaceful methods, such a step, however desirable in itself, would not go far towards securing world-peace or enabling these leagued Powers to reduce their national armaments. This is so obvious that most advocates of the League of Peace urge that the leagued Powers should not confine their undertaking to the peaceful settlement of differences among

---

* From J. A. Hobson (1858–1940). As already noted (see p. 448) Hobson was a close friend of H. N. Brailsford and they held similar views about the need to create a new international institution to prevent war at the conclusion of the First World War. Quoted from *Towards International Government* (London: Allen and Unwin, 1915).

themselves, but should afford a united defence to any of their members attacked by any outside Power which was unwilling to arbitrate its quarrel. A defensive alliance of three such Great Powers (for that is what the League of Peace would amount to at this stage of development) would no doubt form a force which it would be dangerous for any nation, or combination of nations, to attack. But it would secure neither peace nor disarmament. Nor would it, as an earnest advocate of this procedure argues,[1] necessarily, or even probably, form a nucleus of a larger League drawing in other nations. A few nations forming such a League would not differ substantially from the other nominally defensive alliances with which the pages of history are filled. Their purely defensive character would be suspected by outside Powers, who would tend to draw together into an opposing alliance, thus reconstituting once more the Balance of Power with all its perils and its competing armaments. Nay, if such a League of Peace were constituted in the spirit of the Holy Alliance of a century ago, or of the resurrection of that spirit which Mr Roosevelt represents in order 'to back righteousness by force' in all quarters of the earth, such an opposition of organised outside Powers would be inevitable. The League of Peace idea, in order to have any *prima facie* prospect of success, must at the outset be so planned as to win the adherence of the majority of the Great Powers, including some of those recently engaged in war with one another. For until there was an absolute preponderance of military and naval strength inside the League, the relief from internal strife would do very little, if anything, to abate the total danger of war, or to enable any country to reduce its armed preparations. Further, it would seem essential that such a League should in its relations to outside Powers assume a rigorously defensive attitude, abstaining from all interference in external politics until they encroached directly upon the vital interests of one or more of its members. Such an encroachment it would presumably treat as an attack upon the League, and would afford the injured member such power of redress as was deemed desirable by the representatives of the Powers forming the League.

"Before entering upon the fuller consideration of the practicability of a League of Nations formed upon these lines, it may be well to set forth in a brief, formal manner the nature of the chief implications which appear to be contained in the proposal. We shall then be in a position to examine *seriatim* the various steps which the advocates of this method of securing world-peace and disarmament desire to take, and the many difficulties which are involved.

"The signatory Powers to the Treaty or Agreement establishing such a League of Peace would undertake:

1. To submit to arbitration or conciliation all disputes or differences between them not capable of settlement by ordinary processes of diplomacy, and to accept and carry out any award or terms of settlement thus attained.
2. To bring joint pressure, diplomatic, economic or forcible, to bear upon any member refusing to submit a disputed matter to such modes of peaceable settlement, or to accept and carry out the award, or otherwise threatening or opening hostilities against any other member.[2]
3. To take joint action in repelling any attack made by an outside Power, or group of Powers, upon any of the members of the League.
4. To take joint action in securing the redress of any injury which, by the general assent of the signatory Powers, had been wrongfully inflicted upon any member of the League."

Notes
1. "Proposals for a League of Peace", by Aneurin Williams MP, p. 5.
2. Many, perhaps most, supporters of a League of Peace would, however, be disposed to apply this police power of the League only in cases where members in contravention of the Treaty actually opened hostilities against another member.

Woolf – The Need for an International Organisation to Prevent War*

"It is possible to say without begging the question that in the last 100 years a system of international relationship has been very rapidly developing with rudimentary organs for regulating the society of nations without warfare. If we are really to transform that '*some sort of international organisation*' into a definite international organis-

---

* From Leonard Woolf (1880–1969). Writer, member of the Bloomsbury Group and husband of Virginia Woolf. After a brief career in the Colonial Service devoted himself to writing on political and international topics. Was for many years joint editor of the *Political Quarterly*. He was editor of *The Intelligent Man's Way to Prevent War* (1933) and author of *The War for Peace* (1940). Quoted from *International Government* (London: Allen and Unwin, 1916).

ation which will commend itself to the disillusioned judgement of statesmen and other 'practical' men, we must build not a Utopia upon the air or clouds of our own imaginations, but a duller and heavier structure placed logically upon the foundations of the existing system. I, therefore, propose to analyse the most important parts of the existing system, in order to see in what respects it has, during the last century, succeeded and failed in preventing war.

"Before proceeding to this task it will be advisable to answer a preliminary objection which in the present temper of the world is bound to occur to one's mind at various points of the enquiry. Systems and machinery, it is said, are not the way to prevent war, which will only cease when men cease to desire it: Europe, relapsed today into barbarism, shows that men will never cease to desire it: we must face the fact that International Law and Treaties and Arbitration will never prevent these periodical shatterings of our civilisation: one week in August 1914 was sufficient to sweep away the whole elaborate progress of a century. One meets this train of reasoning continually at the present time. It is woven out of pessimism and two fallacies. The first fallacy is the historically false view which men invariably take of the present. It is almost impossible not to believe that each today is the end of the world. Our own short era seems invariably to be in the history of the world a culmination either of progress or dissolution. But in history there are really no culminations and no cataclysms; there is only a feeble dribble of progress, sagging first to one side and then to the other, but always dribbling a little in one direction. Thus the French Revolution was for everyone in it the end or the beginning of the world. The aristocrat dragged through the streets of Paris to the guillotine saw himself perishing in a holocaust of all Law, Order, Beauty and Good Manners; the men who dragged him saw only the sudden birth of Justice and absolute Liberty. Both were wrong, just as both would have been wrong if they had suddenly found themselves transported some thirty years on into the Paris of the second decade of the nineteenth century, for the aristocrat would have seen the culmination of his hopes and the Red of his despair. In each case it was only a little sag in the progress of history, first to this side and then to that, though the main stream was dribbling slowly in the direction of Liberty, Equality, Fraternity. So with this war. Its tremendous importance to us produces in us a delusion that in the history of the world it is tremendously important. But it is neither the beginning nor the end of anything; it is just a little sagging to one side, to violence and stupidity and barbarism, and in ten or fifteen or twenty years' time there will be a sagging to the other side, to what we dimly recognise as progress and civilisation.

"The other fallacy is of the same nature as that dreary assertion that you cannot make men good by Act of Parliament. In one sense the assertion is a truism, and in another it is simply false. It is true that human society is so simple that if a majority of men want to fight, no International Law, no treaties or tribunals will prevent them; on the other hand, society is so complex that though the majority of men and women do not want to fight, if there are no laws and rules of conduct, and no pacific methods of settling disputes, they will find themselves at one another's throats before they are aware of or desire it.

• • •

". . . The cosmopolitan or International State implies a cosmopolitan or international patriotism; it is, therefore, useless at present to disturb its long rest upon the dusty shelf reserved in libraries for Utopias. But that does not mean that there are no practical steps which can be taken for preventing war by improving the machinery of international relationship. We can do something by providing that the complications of modern existence do not, merely because they are complicated, tie us into inextricable international knots, and still more by developing and extending that international machinery which has in the past encouraged and given scope to those factors in human society which have tended to the drawing together of nations and the pacific settlement of international disputes.

"Now, there are two such factors of the greatest importance. One is the growth of International Law and of the principle that the relations of States shall be regulated by general rules of conduct. Society, the whole system of European civilisation, all that we are accustomed to regard as good in our way of life, our hopes and our ideals, have grown about and depend upon the governing of human relationship by law and general rules and morality. The last two years have shown that it would be as easy to destroy that civilisation by attempting to regulate international relationship merely by erratic violence and brute force as it would be within a State to destroy society by abandoning it to lawlessness. We have, in fact, reached the point in the history at least of Europe where continued progress depends upon the growth of International Law and morality as certainly as upon the policeman in Piccadilly Circus and all that he stands for. The binding force of law where law exists, and the binding force of contracts where contracts exist, are the foundations of a stable system of international relationship. But the last 1915 years seem to show that such a system is not going to spring into sudden and full-blown existence by a special act of creation on the part of the Deity. It requires for its operation in this complex world humanly devised and consciously devised machinery. The conception of an International Authority . . . simply recognises these facts. It aims only at providing the machinery without which the system will remain 'in the air'. It presumes merely that nations are to be bound by law where law exists, by contracts where contracts exist, by the bare minimum of international good faith. It would apply legal machinery only to legal international differences, to those disputes which are concerned with rules of law and conduct to which the disputing nations have themselves subscribed, and with contracts to which they have themselves agreed. It proposes, therefore, that the reference of such legal differences and disputes for decision to a legal tribunal should be compulsory. Again, by extending and elaborating International Conferences, it would provide machinery for making International Law of wider application and of greater precision. On the one side it would strengthen the obligation, on the other side extend the range, of International Law.

"The other factor is the growth of the principle which denies the right of any one nation, and asserts the right of the nations collectively, to settle questions which imperil the peace of the world. The world is so closely knit together now that it is no longer possible for a nation to run amok on one frontier while her neighbour on the other is hardly aware of it. We are so linked to our neighbours by the gold and silver wires of commerce and finance – not to speak of telegraph wires and steel rails – that a breeze between the Foreign Offices of Monrovia and Adis Ababa would be felt the same day in every Foreign Office from Pekin to Washington, and every war threatens to become a world war. And the closer the interconnections of international life become, the more necessary becomes this principle to save international society from dissolution. And one must face the fact that what stands in the way of the acceptance of this principle in the regulation of international affairs is the diplomatic, governmental and, to a less extent, popular view of the independence and sovereignty of States."

Zimmern – The League as an Experiment in International Co-operation*

"The best way of approaching the study of the League of Nations at its present stage is to think of it as a particular method for carrying on relations between states. This method was devised at the close of the World War in the hope that it would conduce to a better understanding, particularly between the Great Powers, than had existed in the years before 1914.

"Whatever else may be thought about the war, it cannot be denied that it involved a failure of the older methods, of what is often comprehensively called 'the old diplomacy'. The men who, in 1919, brought the League of Nations into existence aimed at providing machinery which would, so far as is humanly possible, prevent the recurrence of such a catastrophe. They did not indeed imagine that machinery would ever count for more than human motive or that the procedure enshrined in the Covenant would prove either fool-proof or knave-proof. But they were resolved to ensure that statesmanship in the post-war world should be provided with the best safeguards that could be devised to restrain reckless or criminal policies in international affairs and that, should a breakdown nevertheless occur, it should be in no way attributable to the lack of adequate machinery or to technical defects in its working.

"The states which have adopted this new method of intercourse are 'members of the League of Nations'. They include the overwhelming majority of the sixty-odd states which are eligible for membership. The few which do not form part of this company incur the disadvantage of being unable to make full use of the new League method. Several of them have, however, shown their appreciation of its value by arranging to make use of it for a number of purposes without assuming the obligations of direct membership. Broadly speaking, therefore, we may say that the new method has justified itself in the working and that there is every likelihood that it will become a

* From Sir Alfred Zimmern (1879–1957). Originally a teacher of ancient history and student of Greek civilisation, he became increasingly interested in foreign affairs. During the First World War he joined the intelligence department of the Foreign Office and helped to establish the Royal Institute of International Affairs (Chatham House). Became the first professor of international politics at Aberystwyth, then director of the School of International Studies in Geneva, before returning to Oxford as Professor of International Relations in 1930. Quoted from *The League of Nations and the Rule of Law, 1918–1935* (London: Macmillan, 1936).

permanent part of the political arrangements of mankind.

"The fact that the founders of the League were, on the whole, successful in their plan of organisation makes it all the more unfortunate that their work should be mis-described in its English title. For 'the League of Nations' is a misnomer – a fact which has given rise to much confusion of thought in the English-speaking world. Neither the word 'League' nor the word 'Nations' is accurate. The term 'League', with its philanthropic and humanitarian associations, suggests common action by a band of crusaders and enthusiasts *against* some other party or group or cause. It implies a certain *exclusiveness*, derived from a common attachment to certain particular principles or doctrines. But the essential underlying idea of the League of Nations is its *inclusiveness*. It is a new method or model for *all* states and its membership is intended to be universal – is, so to speak, potentially universal. It is framed to be an all-embracing association. This is much more clearly expressed in the French term 'Society' (*Société des Nations*). Much misunderstanding as to aims and methods would have been prevented if this discrepancy between the French and English titles had been avoided. As it is, the English-speaking world must accustom itself to thinking of the League as being no less, and no more, than an all-inclusive association.

"This leads us on to the second part of the title. Of what is this association composed? What are its constituent units? Both texts give the same answer – *Nations*. Both are mistaken. They both misrepresent the membership of the League. Here again is a fruitful cause of confusion.

"The term 'nation' opens out a large theme for discussion, into which this is not the place to enter. But one thing is quite certain. The members of the League are not nations but states. Membership of the League has nothing whatsoever to do with nationality or nationhood. It is concerned simply and solely with statehood – that is to say with *political* status. This will be clear at a glance to anyone who consults the list of the actual members of the League. He will find there 'the British Empire' and 'the United Socialist Soviet Republics', which are certainly neither of them nations, in any sense of that word: and he will look in vain for other names, such as 'Scotland' and 'Wales', which should certainly find a place in any true 'association of nations'.

• • •

"[T]he League of Nations was never intended to be, nor is it, a revolutionary organisation. On the contrary, it accepts the world of states as it finds it and merely seeks to provide a more satisfactory means for carrying on some of the business which these states transact between one another. It is not even revolutionary in the more limited sense of revolutionising the methods for carrying on interstate business. It does not supersede the older methods. It merely supplements them. The old methods still go on, and were intended by the framers of the Covenant to go on, side by side with the new. We shall not therefore be able to understand exactly how the League of Nations has improved, or attempted to improve, upon the previous system until we have examined this in itself, in its pre-war form. . . .

"We shall be concerned throughout with methods of co-operation *between states*, whether by means of the League or in other ways. This is only a very small part of the field of *international relations*. To understand international relations in their full extent involves not merely a knowledge of the relations between states but also of the relations between *peoples*. Moreover, it involves not merely a knowledge of the relations *between* peoples but a knowledge of the *peoples themselves*. Both these large subjects lie outside our present scope. But the reader should constantly bear them in mind; for without some general background of knowledge in these fields the study of methods will be unintelligible and may even be misleading and dangerous. The study of the relations between X and Y presupposes some knowledge at least of X and Y in themselves. The League of Nations is not a patent method of interstate co-operation applicable to all states at any moment of history. It is a particular method which is being attempted at a particular moment of history when there are certain principal Powers with clearly marked characteristics and policies. The method of this book must be, in the main, a method of analysis: for what we are concerned with is a problem of political science. As we shall be studying this problem in the concrete and watching the attempts made to deal with it in particular circumstances, we shall be compelled at times to adopt the narrative form. But the record thus unfolded is not history: it is a mere episode against the background of history – unintelligible without a knowledge of the larger issues of policy involved and of the still larger problems of the relations between *peoples* and of the interaction of the cultures, traditions, attitudes, ingrained ways of thinking and feeling, which constitute the raw material of policy."

30 The Balance of Power in the Modern World

After the First World War, the "balance of power" was increasingly identified with the alliance system; and both were widely condemned as responsible for the outbreak of that conflict.

This was the view taken by Woodrow Wilson, and it became accepted wisdom in the postwar period. Since it was widely believed that the balance of power system had been a major cause of the war, it was hoped it would now be replaced by the new system of "collective security". Under this it was not a balance, but a *preponderance*, of power that would be mobilised against any state which threatened the peace: a preponderance maintained from the beginning against Germany, which was most widely expected to represent such a threat in the succeeding period. The hope that this system of collective action might be made to work effectively for a time allowed thoughts of a balance, and alliances to maintain it, to be put on one side. Only when the new system had demonstrably failed did Britain and France, in rearming themselves, and in giving guarantees to Poland and Rumania in the spring of 1939, belatedly seek to preserve peace through the maintenance of a new balance against Hitler. But their reluctance to bring in the Soviet Union to strengthen that balance shows clearly the difficulties of making such a system work at a time of deep ideological division: a difficulty that was to prove still greater at the conclusion of the forthcoming conflict.

The need for flexibility, if the balance of power was to be maintained, had been demonstrated much earlier in the century. By 1900 Germany had unquestionably become the strongest and the most rapidly expanding power in the continent. Although British statesmen seriously considered an alliance with Germany, which would have tilted the balance still further in her favour, Germany's competitive naval-building and her trouble-making in Morocco finally induced a rethinking of policy. The question was deeply debated in the British Foreign Office. At the beginning of 1907 Sir Eyre Crowe, one of the officials most concerned about German ambitions, drafted a memorandum on British policy drawing attention to the dangers and calling for a shift in attitudes. He was, however, by no means hawkish in his recommendations. He believed that Britain should not resist a legitimate growth in Germany's power and influence, including even a "healthy expansion" in her economic and naval strength. Only an attempt at "universal preponderance", threatening the balance of the continent, should, be suggested, be checked. This then was a call for containment, but not for a stubborn resistance to any change in the balance of forces.

After the Second World War it was the Soviet Union that was seen (at least in the West) as the main potential threat to the peace. As a result there were similar debates, in the nation which had by then replaced Britain as principal world power, about the best way of meeting that threat. There too foreign officials were concerned to consider what policies should be adopted to prevent the Soviet Union from pursuing the expansionary policies of which she had already given evidence in Eastern Europe. George Kennan, a State Department official with considerable experience of the Soviet Union, was permitted to publish an article (under a pseudonym) in the US journal *Foreign Affairs*, which set out a semi-official view on the subject. This suggested that the Soviet government, though cautious and pragmatic in its approach and in no hurry for quick results, would seek to exert "unceasing, constant pressure towards the desired goal". The main element of any US policy towards the Soviet Union must therefore be that of a "long-term, patient but firm and vigilant containment of Russia's expansive tendencies". This did not demand histrionics, threats or blustering, but the "adroit and vigilant application of counter-force at a series of constantly shifting geographical and political points, corresponding to the shifts and manoeuvres of Soviet policies".

The general acceptance of this goal of "containment", subsequently implemented in the creation of NATO and the successive "doctrines" of Presidents Truman (in the Near East), Eisenhower (in the Middle East) and Nixon (in the Far East), implied a recognition that the balance of power still had a part to play in international politics. That view was also, not surprisingly, held by exponents of the "realist" school of international relations who flourished at this period. Hans Morgenthau, the most distinguished of the realist writers, believed a balance of power would occur whether or not it was adopted as a conscious policy. He held that the balance of power and the policies that maintain it, are "inevitable" and are "an essential stabilising factor in a society of sovereign nations". It was indeed, in his view, only a particular manifestation of a "general social principle", operating not only among states but in other societies as a means of preserving the autonomy of the component parts. Balance is maintained because it is in the interest of each state to maintain it: either by directly opposing the power of another state, by containing its influence in third states, or by creating alliances in opposition to it and its own allies. Collective security, rather than abolishing the balance of power, had merely reorganised it, by creating *ad hoc* alliances against particular states in particular circumstances. In one way or another a balance must always come about and this must operate beneficially to the society of states as a whole.

This idea that the balance of power is an automatic process implies that power is an objective factor, which is measurable by states and so can influence their conduct in predictable ways. But states will not necessarily easily agree on what distribution of power or territory constitutes a "balance" at any one time. The action which one state takes to *restore* the balance may be taken by others as an action which *disturbs* it. It is not always clear where particular states should be placed in relation to the balance: on which side, for example, should Italy, Bulgaria or Rumania have been placed before war broke out in 1914, or China today? The relative strength attributed to each state may be judged differently by different states. Finally, even if differences of judgement of this kind could be eliminated, and a consensus established, it does not necessarily follow that peace will be restored. Even where a rough balance of power is generally agreed to exist (as before the First World War) this will not necessarily be sufficient to deter war. A state sufficiently determined on war may even undertake war against a great preponderance of power, as when Frederick the Great invaded Saxony, with most of the rest of Europe ranged against him in 1756, or when Hitler addéd the Soviet Union to his existing enemies in 1941, or when Japan added the US and Britain to hers at the end of the same year.

Some writers on the balance of power on these grounds showed themselves more dubious about the automaticity of the balance of power process, whether as a means of maintaining peace or ensuring stability. Inis Claude, for example, in the passage below, showed that even defenders of the principle of the balance of power do not necessarily claim that it maintains the peace, only that it prevents domination by particular powerful states, which they frequently regard as the only test by which it should be judged. Others have seen it as a source of stability, or as a means by which wars can at least be localised; but often it has not achieved these aims either. Nor do balance of power policies even preserve equilibrium, since each side has a subjective view of what constitutes a balance, and since, in the final resort, the balance can only be secured by war or the threat of war. Thus, in practice, the balance has not in the long term proved an effective means of safeguarding security.

Others were concerned about the ambiguity of the phrase, which was often used in a variety of meanings: the existing balance or the balance to be achieved, an equal balance or a favourable balance, a policy or a principle. So, in the passage quoted below, Martin Wight distinguishes nine separate meanings given to the term "balance of power", including the existing distribution of power (whether balanced or not), a favourable balance, a position of special advantage, or even a preponderance of power. If both sides, in demanding "balance", seek a balance favourable to themselves, the attempt to secure a balance may be self-defeating. Wight therefore casts doubt on the idea – such as Morgenthau had put forward – that the balance is an automatic process (the ninth in his list of meanings of "balance of power" (see p. 490)). On the contrary he sees as much evidence that major powers seek to secure *predominance*, especially in particular regions of concern to them, as that they seek a constant world-wide balance.

The judgements made about the balance of power, therefore, in recent as in earlier times, have depended on what is demanded of it. Pessimistic observers, concerned only to see that no state should be allowed to win excessive power, and willing to see war – or the threat of war – used to prevent this, have emphasised the importance of the principle, whether they see it as an inevitable process or as a desirable policy. Observers who are more demanding, however – who have sought, that is, to find the means of establishing a more peaceful, as well as a more stable international system – have been more doubtful about its value. They question if there is any automatic process at work (if only because states often wish to join a stronger rather than a weaker state, or because they are inhibited by ideological sympathies from switching from one side to another). They are sceptical of policies designed to promote the balance of power, since they see them as often a rationalisation for the desire to establish a superiority of power. Above all, they have doubted the capacity of the principle to promote peace within the system, since under that principle it is often only by war, or at least the threat of war, that the balance can be maintained.

*   *   *

Crowe – The Containment of Germany*

History shows that the danger threatening the independence of this or that nation has generally arisen, at least in part, out of the momentary predominance of a neighbouring State at once militarily powerful, economically efficient, and ambitious to extend its frontiers or spread its influence, the danger being directly proportionate to the degree of its power and efficiency, and to the spontaneity or 'inevitableness' of its ambitions. The only check on the abuse of political predominance derived from such a position has always consisted in the opposition of an equally formidable rival, or of a combination of several countries forming leagues of defence. The equilibrium established by such a grouping of forces is technically known as the balance of power, and it has become almost an historical truism to identify England's secular policy with the maintenance of this balance by throwing her weight now in this scale and now in that, but ever on the side opposed to the political dictatorship of the strongest single State or group at a given time.

If this view of British policy is correct, the opposition into which England must inevitably be driven to any country aspiring to such a dictatorship assumes almost the form of a law of nature . . .

By applying this general law to a particular case, the attempt might be made to ascertain whether, at a given time, some powerful and ambitious State is or is not in a position of natural and necessary enmity towards England; and the present position of Germany might, perhaps, be so tested. Any such investigation must take the shape of an inquiry as to whether Germany is, in fact, aiming at a political hegemony with the object of promoting purely German schemes of expansion, and establishing a German primacy in the

---

* From Sir Eyre Crowe (1864–1925). British Foreign Office official who spent the bulk of his career within the Foreign Office and ended as its senior official. Though born and brought up in Germany and having a German wife, this did not prevent him from becoming, together with other Foreign Office officials, an advocate of a more active effort by Britain to restrain Germany's expansive policies. This memorandum, which is known to have influenced Sir Edward Grey, British Foreign Secretary, was shortly to be followed by the British–Russian understanding of 1907. In 1914 forcefully demanded that Britain should stand by her partners in the Entente against Germany. Quoted from "Memorandum on the Present State of British Relations with France and Germany, 1 January 1907".

world of international politics at the cost and to the detriment of other nations. . . .

• • •

"So long as England remains faithful to the general principle of the preservation of the balance of power, her interests would not be served by Germany being reduced to the rank of a weak Power, as this might easily lead to a Franco-Russian predominance equally, if not more, formidable to the British Empire. There are no existing German rights, territorial or other, which this country could wish to see diminished. Therefore, so long as Germany's action does not overstep the line of legitimate protection of existing rights she can always count upon the sympathy and good-will, and even the moral support, of England.

"Further, it would be neither just nor politic to ignore the claims to a healthy expansion which a vigorous and growing country like Germany has a natural right to assert in the field of legitimate endeavour. . . . It cannot be good policy for England to thwart such a process of development where it does not directly conflict either with British interests or with those of other nations to which England is bound by solemn treaty obligations. If Germany, within the limits imposed by these two conditions, finds the means peacefully and honourably to increase her trade and shipping, to gain coaling stations or other harbours, to acquire landing rights for cables, or to secure concessions for the employment of German capital or industries, she should never find England in her way.

"Nor is it for British Governments to oppose Germany's building as large a fleet as she may consider necessary or desirable for the defence of her national interests. It is the mark of an independent State that it decides such matters for itself, free from any outside interference, and it would ill become England with her large fleets to dictate to another State what is good for it in matters of supreme national concern. Apart from the question of right and wrong, it may also be urged that nothing would be more likely than any attempt at such dictation, to impel Germany to persevere with her ship-building programmes. And also, it may be said in parenthesis, nothing is more likely to produce in Germany the impression of the practical hopelessness of a never-ending succession of costly naval programmes than the conviction, based on ocular demonstration, that for every German ship England will inevitably lay down two, so maintaining the present relative British preponderance.

"It would be of real advantage if the determination not to bar

Germany's legitimate and peaceful expansion, nor her schemes of naval development, were made as patent and pronounced as authoritatively as possible, provided care were taken at the same time to make it quite clear that this benevolent attitude will give way to determined opposition at the first sign of British or allied interests being adversely affected. This alone would probably do more to bring about lastingly satisfactory relations with Germany than any other course.

"It is not unlikely that Germany will before long again ask, as she has so often done hitherto, for a 'close understanding' with England. To meet this contingency, the first thing to consider is what exactly is meant by the request. The Anglo-French *entente* had a very material basis and tangible object – namely, the adjustment of a number of actually-existing serious differences. The efforts now being made by England to arrive at an understanding with Russia are justified by a very similar situation. But for an Anglo-German understanding on the same lines there is no room, since none could be built up on the same foundation. . . . Into offensive or defensive alliances with Germany there is, under the prevailing political conditions, no occasion for England to enter, and it would hardly be honest at present to treat such a possibility as an open question. British assent to any other form of co-operation or system of non-interference must depend absolutely on circumstances, on the particular features, and on the merits of any proposals that may be made. All such proposals England will be as ready as she always has been to weigh and discuss from the point of view of how British interests will be affected. Germany must be content in this respect to receive exactly the same treatment as every other Power."

Kennan – The Containment of the Soviet Union*

"[T]he Kremlin is under no ideological compulsion to accomplish its purposes in a hurry. Like the Church, it is dealing in ideological

* From George Kennan (1904–). US State Department official 1927–63, specialising in Soviet affairs, and finishing as US Ambassador in Moscow for over ten years. Since his retirement has written extensively on international affairs, especially

concepts which are of long-term validity, and it can afford to be patient. It has no right to risk the existing achievements of the revolution for the sake of vain baubles of the future. The very teachings of Lenin himself require great caution and flexibility in the pursuit of Communist purposes. Again, these precepts are fortified by the lessons of Russian history: of centuries of obscure battles between nomadic forces over the stretches of a vast unfortified plain. Here caution, circumspection, flexibility and deception are the valuable qualities; and their value finds natural appreciation in the Russian or the oriental mind. Thus the Kremlin has no compunction about retreating in the face of superior force. And being under the compulsion of no timetable, it does not get panicky under the necessity for such retreat. Its political action is a fluid stream which moves constantly, wherever it is permitted to move, toward a given goal. Its main concern is to make sure that it has filled every nook and cranny available to it in the basin of world power. But if it finds unassailable barriers in its path, it accepts these philosophically and accommodates itself to them. The main thing is that there should always be pressure, unceasing constant pressure, toward the desired goal. There is no trace of any feeling in Soviet psychology that that goal must be reached at any given time.

"These considerations make Soviet diplomacy at once easier and more difficult to deal with than the diplomacy of individual aggressive leaders like Napoleon and Hitler. On the one hand it is more sensitive to contrary force, more ready to yield on individual sectors of the diplomatic front when that force is felt to be too strong, and thus more rational in the logic and rhetoric of power. On the other hand it cannot be easily defeated or discouraged by a single victory on the part of its opponents. And the patient persistence by which it is animated means that it can be effectively countered not by sporadic acts which represent the momentary whims of democratic opinion but only by intelligent long-range policies on the part of Russia's adversaries – policies no less steady in their purpose, and no less variegated and resourceful in their application, than those of the Soviet Union itself.

"In these circumstances it is clear that the main element of any United States policy toward the Soviet Union must be that of a

US–Soviet relations and international politics in the nineteenth century. Other works include *Realities of American Foreign Policy* (1954), *On Dealing with the Communist World* (1963) and *The Nuclear Delusion* (1982). Quoted from "The Sources of Soviet Conduct", *Foreign Affairs*, July 1947.

long-term, patient but firm and vigilant containment of Russian expansive tendencies. It is important to note, however, that such a policy has nothing to do with outward histrionics: with threats or blustering or superfluous gestures of outward 'toughness'. While the Kremlin is basically flexible in its reaction to political realities, it is by no means unamenable to considerations of prestige. Like almost any other government, it can be placed by tactless and threatening gestures in a position where it cannot afford to yield even though this might be dictated by its sense of realism. The Russian leaders are keen judges of human psychology, and as such they are highly conscious that loss of temper and of self-control is never a source of strength in political affairs. They are quick to exploit such evidences of weakness. For these reasons, it is a *sine qua non* of successful dealing with Russia that the foreign government in question should remain at all times cool and collected and that its demands on Russian policy should be put forward in such a manner as to leave the way open for a compliance not too detrimental to Russian prestige.

"In the light of the above, it will be clearly seen that the Soviet pressure against the free institutions of the western world is something that can be contained by the adroit and vigilant application of counter-force at a series of constantly shifting geographical and political points, corresponding to the shifts and manoeuvres of Soviet policy, but which cannot be charmed or talked out of existence. The Russians look forward to a duel of infinite duration, and they see that already they have scored great successes. It must be borne in mind that there was a time when the Communist Party represented far more of a minority in the sphere of Russian national life than Soviet power today represents in the world community.

"But if ideology convinces the rulers of Russia that truth is on their side and that they can therefore afford to wait, those of us on whom that ideology has no claim are free to examine objectively the validity of that premise. The Soviet thesis not only implies complete lack of control by the west over its own economic destiny, it likewise assumes Russian unity, discipline and patience over an infinite period.

•   •   •

"It is clear that the United States cannot expect in the foreseeable future to enjoy political intimacy with the Soviet regime. It must continue to regard the Soviet Union as a rival, not a partner, in the political arena. It must continue to expect that Soviet policies will reflect no abstract love of peace and stability, no real faith in the possibility of a permanent happy coexistence of the Socialist and capitalist worlds, but rather a cautious, persistent pressure toward the disruption and weakening of all rival influence and rival power.

"Balanced against this are the facts that Russia, as opposed to the western world in general, is still by far the weaker party, that Soviet policy is highly flexible, and that Soviet society may well contain deficiencies which will eventually weaken its own total potential. This would of itself warrant the United States entering with reasonable confidence upon a policy of firm containment, designed to confront the Russians with unalterable counter-force at every point where they show signs of encroaching upon the interests of a peaceful and stable world.

"But in actuality the possibilities for American policy are by no means limited to holding the line and hoping for the best. It is entirely possible for the United States to influence by its actions the internal developments, both within Russia and throughout the international Communist movement, by which Russian policy is largely determined. This is not only a question of the modest measure of informational activity which this government can conduct in the Soviet Union and elsewhere, although that, too, is important. It is rather a question of the degree to which the United States can create among the peoples of the world generally the impression of a country which knows what it wants, which is coping successfully with the problems of its internal life and with the responsibilities of a World Power, and which has a spiritual vitality capable of holding its own among the major ideological currents of the time. To the extent that such an impression can be created and maintained, the aims of Russian Communism must appear sterile and quixotic, the hopes and enthusiasm of Moscow's supporters must wane, and added strain must be imposed on the Kremlin's foreign policies. For the palsied decrepitude of the capitalist world is the keystone of Communist philosophy. Even the failure of the United States to experience the early economic depression which the ravens of the Red Square have been predicting with such complacent confidence since hostilities ceased would have deep and important repercussions throughout the Communist world.

"By the same token, exhibitions of indecision, disunity and internal disintegration within this country have an exhilarating effect on the whole Communist movement. At each evidence of these tendencies, a thrill of hope and excitement goes through the Communist world; a new jauntiness can be noted in the Moscow tread; new groups of foreign supporters climb on to what they can only view as the band wagon of international politics; and Russian pressure increases all along the line in international affairs.

"It would be an exaggeration to say that American behaviour unassisted and alone could exercise a power of life and death over the Communist movement and bring about the early fall of Soviet power in Russia. But the United States has it in its power to increase enormously the strains under which Soviet policy must operate, to force upon the Kremlin a far greater degree of moderation and circumspection than it has had to observe in recent years, and in this way to promote tendencies which must eventually find their outlet in either the break-up or the gradual mellowing of Soviet power. For no mystical, Messianic movement – and particularly not that of the Kremlin – can face frustration indefinitely without eventually adjusting itself in one way or another to the logic of that state of affairs.

"Thus the decision will really fall in large measure in this country itself. The issue of Soviet-American relations is in essence a test of the over-all worth of the United States as a nation among nations. To avoid destruction the United States need only measure up to its own best traditions and prove itself worthy of preservation as a great nation.

"Surely, there was never a fairer test of national quality than this. In the light of these circumstances, the thoughtful observer of Russian–American relations will find no cause for complaint in the Kremlin's challenge to American society. He will rather experience a certain gratitude to a Providence which, by providing the American people with this implacable challenge, has made their entire security as a nation dependent on their pulling themselves together and accepting the responsibilities of moral and political leadership that history plainly intended them to bear."

Morgenthau – The Balance of Power as an Automatic Stabiliser*

"The aspiration for power on the part of several nations, each trying either to maintain or to overthrow the status quo, leads of necessity

* From Hans Morgenthau (1904–). (For biographical details see p. 287.) Quoted from *Politics among Nations* (New York: Harper and Row, 1948).

to a configuration that is called the balance of power[1] and to policies that aim at preserving it. We are using the term 'of necessity' advisedly. For here again we are confronted with the basic misconception that has impeded the understanding of international politics and has made us the prey of illusions. This misconception asserts that men have a choice between power politics and its necessary outgrowth, the balance of power, on the one hand, and a different, better kind of international relations on the other. It insists that a foreign policy based on the balance of power is one among several possible foreign policies and that only stupid and evil men will choose the former and reject the latter.

"It will be shown in the following pages that the balance of power in international affairs is only a particular manifestation of a general social principle to which all societies composed of a number of autonomous units owe the autonomy of their component parts; that the balance of power and policies aiming at its preservation are not only inevitable but are an essential stabilising factor in a society of sovereign nations; and that the instability of the international balance of power is due not to the faultiness of the principle but to the particular conditions under which the principle must operate in a society of sovereign states. . . .

ALLIANCES VS. COUNTERALLIANCES

"The struggle between an alliance of nations defending their independence against one potential conqueror is the most spectacular of the configurations to which the balance of power gives rise. The opposition of two alliances, one or both pursuing imperialistic goals and defending the independence of their members against the imperialistic aspirations of the other coalition, is the most frequent configuration within the system of the balance of power.

"To mention only a few of the more important examples, the coalitions that fought the Thirty Years' War under the leadership of France and Sweden on the one hand, and of Austria on the other, sought to promote the imperialistic ambitions especially of Sweden and Austria and at the same time to keep the ambitions of the other side in check. The several treaties settling the affairs of Europe after the Thirty Years' War tried to establish a balance of power serving the latter end. The many coalition wars that filled the period between the Treaty of Utrecht of 1713 and the first partition of Poland of 1772 all attempted to maintain the balance that the Treaty of Utrecht had established and that the decline of Swedish power as well as the rise of Prussian, Russian, and British strength tended to disturb. The frequent changes in the alignments, even while war was in progress, have startled the historians and have made the eighteenth century appear to be particularly unprincipled and devoid of moral considerations. It was against that kind of foreign policy that Washington's Farewell Address warned the American people.

"Yet the period in which that foreign policy flourished was the golden age of the balance of power in theory as well as in practice. It was during that period that most of the literature on the balance of power was published and that the princes of Europe looked to the balance of power as the supreme principle to guide their conduct in foreign affairs. It is true that they allowed themselves to be guided by it in order to further their own interests. But, by doing so, it was inevitable that they would change sides, desert old alliances, and form new ones whenever it seemed to them that the balance of power had been disturbed and that a realignment of forces was needed to re-establish it. In that period, foreign policy was indeed a sport of kings, not to be taken more seriously than games and gambles, played for strictly limited stakes, and utterly devoid of transcendent principles of any kind.

"Since such was the nature of international politics, what looks in retrospect like treachery and immorality was then little more than an elegant manoeuvre, a daring piece of strategy, or a finely contrived tactical movement, all executed according to the rules of the game, which all players recognised as binding. The balance of power of that period was amoral rather than immoral. The technical rules of the art of politics were its only standard. Its flexibility, which was its peculiar merit from the technical point of view, was the result of imperviousness to moral considerations, such as good faith and loyalty, a moral deficiency that to us, seems deserving of reproach.

"From the beginning of the modern state system at the turn of the fifteenth century to the end of the Napoleonic Wars in 1815, European nations were the active elements in the balance of power. Turkey was the one notable exception. Alliances and counter-alliances were formed in order to maintain the balance or to re-establish it. The century from 1815 to the outbreak of the First World War saw the gradual extension of the European balance of power into a worldwide system. One might say that this epoch started with President Monroe's message to Congress in 1823, containing what is known as the Monroe Doctrine. By declaring the mutual political independence of Europe and the Western Hemisphere and thus dividing the world, as it were, into two political systems, President Monroe laid the groundwork for the subsequent transformation of the European into a worldwide balance-of-power system.

"This transformation was for the first time clearly envisaged and formulated in the speech George Canning made as British Foreign Secretary to the House of Commons on 12 December 1826. Canning had been criticised for not having gone to war with France in order to restore the balance of power which had been disturbed by the French invasion of Spain. In order to disarm his critics, he formulated a new theory of the balance of power. Through the instrumentality of British recognition of their independence he included the newly freed Latin-American republics as active elements in the balance. He reasoned thus:

'But were there no other means than war for restoring the balance of power? – Is the balance of power a fixed and unalterable standard? Or is it not a standard perpetually varying, as civilisation advances, and as new nations spring up, and take their place among established political communities? The balance of power a century and a half ago was to be adjusted between France and Spain, the Netherlands, Austria, and England. Some years after, Russia assumed her high station in European politics. Some years after that again, Prussia became not only a substantive, but a preponderating monarchy. – Thus, while the balance of power continued in principle the same, the means of adjusting it became more varied and enlarged. They became enlarged, in proportion to the increased number of considerable states – in proportion, I may say, to the number of weights which might be shifted into the one or the other scale. . . . Was there no other mode of resistance, than by a direct attack upon France – or by a war to be undertaken on the soil of Spain? What, if the possession of Spain might be rendered harmless in rival hands – harmless as regarded us – and valueless to the possessors? Might not compensation for disparagement be obtained . . . by means better adapted to the present time? If France occupied Spain, was it necessary, in order to avoid the consequences of that occupation – that we should blockade Cadiz? No. I looked another way – I saw materials for compensation in another hemisphere. Contemplating Spain, such as our ancestors had known her, I resolved that if France had Spain, it should not be Spain *"with the Indies"*. I called the New World into existence, to redress the balance of the Old.'[2]

"This development toward a worldwide balance of power operating by means of alliances and counteralliances was consummated in the course of the First World War in which practically all nations of the world participated actively on one or the other side. The very designation of that war as a 'world' war points to the consummation of the development.

"In contrast to the Second World War, however, the First World War had its origins exclusively in the fear of a disturbance of the European balance of power, which was threatened in two regions: Belgium and the Balkans. Belgium, located at the northeastern frontier of France and guarding the eastern approaches to the English Channel, found itself a focal point of great power competition, without being strong enough to participate actively in that competition. That the independence of Belgium was necessary for the balance of power in Europe was axiomatic. Its annexation by any of the great European nations would of necessity make that nation too powerful for the security of the others. This was recognised from the very moment when Belgium gained its independence with the active support of Great Britain, Austria, Russia, Prussia and France. These nations, assembled at a conference in London, declared on 19 February 1831, that 'They had the right, and the events imposed upon them the duty to see to it that the Belgian provinces, after they had become independent, did not jeopardize the general security and the European balance of power'.[3]

"In furtherance of that aim, in 1839 the five nations concerned concluded a treaty in which they declared Belgium to be 'an independent and perpetually neutral state' under the collective guaranty of the five signatories. This declaration sought to prevent Belgium forever from participating, on one or the other side, in the European balance of power. It was the German violation of Belgium's neutrality which in 1914 crystallised the threat to the balance of power emanating from Germany and enabled Great Britain to justify its participation in the war on the side of France, Russia and their allies.

"The concern of Austria, Great Britain and Russia in the preservation of the balance of power in the Balkans was concomitant with the weakening of Turkish power in that region. The Crimean War of 1854–6 was fought by an alliance of France, Great Britain and Turkey against Russia for the purpose of maintaining the balance of power in the Balkans. The alliance treaty of 13 March 1854, declared 'that the existence of the Ottoman Empire in its present extent, is of essential importance to the balance of power among the states of Europe'. The subsequent rivalries and wars, especially the events that led to the Congress of Berlin of 1878 and the Balkan wars of 1912 and 1913, are all overshadowed by the fear that one of the nations mainly interested in the Balkans might gain an increase in power in that region out of proportion to the power of the other nations concerned.

"In the years immediately preceding the First World War, the balance of power in the Balkans increased in importance; for, since the Triple Alliance between Austria, Germany, and Italy seemed approximately to balance the Triple Entente between France, Russia, and Great Britain, the power combination that gained a decisive advantage in the Balkans might easily gain a decisive advantage in the over-all European balance of power. It was this fear that motivated Austria in July 1914 to try to settle its accounts with Serbia once and for all, and that induced Germany to support Austria unconditionally. It was the same fear that brought Russia to the support of Serbia and France to the support of Russia. In his telegraphic message of 2 August 1914, to George V of England, the Russian tsar summed the situation up well when he said that the effect of the predominance of Austria over Serbia 'would have been to upset balance of power in Balkans, which is of such vital interest to my Empire as well as to those Powers who desire maintenance of balance of power in Europe. . . . I trust your country will not fail to support France and Russia in fighting to maintain balance of power in Europe.'[4]

"After the First World War, France maintained permanent alliances with Poland, Czechoslovakia, Yugoslavia and Rumania and, in 1935, concluded an alliance – which was, however, not implemented – with the Soviet Union. This policy can be understood as a kind of preventive balance-of-power policy which anticipated Germany's comeback and attempted to maintain the status quo of Versailles in the face of such an eventuality. On the other hand, the formation in 1936 of an alliance between Germany, Italy and Japan, called the Axis, was intended as a counterweight against the alliance between France and the Eastern European nations, which would at the same time neutralise the Soviet Union.

"Thus the period between the two world wars stands in fact under the sign of the balance of power by alliances and counteralliances, although in theory the principle of the balance of power was supposed to have been superseded by the League-of-Nations principle of collective security. Yet, actually, collective security . . . did not abolish the balance of power. Rather it reaffirmed it in the form of a universal alliance against any potential aggressor, the presumption being that such an alliance would always outweigh any potential aggressor. Collective security differs, however, from the balance of power in the principle of association by virtue of which the alliance is formed. Balance-of-power alliances are formed by certain individual nations against other individual nations or an alliance of them on the basis of what those individual nations regard as their separate national interests. The organising principle of collective security is the respect for the moral and legal obligation to consider an attack by any nation upon any member of the alliance as an attack upon all members of the alliance. Consequently, collective security is supposed to operate automatically; that is, aggression calls the counter-alliance into operation at once and therefore, protects peace and security with the greatest possible efficiency. Alliances within a balance-of-power system, on the other hand, are frequently uncertain in actual operation, since they are dependent upon political considerations of the individual nations. The defection of Italy from the Triple Alliance in 1915 and the disintegration of the French system of alliances between 1935 and 1939 illustrate this weakness of the balance of power."

Notes
1. The term "balance of power" is used in the text with four different meanings: (1) as a policy aimed at a certain state of affairs, (2) as an actual state of affairs, (3) as an approximately equal distribution of power, (4) as any distribution of power. Whenever the term is used without qualification, it refers to an actual state of affairs in which power is distributed among several nations with approximate equality.
2. *Speeches of the Right Honourable George Canning* (London, 1836), VI, pp. 109–11.
3. *Protocols of Conferences in London Relative to the Affairs of Belgium* (1830–1), p. 60.
4. *British Documents on the Origins of the War, 1898–1914* (London: His Majesty's Stationery Office, 1926) XI, p. 276.

Claude – The Balance of Power's Failure to Secure Peace*

"The concept of the balance of power is relevant to the problem of the management of power in international relations. In this context, it must be considered as a system, an arrangement within which independent states operate autonomously, without the controlling direction of a superior agency, to manipulate power relationships among themselves. It is thus a decidedly decentralised system; power and policy remain in the hands of its constituent units.

"The balance of power system should not be confused with equilibrium. It *may* operate in such fashion as to produce and stabilise a situation of equilibrium, but it does not necessarily do so. Some of the states which compose the system may adopt the policy of promoting equilibrium, but this is dependent upon the exercise of judgement by their leaders. There have been occasions when statesmen have collaborated in the deliberate effort to produce equilibrium, and British diplomatic history in particular includes a long record of conscious endeavour to keep the power of continental states balanced in the literal sense. More normally, states give evidence of the desire to possess power superior to that of their rivals or potential enemies, whether for the purpose of attacking the status quo or of buttressing their sense of security against attack. Given the difficulty of making precisely accurate appraisals of the power situation, statesmen seldom feel comfortably secure without having a marginal excess of power at their disposal. The system breeds competition; it is pervaded by a spirit of rivalry.

"Conceivably, equilibrium may emerge as the unwilled by-product of competitive strivings for favourable disequilibrium, but most statesmen are quite sensibly inclined to regard it as their duty to take matters involving the security of their countries into their own hands rather than leave them to the inscrutably mechanistic workings of an invisible hand. Historians of philosophic bent may assure us of inexorable-equilibrium-in-the-long-run, but in the long run we are all dead, and the floor of history may well be strewn with the corpses of nations struck down in that crucial 'meanwhile' interval between the immediate present and the indeterminate future. Only the most Utopian brand of statesmanship fails to acknowledge the obligation

---

* From Inis Claude (1922–). (For biographical details see p. 305.) Quoted from *Power and International Relations* (New York: Random House, 1962).

to focus its skill on the problems of the meanwhile.

"The balance of power system is aptly characterised as an *alliance* system. States struggling for what they regard as appropriate places in the distribution of power discover readily enough that they can enhance their power not only by the 'natural' method of building up their own resources, but also by an 'artificial' method of linking themselves to the strength of other states. Indeed, this is the only method available to the bulk of states in the actual circumstances of modern history. Small states obviously cannot hope individually to balance, much less over-balance, their great power neighbours; the only active course open to them in the quest for security within a balance of power system is to seek a position in a grouping of states which, considered as a collectivity, assumes the role of a major participant in the struggle for power. The alliance technique is not, of course, a monopoly of the weak states. The making, breaking and shifting of alliance ties is a central feature of the process of man-oeuvring for position which is the essence of the internal operation of a balance of power system.

"The results of a balance of power system are too heavily dependent upon contingencies to be postulated *a priori*. While the balance of power system may have inherent features and tendencies, it has no inherent results. What men will try to do within the system, and what consequences will flow from their efforts, can be determined only by observation, not by assertion.

"The balance of power system is a concrete reality of history, not a mere abstract construct. Hence, it has an objective record of performance, even though the reading of that record always reflects the subjective peculiarities of the readers. In my judgement, the record is neither so good as champions of the system aver, nor so bad as critics of the Wilsonian stripe insist. Over considerable stretches of time, the system produced management of international power relations which was tolerably – indeed, in retrospect, delightfully – effective. Unfortunately, the small black marks which dot the record were occasionally supplemented by enormous black marks. World War I was a stroke in the boldest of black-faced type; it made sense for Wilsonians to characterise this as a collapse of the system, not to shrug it off as a mere lapse of the system. The war of 1914–1918 was to the scheme of laissez-faire in international politics as the depression of 1929 was to the scheme of laissez-faire in the economic realm; insistence on returning to the good old way of running things in the faith that it was fundamentally sound came from doctrinaires, not realists, whatever they called themselves. The urge to tamper with the system which had failed so disastrously was a sign of hopeful realism, not foolish Utopianism.

"Yet the débâcle of the First World War was not so much a piece of evidence that the balance of power system had been overrated as a peace-keeping mechanism in the nineteenth century, as a warning that it should not be relied upon to maintain international order in the twentieth century. If the fact of failure is permitted to stimulate inquiry into the causes of failure, we may gain insight into the necessary conditions for the successful operation of a balance of power system.

"It appears that a balance of power system requires that effective power be diffused among a substantial number of major states. The control of the policy of the participating units should be vested in skilled professional players of the diplomatic game, who should be largely free to engage in discretionary manoeuvres, manipulate alignments and adjust policy to challenges and opportunities with secrecy and dispatch. There should be no ideological impediments to arrangements for compensatory adjustment of power relations by the leading statesmen. International decision-makers should have both the freedom and the will to make their decisions on the basis of power calculations alone. The elements constituting national power should be simple enough to permit reasonably accurate estimates of the relative strength of states, and stable enough to permit such estimates to serve for some period of time as the basis of policy. The implications of war should be serious enough to stimulate preventive measures, but mild enough to enable statesmen to invoke the threat, and on occasion the actuality, of force in support of policy. War should be imaginable, controllable, usable. Underneath the prudent mistrust of powerful states and the built-in rivalry of the system, there should be a broad consensus among statesmen that the objectives of war should be limited and the essential pluralism of the system unchallenged; hegemonic ambitions should be moderated by the sense of common interest in preserving the system, limited by technological impediments to universal conquest, and frustrated by the flexibility of combination afforded by the alliance technique. Finally, it is highly desirable, if not indispensable, that some major power should be in a position to play the role of holder of the balance, contributing to the stability of the system by adapting its policy to the requirements posed by recurrent thrusts of ambition and alterations of power ratios.

"As indicated by the references above to the essential role of war and the threat of war, this is not a formula for perfect peace, but rather for reasonable stability and order with no more than moderate use of violent techniques by the states involved in the system. Nor is it the blueprint of an automatically operative system, achieving stabilisation through a process unaffected by the contingencies of human behavior. It is rather a description of the setting which would seem to present minimum difficulties and maximum opportunities for the effective regulation of power relationships among states by their leaders.

"One can neither spot an historical moment when this combination of circumstances existed without qualification, nor discover a point in time when all the requisite conditions suddenly disappeared. However, it is clear that the suitability of the world for the operation of the balance of power system has been steadily diminishing for well over a century. The rise of democracy has infringed the freedom of the statesman to base his policy upon coolly rational calculations of the power situation; the free hand of the diplomatist has been tied behind his back by the demands of the public which he represents. The rise of nationalism has limited the political feasibility of carving up the map with single-minded concern for the realisation of a desired power ratio among states. Ideological passions have undermined the possibility of holding rivalry and ambition within bounds of moderation; the rigidity of ideological divisions has reduced the flexibility of combination and recombination within the system. The technological revolution has annihilated the objective limitations of military destructiveness, minimised the possibility of measuring the relative strength of states with a reasonable degree of accuracy, and introduced the danger that drastic alterations of power relationships may occur suddenly and secretly. The concentration of overwhelming strength in two super-powers and the lack of a state qualified for the role of balancer represent a formidable maladjustment of the basic political structure of the world. In short, all the most fundamental tendencies affecting the political realm in recent generations run counter to the requirements of a workable system of balance of power. There is nothing to indicate that the global setting is likely to become more, rather than less, appropriate to the operation of a balance system.

"All this does not mean that the balance of power can be dismissed as an outmoded system, a relic of the past which is already tending to become a mere historical curiosity. For the balance of power system is not one which exists only if instituted by deliberate choice; rather, it is the system which exists unless and until superseded by a consciously erected alternative. Given a pattern of independent states existing in mutual contact and relationship, those states manipulate the distribution of power among themselves, and share in the decentralised management of the system, in the absence of an institution equipped to exercise central direction. Twentieth-century efforts to replace the system have at most introduced modifications of its operative mechanism; today, the balance of power system exists by default."

Wight – Diverse Meanings of the Balance of Power*

"This paper will try to show that 'the balance of power' has had the following distinct meanings in international politics:

1. An even distribution of power.
2. The principle that power ought to be evenly distributed.
3. The existing distribution of power. Hence, any possible distribution of power.
4. The principle of equal aggrandisement of the Great Powers at the expense of the weak.
5. The principle that our side ought to have a margin of strength in order to avert the danger of power becoming unevenly distributed.
6. (When governed by the verb 'to hold':) A special role in maintaining an even distribution of power.
7. (Ditto:) A special advantage in the existing distribution of power.
8. Predominance.
9. An inherent tendency of international politics to produce an even distribution of power.

It is the fascination of the subject that these senses are difficult to disentangle, and almost any sentence about the balance of power, as this paper will perhaps illustrate involuntarily more than deliberately,

* From Martin Wight (1913–72). (For biographical details see p. 284.) Quoted from "The Balance of Power", in H. Butterfield and M. Wight (eds), *Diplomatic Investigations* (London: Allen and Unwin, 1966).

is likely to imply two or more meanings at the same time.

"The original application of the metaphor of the balance to international politics is in the sense of *an even distribution of power*, a state of affairs in which no Power is so preponderant that it can endanger the others. Let us call this sense 1. This is the primary meaning of 'the balance of power', to which there is always a tendency to return. If there are three or more weights that are thus considered as balanced (as with the five major Powers of Italy between 1454 and 1494, or the five Great Powers that formed the Concert of Europe in the nineteenth century) it may be called a multiple balance. If there are only two weights in consideration (as with the Habsburgs and France in the sixteenth and seventeenth centuries, Britain and France in the eighteenth, the Triple Alliance and the Triple Entente before 1914, or America and Russia since 1945) it may be called a simple balance. . . .

"Almost insensibly, the phrase passes from a descriptive to a normative use. It comes to mean (2) *the principle that power ought to be evenly distributed*. When during the American Revolutionary War George III was seeking the assistance of Catherine the Great, she replied: 'Her ideas perfectly correspond with his, as to the balance of power; and she never can see with indifference any essential aggrandisement or essential diminution, of any European state take place'. The *Manchester Guardian* wrote in 1954: 'If there is to be coexistence there must be a balance of power, for if power is unbalanced the temptation to communism to resume its crusade will be irresistible.' In each of these quotations sense 2 can be seen emerging out of sense 1. In 1713 the phrase was written into the Treaty of Utrecht to justify the perpetual separation of the crowns of France and Spain: 'for the end that all care and suspicions may be removed from the minds of men and that the Peace and Tranquillity of the Christian World may be ordered and stabilised in a just Balance of Power (which is the best and most solid foundation of mutual friendship and a lasting general concord)'. Thenceforward, for two hundred years, the balance of power was generally spoken of as if it were the constituent principle of international society, and legal writers described it as the indispensable condition of international law. . . .

"But it is the trouble about international politics that the distribution of power does not long remain constant and the Powers are usually in disagreement on its being an even distribution. Most arrangements of power favour some countries, which therefore seek to preserve the *status quo*, and justify it as being a true balance in the sense of an equilibrium; and are irksome to other countries whose policy is accordingly revisionist. Just as such phrases as 'the hereditary system' or 'property' ceased to have a sacrosanct ring in domestic politics when they were uttered by men of the self-made or unpropertied classes, so 'the balance of power' loses its connotation of being grounded on morality and law when it is uttered by representatives of Powers that believe themselves at a disadvantage. This linguistic process can be seen at work in a discussion between Cripps and Stalin in Moscow in July 1940. Cripps had been sent to Moscow as British ambassador with the task of persuading Stalin that Germany's conquest of Western Europe endangered Russia as well as Britain. 'Therefore both countries', he argued, 'ought to agree on a common policy of self-protection against Germany and on the re-establishment of the European balance of power.' Stalin replied that he did not see any danger of Europe being engulfed by Germany. 'The so-called European balance of power', he said, 'had hitherto oppressed not only Germany but also the Soviet Union. Therefore the Soviet Union would take all measures to prevent the re-establishment of the old balance of power in Europe.' Similarly Hitler to Ciano in 1936: 'Any future modifications of the Mediterranean balance of power must be in Italy's favour.' Here the phrase has lost any sense of an even distribution of power, and has come to mean simply (3) *the existing distribution of power*. . . .

"So far we have been considering 'the balance of power' roughly as a description of a state of affairs; it is now necessary to consider it as a policy; though it will be clear that the two conceptions are inseparable. The principle that power ought to be evenly distributed, raises the question, By whom? There seem to be three possible answers. (*a*) It may be said that the even distribution of power will take place through the combined skill and effort of all the Powers concerned, or, in the case of a simple balance, of *both* the Powers or coalitions concerned. (*b*) It may be said that the even distribution of power will be the responsibility of a particular Power, which is said 'to hold the balance'. This answer presupposes a multiple balance. Where there is a truly simple balance, a holder of the balance is excluded. The holder of the balance is, *ex hypothesi*, a third force; he may be *tertius gaudens*. (*c*) It may be said, again, that the even distribution of power will come about, over the widest field and in the long run, through a fundamental law or tendency of political forces to fall into equilibrium. Let us consider these answers in turn.

"First, the argument that the maintenance of an even distribution of power can take place through the combined skill of all the Powers. If the broad test of an even distribution of power is the absence of a grand alliance against a Power aiming at universal monarchy, then there was such an even distribution from the defeat of Louis XIV to the French Revolution and from the defeat of Napoleon to the First World War. (Suitable qualifications must be made for the anti-British coalition in the American Revolutionary War, and the partial alliance against Russia in the Crimean. And by such a broad test, conflicts on the scale of the Polish Succession, Austrian Succession and Seven Years Wars have to be rated as incidents in preserving an even distribution of power – a generous proviso.) The maintenance of a multiple balance of power during these periods must in some degree be attributed to the skill of the Powers concerned; but allowance must be made for external circumstances, especially the opportunity for expansion outside Europe. And it cannot be overlooked that these periods of multiple balance came to centre upon questions of partition – of Poland and Turkey at the end of the eighteenth century, of Turkey, Africa and China at the end of the nineteenth. The balance of power, in effect, came to mean (4) *the principle of equal aggrandisement of the Great Powers at the expense of the weak.*

• • •

"In the circumstances of a simple balance, when each of two Powers or coalitions is trying to maintain an even distribution of power between them by a competition in armaments or a diplomatic struggle for alliances, the idea of the balance of power as equality of aggrandisement tends to be eclipsed (though it may still have a place) by another idea of the balance of power (which may also appear in the circumstances of a multiple balance). This is (5) *the principle that my side ought to have a margin of strength, in order to avert the danger of power becoming unevenly distributed.* Here the word balance acquires the sense it has in the phrases 'balance of trade' or 'bank balance', i.e., not an equality of assets and debits but a surplus of one over the other. And here the contradiction between the subjective and objective estimates of the balance of power, between a political position as seen from the inside and as seen from the outside, becomes acute. When Dean Acheson first formulated the policy of 'negotiating from a position of strength', he apparently meant a levelling up of America's strength to an equality with Russia's, the restoration of an equipoise; but the phrase was equivocal from the start, and quickly acquired the sense of possessing a margin of strength. . . .

"The fullest transformation of the idea of the balance of power seems to arise out of the notion of 'holding the balance'. The Power that 'holds the balance' is the Power that is in a position to contribute decisive strength to one side or the other. . . . This is the traditional conception, expressed in the simple terms. . . . Here, to hold the balance of power means, (6) *possessing a special role in maintaining an even distribution of power*.

"It became part of the traditional British doctrine on the matter that a holder of the balance was essential to the very idea of the balance of power.

•   •   •

"Who holds the balance? There are good grounds for the traditional British belief that it has been peculiarly Britain's role to hold the balance of Europe. From 1727 down to 1868 (with one or two lapses) the annual Mutiny Act described the function of the British army as 'the preservation of the balance of power in Europe'. To hold the balance has been a policy suited to an insular Power enjoying a certain detachment from Continental rivalries. But there have been other Powers with a degree of geographical detachment, particularly Russia. At the end of the War of the Austrian Succession the Tsaritsa Elizabeth controlled the balance of Europe. In the American Revolutionary War Catherine the Great held the balance between Britain and the anti-British coalition of France, Spain and Holland. In the War of the Bavarian Succession she was in a similar position, courted by both Austria and Prussia, and assuming the role of the protectress of the German constitution, hitherto played by France. Likewise, between March and September 1939 Stalin held the balance between the Western Powers and the Axis. In other words, a Power holds the balance only so long as it does not commit itself; and when it has committed itself, there is a new situation in which the balance will probably be held by another Power.

•   •   •

"When an English politician in 1704 rejoiced that the battle of Blenheim 'has given the balance of Europe into the Queen's hands', he meant that it had made England the strongest Power on the continent, with a freedom of action greater than that of other Powers. Canning's doctrine that Britain should hold the balance between the conflicting ideologies on the Continent was similar. As he wrote to his friend Bagot, the British ambassador at St Petersburg, soon after the enunciation of the Monroe Doctrine, 'The effect of the ultra-liberalism of our Yankee co-operators, on the ultra-despotism of our Aix la Chapelle allies, gives me just the balance that I wanted.' But this was Canning's private comment on what he afterwards publicly described as calling 'the New World into existence to redress the balance of the Old', and it contains perhaps a flavour of sense 5, that my side ought to have a margin of strength. Continental Powers have always noted that while Britain traditionally claimed to hold the balance of Europe with her right hand, with her left hand she was establishing an oceanic hegemony which refused for two centuries to admit any principle of equilibrium. Thus, from possessing a special role in maintaining an even distribution of power, holding the balance imperceptibly slides into (7) *possessing a special advantage in the existing distribution of power.*

• • •

"It will be seen that the idea of the balance of power as a description of a state of affairs tends to slip away from the meaning of an even distribution to that of any possible distribution of power; and that the idea of the balance of power as a policy tends to slip away from the meaning of a duty or responsibility for preserving an even distribution to that of enjoying a margin of strength or some special advantage. By these routes the balance of power comes to mean possessing a decisive advantage, or (8) *Possessing predominance.* In this sense Chester Bowles wrote in 1956 that 'the two-thirds of the world who live in the undeveloped continents . . . will ultimately constitute the world balance of power'. In this sense Bonaparte wrote to the Directory in 1797: *'Nous tenons la balance de l'Europe; nous la ferons pencher comme nous voudrons.'*[1] And more dramatically, the Kaiser, visiting England for Queen Victoria's funeral in 1901, told Lord Lansdowne that the traditional English policy of upholding the balance of power was exploded: *'Die* balance of power *in Europa sei ich.'*[2] Here at last the word balance has come to mean the opposite of its primary diplomatic sense: equilibrium has become preponderance, balance has become overbalance. Or, if you prefer, the word has returned to its still earlier pre-diplomatic sense of authoritative control. And the verbs that govern the phrase pass from possession to identification: from holding, through inclining, to 'constituting' or 'being'.

"There remains to be considered the third answer to the question, By whom is power to be evenly distributed? 'The balance of power' sometimes implies an assertion that the groupings of Powers fall into ever-changing but ever reliable conditions of equilibrium. Thus it means (9) *an inherent tendency of international politics to produce an even distribution of power*. This asserts a 'law' of international politics that underlies and reinforces the 'principle' of the balance of power in sense 2; so that even if Powers neglect or repudiate the principle, the law will be seen at work overruling them. . . .

"The law of the balance of power has a certain fascination and credibility in relation to Western international history since the beginning of the sixteenth century. 'The balance of power', said Stubbs in 1880, 'however it be defined, i.e., whatever the powers were between which it was necessary to maintain such equilibrium, that the weaker should not be crushed by the union of the stronger, is the principle which gives unity to the political plot of modern European history.' (Here the usage seems nearer sense 9 than sense 2.) But it is necessary to take account of contrary indications. It has often been remarked that, while international society has widened from Western Europe to cover the whole world, there has been a steady reduction in the number of Great Powers, from the eight of the years before 1914 to the Big Two of today. Though the field of the balance of power expanded, the number of decisive weights has decreased. The precedent of earlier states-systems, such as that of ancient China before the establishment of the Ts'in empire, and of the Hellenistic world before the Roman Empire, have also been noted. Barraclough has argued, following Dehio, that the law of the balance of power has been good for Europe, but that 'outside Europe, the principle of preponderant Powers is securely established'. This seems an over-simplification. On the one hand, within Europe (if it be considered by itself) the balance of power has worked itself out by 1945, with the partition of the continent between the two remaining Great Powers, both of them extra-European. On the other hand, outside Europe the operation of the balance of power is evident enough. In North America there was a kind of balance of power between Spanish, English, French and Indians for two hundred years before the infant United States became predominant. In India there was a balance of power between English, French and various succession states of the Mogul Empire for a hundred years before Britain became predominant. In China there was a balance of power between all the Western Great Powers, except Austria-Hungary and Italy but including Japan, for a hundred years before it was overthrown by Japan. In the Middle East there was a balance of power – the Eastern Question was one of the most famous essays in the balance of power – for more than a hundred years before Britain acquired in 1919 the lion's share of the Ottoman Empire. And in Africa, a balance was achieved between French and British power which continued until the emancipation of the African states in the past couple of years. In all these regions, as well as in the world as a whole, the balance of power is discernible. But *equally* discernible is 'the principle of preponderant Powers', so that it may be wondered whether the two are not complementary. It has been argued in this paper that the very idea and language of the balance of power has a mobility that tends, so to speak, to defeat its own original purpose, so that the phrase comes to mean predominance instead of equilibrium. And if political 'laws' are in question, it may be wondered whether there may not be another law of international politics besides the balance of power, slower in operation and ultimately overriding it: a law of the concentration or monopoly of power."

Notes

1. G. M. Trevelyan, *Blenheim* (London: Longmans, 1930) p. 419.
2. Letter of 22 January 1824 (*George Canning and his Friends*, ed. J. Bagot (London: John Murray, 1909) vol. II, pp. 217–18).

31 A System of Functional Co-operation

Those who were sceptical whether a more stable international system could be established on the basis of traditional balance of power politics looked rather to the creation of a system based on co-operation among states. Even before the Second World War there were proposals for expanding the scope of such co-operation. The League of Nations itself, in partial recognition of this concept, commissioned the Bruce Report, published on the eve of the Second World War, to examine ways in which its economic and social activities could be improved. The underlying purpose was to provide a better framework for international co-operation which might also serve to promote peace.

During the course of the Second World War, the notion that functional co-operation might be easier to promote than political co-operation, and that it might indeed stimulate the latter, came to be more widely put forward. In his book *A Working Peace System* David Mitrany suggested that the best way of developing international organisation in the future was to make it above all a system of practical co-operation in various functional fields. Any organisation that was primarily political, as the League had been, was bound to be wracked by divisions since it would be specifically designed to deal with contentious political conflicts. But there were many areas where states had common interests and could be expected to work reasonably harmoniously together to promote them. A number of organisations had been established, from the nineteenth century onwards, to promote joint activity in the field of posts, telegraphs, health and the control of drugs. As the world shrank further in size, close co-operation would be needed in many other spheres. This need not always be on a world-wide basis: sometimes regional or continental organisations would be more appropriate. Any arrangements made needed to be flexible and therefore should not be determined irrevocably in advance. No major derogation of sovereignty need be demanded. But, by working more closely together, states might in practice be willing to transfer power for limited purposes to international executive agencies; and by these means it might be possible to establish a "working peace".

The development of the international system in the years after 1945 did not altogether substantiate this thesis. A number of functional organisations were set up on the lines proposed and in some spheres international co-operation developed rapidly. But this did not have the effect, at least over the short-term, that writers of this school had suggested. Functional organisations proved to be almost as subject to political disputes as purely political bodies: nearly all the UN's specialised agencies experienced serious disputes on membership, programmes, and above all on budgets. There was little visible "spill-over" from peaceful functional activities to the political field. On the contrary the intensity of the cold war remained largely undiminished by the growth of the new specialised agencies. Finally, and above all, functional co-operation did not serve, as had been hoped, to promote world peace: wars after 1945 were frequent and they often took place between states which were in theory co-operating in active membership of functional organisations.

There was perhaps more to be hoped from the functional co-operation established at the regional level. This developed rapidly during these years, and, especially in western Europe, did seem to affect political attitudes. This led to new attempts to study that process and to consider the conditions which were most favourable towards it. Deutsch and his colleagues, for example, in *Political Community in the North Atlantic Area*, undertook a study of the process of integration which had taken place within and between the states of western Europe and North America. They studied the process of political unification which had occurred in the US, Great Britain, Germany, Italy and Switzerland, as well as the failed unions between England and Ireland, Norway and Sweden, and within the Hapsburg empire. Their findings tended to discredit some traditional beliefs: for example that modern means of communication hastened the process of integration, that a snow-balling effect took place so that successful growth would steadily accelerate, that the need to maintain law and order within a particular territory had been a major force for integration. They found too that ethnic or linguistic unity, strong economic ties and foreign military threats were not usually important factors in promoting integration. Their principal positive conclusions are summarised in the passages quoted below. They found that where there already existed a "security community" (within which war was no longer considered to be likely) the conditions for integration were likely to be favourable (though they found it made little difference whether this was within a single state or two or more states living harmoniously together). They suggested too that the period during which the initial process of integration occurred could be a long one; during that time the process might either be carried steadily forwards or be reversed once more for a period. In many cases integration took place around a particular core state or area, often more advanced than the surrounding units. But perhaps most significant was their suggestion that the essential condition of integration was not political or administrative structure but a psychological state: a sense of "mutual sympathy and loyalty", the existence of "we-feeling, trust and mutual consideration", of "partial identification in terms of self-images and interests".

The basis for integration is found here in subjective attitudes, rather than in institutions promoting practical co-operation, such as Mitrany had favoured. Changing attitudes are found to promote co-operation, that is, rather than vice versa. But there continued to be interest in the traditional functionalist approach. In his book *Beyond the Nation State*, E. Haas sought to test those theories by means of a detailed study of one of the oldest and largest of the specialised agencies of the UN, the International Labour Organization (ILO). In the light of his study he proposed certain modifications and refinements of the ideas put forward by the early functionalists. He contested the distinction between policies devoted to maximising welfare and those devoted to maximising power, showing that power was usually a means rather than an end, including the means of promoting welfare. He believed that integration was likely to be achieved when governments learned to perceive their self-interest in a new way, and so to adopt new rules of conduct, rather than by learning through co-operation that welfare was more important than power. Integration could be promoted by non-governmental organisations and actors. But this was more likely to occur at the regional than at the world level: in world bodies unofficial representatives would probably act in much the same way as those of governments, while, conversely, government experts would themselves reach decisions having an integrative effect in many areas of a technical kind. Finally, though loyalties could be gradually transferred to international organisations if they satisfied certain functional needs effectively, such a transference was not inevitable since loyalties were often emotional and traditional rather than rational.

All of these writers, though presenting different conclusions, were concerned to examine the conditions in which co-operation among states can best be promoted. They recognised that political disagreements will often inhibit substantial institutional changes, especially those which might seem to represent too great an encroachment on sovereignty. But they believed that by promoting co-operation in peripheral areas it might be possible gradually to bring into being a new kind of international system within which political differences too would eventually be resolved by peaceful means.

* * *

Mitrany – Functional Co-operation as the Road to Peace*

"The problem of our generation, put very broadly, is how to weld together the common interests of all without interfering unduly with the particular ways of each. It is a parallel problem to that which faces us in national society, and which in both spheres challenges us to find an alternative to the totalitarian pattern. A measure of centralised planning and control, for both production and distribution, is no longer to be avoided, no matter what the form of the state or the doctrine of its constitution. . . .

"That is fully as true for the international sphere. It is indeed the only way to combine, as well as may be, international organisation with national freedom. We have already suggested that not all interests are common to all, and that the common interests do not concern all countries in the same degree. A territorial union would bind together some interests which are not of common concern to the group, while it would inevitably cut asunder some interests of common concern to the group and those outside it. The only way to avoid that twice-arbitrary surgery is to proceed by means of a natural selection, binding together those interests which are common, where they are common, and to the extent to which they are common. That functional selection and organisation of international needs would extend, and in a way resume, an international development which

---

* From David Mitrany (1888–1975). Born in Romania but educated in Britain where he spent most of the rest of his life. Avid internationalist, he wrote and lectured widely on international and other questions. Worked for many years as international adviser to the Unilever company. His works include *The Progress of International Government* (1934) and *Marx against the Peasant* (1951). Quoted from *A Working Peace System* (London: Royal Institute of International Affairs, 1943).

has been gathering strength since the latter part of the nineteenth century. The work of organising international public services and activities was taken a step further by the League, in its health and drug-control work, in its work for refugees, in the experiments with the transfer of minorities and the important innovations of the League loan system, and still more through the whole activity of the ILO. But many other activities and interests in the past had been organised internationally by private agencies – in finance and trade and production, etc., not to speak of scientific and cultural activities. In recent years some of these activities have been brought under public national control in various countries; in totalitarian countries indeed all of them. In a measure, therefore, the present situation represents a retrogression from the recent past: the new turn toward self-sufficiency has spread from economics to the things of the mind; and while flying and wireless were opening up the world, many old links forged by private effort have been forcibly severed. It is unlikely that most of them could be resumed now except through public action, and if they are to operate as freely as they did in private hands they cannot be organised otherwise than on a non-discriminating functional basis.

"What would be the broad lines of such a functional organisation of international activities? The essential principle is that activities would be selected specifically and organised separately – each according to its nature, to the conditions under which it has to operate, and to the needs of the moment. It would allow, therefore, all freedom for practical variation in the organisation of the several functions, as well as in the working of a particular function as needs and conditions alter. . . . [S]ubsidiary regional arrangements could. . . . be inserted at any time and at any stage where that might prove useful for any part of a function. Devolution according to need would be as easy and natural as centralisation, whereas if the basis of organisation were political every such change in dimension would involve an elaborate constitutional rearrangement. Similarly, it could be left safely to be determined by practical considerations whether at the points where functions cross each other – such as rail and river transport in Europe or civil flying in Europe and America – the two activities should be merely co-ordinated or put under one control.

•   •   •

"Here we discover a cardinal virtue of the functional method – what one might call the virtue of technical self-determination. The functional *dimensions*, as we have seen, determine themselves. In a like manner the function determines its appropriate *organs*. It also reveals through practice the nature of the action required under the given conditions, and in that way the *powers* needed by the respective authority. The function, one might say, determines the executive instrument suitable for its proper activity, and by the same process provides a need for the reform of the instrument at every stage. This would allow the widest latitude for variation between functions, and also in the dimension or organisation of the same function as needs and conditions change. Not only is there in all this no need for any fixed constitutional division of authority and power, prescribed in advance, but anything beyond the original formal definition of scope and purpose might embarrass the working of the practical arrangements.

• • •

"*Epilogue.* Peace will not be secured if we organise the world by what divides it. But in the measure in which such peace-building activities develop and succeed, one might hope that the mere prevention of conflict, crucial as that may be, would in time fall to a subordinate place in the scheme of international things, while we would turn to what are the real tasks of our common society – the conquest of poverty and of disease and of ignorance. The stays of political federation were needed when life was more local and international activities still loose. But now our social interdependence is all-pervasive and all-embracing, and if it be so organised the political side will also grow as part of it. The elements of a functional system could begin to work without a general political authority, but a political authority without active social functions would remain an empty temple. Society will develop by our living it, not by policing it. Nor would any political agreement survive long under economic competition, but economic unification would build up the foundation for political agreement, even if it did not make it superfluous. In any case, as things are, the political way is too ambitious. We cannot start from an ideal plane but must be prepared to make many attempts from many points, and build things and mend things as we go along. The essential thing is that we should be going together, in the same direction, and that we get into step now. Action at the end of the war will fix the pattern of international relations for many years to come, and in the conditions that will prevail then it is less than likely that we could hold a peace conference of the habitual kind. Frontiers must be settled, and there may be some changes; as no change can satisfy both sides, all one can hope is that frontiers will appear less important and more acceptable as we organise common action across them. But for this to be possible, frontiers must be fixed in advance or at least in the actual armistice, or there will be conflict; and if plans for common action are not prepared in advance, there will be chaos – the chaos of many competing and conflicting local actions. Could a returning Czech or Greek or Polish government tell its people to be patient and wait till a distant conclave works out plans for reconstruction?

"Co-operation for the common good is the task, both for the sake of peace and of a better life, and for that it is essential that certain interests and activities should be taken out of the mood of competition and worked together. But it is not essential to make that co-operation fast to a territorial authority, and indeed it would be senseless to do so when the number of those activities is limited, while their range is the world. 'Economic areas do not always run with political areas', wrote the *New York Times* (26 February 1943) in commenting on the Alaska Highway scheme, and such cross-country co-operation would simply make frontiers less important. 'Apply this principle to certain European areas and the possibilities are dazzling.' If it be said that all that may be possible in war but hardly in peace, that can only mean that practically the thing is possible but that we doubt whether in normal times there would be the political will to do it. Now, apart from everything else, the functional method stands out as a solid touchstone in that respect. Promissory covenants and charters may remain a headstone to unfulfilled good intentions, but the functional way is action itself and therefore an inescapable test of where we stand and how far we are willing to go in building up a new international society. It is not a promise to act in a crisis, but itself the action that will avoid the crisis. Every activity organised in that way would be a layer of peaceful life; and a sufficient addition of them would create increasingly deep and wide strata of peace – not the forbidding peace of an alliance, but one that would suffuse the world with a fertile mingling of common endeavour and achievement."

Deutsch *et al.* – The Process of Integration among States*

"The closer we get to modern conditions and to our own time, the more difficult it is to find any instances of successful amalgamation of two or more previously sovereign states. Thus far we found not a single full-fledged modern social-service state that has successfully federated or otherwise merged with another. (The security-community among the Scandinavian countries has been deepening gradually through limited functional amalgamation, but it has remained essentially pluralistic, since the bulk of its most important functions have not been amalgamated. Its common laws must be adopted by national legislatures, its common parliamentary body can only make recommendations, and it has no common defence forces, police or controls over the political and economic systems of its members.) . . .

"Most countries in the world today devote a larger part of their resources to their domestic economies, and a smaller part to their foreign trade, than they did a half-century ago. Discrepancies between average incomes in different countries, and between national levels of the real wages of labour, do not seem to have become smaller during the last forty or fifty years. Indeed, they may even have increased. Peaceful and voluntary migration across international boundaries, which was still characteristic of the world before 1914, has largely come to an end. In most countries, there has been a considerable decline in the share of foreign mail among the total volume of letters written: and this decline has in general been larger than what would have corresponded merely to the decline in international migration. A large sample count of the share of references to foreign research in major scientific journals in several of the leading countries of the world between 1894 and 1954 offers no evidence in favour of any clearcut increase in internationalism in the world of science during that period. The increase in the political and administrative obstacles to the movement of persons, goods and capital across national boundaries in recent decades is too well known to require documentation. All these data leave us with the impression that men will have to work toward the building of larger security-

---

* From K. W. Deutsch (1912–). (For biographical details see p. 308.) Quoted from *Political Community and the North Atlantic Area* (Princeton, N.J.: Princeton University Press, 1957).

communities without the benefit of any clear-cut automatic trend toward internationalism to help them.

"Another popular belief that our findings make more doubtful is that the growth of a state, or the expansion of its territory, resembles a snowballing process, or that it is characterised by some sort of bandwagon effect, such that successful growth in the past would accelerate the rate of growth or expansion of the amalgamated political community in the future. In this view, as villages in the past have joined to make provinces, and provinces to make kingdoms, so contemporary states are expected to join into ever-larger states or federations. If this were true, ever-larger political units would appear to be the necessary result of historical and technological development. Our findings do not support this view. . . .

"Generally, we found that successful amalgamation of smaller political units in the past tended to increase both the resources and the integrative skills of the governments of the larger units that resulted. We further found, however, that such amalgamations also may increase the degree of the preoccupation with domestic affairs and reduce the ability of those governments to respond promptly and effectively to the needs and interests of governments and people outside the national borders. This ability of governments to respond to the interests of 'outsiders' has always been important, but it has become even more important in our own time.

●   ●   ●

"Another popular notion is that a principal motive for the political integration of states has been the fear of anarchy, as well as of warfare among them. According to this view, men not only came to look upon war among the units concerned as unpromising and unattractive, but also as highly probable. For they came to fear it acutely while believing it to be all but inevitable in the absence of any strong superior power to restrain all participants. Consequently, according to this theory, one of the first and most important features of a newly amalgamated security-community was the establishment of strong federal or community-wide laws, courts, police forces, and armies for their enforcement against potentially aggressive member states and member populations. Beliefs of this kind parallel closely the classic reasoning of Thomas Hobbes and John Locke; and some writers on federalism, or on international organisation, have implied a stress on legal institutions and on the problem of coercing member states. Our findings suggest strong qualifications for these views. The questions of larger-community police forces and law enforcement, and of the coercion of member states, turned out to be of minor importance in the early stages of most of the amalgamated security-communities we studied.

•   •   •

"This stress on the supposed importance of the early establishment of common laws, courts and police forces is related to the suggestion that it is necessary to maintain a balance of power among the member states of a larger union or federation, in order to prevent any one state from becoming much stronger than the others. There is much to be said for this point of view: if a member state is far stronger than all the rest together, its political élite may well come to neglect or ignore the messages and needs of the population of the smaller member units, and the resulting loss of responsiveness may prevent integration or destroy it. The evidence from our cases suggests, however, that not merely amalgamation, but also responsiveness and integration can all be achieved and maintained successfully without any such balance of power among the participating states or political units. . . .

"Contrary to the 'balance of power' theory, security-communities seem to develop most frequently around cores of strength. . . . But military conquest appeared to be the least effective among a large number of methods by which amalgamation was pursued in the cases we studied: amalgamation failed to become integration in more than half of the situations in which military conquest was used to promote it.

"A series of negative findings such as those outlined above can at most clear the ground for a better understanding of the positive nature of the integrative process.

". . . . Among our positive general findings, the most important seems to us that both amalgamated security-communities and pluralistic security-communities are practicable pathways toward integration. In the course of our research, we found ourselves led by the evidence to attribute a greater potential significance to pluralistic security-communities than we had originally expected. Pluralistic security-communities turned out to be somewhat easier to attain and easier to preserve than their amalgamated counterparts. . . .

THE STRENGTHS OF PLURALISM

"The somewhat smaller risk of breakdown in the case of pluralistic security-communities seems indicated by an examination of the relative numbers of successes and failures of each type of security-community. We can readily list a dozen instances of success for each type. . . .

"On the other hand, we find a sharp contrast in the number of failures for each type. We have found only one case of a pluralistic security-community which failed in the sense that it was followed by actual warfare between the participants, and it is doubtful whether a pluralistic security-community existed even in that case: this was the relationship of Austria and Prussia within the framework of the German Confederation since 1815. As members of the Confederation, the two countries were not supposed to prepare for war against each other, but appropriate military preparations were made and war between them was considered a serious possibility on several occasions after the 1840's. The actual war between them in 1866, however, lasted only seven weeks. It was followed by an unusually moderate peace as far as Austria was concerned. In 1879 Germany and Austria concluded an alliance which eventually was expected to be permanent, and Austria and Germany thus became a pluralistic security-community. In contrast to this single instance of failure of a pluralistic security-community, we can readily list seven cases of amalgamated security-communities that failed: the United States in 1861; England–Ireland in 1918; Austria–Hungary in 1918; Norway –Sweden in 1905; Metropolitan France with a series of revolutions and wars between 1789 and 1871; Metropolitan France and Algeria in the 1950s; and Spain including the Catalan and Basque populations in the 1930s. A number of these wars were fought with a bitterness that might have proved fatal to both contestants if they had possessed present-day weapons of mass destruction.

"On balance, therefore, we found pluralistic security-communities to be a more promising approach to the elimination of war over large areas than we had thought at the outset of our inquiry. . . .

• • •

THE THRESHOLDS OF INTEGRATION

"Our second general finding concerns the nature of integration. In our earliest analytical scheme, we had envisaged this as an all-or-none process, analogous to the crossing of a narrow threshold. On the one side of this threshold, populations and policy-makers considered warfare among the states or political units concerned as still a serious possibility, and prepared for it; on the other side of the threshold they were supposed to do so no longer. We expected to apply two broad kinds of tests to the presence or absence of integration – that is, the existence or nonexistence of a security-community – among particular states or territories.

"One of these tests was subjective, in terms of the opinions of the political decision-makers, or of the politically relevant strata in each territory. These had to be inferred from many kinds of historical evidence in the past, or from samples or surveys in present-day situations obtained by well-known methods of studying public opinion. Did influential people in all parts of the wider area believe that a firm sense of community existed throughout its territories? And did the political élites throughout the wider community believe that peaceful change within this wider group had become assured with reasonable certainty for a long period of time?

"The other kind of test was essentially objective and operational. It replaced the recording of opinions by the measurement of the tangible commitments and the allocation of resources with which people backed them: how large preparations were made specifically for the possibility of war against any other group within the wider community? Consider a case in which the maintenance and indoctrination of troops, and the building and upkeep of fortifications and other strategic facilities, suggested possible military action against some particular smaller political unit, whether a state, a people or a territory. If such military action was considered a sufficiently practical possibility to warrant a significant allocation of resources, then there may have existed some other kind of political community, but not a security-community, between the two political units in question.

"We found, as expected, that these tests by opinions and by allocations usually coincided in their results, but that they tended to differ in marginal cases. For example, a war between two states might still be considered possible by some of their leaders, even though no significant preparations for it were being made by either side; and routine preparations for defence of a border might continue even though conflict across it might already appear unthinkable. Even in such rare instances, however, we expected that the achievement of a security-community would involve something like the crossing of a threshold, from a situation where war between the political units concerned appeared possible and was being prepared for, to another situation where it was neither. It was the crossing of this threshold, and with it the establishment of a security-community, that we called integration; and it is in this sense that we are using the term in this book.

"Somewhat contrary to our expectations, however, some of our cases taught us that integration may involve a fairly broad zone of transition rather than a narrow threshold; that states might cross and recross this threshold or zone of transition several times in their relations with each other; and that they might spend decades or generations wavering uncertainly within it."

Haas – The Limits to Functional Co-operation*

"In what fields, then, can we expect the functional process of integration to continue, with or without the help of law? Despite heterosymmetry, we expect both learning and new convergences of separate aims to continue. Despite the absence of strong international influences pushing the evolution of pluralism at the national level – and the resultant international democratic welfare pluralism envisaged by Myrdal – certain new powers may accrue to the United Nations on the basis of newly converging conceptions. *There will be a continued drift toward supranationality*, though no federal millennium is in the offing. Economic planning, local military operations and *ad hoc* disarmament will provide the functions.

"Economic planning is obviously the chief candidate for integrative functions in the future system. In principle, it is of appeal everywhere, and the intensified practice of international assistance in national and regional development would give us the necessary organisational task to maximise integrative consequences. A closer look, however, will reveal that matters are not so simple, another reason why Myrdal's enthusiasm for this function should not be allowed to be wholly infectious.

"The present international structures do a great deal of 'planning' in the course of administering aid programmes. However, each agency does its own 'planning' in the context of its particular task, organisational dynamic, leadership and clientele. The IBRD has evolved a sophisticated technique for judging national development

* From E. Haas (1924–). Born in Germany, educated at Columbia University, has taught for many years at Columbia and Berkeley. Interested in international organisations, the effect of membership on national policy and the relationship between domestic and international politics. Works include *The Uniting of Europe: Political, Social and Economical Forces, 1950–1957* (1958), *Tangle of Hopes: American Commitments and World Order* (1969) and *The Web of Interdependence, the US and International Organisations* (1970). Quoted from *Beyond the Nation-State: Functionalism and International Organisation* (Stanford, Conn.: Stanford University Press, 1964).

plans, and for scrutinising the feasibility of national projects, before making loans. It compels under-developed countries to consider the interrelations of tax rates, investment incentives, the cost of raw materials and future markets, and to come up with specific estimates before funds are advanced. The Bank has its loan officers stationed throughout the world as an advance guard of sound financial policy; this makes the recipient countries permeable to centralised financial planning. The IMF has stringent doctrines of short-run financial viability that govern its support programmes for national currencies, doctrines that are sometimes enforced over the bitter protest of the recipient governments. International commodity agreements 'plan' the flow and the price of primary products, and thus impose a species of centralised direction on agricultural and mineral production and marketing.

"The point of concern to us, however, is the fact that although all these efforts involve a drift toward supranationality at the subsystemic level, they do *not* integrate the units that make up the system. These are *ad hoc* approaches to planning. They do not consistently take into consideration political stability, the rate of social mobilisation, the relationship of social mobility to internal demand or world demand. Each agency plans in a restricted context, with relatively little ability (either technical or political), to concern itself with the socio-economic factors of interest to other agencies. The partial and *ad hoc* character of this planning stands sharply revealed in the dissatisfaction surrounding the first few years of the Alliance for Progress. This effort was self-consciously designed to unite these various contexts in one coherent social and political planning effort. Instead of resulting in one supranational institution, however, responsibility was split among agencies of the US government, the Inter-American Development Bank, the Committee of Nine of the Organisation of American States, and the Inter-American Economic and Social Council, which was to act as a general review body. Given considerable diffusion of authority and much dissensus among recipients and donors about what was to be achieved, the main recipient governments still found it preferable to put direct pressure on the US government. One of the main difficulties was lack of agreement about what constituted acceptable criteria of success, and about what should be done, by way of more supranationality, to obtain and meet them.

"Such criteria have been proposed and even implemented by certain international agencies, notably the IBRD. They usually involve considerations of efficiency and consistency in the allocation of resources for development. One experienced administrator of aid proposes to unite these contexts by having all national plans based on the following criteria and calculations:

1. The need for outside assistance. This involves (a) establishing a desirable or appropriate rate of development, which can be stated in terms of a specific percentage increase in per-capita income, and (b) the potential ability of a country to contribute to the achievement of this rate, which is reflected to some extent in its absolute level of per-capita income and its past performance in supporting development.
2. A country's own effort with respect to development. This consideration may generally be best satisfied by an examination of where and to what extent a country increases its development effort with outside assistance.
3. A country's ability to use outside assistance, both in terms of physical capacity and maximum returns for outside resources.

But the point remains that these criteria are to be applied within nations and by national officials acting in consultation with international advisers. If successful they would merely increase the viability of each nation; they would result in less permeability and more national self-consciousness.

"Precisely the same conclusion could be advanced if we were to assume that the formulation and application of rigorous planning criteria be entrusted wholly to international agencies. In fact, the United Nations Special Fund seeks to approximate that aim. It insists that funds earmarked for its 'pre-investment' technical and resource aid be justified in terms of overall economic development planning. A very high premium is put on the requirement that the recipient country match the efforts of the Special Fund personnel in surveying resources, establishing training centres, and seeing the economy as a whole. If successful, these efforts will *not* make the developing countries more penetrable to international influences; on the contrary, they will be in a better position to live up to the ideological pressures associated with integral nationalism. In fact, the Special Fund's approach might be expected to be more palatable to a mobilisation system than to a partially mobilised Latin American nation. In short, international economic aid based on coherent rather than *ad hoc* planning, even if it were to be achieved by a large and powerful UN economic development fund, will not automatically lead to

accelerated integration. Even 'country programming' as now practised by the UN family, though an administrative improvement over
the earlier *ad hoc* approach, will make no appreciable difference as
far as integration is concerned.

"In what sense, then, can economic planning be considered as
functional? We predict that requests for economic aid will multiply in
the future, and that the two superpowers will feel increasingly compelled to make assistance available through UN channels, thus implying a short-run growth in the powers of international agencies.
Such aid will advance international integration only if the problems
and challenges remaining after one immediate problem is solved
become of greater concern to the actors than the initial development
problem. The principle is what Albert Hirschman calls 'unbalanced
growth'. New co-operative and integrating efforts are deliberately
induced by stimulating an original decision that will unsettle more
than it will solve. It involves the conscious planning of consequences
unintended by the national actors, but compelling these élites to
undertake new planning later in order to deal with the unintended
consequences of their earlier purposes. The implications, of course,
would be that the purposes growing out of these consequences could
be met only with an increased international task and appropriate
supranational institutions. One obvious example – among many
possible ones – would be a new power for the FAO to set and change
commodity prices in line with minimum earnings considered desirable (and determined earlier by the IBRD) for purposes of supporting a given rate of local investment.

"Would such a bundle of guile require the extraordinary manipu-
latory skills and supreme virtues of the Saint-Simonian expert whose
role we downgraded earlier? For perfect consistency and predictable
success, we would have to make an assumption in his favour. A
public international technocracy would seem required to give institutional reality to Myrdal's vision or to the functional logic. Hence,
for the reasons indicated earlier, it is idle to expect the full-fledged
evolution of such a body of men or institutions. What is more
reasonable, however, is to expect the continuation of a learning
process among national élites and international officials. This will
make possible the occasional evolution, more accidental than
planned, of the kinds of unintended consequences that are bound to
flow from the present *ad hoc* pattern of economic development. But
it would be too much to expect such unwilled results consistently to
support the trend toward supranational integration.

"The same conclusion applies to the field of disarmament. An international function in this field is likely in view of the output pattern that flows from the converging aims of the two superpowers and of the non-aligned. The degree of institutional drift toward supranationality will depend on the degree of international inspection and conciliation built into efforts at disarmament and arms control. A test-ban agreement that excludes underground explosions has no integrating consequences of this sort. But monitoring devices set up to check on such explosions, corps of inspectors to examine denuclearised zones, communications satellites to check on national forays into space, or to determine the existence of orbiting bombs, would have a definite integrating consequence. An agreement for general disarmament, obviously, would have an even greater institutional impact and would push us far toward national permeability in terms of military aims. But even if we assume no such dramatic development, and limit the projection to what the next system makes likely, some *ad hoc* integrating results remain.

"United Nations military operations that are designed to stop or contain local wars fought with conventional weapons fulfil a similar purpose. The command and logistical apparatus built up to support them, and the authority of UN personnel in deploying them, imply an institutional development of some magnitude. The output pattern of the future system will advance these developments further, despite – or, perhaps, because of – the ideological heterogeneity of its regimes. Such developments, though, do not imply the birth of an international army that would take the place of national military establishments. They constitute merely another nibble at the structure of the self-confident national state.

"The chances for expanding the human rights function, however, are far cloudier. For reasons already indicated, the legal and political developments that favoured the growth of a UN task in this field are closely associated with the output pattern of the current system. The function has not yet acquired the capacity for self-sustained growth in the hands of international institutions able to penetrate the national state. The inputs which favoured the confrontations and compromises that gave rise to the function are likely to undergo great change as the Cold War grows less pronounced and decolonisation is completed. Integral regimes of the future will have reason to resent and oppose international efforts to make them observe the general human rights standards enshrined in the UN Universal Declaration. The Western democracies will have less reason than before to press them on this matter. Moreover, they will have less compulsion to attack the Soviet bloc in this context. Far more likely, new functions will flow from areas of interdependence that can be considered metapolitical from the outset, such as the exploitation of new natural resources in a global setting dominated by concern over the population explosion.

"Heterosymmetry, then, implies the continuation of the present *ad hoc* pattern of international integration. We have no reason to suppose that the autonomy of subsystems, so marked in the present era, will be less pronounced in the future. Integration must be expected to proceed in line with the forces here outlined, without significant acceleration over the present rate. We have no reason to expect the successful co-ordination of all such impulses in one system-dominant supranational structure. New agencies will flower or wither in proportion to their ability to meet the purposes of actors, and to upgrade the joint interest by profiting from new convergences of inputs. Integration will come about in the same unplanned and almost accidental fashion that has dominated in the past. The new system will be looser than the one now familiar to us. There will be fewer functions calling for mutual accommodation and therefore less leverage for actors to influence one another, though some of the functions will relate more heavily to world peace and military stability than in the present system. Actors will be more numerous, and their regional blocs less cohesive. But the reduction in inputs implies a lessening of the volume of bargaining and of the integrative compromises possible.

"The lesson is clear. Neither Functionalism nor functional analysis can bring international order out of the chaos of national confrontation. Neither a commitment to welfare nor a desire to use the analytical properties of national egotism can build the *civitas dei* or the *civitas maxima*. But functional analysis can tell us in which direction the faint ripples of common concerns are likely to spread. Even chaos becomes bearable when its constituents and their movement are understood."

32 The International System

In the US, international relations has traditionally been studied as a branch of political science. One effect has been that it has been strongly influenced by the fashions which dominated political science in that country at any one moment. We have already seen how the "behavioural approach", which dominated most branches of the social sciences in the early postwar years in that country, also affected the study of international relations. Another movement which exercised a strong influence on all branches of the social sciences was the so-called "systems" approach.

"General Systems Theory" originated outside the social sciences altogether. It emerged in the US during the 1940s and 1950s largely as a tool of engineering science: as a means of analysing operational requirements, the most efficient allocation of resources and the system of organisation which would prove most economic and efficient. By the early 1950s a few key concepts from that theory were being applied within the social sciences.

So, for example, Talcott Parsons made extensive use of the idea of "systems" in his writing on sociology. In his book *The Social System* (1952) he was mainly concerned with the functioning of the "system" represented by society as a whole. But he sees this general social system as being closely interconnected with other systems with which it is interrelated: in the first place with the cultural "system" and the "system" of the individual personality, but also with many other systems and subsystems of various kinds related to each of these. For example, in the passage quoted below, apart from the three main systems already mentioned, he speaks of an actor-situation "system", a "system" of expectations and a "system" of interaction. Used in this broad way the idea of system does not seem to mean much more than any set of relationships, whether stable or unstable. Though Parsons claims to adopt a "voluntaristic" approach, allowing for free choice by individuals, the general picture presented is a highly mechanistic one; and he employs images derived directly from the field of engineering – equilibrium, control mechanism, maintenance, feedback, adaptation, allocation and processing of resources, static and dynamic analysis, homeostatic control and so on. The implica-

516

tion of this imagery – whatever the protestations to the contrary – is that the individual is conditioned and controlled by the system, rather than vice versa.

This approach came soon to be applied to the world of politics. Shortly after the publication of *The Social System*, David Easton published his *The Political System*, describing the way in which political demands were processed by the system and converted into political outputs of various kinds. In the following years he carried these ideas further in *A Framework of Political Analysis* and, especially, in his *A Systems Analysis of Political Life* an extract from which is reproduced below. Like Parsons he conceives of a whole set of different "systems", each influencing one another. Thus the political system is influenced by a range of other "systems" and "subsystems". The chart which forms part of the passage quoted below records more than a dozen different such systems and subsystems, national and international, all of which form a part of the "total environment of a political system". The main "inputs" of the system are "demands" (for change) and "support" (for the existing system), which are converted by the political process into "outputs" of various kinds, usually decisions and actions by authorities. Through a process of "feedback" the authorities are able to inform themselves of the effect of earlier decisions and actions and so to maintain the entire system in a state of appropriate equilibrium. The "flow-model" included with the passage quoted below, shows how this theoretical mechanism is supposed to operate.

The systems approach was soon applied in the field of international relations. In 1955 Charles McClelland published an article on the "application of general systems theory in international relations". Later he elaborated this in his book *Theory and the International System*. In the passage from this quoted below he suggests that the idea of the international system is useful as the image of a "complicated framework of relationships which is formed through the process of interaction". The state of the system at any one time reflects a set of prevailing conditions and will manifest "characteristics of structure and process". To determine how the system works it is necessary to know the answer to a number of questions including, for example, the relationships of the "components" to the "ensemble" and the "performance of the system". But the state of a system is determined not only by its structure: it is the "resultant of the interacting behaviour of all its constituent parts". Thus a description of structure must include a consideration of the part played by the policy positions and the actions of individual states. But he refuses to accept that the question whether the state of the system dictates the actions of the units or vice versa (which to many observers seems crucial in considering the validity of the systems approach) is relevant. He believed that this is merely a question of analytical choice for the observer and is insignificant for "systems theory".

But the classic application of the systems approach to international relationships was in Morton Kaplan's *System and Process in International Politics* which appeared in 1957. In this he set out six theoretical models of possible international systems: the "balance of power" system, the loose bi-polar system, the tight bi-polar system, the universal system, the hierarchical system in its directive and non-directive forms, and the unit-veto system. Only the first two were said to have had historical counterparts, the rest being only "heuristic models". Within each system the "actors" (states) reacted to each other according to built-in "rules" of behaviour and power relationships. Like Parsons and Easton, Kaplan describes these systems by use of terms taken from the field of engineering science: input, output, feedback, negative feedback, stable and unstable equilibrium, homeostatic control, parameter values, operational rules, capability variances and information variables.

The ideas set forth by Kaplan, presented in highly abstract style, provoked considerable debate. Some held that the six models described represented valuable archetypes which, even if they did not accurately depict historical systems, could be the stimulus to further research, while others saw them as purely fictitious creations, which, since they bore only a passing resemblance to any system of international relationships which had ever actually existed, were unable to cast much light on the way in which real states operated in the real world. The systems approach generally was seen by many as applying a *metaphor* to the area of society in which the writer was interested; Parsons, Easton and Kaplan each compared different aspects of society to a mechanical system, or more accurately *described* them as such a system, using the terms and concepts appropriate to engineering science. The question that arose was whether this added to understanding of the reality in which each writer was interested. Some held that the mechanical image was inappropriate to the social processes to which it was applied – whether the human society of Parsons, the political process of Easton or the international relations process of Kaplan. The behaviour and responses of large numbers of human beings, it was said, each unique, and each interrelating in highly complex ways with each other, could not be represented without gross simplification by this mechanical image. The approach implied that humans (or politicians or states) reacted in a mechanistic way to the environment in which they found themselves; and it therefore seemed to underestimate the unpredictable, and even irrational, way in which humans or groups of humans or states could react in certain circumstances. At the same time it underplayed differences between the "actors", attributing to them a uniformity of response and behaviour which was rarely to be found in the real world. Finally and most damagingly of all, the systems approach, it was objected, was anyway tautological: just as the computer can only reproduce the information which had already been fed into it, so the systems approach can only tell us about the way states (or individuals) will behave if they conform to the rules of behaviour which have been ascribed to them by the proposed system (which may or may not correspond with the way in which real states behave in real situations). If the concern was to understand the way real states in fact behaved, such observers suggested, it might be better to study the reality rather than the invented model. Doubts of this kind about the validity of the approach are put forward in the last of the excerpts in this section, taken from Stanley Hoffmann's *Contemporary Theory in International Relations*: one of the most incisive criticisms to be made of the systems model.

* * *

Parsons – Interaction within a Social System*

"The situation is defined as consisting of objects of orientation, so that the orientation of a given actor is differentiated relative to the different objects and classes of them of which his situation is composed. It is convenient in action terms to classify the object world as composed of the three classes of 'social', 'physical' and 'cultural' objects. A social object is an actor, which may in turn be any given

* From Talcott Parsons (1902–). Highly influential US sociologist who has taught mainly at Amhurst College and Harvard. His first book *The Structure of Social Action* (1937), much influenced by Max Weber, established his reputation as an innovative thinker. Other works include *Sociological Theory and Modern Society* (1967) and *The System of Modern Societies* (1971). Quoted from *The Social System* (London: Routledge and Kegan Paul, 1952).

other individual actor (alter), the actor who is taken as a point of reference himself (ego), or a collectivity which is treated as a unit for purposes of the analysis of orientation. Physical objects are empirical entities which do not 'interact' with or 'respond' to ego. They are means and conditions of his action. Cultural objects are symbolic elements of the cultural tradition, ideas or beliefs, expressive symbols or value patterns so far as they are treated as situational objects by ego and are not 'internalised' as constitutive elements of the structure of his personality.

"'Action' is a process in the actor-situation system which has motivational significance to the individual actor, or, in the case of a collectivity, its component individuals. This means that the orientation of the corresponding action processes has a bearing on the attainment of gratifications or the avoidance of deprivations of the relevant actor, whatever concretely in the light of the relevant personality structures these may be. Only in so far as his relation to the situation is in this sense motivationally relevant will it be treated in this work as action in a technical sense. It is presumed that the ultimate source of the energy or 'effort' factor of action processes is derived from the organism, and correspondingly that in some sense all gratification and deprivation have an organic significance. But though it is rooted in them the concrete organisation of motivation cannot for purposes of action theory be analysed in terms of the organic needs of the organism. This organisation of action elements is, for purposes of the theory of action, above all a function of the relation of the actor to his situation and the history of that relation, in this sense of 'experience'.

"It is a fundamental property of action thus defined that it does not consist only of *ad hoc* 'responses' to particular situational 'stimuli' but that the actor develops a *system* of 'expectations' relative to the various objects of the situation. These *may* be structured only relative to his own need-dispositions and the probabilities of gratification or deprivation contingent on the various alternatives of action which he may undertake. But in the case of interaction with social objects a further dimension is added. Part of ego's expectation, in many cases the most crucial part, consists in the probable reaction of alter to ego's possible action, a reaction which comes to be anticipated in advance and thus to affect ego's own choices.

"On both levels, however, various elements of the situation come to have special 'meanings' for ego as 'signs' or 'symbols' which become relevant to the organisation of his expectation system. Especially where there is social interaction, signs and symbols acquire common meanings and serve as media of communication between actors. When symbolic systems which can mediate communication have emerged we may speak of the beginnings of a 'culture' which becomes part of the action systems of the relevant actors.

"It is only with systems of interaction which have become differentiated to a cultural level that we are here concerned. Though the term social system may be used in a more elementary sense, for present purposes this possibility can be ignored and attention confined to systems of interaction of a plurality of individual actors oriented to a situation and where the system includes a commonly understood system of cultural symbols.

"Reduced to the simplest possible terms, then, a social system consists in a plurality of individual actors interacting with each other in a situation which has at least a physical or environmental aspect, actors who are motivated in terms of a tendency to the 'optimisation of gratification' and whose relation to their situations, including each other, is defined and mediated in terms of a system of culturally structured and shared symbols.

"Thus conceived, a social system is only one of three aspects of the structuring of a completely concrete system of social action. The other two are the personality systems of the individual actors and the cultural system which is built into their action. Each of the three must be considered to be an independent focus of the organisation of the elements of the action system in the sense that no one of them is theoretically reducible to terms of one or a combination of the other two. Each is indispensable to the other two in the sense that without personalities and culture there would be no social system and so on around the roster of logical possibilities. But this interdependence and interpenetration is a very different matter from reducibility, which would mean that the important properties and processes of one class of system could be theoretically *derived* from our theoretical knowledge of one or both of the other two. The action frame of reference is common to all three and this fact makes certain 'transformations' between them possible. But on the level of theory here attempted they do not constitute a single system, however this might turn out to be on some other theoretical level.

"Almost another way of making this point is to say that on the present level of theoretical systematisation our dynamic knowledge of action-processes is fragmentary. Because of this we are forced to use these types of empirical system, descriptively presented in terms of a frame of reference, as an indispensable point of reference. In relation to this point of reference we conceive dynamic processes as 'mechanisms' which influence the 'functioning' of the system. The descriptive presentation of the empirical system must be made in terms of a set of 'structural' categories, into which the appropriate 'motivational' constructs necessary to constitute a usable knowledge of mechanisms are fitted.

• • •

"[A]cts do not occur singly and discretely, they are organised in systems. The moment even the most elementary system-level is brought under consideration a component of 'system integration' must enter in. In terms of the action frame of reference again this integration is a selective ordering among the possibilities of orientation. Gratification needs have alternatively possible objects presented in the situation. Cognitive mapping has alternatives of judgement or interpretation as to what objects are or what they 'mean'. There must be ordered selection among such alternatives. The term 'evaluation' will be given to this process of ordered selection. There is, therefore, an evaluative aspect of all concrete action orientation. The most elementary components of any action system then may be reduced to the actor and his situation. With regard to the actor our interest is organised about the cognitive, cathectic and evaluative modes of his orientation; with regard to the situation, to its differentiation into objects and classes of them."

Easton – Interaction within a Political System*

"A systems analysis promises a more expansive, more inclusive and more flexible theoretical structure than is available even in a thoroughly self-conscious and well-developed equilibrium approach. To do so successfully, however, it must establish its own theoretical imperatives. Although these were explored in detail in *A Framework for Political Analysis*, we may re-examine them briefly here, assum-

---

* From David Easton (1917–). Canadian-born political scientist. Studied at Harvard, later professor at Chicago University. Best known for *The Political System* (1953), in which he applied the systems approach to the study of the domestic political process. Other works include *A Systems Analysis of Political Life* (1967) and (as editor) *Variations of Political Theory* (1966). Quoted from *A Systems Analysis of Political Life* (New York: Wiley, 1965).

ing, however, that where the present brevity leaves unavoidable ambiguities, the reader may wish to become more familiar with the underlying structure of ideas by consulting this earlier volume. In it, at the outset, a system was defined as any set of variables regardless of the degree of interrelationship among them. The reason for preferring this definition is that it frees us from the need to argue about whether a political system is or is not really a system. The only question of importance about a set selected as a system to be analysed is whether this set constitutes an interesting one. Does it help us to understand and explain some aspect of human behaviour of concern to us?

"To be of maximum utility, I have argued, a *political* system can be designated as those interactions through which values are authoritatively allocated for a society; this is what distinguishes a political system from other systems that may be interpreted as lying in its environment. This environment itself may be divided into two parts, the intra-societal and the extra-societal. The first consists of those systems in the same society as the political system but excluded from the latter by our definition of the nature of political interactions. Intra-societal systems would include such sets of behaviour, attitudes and ideas as we might call the economy, culture, social structure or personalities; they are functional segments of the society with respect to which the political system at the focus of attention is itself a component. In a given society the systems other than the political system constitute a source of many influences that create and shape the conditions under which the political system itself must operate. In a world of newly emerging political systems we do not need to pause to illustrate the impact that a changing economy, culture or social structure may have upon political life.

"The second part of the environment, the extra-societal, includes all those systems that lie outside the given society itself. They are functional components of an international society or what we might describe as the supra-society, a supra-system of which any single society is part. The international political systems, the international economy or the international cultural system would fall into the category of extra-societal systems.

"Together, these two classes of systems, the intra- and extra-societal, that are conceived to lie outside of a political system may be designated as its total environment. From these sources arise influences that are of consequence for possible stress on the political system. The total environment is presented in Figure 1 as reproduced

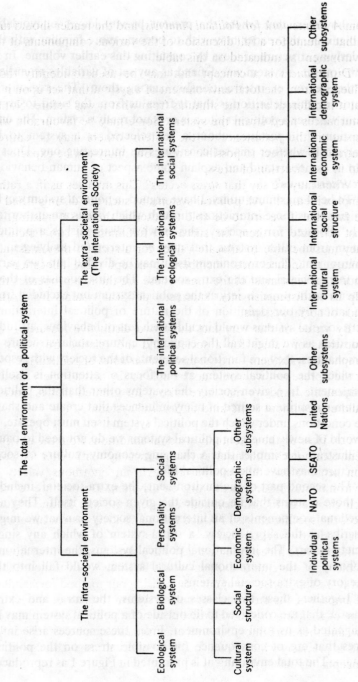

FIGURE 1: Components of the total environment of a political system

The total environment of a political system

The extra-societal environment (The International Society)

- Other subsystems
- International demographic system
- International economic system
- International social systems
  - International social structure
  - International cultural system
- The international ecological systems
- The international political systems
  - Other subsystems
  - United Nations
  - SEATO
  - NATO
  - Individual political systems

The intra-societal environment

- Ecological system
- Biological system
- Personality systems
- Social systems
  - Economic system
  - Demographic system
  - Social structure
  - Cultural system
  - Other subsystems

from *A Framework for Political Analysis*, and the reader should turn to that volume for a full discussion of the various components of the environment as indicated on this table.

"*Disturbances* is a concept that may be used to identify those influences from the total environment of a system that act upon it so that it is different after the stimulus from what it was before. Not all disturbances need strain the system. Some may be favourable with respect to the persistence of the system; others may be entirely neutral with respect to possible stress. But many can be expected to lead in the direction of stress.

"When may we say that *stress* occurs? This involves us in a rather complex idea. . . . All political systems as such are distinguished by the fact that if we are to be able to describe them as persisting, we must attribute to them the successful fulfilment of two functions. They must be able to allocate values for a society; they must also manage to induce most members to accept these allocations as binding, at least most of the time. These are the two properties that help us to distinguish most succinctly political systems from other kinds of social systems.

"By virtue of this very fact these two distinctive features – the allocations of values for a society and the relative frequency of compliance with them – are the *essential variables* of political life. But for their presence, we would not be able to say that a society has any political life. And we may here take it for granted that no society could exist without some kind of political system. . . .

• • •

". . . How do the potentially stressful conditions from the environment communicate themselves to a political system? After all, common sense alone tells us that there is an enormous variety of environmental influences at work on a system. Do we have to treat each change in the environment as a separate and unique disturbance, the specific effects of which for the political system have to be independently worked out?

"If this were indeed the case, as I have shown in detail before, the problems of systematic analysis would be virtually insurmountable. But if we can devise a way for generalising our method for handling the impact of the environment on the system, there would be some hope of reducing the enormous variety of influences into a relatively few, and therefore into a relatively manageable number of indicators. This is precisely what I have sought to effect through the use of the concepts 'inputs' and 'outputs'.

"How are we to describe these inputs and outputs? Because of the analytic distinction that I have been making between a political system and its parametric or environmental systems, it is useful to interpret the influences associated with the behaviour of persons in the environment or from other conditions there as *exchanges* or *transactions* that cross the *boundaries* of the political system. Exchanges can be used when we wish to refer to the mutuality of the relationships, to the fact that the political system and those systems in the environment have reciprocal effects on each other. Transactions may be employed when we wish to emphasise the movement of an effect in one direction, from an environmental system to the political system, or the reverse, without being concerned at the time about the reactive behaviour of the other system.

"To this point, there is little to dispute. Unless systems were coupled together in some way, all analytically identifiable aspects of behaviour in society would stand independent of each other, a patently unlikely condition. What carries recognition of this coupling beyond a mere truism, however, is the proposal of a way to trace out the complex exchanges so that we can readily reduce their immense variety to theoretically and empirically manageable proportions.

"To accomplish this, I have proposed that we condense the major and significant environmental influences into a few indicators. Through the examination of these we should be able to appraise and follow through the potential impact of environmental events on the system. With this objective in mind, I have designated the effects that are transmitted across the boundary of a system toward some other system as the *outputs* of the first system and hence, symmetrically, as the *inputs* of the second system, the one they influence. A transaction or an exchange between systems will therefore be viewed as a linkage between them in the form of an input-output relationship.

DEMANDS AND SUPPORTS AS INPUT INDICATORS

"The value of inputs as a concept is that through their use we shall find it possible to capture the effect of the vast variety of events and conditions in the environment as they pertain to the persistence of a political system. Without the inputs it would be difficult to delineate the precise operational way in which the behaviour in the various sectors of society affects what happens in the political sphere. Inputs will serve as *summary variables* that concentrate and mirror everything in the environment that is relevant to political stress. Thereby this concept serves as a powerful tool.

"The extent to which inputs can be used as summary variables will depend, however, upon how we define them. We might conceive of them in their broadest sense. In that case, we would interpret them as including any event external to the system that alters, modifies or affects the system in any and every possible way. But if we seriously considered using the concept in so broad a fashion, we would never be able to exhaust the list of inputs acting upon a system. Virtually every parametric event and condition would have some significance for the operations of a political system at the focus of attention; a concept so inclusive that it does not help us to organise and simplify reality would defeat its own purposes. We would be no better off than we are without it.

"But as I have already intimated, we can greatly simplify the task of analysing the impact of the environment if we restrict our attention to certain kinds of inputs that can be used as indicators to sum up the most important effects, in terms of their contributions to stress, that cross the boundary from the parametric to the political systems. In this way we would free ourselves from the need to deal with and trace out separately the consequences of every different type of environmental event.

"As the theoretical tool for this purpose, it is helpful to view the major environmental influences as coming to a focus in two major inputs: demands and support. Through them a wide range of activities in the environment may be channelled, mirrored and summarised and brought to bear upon political life, as I shall show in detail in the succeeding chapters. In this sense they are key indicators of the way in which environmental influences and conditions modify and shape the operations of the political system. If we wish, we may say that it is through fluctuations in the inputs of demands and support that we shall find the effects of the environmental systems transmitted to the political system."

McClelland – The Use of System Analysis*

"It is one thing to state a theory and thereby achieve an abstract description of some aspect of the world, and it is something else to use a theory.

"The idea of the international system is abstract, descriptive and theoretical. It contributes a perspective. The international system constitutes an expression to stimulate thoughts about a certain generalised image. Thus, the nations of the world are conceived to be in contact and association in a complicated framework of relationships, which is formed through the process of interaction. The nation is thought of as a complex of interrelated physical and human activities. One portion of its complex of activities is seen turning inward for maintenance, support and other purposes of the nation itself, while another portion is directed abroad into the international environment.

"Something similar to a metabolic principle governs the internal–external division of a nation's activities. In order to sustain itself, the nation diverts inward much of its energies, resources and organisation, but this pursuit of its national interest requires also a certain amount of exchanging with its environment. The latter phenomenon of exchange between nations gives rise to the idea of international relations and also provides its main data source. Exchange consists of fundamental functions of drawing in and transmitting outward a variety of materials and effects. In other words, a nation's international behaviour, in the system perspective, is a two-way activity of taking from and giving to the international environment. All the giving and taking, when considered together and for all the national actors, is called the international system.

"At any time in history, the international system is in a particular state. The state of the system has a form, reflects a set of prevailing conditions and manifests characteristics of structure and process. Over a period of time, the international system is conceived to move from one state to another state. Its motions, however complex they are found to be, are the phenomena that become the objects of

---

* From Charles McClelland. For many years professor of international relations at the University of Southern California. Interested in patterns of interaction in international relations, and quantitative studies of the structure of the international system. His principal book on international relations is *Theory and the International System*, from which this extract is taken, but he is also the author of many articles in journals of international affairs. Quoted from *Theory and the International System* (New York: Macmillan, 1966).

investigation. In a system orientation, virtually all the aspirations and all the intellectual problems of knowledge for international relations are bound up in the basic question: How does the international system work?

"The specifications of what needs to be done in theory and research to answer the question are, on the general conceptual level, plain and straightforward. First, it needs to be shown in detail what each component of the international system contributes in the give to–take away process of a particular moment of time. Second, with time still stopped, it is necessary to trace out the configuration of the system and to establish the nature of the ensemble. Third, the task is to follow the development and change in both the components and the ensemble of the system over time in order to understand the systematic performance, the fluctuations and the trends as the system moves from state to state. Fourth, useful knowledge will be expected to develop from the concentration of attention on all the foregoing tasks and problems with the primary purpose of controlling the performances of the system. The knowledge to control might appear to be the ultimate accomplishment. A fifth goal in the study of international relations is likely to be that of acquiring an understanding of what may be done – of developing effective procedures – when two or more contrary efforts to control the international system are being exerted at the same time.

"The proposition that the behaviour of the international system is determined by its structure has more to it than meets the eye. Complaints have been raised against too great a preoccupation with the effects on international relations that are thought to arise from bipolar or multipolar alignments of great powers and with bloc arrangements in international politics. A slighting of the influence on international relations created by the policy positions of single national states is said to develop from the heavy attention being given to the structure of the international system. This is a criticism that is worth examining from the system viewpoint. A firm understanding of the linking of subsystems to the system would appear to remove the cause of the complaint.

"The conception that has been presented in this discussion is that the system, including the state it is in and its various properties and characteristics, is the *resultant* of the interacting behaviour of all its constituent parts. Thus, a description of the structure of the international system at a given time would include the consideration of the part played by the policy positions and the actions of individual nation states. The question of overall system versus national actor appears to be more an issue of analytical choice faced by the observer or investigator than a problem in system theory. That there is a distinction to be drawn between theory and system analysis is the main message in this chapter. Theory describes and circumscribes the conditions of system complexity and interrelatedness, but analysis must cope directly with these factors. The work of analysis is the application of techniques to materials. Thus, when we turn from generalised and abstract descriptions of international relations in terms of systems concepts to the methods and procedures of analysing data, we are entering a different realm. How the system orientation can be used in studying international relations can be discussed most profitably by the consideration of matters of technique and application.

THE TOOL OF SYSTEM ANALYSIS

"System as a method appears to have only one contribution to make to analysis. This contribution is the procedure for the orderly shifting of perspective from level to level and for the sequence of redefinitions of system and subsystems. The later discussion will show several applications of the shift of level contribution and it will make apparent that the procedure is useful but does not displace other existing research techniques. In general, system analysis is neutral with respect to the employment of any of a number of alternative approaches to inquiry. Neither system concepts nor system analyses establish requirements for the use of either behavioural or traditional modes of research. Historical, comparative, statistical, experimental and simulative approaches can be used in the work of system analysis one at a time or in combinations. It is a mistaken notion that system analysis must involve the quantification of data, although it is true that these operations are compatible. Historical narratives that depend greatly on artistic reconstructions of the relationships in past events could be cast in the mould of system analysis and could be organised according to the shift of level technique.

• • •

". . . System analysis is a technique for slicing into a system complex in a particular direction and for a particular purpose. The researcher is confronted by decisions on which way to make the cut, not simply at the beginning of the problem but frequently at each of a number of its branching points. Thus, it should be clear that the generalised theorising about the international system, with its broad sweep and its synthesising attributes, produces sharp contrasts when it is compared with system analysis, which is differentiated by a narrowness of objective and a specificity in approach. The two are interdependent but the gulf is wide with respect to differences in orientation.

"System analysis has proven to be effective in many fields where there are demanding and concrete problems of managing complex relationships among many processes. The building of a new missile that will be guaranteed to work, that is to be constructed against a fixed schedule of time and costs, and that will incorporate a mixing together of new and old types of equipment and will involve, therefore, the designing, planning and fabricating of some elements that, at the outset, are only ideas in somebody's mind is an example of a problem that has been attacked very successfully through multiple-system analysis. One may be very sceptical about the idea that directing the transformations of the international system is anything like the constructing of a new missile. It can be insisted that the mobilising of international activities for the national development of underdeveloped countries has no possible relationship to the planning of industrial processes for making some apparatus, parts of which are not even on the drawing boards."

Kaplan – Six Types of International System*

PRIMITIVE CONCEPTS OF THE INTERNATIONAL SYSTEM

"The international system has among its subsystems a set of actors. These actors will be called international actors and will remain undefined. The set of international actors will be divided into the subsets 'national actors' and 'supranational actors'. These also will be undefined. An extensional or 'pointing' reference, however, will be

---

* From Morton Kaplan (1921–). Influential US writer on international politics who has taught mainly at Chicago University. Best known for his *System and Process in International Politics* (1957) which applied the systems approach to international relations. Has undertaken a strenuous defence of the "scientific" approach to international relations studies against those advocating a more traditional approach, such as Hedley Bull. Other works include *Macro Politics: Selected Essays in the Philosophy and Science of Politics* (1970). Quoted from *System and Process in International Politics* (New York: Wiley, 1957).

offered. The United States, France and Italy are examples of national actors. The subset of supranational actors will itself be broken into subsets of bloc actors and universal actors. NATO and the Cominform are examples of bloc actors. The United Nations is an example of a universal actor.

"International action is action taking place between international actors. International actors will be treated as elements of the international system. Their internal systems will be parameters for the international system; their outputs will be behaviour of the international system. However, in the chapter on the international actors, the systems of the international actors will be treated as differentiated systems; the international system will then be treated as a parameter for these systems of action.

"Thus, it is important to examine both what happens to the international system as changes occur inside the systems of the international actors and to examine how the behaviour of the international actors is modified as the international system undergoes change.

• • •

"The essential rules of these systems will either be specified or treated generally. The types of actors who participate in the systems and other characteristics of the systems will be described. The parameter values necessary to the stability of each system will receive general treatment. The step-level functions, that is, the parameter values, which transform each system will be illustrated and will be linked to the type of transformation they are likely to induce. In effect, this spells out the implicit transformation rules of the system. Finally, the expectations for stability of each of the systems will be discussed.

"The various international systems as discussed in this chapter are heuristic models. Except for the first two systems, the international systems described have never had historical counterparts.

"The analysis of systems without historical counterparts has definite value. In the first place, the models of international systems with historical counterparts contain predictions that new kinds of international systems will arise if certain conditions hold. Therefore a statement of the characteristics of international systems without counterparts is necessary if models of existing systems are properly to be subject to confirmation. In the second place it is desirable to make predictions about how such international systems will behave if they do arise. Unless this is done, predictions concerning the transformation of existing systems will be too loose for proper confirmation.

"The 'balance of power' and loose bipolar system models are simpler than their objective referents. It is possible that important essential rules have been left out of account through ignorance. If so, these defects should be revealed by efforts to apply the models. Simplicity in the model has the important initial function of presenting system relations in their clearest and starkest forms.

"If theorising stops – rather than starts – with overly simple models, there will, of course, be no progress and even no really operational knowledge. The real test is: Do the simplifications aid progress in research, or do they obscure important relationships and thereby detour science into the study of interesting puzzles?

THE 'BALANCE OF POWER' SYSTEM

"The term 'balance of power' is placed in quotation marks because, interpreted literally, any state of international equilibrium represents a balance of power. In this sense the term is tautologous and even trivial. It fails to convey information about what will happen or about what an actor should do. However, the term 'balance of power' has been used in the literature and makes intuitive sense if it is applied to the description of the international system that persisted throughout the eighteenth and nineteenth centuries and perhaps the early part of the twentieth century.

"The 'balance of power' system is distinguished from other international systems by the following characteristics. It is an international social system without a political subsystem (or, alternatively, with a null political subsystem). The actors within the system are international actors who fall within the subclass 'national actor'. 'Essential' being used as an undefined term, the number of essential actors in such a system must be at least five and preferably more.

"Extensionally, in the pre-World War I period England, France, Germany, the Austro-Hungarian Empire, Italy and the United States fell within the essential national actor category. The labelling of the essential national actors is without importance, but the existence of a minimum number of actors falling within that class is of vital importance to the system.

"Although no political system exists in the 'balance of power' international system, the national actors act individually in a complementary manner and thereby implement the essential rules of the 'balance of power' system. These rules describe the characteristic behaviour of the actors. They are universalistic in character.[1]

"The 'balance of power' system is characterised by the following essential rules:

1. Act to increase capabilities but negotiate rather than fight.
2. Fight rather than pass up an opportunity to increase capabilities.
3. Stop fighting rather than eliminate an essential national actor.
4. Act to oppose any coalition or single actor which tends to assume a position of predominance with respect to the rest of the system.
5. Act to constrain actors who subscribe to supranational organising principles.
6. Permit defeated or constrained essential national actors to re-enter the system as acceptable role partners or act to bring some previously inessential actor within the essential actor classification. Treat all essential actors as acceptable role partners.

"The first essential rule states that each essential national actor is to increase its capabilities. However, this is to be accomplished, if possible, without the costs entailed by war and also without the possible disequilibrating consequences war may have for the 'balance of power' system.

"The second essential rule states that the primary obligation of each essential national actor is to itself. It implies that unless an essential national actor is capable of protecting its own interests, those interests are unlikely to prevail. Therefore capabilities are to be increased even at the price of war.

"The first two essential rules seemingly are egoistic prescriptions of the Hobbesian variety. They accord with the 'war of all against all'. However, they also agree with classic philosophic standards. If there are practical limits to the size of the just community, the possibility of a just ordering between communities – although desirable – must be subordinated to the prudential necessity of being strong enough to protect oneself against possible enemies.

"The third essential rule corresponds with the classic standard and not with the Hobbesian. The essential national actor should not so expand that it outgrows the optimal size of the just and lawful community. It also corresponds with the bonds relating legitimate dynastic regimes and with the character of modern national territorial states. Expansion beyond certain limits clearly would be inconsistent with nationality or exclusiveness.

"The fourth and fifth rules are merely rational rules necessary to maintain the international action system. A predominant coalition or an essential national actor which became predominant or which aspired to establish a political hegemony over other essential national actors would constitute a threat to the interests of the national actors who did not belong to the coalition. Moreover, if a coalition were to succeed in establishing hegemony over the international system, the dominant member(s) of the coalition would then also dominate the lesser members of the coalition. Coalitions therefore tend to be counterbalanced by opposing coalitions when they become threatening to non-members and to become fragile when they threaten the interests of some of their own members. In the last case, the threatened members find it advantageous either to withdraw into neutrality or to join the opposed coalition. These rules are also interwoven with the third rule. It is necessary to limit one's objectives and not to eliminate other essential national actors so that one may be able, if necessary, to align oneself with them in the future.

"The sixth rule states that membership in the system is dependent only upon behaviour which corresponds with the essential rules or norms of the 'balance of power' system. If the number of essential actors is reduced, the 'balance of power' international system will become unstable. Therefore, maintaining the number of essential national actors above a critical lower bound is a necessary condition for the stability of the system. This is done best by returning to full membership in the system defeated actors or reformed deviant actors.

"Although any particular action or alignment may be the product of 'accidents', that is, of the set of specific conditions producing the action or alignment, including elements such as chance meetings or personality factors, a high correlation between the pattern of national behaviour and the essential rules of the international system would represent a confirmation of the predictions of the theory."

Note
1. In the historical "balance of power", dynastic relations and common cultural and political institutions facilitated the play of the system. Thus there was a wider ascriptive base within which the universalistic pattern characteristic of the system operated. This ascriptive base gave rise to an expectation that the roles of the system would be filled and the norms of the system obeyed. In a sense, however, this ascriptive base is accidental to the system, for the system would operate in any situation in which the proper expectations were present. The essential determinants of the "balance of power" are thus the universal norms rather than the ascriptive base, for indeed the same ascriptive base would be completely consonant with a totally different international system while a completely different ascriptive base could be completely consonant with a "balance of power" system.

Hoffmann – The Weaknesses of Systems Theory*

"Not only are the purposes and methods of systems scientism open to criticism, but the results achieved so far are also questionable, on three counts. First, the map these efforts produce does not allow us to recognise the landscape. Precisely because they aim at a high level of generality and use tools coming from other disciplines, these systems do not capture the stuff of politics. The political patterns they study are always reduced to something else, because their enterprises are built on the shaky foundations of metaphors taken too seriously. 'We cannot think creatively without metaphors, but any metaphor is in danger of becoming a categorical imperative.'[1] It is significant that mechanics provide the dominant metaphor or the model which commands the vocabulary of the social scientists discussed here – a tendency which can be traced back to Pareto and Durkheim, and even further to the sixteenth and seventeenth centuries. Mechanism today has a new aspect which reflects the sophistication of modern technology: both in Mr Kaplan's and in some of Mr Deutsch's earlier works, men and societies are reduced to communication systems, without much concern for the substance of the 'messages' these networks carry. Maybe communications theory will prove to be the common framework for efforts that seek to interpret the behaviour of all systems 'from atomic particles to galaxies', from viruses to planets. But this is not what we are interested in here. The definition of values as the operating preferences according to which certain messages are transmitted first is a fine example of a statement which may be useful for cybernetics, but is merely tautological in international relations.

"In addition to communications theory Mr Kaplan has transplanted into alien soil some aspects of structural-functional theory. Even though he starts with one good idea, and one sound warning: the idea that there are various types of international systems, and the warning that these types are not integrated social systems, he soon forgets the warning and overextends the idea. He borrows his vocabulary from a discipline whose model is the integrated society. Concepts which fit such a model (and which are even within their own

* From Stanley Hoffmann (1928–). (For biographical details see p. 299). Quoted from *Contemporary Theory in International Relations* (Englewood Cliffs, N.J.: Prentice-Hall, 1960).

realm open to the challenge that most living societies cannot be analysed in so simplified and static a way) do not fit at all the small international milieu characterised by 'the extraordinary diversity of national situations'. Such heterogeneity vitiates an abstract discussion in terms of general 'role functions'. For the specialist in international relations, from the viewpoint of the 'total system', the differences between the basic units are as important as the similarities; the opposite is true when the sociologist looks at the actors playing a role in the social system. Mr Kaplan's roles, systems and processes are assumed but not examined.

"Consequently 'sociologism' operates here too – in the most unlikely field. Systems are discussed as if they had a compulsive will of their own; the implicit God, Society, who gave its stuffy oppressiveness to the universe of Comte and Durkheim, is again at work, under the incognito of System. Each system assigns roles to actors; the structure of the system sets its needs, its needs determine its objectives, and 'the objectives of a system are values for the system'. The old and mistaken habit of treating social facts like things is back again. It is not too surprising that the only processes discussed are processes of maintenance, integration and disintegration; for the implied supreme value is stability: mechanical stability, since purposes and values other than preservation of the system are left out. It is the usual penalty for the double attempt to drive the consideration of values out of the subject matter, and to present a value-free theory: the status quo becomes an empirical and normative pivot. For only the closed society can be compared to an organism, or dealt with in terms which assume a closed system. International systems are always open and moving – at least sufficiently to force us to abandon the model and the vocabulary of the closed system. Such a model, which starts with the hypotheses of integration and equilibrium, proves totally unable to account for patterns of change and conflict, and tends to treat as disturbances the processes of change which are, in world affairs, certainly more a rule than an exception.

"Second, the inadequacy of the results can be shown by pointing to their inability to *explain* world politics. On the one hand, excessive use of Occam's razor (i.e., a desire to reduce the theory to as few hypotheses as possible, and to prefer a single hypothesis to a complex one, because such simplicity makes a theory easier to use even though it might imply sheer formalism) and the tendency to reduce politics to what it is not, entail a loss of such vital elements as institutions, culture and the action of individuals as autonomous variables rather than social atoms. As in the 'realist' theory, Mr Kaplan's emphasis on international systems also involves a neglect of the domestic determinants of the 'national actors', and his model of 'action' leaves out the forces of change operating within or across the 'actors'. On the other hand, the striving for total objectivity (which almost means the reduction of subjects to objects), the desire to retain mainly measurable elements and the effort to build 'systems' combine in the production of models in which many variables are interrelated, but where no hierarchy is established among the variables. The principle of 'indetermination' is followed with rigorous 'scientism', as if it were compatible with the goal of predictability. It does not allow us to determine first what variables will be submitted to the standard scientific methods of verification and validation which determine whether these variables will be included in or excluded from our scheme; nor does it allow us to decide later whether the correlations we have discovered are meaningful or relevant or not.

"Furthermore all the variables tend to be treated alike; it is only in their weight that they differ; factors which limit the range of political choices and affect the decision which is ultimately made among such alternatives are treated as if they were of the same kind as those decisions themselves: hence the mechanistic aspect of the models, concatenations of functions and correlations which distort reality far more than they account for it. Here, whatever its ambiguities, obscurities and perils, the need for the method of 'understanding' stressed by Max Weber cannot be denied. We must interpret the correlations we have established; we must present hypotheses as to what variables are the most significant, and how the various correlations discovered between isolated phenomena are interrelated in the area which we try to explain. Otherwise we will end with overstuffed boxes, or with static schemes or, at best, with comparative statics. What is hidden behind the building of 'indetermined' schemes is the belief or wish that a correct scientific analysis of a field would reveal all by itself the truth about the field. The subject, if it is submitted to the proper type of scrutiny, will divulge its essence without making it necessary for the specialist to do any interpreting of his own – and to run the frightful risks of subjectivity implied. All he needs is the most advanced form of scientific equipment. Without it, he would be lost; with it, the subject will obligingly disclose its true structure and its laws.

"Thirdly, the inadequacy of the results of 'systems theory' is also revealed, more indirectly but no less effectively, by the strange underground connection which exists between this theory and a particularly objectionable form of policy scientism. A view of the social universe as the interplay of impersonal forces, the lack of concern for the substance of politics, the procedural and mechanical analogies, the implied norm of stability lead the social scientist almost inevitably to a therapeutic and manipulative approach – to the belief that the control of the variables he has identified would push society in the direction he, or social 'élites', deem desirable. The connection between the cool and detached objectivity of the theorist and the '*engagement*' of the policy scientist is often made through another set of metaphors: metaphors about the health and sickness of societies and systems. This is another part of Durkheim's heritage, another consequence of the assumption of equilibrium and integration as the norm: for what disturbs or denies the norm tends to be treated as abnormal. This is a way of arguing which can hardly have any claim to scientific positivism, for it is neither consistent with the pretence of value-freedom, nor does it make sense analytically as long as we do not know the laws of change from one system to another.

"Indeed, it is a course which leads to highly unscientific results. On the one hand, precisely because the schemes established by systems theorists are static and not explanatory, when these writers want to suggest policies, they tend to jump from the extreme of indetermination to the extreme of 'single-trend' analysis. They suddenly give crucial importance to one factor, without realising that such a decision postulates both the existence of a general law which states 'what kind of change in human culture will regularly follow upon specific changes' in the selected factor, and the possibility of isolating this factor. On the other hand, reliance on system and method is so great that there is a tendency to assume that the 'laws of equilibrium' of the system or the methods of scientific analysis will set by themselves the objectives to be attained. What happens instead is that the scientist mistakes for the objectives of his scientific system, the objectives of the social system in which he lives and which, not infrequently, he has more or less unconsciously taken as a point of departure for his system-building; the 'nationalist celebration' is one of the most curious practical consequences of systems theory. The result is bound to be either very dubious advice, or a considerable number of platitudes, all predicated on the fancy conception of the social scientist as an all-knowing, though democratic, brain-washer."

Note
1. David Riesman, "Some Observations on the 'Older' and the 'Newer' Social Science", in Leonard D. White (ed.), *The State of the Social Sciences*, Chicago, Ill., 1956, p. 338.

33 Transnational Relations

One of the criticisms raised against the systems approach was that it ignored informal factors within international relations. It tended to conceive of states as homogeneous wholes, each reacting to the other according to their relative power, or to the built-in behaviour mechanisms which were attributed to them. It thus underestimated, so it was said, the diffuseness and unpredictability of international relations, which depended in the final resort on the attitudes, feelings and decisions of individual human beings interacting in many different ways. In particular, it excluded the growing importance of non-governmental contacts and relationships, which in many cases influenced, distorted or even conflicted with the relations between governments themselves.

Because of the growth of these contacts there was in the late 1960s a growing interest in "transnational" relations: relationships of many kinds which took place across national boundaries between organisations, groups and individuals that were not states or the official representatives of states. The importance of these contacts, and the way they could influence or even change official relationships, had long been recognised. For example Sir Alfred Zimmern, in the passage quoted above (p. 466), had especially emphasised the distinction between relations among states and relations among individuals, seeing inter-governmental relations as only "a small element within the total relationships among many peoples". In the same way functionalist writers had often stressed the importance of non-official contacts outside the system of political relations among governments (though their main interest was in the less political contacts among governments).

After the Second World War the importance of non-governmental contacts became increasingly apparent. Large transnational corporations extended their activities across the globe; associations of employers, unions, special interest groups, scientists and other specialists, working in similar areas, proliferated and expanded. Individuals travelled from country to country on a scale many times greater than before. These contacts were sometimes closely related to relations between governments, or even directly controlled by them. But often they were not, yet they nearly always had some influence on relations among states, and themselves formed a part of the entire context of international relations.

Such contacts therefore became of increasing interest to students of international affairs. Some believed that modern means of communication, shrinking the size of the world, had transformed international relationships and the character of the modern state. The traditional "billiard-ball" image of the state, self-sufficient and self-directing, but involved in occasional collisions with other equally self-enclosed states, now had to be discarded. This thesis was put forward by J. H. Herz, the US political scientist, in his book *International Politics in the Atomic Age*. In his view the traditional impermeability which states had enjoyed within their own frontiers, symbolised by the "hard shell" of their defensive perimeters, was now destroyed. In the modern world states had become vulnerable to economic blockade, which in former days had been ineffective; were open to ideological and political penetration, through broadcasting, the printed word and personal contacts, in a way they had never been before; were subject to air attack; above all were vulnerable to possible atomic war. The type of security which states had traditionally enjoyed within their own frontiers was therefore now destroyed. They were obliged to extend their control over much wider areas: areas no longer restricted by political frontiers. Finally, ideological allegiance became more important than territorial citizenship in influencing political actions and state capabilities. An entirely new type of world had therefore been created.

European writers were also struck by the effect of transnational relationships on the traditional conduct of international affairs. In his book, *Paix et guerre entre les nations*, first published in 1962, Raymond Aron, the French sociologist, contrasted the *international* system, consisting of interactions of states, with *transnational* society, consisting of the interactions of individuals. Transnational society was manifested in commercial exchanges, migration, common beliefs, associations which transcended frontiers, even transnational ceremonies and competitions (such as the Olympic Games). He gave as an example of a flourishing transnational society pre-1914 Europe, linked by relatively free commercial exchanges and a common gold standard, international political parties, generally free migration, shared beliefs and political doctrines; and pointed out that flourishing and harmonious relations among individuals of this kind can co-exist with hostile relationships among states. Against this the Europe of the iron curtain years, immediately after the Second World War, was not a genuinely transnational society, since such inter-personal links scarcely existed. A transnational society could be sustained by customs, conventions and even laws (in the form of private international law). These were themselves normally subordinated to the law which exists between states: public international law. But that law, though it reflected the will of the states, could not be enforced, since there existed no enforcement agency. Thus the only ultimate sanction of war, which itself was a transgression of the law.

At the end of that decade the same phenomenon – growing non-official contacts between states – attracted new attention. In 1970 a special edition of the journal *International Organisation*, edited by Joseph Nye and Robert Keohane, was devoted to the question. In this a number of writers addressed such themes as the transnational activities of multinational corporations, international banks, labour unions, airlines, non-governmental organisations, revolutionary groups, the Catholic Church, the Ford Foundation and scientific unions. In their introduction, part of which is reproduced below, the editors noted the effects which transnational interaction (defined as the "movement of tangible or intangible items across state boundaries when at least one actor is not an agent of a government or an inter-governmental organisation") may have on traditional relationships among states. Apart from the general effect of increasing mutual knowledge and awareness, there were a number of other consequences. Changes of attitude might be brought about which would eventually affect government policies; a more pluralist international system was created in which groups and states become linked with groups having common interests in other states; domestic politics was partly internationalised; relations of dependence and interdependence were sometimes established, especially in the commercial and monetary fields; and non-governmental organisations began to become a new instrument by which the government of one state might exercise influence within another. Above all, the forces that were significant in international politics changed: non-governmental organisations became a new kind of actor within the system, operating largely independently of governments.

These writers, therefore, were reflecting an increasingly visible reality of the contemporary world scene. By pointing out the importance of new kinds of "actors" they showed that the relationships within international society are considerably more complex than the traditional "billiard ball" models, concentrating on relationships between homogeneous "states", had suggested.

*   *   *

Herz – The Decline of the Territorial State*

"In view of the tremendous role nation-states – or at least several of them – play in the world today, talking about the 'decline' of states manifestly would be absurd. What is referred to in the title of this chapter ["The Decline of the Territorial State"] is the decline of that specific element of statehood which characterised the units composing the modern state system in its classical period, and which I called their 'territoriality' or 'impermeability'. The 'model-type' international system built upon units of this structure was that of a plurality of countries – at first all European – bound together by certain common standards, different but not too different in power, all enjoying a certain minimum of protection in and through that system. They would quarrel, try to diminish each other, but they would hardly ever suffer one of theirs to be extinguished. In their quarrels, which they called wars, they would attack each other, but their fortress-type shells of defence could be breached only by frontal assault and thus even the smaller powers had a goodly chance to resist and survive. Self-contained, centralised, internally pacified, they could rely on themselves for a high degree of external security.

"Beginning with the nineteenth century, certain trends emerged which tended to endanger the functioning of the classical system. Directly or indirectly, all of them had a bearing upon that feature of the territorial state which was the strongest guarantee of its independent coexistence with other states of like nature: its hard shell, that is, its defensibility in case of war.

•   •   •

"Total war, as distinguished from both kinds of traditional war, limited and unlimited, is involved with developments in warfare which enable belligerents to overleap or by-pass the traditional hard-shell defence of states. As soon as this happens, the traditional relationship between war, on the one hand, and territorial sov-

---

* From J. H. Herz (1908–). Professor of Government at the City College of New York. His early interests were in the field of political philosophy and it was from this standpoint that he approached international topics, including the controversies surrounding the "realist" approach: for example in *Political Realism and Political Idealism* (1951). In his later writing he somewhat modified the thesis expressed in this extract. Quoted from *International Politics in the Atomic Age* (New York: Columbia University Press, 1959).

ereignty and power, on the other, is altered decisively. Arranged in order of increasing effectiveness, these new factors may be listed under the following headings: (a) possibility of economic blockade; (b) ideological-political penetration; (c) air war; and (d) atomic war. . . .

• • •

"Prior to the industrial age the territorial state was largely self-contained ('self-sufficient'), economically as otherwise. Although one of the customary means of conducting limited war was to try to starve fortresses into surrender, this applied only to the individual links in the shell, and not to entire nations in order to avoid breaching the shell. When some authors refer to economic blockade of entire countries as the 'traditional' means of English warfare, this is hardly correct, for, prior to the twentieth century, attempts undertaken in this direction proved rather ineffective, as witness the Continental Blockade and its counterpart during the Napoleonic era. The Industrial Revolution changed all this, for it made countries like Britain and Germany increasingly dependent on imports. This meant that in war they could survive only by controlling areas beyond their own territory, which would provide them with the food and raw materials they needed. The Germans managed by overrunning food-surplus and raw-material producing areas in the initial stages of both world wars, and the British, of course, by keeping the sea lanes open through superior naval power.

"In peacetime, economic dependency became one of the causes of a phenomenon which itself contributed to the transformation of the old state system: imperialism. Anticipating war, with its new danger of blockade, countries strove to become more self-sufficient through enlargement of their areas of control. I do not mean to imply that the complex phenomenon of imperialism was exclusively or even chiefly caused by economic interdependence and its impact on war. Clearly, the earlier stage of capitalist industrialism as such had already supplied various motives for expansion, especially in the form of colonialism. But an economic determinism which sees the cause of imperialist expansion only in the profit motive and the ensuing urge for markets or cheap labour overlooks the additional, and very compelling, motivation that lies in power competition and the urge for security in case of war. To the extent that the industrialised nations lost self-sufficiency, they were driven into expansion in a – futile – effort to regain it. Today, if at all, only the control of entire continents enables major nations to survive economically in major wars. This implies that hard-shell military defence, if it is to make any sense, must be a matter of defending more than one single nation; it must extend half way around the world. This, in turn, affects the status of smaller nations, whether they are included in the larger defence perimeter or not. If they are, they tend to become dependent on the chief power in the area; if they are not, they may become 'permeable' precisely because of the possibility of economic blockade.

• • •

"With the emergence of political belief systems and ideological creeds in our century, however, nations have become susceptible to undermining from within. Although, as in the case of economic blockades, wars have not yet been won solely by subversion of loyalties, the threat has affected the coherence of the territorial state ever since the rise to power of a regime that claims and proclaims to represent not the cause of one particular nation, but that of all mankind, or at least its exploited or suppressed 'masses'. Bolshevism from 1917 on has provided the second instance in modern history of world-revolutionary propaganda. Communist penetration tactics were subsequently imitated by Nazi-Fascist regimes, and eventually even by the democracies. To be sure, neither Nazi-Fascist propaganda directed to the democracies nor democratic counterpropaganda directed to populations under totalitarian regimes were by themselves sufficient to defeat an enemy in the Second World War; but individual instances of 'softening up' countries and then gaining control with the aid of a subversive group within occurred even then. Such tactics have, of course, become all too familiar during the cold war. It is hardly necessary to point out how a new technological development and a new technique of penetration – radio broadcasting – has added to the effectiveness of political penetration through psychological warfare. The radio has rendered units accessible to propaganda and undermining from abroad, which formerly were impenetrable not only in a political but also in a technical sense. Examples abound, from what was probably one of its first effective uses – Nazi radio broadcasting to the Saar during the plebiscite campaign of 1934–5 and to Austria in the summer of 1934 – down to the present Nasserite propaganda throughout the Near East.

"Thus, new lines of division, cutting horizontally through state units instead of leaving them separated vertically from each other at their frontiers, have now become possible. Under such political-ideological alignments, 'aliens' may turn out to be friends, citizens, more treacherous than 'enemy aliens'; 'friendly' prisoners of war may have to be distinguished from hostile ones, as, in the Second World War in the case of German or Italian PWs, or, more recently, in Korean prison camps; 'refugees' may be revealed as spies or 'agents', while 'agents' may deliver themselves up as refugees; the Iron Curtain is crossed westward by those who feel that this is the way to escape 'slavery', while others cross it eastward to escape 'oppression' or 'discrimination'. How even in peacetime such a new type of loyalties (or disloyalties) can be utilised to weaken the internal coherence and therewith the 'impermeability' of nations is vividly portrayed by the statements of French and Italian Communist leaders calling upon their compatriots to consider the Soviet Union a brother instead of an enemy in case of war. And during actual war, political-ideological fissures can be utilised to counter the effects of newly developed means of attack by rendering it more difficult to 'pacify' territory 'conquered' in the traditional manner of breaching the outer defence wall. Guerrilla warfare then becomes another means of rendering obsolete the classical way of defeating an enemy through defeating his traditional armed forces. Using planes to establish communication with guerrilla forces behind enemy lines, or to drop them supplies or advisers, illustrates the combined effect which political-ideological strategy and air war may have upon the customary type of classical warfare.

"*Air war*, of all the new developments and techniques prior to the atomic age, is the one that has affected the territoriality of nations most radically. With it, so to say, the roof blew off the territorial state."

Aron – Transnational Society and International Systems*

TRANSNATIONAL SOCIETY AND INTERNATIONAL SYSTEMS

"International systems, as we have said, are comprised of units that have regular diplomatic relations with each other. Now such relations

---

* From Raymond Aron (1905–84). French sociologist and prolific author on a wide variety of social and political themes. His principal contribution to international

are normally accompanied by relations among individuals, who make up the various units. *International systems are the inter-state aspect of the society to which the populations, subject to distinct sovereignties, belong.* Hellenic society or European society in the fifth century BC or in the twentieth century AD are realities that we shall call transnational, rather than inter- or supranational.

"A transnational society reveals itself by commercial exchange, migration of persons, common beliefs, organisations that cross frontiers and, lastly, ceremonies or competitions open to the members of all these units. A transnational society flourishes in proportion to the freedom of exchange, migration or communication, the strength of common beliefs, the number of non-national organisations and the solemnity of collective ceremonies.

"It is easy to illustrate the vitality of transnational society by examples. Before 1914 economic exchanges throughout Europe enjoyed a freedom that the gold standard and monetary convertibility safeguarded even better than legislation. Labour parties were grouped into an International. The Greek tradition of the Olympic Games had been revived. Despite the plurality of the Christian Churches, religious, moral and even political beliefs were fundamentally analogous on either side of the frontiers. Without many obstacles a Frenchman could choose Germany as his place of residence, just as a German could decide to live in France. This example, like the similar one of Hellenic society in the fifth century, illustrates the relative autonomy of the inter-state order – in peace and in war – in relation to the context of transnational society. It is not enough for individuals to visit and know each other, to exchange merchandise and ideas, for peace to reign among the sovereign units, though such communications are probably indispensable to the ultimate formation of an international or supranational community.

"The contrary example is that of Europe and the world between 1946 and 1953 (and even today, although since 1953 a certain transnational society, over the Iron Curtain, is being reconstituted). Commercial exchanges between Communist nations and the nations of Western Europe were reduced to a minimum. In so far as they existed, they pertained only to states (at least on one side). The

relations literature is the massive and influential *Paix et guerre entre les nations*, from the English translation of which this extract comes. Other works include *On War* (1959), *Main Currents in Sociological Thought* (1965–8), and *The Imperial Republic: The US and the World, 1945–73* (1975). Quoted from *Peace and War: A Theory of International Relations* (London: Weidenfeld and Nicolson, 1966).

'Soviet individual' had no right to deal with a 'capitalist individual', except by intermediary of public administration. He could not communicate with him without becoming suspect. Inter-individual communications were generally forbidden unless they were the express of inter-state communications: officials and diplomats chatted with their Western colleagues, but essentially in the exercise of their functions.

"This total rupture of transnational society had a truly pathological character: subsequently the Soviet Union has been represented in scientific congresses as in athletic competitions, receives foreign tourists and allows several thousand Soviet citizens to visit the West each year, and no longer strictly forbids personal contacts with Westerners. Russian wives of English aviators have been able to rejoin their husbands. Commercial exchanges have gradually broadened. Yet it is doubtful if this restoration of transnational society has modified essentials: heterogeneity, with regard to the principle of legitimacy, the form of the state and the social structure, remains fundamental. The Christian community has only a limited scope because political faith is stronger than religious faith, the latter having become a strictly private matter; lastly, no organisation, whether political, syndical, or ideological, can unite Soviet and Western citizens unless it is in the open or clandestine service of the Soviet Union. The heterogeneity of the inter-state system irremediably divides transnational society.

"In every period, transnational society has been regulated by customs, conventions or a specific code. The relations that the citizens of a nation at war were authorised to maintain with the citizens of the enemy state were controlled by custom rather than by law. Conventions among states specified the status of the citizens of each established on the territory of the other. Legislation made legal or illicit the creation of transnational movements or the participation in those professional or ideological organisations intended to be supranational.

•   •   •

"States have concluded many agreements, conventions or treaties, some of which concern *transnational society*, while others concern both that and the *international system*. To the first category belong, for instance, postal conventions, those conventions relative to hygiene, to weights and measures; to the second belong questions of maritime law. In the collective interest of states and not of individuals alone, international conventions control the utilisation of seas or rivers, the means of transportation and of communication. The extension of international law expresses the broadening of the collective interests of transnational society or of the international system, the increasing need to submit to law the coexistence of human collectivities, politically organised on a territorial basis, on the same planet, upon the same seas and under the same sky.

"Yet does international law thereby modify the essence of interstate relations? Controversies relating to international law[1] ordinarily occur on an intermediary level between positive law on the one hand and ideologies or philosophies on the other, a theoretical level that might be called, to borrow the expression of F. Perroux, 'implicitly normative'. The obligations of international law are those which result from treaties signed by states or from custom. On the other hand, 'the right of peoples to self-determination', 'the principle of nationalities', 'collective security' are vague formulas, ideologies that influence statesmen, eventually even the interpretation jurists make a positive law. It cannot be said that they serve as the basis of a system of norms, that they involve, for states, specific privileges or duties. Now the jurist who seeks to define the nature of international law attempts to put positive law in a conceptual form, to discover its specific meaning. But this interpretation is not included in positive law itself. The latter allows various interpretations. Juridical theory, even more than economic theory, conceals an element of doctrine. It brings to light the meaning of juridical reality, but this apparent discovery is also an interpretation, influenced by the theoretician's idea of what international law should be.

• • •

"If treaties are the source for international law, it is because the subjects of the law are states. But by the same token, major historical events, those by which the states are born and die, are external to the juridical order. The Baltic states have ceased to exist, they are no longer subjects of law; nothing the Soviet Union does on the territories that, in 1939, were subject to the Estonian or Lithuanian sovereignty any longer relates to international law, at least in the eyes of those of the states that have ceased to 'recognise' Estonia, Lithuania and Latvia (that is, almost every state). When a state is crossed off the map of the world, it is the victim of a violation of international law. If no one comes to its aid, it will soon be forgotten and the state that has delivered the *coup de grâce* will be no less welcome in the assemblies of so-called peaceful nations. Ideologies scarcely permit us to affirm or deny, in the abstract or even in specific circumstances, that certain peoples have or do not have the right to constitute themselves into a nation. In other words, even the un-biased observer often hesitates to assert that a specific violation of the territorial status quo is just or unjust, conforms to or violates, in the long or short run, the interest of the nation directly involved, or of the international community.

"The laws of states come into effect, one might say, the day the states themselves are recognised. Non-organised rebels do not ben-efit from any legal protection. The legitimate authority treats them as criminals and must treat them as such if it wishes to preserve itself. If the rebels are organised and exercise authority over a part of the territory, they obtain certain belligerent rights; the situation becomes that of a civil war and, in practice, the distinction tends to be effaced between 'legitimate authority' and 'rebels', which appear as two rival governments, the outcome of the war deciding the legality or illegal-ity of the belligerents. International law can merely ratify the fate of arms and the arbitration of force. In a few years the Algerian FLN changed from a band of 'rebels' to 'a government in exile'. In a few more, in the name of national sovereignty, it functioned freely within the frontiers of an independent Algeria.

"Jurists have elaborated the rules that are to be imposed upon states or that the latter ought to impose in case of civil war. In fact, practice varies, even in modern times, as a result of many circum-stances. There are, as we have seen, two extreme cases: the hom-ogeneous system can lead to the Holy Alliance, to the common defence of the established order, to the repression by the French army of the Spanish Revolution of 1827 or by the Russian army of the Hungarian Revolution of 1848. On the other hand, in a hetero-geneous system, each camp supports the rebels opposing a regime favourable to the enemy camp. The rules of 'non-intervention' were elaborated and more or less applied during intermediate periods, when neither powers nor revolutionaries had partisans across the frontiers. If there exists neither a popular nor a royal *internationale*, states abstain from siding with the sovereign or the rebels, because in fact the victory of the one or the other does not profoundly affect them.

"Juridical norms need to be interpreted. Their meaning is not always evident and their application to a specific case leads to controversy. Now international law does not determine the organ that, in regard to interpretation, holds the supreme power. If states have not promised to submit their cases to the International Court of Justice,[2] each signatory actually reserves the right of interpreting the treaties in its own way. As states have different juridical and political conceptions, the international law to which they subscribe will involve contradictory interpretations, will be split, in fact, into many orders, based on the same texts but leading to incompatible results.

"Moreover, states need only fail to 'recognise' the same states or the same governments, to reveal the scope of these incompatible interpretations. Supposing that states agree on their conduct with regard to 'rebels' or 'legal government', it is enough that a group of men be rebels in the eyes of some and, in the eyes of others, represent the legal authority, for the juridical order, embracing a heterogeneous system, to reveal its internal contradiction. States will not attach the same descriptions to the same situations of fact. The FLN was treated as a 'band of rebels' by some, as a legal government by others. The government of the German Democratic Republic is a 'so-called government' or an 'authentic government'. The crossing of the 38th Parallel by the North Korean armies was a 'civil-war episode' or an 'act of aggression'.

"It will be objected that such interpretations are not probable to the same degree, and there is no denying the fact. The Korean demarcation line had been drawn by agreement between the Soviet Union and the United States. The FLN 'rebels' exerted no regular power over any part of the Algerian territory in 1958. Objectively, to an observer applying traditional criteria unburdened by ideology, one interpretation would be preferable to another. But why should states apply this interpretation if it is not favourable to their undertakings? States are anxious to maintain the juridical order that suits their common interest when they recognise each other's regimes. But this reciprocal recognition is limited, in a heterogeneous system, by ideological rivalry. Each camp seeks not necessarily to destroy the states in the other camp, but to weaken or overthrow their regimes: juridical interpretation, even when it is concretely improbable, is utilised as an instrument of subversive war, a means of diplomatic pressure.

"Lastly, supposing that the community of states is in agreement as to the true interpretation (in Hungary, the legal government was that of Imre Nagy, the insurrection was staged by the people and not by foreign agitators or American agents), it is still necessary to punish or constrain the state violating the law. Here, too, international law differs, on an essential point, from municipal law. The only effective sanction against the state that has committed the illicit act is the use of force. The guilty state also possesses arms, it does not agree to submit to the judgement of an arbitrator or to the vote of an assembly. Hence an effort to enforce the law will involve a risk of war. Either Gribouille or Gandhi: to punish the violators of the law, a war is precipitated which it was the law's function to forestall; or else the injustice is merely proclaimed and endured, although the conquerors are usually less sensitive to non-violence than the British of the twentieth century.

"Does this international law, which involves neither indisputable interpretation nor effective sanction, which applies to subjects whose birth and death it is limited to certifying, which cannot last indefinitely but which cannot be revised, does this international law belong to the same genre as municipal law? Most jurists reply in the affirmative, and I shall not contradict them. I prefer to show differences between kinds rather than deny membership in the same genre."

Notes

1. We do not add in each case the word *public*. But it is understood that the international law to which we henceforth refer is what jurists call public international law.
2. Or if they remain judges of the application of such a promise.

Nye and Keohane – Transnational Relations and World Politics*

"Students and practitioners of international politics have traditionally concentrated their attention on relationships between states. The state, regarded as an actor with purposes and power, is the basic unit of action; its main agents are the diplomat and soldier. The interplay of governmental policies yields the pattern of behaviour that students

---

* J. S. Nye (1937–). Educated at Princeton, Oxford and Harvard Universities, subsequently professor at Harvard, served as Assistant Under-Secretary of State during the Carter administration. Interested in transnational relations and international politics and organisations. His books include *Pan-African and East African Integration* (1966) and *Power and Interdependence* (with R. O. Keohane) (1977).

   R. O. Keohane (1941–). Studied at Harvard and subsequently taught at Swarthmore and Stanford Universities. Interested in international organisation, international economic relationships and international regimes. Other works include *Power and Interdependence* (with J. S. Nye) (1977), and *After Hegemony* (1984).

   Quoted from *Transnational Relations and World Politics* (Cambridge, Mass.: Harvard University Press, 1970).

of international politics attempt to understand and that practitioners attempt to adjust to or control. Since force, violence and threats thereof are at the core of this interplay, the struggle for power, whether as end or necessary means, is the distinguishing mark of politics among nations. Most political scientists and many diplomats seem to accept this view of reality, and a state-centric view of world affairs prevails.

"It is obvious, however, that the interactions of diplomats and soldiers do not take place in a vacuum. They are strongly affected by geography, the nature of domestic politics in the various states and advances in science and technology. Few would question that the development of nuclear weapons has dramatically altered the nature of twentieth-century international politics or deny the importance of internal political structure for relations between states. From the state-centric perspective geography, technology and domestic politics comprise aspects of the 'environment' within which states interact. They provide inputs into the interstate system but for considerations of analytic convenience are considered to be outside the system.

"The environment of interstate politics, however, does not include only these powerful and well-known forces. A good deal of inter-societal intercourse, with significant political importance, takes place without governmental control. For example, among the major Western countries this includes most trade, personal contact and communication. Furthermore, states are by no means the only actors in world politics. Arnold Wolfers noted more than a decade ago that 'the Vatican, the Arabian-American Oil Company, and a host of other nonstate entities are able on occasion to affect the course of international events. When this happens, these entities become actors in the international arena and competitors of the nation-state. Their ability to operate as international or transnational actors may be traced to the fact that men identify themselves and their interests with corporate bodies other than the nation-state.'

"How do transnational interactions or organisations affect interstate politics? At the most general level our contention is that these transnational relations increase the sensitivity of societies to one another and thereby alter relationships between governments. . . .

"We can become more specific by suggesting five major effects of transnational interactions and organisations, all with direct or indirect consequences for mutual sensitivity and thereby for interstate politics. Four of these may result from transnational interactions even without the presence of transnational organisations, although transnational organisations may produce them as well; the fifth effect necessarily depends on the presence of transnational organisations as autonomous or quasi-autonomous actors. We summarise these effects under the following headings: (1) attitude changes, (2) international pluralism, (3) increases in constraints on states through dependence and interdependence, (4) increases in the ability of certain governments to influence others, and (5) the emergence of autonomous actors with private foreign policies that may deliberately oppose or impinge on state policies. Our categorisation does not pretend to be exhaustive or definitive but is rather designed systematically to suggest some effects of transnational relations on interstate politics.

"Transnational interactions of all types may promote *attitude changes* which may have possible consequences for state policies. . . . [F]ace-to-face interactions between citizens of different states may alter the opinions and perceptions of reality of élites and non-élites within national societies. Transnational communication at a distance, transmitted either electronically or through the printed word, may also promote attitude changes. Similar results may follow, although probably less directly, from transnational transportation, travel and finance. World peace may not, as the IBM slogan has it, come through world trade, but buying a Toyota or a Fiat may very well influence one's attitudes toward Japanese or Italians.

"New attitudes can also be fostered by transnational organisations as they create new myths, symbols and norms to provide legitimacy for their activities or as they attempt to replicate Western beliefs, life-styles or social practices elsewhere in the world. . . .

" . . . What is clear to anyone, however, is that the attitudes produced by transnational relations will not necessarily lead to either universal concord or to the continued growth of transnational relations themselves.

"A second effect of transnational relations is the promotion of *international pluralism*, by which we mean the linking of national interest groups in transnational structures, usually involving transnational organisations for purposes of co-ordination. [There has been a] rapid growth of international nongovernmental organisations which link national organisations having common interests. After their creation these transnational organisations may stimulate the creation of new national affiliates and thus contribute to the internationalisation of domestic politics. But transnational organisations themselves are apparently the product of increasing specialisation of societies combined with the phenomena of transnational communication, travel and transportation which allow people to perceive the possibilities for transnational organisations and to implement their visions. . . .

"It is interesting to note that the first two suggested effects of transnational relations are similar to those that have been most frequently observed by students of European integration. The 'cybernetic' school of theorists has stressed the effect of transactions on mass attitude changes, whereas the 'neo-functionalist' approach emphasises the roles of interest groups and élites, or international pluralism.[1] Theorists of both varieties attempt to specify certain effects of transnational relations that are likely to constrain governments and make their policies more co-operative.

③ "A third effect of transnational relations, the creation of *dependence and interdependence*, is often associated with international transportation and finance. . . . [A]s we have suggested above, one may also become dependent on a transnational communication network or on transnational travel. Even totalitarian states, if their governments want to keep pace scientifically, may have to allow their scientists to read foreign journals and to participate in international conferences. States may also become dependent on transnational organisations, particularly if those organisations provide something – goods, services, information, managerial skills, religious legitimacy – that they need.

"Dependence is translated into policy most directly when certain policies which a government might otherwise follow become prohibitively costly. Integration into a world monetary system may make it impossible for a state to follow an autonomous monetary policy without drastic changes in its economy; dependence on foreign companies for technology, capital and managerial skill may deter less-developed countries from following highly nationalistic and socialistic economic policies. Where transnational organisations become important within a host society, they may alter the patterns of domestic interests so that certain governmental policies become prohibitively costly politically even if they might be feasible economically. Furthermore, new actors, such as multinational enterprises, with new patterns of behaviour may raise difficulties for bureaucratised governments that tend to follow standard operating procedures when reacting to change. Following an effective policy toward a new transnational actor may therefore be too costly on bureaucratic grounds.

important issue →

"Coping with dependence and interdependence raises special problems for large states. Small or weak states may well be able to make their decisions solely by considering the costs and benefits of various alternative policies to themselves, taking into account, of course, the probable reactions of other states. More powerful states, however, must also consider the effects of their own policies on the system of transnational relations. In so far as the state benefits from a particular set of linked transnational arrangements, it will need to exercise care lest a reversion to autonomy in one area sets off retaliatory measures by other large states that could – quite apart from their direct effects on the first state – destroy the entire system. Yet, only if statesmen perceive both interdependence and system-fragility will they allow considerations such as these to constrain their actions. Perceptions of transnational relations by governmental élites are therefore a crucial link between dependence or interdependence, on the one hand, and state policies on the other.

effects of interdependence →

(4) "We have just noted that transnational relations may make all states dependent on forces that none of them controls. But they may have a less evenhanded result as well by creating *new instruments for influence* for use by some governments over others. Among powers of roughly equal weight both sides may be able to take advantage of these instruments, as in the use of the Pugwash Conferences on Science and World Affairs by the United States and the Union of Soviet Socialist Republics to explore questions of arms control. But among unequal states transnational relations may merely put additional means of leverage into the hands of the more powerful states, located at the centre of the transnational networks, to the disadvantage of those which are already weak.

"Governments have often attempted to manipulate transnational interactions to achieve results that are explicitly political: the use of tourists as spies or the cultivation of sympathetic ethnic or religious groups in other states are examples of such 'informal penetration'.[2] Governments may also seek, however, to direct the flow of economic transactions to their own politico-economic ends. Through the use of tariff and quota policies powerful governments may attempt to affect the flow of international trade – for example, they can discourage manufacturing in less developed countries by levying higher tariffs on imports of processed and semiprocessed goods than on raw materials. . . . [G]overnments may try to produce changes in international monetary arrangements by unilateral or multilateral action. In so far as states become dependent on one another, some states may acquire new means by which to influence others.

"Transnational organisations are particularly serviceable as instruments of governmental foreign policy whether through control or willing alliance. This has been evident in the use of United States-based multinational business enterprises by the American government. Thus, in the mid-1960s the United States sought to retard the development of France's nuclear capability not by sending an ultimatum or launching a war but by forbidding IBM-France to sell certain types of computers to the French government. The United States has also used its influence over United States-based multinational enterprises as a means of internationalising its embargoes against the People's Republic of China (Communist China) and Cuba.[3] . . .

5 "The fifth effect of transnational relations on interstate politics depends on the presence of transnational organisations as *autonomous* or quasi-autonomous *actors* in world politics. . . . [S]uch organisations – revolutionary movements, trade unions, multinational business enterprises, and the Roman Catholic church among others – [can] maintain private foreign policies. In some cases these organisations possess enormous resources: In 1965 some 85 business enterprises each had annual sales larger than the gross national products of some 57 voting members of the United Nations.[4] . . . [I]n the monetary field the resources in the hands of some twenty banks can, at least in the short run, render nugatory the efforts of national monetary authorities even in very powerful countries. Thus, autonomous transnational organisations are potential and sometimes actual opponents of governmental policy in a wide variety of areas – whether the policy is liberalising divorce in Italy, living at peace with Israel in the Middle East, enforcing economic plans in France, or maintaining a strong balance-of-payments position in the United Kingdom. The conflict between government and transnational organisations may reflect the policies of a home government standing behind the transnational organisation, but it may also result from differences between the policies of a host government and those of a transnational organisation, without the home government, if any, becoming involved in the dispute.

"Where home governments are involved, the presence of transnational organisations may exert a distinctive effect on the interstate relations that develop. Thus, it would be difficult to understand British–Iranian relations during 1951–53 or American–Cuban relations between 1959 and 1961 without appreciating the role of certain international oil companies in both situations. In these cases actions by the oil companies almost certainly aggravated existing interstate conflicts. It is possible, however, for a transnational organisation also to facilitate good relations between states; certainly, these same oil companies have tried to foster co-operation between the United States and the Arab world. Their efforts have, in turn, been partially foiled by a very powerful transnational force – namely, Zionism – which has worked effectively for good American relations with Israel even at the expense of United States relations with Israel's adversaries. Not only may a struggle between transnational organisations, or between transnational organisations and states, lead to interstate conflict; interstate conflict, such as the Arab–Israeli conflict, may lead to struggles for influence among transnational organisations or movements. The interrelationships are complex and often reciprocal, but they can hardly be ignored."

Notes

1. See Peter J. Katzenstein, "Hare and Tortoise: the Race toward Integration", *International Organisation*, vol. 25, no. 211 (Spring 1971) pp. 290–5.
2. See Andrew M. Scott, *The Revolution in Statecraft: Informal Penetration*, Random House Studies in Political Science, 551 (New York: Random House, 1965); and Richard W. Cottam, *Competitive Interference and Twentieth Century Diplomacy* (Pittsburgh, Pa.: Pittsburgh University Press, 1967).
3. For a discussion of some of the controls used by the United States for these purposes see Jack N. Behrman, *National Interests and the Multinational Enterprise: Tensions among the North Atlantic Countries* (Englewood Cliffs, N.J.: Prentice-Hall, 1970) ch. 7, pp. 101–13.
4. G. Modelski, "The Corporation in World Society", in The Year Book of World Affairs, 1968 (London: Stevens, for the London Institute of World Affairs, 1968) pp. 64–79.

34 The World Society Approach

Some writers on international relations wished to carry the emphasis on transnational contacts still further. Those we have just considered saw non-governmental relationships – between individuals, groups, parties and corporations – as an increasingly significant factor *influencing* relations among states as a whole, but never saw them as replacing the dominant place in international relations occupied by states and their governments. There were others, however, who sought to downplay the significance which states and their governments had traditionally occupied in the study of international relations. They began to place the main focus of their analysis on relationships among non-governmental groups.

This approach to the study of international relations was put forward most prominently by John Burton in a number of his writings and especially in his book *World Society* which appeared in 1972. Part of his thesis was similar to that of the transnational writings which had appeared in the previous few years. He too was concerned to emphasise the rapid growth of non-state relationships. Many developments in the modern world, he pointed out, in culture, science, technology, the media and political thinking, took place across national boundaries and irrespective of them. With the decline in distance developments which might once have had a purely domestic impact, such as revolutions and civil wars, now had an effect that was international as well as national. The distinction between the purely domestic and the international thus progressively declined in importance. Boundaries between states, which were only one of many kinds of boundaries existing between groups of various sorts, thus also became less significant. Perceptions of the world, which mattered most, were therefore changing all the time, so that questions of human rights, racial discrimination and economic development had become more important to most individuals than questions relating to state power. Thus the separate "cobwebs" of relationships established between individuals and groups of different kinds, often transcending state boundaries, became more worthy of research and understanding than relations between states themselves.

Under this way of looking at the world there was clearly a special importance in analysing in detail the various kinds of relationship undertaken between non-governmental groups. C. R. Mitchell, a follower of Burton, sought to undertake an analysis of "relationships" in a volume produced to explore Burton's ideas. He believed that "the structure of the global system" is the pattern of relationships that exist at any one time, and identified six different meanings which can be attributed to the term (though it may be doubted if these are exhaustive). He concludes that the most common meaning given to the term in the world society literature is something like "exchange", "transaction" or "interactions", though it is sometimes used to mean the "possession of shared attributes". His main concern, however, is to stress, like other followers of Burton, the distinction between "legitimised" relationships, being those which rest on a basis of consent, and "non-legitimised" relationships, which are those based on coercion. In his eyes (and those of others of this school) only the former can be regarded as "normal". While earlier writers, they suggested, had been prepared to accept coercive relationships as a normal feature of international society, henceforth only those which were freely entered into on both sides could be regarded as "legitimised".

There were other writers who were increasingly interested in examining the relations between individuals and groups in world society, rather than continuing to study those between states. Some argued that there existed a greater common interest between particular groups and classes in different national states than there were between opposing groups and classes within states. This was a thesis frequently put forward by Marxist writers, and by non-Marxists particularly interested in north–south relations: it was, for example, suggested that workers in the Western world had a common interest with those in developing countries in opposing the exploitation of capitalist multinational corporations, or of imperialistic western governments, and should join in common action against them. Others were interested in a sociological analysis of world society to examine how far, for example, industrialisation, following a common pattern in many different states, had altered traditional social values and created the beginnings of a world-wide class structure. World society was seen as a single interrelated entity, which should be subjected to similar kinds of analysis to that which individual national societies had received in the past. Ralph Pettman, in his *State and Class: A Sociology of International Affairs*, attempted to analyse relationships in world society on this basis. He considered, for example, the growth of an international consciousness, the advent of global norms, the sociology of international law and the sociology of world conflict. In the passage quoted below he sets out his reasons for believing that the world can be studied as a single interrelated society, drawing a contrast between a "pluralist" view, accepting that states, because of the loyalties which they can command, remain the most important grouping existing within world society, and what he calls the "structuralist" perspective, which perceives world society "in terms of the horizontally arranged hierarchies that run across geographic boundaries".

All of these writers, therefore, saw national boundaries as an increasingly irrelevant factor dividing individuals within world society. The fundamental question which the approach raised was whether an analysis under which boundaries between states, and the actions that are taken by states, were relegated to that secondary role could be reconciled with the realities of state power in the modern world.

* * *

Burton – International Relations and World Society*

"It is because of the past preoccupation with relations between nations that 'International Relations' is the title that is usually given to the discipline concerned with the study of world politics and world society. It is an unfortunate title for our present purposes. States sometimes comprise different national groups, such as English, Irish, Scots and Welsh in the state of the United Kingdom. If we were concerned only with relations among the 150 or so independent political units of today, 'inter-state' would be a more appropriate term than 'inter-national' relations. The general idea that most of us have of world society is one that is based on maps of the world which

---

* From John Burton (1915–). Originally an Australian government official, he became Professor of International Relations at University College, London, where he became influential especially because of his development of the "world society" approach which he expounded in his book of that name. Also author of *International Relations, a General Theory* (1965) and *Systems, States, Diplomacy and Rules* (1968). Quoted from *World Society* (Cambridge: Cambridge University Press, 1972).

emphasise state boundaries, on historical studies which concentrate on relations among governments. We are familiar with a set of national symbols, customs and institutions that make us feel different from peoples in other states. For this reason we think about world affairs as though they were confined to relations between states. But the study of world society is not confined to relations among states or state authorities. There are important religious, language, scientific, commercial and other relationships in addition to a variety of formal, non-governmental institutions that are world-wide.

"This is not just a matter of choosing between different words. We are choosing an approach when we choose to speak of world society and not inter-national relations. The study of world society is a much wider study than the relations of units within it. It is, of course, possible and useful to study inter-state trading relations and inter-governmental institutions of various kinds. It is also possible and useful to make comparative studies of the ways in which different governments behave and how their different institutions function. But these studies based on states cannot give us that understanding we seek of world society, and in particular its processes and trends. Obviously, any separation of domestic politics and world politics is arbitrary and probably misleading. For example, these state studies cannot tell us much about the nature of conflict among communities that originates within states and spills over into world society. The political and social life of people within states, which is always altering with changed thinking and new technologies, influences relations among states. This is clear where there are sudden and fundamental changes such as have taken place this century in Russia and in China. Less dramatic internal political and social changes are altering relations among states year by year. Indeed, it is because this is so that the more powerful states such as the United States of America and the Union of Soviet Socialist Republics endeavour to influence these changes in other states.

"State boundaries are significant, but they are just one type of boundary which affects the behaviour of world society. There are local municipal boundaries such as those of the Greater London Council, which include more people than do many states, and in which administrative functions are carried out such as those that occur within small states. At the other end of the scale there are boundaries that include several states, such as those of the European Common Market and the Organisation of African Unity. There are also non-geographical boundaries to be taken into account. These are based on functions, for example, the boundaries that separate the work of the World Health Organisation from the Food and Agricultural Organisation. These cut across geographical or state boundaries. The world geographical map depicting states cannot show these – but they exist and an image of world society is not complete without them.

"If states controlled all world activities even to the limited extent that they control the activities of an inter-state institution like the World Health Organisation, then one could extend the idea of inter-state relations to include all activities in world society. But there are many transactions in addition to those initiated and regulated by governments within states that cut across state boundaries. Indeed, new ideas and philosophies cut across state boundaries sometimes despite attempts by governments to prevent this happening. There is now one world of science. No state can afford to cut itself off from scientific and technological developments. It is not possible to import just a selection of scientific thoughts. From our own studies we know how knowledge in one subject relates to knowledge in another. Natural science and political thought cannot be separated because the one employs the methodologies and thinking of the other, and developments in the one field lead to developments in the other. Technological inventions change political and social life wherever they occur. The working life of a factory worker in a developed socialist country is little different from the life of a factory worker in another industrialized country. Similarly, administrations and cultures tend to converge with the spread of ideas, and this will occur even more rapidly when television is as widely received as radio is now.

"If we employ the term 'world society' instead of 'international relations', if we approach our study in this global way instead of the more traditional 'national' way, we will tend to have a wider focus, to ask questions that are more fundamental and important to civilisation, and be able to assess better the relevance of our own national behaviour to the wider world environment.

•   •   •

"The conventional map of the world is a physical one: it shows geographical relationships, over which are sometimes drawn political boundaries. It does not tell us much about processes or behaviour. The same proportional space and importance are given to seas and deserts as are given to ports and cities. There do exist diagrammatic maps that tell us where populations are concentrated, where resources are to be found, how many newspapers are read and other

information such as this. But even these do not give us much information about behaviour, or more particularly, about transactions and
links that exist. We are familiar with maps of the world showing air
and shipping routes. What we really need to have, either in map form
or conceptually, is an image of world society that shows behaviour by
showing these linkages. If we could superimpose on successive sheets
of transparent paper air-passenger movements per week, telegraphic
flows, ethnic and language relations, movements of scholars, technical advisers, migration, tourism, and all other transactions, we would
begin to build up a picture of relationships which would help to
explain behaviour in world society far better than traditional maps.
Maps were designed to show people how to get from point *A* to point
B. They are useful for this purpose. But they have been used for
purposes other than this. They have had the effect of creating in our
minds this geographical image of world society. What we need is a
map or concept that tells us something about behaviour. The difference is like the difference between a set of photos of a car showing its
headlamps and other details, and the type of diagram an electrical
engineer would draw showing the wiring links within the electrical
system. We cannot understand a car by looking at it. Its processes
need to be analysed, and then we can understand it, and remedy any
failures.

"If we had been brought up with such maps on the wall, if we were
not so consciously aware of states whenever we looked at a map of
the world, and best of all, if we had never seen an ordinary map of
the world, we would think far more in terms of world society and far
less in terms of a system of states. We would approach closer to a
realistic model of world society. . . .

"Which is the more representative model of the world – the world
of continents, islands and states or the world of transactions? This is
not a superficial question. There are two different models or images
presented. If we adopt the nation-state one we will use the language
of relations between states and their relevant power, and have one
set of solutions to problems of conflict and world organisation. If we
adopt the transactions one we will use a different language to describe world society, and have a different set of solutions to world
problems. For example, we will be greatly concerned with political
and social conditions within states because it is these which, in this
model, determine relationships in world society, including relations
between states.

"Let us dwell on this a little more. The model we have at the back of our minds determines our interpretation of events, our theories and our policies. For example, the billiard-ball model is a power model – world society is seen to be organised by the relative power of each unit. There are matters of domestic jurisdiction of no concern to others, not even the United Nations. There are legal political entities that have a right to protect themselves and to expect assistance from others, including the United Nations, if they are threatened, even though they have no popular support – no legitimised status. Collective security is the means of preventing 'aggression'. Economic development is the means to social and political stability.

"The model depicting transactions invites a different approach to world problems. The source of conflict between states is in internal politics, in failures by states to adjust to altering conditions, in the struggle of states to preserve their institutions, and in the conflict between states and systems that cut across state boundaries. Conflict cannot be prevented by external coercion, or by great power threats. Communal conflict – race, religious, ideological – invites sympathies across state boundaries and promotes international conflict. The role of authorities is to assist in the making of adjustments to altering conditions so that conflict between interests within the state, and the wider world systems, do not occur. Development and stability must rest on internal conditions or political organisation, that is, a high degree of participation so that authorities are strongly legitimised. In accordance with this model, a form of world government cannot rest on collective security, and must be based on the transactions inherent in functional organisations that are, by their nature, universal in potential membership. Viable political units can be very small, provided there is a high level of transactions with the wider environment. Communications, and not power, are the main organising influence in world society.

"There is an important practical question raised here. An image of world society that comprises separate state entities, each potentially hostile to others, leads understandably to defensive policies. Is the image a realistic one, or are the conflicts that occur and seem to validate the image merely the consequences of our having this image? An image of world society that depicts transactions, controlled and regulated by local state and international authorities, with a view to securing the maximum benefits from interdependence without loss of security, leads reasonably to integrative policies. Is the image a realistic one, or are the functional arrangements, world corporations and other evidences that seem to validate the image merely the consequence of us having this image? It is possible that the cobweb image is the realistic one, except in so far as lack of confidence has created the one comprising separate and fearful entities. Thus created it becomes part of our perceived reality."

Mitchell – Relationships within World Society*

"Probably the area in which the study of international relations generally has moved furthest away from the state-centric model has been in the development of a whole list of non-state actors that participate in and affect international politics. This trend reflects the realisation that, while national governments remain a potent influence within some parts of the global system, other elements have become equally, and in some cases more, influential. . . .

"In some ways, . . . arguments about what types of entity might form elements in the transnational systems making up world society are peripheral to [the world society] approach's main contribution to innovatory thinking. The crucial concept is less the entities engaged in a particular network of relationships and more the nature, and changing nature, of those relationships themselves. In all work on the world society approach, existing and altering relationships are the key focus of attention. The *structure* of the global system consists of the patterns of relationships that exist at any one time. *Processes* in that system consist of the manner in which these relationships change and evolve naturally, are deliberately altered, or are completely severed as when a boundary is imposed or reactivated and existing interaction prevented. In many senses, the *relationship* is the unit of analysis in the world society approach, and a clear delineation of the nature and classification of relationships is an important part of refining that approach.

•   •   •

". . . Efforts to characterise relationships, or at least to differentiate between them, are familiar in any work on international politics.

---

* From C. R. Mitchell. A lecturer at the City University, London. A follower of John Burton and the "world society" school. This contribution comes from a collective work dedicated to Burton, devoted to expounding that approach. Author of *The Structure of International Conflict* (1981). Quoted from "World Society a Cobweb: States, Actors and Systemic Processes", in M. Banks (ed.), *Conflict in World Society* (Brighton, Sussex: Harvester, 1984).

Usually, these use some crude and often ambiguous 'main quality' approach, classifying networks of relationships as 'military', 'political', 'economic', 'social', 'ideological' without bothering to specify clearly what criteria are used to distinguish one type of relational network from another.

"Such ways of characterising relationships obviously play a part in the world society approach, but in many ways the extension of the approach into prescriptive analysis (one of its great strengths) is based on the concept of relationships that possess the quality of being *legitimised*. This conception is a central feature. It also suggests that some networks of relationships are durable and can exist in their own right, while others are imposed and only kept in existence by the coercive and ultimately self-defeating efforts of those entities with some usable political power or economic resource.

"Several points need to be noted about this concept of *legitimised relationships*. The first, frequently stressed by all who use a world society approach, is that legitimised relationships are not the same as 'legal' or 'legalised' relationships. The latter are frequently established by force and maintained through coercion or the threat of sanctions by the stronger against the weaker (many 'peace' treaties are of this nature). The whole point about legitimised relationships is that the entities involved in them accept them as being beneficial and, in some profound sense, 'right'. This conception can, paradoxically, include some relationships that are objectively or statistically unequal or one-sided, and others which involve the use of authority to cause elements to act in ways which, frequently, they would rather not. The point about this latter circumstance is that the action occurs, and the relationship is valued and retained, not because of any coercive element, but because the right of one element to demand conformity is recognised by the conforming units. A chairman is obeyed because he *is* chairman. His role is recognised as necessary and (even) beneficial. Hence, it is accepted, even when he demands conforming behaviour from members of his committee or cabinet. In slightly different terms, the crucial factor about a legitimised relationship is *its acceptance by those involved*. Legitimacy is not necessarily the same as symmetry or equality, although empirically there seems to be a close connection between the two concepts (especially in societies where egalitarianism is a major value).

"The second point about relationships which possess legitimacy is that they tend to be self-sustaining, through their acceptability and because they fulfil some strong need for those involved. In contrast, non-legitimised relationships are those which are not acceptable to some of those involved and which thus contain elements of coercion or threat. The latter are maintained less because they are self-supporting than because the satisfied possess the means of imposing sanctions for ending the relationship on the dissatisfied, while the dissatisfied do not. Hence, according to Burton, a non-legitimised relationship contains strong elements of power without which the relationship would change or terminate because it fails to fulfil the needs of all those involved, and is unacceptable to some of them. The world society approach, therefore, makes a clear and important distinction between relationships among elements that are legitimised and those which are 'power' relationships involving overt or covert coercion.

"Classifying relationships into those which are legitimised and those which are not returns us to the question of criteria. In seeking legitimacy, how one categorises a particular relationship involves no recognition of some quality *inherent in the relationship itself*. Characterising a relationship as 'legitimised' or 'non-legitimised' involves an assessment of the views, feelings or attitudes of the entities involved. This goes some way towards explaining how relationships can change radically over time without any apparent alteration in their fundamental structure as, for example, colonial and imperial relationships gradually altered. What is acceptable to entities at one point in time can, with changes in the views and values of one or other of them, become wholly non-legitimised at a later period. Legitimacy is in the eye of the beholder – or, perhaps more accurately, in the eyes of those involved.

"A final point about classifying relationships into *legitimised* and *non-legitimised* categories is that one uses a totally different starting point from conventional analyses to ask questions about the fundamental nature of global society and what are its aberrations. For example, the world society approach begins by assuming that legitimised relationships should be regarded as a 'norm', in both a statistical and a prescriptive sense. In other words, in contemporary global society it is usual to find networks of relationships that are accepted by those involved and are thus both functional for the elements interacting, and self-supporting because of the mutually recognised benefits conferred by the transactions involved. The legitimised relationship is the norm, in the sense that the sheer number of such relationships far outweighs non-legitimised relationships involving power and coercion.

"The contrast between this assumption and that customarily underlying power political, state-centric approaches hardly needs emphasising. In conventional analysis, it is assumed that coercive relationships are the norm. They are inevitable, given the structure of the inter-state system. Peace, accepted authority, legitimised exchanges and lack of coercion are the exceptions which are curiosities to be explained. In the world society approach, these latter phenomena are held to be normal, and the task becomes one of explaining the unusual circumstances that turn elements away from customary patterns of interaction and necessitate their behaving in some abnormal way. A whole new perspective emerges from such a simple reversal of assumptions.

"Moreover, the world society approach also posits that legitimised relationships are the norm in a prescriptive sense; that is to say, the search for peace and a harmonious global society can best begin by rejecting the conception that stability and absence of violence can most surely be assured by the use of threats, coercion and deterrence. These are the very signs that existing relationships are non-legitimised and will inevitably lead to further conflict and violence so that their continued use will inevitably be counter-productive. What is needed is a search for ways of changing existing coercive relationships into those acceptable to elements involved. This would remove the need for threat systems to ensure continuation, or 'stability', to use the polite euphemism. In the best of all possible worlds, relationships would be entirely legitimised and durable because of this fact. (As can be seen, there is a strong infusion of anarchist assumptions in the world society approach.)

"It is acknowledged by scholars who use this approach that such a complete Utopia is unlikely to be attainable. Even moving in the direction of fewer coercive and more legitimised interactions and exchanges presents major practical problems, not least in convincing decision makers of the long run counterproductive nature of coercion and the use of power to maintain relationships that are unacceptable to others. However, world society analysis does at least offer an alternative guide for action, a way out of the logical and empirical *impasse* that the use of state-centric, power political ideas produces, where the very factors that are supposed to produce security, stability and absence of overt violence frequently give rise to the very opposite."

Pettman – World Society as a "System"*

"What is this world society that the cultural consequences of industrialisation and modernisation help us define? What are its conceptual competitors?

"The most conspicuous and the most widely noted unit in global affairs is that of the 'state'. The contemporary complement of diverse bodies we collect together under this label make up in their manifold interrelations the 'state system' so called. Though opinion differs about their significance and their desirability we may also note now many non-state actors with quasi-autonomous global interconnections of their own. When we add in these so-called 'transnationals'[1] we discern a more general social cosmos that surrounds the central network of states; we expand our understanding of the ways in which human society seems to be arranged.

"It is useful to think at first in terms of a continuum, of a scale along which increasingly more intimate social relationships occur; to picture the world initially as a 'system', growing progressively more 'social' as we examine in greater detail the various qualities that global interactions display. A *system* of states, their representatives in touch with each other on a more or less regular basis who feel they must not only account for the behaviour of some at least of their confrères but also accommodate the fact of the system as a whole, is one fundamental facet of world affairs. The concept of a 'system' is used here in its technical sense to mean a number of units alike enough to form a set and sufficiently independent for a change in the state of one unit to cause repercussions for others. They operate within a boundary that marks the major discontinuities in the transactions and traffic between them and their environment. As such, the *inter-state* system is 'closed' since the interactions fall entirely within the system boundaries, which are the world. One can still discriminate between a global set of countries as an *energy* system or as an *economic* system for example, and these separate systems can be seen as part of each other's environment. In this sense the system of states is not closed but 'open'.

---

* From R. Pettman. Studied at the London School of Economics before becoming a research Fellow in the Department of International Relations in the Australian National University in Canberra. His book *Human Behaviour and World Politics*, described as a "transdisciplinary" introduction, discusses, *inter alia*, futurology, cybernetics, bio-politics and psycho-politics. Quoted from *State and Class: A Sociology of International Affairs* (London: Croom Helm, 1979).

"Depicting the world in terms of a collection of discrete bodies whose only point of contact is some generalised idea of 'interaction' does not carry us very far, however. Certain 'behaviouralist' analyses of the 1950s and 1960s attempted to move beyond the concept of a 'states' system and to confront human-kind as a single mass of four or five thousand million people, organised for some purposes into states but for others into interrelated economic, scientific, cultural, ideological and religious sets that might not be so apparent but are still real. Less explicit regularities and less formalised non-state collectivities were seen to emerge that might well be concentrated into territorial and administrative conclaves called 'states', but were also dispersed beyond them. The world was made up, in this view, of universal networks covering many parts of it, plus regional interactions and those of more localised entities such as the family – the whole being infinitely complex and confused.

"A set of relationships, a system that is, can be abstracted from the human totality by analytic means, but the persons involved in one set are often involved in others. An oil magnate, for example, a member of a sectional trading and resource network, may also belong to a regional set of an ethnic or cultural kind. Separating out a system becomes a process of reduction. Rather than identifying people as such as they interact with each other, we highlight for the purpose of the enquiry the set of relevant roles particular individuals play under specified circumstances. The world then appears

like millions of cobwebs superimposed one upon another, covering the whole globe . . . Each separate cobweb . . . represent[ing] a separate system – trade flows, letters exchanged, tourist movements, aircraft flights, population movements and transactions in ideas, cultures, languages and religions, traffic flows within towns and social interactions within village communities.[2]

• • •

". . .'World society' is structured not only in terms of states and trans-state entities but also in terms of socio-economic classes. Which is not to assert that the process of global integration has proceeded at different depths, with one or the other phenomenon historically prime. We are simply dealing with two aspects of one extraordinary event, that is, the rise and dissemination of the industrial mode of production by both capitalist and collectivist means. State formation and class formation are the competing and the complementary social consequences of this process on a world scale. We have two dimensions to account for, both of which detail the singular development of a sense of coalescence, and of conflict too.

"The vision implicit here is not new. Those with an interest in the process of law have frequently been led to extend their feeling for the network of rules that knit societies together to global society as a whole. Though the advent of nation-states has made this generalising feeling more difficult to sustain, the Grotian notion of one human grouping under 'natural' edicts of some kind has been restated in a modernised form many times. Grotius himself transmitted a tradition that reached back to the Stoics; to the Platonic idea of an overarching body of ultimate values that all might apprehend if they could only be brought to recognise them. These values were considered to be a phenomenon apart, an 'impersonal system of pure ideas',[3] and for two millennia the concept of such a system has remained an emergent principle of world affairs. In its differing European modes it has helped sustain the expectation, entirely unreasonable perhaps, but a powerful picture none the less, that there must ultimately arise one cultural framework to which all people can refer, and maybe a single political system along with it. The rulers of the Roman Empire drew heavily on just such a sense of unification, of that part of the world at least that lay within their ken, and Cicero in particular was concerned to advance and defend very general notions of justice and peace. The Church that won the patronage of Rome adopted the same imperial outlook, though the attempt to establish a spiritual cosmos of Christian citizens failed finally to stall the process of schism, or to contain more secular conflicts, or indeed, to carry the day against the equally potent universalising force of Islam. Non-religious philosophers, generalising from their diverse understanding of the history of the human enterprise, came to locate the potential for global coalescence in other places, but the urge to define a fundamental set of ideas for all persons everywhere and for the world society immanent in that concept has remained much the same.

"We can move toward this vision, as I have mentioned already, from the idea of separate interacting states, or from our image of a plethora of pre-capitalist social formations and the growth of a world capitalist economy and within it a global class system, in particular, a global bourgeoisie. Different methodological paradigms have been evolved to interpret these two perceived processes, and any theory of world society can be classified in terms of one or the other arena of analytic discourse and its shifting and fashionable concerns. I refer in fact to what I call the 'pluralist' and the 'structuralist' approaches, though I do not mean to suggest that these are the only ways of approaching the abiding issues in world affairs or that there has been no traffic in ideas from one arena to the other. On the contrary, throughout the history of the study of the subject we find a confused and contentious debate between the two. Within each approach, furthermore, there are important differences of emphasis and argument. But the distinctions stand, and I would maintain that they draw our attention to the major divisions of analytic interest in the social field.

"A *pluralist* view of the world grants the groups – most obviously the states – of which the world is composed a quite distinctive status. Such groups are seen to be the ultimate and preferred source of self-identification and command. 'Pluralism' depicts a world divided into a multitude of states of unequal size but equally dedicated to the pragmatic pursuit of their interests and moral desires, joined in strategic alliance, the balance of power forming and reforming, and the conflicts between blocs of states potentially domesticated in the shared interests of all. A *structuralist* perspective confronts global politics in terms of the horizontally arranged hierarchies that run across geographic boundaries, throwing into high relief the pattern whereby 'overdeveloped' states reproduce characteristic socio-economic and political forms within 'underdeveloped' ones in terms of the uneven spread of the industrial mode of production, the uneven and complex character of the class systems that have grown up in its wake, and the current global division of labour.

•   •   •

"What of the concept of 'world society'? *Pluralist* scholars, confronted by analytic attempts to accommodate the actors other than 'states' which now tread the global stage, are apt to proclaim a return to the notion already introduced and common to the history of Western political thought of one potential political entity embracing all humankind. In doing so they tend to underplay the advent of more novel events. They embrace the sort of analysis that identifies the twentieth century with the seventeenth century, for example, without due consideration for the fact that the Industrial Revolution has intervened, an event of paramount significance which marks, in one analyst's words, 'the most fundamental transformation of human life in the history of the world recorded in written documents'.

"This point can be applied to our understanding of the state. Thus it has been argued that: 'The modern highly complex large-group

574 Basic Texts in International Relations

society is . . . only possible upon the basis of modern technology, and any comparison with social groups like the states of the 19th century is in reality entirely misleading.'[4] Though such things as the balance of power can be found wherever systematic circumstances allow them, whoever selects to see the notion of 'world society' as a *revival*, as a return to an earlier set of conceptions, will still have to account for the much changed circumstances of an industrialised world. Whether in the end he or she decides to retain the label or call what is happening by a different name, such identity as exists must be established in detail – it cannot be assumed.

" 'Structuralist' contributors can be equally one-eyed. Preoccupied with the patterns of global class, they tend to downplay the fact of the state and the independent force the notion of nationalism and its proliferating ideological progeny exert upon world affairs. The contemporary approach is a universalist one and the state system, in Marxist/Leninist terms in particular, is seen as the political product of and vehicle for a pervasive process of socio-economic 'exploitation'. One should add, however, that this is a caricature, and that structuralist theorists have also been led to more sophisticated attempts to accommodate the fact of states and of statehood. Many scholars from peripheral countries are hostile not so much towards Western claims that (in 'pluralist' terms) an integrated world society of states may be seen to be developing or ought to be doing so, but rather towards the fact that to them, in 'structuralist' terms, it already exists. They then attack the process of rationalisation, common in the West, which portrays the contemporary world hierarchy as beneficial or inevitable or fit to be defended for other reasons. Which has led them in turn to define development strategies as often as not in terms of self-reliance, and to advocate the attempt to rescue a modicum of economic and political sovereignty from their penetrated or neo-colonised plight by neo-mercantilist or other such means."

Notes

1. The usual list includes multinational business corporations, international trade unions, professional bodies, educational, religious and cultural organisations and political parties.
2. J. Burton, *Systems, States, Diplomacy and Rules* (London: Cambridge University Press, 1968) p. 8. Also *World Society* (London: Cambridge University Press, 1972) pp. 35–45.
3. F. Znaniecki. *Modern Nationalities: A Sociological Study* (Urbana, Ill.: University of Illinois Press, 1952) p. 174.
4. E. Hobsbawn, *Industry and Empire* (London: Weidenfeld and Nicolson, 1968) p. 1.

35 The International Society Approach

The "world society" approach had presented an image of a world in which relations between individuals were more important than those between states. To some extent this appeared to reflect a moral attitude. Relations between states included the worst features of the international scene – warfare, imperialism, economic exploitation, domination and dependence – and so were seen as bad. Therefore, it was implied, relations between individuals and groups, which lacked these features, were good ("legitimate"). But this raised the underlying question: did this approach, whether or not it conjured up a picture of a more attractive world, accurately describe the *reality* of the world as it exists today? In other words, was the power and influence of states perhaps greater in the real world than some of these writings suggested? Because governments dispose of armed force which is far greater than that available to non-official groups, because governments control, more or less directly, the economic relations which can be conducted by their nationals with other states, because they represent their people in international organisations of all kinds, which themselves exert a significant influence on relationships (among peoples as well as among governments), did not the decisions and actions of governments have an impact on world affairs – including the relationships undertaken by individuals and groups – far greater than the decisions and actions of any other entities on the world scene? Even if it was true, therefore, that unofficial contacts of many kinds, especially those undertaken by large business corporations, were more significant than ever before – and would probably become more so still – did not national states remain the most important single feature of international society, if only because they so strongly influenced, or even controlled, every other kind of relationship which could be undertaken? And that being so, must not their relations with each other remain at the centre of the study of international relations?

Partly because of doubts of this kind, other writers, again mainly European, adopted a somewhat different approach. They too recognised the increasingly close relationships across frontiers which had been brought about by modern means of communication. They too rejected the obsessive concern with power and power relationships which the "realists" had adopted, as well as the mechanistic image put forward by system analysts. They too accepted that states had become joined within an increasingly closely interrelated international society. But unlike those of the world-society school, they acknowledged the primary importance of state actions and decisions in the working of that society.

This might be termed the "international society" approach. Such writers recognised that the international system had many of the features of a small-scale society, and that it might therefore be studied by methods not unlike those used by sociologists in studying small-scale societies. Thus Raymond Aron, himself in origin a student of sociology, had already in the 1950s advocated, as a tool in the study of international relations, some form of "historical sociology". In the passage below he presents arguments in favour of this approach to the discipline. His aim is, in the first place, not so much to apply the techniques of sociology to the society of states as a whole, but to undertake sociological analysis of *individual* national societies, with a view to determining which type is most frequently associated with particular kinds of foreign policy. This approach might, for example, be able to show whether states with a particular kind of political system, decision-making system or political doctrines, were associated with particular kinds of policy. Again attempts could be made to show whether changes in the economic system of a state influenced its conduct of diplomacy; or whether demographic pressures, or high levels of unemployment, are associated with particular types of policy. Historical sociology might also be of value in comparing different *systems* of international relations, as distinguished by the type of diplomatic relations undertaken within them, the power relationships between the members, the military technology available, the nature of the state system, the influence of domestic political pressures and the nature of foreign policy aims, together determining which factors influenced the incidence of war.

Other writers have been interested in the use of sociology to analyse the society of states as a whole. Though they recognised that sociological analysis could be applied to "world society" conceived as a single unit, and disregarding national boundaries, they found it more useful, given the dominant role played by states, the superior power available to them and the strong loyalty still afforded to them, to analyse the *international* (rather than the world) society: that is, the society of states. Because that society contains many features found in the small-scale societies that are studied by anthropologists and sociologists – a regular pattern of relations among their members, established forms of intercourse, a system of stratification, traditional institutions, norms of conduct, acknowledged procedures for resolving disputes, even sometimes an embryonic system of authority – similar concepts and techniques may be useful in analysing the way each such society operates. Thus the second extract in this section suggests the way a number of these concepts – authority, legitimacy, status, class, socialisation, social structure, social norms, institutions and ideology – can be applied within the wider society of states.

Hedley Bull also believed that the society of states shows many of the characteristics of a smaller society, even if it is a society of an anarchical kind: that is, a society without government. In his book *The Anarchical Society*, he explored a number of features of this apparent paradox: the degree to which there can exist an international law within such a society; the conflict between order and justice in a system where justice is maintained by self-help and group action; the role of great powers, and of the balance of power between them, in maintaining an international order; and similar questions. In the passage below he compares this anarchical international society with primitive societies, which are equally without government or any centralised political institutions. He shows that in both cases conformity to the rules by which order is maintained comes about by conditioning and inertia, rather than through the sanctions which a national government can exercise, and that in both cases a condition for maintaining order is a recognition among the society's members of a primitive system of rules. The only ultimate sanctions for punishing violation of the rules is the unilateral use of force, whether by individuals or groups acting together, which, within such a society, is seen as a legitimate way of protecting the rights of the members. He recognises, none the less, that there exist important differences between the two types of society: the lack of any territorial basis of authority in primitive societies, the lack of cultural homogeneity in international society, and the lack of any religious authority, myth or magic, to sustain the social order in the latter case. Against this, there exist in international society various special factors which help to sustain order, not usually available in primitive societies: the possibility of a balance of power among the members, the potential for mobilising the common interest of member-states in stable coexistence, the formulation of rules of conduct, and the existence of primitive institutions for maintaining order.

Each of these writers, therefore, like those in the previous group, is concerned with world society; but they conceive of it in a different way. They recognise the importance of non-state transactions and relationships (though often they are concerned mainly with their importance as an influence on the behaviour of governments). But they believe that the actions which are of primary importance in determining the character of the society and the welfare of individuals within it are those which are undertaken by and between governments. And they therefore devote their primary attention to the interactions which take place between governments and states within the common international society to which they all belong.

* * *

Aron – Historical Sociology*

"Political scientists have a tendency to simplify in two respects, both of which are dangerous. The first simplification is that of the historical school, which would end by describing the vicissitudes of international relations without explaining them; while the second is that of the 'realist' school, which tends to hypostasise the States and their so-called national interests, to attribute to those interests a sort of patency or permanence, and to regard events as reflecting nothing but the calculation of power and the compromise necessary to achieve a balance.

"The mere story of events teaches us nothing unless it is given form and meaning by reference to concepts; unless it entails an effort to distinguish the essential from the subsidiary, and deep-lying trends from accidents; and unless it seeks to compare the means, differing from age to age, by which international relations and wars are conducted. The realistic simplification is liable to distort the real psychology of the rulers, and to lead to neglect of certain factors which are sometimes of decisive importance, such as the influence of

---

* From Raymond Aron (1905–84). (For biographical details see p. 546.) Quoted from "Historical Sociology as an Approach to International Relations", in *The Nature of Conflict* (Paris: UNESCO Publications Centre, 1957).

systems of government and ideologies on the conduct of diplomatic affairs and the character of conflicts or wars. . . .

"Let us for example consider the fifth and sixth headings – the influence of domestic policy on the foreign policy of States, and the view that the rulers take of foreign policy. All branches of social study can play their part in clarifying these questions. If, for instance, we were seeking to clarify the present situation, we should begin by investigating the question of how decisions concerning foreign policy are taken in a particular country and under a particular system of government (e.g., in the United States of America). Naturally we should not confine ourselves to elucidating the constitutional rules, but should seek to understand the real office and the real influence of the President, his advisers, the National Security Council, the armed forces, the press, public opinion – or at least what goes by that name – and so on. This type of study is within the sphere of political science (or political sociology, for the name matters little); it is obviously easier to carry out in a democratic country than in authoritarian or totalitarian countries (it was only afterwards that we learnt how decisions were taken in the Third Reich). The information it furnishes gives us only part of the picture and may not remain true indefinitely. The part played by the President in the United States of America changes with the individuals who hold that office. The more concrete and the more detailed the study, the more likelihood there is of arriving at the truth, but the truth arrived at may be made up of so many unrelated particles as to be useless for practical purposes.

"When we consider the foreign policy of the Soviet Union, two types of investigation come to mind. An attempt might be made to analyse the process by which decisions are reached, the relations between the various authorities (what influence, if any, is exercised by the military? what individual influence is exercised by a particular member of the Politburo or the Praesidium?). This type of analysis, as applied to contemporary phenomena in the Soviet Union, is more or less useless because we have so little information to go on. On the other hand, we can make an analysis of the system of thought and action characteristic of the Communists since 1917. We can discover this system by studying the writings of Communists and their conduct and, as a result of this analysis, we can predict with a reasonable probability of accuracy how the leaders of the Soviet Union will act in given circumstances (specialists explained in advance, for instance, why the leaders of the Soviet Union would immediately reject the Marshall Plan offer, why they would not attempt an invasion of

Western Europe at a time when that part of the continent was completely disarmed, etc.). As prediction has always been regarded as one of the tests of success in science, the studies which make such prediction possible must be admitted to have some scientific value.

"Could similar studies be undertaken on other countries? The results would doubtless not be exactly similar, because American statesmen do not follow so rigid a doctrine as Soviet statesmen. There is no common doctrine to which the whole American political class subscribes; there are schools with different ideas about the part to be played by the United States (in the Soviet Union, the most that can be said is that there are 'trends' within the Bolshevik party, but these trends are always subordinate to the same body of doctrine). The result is that the world is uncertain about the main lines of the United States' foreign policy. In 1914 the Americans were scarcely expected to intervene in 1917; in 1939, the Germans feared they might intervene, the French and the British hoped that they would, but neither side was sure. A less important decision, such as the American intervention in Korea, was probably a surprise to the members of governments most directly concerned.

"The degree of predictability in a country's foreign policy is a matter of fact which can be objectively observed. This fact, in its turn, requires explanation. Investigations may follow two different lines: Is the fact attributable to the special characteristics of the nation or to its system of government? To what extent is it attributable to the nation and to what extent to democracy? It is impossible to answer these questions without having recourse to the most distinctive method of historical sociology – comparative study. A comparison may be made of the way in which foreign policy is determined in the United States of America or Great Britain, of the differing parts played by Congress and Parliament, and of the influence of the press. In the same way, we may show – or at least attempt to show – the special conditions imposed in the conduct of foreign policy by a democratic form of government (the policy-makers probably have less tactical freedom). Lastly, an investigation may be made, on the basis of past history, into the conceptions of national interest of which we hear so much. Is it true that national interest is always the same, however the form of government may change? To what extent is Soviet diplomacy, in the long run, similar to that conducted by Czarist Russia or to that which would have been conducted by a democratic Russia? The method of historical comparison can and must be used to test the correctness of the theories advanced to explain phenomena by reference to geography, population or economics.

"There are diplomatic traditions in all countries, allegedly based upon the lessons of history. On analysis, these lessons turn out to represent no more than the relative permanence, or the repetition, of certain typical groupings of powers. On the assumption that we have a diplomatic field of given scope and that the same States remain in this field, certain situations are obviously bound to recur. France will seek the support of the power situated to the east of the neighbouring, rival power and so the tradition of the pincer alliance grows up. In a balance of power policy, this tradition is good only if several conditions are fulfilled. The diplomatic field must not be altered (when Europe becomes part of a world-wide field, the constants of yesterday cease to be applicable); the strength of the principal parties must remain approximately the same (if the eastern country becomes as strong, by itself, as all the others together, the pincer alliance is undesirable for the very reasons which previously commended it. Rules of caution based on experience are often dangerous, because they are formulated without any exact definition of the conditions in which they are applicable.

"The same criticism applies to allegedly scientific general propositions. Most general statements about the factors determining foreign policy are mistaken for two reasons: they tend to establish 'causes' where, at most, there are trends, and they do not take account of all the factors involved but exaggerate the influence of those that are considered.

Let us take, for example, the geographical determinants of foreign policy. The usual clichés about the 'need for an outlet to the open seas' or the 'mastery of the seas and the balance in Europe in relation to an insular position' sum up certain contingent factors. The importance that the Russian leaders attribute to free access to the sea depends on strategic considerations which alter with changes in the methods of warfare, and on the importance accorded to the problems of war as compared with those of peace. Czarist Russia was much more concerned about Constantinople and the Dardanelles than Soviet Russia (the former secured undertakings in 1915, the latter asked for no such undertakings during the hostilities of 1941–5).

• • •

"Similarly, when we seek to determine the influence of the 'economic factor', we shall find that it comes under our first set of headings, as one of the causes of change in the technique of warfare, the relative strength of the parties (since economic progress or decline entails an increase or a decrease in the strength of the nations), or change in the area of diplomatic relations, whose possible size is partly determined by the available means of transport. From another point of view, efforts can and should be made to discover how far the economic system and, more precisely, those in charge of the economy, influence the conduct of diplomacy. General propositions must therefore, at all events, be checked against experience.

"The method of historical comparison is simple enough in theory but complicated in practice. In theory, it is a question of drawing attention to both similarities and differences between two given situations; this calls for a conceptual system by which to recognize the principal determinants. A strict comparison between the conduct of foreign policy in Great Britain and the United States of America, for example, presupposes a knowledge of the main factors exerting an influence in both countries. But such a knowledge must be based on study of the facts quite as much as on theory. We must therefore turn constantly from study of the facts to structural analysis or investigation of the principal determinants, and vice versa.

"No comparison can cover the whole field: in other words, we always seek to determine the consequences of a particular phenomenon, such as the existence of a certain pattern in the relative strengths of countries. What are the effects of a bipolar structure? To what extent do we find the same developments in the Peloponnesian War and in the present conflict between the Soviet bloc and the free world? Or again, to what extent do we find similarities between periods in which the wars between States have been of a religious or ideological character?

"The danger of such comparisons – and, still more, of the conclusions that we may claim to draw from them – is that the similarities are found only in certain features and the differences are so considerable that we cannot hope for more than a moderate prospect of being right in our forecasts or in the advice we give. There are cases in which two great coalitions have engaged in a war to the death, and others in which they have resigned themselves to coexistence on a more or less warlike footing. There have been centuries in which wars of religion have ended in compromise peaces, obliging men holding apparently incompatible convictions or fanatical beliefs to tolerate one another within the boundaries of the States, and at the same time defining the regions or nations in which one or other doctrine has triumphed. Analogies are ready to hand, but the question is whether the differences do not reduce the value of the analogies.

•   •   •

"What is the logical way to approach the problem of causality? In the first place, it seems to me, we may look for the immediate or sufficient cause of a particular war in population phenomena. In most cases, the demographic cause, assuming that there is such a cause, is not the only one, but is reinforced or weakened by the psychology of the leaders and the people, as expressed in a particular manner in a given historical situation. The wars which seem to be directly due to demographic factors are the variety in which colonies are founded by men who no longer have the necessary resources for life in their country of origin.

"Secondly, we may compare the foreign policy of a nation at times when its population has been very large in relation to its resources with the foreign policy of that same nation at times when it is less so. This type of comparison will give us results which may be somewhat doubtful, for, on the assumption that over-populated countries pursue more aggressive policies than under-populated countries – which seems often to be the case – the state of affairs can be explained quite as well by reference to the general situation and calculations regarding the balance of power as by reference to the demographic position.

"Again, we may consider a particular period of history as a whole – a given century in a given civilisation – and gauge the frequency of wars and the mode of international relations by reference to population pressure. It is possible – indeed probable according to certain studies, though the truth of the conclusions drawn is not yet proved – that wars are more frequent in periods of over-population and less frequent in periods of relative depopulation but, in this case, it would seem that wars in the strict sense should be considered in conjunction with civil wars and manifestations of violence. It would appear that manifestations of violence increase in periods of over-population, and the increased frequency of war often coincides with increased frequency of civil conflict. If this is so, however, the periods when there have been great wars might coincide with periods of domestic upheaval, either moral or political. Such upheavals are sometimes, but not inevitably, a consequence of over-population. Over-population would therefore be one of the possible causes, but not the only possible cause, of a 'high incidence of war'."

Luard – International Sociology*

"At first sight there are such huge differences between world society and a domestic social system that it might seem meaningless to attempt to analyse it according to traditional sociological techniques. Its size, its complexity, its diffuseness, its lack of recognised authority or social cohesiveness, its lawless and violent character, all seem to remove it to a different realm altogether.

"All these differences, though they are real, on examination prove to be differences of degree rather than of kind. Its size is self-evidently greater than that of any individual state, but not disproportionately larger: if it is possible to apply sociological techniques to a nation such as China, with 800 million people of many races, provinces and cultures, it is not self-evident that they cannot be used in a society whose population is only about four times that size and whose distances, in travelling time, are far smaller than were those of China only two or three decades ago. It is complex and diffuse, certainly, but this is true of all modern large-scale industrial societies – world society is far less different in kind from the US than the US is from the small-scale primitive societies studied by anthropologists. It is subdivided into relatively enclosed and heterogeneous compartments, but this again is true of a number of national societies, particularly federal states such as Switzerland, the Soviet Union and Yugoslavia. It is lawless and violent, certainly, but so are many national states and many primitive societies, to only a slightly lesser extent. There is no widely accepted consensus concerning how this society should be ordered, but this too is true of many modern societies where there is widespread dissension on basic values. There is no authority capable of law enforcement, but this is equally so in a large proportion of primitive societies, which may have procedures for *pronouncing* on violations of order but no means for ensuring the fulfilment of those pronouncements. There is little social cohesiveness, but this too is the case in very many societies, especially large modern states, in which there are many subcultures and subgroups sharing few common beliefs.

"There are of course significant differences between world society and the type of society mainly studied by sociologists. In most national societies, even where there is no basis of common *values*,

---

* From Evan Luard (1926–). (For biographical details see p. 317.) Quoted from *Types of International Society* (New York: Free Press, 1976).

there exists at least a limited consensus concerning how disputes and differences on such points should be *resolved*; at the lowest there is a willingness most of the time to live and let live. In the world society even this is sometimes lacking. However, in this respect, too, the difference is only marginal. On the one hand, even within national societies, there are today significant groups (minority ethnic groups, revolutionary political movements and others) who are no longer prepared to accept the traditional norms and traditional means of resolving differences – who will no longer live and let live, who use violence to express their discontents. On the other hand, in the international society there is increasing acknowledgement, at least in large sections of it, of the illegitimacy of violence as a means of securing change, even an embryonic willingness to concede the legitimacy of international understandings as the means for determining certain issues. Authority is undoubtedly weaker and more widely challenged in the international society than in the national, but this is a difference of degree rather than of kind. In certain specific areas – for instance, the allocation of broadcasting frequencies, the drawing up of international health regulations, the maintenance and enforcement of international navigation standards, the determination of international monetary problems – a considerable degree of authority has already been vested in international bodies, with virtually no dissent; conversely, authority in national states is also sometimes disputed. Integration may still be much weaker in the international society than in the national, and may be growing more slowly, but it is none the less increasing rapidly, since many of the same factors (trade, travel and communications) which bring it about at the national level also operate within the wider society.

"Thus, though this is perhaps an unusual, indeed a unique, type of society, it is a society none the less, and not so dissimilar to smaller societies that some traditional sociological concepts may not have some relevance to it. Let us then consider the applications which some of these concepts may have in this sphere.

"If we accept the thesis that there exist 'societies' of states with their own traditions, rules, expectations and institutions, and that they should be studied on this basis, which are the concepts which will be of special importance to us in examining these societies?

"Before analysing the key social factors that will concern us in this study, let us first look at some general sociological ideas. To some extent almost all the concepts devised by sociologists for the study of smaller societies, can be used in examining international societies.

"For example, the concept of *authority* has relevance for us, though its application here is limited. Within most international societies, including even that of the present day, international authority has been so weak in relation to that of the members of society (the nations) that its significance is questionable: the characteristic of international societies is that power is decentralised there. The difference is not an absolute one, however. There are many primitive societies in which there is no central authority with powers of enforcement. Conversely, even in the international society, lip service at least is paid today to the authority exerted by world bodies: in Article 25 of the UN Charter almost all states of the world have expressly acknowledged the authority of the UN and their own obligation to obey its decisions under certain circumstances. Authority within an international society is not unlike that of a body of elders, or a revered chief, within a primitive society, whose influence is based largely on intangible factors, involving respect for the office, rather than on the ability to call on armed power to enforce his judgements. The authority which is exerted within a diffused and highly decentralised society is different from that to which we are accustomed in tightly organised national states, but it is a type of authority none the less. And the same methods of analysis which have shown their value at the national level may have their application here too.

"The concept of *legitimacy* also has its application within the international society. It has indeed been applied for centuries in the relations *between* states. Governments acknowledge the legitimacy of other governments by entering into diplomatic relations with them. The international society, equally, accords or denies legitimacy to particular governments by its decisions concerning membership of international organisations. The eagerness with which this is demanded by certain governments (and opposed by others) is an indication of the importance such decisions hold in their eyes as a mark of legitimacy. A nation that has been admitted as a member of the UN can be regarded as a bona fide member of the international system, even if individual governments continue to boycott it. It provides, in a sense, a definition of membership of the international society, a mark of respectability. And the fact that it is a mark which is valued and acknowledged, that membership in such organisations is almost universally desired, is evidence not only of the legitimacy of the member governments in the eyes of others, but of the legitimacy of the organisations themselves in the eyes of all.

"Again the concept of *status* operates within the international society as in smaller ones. A large and powerful state will normally be accorded a certain position of dominance in its dealings with others. The five largest European states in the earlier nineteenth century became 'the powers', accorded by the rest a special position within society and coming together at frequent intervals to resolve the important issues of the day. Similarly in the League Council, in the UN Security Council, and the corresponding councils of many of the specialised agencies, a permanent seat has been accorded to the largest and most-developed states: a visible symbol of status that is coveted by others. But status may be acquired by means other than power or size. During the Chou dynasty in China, the Chou state possessed, as we shall see, a revered status and authority that was disproportionate to its power or importance: status was based on the traditional authority of the dynasty. In the middle ages the Pope had a status that was not dependent on military power but on spiritual authority. And in modern times nations may acquire status through liberal sentiments (Sweden or Canada), wealth (Saudi Arabia or Iran), technology (the US), generosity (the Scandinavians and the Netherlands), benevolent neutrality (Switzerland or Ireland), or for other reasons.

"But *class*, among nations as among individuals, does not necessarily correspond to status. Class is related above all, in the international society, to the size of a state, especially its military power or, sometimes, its wealth. Traditionally nations have been divided into 'great' powers and small. The great powers have been those able to coerce the smaller. Today wealth has become more significant than before, though primarily because of the influence it brings. And because nations at a similar level of economic development have not only a common economic status, but a common *interest*, for example in relation to the policies of international organisations, or on questions of trade and development, they become increasingly organised, like classes within states, to struggle for their common interests within the international society. So the Group of 77 is created in the UN to struggle for the rights of the poor. Such a class division, in modern times at least, has displaced divisions of other sorts, based on ideological or historical association. The class struggle is in a sense fought out at the world level, and becomes in the international society as dominant and overriding a concern as it had been in national societies.

"Another factor of importance, in international as in domestic societies, is the socialisation that takes place within them. On the international level the socialisation forces are very weak. Unlike the socialisation which occurs within states, where the individual is directly influenced by parents and peer groups, by priests and peda-gogues, by the press and other media, it is here mainly indirect. Images of an international society existing beyond the national are only gradually instilled. The idea of an international authority is one which emerges for the individual only slowly in the course of reading about international events generally. In so far as they occur at all, these conceptions of the international society arise much later in life, usually in adolescence or even after adulthood, and for this reason make a far smaller impact than the conceptions of the nation instilled in early life. Slowly, and then mainly among a small élite, through the reading of speeches, news, history, or today through the viewing of films and television, a vague conception of an international society, and of the kinds of national conduct within it which are acceptable or taboo, begins to be formed. In so far as any explicit instructions, dos and don'ts, are made on such questions – for example, by inter-national bodies or law courts – they are made only indirectly, to governments in the first place, rather than to individuals, and for this reason too are weaker in effect. Moreover, in so far as any idea of an international society with purposes and norms of conduct of its own is established, it is only superimposed on loyalties and attitudes toward the national state which have already been far more deeply im-printed. Finally, the lack of any visible sanction which can be wielded by the international society to secure compliance with its norms also means that its perceived authority is weak. For all these reasons, socialisation of individuals into the wider society is much feebler and more indirect than that which occurs within national states. Yet it none the less occurs. And with the increasing number and saliency of international communications – for example, press items and tele-vision programmes relating to foreign opinion and to decisions by international bodies – socialisation into the international society is constantly being marginally strengthened.

"Resulting from this socialisation process are the *attitudes* and *loyalties* of individuals toward the wider society. These will be drawn partly from the domestic scene within, and partly from the inter-national stage without. Because the impressions derived from these sources are generally similar for individuals within the same nation, attitudes and loyalties will be somewhat similar for all its members, though there will be variations according to the psychological factors we examined earlier, and to education and position. Thus it is collective motives, collective ambitions, collective desires for revenge or justification, instilled by a common socialisation and a common national experience, that are often the essential factors within the international society. The attitudes and motives of individual decision-makers will usually reflect the attitudes and motives of their population, not so much because they are controlled or directly influenced by those populations, but because they share the common sentiments and views of a people to which they themselves belong. Thus, though many of the international *events* which are perceived are the same for all nations – the murder of an Austrian archduke, the invasion of the Rhineland, the war in Vietnam – because of differences in the domestic environment in each state, different speeches by different statesmen, different editorials in the press, different initial prejudices and sympathies, *perceptions* of them, reactions and long-term attitudes, will vary considerably from one population to the next, even where interests do not radically differ.

"These are only a few examples of some concepts which have been used by sociologists in analysing small-scale societies and which have a clear applicability to the society of states as well. Those mentioned so far, however, are of a relatively general kind. They are unlikely to provide the key ideas we need to guide us in our analysis of individual international societies. A systematic study will have to be more clearly focused on those social factors that are of special importance in determining the character of the society as a whole.

"It is a *series* of such factors that we are seeking. It has long been recognised among anthropologists that no single category, material culture, institution or kinship system can alone give an adequate understanding of the essential nature of each society. The significance of the material equipment can be totally transformed according to the type of social organisation, religious beliefs, kinship system, system of authority, above all the dominant value structure. Similarly, the significance of the power relationships within international societies, or relative technical development, will depend on the basic motives and objectives of the units, the type and effectiveness of the norms established, the communication system, the interrelationships normally existing among members, and above all the value system currently held. It is thus no more possible to distinguish and classify different types of *international* society according to a single factor, such as power relationships ('balance of power', bipolar or multipolar), communications systems, decision-making procedures and so on, than it is to classify primitive societies according to a single factor, such as material equipment or kinship system. It is the mix among the various elements within each society which will give it its specific character."

Bull – Order and Anarchy in International Society*

"Order within the modern state is the consequence, among other things, of government; order among states cannot be, for international society is an anarchical society, a society without government. But primitive stateless societies also present this spectacle of 'ordered anarchy', and it is worth considering the resemblances and differences between the ways in which order is created and maintained in the one case and in the other.

• • •

"Primitive anarchical societies clearly have important resemblances to international society in respect of the maintenance of order. In both cases some element of order is maintained despite the absence of a central authority commanding overwhelming force and a monopoly of the legitimate use of it. In both cases, also, this is achieved through the assumption by particular groups – lineage and locality groups in primitive stateless societies, sovereign states in international society – of the functions which, in a modern state, the government (but not the government exclusively) carries out in making rules effective. In primitive anarchical society, as in international society, order depends upon a fundamental or constitutional principle, stated or implied, which singles out certain groups as the sole bodies competent to discharge these political functions. In both

---

* From Hedley Bull (1932–85). Australian-born, studied and taught at the London School of Economics and Australian National University in Canberra, before becoming Professor of International Relations in Oxford. His principal contribution to the literature of international relations is *The Anarchical Society*, from which this extract is taken. Deeply critical of the "scientific" method in much contemporary US writing on international relations. Other works include *The Control of the Arms Race* (1961) and (as editor) *Intervention in World Politics* (1983). Quoted from *The Anarchical Society* (London: Macmillan, 1977).

societies the politically competent groups may legitimately use force in defence of their rights, while individuals and groups other than these must look to the privileged, politically competent groups for protection, rather than resort to force themselves.

"In primitive anarchical societies, as in international society, the relations between these politically competent groups are themselves circumscribed by a structure of acknowledged normative principles, even at times of violent struggle. But in both there is a tendency, during these periods of struggle, for the structure of rules to break down, and the society to fall apart to such an extent that the warring tribes or states are better described as a number of contending societies than as a single society. Finally, in both primitive anarchical society and modern international society there are factors operating, outside the structure of rules itself, inducing the politically competent groups to conform to them. These include the factors of mutual deterrence or fear of unlimited conflict, the force of habit or inertia, the long-term interests they have (consciously rationalised in the modern world, and intuitively felt in primitive society) in preserving a system of collaboration, whatever their short-term interest in destroying it.

•   •   •

"The maintenance of order in world politics depends, in the first instance, on certain contingent facts which would make for order even if states were without any conception of common interests, common rules or common institutions – even if, in other words, they formed an international system only, and not also an international society. A balance of power, for example, may arise in an international system quite fortuitously, in the absence of any belief that it serves common interests, or any attempt to regulate or institutionalise it. If it does arise, it may help to limit violence, to render undertakings credible or to safeguard governments from challenges to their local supremacy. Within international society, however, as in other societies, order is the consequence not merely of contingent facts such as this, but of a sense of common interests in the elementary goals of social life; rules prescribing behaviour that sustains these goals; and institutions that help to make these rules effective.

COMMON INTERESTS

"To say that *x* is in someone's interest is merely to say that it serves as a means to some end that he is pursuing. Whether or not *x* does serve

592 Basic Texts in International Relations

as a means to any particular end is a matter of objective fact. But whether or not x is in his interest will depend not only on this but also on what ends he is actually pursuing. It follows from this that the conception of interest is an empty or vacuous guide, both as to what a person does do and as to what he should do. To provide such a guide we need to know what ends he does or should pursue, and the conception of interest in itself tells us nothing about either.

"Thus the criterion of 'national interest', or 'interest of state', in itself provides us with no specific guidance either in interpreting the behaviour of states or in prescribing how they should behave – unless we are told what concrete ends or objectives states do or should pursue: security, prosperity, ideological objectives or whatever. Still less does it provide us with a criterion that is objective, in the sense of being independent of the way state ends or purposes are perceived by particular decision-makers. It does not even provide a basis for distinguishing moral or ideological considerations in a country's foreign policy from non-moral or non-ideological ones: for x can be in a country's interest if it serves as a means to a moral or ideological objective that the country has.

"However, the conception of national interest or interest of state does have some meaning in a situation in which national or state ends are defined and agreed, and the question at issue is by what means they can be promoted. To say that a state's foreign policy should be based on pursuit of the national interest is to insist that whatever steps are taken should be part of some rational plan of action; an approach to foreign policy based on the national interest may thus be contrasted with one consisting simply of the uncritical pursuit of some established policy, or one consisting simply of unconsidered reactions to events. A policy based on the idea of the national interest, moreover, may be contrasted with one based on a sectional interest, or one based on the interests of some group wider than the state, such as an alliance or international organisation to which it belongs. To speak of the national interest as the criterion at least directs our attention to the ends or objectives of the nation or state, as against those of some other group, narrower or wider.

"The maintenance of order in international society has as its starting-point the development among states of a sense of common interests in the elementary goals of social life. However different and conflicting their objectives may be, they are united in viewing these goals as instrumental to them. Their sense of common interests may derive from fear of unrestricted violence, of the instability of agreements or of the insecurity of their independence or sovereignty. It may have its origins in rational calculation that the willingness of states to accept restrictions on their freedom of action is reciprocal. Or it may be based also on the treatment of these goals as valuable in themselves and not merely as a means to an end – it may express a sense of common values as well as of common interests.

[handwritten margin note: Bradney to allude to this with "republicanism". It also touches on norms & rules.]

RULES

"In international society, as in other societies, the sense of common interests in elementary goals of social life does not in itself provide precise guidance as to what behaviour is consistent with these goals; to do this is the function of *rules*. These rules may have the status of international law, of moral rules, of custom or established practice, or they may be merely operational rules or 'rules of the game', worked out without formal agreement or even without verbal communication. It is not uncommon for a rule to emerge first as an operational rule, then to become established practice, then to attain the status of a moral principle and finally to be incorporated in a legal convention; this appears to have been the genesis, for example, of many of the rules now embodied in multilateral treaties or conventions concerning the laws of war, diplomatic and consular status, and the law of the sea.

[handwritten margin note: But, common interests do not provide guidance as to the correct behavior. Rules do this.]

"The range of these rules is vast, and over much of this range they are in a state of flux. Here we shall mention only three complexes of rules that play a part in the maintenance of international order.

"First, there is the complex of rules that states what may be called the fundamental or constitutional normative principle of world politics in the present era. This is the principle that identifies the idea of a society of states, as opposed to such alternative ideas as that of a universal empire, a cosmopolitan community of individual human beings, or a Hobbesian state of nature or state of war, as the supreme normative principle of the political organisation of mankind. It is emphasised elsewhere in this study that there is nothing historically inevitable or morally sacrosanct about the idea of a society of states. Nor does this idea in fact monopolise human thought and action, even in the present phase; on the contrary, it has always had to do battle with competing principles, and does so now. Order on a world scale, however, does require that one or another of these basic ideas

[handwritten margin symbol: (1)]

should be clearly in the ascendancy; what is incompatible with order on a world scale is a discord of competing principles of universal political organisation.

"On the one hand, the idea of international society identifies states as members of this society and the units competent to carry out political tasks within it, including the tasks necessary to make its basic rules effective; it thus excludes conceptions which assign this political competence to groups other than the state, such as universal authorities above it or sectional groups within it. On the other hand, the idea of international society identifies the relationship between the states as that of members of a society bound by common rules and committed to common institutions; it thus excludes the conception of world politics as a mere arena or state of war.

"This fundamental or constitutional principle of international order is presupposed in ordinary state conduct. The daily actions of states – in arrogating to themselves the rights or competences of principal actors in world politics, and in combining with each other to this end, in resisting the claims of supra-state or sub-state groups to wrest these rights and competences from them – display this principle and provide evidence of its central role. The principle is contained in a number of basic rules of international law. Thus it has been the predominant doctrine that states are the only or the principal bearers of rights and duties in international law; that they alone have the right to use force to uphold it; and that its source lies in the consent of states, expressed in custom or treaty. The principle, however, is prior to international law, or to any particular formulation of international law; it is manifest in a whole complex of rules – legal, moral, customary and operational. It is not a static principle, but is subject to constant development. In the formative stages of international society, it had to meet the challenge of doctrines which proclaimed the right of individuals and of groups other than the state to a place in universal political organisation; and at the present time it faces a similar challenge.

"Second, there are what may be called 'the rules of coexistence'. Given the guidance supplied by the constitutional principle as to who are the members of international society, these rules set out the minimum conditions of their coexistence. They include, first of all, the complex of rules which restrict the place of violence in world politics. These rules seek to confine the legitimate use of violence to sovereign states and to deny it to other agents by confining legitimate violence to a particular kind of violence called 'war', and by treating war as violence that is waged on the authority of a sovereign state. Furthermore, the rules seek to limit the causes or purposes for which a sovereign state can legitimately begin a war, for example by requiring that it be begun for a just cause, as maintained by the natural-law doctrines of the formative era of the states system, or by requiring that it be begun only after certain other procedures had been tried first, as insisted by the Covenant of the League of Nations. The rules also have sought to restrict the manner in which sovereign states conduct war, for example by insisting that war be conducted in a way proportionate to the end pursued, or in such a way as to spare non-combatants, or so as to employ no more violence than necessary. In addition, the rules have sought to restrict the geographical spread of a war, by establishing the rights and duties of neutrals and belligerents in relation to one another.

"There is a further complex of rules of coexistence which prescribes the behaviour appropriate to sustain the goal of the carrying out of undertakings. The basic rule *pacta sunt servanda*, sometimes seen as a presupposition of the law of nations, and sometimes as a first principle of it, established the presumption on which alone there can be point in entering into agreements at all. Subordinate or qualifying rules concern whether or not good faith need be kept with heretics or infidels, whether or not agreements remain valid in changing circumstances and who is the judge as to whether or not they have changed, whether or not and in what sense agreements are valid that are imposed by force, what the circumstances are in which a party to an agreement can be released from it, what are the principles according to which agreements should be interpreted, whether or not and to what extent a new government succeeds to the obligations of its predecessors, and so on.

"The rules of coexistence also include those which prescribe behaviour that sustains the goal of the stabilisation of each state's control or jurisdiction over its own persons and territory. At the heart of this complex of rules is the principle that each state accepts the duty to respect the sovereignty or supreme jurisdiction of every other state over its own citizens and domain, in return for the right to expect similar respect for its own sovereignty from other states. A corollary or near-corollary of this central rule is the rule that states will not intervene forcibly or dictatorially in one another's internal affairs. Another is the rule establishing the 'equality' of all states in the sense of their like enjoyment of like rights of sovereignty.

"Third, there is the complex of rules concerned to regulate co-operation among states – whether on universal or on a more limited scale – above and beyond what is necessary for mere coexistence. This includes the rules that facilitate co-operation, not merely of a political and strategic, but also of a social and economic nature. The growth in this century of legal rules concerned with co-operation between states in economic, social, communications and environmental matters exemplifies the place of rules of co-operation. . . .

"Rules of this kind prescribe behaviour that is appropriate not to the elementary or primary goals of international life, but rather to those more advanced or secondary goals that are a feature of an international society in which a consensus has been reached about a wider range of objectives than mere coexistence. Nevertheless, these rules may be said to play a role in relation to international order, inasmuch as the development of co-operation and consensus among states about these wider goals may be expected to strengthen the framework of coexistence.

"This is not the place to expound these three complexes of rules in full, or to examine the problems of interpreting them or reconciling the conflicts between them. Nor is it appropriate here to consider which of them has the status of law, which the status of moral rules, which should be seen as customary or as operational rules, nor to trace the historical evolution through which these rules have passed from one of these embodiments to another, and sometimes back again. It is sufficient to note that the vast and changing corpus of rules and quasi-rules, of which those cited are part of the central core, provide the means whereby international society moves from the vague perception of a common interest to a clear conception of the kind of conduct it requires."

Conclusions: The Changing Conception of International Society

A collection of readings of the kind assembled here can never hope to be comprehensive. The range of writing (and speaking) on international affairs is so voluminous and so diverse that it would never be possible, even in a volume of this length, to provide more than a cursory glimpse of the total. The extracts chosen for this collection include some of the best-known passages written on the subject and most of the best-known authors, as well as a few less familiar writers. They have been selected to provide a reasonably representative cross-section of the ideas put forward on these questions over the years, representing diverse schools of thought and different nationalities.[1]

The way the volume is organised may give the impression of a more logical and progressive development in thinking about international affairs than has in fact occurred. In many cases the thoughts which have been expressed on such matters have derived from the personal viewpoints of the writers, who have not conveniently grouped themselves into "schools" in the way that the collection might sometimes suggest. But, even making allowances for an artificially imposed coherence of this kind, it is possible to detect some kind of pattern in the way ideas about international relationships, and the international society within which they occur, have developed.

There is, first, a consistent evolution in the way the subject is approached in different ages. The focus of attention has changed: moving outwards from individual to state to system of states. In earlier times the main interest was in the attitudes of individuals. States were still in the process of formation and armed conflict occurred as often between various groups within the state as it did between states themselves. This ubiquity of warfare between rival religious faiths, between monarchs and revolting nobles, cities and peasants, as well as between states, made it reasonable to attribute responsibility for that phenomenon to all humans, and not only to those who controlled the affairs of a state. Even among states relationships were almost entirely in the hands of a few individuals, autocratic rulers who determined almost single-handedly government policies. Thus judgements about human nature in general, rather than about the policies of rulers or governments, were those that appeared relevant. Whether human beings were "good" or "bad" (as was debated by ancient Chinese philosophers), whether humans were aggressive or pacific by nature (as debated by modern psychologists), had a significance for international relations, since it would determine the way individual rulers conducted the policies of their own states. But as the control of policy came to be more widely distributed, and decision-making more institutionalised, the actions of states no longer depended on the attitudes of a few individuals. Increasingly, therefore, over time it came to seem more reasonable to focus attention not so much on the character of individual humans as on the way states were organised, decision-making machinery and their dominant foreign policy goals. Finally, as states extend into lasting relationships with other states, and established conventional patterns of behaviour of joint institutions, attention moved out once more to the system of states as a whole.

But whether the focus of attention was individuals, states or the system of states, there was another contrast in the views put forward. In all ages there have been some writers who have emphasised a natural *conflict* of interests – whether between individuals or states – and others who have believed on the contrary that a *harmony* of interests existed, or at least could be created if only the right institutions were established. This is comparable to the contrast to be found among writers on social and political affairs: between those who have assumed a natural conflict of interests between individuals and classes within the state (such as Hobbes, Marx, Sorel and contemporary Marxist writers, for example), and those who assume (like Locke, Rousseau, Comte, Durkheim and many modern sociologists such as Talcott Parsons) that, though conflict may occur, it is possible to create political and social institutions that will establish a harmoniously functioning community. Writers on international affairs can be divided in a similar way. Among them too some have assumed a natural state of conflict, between states or individuals or both, within the international community. Sometimes this judgement results (as for the legalist writers in ancient China or for Machiavelli) from the experience of endemic warfare in the international society they knew; sometimes from a cynical or conservative turn of mind; sometimes from a deliberately adopted position, designed as a warning against excessively idealistic or conciliatory policies (as for the realist writers of the 1930s and 1940s). This assumption of conflictual relationships often results in an emphasis on power factors and on the importance of the balance of power, either as an automatic process or as a desirable policy. And it implies a belief that these fundamental antagonisms will frustrate any attempt to establish a truly co-operative system of relations among states.

In contrast are those writers who, though they recognise the existence of disagreement and conflict among states, have not seen this as an *inevitable* feature of international society. They have believed it might be possible to create a more integrated and harmonious world community: either through the creation of new institutions (such as those advocated by Penn, Bentham, Kant and by their successors in recent times), or through the adoption by governments of more enlightened policies – disarmament, better communication and understanding with other states, conciliatory foreign policies and world community. Such writers have been inclined to downplay the role of "power" and "power politics" in relation to other features of international relationships. They believe that the existing patterns of national behaviour are not immutable but can be changed. And they have stressed the possibility, as well as the desirability, of co-operative relationships and effective international institutions. This difference of view, between those who have seen conflict as a central feature of international society, and those who have seen it rather as an incidental feature which, by appropriate means, might be moderated and contained, is a fundamental division among those who have thought and written on this subject through the ages.

This division is related to another: between different *images* of other states, held at different times by different authors. All writers on international affairs view the world from a central position occupied by their own state, surrounded by a circle of others, more or less numerous. Other states may be seen as like or unlike, rivals or partners, friends or enemies. Writings on international affairs nearly always imply some view of the character of other states. Those who think in terms of a natural conflict of interests among states have tended to see other states as unlike their own: potentially aggressive, or at least as opponents, who need to be checked, outwitted, if necessary defeated, to protect their own interests. This view is naturally to be found especially during periods of widespread conflict, intense nationalism, and in periods when direct contact with other states was limited, so that it is easier to maintain traditional stereotypes (the aggressive German or Japanese or Russian, or even the deplorable character of foreigners in general). The greater the degree of direct contact which has existed, the more difficult it has been to sustain these pictures of hostile and wicked enemies; and the more realistic has appeared the possibility of establishing a more peaceful and constructive relationship with other states. Among writers on international affairs this change of attitudes is reflected in the contrast between the approach of Machiavelli, taking for granted the hostile intentions of opponents (even close neighbours), and so concerned to describe the way they can be outwitted, and that of, for example, David Hume, seeing people as a mixture of good and bad qualities, often distrustful of each other, but capable of living in amity if the right conditions are established; or, in more recent times, between the approaches of von Moltke and the nationalist writers of the late nineteenth-century proclaiming the inevitability of war and the forthcoming triumph of their own states, and that of foreign office officials, such as Crowe and Kennan, with a wide knowledge of other states, seeking to understand the aspirations and fears of their opponents, and so the best way of encouraging them towards more constructive relationships or between the somewhat naïve image of state motives projected by the "realists" of the 1930s and 1940s (many of them based in the isolated and isolationist US), and the more balanced viewpoint favoured by some of their critics (American and European) two or three decades later.

Another important distinction concerns differing areas of attention. Many of the early writers were advisers to rulers and were therefore inevitably concerned with the way a *particular* state should conduct itself (even if the proposed policy was based on judgements about the way states generally behaved). Not all early writers were so narrowly focused in their approach. Thucydides was able to write an objective account of the Peloponnesian war from a synoptic viewpoint, unaffected by partiality for any single city: and his history therefore presented a balanced picture of international relationships generally in his time; just as the Chinese historian Ssu Ma-chien did of the warring states period in China. But that attitude was, until recent times, exceptional. In Europe such writers as Machiavelli and Bodin had an entirely state-centric view of the world, and there is little attempt by either to make judgements about the nature of the international system as a whole. Only as the concept of the "balance of power" emerges, not as a policy but as a desirable end-state for all nations – as advocated, for example, by Fénelon (pp. 384–6 above) – does attention broaden to the needs of the community of states as a whole. Even then, as we saw, the balance was normally viewed in highly subjective terms, so that the concept was used usually as a justification for the actions that states anyway wanted to take, rather than as a restraint on those actions. The writings of international lawyers were, in theory at least, concerned with the needs of international society as a whole, but they too were on occasion inclined (like their successors until the present day) to favour those rules which were most favourable to their own states: so that, for example, Grotius, as a Dutchman by birth, was highly favourable to the freedom of the seas while Selden, the Englishman, opposed the principle, each reflecting the interests of their own state at their time.

It was above all in the nineteenth century, with the emergence of the conception of "Europe", having its own needs above and beyond those of its individual member states, that a wider focus emerged. The idea that the nation had a duty to the international community to which it belonged then became widely accepted. The declaration that "Europe too has its rights which the social order has created" expressed an explicit recognition that states were one of another and could not conduct their affairs on the basis of "sovereignty" alone. This principle of community needs came to be enshrined in the principle of multilateralism – that every settlement needed to be agreed among all the major powers: a notion that was to have a continuing influence on the conduct of international relations in future years. Writings on international relations reflected this acceptance of the needs of the wider community. So it has come about that in the present day a large proportion of writers on international relations (other than those who continue to see it as their task to proffer advice on policy to their own government or their own alliance) focus their attention on this wider entity – the society of states as a whole. And it seems possible that in the coming decades there may be a reversion to the type of writing – such as much in this volume – which more clearly reflects preferences concerning the types of international society, and therefore of national policy, the writer believes to be desirable.

There was another contrast: between those who stressed the essential likeness among states and those who emphasised their unlikeness. If the interests of the writer (as for many of those featured in

Part Two of this collection) was at the level of the state, then the study almost inevitably focused on the dissimilarities between states. Thus those who looked at the effect of geography on state behaviour (such as Montesquieu), those who believed in the importance of the political system (such as Paine and Cobden), or of class structure (such as Kautsky and Lenin) or of the character of the rulers (such as the ancient Chinese writers) in influencing state behaviour, by placing states into categories, almost inevitably emphasised their differences. Against this, those who were mainly interested in systems of states tended to underplay the differences among the individual states. Their common membership of a common system appeared more important than differences in the aims or situation of each; placed them in the same category rather than in different ones. Thus, for example, the "systems" approach, though it distinguished between states according to their relative power, generally ignored most other differences in a state's situation or policies: because every state was influenced by the nature of the system, they would behave in similar ways in similar situations. So too the Utopian writers, describing desirable international institutions, implied that all states alike would respond similarly to the benevolent influence of those institutions. Advocates of the balance of power likewise implied that all states would be equally responsive to power balances. Among such writers differences between states – in geographical situation, political system, historical experience, traditional orientation, and even in size and population – were frequently discounted. Differences between states and types of state appeared less important in such approaches than differences in types of system.

Such differences reflect varying views about which are the significant *actors* in international relations. Early writers, as we have seen, were often concerned with individuals, especially the rulers with whom states were frequently identified. During the nineteenth century, the age of nationalism, the actors were the nations – Germany, France, Russia, Austria, Hungary – increasingly personified as distinct entities, having a personality, even (as Hegel would have said) a soul. The particular individuals, groups and classes within each of these entities were rarely seen as having a distinct role to play in international affairs. The "nation" was believed to have a cohesive power which made its component parts irrelevant. This was reflected, in writing on international affairs, in the so-called "billiard-ball" approach, in which the units were conceived as single, homogeneous entities, having their own weight and momentum, coming into regular collision with other entities of essentially similar type. Such bodies had hard outer casings, and the differences *within* each – the views and actions of particular groups, parties or individuals – were discounted. In more modern times the systems approach equally usually saw the states, each seen as an undifferentiated whole, as the essential factor, categorised according to the power to be attributed to it, and the balances of power which resulted for the system as a whole. At the opposite extreme the world society approach has seen the essential actors within international relationships as individuals and groups, interrelated with each other across national borders, and establishing relationships of their own, largely independent of the relationships between states: in consequence of these trans-frontier contacts, economic, cultural and ideological relationships become as important as those based on power, and international trade unions, multinational corporations, associations of scientists and similar bodies become as significant actors as states and groups of states. Other writers fall between these extremes. Some would see particular interest-groups – for example, the military-industrial complex, political movements, foreign office officials – as being significant actors; but in many cases they are seen as significant because of the influence they have on the actions of *states*, which remain the primary actors. While most would accept that transnational (non-state) influences are more significant than in any earlier times, they do not necessarily believe that this has transformed the character of international relations. Some would hold that the increase in the significance of non-state influences has been accompanied by an equal increase in the power and authority of governments, both within and outside their own borders. Under this view political events within states and relationships between states alike are influenced and controlled by governments today as much as, and perhaps even more than, in any earlier time. Under this view states *remain* the most significant actors within international society, though the various forces operating to influence their actions, both within their own borders and outside, are more complex and diverse than in any earlier period.

A final distinction that can be drawn between writers on international topics, from all ages, concerns the nature and underlying purpose of their approach. At all times there have been some writers whose aim was primarily dogmatic, moral and prescriptive; whose main concern was to change the world rather than to explain it. But there have been others whose aim was empirical, analytical and descriptive: concerned to examine the world as it is, rather than as it should be. While such writers as Mo Tzu, Erasmus, Rousseau, Norman Angell, Woodrow Wilson, to take a few names almost at random, were concerned above all to persuade, to advocate a change in conduct or institutions, in order to bring about a different world, normally one more peaceful and harmonious than that in which the writer lived, others – Han Fei-tzu, Machiavelli, Hobbes, Frederick the Great, Hans Morgenthau, for example – were concerned with describing, often with ruthless realism, the existing world and the international behaviour to be found within it, so as to identify appropriate responses to that situation. This division is not clear-cut. Though it is superficially convenient to label some writers as "Utopian" and others as "Realists", the distinction is a somewhat crude one. Those who have prescribed particular forms of conduct to governments have nearly always based those prescriptions in part on assumptions about the way the world operated at present; while those whose purpose was mainly analytical and descriptive have often formed conclusions about the type of policy required in the light of their analysis. But it is probably true to say that over the years there has been some movement from the prescriptive to the descriptive, from the normative to the "scientific". Especially since 1945 many scholars have tended to seek a "value-free" approach, which avoided adopting any preference for one set of outcomes or future world over another. The so-called behavioural approach has concentrated on analysing and describing *existing* conduct, rather than imagining or anticipating possible *alternative* conduct. It has been accompanied, especially in the US, by the development of so-called "quantitative" techniques, which have effectively confined research to those areas of reality which could easily be measured. The "scientific" method has demanded the testing of previously stated hypotheses, usually set out in highly abstract terms, in order to arrive at a "theory" which can be used for predictive and even for policy purposes. However commendable that objective in avoiding hidden bias, based on subjective preconceptions or desires, its effect can be to restrict, and even impoverish the scope of the studies undertaken. And it seems possible that in the coming decades there may be a reversion to the type of writing – such as much in this volume – which more clearly reflects preferences concerning the types of international society, and therefore of national policy, the writer believes to be desirable.

Whether or not this occurs, it is to be hoped that the literature continues to display the diversity of approach which has been demonstrated in the past. The worst possible outcome would be for thinking to become congealed into the moulds dictated by current academic fashion. The wider the variety of approaches to the subject adopted the greater the chance that our understanding of the complex and ever-changing relationships which occur within international society may be increased. If this volume contributes to providing some idea of the rich variety of thinking which has taken place over previous centuries on this vital and all-absorbing subject it will have served its purpose.

Note
1. The editor is well aware that he has omitted many significant present-day writers on international relations and hopes to remedy this deficiency by producing, at a later date, a set of modern texts which will represent contemporary authors more adequately.

Index